S0-ASP-827

CHRIST
AND HIS CHURCH
IN THE BOOK OF
PSALMS

CHRIST AND HIS CHURCH IN THE BOOK OF PSALMS

by

Andrew A. Bonar

KREGEL PUBLICATIONS
Grand Rapids, Michigan 49501

CHRIST AND HIS CHURCH IN THE BOOK OF PSALMS
Published in 1978 by Kregel Publications,
a division of Kregel, Inc. All rights reserved.

Library of Congress Cataloging in Publication Data

Bonar, Andrew Alexander, 1810-1892.
  Christ and His Church in the Book of Psalms.

  Reprint of the 1861 ed. published by R. Carter,
New York.

  1. Typology (Theology). 2. Bible. O.T.
Psalms — Criticism, interpretation, etc.
3. Church — Biblical teaching. I. Title.
BT225.B6 1978   223'.2'06   78-5692
ISBN 0-8254-2230-2

Printed in the United States of America

PREFACE

FEW of the Books of Scripture are richer than the *Book of Psalms,* that *" Hymn-book for all times,"* as it has been called. " There," says Luther, " you look right down into the heart of saints, and behold all manner of joys and joyous thoughts toward God and his love springing lustily into life ! Again, you look into the heart of saints as into death and hell ! How gloomy and dark their mournful visions of God." Another has said, " The Psalms teach me to prize a much tried life." And Tholuck (who gives these quotations) remarks, " Songs which, like the Psalms, have stood the test of three thousand years, contain a germ for eternity."

The Psalms are for all ages alike—not more for David than for us. Even as the cry, " *It is finished !"* though first heard by the ear of John and the women from Galilee, who stood at the cross, was not meant for them more truly than for us ; so with the Psalms

The writers were prepared by God, through personal

and public circumstances, for breathing forth appropriately the mind of Him who used them. *Irving,*
in his preface to *Horne* on the Psalms, has spoken some
most valuable truths on this subject. He remarks
that the Psalms, like the prophetic writings, " *arose by
the suggestion of some condition of the Church,* present
in the days of the prophets, as the particular case.
But passing beyond this in time, and passing beyond
it in aggravation of every circumstance, they give as
it were a consecutive glance of all the like cases and
kindred passages in the history of the Church, and
bring out the general law of God's providence and grace
in the present, and in all the future parallel cases."
The Psalmist, however, was not to be an automaton,
nor his readers mere lookers on or listeners to what
the automaton gives forth. " *Therefore, God moulded
his man to his purpose, and cast him into the conditions
that suited his ends.* And still he was a man, acted on
by course of nature, and manifest to the people as a
fellow-man, through whom, indeed, they heard soul-
stirring truths, uttered with ear-piercing words, but
suited to their case, and thrust in their way, and
spoken to their feelings, and pressed on their con-
sciences, and riveted there by the most mighty sanc-
tions of life and death, present and eternal." " And
asTHE WORD which was in the beginning took not
voice, nor intelligence, but flesh, human flesh, and the
fulness of the Godhead was manifested bodily ; so
when that same Word came to the fathers by the pro-

phets, and discovered a part of his fulness, it was through their flesh, or their humanity—that is, through their present condition of spirit, and mind, and body, and outward estate."

It was for this end that God led David the round of all human conditions, that he might catch the spirit proper to every one, and utter it according to the truth. " He allowed him not to curtail his being by treading the round of one function ; but by a variety of functions he cultivated his whole being, and filled his soul with wisdom and feeling. He found him objects of every affection. He brought him up in the sheep-pastures, that the groundwork of his character might be laid through simple and universal forms of feeling. He took him to the camp, that he might be filled with nobleness of soul, and ideas of glory. He placed him in the palace, that he might be filled with ideas of majesty and sovereign might. He carried him to the wilderness and placed him in solitudes, that his soul might dwell alone in the sublime conception of God and his mighty works. And he kept him there for long years, with only one step between him and death, that he might be well schooled to trust and depend upon the providence of God. And in none of these various conditions and vocations of life did He take from him His Holy Spirit. *His trials were but the tuning of the instrument with which the Spirit might express the various melodies which He designed to utter by him for the consolation and edification of spiritual men.*

John the Baptist, having to be used for rough work, was trained in the desert. . . . . Every one hath been *disciplined by the providence of God,* as well as *furnished in the fountains of his being,* for that particular work for which the Spirit of God designed him."

The literal and historical sense is in the highest degree profitable ; as Calvin, and Venema, and Matthew Henry, and others, have shewn. But our principle is, that having once found the literal sense, the exact meaning of the terms, and the primary application of the Psalm, we are then to ask what the Holy Spirit intended to teach in all ages by this formula. Bishop Horne speaks of such study as being like a traveller's ascent to an eminence, " neither unfruitful nor unpleasant," whence he gets an extensive prospect lying beyond, and stretching away to the far distance. Bishop Horsley quotes 2 Sam. xxiii. 3, " *The Spirit of Jehovah spake by me, and His word was in my tongue*" —and adds, " If David be allowed to have had any knowledge of the true subject of his own compositions, that subject was nothing in his own life, but something put into his mind by the Holy Spirit of God." This is so far true ; but at the same time let us hold (as stated above) that what the Spirit put into David's mind, or the mind of any other writer, was done not abruptly, but in connection with the writer's position. Even as our Lord's sayings for all ages were not uttered at random in any circumstances, but were always connected naturally with some present passing event or incident.

" Jesus *answered* and said," is true of them all : he strang his pearls on the thread of passing occurrences or conversations. And even so is it with the Psalms. They take their rise in things local and temporary, but they pass onward from the present into the ages to come.

Now, in the early ages, men full of the thoughts of Christ could never read the Psalms without being reminded of their Lord. They probably had no system or fixed theory as to all the Psalms referring to Christ ; but still, unthinkingly we might say, they found their thoughts wandering to their Lord, as the one Person in whom these breathings, these praises, these desires, these hopes, these deep feelings, found their only true and full realization. Hence Augustine (Psa. lviii.) said to his hearers, as he expounded to them this book, that " the voice of Christ and his Church was well-nigh the only voice to be heard in the Psalms"—" *Vix est ut in Psalmis inveniamus vocem nisi Christi et Ecclesiae ;*" and on another occasion (Psa. xliii.), " Everywhere diffused throughout is that man whose Head is above, and whose members are below. We ought to recognise his voice in all the Psalms, either waking up the psaltery or uttering the deep groan—rejoicing in hope, or heaving sighs over present realities." Tertullian (quoted by Horne) says, " Omnes poene Psalmi Christi personam sustinent."

We set out with laying down no other principle of interpretation in regard to the speakers in these sacred songs, than this one,—viz., we must consider this book as "*not of private interpretation,*" (2 Peter i. 20). Its utterances did not originate with the authors themselves. It is one of those writings which "holy men of God spake as they were moved by the Holy Ghost;" and therefore it is decidedly erroneous to suppose, that because David, or any other, was the author, that therefore nothing is spoken of, or sung, but matters in which they were mainly or primarily concerned. "*Not unto themselves, but unto us they did minister,*" is true here also, (1 Pet. i. 12). We cannot err far, therefore, if with Amyrauld we keep "our left eye on David, while we have our right eye full on Christ." In some instances, *the Head exclusively* speaks, or is spoken of, and in a few others *the Members alone;* but generally, the strain is such in feeling and matter, that the Head and Members together can use the harp and utter the song. And so important are these holy songs, that nearly fifty of them are referred to in the New Testament, and applied to Christ.

Hengstenberg has evidently felt, in spite of his dread of admitting Messiah into the Psalms too often, that *one individual* was very generally present to the writer's mind. He is constrained to admit that reference is made to some *ideal* perfect one, or some *ideal* righteous one, who is the standard.* Unwittingly he thus

---

* Another German writer, Baehr, treats *the Cherubim* somewhat in the same manner. He says that the cherub is "the image of the creature in its highest form—an *ideal creature.*" What is this *idea* of perfection in the *creature*, but

grants the fact, that none can read those songs of Zion without being led to think upon some one individual as the ever-recurring theme. And as the Scriptures do not speak in the style of philosophy, we may safely say, that the reference in all these cases is not to any abstract *ideal* person, but to the real *living One*, in whom all perfections meet, and against whom all the plots and malice of hell have ever been directed—*Messiah, the Righteous One.*

There is in almost every one of all these Psalms something that fitted them for the use of the past generations of the Church, and something that fits them admirably for the use of the Church now ; while also there is diffused throughout a hint for the future. There is, we might say, a *past*, a *present*, and a *future* element.* Few of them can be said to have no pro-phetic reference, no reference to generations or events yet to arise,—a circumstance that gives them a claim upon the careful study of every one who searches into the prophetic records, in addition to the manifold other claims which they possess.

---

just the *Redeemed Church ?* And why are men reluctant to leave the abstrac-tions of philosophy for the realities of revelation ?

* Dr Allix does not hesitate to apply them very specially to the Church in these latter days. Thus he says of the first Psalm, " It containeth both the de-scription of the happiness which the faithful Christians who apply themselves to their duty shall enjoy, as also those who with patience wait for the promises made unto them when Jesus Christ will come to reign upon the whole earth ; and the misery of those who are of Antichrist's side, and who laugh at his coming "

The substance of these Notes (for they are no more than notes) appeared originally in the " *Quarterly Journal of Prophecy.*"   They are meant to help those who delight to search the Scriptures.   There are also gleanings from many fields here and there presented to the reader ; for the Author has consulted writers on the Psalms of all different shades of opinion, even where he simply states the conclusion at which he has arrived as to the true sense of the passage.

Christt and His Church
in the
Book of Psalms

Psalm 1

1 BLESSED is the man that walketh not in the counsel of the ungodly.
Nor standeth in the way of sinners, nor sitteth in the seat of the scornful.
2 But his delight is in the law of the Lord;—and in his law doth he meditate day and night.
3 And he shall be like a tree planted by the rivers of water,
That bringeth forth his fruit in his season;
His leaf also shall not wither;—and whatsoever he doeth shall prosper.
4 The ungodly are not so : but are like the chaff which the wind driveth away.
5 Therefore the ungodly shall not stand in the judgment,
Nor sinners in the congregation of the righteous.
6 For the Lord knoweth the way of the righteous:—but the way of the ungodly shall perish.

THE first sound of the harp of the sweet singer of Israel* The Theme might well be thought strange in a world lying in wickedness. It celebrates the present happiness of that man who has fellowship with God, and no fellowship with the ungodly. Behold the man ! his eye arrested, not by the things of earth, but by what has been sent down from heaven—"the law of the Lord." He has found the "river of living water;" he is like a

---

* David's name is prefixed to *seventy-three* Psalms; but he is understood to be the penman of *thirty* others that bear no title.

1

tree—like some palm or pomegranate-tree,*—laden with fruit, or like that tree of life in Rev. xxii. 2, that yieldeth its fruit every month, and yieldeth fruit of all variety. "Every bud of it grows into a grain," says the Targum, on the words "all that he doeth shall prosper," taking עָשָׂה as it is used in Gen. vii. 11, 12. "He is the very contrast to the barren fig-tree, withered by the curse," says a modern interpreter.

Perhaps this comparison to the *tree and the streams* should carry us back to Eden, and suggest the state of man holy and happy there. Redeemed man rises up again to Eden-blessedness. Is it the fact of its occurrence in this Psalm, or is it simply the expressiveness of the similitude, that has led to its repetition in Jer. xvii. 8?

Historical allusion.

But, besides, we are carried back to *Joshua* by the language used regarding the man's prosperity. Joshua's career was one of uninterrupted prosperity, except in one single case, when he forgot to consult the Lord; and the Lord's words to him were these :

> "This book of *the law* shall not depart out of thy mouth,
> But thou shalt *meditate therein day and night*,
> That thou mayest observe to do according to all that is written therein ;
> For then thou shalt *make thy way prosperous*,
> And then thou shalt have good success."—(Josh. i. 8.)

Perhaps this reference to the days of Joshua made this Psalm the more appropriate as an introduction to the whole book. It connected these ancient days with other generations. It sang of the same Lord, acting toward all men on the same principles. It sang of a race who had come to possess the land of Canaan, who acted on the holy maxims that guided Joshua when he took possession—a race of men guided by the revealed will of Jehovah.

Prophetic reference.

The ungodly are not thus prosperous,—they are not as "trees by the river side." They are as "*chaff*," ready to be driven away in the day of wrath, and unable to resist the slightest breath of Jehovah's displeasure (Dan. ii. 35 ; Matt.

---

* *Stanley* (Pal. and Sinai, p. 145) thinks the *oleander* referred to. It grows common and abundant by river-sides in the East. But the oleander does not bear fruit.

iii. 12, the " day of decision"). Hence they cannot " *stand.*" Even as in Rev. vi. 17, the cry of the affrighted world— kings, captains, rich men, mighty men, bond, free—is, " The great day of his wrath is come, and who shall be able to *stand ?*" For the " Lord *knoweth* the way of the righteous." Our Lord may have referred to this passage in his memorable expression so often used (Matt. vii. 23 ; Matt. xxv. 12 ; Luke xiii. 27), "*I never knew you—I know you not.*" O the happiness, then, of the godly ! happy now, and still happier in that day which now hastens on, when the Husbandman shall separate "the chaff" from the wheat, and the kingdoms of earth be broken in pieces " like the chaff of the summer threshing-floor," and " the wind shall carry them away." O the folly of those who " *sit in the seat of the scorners,*" and ask in these last days (2 Pet. iii. 3), " Where is the promise of his coming ?"

We have noticed that our Lord seems to quote one of the expressions of this Psalm ; and let us see how we may suppose it all read by him in the days of his flesh. We know He read it ; his delight was in the law of the Lord ; and often has he quoted the book of Psalms. As he read, it would be natural to his human soul to appropriate the blessedness pronounced on the godly ; for he knew and felt himself to be indeed *The godly,* who "had not walked in the counsels of the ungodly, nor stood in the way of sinners, nor sat in the seat of the scornful." He felt himself able to say at all times, " Thy law is within my heart !" Was He not the true palm-tree ? Was He not the true pomegranate-tree ? Can we help thinking on Him as alone realizing the description in this Psalm ? The members of his mystical Body, in their measure, aim at this holy walk ; but it is only in him that they see it perfectly exemplified. " *His leaf never withered ;*" " he did no sin, neither was guile found in his mouth" (1 Peter. ii. 22) ; " *he yielded his fruit in its season,*" obeying his mother Mary, and being found about his Father's business ; going up to the feast " when his hour was come," and suffering, when the time appointed came ; everything " in *season.*" And " *all he did prospered ;*" he finished the work given him to do (John xvii. 4), and because

Used by Christ, the Head.

of his completed work, "therefore God hath highly exalted him," (Philip. ii. 8, 9).

Used by the members. We who are his members seek to realize all this in our measure. We seek that everything in us should be to the glory of God—heart, words, actions—all that may adorn the gospel, as well as all that is directly holy. Having the imputed righteousness of this Saviour, we earnestly long to have his holiness imparted too; though conscious that He alone comes up to the picture drawn here so beautifully. In either view, we may inscribe as the title of this Psalm,

The blessed path of the Righteous One.

Psalm 2

1 WHY do the heathen rage, and the people imagine a vain thing?

2 The kings of the earth set themselves, and the rulers take counsel together, Against the Lord, and against his anointed, saying,

3 Let us break their bands asunder, and cast away their cords from us.

4 He that sitteth in the heavens shall laugh:—the Lord shall have them in derision.

5 Then shall he speak unto them in his wrath, and vex them in his sore displeasure.

6 Yet have I set my king upon my holy hill of Zion.

7 I will declare the decree:—the Lord hath said unto me, Thou art my Son; this day have I begotten thee.

8 Ask of me, and I shall give thee the heathen for thine inheritance, And the uttermost parts of the earth for thy possession.

9 Thou shalt break them with a rod of iron; Thou shalt dash them in pieces like a potter's vessel.

10 Be wise now therefore, O ye kings: be instructed, ye judges of the earth.

11 Serve the Lord with fear, and rejoice with trembling.

12 Kiss the Son, lest he be angry, And ye perish from the way,—when his wrath is kindled but a little. Blessed are all they that put their trust in him.

Referred to Acts 13 WE have a quotation from this Psalm in Acts xiii. 33, where recent criticism reads, "As it is written in the *first* Psalm." It is not unlikely that it had at one time been considered as a second part of Psalm i., instead of standing as a separate hymn of praise. But, at all events, it is an appropriate advance upon the preceding, inasmuch as it places before us the Righteous One in a new position. The view taken of Messiah by the world and by Jehovah is the theme ; our eye is fixed on the purpose of Jehovah, triumphantly accomplished in Messiah's glory, in spite of all opposition. Nor let us forget the quotation of ver. 1, 2, in Acts iv. 23, which countenances us in asserting that it speaks of the fierce enmity of the world to the Righteous One from the period of his First coming onward to his Second appearing. The nations, or Gentiles (גוֹיִם), have raged, and the tribes of Israel (לְאֻמִּים) have agreed in hostility to the Lord's Messiah, ever since the day when Jew and Gentile met at Calvary to kill the Prince of life ; and their rage is not evaporated, but shall be manifested more fiercely still when the beast and the false prophet lead on their hosts to Armageddon. It is quoted with reference to that day in Rev. ii. 27, xi. 18 ; and xix. 15, quotes " the rod of iron," from ver. 9.

Perhaps the expression used so frequently in the epistles, *"fear and trembling,"* is taken from ver. 11. It is used in exhortations to servants (Ephes. vi. 5) regarding duty ; in Philip. ii. 13, to all believers engaged in striving for holiness ; while in 1 Corinth. ii. 3, Paul describes his state of mind in his ministry at Corinth by these terms. May there not be a reference in all these, and similar passages, to our Psalm ? It is as if it had been said, Remember our instructions for serving our King Messiah, in prospect of his glorious coming and kingdom—" Serve the Lord with fear, and rejoice with trembling." *Referred to in The Epistles.*

Even the Jews are pretty nearly agreed that no other than Messiah is the theme of the sweet singer of Israel here. *" Anointed"* is considered as decisive—it is *Messiah, Christ.* By some readers, however, the introduction of Christ by the name of " *Son,*" in ver. 7, and then in ver. 12, (where the rarer term בַּר occurs, probably because poetical and lofty, as in Prov. xxxi. 2,) has been thought abrupt. But, abrupt as it may seem, there is no doubt hanging over the application. Messiah is " *my Son,*" and so exclusively pre-eminent in this, that Jehovah, pointing to him, calls on all men to honour *Referred to in the Gospel.*

the Son even as they honour the Father—"Kiss *the Son*." Had not our Lord this very passage in his eye when he spoke these words (John v. 23): "The Father hath committed *all judgment* to the Son, that all men should honour the Son even as they honour the Father?" And it is thus we can understand how the term "*Father,*" as applied to Godhead, broke upon the ear of Israel without exciting surprise, when John the Baptist (John i. 18), spoke of the "only begotten *Son* who is in the bosom of *the Father.*" Son and Father are co-relative terms, and would be so understood by John.

Referred to in the Apocalypse.

Whether, with Hengstenberg and most other interpreters, we render ver. 12, "*A little while and his wrath shall be kindled,*" or retain the common version, there is, no doubt, a reference to this verse in Rev. vi. 16, 17: "The *wrath* of the Lamb, . . . and who shall be able to *stand?*" And if the former rendering be adopted, as we believe it ought, then there is a tacit reference to this passage in the New Testament expression, Rev. xxii. 7, "I come quickly." It is as if he said, Come quickly to that Saviour for eternal life ; for lo ! he cometh quickly to deal with all who obey not the Gospel. Opposition ends in ruin ; submission brings a blessedness, the fulness of which shall be known only on the day of wrath.

The scope.

But let us examine the contents of this rich and lofty Psalm. The plan of it is simple, but very grand. Messiah, on the morning when he broke the bands of death, is contemplating our world lying in wickedness. He beholds a sea of raging hatred and hostility dashing its angry waves on the throne of God and his anointed One.* He hears their scornful words, "Let us break their bands asunder," and marvels at their infatuation. For, lo ! in the heavens above, Jehovah sits in long-suffering calmness, till their stubborn and long-lasting enmity compels him to arise against them. He "*troubles them*" (ver. 5) as he did the Egyptians at the Red Sea, and referring to their haughty words, declares (ver. 6) "They on their part so speak, and I (אֲנִי) in spite of them, have set my king in Zion." They may try to make Rome, or

---

* We might notice a reference to 1 Sam. ii. 10, the original source of " *anointed,*" if not of " *king,*" also in connexion with " *anointed.*"

any other city, their metropolis, and may set up a head to themselves, but Jehovah will set up his King, and make Zion —the platform of Jerusalem—his metropolis, as certainly as he set David on the throne and made Zion his capital. From that city of the greater than David has gone and shall again go forth the law. Yes, says Messiah, I will proclaim Jehovah's resolution or decree ; He has said to me, "*Thou art my Son.*" At his resurrection (Rom. i. 3) he was saluted as "*Son,*" because appearing then in his own proper array ; no more hid in humiliation. He had been *Son* from eternity, but having dived under our ocean of sin and misery, his sonship seemed obscured till he emerged at his resurrection on the third day. (Acts xiii. 33.) And even so again, when he appears in glory at his coming, investing his own with their resurrection-dress (their proper clothing as adopted sons), the long-unseen Son of God shall be saluted as "*My Son*" by the Father as he places him on his visible throne. At what time that manifestation shall occur depends on his own request (ver. 8)—a request which he shall prefer whenever his purposes are ripe—and then He arises to shake terribly the earth. Does the reader not recognise in ver. 10, the voice of the tender, long-suffering, compassionate Saviour? It resembles his mode of expostulation in Proverbs i. 23, in prospect of that "*laugh*" which is the extreme opposite of pity, and which is referred to in Prov. i. 26, as used by himself against his unyielding foes, even as it is here by the Father. (Ver. 4.) Come, then, great and small, fall upon his neck, and be reconciled now. Be well pleased with him with whom the Father is well pleased ; "Kiss the Son,"— this is saving faith. For, "Yet *a little while and his wrath shall be kindled.*" (Ver. 12.) Behold, he comes quickly ! Blessed are all they who put their trust in him.

It is not, then, to be forgotten that the time when Messiah utters these strains is supposed to be the time of his *resurrection.* This seems to be declared to us in Acts xiii. 33. He had felt the united assault of earth and hell, but had proved all to be vain ; for He that sat in heaven had gloriously raised him from the dead, and his enemies had sunk to the ground as dead men. We might imagine this Psalm poured forth by him as he stood in Joseph's garden, beholding the empty sepulchre on the one hand, and the glory at the right hand of the Father on the other. It is thus we easily understand the words in ver. 7: " *This day* have I begotten thee ;" the Father declaring him his " *only begotten*," by raising him from the dead, and doing this as a pledge of his farther exaltation,—placing him (ver. 8) in the position of *Intercessor*, ere he shall arise to return as acknowledged Conqueror and King.

Connection with the preecding Psalm.

Glancing back now upon Psalm i., in connection with this more lofty and triumphant song, we see how appropriately the book of Israel's sacred songs has begun. It has sketched to us the calm, holy path of the righteous, and then the final results in the day of victory, when the Anointed shall have put down all enemies, and the way of the ungodly shall have perished. We shall meet with these topics continually recurring in the course of the book; it was good, then, to present an epitome at the outset.

Glancing, also, at particular expressions in both psalms, we see, at the beginning and end, links of connection with the preceding, in such expressions as ver. 1, "*meditating* a vain thing," in contrast to the *meditating* on the law (Psa. i. 3), while " the way of the ungodly shall *perish*," in Psalm i. 8, is brought to mind when we read in ver. 12 of " their *perishing from the way.*" It carries our thoughts to Joshua xxiii. 16. as Psa. i. 3 did to Joshua i. 8. And does not the Baptist get his expression, " chaff he shall burn with unquenchable fire" (Matt. iii. 12) by joining Psa. i. 4, and ii. 12 ?

Used by Christ.

Our Lord, when on earth, might read this Psalm as his history,—the Righteous One, who ever meditated on the law of the Lord, and kept aloof from the vain meditations of the heathen, opposed by men who could not submit to the restraints of holiness, but in spite of all, exalted at length to honour. For here we have Messiah, (the head of every one who seeks Jehovah's face), exhibited in his majesty, and in full prospect of final triumph. The subject of the whole may thus be said to be the assertion of " the righteous One's claims to the throne." Some one has proposed to entitle it rather, " *The eternal decree*," in reference to ver. 6, of which the Psalm might be spoken of as the development. But inasmuch as the Eternal decree forms only one topic, while the burden is Messiah himself directly, it is undoubtedly more exact and descriptive to give as its title,

The certainty of the Righteous One's exaltation to the throne.

Psalm 3

A Psalm of David, when he fled from Absalom his son.

1 LORD, how are they increased that trouble me! many are they that rise up against me.
2 Many there be which say of my soul, There is no help for him in God. Selah.
3 But thou, O Lord, art a shield for me; my glory, and the lifter up of mine head.
4 I cried unto the Lord with my voice,—and he heard me out of his holy hill. Selah.
5 I laid me down and slept ;—I awaked ; for the Lord sustained me.
6 I will not be afraid of ten thousands of people,—that have set themselves against me round about.
7 Arise, O Lord ; save me, O my God !
   For thou hast smitten all mine enemies upon the cheek-bone :
   Thou hast broken the teeth of the ungodly.
8 Salvation belongeth unto the Lord:—thy blessing is upon thy people. Selah.

THERE is strong evidence for the genuineness of the titles of the Psalms ; they occur in all the Hebrew Manuscripts.* This Psalm was written by David, " when *he fled from Absalom his son.*" The Holy Ghost may have used these circumstances in David's lot, as an appropriate occasion on which to dictate such a hymn of hopeful confidence in the Lord. *The title.*

The connection with Psalm ii., is natural, whether we look to David's case when he penned it, or to the more general circumstances referred to throughout. When the men of Israel refused David as "King in Zion," (God's chosen type of a greater King), it was natural for him to raise the cry to the Lord, *The connection with the preceding.*

* There are only *thirty-three* of the Psalms that have no title at all, and these are called by the Jews, "Orphan Psalms."

" Lord, how are they increased that trouble me." (Compare
2 Sam. xv. 12.) And not less natural is it to place this cry
next to the closing verses of Psalm ii., a Psalm wherein we
were told how men despised His call and plotted against Jehovah and his Christ. Hengstenberg has remarked :—" It is
certainly not to be regarded as an accident that Psalms the
third and fourth follow immediately the first and second. They,
as well as Psalm second, are occupied with a revolt against
the Lord's Anointed. And when, in ver. 8, the enemy is
spoken of as *' smitten on the cheek-bone, and his teeth broken,'*
there is the same tone of conscious safety, mingled with contempt of their efforts, as in the *' laugh'* of Psalm ii."

A Psalm for all ages.
It is a Psalm that may be found as suitable and needful in
the latter days, as when David wrote it. When waves of sorrow and calamity are dashing over the ship of the Church, it
may borrow from this Psalm that ground of hope which long
ago Jonah borrowed from it in his strange trial, *" Salvation is
of the Lord,"* (Jonah ii. 9.) " Affliction and desertion are
two very different things, but often confounded by the world,"
and confounded too " by the fearful imaginations of our own
desponding hearts, and the suggestions of our adversary."—
Horne.

Used by the Head.
This seems to be a *morning hymn* (ver. 5.) And so Horsley
hesitates not to call it " A prayer of Messiah, in the character
of a Priest, coming at an early hour to prepare the altar of
burnt-offering for the morning sacrifice." Every member of
Christ may use it ; and we can easily see how the Head himself could adopt it as his own. We feel as if sympathy were
more sure to us, when we know that the Lord Jesus himself
once was in circumstances when such a morning hymn expressed his state and feelings ; for now every believer can say,
" My Head once used this Psalm ; and while I use its strains,
his human heart will recall the day of his humiliation, when
himself was comforted thereby."

Who more truly than he could say of his foes, *"How many!"*
since it was " *the world*" that hated him. (John vii. 7.) On
the cross, did they not upbraid him with the taunt, " There is
no salvation for him in God," (ver. 2), when they cast in his

teeth, "*If he will have him*" (Matt. xxvii. 43) ; saying it not only *of* him, but *to* him ? But (as in Psalm xxii.,) he cried unceasingly in the Father's ear the more his foes reviled—" *I cry—he heareth.*" Often he retired to the Mount of Olives, and either amid its olives or at Bethany, "lay down and slept," after enduring the contradiction of sinners all day long ; yes, even after such a day as that whereon they took up stones to stone him. He foresaw the ruin of these foes, (ver. 7), when the Lord should arise.* What a victory ! and all the glory of it belonging to the Lord, and all the blessing to his people ! (ver. 8.)

A believer can take up every clause, and sing it all in sympathy with his Head ; hated by the same world that hated him ; loved and kept by the same Father that lifted up his head ; heard and answered and sustained as he was, and entering on with him final victory in the latter day. It was fitting to put the arresting mark, "*Selah,*" at ver. 2, where the foes are spoken of ; at ver. 4, where the cry and its answer are declared ; and at ver. 8, where the final result appears. "*Selah,*" whatever be its etymology,† marks a proper place to pause and ponder. (*Hengstenberg.*) Here each Selah stops us at a scene in which there is spread before our eyes sufficient for the time ; *first,* the host of foes, as far as eye can reach ; *next,* the one suppliant crying into the ears of the Lord of hosts ; and, *lastly,* that one suppliant's secure repose, certain of present safety and future triumph. May we not, then, justly entitle this Psalm,

Used by the Members.

The three Selahs, v. 2, 4, 8

The Righteous One's safety amid foes ?

---

* The English Prayer-Book translation is, "Up, Lord, and help me;" reminding us of the sudden unexpected rise of the Guards at Waterloo, after long and patient waiting for the seasonable moment.

† Gesenius' [Gramm. § 93,] thinks that in סֶלָה the ָה is *motion towards*, *q. d. ad silentium ;* and in that case the root is related to שָׁלָה, to be still.

Psalm 4

To the chief Musician on Neginoth, A Psalm of David

1 HEAR me when I call, O God of my righteousness .
Thou hast enlarged me when I was in distress ;
Have mercy upon me and hear my prayer.
2 O ye sons of men, how long will ye turn my glory into shame ?
How long will ye love vanity, and seek after leasing ?   Selah.
3 But know that the Lord hath set apart him that is godly for himself:
The Lord will hear when I call unto him.
4 Stand in awe and sin not :
Commune with your own heart upon your bed, and be still.   Selah.
5 Offer the sacrifices of righteousness,—and put your trust in the Lord.
6 There be many that say, Who will shew us any good ?
Lord, lift thou up the light of thy countenance upon us.
7 Thou hast put gladness in my heart,
More than in the time that their corn and their wine increased.
8 I will both lay me down in peace and sleep :
For thou, Lord, only makest me dwell in safety.

The title.

THERE is no solid reason for doubting the genuineness of those titles, or inscriptions, that are prefixed to many of the Psalms. They are as ancient as the text of the Psalms themselves.   The ancient versions prove that they are no modern addition.   If, then, we may put confidence in them, why is it that so frequently these fragmentary marks are so obscure ?   Every one feels their obscurity ; for to this day no criticism has succeeded

Neginoth.

in satisfactorily shewing the true sense of " On *Neginoth*," and similar terms.   *Musical instruments* are almost always referred to in these terms ; but these joyful instruments of holy service have been lost in the ruin of Israel's temple.   It is somewhat, however, for us to know that the times of the *true* David and Solomon were typified, as to their manifold streams of joy, by the " *Neginoth*," " *Sheminith*," and similar forms of the harp and psaltery.

The Psalm before us, describing the chief good, was one sung on Zion, in the tabernacle, and afterwards in the temple, on the " *Neginoth*," some stringed instrument, played upon by the stroke of the fingers, or of the musician's plectrum.   Its theme calls for a joyous instrument.

It is the first Psalm we have found inscribed, " *To the Chief* The chief *Musician,*" and there is an interesting propriety in this being musician. the first so inscribed. For, its subject being throughout Jehovah as the chief good —Israel's true blessedness—what more fitting than to give it to be sung in the midst of all the people by Asaph, the leader of the sacred music in the days of David ? (1 Chron. xvi. 5.)* May we not suppose that the " *Chief Musician"* occupied a high place in the typical economy ? Was he not used by the Lord to represent to Israel Him who is to lead the praise of the great congregation ? (Psalm xxii. 25.) When he sang such deeply melancholy Psalms as the twenty-second was the scene not fitted to bring into the minds of God's people the idea of the suffering Saviour, passing from the unutterable groanings to the joy unspeakable ?

This Psalm takes a survey of earth's best enjoyments—the sons of men revelling in the plenty of corn and wine, the The scope of joy of harvest and of vintage. Their mirth is loud, their the Psalm. mockery of less mirthful ones than themselves is keen, vanity is their pursuit, false joys their fascinations. To such a gay multitude our Psalm represents One approaching who has come from weeping in secret places. (Ver. 1.) Entering their circle, this Righteous One calls upon them to consider their ways : " *O ye sons of men,*" is his cry, " *how long will ye turn my glory into shame ? How long will ye love vanity and seek after lies ?*"† When will you leave broken cisterns ? When will you turn from the golden calf back to the God of Israel, your glory ? A pause ensues—" *Selah"* marks it. It is the silence of one who waits for the effect of his expostulation ; but there is no response, and he lifts up his

---

* There are fifty-three Psalms which bears this inscription, " To the Chief Musician." The word מְנַצֵּחַ never means " Conqueror," as some have wished to render it. It means always "standing over," as a foreman, and is used only of the arrangements made in regard to the Levites in their courses. (See Hengstenberg, who confesses this by Hab. iii. 19.)

† It has been observed, that, for the sake of all ages, the psalmist is led by the Holy Ghost to use terms such as "*glory*," a term which describes whatever man values ; "*lies*," which may include under it every degree and species of deception ; and "*vanity*," expressive of all those earthly, unsatisfying objects sought after by rich and poor.

voice again, and leaves his testimony among them : " *But know the Lord hath set apart the godly for himself.*" The Lord keeps the godly ; each such man is like the witnesses of Revelation xi. 6 : " These have power to shut heaven, and to smite the earth ;" for " *The Lord heareth when I call upon him.*" Well then may the sons of men give ear. " Stand in awe—consider —flee to the atoning sacrifices appointed by the *God of my righteousness*" (ver. 1). Having so done stay yourselves on Him ; for I testify that the experience of all who have tried this plan of happiness has been such that they can answer the question, " *Who can shew us any good ?*" by an upward look to Jehovah, "*Lord, lift thou on us the light of thy countenance !*" Yes, (says the speaker to his God, to whom he had cast his upward glance, and by whose look of love he seems riveted,) no sooner did my prayer ascend than the answer came ; no sooner did I look to Him than the sun broke through the dark clouds. " Thou *hast put more gladness in my heart than in the time when their corn and wine abound. I lay me down and sleep in peace ; for thou, Lord,* (giving me the full portion of Israel dwelling in their land of corn and wine, with its heavens dropping dew, Deut. xxxiii. 28,) *makest me to dwell in safety, all alone !*"

There is an undoubted allusion in the last verse, in the לְבָדָד לָבֶטַח to the blessing of Moses in Deut. xxxiii. 28, where Israel's final destiny is declared to be " dwelling בֶּטַח בָּדָד. in undisturbed security alone," and needing none to help or bless them but Jehovah. In this Psalm the godly one anticipates that blessedness as yet to be his portion, and so we see him fixing his eye on the *future,* even while at present his gladness is greater far than all earth can yield. The vanity of the sons of men is all the more clearly seen in the additional light of the coming glory.

Used by the Head.

We can easily understand how any true child of God can use these words—they so exactly delineate his state of feeling both toward his God, and toward his fellow-men. But in no lips could they be so appropriate as in His "who spake as never man spake." Indeed, is there not throughout a tone like that of "*Wisdom*," in Proverbs i. and viii. ? The party addressed is the "sons of men," as there ; and there is the same expostulatory and anxious voice, "*How long, ye simple ones ?*" (i. 22). "*Hear, for I will speak of excellent things,*" (viii. 6). We might imagine 'every syllable of this precious Psalm used by our Master some evening, when about to leave the Temple for the day, and retiring to his wonted rest at Bethany, (ver. 8), after another fruitless expostulation with the men of Israel. And we may read it still as the very utterance of his heart, longing over man, and delighting in God.

Used by the members.

But further, not only is this the utterance of the Head, it is also the language of one of his members in full sympathy with him in holy feeling. This is a Psalm with which the righteous may make their dwellings resound, morning and evening, as they cast a sad look over a world that rejects God's grace. They may sing it while they cling more and more every day to Jehovah, as their all-sufficient heritage, now and in the age to come. They may sing it, too, in the happy confidence of faith and hope, when the evening of this world's day is coming, and may then fall asleep in the certainty of what shall greet their eyes on the Resurrection morning-

> Sleeping embosomed in his grace
> 'Till morning-shadows flee.

If, therefore, we were required to state the substance of this Psalm in a few words, we should scarcely err in describing its theme as

The Godly One's Chief Good.

Psalm 5

To the Chief Musician upon Nehiloth, A Psalm of David

1 Give ear to my words, O Lord ; consider my meditation.

2 Hearken unto the voice of my cry, my King, and my God ;—for unto thee will I pray.

3 My voice shalt thou hear in the morning, O Lord ;
In the morning will I direct my prayer unto thee, and will look up.

4 For thou art not a God that hath pleasure in wickedness ; neither shall evil dwell with thee.

5 The foolish shall not stand in thy sight ; thou hatest all workers of iniquity.

6 Thou shalt destroy them that speak leasing :
The Lord will abhor the bloody and deceitful man.
7 But as for me, I will come into thy house in the multitude of thy mercy :
And in thy fear will I worship toward thy holy temple.
8 Lead me, O Lord, in thy righteousness because of mine enemies ;
Make thy way straight before my face.
9 For there is no faithfulness in their mouth ; their inward part is very wickedness ;
Their throat is an open sepulchre ; they flatter with their tongue.
10 Destroy thou them, O God ; let them fall by their own counsels ;
Cast them out in the multitude of their transgressions ;—for they have rebelled against thee.
11 But let all those that put their trust in thee rejoice :
Let them ever shout for joy, because thou defendest them :
Let them also that love thy name be joyful in thee.
12 For thou, Lord, wilt bless the righteous ;
With favour wilt thou compass him as with a shield.

The Title.

ANOTHER song of the sweet singer of Israel, handed over to the " Chief Musician," who was to fit it to be publicly sung

Nehiloth.

" on the *Nehiloth*." This was some one of the many musical instruments now unknown, lost to us ever since Israel hung their harp on the willows, and had their joy turned into mourning *—though generally understood to be a wind instrument, or pipe, of some sort.

Prophetic reference.

There is in it a prophetic element toward the close. In ver. 10, 11, we have something that closely resembles the Apocalyptic scene in Revelation xix. 1, 3, 4. The psalmist so fully

Apparent imprecations on foes.

sympathises in the justice of the doom that is coming on the obstinate and impenitent rebels against God, that he cries aloud, " *Destroy them, O God !*" or, more exactly, " Hold them guilty, and treat them as such." On the other hand, there

---

* The idea of Hengstenberg, that this and some others of the titles convey a mystical meaning, or enigmatical sense, is quite fanciful. He renders this, " *On the lots*," as being a Psalm that exhibits the different lots of righteous and wicked. But is not the *conduct and life* of the two classes exhibited in it, far more than the *lot ?* The objection that אֶל is not used with stringed instruments, is a gratuitous assertion ; probably אֶל is used, instead of עַל, because of some peculiarity in using the instrument. Tholuck remarks, somewhere, that ancient performers were not able to play different tunes on the same instruments, but employed separate instruments for different tunes.

arises at the same moment the shout of the righteous, acquies-
cing with entire satisfaction in their doom : " *And let all those
that put their trust in thee, rejoice ! Let them ever shout for
joy !*" This is their " Halelujah" over the rising smoke of torment—their " Glory and honour to the Lord our God." And
perhaps it is in this manner we are to understand, throughout
the Book of Psalms, all those portions where we find, apparently,
prayers that breathe revenge. They are never to be thought
of as anything else than the *breathed assent of righteous souls*
to the justice of their God, who taketh vengeance on sin. When
taken as the words of Christ himself, they are no other than
an echo of the Intercessor's acquiescence at last in the sentence
on the barren fig-tree. It is as if he cried aloud, "Hew it down
now—I will intercede no longer—the doom is righteous, *destroy
them, O God ; cast them out in* (or, for) *the multitude of their
transgressions! for they have rebelled against thee.*" And in
the same moment ·he may be supposed to invite his saints to
sympathize in his decision ; just as in Revelation xviii. 20 :
" Rejoice over her, thou heaven, and ye holy apostles and prophets !" In like manner, when one of Christ's members, in
entire sympathy with his head, views the barren fig-tree from
the same point of observation, and sees the glory of God concerned in inflicting the blow, he too can cry, "Let the axe
smite !" Had Abraham stood beside the angel who destroyed
Sodom, and seen how Jehovah's name required the ruin of these
impenitent rebels, he would have cried out, " Let the shower
descend—let the fire and brimstone come down !" not in any
spirit of revenge—not from want of tender love to souls—but
from intense earnestness of concern for the glory of his God.

We consider this explanation to be the real key that opens
all the difficult passages in this book, where curses seem to be
called for on the head of the ungodly. They are no more than
a carrying out of Deut. xxvii. 15–26,—" Let all the people
say, Amen," and an entering into the Lord's holy abhorrence
of sin and delight in acts of justice expressed in the " Amen,
hallelujah," of Rev. xix. 3.*

---

* " *Truth*," says one, "is always a form of *Charity* ; or to speak more properly,
Truth is the soul of which *Charity* is but the beautiful, graceful, and lovely

But let us read the whole Psalm. And we may notice that here the words occur, for the first time, " My *King* and my *God.*" On this Augustine remarks, " Recte primo ' *Rex meus,*' et deinde *Deus meus,*' secundum illud quod dictum est, ' Per me itur ad Patrem.'" He that is peculiarly " King" to Israel is on Israel's side, for 1 Sam. viii. 20 shews that the idea included in this term is fighting for his subjects. The blue, (Exod. viii. 15), purple, and scarlet, at the gate of the Tabernacle, and on all its veils, proclaimed, " This is the dwelling of Israel's *King,* as well as Israel's *God.*"

We seem to see One going up to the Tabernacle early, in prospect of the morning sacrifice. It is near the time ; the priest is already at the altar, setting the wood in order, and the Lamb is bound to the altar's horns ; the worshipper's eye and heart are upward,—" Give ear to my words, O Lord, consider my *silent prayer*" (ver. 1), a prayer made up of the " unutterable groanings" (Rom. viii. 26), and which can be heard, as well as presented, while he stands amid the crowd that are gathering in the courts. " My voice shalt thou hear in the morning" (ver. 3), is the expression of a resolution habitually to come before him early,—" My earliest cry shall always be to thee ; in the morning will I direct my (spiritual) offering unto thee, and will look up to that house of prayer where stand the altar and the mercy-seat, and where God is revealed in grace." The altar presents " God reconciling the world unto himself, not imputing unto men their trespasses." Jehovah's look of love is there ; his voice is love from its four horns ; everything tells man of grace.

He is up early, securing the best hour of the day, "like a diligent artificer," (Horne). But how careless are those around this worshipper ; some coming up to the altar to lull their conscience asleep by the formality of a visit to the courts of God ; others hurrying off to their earthly pursuits. This leads him

member. Charity, therefore, is not to be known by soft words and gentle actions, which are oftener the form of policy and courtesy ; but must be sought in the principles of the heart, out of which our words, thoughts, and actions come forth. Is it love to God by which we are moved ? Then it is charity, be its form mildness, or zeal, or the stern inflictions of justice."

to meditate before God on the "world lying in wickedness" (ver. 4–9), interposing his own resolute determination to be unlike that world (ver. 7) by the help of Jehovah (ver. 8). A "*dwelling with God*," which at the lowest means friendly intercourse, is what his righteous soul relishes and revels in the enjoyment of, and the want of this he reckons to be the misery of the ungodly. (Ver 4.) This is the very spirit of the beloved John (1 John. iv. 16),—" He that dwelleth in love, *dwelleth in God*, and God in him ;" and the resemblance is all the closer when we find ver. 7 speak of his coming " *in the multitude of thy mercy*," or "greatness of *thy love*," to worship in Jehovah's " Holy Temple." And then the believer's soul prays to be led by the pillar cloud of divine wisdom, knowing the snares of his foes.

It is after this that he is brought into such deep sympathy with the holy purposes and righteous sentences of Jehovah, in whose love he dwells, as to cry, " *Destroy them*, O God," (ver. 10). And we leave him singing with assured confidence, " For thou, O Lord, wilt bless the righteous ; with favour thou wilt compass him, as with a shield."

It is a Psalm which most certainly Messiah could use ; none could ever use it so fully as He. Think of Him, some morning leaving Bethany early that He may be in time for the morning sacrifice, and breathing forth this Psalm by the way and as He enters the Temple-courts. Every word of it becomes doubly emphatic in his lips, down to the last verse, where we see Him as " *The* Righteous One," encompassed with the Father's love and well-pleasedness. But whether we read it as peculiarly the utterance of Messiah, or as that of one of his members, we may describe this Psalm as being

The Righteous One's thoughts of God and of man while going up to the morning sacrifice.

How Christ our Head would use it.

Psalm 6

To the chief Musician on Neginoth upon Sheminith, A Psalm of David

1 O LORD, rebuke me not in thine anger,—neither chasten me in thy hot displeasure.

2 Have mercy upon me, O Lord; for I am weak: O Lord, heal me; for my bones are vexed.

3 My soul is also sore vexed:—but thou, O Lord, how long?

4 Return, O Lord, deliver my soul:—oh save me for thy mercies' sake !

5 For in death there is no remembrance of thee :—in the grave who shall give thee thanks?

6 I am weary with my groaning!
All the night make I my bed to swim ;—I water my couch with my tears.

7 Mine eye is consumed because of grief;—it waxeth old because of all mine enemies.

8 Depart from me, all ye workers of iniquity ; for the Lord hath heard the voice of my weeping.

9 The Lord hath heard my supplication ;—the Lord will receive my prayer.

10 Let all mine enemies be ashamed and sore vexed:
Let them return and be ashamed suddenly.

The title.

HITHERTO, the harp of Judah, and the sacred instruments of varied chords, have sounded little concerning the Just One's inward sorrows. But now the Psalmist points "the Chief Musician" to the "*Neginoth*," mentioned in Psalm iv., and at

Sheminith.

the same time to "*Sheminith*,"† some eight-stringed instrument, as if both together must be used for a theme so intensely melancholy as these verses handle.

The members of Christ.

We might at once say to the reader, This is not David, it is the Son of David ; the grief is too deep for any other,-

"*You never saw a vessel of like sorrow.*"

---

* This Psalm, and Psalms xxxii, xxxviii, li, cii, cxxx, cxl, and cxlii, seven in all, form "the *Penitential Psalms*"—which in Popish days a penitent was taught to use, as Naaman at Jordan, and the lepers at purification, used a sevenfold washing or sprinkling.

† Augustine has a long passage in which he discusses the question, whether there is any reference to the *Last Day* in the number "*eight ;*" and is inclined to think that the Eternal Day may be meant. Some recent critics find an "*octave*" in the word, and others "*the eighth tune.*" This very obscurity as to the sense of such technical terms, confirms the proof of the indisputable antiquity of the writing, like some of those names in 1 Chronicles, for which we can find no etymology in written Hebrew.

David may have been led by the Holy Ghost to write it when in anguish of soul, as well as suffering of body ; through such a bruised reed the Spirit of God may have breathed. But surely he meant to tell of One greater than David,—"*the Man of sorrows.*" Perhaps David had some seasons of anguish in his wanderings in the wilderness of Judah that furnished a shadow of the grief of Him who was to come, " bearing our griefs and carrying our sorrows.*" Awakened souls experience horror of soul and alarming apprehensions of divine indignation, such as this Psalm expresses. A clear sight of sin, while the face of the Mediator is hid, produces this state of soul. Occasionally, too, believers feel, from peculiar causes, glooms that may be expressed in the words of this Psalm more fitly than any other. And particular clauses in it will express many of a believer's frames, even as ver. 6. " *Lord, how long?*" was Calvin's favourite utterance. Still, it is chiefly of the true David that this is written. We may suppose every word used by Him in some of those nights which He passed in desert places, or in the garden of Gethsemane.

What cries are these ? " *Lord, rebuke me not in thy wrath.*" *The Head.* Is not this the same voice that cried, " Father, if it be possible, remove this cup from me ?" Again : " *Have mercy upon me, O Lord, for I am weak.*" Is not this the same who said, " The spirit indeed is willing, but the flesh is *weak ?*" (Matt. xxvi. 34.) We listen, and again He cries, " *My soul is sore vexed.*" Is it not the voice of Him who, as He entered the garden, spoke with such affecting sadness to his disciples, " My soul is exceeding sorrowful ?" (Matt. xxvi. 38.) Yes, He said, " *even unto death.*" And in this Psalm we hear Him tell some of his forebodings of death. It seems to be the very hour referred to in Heb. vi. 7,—the hour of " strong crying and tears to Him who was able to save him from death." For here are his strong reasonings with God,—" *In death there is no remembrance of thee ; in the grave, who shall give thee thanks ?*" This expostulation undoubtedly is such as a member of Christ could use ; for Hezekiah used it (Isa. xxxviii. 18), pleading that, if taken away, he could do no more for the making known God's name and glory among men. But how peculiarly forcibly it becomes in the lips of Jesus ! If he be given over to death, *i.e.*, left under its power, then neither He, nor any one of all those whom the Father had given Him, can ever give praise. The dark night becomes darker. It is midnight. "*I am weary with my groaning. Mine eye is consumed with grief. It waxes old, because of all mine enemies.*" "The eye is the mirror and gauge of soundness, not merely as respects the soul, but the body also," says a well-known commentator. On his brow, anguish had shed more snows (see. John viii. 57,) than threescore winters, in their natural course, might else have sprinkled there; for inconceivably stupendous must His view of sin have been, and his sense of its loathsomeness, his discovery of its hurt to God and man, and his horror under the wrath due to it. But all at once there is a change. *The angel from heaven strengthens Him.* (Luke xxii. 43.) He is revived by the Father's promise, "I have glorified thee, and will glorify thee again." He sees his foes "confounded and terrified" by the look of that very countenance, which they once could spit upon (ver. 10).

Prophetic reference. It is only at this one point that this Psalm presents anything bearing on the prophetic future. But certainly it does at this turn present us with a glimpse of the *Second Coming* of Him whose First Coming was so full of woe. "The voice of the turtle is heard again," says a German commentator; and truly it is so. For, at ver. 8, the Suffering One sees "the glory that is to follow," and exclaims, "*Depart from me ye workers of iniquity,*" words which are employed by himself in Luke xiii. 27, in describing the terms in which, as judge, He will address the multitudes of the unsaved on the Great Day, when He has risen up and has shut to the door.

Was it not designed that this ending should draw more attention to the beginning? Let the sinner now consider the Suffering One, lest the sentence pass on him, "Depart." Come, and see here what a price was paid for the soul's redemption; and if you have felt anguish of spirit under a sense of deserved wrath, let it cease when you find the Man of sorrows presenting all his anguish as the atonement for your soul. Thus will the reader use aright this most pathetic Psalm, in meditating on which he is shewn—

The comfortless couch of the Righteous One.

Psalm 7

Shiggaion of David, which he sang unto the Lord, concerning the words of Cush the Benjamite

1 O LORD my God, in thee do I put my trust :
   Save me from all them that persecute me, and deliver me :
2 Lest he tear my soul like a lion, rending it in pieces, while there is none
   to deliver.
3 O Lord my God, if I have done this ;—if there be iniquity in my hands ;
4 If I have rewarded evil unto him that was at peace with me ;
   (Yea, I have delivered him that without cause is mine enemy !)
5 Let the enemy persecute my soul, and take it ;
   Yea, let him tread down my life upon the earth,—and lay mine honour in
   the dust. Selah.
6 Arise, O Lord, in thine anger,—lift up thyself because of the rage of mine
   enemies :
   And awake for me to the judgment that thou hast commanded.
7 So shall the congregation of the people compass thee about :
   For their sakes therefore return thou on high.
8 The Lord shall judge the people ! Judge me, O Lord,
   According to my righteousness, and according to mine integrity that is in
   me.
9 Oh let the wickedness of the wicked come to an end ;—but establish the just !
   For the righteous God trieth the hearts and reins.
10 My defence is of God, which saveth the upright in heart.
11 God judgeth the righteous,—and God is angry with the wicked every day.
12 If he turn not, he will whet his sword ;—he hath bent his bow, and made
   it ready.
13 He hath also prepared for him the instruments of death ;
   He ordaineth his arrows against the persecutors.
14 Behold, he travaileth with iniquity,
   And hath conceived mischief, and brought forth falsehood.
15 He made a pit, and digged it,—and is fallen into the ditch which he made.
16 His mischief shall return upon his own head.
   And his violent dealing shall come down upon his own pate.
17 I will praise the Lord according to his righteousness :
   And will sing praise to the name of the Lord most high.

THERE is something like excitement in the style of this Psalm. *The tone and title.*
We do not find in it the calm, deep cries of one in anguish,
but rather, the earnest, almost indignant, appeals of one whose
righteous soul is vexed by a world's opposition.

" *Jehovah, my God, in thee have I put my trust !*
Save me from my persecutors ! " (Ver. 1.)

It is the voice of one who betakes himself to Jehovah as his only Adullam-cave, and who makes his cave of refuge ring with his vehement appeals. Horsley remarks there is in it complaint, supplication, prediction, crimination, commination, and thanksgiving.

Shiggaion. "Shiggaion," though some have attempted to fix on it a reference to the moral aspect of the world as depicted in this Psalm, is in all probability to be taken as expressing the *nature of the composition.* It conveys the idea of something *erratic* (שָׁגָה, to wander), in the style; something not so calm as other psalms; and hence *Ewald* suggests, that it might be rendered, "a confused ode," a Dithyramb. This characteristic of excitement in the style, and a kind of disorder in the sense, suits Habakkuk iii. 1, the only other place where the word occurs.

The Contents. But who was *"Cush the Benjamite?"* None can give a decided answer, though all turn their eye to *Saul,* and seem nearly agreed that his calumnies against David gave occasion for the writing of this Psalm. The Targum hesitates not to say it is *"Saul, the son of Kish."* Hengstenberg concludes that *Cush,* the Ethiopian, is a name for Saul, because of his dark, black hatred of David; others refer the name to some one of Saul's retinue who was as *Ethiopian* in heart as his master. This last conjecture may be the truth; for David had a variety of foes. But at all events, the Holy Spirit made use of some special attack of some one foe as his time for conveying to his servant this song. He is a *"God who giveth songs in the night,"* and he has by this means given to his Church a song which every succeeding generation has felt appropriate in a world lying in wickedness, and which was never more appropriate than in these latter days.

Used by Christ. The true David, no doubt, took it up in the days of his flesh; and often may he have used it as part of his wondrous Liturgy, when alone in the hills of Galilee. The cry in ver. 9,-

> " O let the wickedness of the wicked come to an end !
> And establish the just !
> And the trier of the heart and reins be thou, O God ! "

followed up by ver. 10, *"My defence is in* God who saveth*

---

* Literally, " *My shield is upon God,*" like Psalm lxii. 8, " *My salvation is upon God.*" The idea may be taken from the armour-bearer, ever ready at hand to give the needed weapon to the warrior.

giveth victory to) *the upright in heart*," may remind us of
Him who elsewhere longs for the day of God in the words,
" Till the day break and the shadows flee away, I will get me
to the mountain of myrrh and the hill of frankincense."
From ver. 1 to ver. 5, innocence is pleaded against those   The Contents.
who are adversaries "*without a cause.*" This feature of enmity, "*without a cause,*" seems to have wounded the tender
heart of our David very deeply; for in John xv. 25, we find him
quoting another Psalm where the same words occur, and where
the emphasis lies on " *without a cause.*" The world has hated
him, because it hated the holiness that furnished no cause of
accusation ; and so has it hated his members because of what
resemblance they bear to their unblemished Head. The world's
enmity is ever directed against the only thing in the saints
which they are sure the Lord loves ; and so they can appeal
with their Head against " Those that *without cause* are our
adversaries."

After a *Selah*-pause (see Psalm iv.), the tone changes.
From ver. 6 onward, the future day of retribution comes into
view. What an importunate cry is raised in ver. 6, "*Arise,
O Lord, in thine anger*"—put on that fierce wrath which con-
sumes all before it. " *While thy foes are raging* (as in Psalm
ii. 1), *lift up thyself ;*" and all this because " Thou hast appointed a day in which thou wilt judge the world in righteousness." Had not Paul at Athens (Acts xvii. 31), his eye on this
verse : " *The judgment thou hast ordained ?*"

In ver. 7, we see all the tribes (לְאֻמִּים), gathered round the
Lord's tribunal ; and " *over that congregation,*" or assembly,
the Lord takes his seat—as if they were all met there, waiting
the arrival of the Judge, who does at last appear, and walks up
to his seat in the view of all. Is there not a reference to the
long-expected arrival of one who had gone for a time to a far
country in the word " return ?" (Luke xix. 12.)

And now, ver. 8. " *The Lord judges the nations,*" acting in
all the plenitude of the Judge's office—the office as held by
Othniel, and Ehud, and Gideon, and Samson. As to right and
wrong, he is what an ancient Roman was called, " *Scopulus
reorum*"—every guilty man makes shipwreck on that rock ;

but He is ruler, too, putting earth in order. And when the *Son of David* used this prayer, he was implicitly asking for the day of his own glory—when the Father shall be the Judge by committing all judgment to the Son. (John v. 22, 27.)

The remainder of this judgment-day Psalm presents us with views of the fearful overthrow of the ungodly—all of them doubly emphatic when understood as spoken by Him who had seen the armoury of heaven, "no man having ascended up to heaven, but He that came down from heaven," and who spake what he did know, and testified what he had seen. Whether we apply these verses to each individual sinner, or use them of the great Antichrist—that special ἄνομος, lawless one—the description is so constructed as to apply in terrible grandeur. We see Jehovah's daily anger (ver. 11), which is, in other words, his daily hatred of sin. "Judging righteously, while every day finding cause of anger." We hear him tell, that if yonder sinner return not (ver. 12, "*If a man turn not*"), then there is prepared for him the sword, as well as the bow, *q. d.*, there is the arrow from the bow aimed at his heart to lay him low, like Goliath laid low by the pebble in his forehead, and then the sword to complete the work of death. Let none think of recovering from the wound ; for his instruments are "*instruments of death*," and he "*makes his arrows burning*" (דֹּלְקִים) ; and he shoots his flaming shafts, burning with the fire of Almighty wrath, into their hearts ! All this the sinner has wrought for himself—all this *Antichrist* has wrought for himself—it is the cup he has filled, and filled double.

> "*Behold ! he travailed with mischief,* (אָוֶן)
>
> *And hath conceived misery !* (עָמָל)
>
> *And bringeth forth falsehood !*" (disappointment)

He is precipitated into "the pit" from the height of his prosperity. How brief, yet how comprehensive, is this sketch of his doom ! It is James i. 15 exhibited in each sinner's history, and in the final end of "*That Wicked*" whom the Lord shall destroy by the brightness of his coming.

Ver. 17, is the "*Hallelujah, amen !*" of Rev. xix. 1–4. And is not the whole Psalm one which we may well believe *the*

Head of the Church often used, and which each member uses still when in sympathy with the martyr-band (Rev. vi. 10) ?
In either view it is-

The Righteous One's cry for righteous retribution.

Psalm 8

To the chief Musician upon Gittith, A Psalm of David

1 O LORD our Lord, how excellent is thy name in all the earth!
Who hast set thy glory above the heavens.
2 Out of the mouth of babes and sucklings hast thou ordained strength
Because of thine enemies, that thou mightest still the enemy and the avenger.
3 When I consider thy heavens, the work of thy fingers,
The moon and the stars, which thou hast ordained ;
4 What is man, that thou art mindful of him ?—and the son of man, that thou visitest him ?
5 For thou hast made him a little lower than the angels,
And hast crowned him with glory and honour.
6 Thou madest him to have dominion over the works of thy hands ;
Thou hast put all things under his feet :
7 All sheep and oxen, yea, and the beasts of the field ;
8 The fowl of the air, and the fish of the sea,
And whatsoever passeth through the paths of the seas.
9 O Lord our Lord, how excellent is thy name in all the earth !

PSALM VII. closed with "*The name* of the Most High," and this Psalm commences with it. Who can hesitate to say of this song of Zion, that its subject is no other than "The Name that is above every name ?" For Heb. ii. 6–9 has claimed it for Jesus, and claimed it for him, too, in speaking of his exaltation in the New Earth, "The world to come." Paul, in 1 Cor. xv. 24, refers a clause of it for fulfilment to the day of the Advent : and it is interesting to find our Lord himself quoting ver. 2 in reference to the hosannas that welcomed him as Israel's King on that day when he proved his power over man and over the creatures, riding on the ass amid the shouts of thousands upon thousands. *The name.*

It is not to us of much moment whether the original Psalmist David knew distinctly the glorious burden of his *The title.*

song when the Holy Spirit taught his heart and harp to sing it, and when he gave it over to "the *chief musician*" for temple-use, to be sung or played " on *Gittith.*" *He* may have had as dim a view of its real reference, as *we* have of the reference of the term " Gittith ;" yet that alters not the Holy Spirit's meaning. The most skilful of our critics can do no more than give obscure suggestions as to what the title means ; yet that alters not the certainty that the title " *Gittith*" had its sure and definite meaning in the mind of Him who prefixed it. Our position and that of the original receivers of the Psalm is now reversed. Any singer of the Tabernacle could have told us at once whether *Gittith* meant a " *Gathic air,*" used by those that handled the harp at Gath, or whether it referred to the air of some *vintage-song,* or some joyous *vintage-instrument* (from גַּת) ; while yet they could not have told so surely as a child among us who can put his finger on Heb. ii. 6, 7, 8, that here is the crown that fell from our heads seen on the head of the Second Adam.

The theme.
Led by Heb. ii. 6–9, we find in this Psalm the manifestation of the *Lord's name** in the dominion of the Second Adam, when he reigns over a restored world. It has been said that this Psalm might be called " *Genesis* i. *turned into a prayer ;*" but it is more truly "*the Genesis* i. *of the* NEW *Earth.*" It corresponds to Isaiah xi. 6, 7, in the scene it exhibits.

It contains a general view of God's dealings with earth, from Genesis to Revelation. He whose glory crowns the heavens, chooses earth for a theatre whereon to display " *His name,*"—that is, his character, his very being, of which the name is the manifestation. Amid the ruins of the fall, He finds as sweet notes of praise ascending as from his angelic choirs ; he finds he can confound his foes—all the seed of the serpent, in hell and on earth (Psa. xliv. 16)—by hosannas from " babes and sucklings." While " *He sets his glory above the heavens,*" He finds no less glory to His name on earth. *Glorious grace* appears in choosing *earth* for the place of this manifestation (ver. 1). *Glorious grace* appears again in his

* "Name is the expression of his being, God existing secretly in himself is nameless. *Manifestation* and *name* are inseparable."—*Hengstenberg.*

working amid the feeblest of our feeble race, and in confounding the enemy and avenger by this display (ver. 2). *Glorious grace* is seen dealing with man, the worm (אֱנוֹשׁ, "sorry man"), whose dwelling and whose place in the scale of creation seem so low when compared with *the heavens* by day, lighted up by their blazing sun, or the *moon and stars* by night, in their silent majesty (ver. 4). *Glorious grace* lifts up man from his inferiority to angels (ver. 5). *Glorious grace* gives man exaltation above angels, in giving him a *Head*, to whom that whole world is subject, and on whom it leans. All that was lost in Adam is gathered up in this Head : " Thou madest Him to have dominion—thou hast put all things under his feet." It is a sight that, seen even from afar, raises in the prophetic Psalmist adoring wonder and delight, so that like the "*Amen*" in Rev. vii. 12, that both prefaces and concludes the angelic song, he begins and ends with the rapturous exclamation,—"*Jehovah, our Lord,** *how excellent is thy name in* ALL THE EARTH ! '

One difficulty in the Psalm may be solved by attending to the apostolic use of it in Heb. ii. It is the clause, " Thou hast made him a little lower than the angels." In Exod. xxii. 28, the word signifies "*judges ;*" and so it seems to have been used for other beings who are high and noble, viz., *angels*. For Heb. i. 6 again renders the word, "*angels.*" Some, however, would fain keep אֱלֹהִים in the sense of " God," and explain it to this effect : " Thou madest him want little of God," raising him to a super-earthly dignity. But let it be noted, that these interpretations are all inconsistent with Heb. ii. 6–9. That passage quotes this clause as referring to our *Lord's humiliation*, not to his *exaltation ;* " We see Jesus, who has been crowned (ἐστεφανωμένον) with glory and honour because of his suffering death,—we see this Jesus made a little lower than angels, in

A difficulty.

---

* The English Prayer-book version has it " *our Governor,*" a rendering that suits well with the scope of the whole. Luther's " *Herr unser Herrscher,*" is better than our " Lord our Lord," and than the similar rendering of the Vulgate and Septuagint. The Hebrew has the two distinct appellations יְהֹוָה אֲדֹנֵינוּ. And notice, too, " *How excellent*" אַדִּיר, is the same word as Jer. xxx. 21, " his אַדִּירוֹ noble one."

order to taste death for every one." The "*made lower*" is thus placed beyond doubt as signifying *humiliation;* the comparison being, not how little was between him and God, but how there was a little between him and angels, and that little on the side of apparent inferiority during the days of his humiliation—though only as a scaffolding for his after rising in our nature far beyond every angel.

Christ and his members. One other difficulty remains. At what point does the Psalm leave off the subject of *man in general,* and begin to speak of *man's Head ?* We think it is at the word "*Thou visitest.*" Out of this "*visiting*" emerges nothing less than man's exaltation in his Head ; and this sense of "*visiting*" seems referred to in Luke i. 68. (See Duke of Manchester on Epistle to the Hebrews.)

The still future manifestation of His name. As the "manifesting" Jehovah's "name" was our Lord's unvarying design in all his work at his first coming (John xvii. 6 and 26), so shall it still be his design at his second. Isaiah xxx. 27, introduces that event by, "Behold, the *name of the Lord* cometh." To this, indeed, he may refer, when in John xvii. 26, he says, that he not only "*has*" declared that "name," but that he "*will*" declare it." Have we not a link of connection here ? Our Psalm and that wondrous prayer in which he looked onward to coming glory, both speak much of that "Name." The dominion of the Second Adam shall carry on this discovery to the praise of his glory ; and viewing the Psalm as pointing to this, we may say, that it contains—

The manifestation of Jehovah's name in the dominion of the Son of man.

Psalm 9

To the Chief Musician upon Muth-labben, A Psalm of David

1 I WILL praise thee, O Lord, with my whole heart ;
  I will shew forth all thy marvellous works.

2 I will be glad and rejoice in thee :—I will sing praise to thy name, O thou Most High.

3 When mine enemies are turned back,—they shall fall and perish at thy presence.

4 For thou hast maintained my right and my cause ;—thou sattest in the throne judging right.

5 Thou hast rebuked the heathen,—thon hast destroyed the wicked, Thou hast put out their name for ever and ever.

6 O thou enemy, destructions are come to a perpetual end! And thou hast destroyed cities ;—their memorial is perished with them.

7 But the Lord shall endure for ever :—he hath prepared his throne for judgment.

8 And he shall judge the world in righteousness, He shall minister judgment to the people in uprightness.

9 The Lord also will be a refuge for the oppressed,—a refuge in times of trouble.

10 And they that know thy name will put their trust in thee: For thou, Lord, hast not forsaken them that seek thee.

11 Sing praises to the Lord, which dwelleth in Zion :—declare among the people his doings.

12 When he maketh inquisition for blood, he remembereth them : He forgetteth not the cry of the humble.

13 Have mercy upon me, O Lord ;—consider my trouble which I suffer of them that hate me, Thou that liftest me up from the gates of death :

14 That I may shew forth all thy praise in the gates of the daughter of Zion! I will rejoice in thy salvation.

15 The heathen are sunk down in the pit that they made : In the net which they hid is their own foot taken.

16 The Lord is known by the judgment which he executeth : The wicked is snared in the work of his own hands. Higgaion. Selah.

17 The wicked shall be turned into hell,—and all the nations that forget God.

18 For the needy shall not always be forgotten : The expectation of the poor shall not perish for ever.

19 Arise, O Lord ; let not man prevail :—let the heathen be judged in thy sight.

20 Put them in fear, O Lord, that the nations may know themselves to be but men. Selah.

THE position of the Psalms in their relation to each other is often remarkable. It is questioned whether the present arrangement of them was the order in which they were given forth to Israel, or whether some later compiler, perhaps Ezra, was inspired to attend to this matter, as well as to other points connected with the Canon. Without attempting to decide this point, it is enough to remark that we have proof that the order of the Psalms is as ancient as the completing of the canon ; and if so, it seems obvious that the Holy Spirit wished this book to come down to us in its present order.

Position of the Psalm.

We make these remarks, in order to invite attention to the fact, that as the eighth caught up the last line of the seventh, this ninth Psalm opens with an apparent reference to the eighth :

> "*I will praise thee, O Lord, with my whole heart.*
> *I will show forth all thy marvellous works.*
> *I will be glad and rejoice in thee.* (Comp. Song i. 4 ; Rev. xix. 7.)
> *I will sing to* THY NAME, *O thou Most High.*" (Ver. 1, 2.)

As if "*The Name,*" so highly praised in the former Psalm, were still ringing in the ear of the sweet singer of Israel. And in ver. 10, he returns to it, celebrating their confidence who "know" that "*name,*" as if its fragrance still breathed in the atmosphere around.

Referred to by Isaiah Ch. 25

There is a considerable resemblance, in the commencement, to the song in Isaiah xxv. 1–5. In both we have *praise— praise to his name—wonderful things—enemies, and nations, and cities destroyed*—and the Lord *a refuge* for *the needy, a refuge in times of trouble.* The period in prophetic history, before the view of the prophetic Spirit, is the same in both cases ; the same scene of the final ruin of God's enemies, and of Antichrist, is exhibited ; and the language of our Psalm, like that of Isaiah xxv. 1–5, is that of the past, because the future is to the Lord as sure as if already come and gone.

Alphabetic.

There is an approach to the alphabetic form in the verses of this Psalm, but only in part. We shall have occasion to remark on this point again in Psalm x. and elsewhere.

The title.

It may be in connection with the subject of the Psalm, that it is inscribed "*To the Chief Musician upon Muth-labben.*" None of the titles in this whole book is so obscure as this one. There is a plausible conjecture that עֲלָמוֹת should be the pointing, in which case it might be connected with "*the psalteries on Alamoth,*" 1 Chron. xv. 20 ; and "*Ben,*" of 1 Chron. xv. 18, be referred to in "*Lab-ben ;*" but then the omission of עַל is unaccountable, were this sense intended. There has been an attempt by Grotius, and others, to regard it as an anagram, "עַל נָבָל," on the death of Nabal, or, on the dying of the fool— but this is wholly gratuitous. Probably the title refers to something in the sacred music now unknown, the appropriateness of which to the subject of this Psalm can be conjectured only ; the word מָוֶת, *death*, occurring in it, suggests something sombre and solemn.

From vers. 1–8, there is a sketch of what the Lord is to do when he rises up. " *O enemy*,"—as if like Hos. xiii. 14, looking in the face of Satan, and all that follow him on earth, from Saul down to the last Antichrist. " *O enemy, destructions are at an end.*" The memory of the foe perishes, like the cities which they destroy. In vers. 9–12, we hear what the Lord has been, and is, and shall be to his own, onward to the day when he remembers the cry of souls under the altar (Rev. vi. 10.) Then a cry, like that of the martyrs, arises, vers. 13, 14, and the answer is given in vers. 15–17. After all which, vers. 18–20, sing confidently, and pray boldly to him who is to do such things on behalf of his saints.

The plan.

The speaker may be any member of Christ's body in sympathy with his Head ; but *Christ himself* could utter it as no other could. Hence Augustine, on ver. 13, asks, " Quare non dixit, ' Miserere *nostri*, Domine ?' An quia unus interpellat pro sanctis qui primus pauper pro nobis factus est." Christ on earth delighted to commend his *Father's name*, as ver. 10 does, and to assure disciples that with God there is no casting out of one that has once come in.

Christ and his members.

But to all this every believer responds, and even in ver. 16, every member of Christ may, in full sympathy with the feelings of justice and holiness in our Head, enter into the awful scene. They see the event as if it were already come :

" *The heathen are sunk down into the pit that they made ;*
In the net which they hid is their own foot taken.
The Lord is known by the judgment he executeth !
The wicked is snared in the work of his own hands !
Higgaion ! Selah !

We hear a voice, as from the Holiest, uttering the words, "*Higgaion*," a call to deep reflection or solemn musing,* and " *Selah*," a call to the Chief Musician to pause, that, the

Higgaion—
Selah.

---

* So in Buchanan's version in Latin metre :-
  " O res pectoris altis
      Condenda in penetralibus ! "

music ceasing, the worshippers might for a time meditate and adore. With such silent awe, we may suppose, the hosts of Israel stood for a time, gazing on the dead bodies of the Egyptians, when morning light unveiled them floating on the wave, or cast up as sea-weed on the shore. Not less than this shall be the intensity of interest and awe felt by the saints, when from their cloud they look down on the overwhelmed hosts of Babylon.

In ver. 18 there is an interesting rendering of תִּקְוַת עֲנָוִים, in the English Prayer-book version, "the *patient abiding* of the poor." It reminds us of James v. 7, "Be patient, brethren, unto the coming of the Lord." At the same time, the words more properly express the *earnest expectation* of God's poor ones, who are looking from their state of "oppression" and "trouble" (ver. 9), for the coming of him whose "*name they know*" (ver. 10), to be the Judge of a disordered world. Then truly shall they sing:

> " *The Lord is enthroned for ever.*   (lit. *has sat down,* i.e., *on his throne.)*
> *He has prepared his throne for judgment.*
> *He judges the world in uprightness :*
> *He ministers judgment to the people in uprightness."*   (v. 7, 8).

Of this Psalm, then, we may say that in it we see—

The Righteous One anticipating the setting up of the throne of judgment.

Psalm 10

1 Why standest thou afar off, O Lord ?—why hidest thou thyself in times of trouble ?
2 The wicked in his pride doth persecute the poor :
Let them be taken in the devices that they have imagined.
3 For the wicked boasteth of his heart's desire,
And blesseth the covetous, whom the Lord abhorreth.
4 The wicked, through the pride of his countenance, will not seek after God :
God is not in all his thoughts.
5 His ways are always grievous ; thy judgments are far above out of his sight :
As for all his enemies he puffeth at them.

6 He hath said in his heart, I shall not be moved:—for I shall never be in adversity.

7 His mouth is full of cursing, and deceit, and fraud:
Under his tongue is mischief and vanity.

8 He sitteth in the lurking places of the villages:
In the secret places doth he murder the innocent:
His eyes are privily set against the poor.

9 He lieth in wait secretly as a lion in his den:
He lieth in wait to catch the poor:—he doth catch the poor, when he draweth him into his net.

10 He croucheth, and humbleth himself, that the poor may fall by his strong ones.

11 He hath said in his heart, God hath forgotten: he hideth his face; he will never see it.

12 Arise, O Lord; O God, lift up thine hand: forget not the humble.

13 Wherefore doth the wicked contemn God?
He hath said in his heart, Thou wilt not require it.

14 Thou hast seen it;—for thou beholdest mischief and spite, to requite it with thy hand:
The poor committeth himself unto thee; thou art the helper of the fatherless.

15 Break thou the arm of the wicked and the evil man:
Seek out his wickedness till thou find none.

16 The Lord is King for ever and ever! the heathen are perished out of his land.

17 Lord, thou hast heard the desire of the humble:
Thou wilt prepare their heart, thou wilt cause thine ear to hear:

18 To judge the fatherless and the oppressed,
That the man of the earth may no more oppress.

THERE is much that is prophetic in this Psalm towards its close—the gloom of the present turning the eye forward in search of the coming day-spring. In ver. 16, faith is seen in its strength, singing as if already in possession of anticipated victory and deliverance, " *The Lord is king for ever and ever :* the *heathen are perished out of his land !*" Such confidence and faith must appear to the world strange and unaccountable. It is like what his fellow-citizens may be supposed to have felt (if the story be true) toward that man of whom it is recorded, that his powers of vision were so extraordinary, that he could distinctly see the fleet of the Carthaginians entering the harbour of Carthage, while he stood himself at Lilybæum, in Sicily. A man seeing across an ocean and able to tell of objects so far off! he could feast his vision on what others saw not. Even

The prophetic element.

thus does faith now stand at its Lilybæum and see the long-tossed fleet entering safely the desired haven, enjoying the bliss of that still distant day, as if it was already come.

It is a Psalm for "times of trouble" (ver. 1), like the preceding, (ix. 9). In it we again hear the cry, "*Arise*," addressed to the Lord, as in the preceding (ix. 20). Here, too, *man* is felt as the oppressor (ver. 18), even as in Psa. ix. 19. So much does it resemble the preceding, that the Septuagint have reckoned it a continuation. There is, however, this obvious difference, viz., while the ninth dwells much on the *ruin* of the ungodly, this Psalm dwells much on their *guilt.* Both Psalms also are in some measure alphabetic. (See Hengstenberg.) Both, however, are alphabetic in a very irregular manner. Perhaps it was intended by the fact of irregularity in the first two instances of an alphabetic kind, to teach us not to lay too much stress upon this kind of composition. God occasionally employs all the various ways in which men are wont to express their thoughts, and by which they are wont to aid the memory in retaining them.

The connection with the preceding.

Alphabetic in structure.

The contents.

Three parties are presented to our view in succession. God —the wicked—the righteous. *God* (ver. 1) is seen standing afar off, covering his eyes from the painful sight (הַעְלִים, scil. עֵינָיו), being of purer eyes than to behold iniquity. The *wicked* (vers. 2–11) is seen in all his ungodliness and unprincipled selfishness, practising evil as if no eye regarded. The *righteous* (vers. 12–14) calls God's attention to these scenes, and raises the cry for his interposition. Then, at ver. 15, and onward, the scene suddenly changes. God has come nigh ; "the arm of *the wicked* is broken." In the Hebrew, the first clause is a prayer, "Break thou the arm of the wicked and evil man ;" and the next seems to be the response to that prayer, *q. d.,* "Yes, it shall be broken." "*And thou shalt seek out his wickedness, and find none.*" His extirpation shall be complete, (compare Jer. 1. 20). "*The Lord* is King." He has heard the desire of the humble ; "he has *judged* the fatherless*

* Augustine gives one reason why saints are called fatherless :—"*Pupillus ;* id est, is cui moritur pater hic mundus, per quem carnaliter genitus est ; et jam potest dicere, 'mundus mihi crucifixus est, ego mundo.'"

and the oppressed," *i.e.*, he has acted to them as Othniel, and Gideon, and Samson, and other judges of Israel did when they brought down the foe, and set things to right in the land. Our Master, in the days of his flesh, might see all that is here described verified before him. He saw the buyers and sellers making gain in the courts of the Temple, and probably fulfilling there, Zech. xi. 5, " Blessed be the Lord ; for I am rich,"—even as it is said, ver. 3, " *And whosoever makes gain blesses* (God for it), *and yet despise Jehovah.*" In the Sadducees, he saw before him men of whom it might be said,

Exemplified in Christ's days.

" ' *There is no God,*' in all their thoughts." (ver. 4.)

Their ways were firm (ver. 5, Hengstenberg). They feared no adversity, saying (as the Prayer-book version graphically renders ver. 6), " Tush ! I shall never be cast down." The Pharisees, and Scribes, and Elders furnished abundant exemplification of " *mischief is under his tongue,*" (ver. 7,)—the storehouse, or cellar, that seemed to lie under their tongue, ever providing their lips with plans and suggestions of evil. Their lying in wait, as a lion in his covert, most vividly paints the plots entered into against Christ, and against his disciples afterwards. At the same time, " The servant is not above the master,"—the members of Christ have ever met with the same treatment, and found the world lying in the same wickedness. Any member of Christ can use this Psalm who feels earth's unholiness and atheism, and who is at all like Lot in Sodom, " his righteous soul vexed from day to day by their unlawful deeds." It will be well fitted for those who are on earth when Antichrist practises and prospers ere his final overthrow. In short, it is so comprehensive, that whether used by Christ or by his people, whether in the days of the First Advent, or in the days that precede and usher in the Second, it may be said to be-

Christ's Church in all ages.

*The Righteous One detailing earth's wickedness in antici-
pation of earth's deliverance.*

Psalm 11

To the chief Musician, A Psalm of David

1 IN the Lord put I my trust:—how say ye to my soul, Flee as a bird to your mountain?

2 For, lo, the wicked bend their bow, they make ready their arrow upon the string,
That they may privily shoot at the upright in heart.

3 If the foundations be destroyed, what can the righteous do?

4 The Lord is in his holy temple! the Lord's throne is in heaven:
His eyes behold, his eyelids try, the children of men.

5 The Lord trieth the righteous.
But the wicked and him that loveth violence his soul hateth.

6 Upon the wicked he shall rain snares,—fire and brimstone, and an horrible tempest:
This shall be the portion of their cup.

7 For the righteous Lord loveth righteousness; his countenance doth behold the upright.

The tone and plan of the Psalm.

THE combatants at the Lake Thrasymene are said to have been so engrossed with the conflict, that neither party perceived the convulsions of nature that shook the ground-

> "An earthquake reeled unheedingly away,
> None felt stern nature rocking at his feet."

From a nobler cause, it is thus with the soldiers of the Lamb. They believe, and, therefore, make no haste; nay, they can scarcely be said to feel earth's convulsions as other men, because their eager hope presses forward to the issue at the advent of the Lord.

> " *In the Lord I have put my trust :—how say ye to my soul, Flee, sparrows, to your hill.*" (Sneeringly referring to Zion-hill. *Horsley.*)

They have taken up their position, and who shall ever drive them from it? They refer to a two-fold ground of alarm presented to their thoughts by the foe.

> "*For lo ! the wicked bend their bow,*
> *They place their arrow upon the string*
> *To shoot privily at the upright in heart,*
> *For* (כִּי) *the foundations are destroyed !*
> *The righteous, what can he do ?*"

The enemy may thus array his terrors, as if the Lord's host were a partridge on the mountains. (1 Sam. xxvi. 20.) There

is a sneer at Mount Zion, in ver. 1 it has been suggested ;
but the words may as well mean, they have their secure resort,
their Zoar mountain (Gen. xix. 17), on which they shall stand
and see the rain of " snares, fire, and brimstone " on these men
of Sodom (ver. 6) ; their Judean mountain, where they shall
be safe when the abomination of desolation appears (Matt. xxiv.
16). It is this—*the Lord himself.* Though all the pillars of
social and religious order were destroyed, still -

> " *The Lord is in his holy temple ;*
> *The Lord's throne is in heaven !* "

The enemy has not reached up to this fortress ; he has not
shaken this sure defence.* On the other hand, the Lord is preparing to make a *sortie* in behalf of his own. He is surveying,
in preparation for this burst of judgment.

> " *His eyes behold*"

Nay, more, he is in the position of one who contracts his eye-
brows and fixes his eyelids in order to discern accurately the
mark he aims at ;

> " *His eyelids try the children of men.*
> *The Lord trieth the righteous.*"

And the result is interposition in behalf of his own ; for in the
trial he discovers the difference between the principles of the
two hostile parties, and now makes it known :

> " *The wicked, and him that loveth violence, his soul hateth.*
> *Upon the wicked he shall rain snares, fire, and brimstone :*
> *And an horrible tempest* (a wrath-wind) *shall be the portion of their cup.*"

All that came upon Sodom and Gomorrah shall be realized at
the Lord's appearing "in flaming fire," (2 Thess. i. 8). At the
very time, perhaps, when men imagine they have got the
righteous in their snares, the Lord comes and his net is spread
over them ; his " *snare*" suddenly starts up (Luke xxi. 35) and
they are taken ; caught unexpectedly in a net whose meshes
they can never break ; seized by the hands of the living
God, and doomed to "the vengeance of eternal fire," as the
" *portion of their cup.*" It is the measured, just, and due
amount of wrath for their sins ; for it is called a cup-portion,

---

* " Shall the pillars be brangled," says Leighton somewhere, " because of the
swarms of flies upon them ?"

"Ne quid præter modum atque mensuram, vel in ipsis pecca-
torum suppliciis per divinam providentiam fieri arbitremur."
(August.) All this proceeds from the rectitude of Jehovah's
character :

> " For righteous is the Lord ; he loveth righteousness ;
> His countenance doth behold the upright."

His righteousness sees it meet thus to visit the ungodly with a
Sodom-doom ; and on the other hand, to *look with favour* on
his Abrahams at Mamre, and no longer "*hide himself,*" as in
Psalm x. 4. It is somewhat remarkable that in ver. 7 the Hebrew uses the plural for " *His countenance.*" Critics are content to call this use of כָּנִימוֹ, " THEIR countenance," by the
name *pluralis majestatis;* and to say that it may express perfection, or greatness, in Him of whom it is used. But if we admit
of a reference to the Trinity in Gen. i. 26, why not here ? The
countenance of the *Godhead*—Godhead in all its fulness—each
person of the Godhead—shall give a look of delighted approval.
" With a countenance full of paternal affection he beholds them
in the midst of their sorrows, until, admitted through mercy to
the glory from which he excludes the wicked, they behold that
countenance which has always beheld them." (Horne.)

Christ using this Psalm.

Our Lord might sing this Psalm at Bethany on such occasions as that mentioned in Luke xiii. 31, 32, when they came
and said, " Get thee out hence, for Herod will kill thee." And
he has left it for us, that we may use it, as no doubt *David*
used it when it was first given to the Church, in times of danger
and threatening. Dr Allix would apply it specially to the
Church after she fled into the wilderness ; comparing ver. 2,
with Rev. xiii. 14. It applies with almost equal fulness to all
these cases, and yet also to an individual believer's case when
tempted, like that good man who said, "Sirs, it is a great thing
to believe that there is a God !" It exhibits to us-

The Church.

The Righteous One's faith under apparent disaster.

Psalm 12

To the chief Musician upon Sheminith, A Psalm of David

1 HELP, Lord ; for the godly man ceaseth ;
  For the faithful fail from among the children of men !
2 They speak vanity every one with his neighbour :
  With flattering lips and with a double heart do they speak.
3 The Lord shall cut off all flattering lips, and the tongue that speaketh
  proud things :
4 Who have said, With our tongue will we prevail; our lips are our own ;
  who is lord over us ?
  For the oppression of the poor, for the sighing of the needy,
  Now will I arise, saith the Lord ;
  I will set him in safety from him that puffeth at him.
6 The words of the Lord are pure words :
  As silver tried in a furnace ot earth, purified seven times.
7 Thou shalt keep them, O Lord, thou shalt preserve them from this generation for ever.
8 The wicked walk on every side, when the vilest men are exalted.

A PSALM for all ages, as well as for David's time. Elijah could   *The Title.*
sing it, Jeremiah could sing it, and never was there a time when
this Psalm was more appropriate than in our own day. Though
written by David, and handed over to his " Chief Musician,"
and though the *"Sheminith's"* now unknown strings were
touched by the fingers of a Levite whose heart could sigh in
sympathy with its strain of sad foreboding and present gloom,
it is, at the same time, quite a Psalm for the last days. The
Lord is called upon to arise, for the godly perish. You see a
little band gathered under the floating banner of their King,
who had promised to come to their help in due time. One after
another sinks down, wearied and worn, while the remaining
few, at each such occurrence, cry to their King-

" *Help, Lord !* " (Ver. 1.)

This is the cry that ascends from the saints, as one after   *The Contents.*
another of their number is successively gathered to the tomb ;
while, " *I will arise,*" (ver. 4,) is the response that faintly
reaches their ear.

" *Help, Lord !*" is their cry as they witness the increase of
bold infidelity, (ver. 2), and hear such mutterings of boastful
pride as these :

> " *Through our tongues we are strong.*
>   *Our lips are with us, (i. e., are our help.—*Hengstenberg.)
> " *Who is lord over us ?*" (Ver. 2, 3.)

The power of human talent and the grandeur of man's intellect are boasted of; while ver. 2, shews that these same persons flatter each other into deceitful peace, and are living without regard to the holy law of love. Meanwhile, the remnant who sigh in secret to the Lord—a remnant hated and often in danger (ver. 5)—are sustained by the sure word of promise. They tell their hope and faith in ver. 6, when they describe " *Jehovah's words :*"

> " *The words of the Lord are pure words :*
>   *As silver tried in a furnace of earth,**
>   *Purified seven times.*"

All He has spoken about the Woman's Seed from the beginning ; all He has spoken of Him in whom all nations shall be blessed ; all He has spoken of David and David's seed ; all is sure, all shall come to pass. And so they sing, (ver. 7), " Thou shalt keep them (*i. e.,* thine own), and shalt preserve them from this generation,"—a generation so corrupt and evil that one may say of it-

> " *The wicked walk on every side ;*
>   *Vileness is held in honour by the sons of men.*"

The future. How descriptive of the latter days ! How like the times of which Peter speaks, when men shall " speak great swelling words of vanity," (2 Peter ii. 18), and shall boldly ask, " Where is the promise of his coming ?" (iii. 4.) How descriptive, too, of the consolation of the saints ; for Peter tells us that this shall be their comfort, " The Lord is not slack concerning his promise," (ver. 9) ; and " according to His promise" they shall continue looking for the New Heavens and New Earth, (ver. 13). They know that the "*words of the Lord are pure words.*" They cannot fail.

David's time. Some of the features of this scene are to be found in all the conflicts that have risen between the woman's seed and the

---

* The original is difficult. Hengstenberg's rendering gives additional force to the comparison,—" the *purified silver of a lord of earth*"—the fine silver of some prince. Such is God's promise ; no dross in it ; no exaggeration ; no deceit.

serpent's. At the same time, the times of David when he was
a persecuted man, though anointed to the kingdom, were such
that they might be compared to the days that precede the coming of the Son of man. The flatterers of Saul hated David's
person and David's principles ; and could not fail to try to cast
contempt on "*the Lord's words*" in regard to him and his seed.
Such, also, were the days of the true David, our Lord, when He
appeared in our world as the Lord's anointed. We can easily   Christ's time.
see how the proud Pharisees, Scribes, and Sadducees, might
be characterised by vers. 2, 3 ; and not less how, on such an
occasion as the *Baptist's death,* Jesus could use ver. 1.   Let
us follow the Baptist's disciples, who have just buried their
master. They walk along in silent sadness ; for a witness to
the truth has perished. They seek out Jesus (Matt. xiv. 12),
and tell Him all that the foes of God have done. Jesus hears
and sympathises ; and may we not imagine the whole company
of disciples, with the master as " chief musician," sitting down
in the solitary place (ver. 13), and making it echo with the
plaintive cry,-

> "*Help, Lord, for the godly man ceaseth,*" &c.

The Church's eye, anointed with eye-salve, has ever since   Our time.
been able to discern in the world resemblances to the same
state of things ; and never more clearly than now.   Hence
David, and David's Son, and the seed of David's Son, have
ever found the strain of this song fitted to express what the
world made them feel.   Horsley entitles it, " Of free thinkers ;
their cunning, audacity, and final excision." But this is only
one aspect of it. It is rather,

*The Righteous One's consoling assurance that the Lord's
word, though mocked at, shall not fail.*

Psalm 13

To the chief Musician, A Psalm of David

1 How long wilt thou forget me, O Lord ? for ever?
  How long wilt thou hide thy face from me ?
2 How long shall I take counsel in my soul,—having sorrow in my heart
    daily?
  How long shall mine enemy be exalted over me ?

> **3** Consider and hear me, O Lord my God : lighten mine eyes, lest I sleep the sleep of death ;
> **4** Lest mine enemy say, I have prevailed against him ;
> And those that trouble me rejoice when I am moved.
> **5** But I have trusted in thy mercy ;—my heart shall rejoice in thy salvation.
> **6** I will sing unto the Lord, because he hath dealt bountifully with me.

The tone. HERE is what has been called "the *Righteous One's pathetic remonstrance.*" The darkness may be felt ; the time seems long ; the night wears slowly away ; hope deferred is making the heart sick ; heaviness hangs on the eyelid of the watcher.

> "*How long, O Lord, will thou forget me still ?*
> *How long wilt thou hide thy face from me ?*
> *How long shall I lay up counsel in my soul—sorrow in my heart daily ?*
> (Storing up plans of relief which all end in sorrow.)
> *How long shall the enemy exalt himself over me ?*"

David. When David wandered in Judea, and mused on the long-deferred promise of the Throne of Israel, he might use these words first of all. When he saw no sign of Saul's dominion ending, and no appearance of the Seed of the Woman, he was in such circumstances as fitted him to be the instrument of the Holy Ghost in writing for all after-times words which might utter the feelings of melancholy weariness.

Christ. The Son of David came in the fulness of time. Many a night of darkness He passed through. Sometimes the very shades of death bent over Him. "My soul is exceeding sorrowful even unto death !" Could He not most fitly take up ver. 4, as He carried his cross along the "Via Dolorosa ?" Who more fitly than he might appeal,

> "*Consider, hear me, O Lord my God (Eli ! Eli !)*
> *Make mine eyes glisten with joy,*
> *Lest I sleep in death !*
> *Lest mine enemy say, I have prevailed against him,*
> *Lest those that trouble me rejoice when I am moved !*"

High Priests, Governors, Scribes, Pharisees, Herodians, Sadducees, common priests and common people, were all on the eve of shouting triumph if He rose not from the grave ; and a burst of joy from hell would respond to their derision if He failed to arise, and failed to shew himself King of kings.

But not our Head only, every member of his body also, has found cause oftentimes to utter such complaints and fears. A believer in darkness—a believer under temptation—a believer under the pressure of some continued trial—a believer spending wearisome nights, and lying awake on his couch, may find appropriate language here wherein to express his feelings to God, and all the more appropriate because it is associated with the Saviour's darkness, and so assures us of his sympathy. We take up the harp which He used in Galilee and Gethsemane ; and in touching its strings, do we not recall to our Head the remembrance of "the days of his flesh ?"

Christ's members.

How glorious too, for the Church to join with her Head in the prospects of ver. 5 :

" *But as for me (וַאֲנִי) I have trusted in thy mercy,*" &c.

Leaning on the Father's love amid these sorrowful appeals, He was sure, and in him they are sure, of a day of glory dawning—joy coming in the morning. Verse 6th anticipates not only His own resurrection, but the resurrection of the saints also, and the glory of the kingdom :

" *I will sing unto the Lord, for He hath dealt bountifully with me.*"

Glory much more abounds—joy has set in instead of sorrow, in full tide ; fruition more than realizing the most " ample propositions that hope made" to the weary soul. And this is the blessed issue of what Calvin would perhaps have called, the " QUOUSQUE DOMINE," and which we may call,

The Righteous One's, Lord, how long ?

Psalm 14

To the chief Musician, A Psalm of David

1 THE fool hath said in his heart, *There is* no God.
   They are corrupt, they have done abominable works,—there is none that doeth good.
2 The Lord looked down from heaven upon the children of men,
   To see if there was any that did understand, and seek God.
3 They are all gone aside, they are altogether become filthy :
   There is none that doeth good, no, not one.

4 Have all the workers of iniquity no knowledge ?
Who eat up my people as they eat up bread, and call not upon the Lord.
5 There were they in great fear: for God is in the generation of the righteous.
6 Ye have shamed the counsel of the poor, because the Lord is his refuge.
7 Oh that the salvation of Israel were come out of Zion !
When the Lord bringeth back the captivity of his people,
Jacob shall rejoice, and Israel shall be glad.

David.

As we read these verses, we seem to pass from gloom to deeper gloom ; and when ver. 7 suggests a remedy, it is as if a " spark of light had been struck out from solid darkness." David wrote it under the inspiration of the Holy Ghost, but we know not when ; it may have been in his wilderness-days, when Judah seemed nearly as indifferent to Jehovah as were the realms of the Gentiles. The title " Upon Mahalath," as in Psalm lxxxviii., has been considered by Hengstenberg, to be not a name for a musical instrument, but as meaning " Upon the sickness," the moral sore and sickness described in the Psalm. Perhaps the title of Psalm lxxxviii. favours this view. But after all, some special instrument, used for melancholy subjects, may be meant, and Gesenius has found for it an Ethiopic root signifying, " to sing."

Title.

Christ in it.

Messiah is the speaker far more than David ; for though David could call the sheep of the house of Israel " *my* people," as being given him by the Lord, yet it is Messiah that is wont to speak in this manner. *He* is the shepherd whose voice we recognise here, saying, " They eat up MY people." (ver. 4.) He it is who describes our world's condition—Oh, how unlike the heaven He had left ! But amid the flood, He descries the waters receding. He sees the overthrow of the ungodly (ver. 5), and whence the grand deliverance is to come, (ver. 7.) De-liverance is to appear on the walls of Zion. " Salvation is of the Jews." (John iv. 22.) From Israel comes the Saviour, born at Bethlehem, but crucified, rising, ascending at Jerusalem. Out of Israel too, comes life from the dead to the world, when the Redeemer returns again; for, " Behold, darkness shall cover the earth, and gross darkness the people : but the Lord shall arise upon thee, and His glory shall be seen upon thee. And the Gentiles shall come to thy light, and kings to the brightness of thy rising," (Isaiah lx. 2, 3).

Let us, then, read this Psalm as our Lord's report regarding the state in which earth and its multitudes are found.

(Ver. 1.) O Father, they are denying that thou hast any being. The whole earth is replenished with fools, who say in their heart, " There is no God." They are corrupt ; they are doing abominable deeds ; there is none that doeth good. The contents.

(Ver. 2.) O sons of men, the cry of earth's wickedness came up to heaven. The Lord looked down to see if there were any that understood and sought after God.

(Ver. 3.) Alas ! it is altogether according to the cry, They are all gone aside. They are altogether become filthy. There is none that doeth good : NO, NOT ONE.

(Ver. 4.) Yet they see not their folly. Who has bewitched them ? Have they no knowledge, that they eat up my people, and call not on Jehovah ?

(Ver. 5.) But their damnation slumbereth not. On the very spot where their folly has been wrought I see them trembling. " Terror overtakes them ; for God is among the generation of the righteous."

(Ver. 6.) Where is now your mouth, wherewith ye said, Who is the Lord that we should serve Him ? Is not this the people whom ye despised ? (Jud. ix. 38.) Ye cast shame on the counsel of the poor, because he made the Lord his refuge. Ye scorned the policy of those who made the Lord their wisdom ; but the Lord has now laughed you to scorn.

(Ver. 7.) O let the day dawn and the shadows flee away ! Come quickly, year of my redeemed ! (Isaiah lxiii. 4.)

> " Let Jacob rejoice and Israel be glad,
> At the Lord's bringing back the captivity of His people."

Let the time come when earth shall hear Israel's shouts of joy at the opening of their prison, at the termination of their exile, at the restoration of their long-lost prosperity, at the return of their Shepherd to dwell among them. For when earth shall hear that shout of joy, it shall be a token that now at length has the time arrived when the full accomplishment shall take place of that promise to Abraham, " In thy seed shall all nations of the earth be blessed."

Thus does the true Righteous One survey the world lying in wickedness, and turn his eye toward the dawn of day, every member sympathizing with the Head. We may describe the Psalm as being a setting forth of

The Righteous One's view of earth, and its prospects.

Psalm 15

A Psalm of David

1 Lord, who shall abide in thy tabernacle? who shall dwell in thy holy hill?

2 He that walketh uprightly, and worketh righteousness,
And speaketh the truth in his heart.

3 He that backbiteth not with his tongue, nor doeth evil to his neighbour,
Nor taketh up a reproach against his neighbour.

4 In whose eyes a vile person is contemned;—but he honoureth them that fear the Lord.
He that sweareth to his own hurt, and changeth not.

5 He that putteth not out his money to usury, nor taketh reward against the innocent.
He that doeth these things shall never be moved.

Helper.

WE heard of a "righteous generation" in last Psalm, and here is one of them as a representative of the whole. None can be said to have fulfilled the conditions, or come up to the character here sketched, excepting Christ, if we view the matter in its strictness; although every member of His body lays claim to His imputed obedience, and exhibits a goodly specimen of the effect of this imputation in producing personal holiness. We consider this Psalm as descriptive of our Head in His personal holiness, and of his members as made holy by Him.

It is one thing to state how holiness is attained, and quite another to assert that perfect holiness is possessed. When you describe a worshipper in the Holy Hill as one who is holy, you do not on that account maintain that his holiness was *self-de-*

rived, or that it was his *primary* qualification. Far less do you assert that holiness of character stands in the place of the blood that cleanses the conscience. There are several links in the golden chain, and my pointing to one of these does in no way interfere with my conviction of the necessity of the rest. If I find it said of our Lord :

> "It is Christ that died ;
> Yea, rather, that is risen again.l
> Who is even at the right hand of God !
> Who also maketh intercession for us,"

I may take up one feature of this Redeemer, and may say, " He who saves us is One who is risen again ;" but by so saying I do not deny, but rather necessarily include, the assertion, that He died first of all. So also if I say, " He who is saved is one who has holiness ;" I do not, by saying this, deny that the man has first of all been made clean by the blood : on the contrary, I imply that as a thing of course, necessarily preceding the other. Again, if I say, " That Priest has washed his hands and feet in the *laver,*" I do not deny, but, on the contrary, necessarily imply, that first of all he was at the *Altar,* and touched the blood there. Or, once more, if I read 1 Tim. i. 5,

> " Now the end of the commandment is charity
> Out of a pure heart,
> And out of a good conscience,
> And out of faith unfeigned,"

I may fix on the middle clause and say, the love, or charity, aimed at by the law, is the product of a *" good conscience."* But do I, on account of that statement, at all deny that *" faith unfeigned"* is needful in *order to arrive at a good conscience ?* It is even thus with our Psalm, when received as stating what belongs to the members of Christ. It tells of their *" pure heart;"* but then that pure heart came from *" a good conscience ;"* and that good conscience was the effect of *" unfeigned faith"* in the blood.

It is, however, only our Head that can fully realize the cha- Christ. racter here given. *" Holiness to the Lord"* is on our High Priest's mitre, while we, as inferior priests, go forward in his steps, to dwell in the Tabernacle.* The question is asked, ver. 1, " *Who shall dwell ?*" abide, be a guest for ever, in the palace of our King and God? Verse 2 tells the *outward* purity required, and the *inward* guilelessness. Verse 3, the purity of *word ;* verse 4, *company ;* verse 5, disinterested and self-denied *love to His neighbours ;* ver. 5, *uprightness,* if He once promise he will not " exchange" his promise for anything more convenient to himself, and will not fail to shew the heart of *a brother* in everyday transactions. These are signs of a renewed nature, very rare in our world, and such as manifest the man to be, " though in the world, yet not of the world." In verse 4, we have the key to the difference between such a one and the man of earth. "*He honoureth them that fear the Lord ;*" his heart lies in the company of those who fear Jehovah ; and if so, then he himself prefers Jehovah's company to all besides. He is one who has fellowship with God.

But we must not fail to notice the " *Tabernacle* " and the " *Holy Hill,*" where this man's dwelling shall be for ever. The *Tabernacle* of Moses, which, in David's days, was pitched on the slopes of *Zion-hill,* is the type of greater things. In that figure we see God in the cloud of glory over the mercy-seat, dwelling with men, and the Priest entering in on the atonement-day, to His presence. All this was typical of what is now before us in clearer light. The redeemed go in with the blood of the Redeemer through the rent veil, (for the atonement-day is "*now*") to Him who is in heaven. And when the Lord returns, and the " *Tabernacle of God is with men,*"— when Christ, the true mercy-seat, is here—then shall we go to that Tabernacle, and see Him, on that Holy Hill, where his presence shall be manifested. (See this more at large in Psalm xxiv.) But on that day none shall ascend that Hill, or approach that Tabernacle, who are not " sanctified." On this point Revelation xxi. 27 corresponds with our Psalm—into

---

* As Barclay puts it, with truth though not with poetic taste,

> "Now who is He ? Say if ye can
> Who *so* shall gain the firm abode ?
> Pilate shall say, ' Behold the Man ! '
> And John, ' Behold the Lamb of God!' "

New Jerusalem "there shall in no wise enter anything that defileth or maketh a lie." Over its gate is written, " Without holiness no man shall see God."

Here, then, we have before us a description of

The dweller in the Holy Hill of God.

Psalm 16

Michtam of David

1 PRESERVE me, O God: for in thee do I put my trust.

2 O my soul, thou hast said unto the Lord, Thou art my Lord:
My goodness extendeth not to thee;

3 But to the saints that are in the earth, and to the excellent, in whom is all my delight.

4 Their sorrows shall be multiplied that hasten after another god:
Their drink-offerings of blood will I not offer, nor take up their names into my lips.

5 The Lord is the portion of mine inheritance and of my cup :—thou maintainest my lot.

6 The lines are fallen unto me in pleasant places; yea, I have a goodly heritage.

7 I will bless the Lord, who hath given me counsel:
My reins also instruct me in the night seasons.

8 I have set the Lord always before me:
Because he is at my right hand, I shall not be moved.

9 Therefore my heart is glad, and my glory rejoiceth: my flesh also shall rest in hope.

10 For thou wilt not leave my soul in hell;
Neither wilt thou suffer thine Holy One to see corruption.

11 Thou wilt shew me the path of life :—in thy presence is fulness of joy;
At thy right hand there are pleasures for evermore.

IT is not sin alone that characterises our world. *Misery* goes hand in hand with sin. And hence, as the preceding Psalm set before us One who was *holy* in the midst of a world lying in wickedness, though breathing its air, walking on its highway, handling its objects, and conversing with its inhabitants, so this Psalm exhibits One who is *happy*, truly *happy*, notwithstanding a world of broken cisterns around him, and the sighs borne to his ear on every breeze. This happy One is

Christ in a world of sorrow.

"*the Man of Sorrows*,"—no other than He ! For Peter, in Acts ii. 31, declares, " David speaketh concerning *Him !*"

His members. too.

This happy One (followed in all ages by his chosen ones) walks through many a varied scene, and at every step expresses satisfaction and perfect contentment with the Father's arrangements. In verses 1, 2, he tells, with complacent delight, into whose hands it is he has committed his all : " *Thou art my Lord*,"—my soul has said this with all its strength. And

" *My goodness is not over Thee ;*"

whatever is good or blessed in my lot, makes no pretensions to add anything to thy blessedness, to overshadow thee ; nor do I allow the bliss I enjoy to supersede Him who blesses me.* And does not every member of his body respond to all this ! Who of them does not reply, " My Lord and my God ! thou art the very bower of bliss under which I sit. We are blessed in thee ; but thou needest not us to bless thee !"

Satisfied with his Father as God, and Lord, and Guardian, he is equally so with the sphere within which he must move : " Jesus loved Martha, and her sister, and Lazarus." None on earth, seem to Him so pleasant and " honourable" (אַדִּירִים), (see Psa. viii. 1) as the saints. And not less is He pleased with his separation from all idols and all idolatry. (See ver. 3 and 4.) And does not every member of his body respond, " *Amen !*" gladly recognising their own company as the circle within which is " all their delight." But how instructive and wonderful it is to find, in ver. 5, such entire contentedness with the Lord's doings, and such a recognition of his will. For it was enemies that brought him many a bitter draught to drink, the vinegar and the gall,—it was " not an enemy," but worse far, a perfidious friend, that plunged the dagger into his heart ; and yet in all this he sees the Lord giving him his cup and portion. Nor less remarkable is it to hear, in ver. 6, the Man of Sorrows tell that his lines have fallen to him in pleasant places ! He that had nowhere to lay his head, how happy is He ! What

* As for " goodness," see Psalm cvi. 5, and the equivalent טוֹב of Psalm cxxviii. 5. In the עָלֶיךָ there may be reference to the sky over our head. Such a passage as Psalm cviii. 5 is parallel ; " Great above the heavens"—the heavens not above thee, but thou over them.

a calm contentment sits upon his pensive brow ! Earth and hell are unable to destroy his blessed lot. He has (ver. 7) found communion with his Father, when others sleep,—in the retired valleys and hills of Galilee, on the Mount of Olives, in the wilderness. The presence and care of his Father is a fund of enjoyment in itself. (Ver. 8.) All may be scattered and leave him alone ; but yet he is not alone, for the Father is with him.

Such joys as these still gladden every believer's soul, even as they did refresh the "Author and Finisher of our Faith." He drank of these brooks by the way, " therefore was his heart glad." That he might endure to the end, and *as man* endure, he tasted of needful draughts in his sore undertaking ; and his draughts of refreshment were of the kind which we have seen above. We, too, can taste the same, and we need the same. Nor less do we need what follows in ver. 9, secure confidence in prospect of death, and (ver. 10) the hope of blessed resurrection. Our Head laid his flesh in the Joseph's sepulchre, expecting the future result, a speedy resurrection. His soul was not to be left long separate from his body—out of paradise it was soon to come, and on the third day to rejoin its body ere corruption could begin. But we, too, his members, are as sure of a return of our souls from paradise to join our bodies on the Resurrection Morn, when " this corruptible shall put on incorruption." And thus to the Head and members shall their full satisfaction be realized, and that for ever. He and they shall tread the path of life, and enter into "fulness of joy, pleasures for evermore,"—the blessedness of the eternal kingdom.

Such are the riches of this Psalm that some have been led *Title.* to think the obscure title, "*Michtam*," has been prefixed to it on account of its *golden stores.* For כֶּתֶם is used of the " gold of Ophir," (*e.g.*, Psa. xlv. 10), and מִכְתָּם might be a derivative from that root. But as there is a group of five other Psalms (viz., lvi., lvii., lviii., lix., lx.) that bear this title, whose subject matter is various, but which all end in *a tone of triumph*, it has been suggested that the Septuagint may be nearly right in their Στηλογραφια, as if " A Psalm to be hung up or inscribed on a pillar to commemorate victory." It is, however, more like still that the term, *"Michtam"* (like *"Maschil"*), is a musical term, whose real meaning and use we have lost, and may recover only when the ransomed house of Israel return home with songs. Meanwhile the subject-matter of this Psalm itself is very clearly this—

The Righteous One's satisfaction with his lot.

Psalm 17

A Prayer of David

1 HEAR the right, O Lord, attend unto my cry,
Give ear unto my prayer, that goeth not out of feigned lips.

2 Let my sentence come forth from thy presence ;
Let thine eyes behold the things that are equal.

3 Thou hast proved mine heart ; thou hast visited me in the night;
Thou hast tried me, and shalt find nothing ;
I am purposed that my mouth shall not transgress.

4 Concerning the works of men,
By the word of thy lips I have kept me from the paths of the destroyer.

5 Hold up my goings in thy paths,—that my footsteps slip not

6 I have called upon thee, for thou wilt hear me, O God :
Incline thine ear unto me, and hear my speech.

7 Shew thy marvellous loving-kindness, O thou that savest by thy right hand.
Them which put their trust in thee from those that rise up against them.

8 Keep me as the apple of the eye, hide me under the shadow of thy wings,

9 From the wicked that oppress me, from my deadly enemies, who compass me about.

10 They are enclosed in their own fat : with their mouth they speak proudly.

11 They have now compassed us in our steps :
They have set their eyes bowing down to the earth;

12 Like as a lion that is greedy of his prey,
And as it were a young lion lurking in secret places.

13 Arise, O Lord, disappoint him, cast him down :
Deliver my soul from the wicked, which is thy sword :

14 From men which are thy hand, O Lord,
From men of the world, which have their portion in this life,
And whose belly thou fillest with thy hid treasure :
They are full of children, and leave the rest of their substance to their babes.

15 As for me, I will behold thy face in righteousness :
I shall be satisfied, when I awake, with thy likeness.

The tone. THE same strain again—only here the sin and sorrow of the world are brought together, and the Righteous One is seen lifting his eyes to heaven, as sure conqueror over both. Earth, whether viewed from the top of Peor, or the field of Zophim, is still the same fallen earth ; and not less gratefully does the shout of the King of Jeshurum greet our ears, by whatever cliff of Pisgah it may happen to be echoed back. It is called *A Prayer,* for it consists of strong appeals to God. The title.

While fully *satisfied with his lot,* the Righteous One tells us how little reason there is to be satisfied with the world The plan. wherein his lot was for a time cast. Dissatisfied with man's judgment, he appeals to the Lord, and ver. 1 is equivalent to those two words in his prayer (John xvii. 25), " *O righteous Father.*" Before Him he spreads his cause, expecting (ver. 2, 3) a reversal of the world's sentence. The Father " proved him and could find nothing." Was it to this he referred in John xiv. 30, when telling of Satan's attempt? Mysterious trial! all-perfect righteousness! Heaven and hell have tried it ; and neither the holiness of God, nor the envy of Satan, could detect a flaw. We find him appealing to the Father as to his heart (ver. 3), as to his *words* (ver. 4), and as to his *ways* (ver. 5) —sure of the verdict from the lips of Holiness itself. And, united to Him, each believer may make the same appeal, with the same success, while he is led also, in the very act of so doing, to plant his steps in the footsteps of his all-perfect Surety. In ver. 6, emphasis rests on *I* (אֲנִי) ; " I have called ;" let others do the same.

Still dissatisfied with men, in ver. 6–8 He seems to unbosom himself to the Father, fixing his eye on the marvellous love shewn in redemption, "the tender mercies," or "bowels of mercy," by reason of which the " Dayspring from on high hath visited us," (Luke i. 78).

" *Single out thy lovingkindness, thou deliverer of those that trust.*"

Saints are called "Trusters," (חוֹסִים) and the prayer is, " Set apart (Psalm iv. 3) for me some special mercy. Make it appear in its singular brightness, O thou who deliverest me who trust in Thee, and wilt deliver all others who simply trust in Thee through me !" We, too, may follow Him even into the very secret of the Most High, when in ver. 8 he presses forward and sits down under the wings of majesty and love—at rest in the "God of Israel, under whose wings he has come to trust." And here we may, with our Head, survey the turmoil of human wickedness, beholding (verses 9–14) their assaults, their snares, their lion-like anger, their conspiracies, and, in ver. 14, their luxury and worldly ease.

> "*My soul deliver from the wicked, by thy sword,*
> *From men, by thy hand, O Lord,*
> *From men!*" (Perhaps, frail, dying men, if מְתִים be connected with מוּת to die.)
> "*From the transitory world!*"

Grieved at such scenes, the Righteous One suddenly darts his eye into the future, and anticipates resurrection-glory,—a glory that shall cast human splendour into the shade, and leave the Lord's people without one unsatisfied desire. Our Head sung, in prospect of his resurrection, and we, his members, sing, in prospect of ours,

> "*But as for me I shall behold his face in* RIGHTEOUSNESS." (Ver. 15.)

O righteous Father, O holy Father (John xvii.), I come to thee, and, for ever dead unto sin, and escaped from the world's miry clay, I shall stand before Thee who art righteous in the beauty of pure righteousness. And my dissatisfactions shall be forgotten when entering on that enjoyment,—thou appearing in glory to meet me, and I conformed to the glory that meets me at my rising,

> "*I shall be satisfied when thy likeness awakes*"

This likeness is spoken of in Numb. xii. 8. It is the manifestation of God in his glory. The "glory of the Father" (Rom. vi. 3) met Christ at the sepulchre, and He arose glorious, soul and body. So shall it be with each of his members. Christ our Life, the incarnate manifestation of the likeness of God, shall appear in glory ; and we shall instantly be conformed to Him "seeing Him as He is" (1 John iii. 2). The appearing of that glory, in our dark world, whence it has so long been exiled, seems to be meant by the "*awakening of His likeness.*" Psalm lxxiii. 20 speaks of it again, and attributes to that event the eternal confusion of the worldlings who had their portion and cup full for a season.

It was in the act of singing these words, as they stand in the metrical version, that one of our Scottish martyrs, Alexander Home, passed from the scaffold to glory. With a solemn eye and glowing soul, he was able amid gathered thousands to express his rest and hope in these words,—

> " But as for me I thine own face
> In righteousness shall see ;
> And with thy likeness when I wake
> I satisfied shall be."

And who of all the saints would not join him ? Who would not take up every clause of the whole Psalm ? Who would not sympathize in

The Righteous One's dissatisfaction with a present world ?

Psalm 18

To the chief Musician, A Psalm of David, the servant of the Lord, who spake unto the Lord the words of this song in the day that the Lord delivered him from the hand of all his enemies, and from the hand of Saul : And he said,

1 I WILL love thee, O Lord, my strength.
2 The Lord is my rock, and my fortress, and my deliverer;
   My God, my strength, in whom I will trust ;
   My buckler, and the horn of my salvation, and my high tower.
3 I will call upon the Lord, who is worthy to be praised :
   So shall I be saved from mine enemies.
4 The sorrows of death compassed me, and the floods of ungodly men made
   me afraid.
5 The sorrows of hell compassed me about : the snares of death prevented me.
6 In my distress I called upon the Lord, and cried unto my God :
   He heard my voice out of his temple, and my cry came before him, even
   into his ears.
7 Then the earth shook and trembled ;
   The foundations also of the hills moved and were shaken, because he
   was wroth.
8 There went up a smoke out of his nostrils,
   And fire out of his mouth devoured :—coals were kindled by it.
9 He bowed the heavens also, and came down : and darkness was under
   his feet.
10 And he rode upon a cherub, and did fly : yea, he did fly upon the wings
   of the wind.
11 He made darkness his secret place ;
   His pavilion round about him were dark waters and thick clouds of the skies.
12 At the brightness that was before him his thick clouds passed,—hail-stones
   and coals of fire.

13 The Lord also thundered in the heavens,
And the Highest gave his voice ;—hail-stones and coals of fire.

14 Yea, he sent out his arrows, and scattered them ;
And he shot out lightnings, and discomfited them.

15 Then the channels of water were seen, and the foundations of the world were discovered
At thy rebuke, O Lord, at the blast of the breath of thy nostrils.

16 He sent from above, he took me, he drew me out of many waters.

17 He delivered me from my strong enemy,
And from them which hated me : for they were too strong for me..

18 They prevented me in the day of my calamity :—but the Lord was my stay.

19 He brought me forth also into a large place ;—he delivered me, because he delighted me.

20 The Lord rewarded me according to my righteousness ;
According to the cleanness of my hands hath he recompensed me.

21 For I have kept the ways of the Lord, and have not wickedly departed from my God.

22 For all his judgments were before me, and I did not put away his statutes from me.

23 I was also upright before him, and I kept myself from mine iniquity.

24 Therefore hath the Lord recompensed me according to my righteousness,
According to the cleanness of my hands in his eyesight.

25 With the merciful thou wilt shew thyself merciful ;
With an upright man thou wilt shew thyself upright ;

26 With the pure thou wilt shew thyself pure ;
And with the froward thou wilt shew thyself froward.

27 For thou wilt save the afflicted people ; but wilt bring down high looks.

28 For thou wilt light my candle : the Lord my God will enlighten my darkness.

29 For by thee I have run through a troop ; and by my God have I leaped over a wall.

30 As for God, his way is perfect : the word of the Lord is tried :
He is a buckler to all those that trust in him.

31 For who is God save the Lord ? or who is a rock save our God ?

32 It is God that girdeth me with strength, and maketh my way perfect.

33 He maketh my feet like hinds' feet, and setteth me upon my high places.

34 He teacheth my hands to war, so that a bow of steel is broken by mine arms.

35 Thou hast also given me the shield of thy salvation :
And thy right hand hath holden me up, and thy gentleness hath made me great.

36 Thou hast enlarged my steps under me, that my feet did not slip.

37 I have pursued mine enemies, and overtaken them :
Neither did I turn again till they were consumed.

38 I have wounded them that they were not able to rise :—they are fallen under my feet.

39 For thou hast girded me with strength unto the battle :
Thou hast subdued under me those that rose up against me.

40 Thou hast also given me the necks of mine enemies;
That I might destroy them that hate me.
41 They cried, but there was none to save them:—even unto the Lord, **but**
he answered them not.
42 Then did I beat them small as the dust before the wind:
I did cast them out as the dirt in the streets.
43 Thou hast delivered me from the strivings of the people:
And thou hast made me the head of the heathen:
A people whom I have not known shall serve me.
44 As soon as they hear of me, they shall obey me:
The strangers shall submit themselves unto me.
45 The strangers shall fade away, and be afraid out of their close places.
46 The Lord liveth! and blessed be my rock; and let the God of my salvation be exalted.
47 It is God that avengeth me, and subdueth the people under me.
48 He delivereth me from mine enemies:
Yea, thou liftest me up above those that rise up against me:
Thou hast delivered me from the violent man.
49 Therefore will I give thanks unto thee, O Lord, among the heathen,
And sing praises unto thy name.
50 Great deliverance giveth he to his king; and sheweth mercy to his anointed,
To David, and to his seed for evermore.

THIS is a Psalm of " *The Lord's Servant,*" a title given to one called to specific services for God. It was given into the hands of " *The Chief Musician*" on the day when the Lord had delivered from every foe. The circumstances were peculiar, and so is the style of the song. Thus ver. 1, " *I will love thee*" is expressed by the unusual word אֶרְחָם, which can be expressed only by some such paraphrase as " *My bowels yearn in love to thee.*"* And then the next term, " *My strength,*" חִזְקִי is rare but very expressive, equivalent to, " *Thou who hast held me up firm and fast.*"

It is meant for a greater than David, but David's circumstances furnished an appropriate occasion for giving to the Church a song such as might suit Messiah, and all his members too. David's circumstances, that made him suitable to be the vehicle of this divine communication, have moulded the lan-

* Sternhold had no doubt felt that there was something very energetic in the original, and so he has versified it thus, with considerable success:

" O God, my strength and fortitude
Of force I must love thee;
Thou art my castle and defence
In my necessity."

guage ; but we are not to carry the allusion to his history too far. Some have supposed that there is reference in verses 7–15 to some tempest that helped David's victory on some occasion ; but we may be content with observing that the style is coloured by David's experience. Thus, ver. 2 amplifies the חִזְקִי of ver. 1. "The Lord is my סֶלַע :" my precipitous rock (like 1 Sam. xxiii. 28), which foes find inaccessible. "My מְצוּדָה strong-hold" amid such rocks ; like those of Engedi, 1 Sam. xxiii. 29. "*My deliverer,*" not leaving me simply to the defence of rocks, but himself interposing with his loving arm. "*My God!*" not deliverance only to me, but every thing, my all in all ! "My צוּר," my firm, immoveable rock (Isa. xxvi. 4) who never changes. "*In Him will I trust.*" In such a one as this may I not be satisfied? And when I go forth to the battle field, this Jehovah is "*My Shield;*" and by Him I win victory ; "*The horn of my Salvation!*" And as I return to my encamp-ment on yonder height, such as 1 Sam. xxvi. 13 used to be to me, far above the reach of foes, I sing of Him as "*My High Place,*" the height where I repose secure.

Christ in it. But the Psalm was meant for the Lord Jesus very specially. It presents a singular history of some portions of our Lord's mighty undertakings, all related in such a manner as that his mem-bers (and David among the rest) might often use it for them-selves. In Heb. ii. 13, Paul quotes verse 2 as our Lord's words: "*I will put my trust in him;*" to shew that Christ, as our brother, leant on God, just as we ourselves would lean our weakness on Almighty strength. And again, in Rom. xv. 9, he quotes verse 49, "*I will confess to thee among the Gentiles,*" to shew Christ's deep interest in the world at large. So that we have, by means of these two references,—one from the be-ginning, the other from the close,—the whole Psalm marked out (bracketed within these two quotations) as belonging to *Christ* in a special and direct manner.

It is, then, our Brother who here sings. (Heb. ii. 13.) He begins with telling his younger brethren what his Father ("*His* Father and *ours*") did for him in the day of the sadness of his heart. He is relating some of the hidden things, which are nowhere else recorded, but which fit in to the time of Gethsemane suffering, and the three hours' darkness, and the earth-quake, and the rending of the Temple veil,—things that took place in the view of other spectators than man, when the "prince of the air" was overthrown, and the Father, with his legions of angels, came forward to deliver.

The mention of the "*cherub*" in verse 10 is not to be over- The cherub. looked : "*He rode upon a cherub.*" Like a king or warrior, the Lord is represented as going forth in his chariot ; but he mounts, on that memorable day, a chariot whose coat of arms is *the cherub.* He *goes forth in his cherub-chariot*, and this is sufficient to shew the errand on which he is gone out : it is redemption. For that symbol is the redemption-symbol. *Cherubim* in paradise after the fall ; *cherubim* on the mercy-seat, with their feet touching the blood, and their whole weight on the ark ; *cherubim* on the veil that was rent ;—everywhere *cherubim* (the four living beings of Rev. iv.) represented the Redeemed. How significant to the universe, when Jehovah rose up with the symbol of man's redemption, to go forth to the aid of man's Redeemer.

Let us begin, then. The true Sweet Singer of Israel, the The plan. firstborn among many brethren, stands on the shore of his Red Sea, and sings, in verses 1 and 2, the grace and glory of his God. What a God he is : "My strength, my rock,* my fortress," &c. Then comes the story of his awful conflict. He traverses the field with us, and tells us of his cries that pierced the heavens and the Father's heart (ver. 3–6),—a commentary on Heb. v. 7. But from verse 7 to 15 what a scene of terrific incidents is opened to view ! "The cords" of the hunter "death" were enclosing him ; and the "torrents of Belial" —floods swollen with all the mischief of hell and hellish men, —were sweeping down upon him, when his cry began to be noticed, and the Father rose up. Earth shook—smoke and fire were seen by those same angels who were witnesses of the smoke and fire on Sinai, attesting the majesty of the law ; and the same heavens bowed that bowed when the Law was given,

---

* The clause, "God of my rock," in 2 Sam. xxii. 3, is properly "my rock-God," *i.e.*, my strong, rock-like, God.

the same darkness attended this descent, for now the *Law-ful-filler* was about to present the law fulfilled.   He came with the *cherub*-symbol, inasmuch as there was now to be redemption from the curse of the law.   But there was no abatement of his glory—no obscuring of his majesty ; on the contrary, there was the same covering of darkness, as when the law was given, and thereafter the same brightness shot forth.   Hailstones, too, as when He overcame his enemies at Bethhoron, attested the presence of the same majesty and power: the same thunder uttered its voice, the same lightning-arrows flew abroad.   It was Israel's God in his majesty; yes, the same that laid bare the Red Sea's channel, (verses 14, 15), who then appeared in still greater displays of majesty.   It was a scene not witnessed by mortal eyes, but, no doubt, "seen of angels."

At length the Redeemer was delivered.   "He sent from above, he took me, he drew me out of many waters" (Verses 16–18).   In vain do the scribes and elders triumph, sealing the sepulchre stone, and setting a watch ; in vain does Satan exult, as if he had crushed the woman's seed.

> " *They prevented me*, (*i.e.* got before me, as if between me and my refuge,) *in the day of my calamity.*"

But Jehovah came—resurrection followed, with all its consequences.   He stood in "*a large place ;*" and soon sat down at the right hand of Majesty on high.   And in that hour every member of his body was virtually "raised with Him, and made to sit with Him in the heavenly places,"—in a large room !

And was all this done in conformity with *law and righteousness ?*   The law was honoured then, and is honoured and magnified for ever, by all that the Redeemer wrought.   Vers. 20–26 declares it :

> " *Jehovah rewarded me according to my righteousness*
> " *According to the cleanness of my hands has he recompensed me.*
> " *Because I kept the ways of the Lord*
> " *All his judgments were before me,*
> " *And I did not put away his statutes from me.*"
> " *Yea, I was upright before Him,*" &c.

Henceforth, nothing hinders the application of his redemption-work on the part of God ; and on man's part there is nothing required but the poverty of spirit that is willing to receive *a gift*. Pride, that caused the fall, hinders the rising again of the fallen.

" For thou wilt save the people that are poor,"
" But will bring down high looks," (ver. 27).

Our Brother, having brought us thus far in his history, tells us once more of the Father's love to Him and his people, and how fully the Father, who equipped Him for the former struggle, has equipped him for whatever remains for him to do. (Verses 28–35). The Father loveth the Son, and hath given all things into his hands. He seems suddenly to remind the Father of this, (verses 35, 36), in preparation for what is coming, saying,—

" Thy gentleness hath MADE ME GREAT."

Then follows the final assault (long deferred) upon his unyielding enemies.* (Verses 37–42.) It is evidently the day of his Second Coming ; for we hear the cry (v. 41), when *" there is none to save :"* the Master has risen up and shut to the door. Rocks and mountains cannot shelter foes, any more than could the cave of Makkedah the five kings that fled to it. Our Joshua calls them out, and puts his own foot upon their necks. (V. 40, compared with Josh. x. 24). And then is earth subdued under Him. (Ver. 43, 44, 45). Isaiah lii. 15 is fulfilled : nations coming to Him, as did the Queen of Sheba, attracted by the report of his grace and glory.

---

* The כִּחֵשׁ of v. 45, is the same word used in Ps. lxvi. 3, and lxxxi. 16. It originally expressed "*feigned* obedience," through fear or flattery ; the kind of submission yielded by men to irresistible conquerors. But here we must understand the word to be accommodated to the circumstances of the case, and to express the completeness of the homage rendered to Messiah, arising from the feeling of his irresistible greatness. It is *q. d.* all the homage that was ever given by subdued nations to their conquerors, shall be given to Messiah. The *feignedness* of the submission is not to be considered. Just as in Isaiah viii. 13, " Make Jehovah your *dread*, the object of your *terror*," (מַעֲרִיץ). The allu- sion is to what idolators felt toward their horrid idols : but it is only an allu- sion, *q.d.*, let Jehovah be the object of your heart's reverence,—this is your dread !

The Lord alone is exalted in that day. The glory resounds to Him (verses 46–48) ; and " חַי יְהֹוָה " is the watchword, or congratulatory acclamation (1 Kings i. 25, 31), of all the earth —"*Jehovah liveth !*" Jew and Gentile are seen in union ; for the Deliverer (ver. 49–50) declares his celebration of Jehovah's name among the Gentiles, while he shews kindness " to David and his seed for ever."

Well may we join with all the members of our Head, " made more than conquerors" in Him, and enjoying our share in all these triumphs along with Him,—well may we join in the exclamation of ver. 50,

" *Thou who makest great the salvations of his King !* "

The full, salvation-work wrought out by our appointed King, is called " יְשׁוּעוֹת ; " and these things are all done in the way of might and majesty.

The members of Christ.

But now see how we too may sing all this ; even as David could sing it, as well as David's son. We sing of our deliverances, and remember all the while that the source of them was God's rising up for us in all his power, invisible yet awfully great. And then in ver. 20–27, we, like David, may speak before the Lord of the righteousness we have got, and of the purity He himself has bestowed. It is with our eye on Christ's righteousness imputed, and Christ's Spirit imparted, that we so sing, humbly declaring what He has wrought for us. As for ver. 28–36, they tell our experience to the life ; and as for ver. 37–45, they tell, in our case, of the day when we shall share with our Head, in bruising Satan under our feet, and when Rev. iii. 9 shall be fulfilled. What are we that we should be called upon to join in such a song ! What are we, Lord, that thy Son should be our elder brother, and work all this for us ! Enable us for evermore to love, serve, glorify, and follow fully that *Saviour* who *was saved* when he took our place ! And never may we sing this Psalm but with burning love to Him, as we think of

The Righteous One saved and glorified.

Psalm 19

To the chief Musician, A Psalm of David

1 THE heavens declare the glory of God ; and the firmament sheweth his handywork.
2 Day unto day uttereth speech, and night unto night sheweth knowledge.
3 There is no speech nor language, where their voice is not heard.
4 Their line is gone out through all the earth, and their words to the end of the world.
   In them hath he set a tabernacle for the sun,
5 Which is as a bridegroom coming out of his chamber,
   And rejoiceth as a strong man to run a race.
6 His going forth is from the end of the heaven, and his circuit unto the ends of it:
   And there is nothing hid from the heat thereof.
7 The law of the Lord is perfect, converting the soul :
   The testimony of the Lord is sure, making wise the simple :
8 The statutes of the Lord are right, rejoicing the heart:
   The commandment of the Lord is pure, enlightening the eyes :
9 The fear of the Lord is clean, enduring for ever :
   The judgments of the Lord are true and righteous altogether.
10 More to be desired are they than gold, yea, than much fine gold :
   Sweeter also than honey and the honeycomb.
11 Moreover by them is thy servant warned : and in keeping of them there is great reward.
12 Who can understand his errors? cleanse thou me from secret faults.
13 Keep back thy servant also from presumptuous sins ;—let them not have dominion over me :
   Then shall I be upright, and I shall be innocent from the great transgression.
14 Let the words of my mouth, and the meditation of my heart,
   Be acceptable in thy sight, O Lord, my strength, and my redeemer.

STANDING on the platform of earth, but looking away from *The plan.* what in it is merely man's work, the eye of him that speaks in this Psalm has rested first on the *glorious heavens,* and then on the *law* that reveals *Him who dwelleth in the heavens.* *Law* is here equivalent to *Revelation;* it is תּוֹרָה ; that is, what he teaches.

There will be a time when, under the seven-fold light of the New Heavens that will stretch their canopy over a New Earth, it may be said yet more emphatically than now, that " without voice, or articulate sound,"

" The heavens are telling the glory of God."
" Day unto day pours out a gushing stream of speech," &c.

And then, too, shall we be better able to read that glorious *law,* that tells of Jehovah,—for we shall see better then than we do now how *" perfect"* it is, how *" sure,"* never failing in threatening or promise, how *" right,"* how really *" eternal ;"* better than *" gold ;"* and what a future as well as present *" reward"* there is in keeping it ! But why should we not even now reach far into the understanding of all this ? His *"'Law," i. e.* his revelation of his will (תּוֹרָה, teaching), is *"perfect,"* or entire, wanting nothing ; and so it can furnish the soul that needs to be *" restored"* with what suits its case. His *" testimony," i.e.* his *witness,* (with a tacit reference to the Tabernacle of Witness), or declaration of what is really good and evil, sweet and bitter, is *" sure,"* worthy to be trusted as true, not being like the speculations and systems of philosophy ; and so it is the very thing for the man who is easily misled, and who hitherto has had no decided principles, *" the simple."* His *" statutes"* (פִּקּוּדִים) are always according to rectitude. These His special charges in special circumstances (such as that at Sinai, not to touch the mountain), are *" right,"* being wisely accordant with circumstances; and so, instead of being grievous, they become the occasion of gladness. His commandment (מִצְוָה), every single precept of the whole Moral Law (Rom. vii. 12), is *" pure,"* clear, fair, (בָּרָה Song vi. 9, 10), and so is a heart-cheering object, and would impart to the man who kept it (who dipt his rod in this honey, 1 Sam. xiv. 27), cheerfulness and vigour of mind, arising from clearness of conscience and freedom from gnawing corruption. (*"Enlighten the eyes,"* means *invigorate ;* see Ezra ix. 8, &c.) His *" fear"* is the solemn impression made by God's perfections on the soul, as on Jacob at Bethel. Instruction in regard to this is in its nature *" clean"* (טְהוֹרָה Levit. xiii. 17), there is in it no defilement condemned by the law to be cast out, no pollution, and therefore nothing that requires removal, " standing *fast for ever."* In a word, His *" judgments," i. e.* His decisions as to our duty, and his modes of dealing or providential actings, following out his decisions, are all according to "*truth*," not capricious : firm principle guides them, "*they are thoroughly righteous.*"

There was once one in our world who used this Psalm, and   Christ. was guided by it to gaze on the glory of God, in the heavens and in the law. Our Lord and Saviour loved his Father's *works* and *word.* Often did He sit on the high mountains of the land of Israel, or look abroad over its broad plains, and then turn upward to the blue canopy over all, to adore his Father. Often did He unrol "the volume of the Book," or sit listening to its words read in the synagogue. He saw evil on every side ; his own holy soul was the only ark which this deluge had not overtaken ; and, with this in full view, He might often pray, "*keep me clear from secret faults*," (v. 12), as well as "*from presumptuous sin*," in a world where none are free from sin, and few care to know that they do sin ; and thus shall I be found,

"*Upright and innocent from transgression that abounds.*"*

We can easily imagine our Master thus using these two wit-   The members. nesses to his Father's glory. Let us trace His steps ; let us turn our eye from vanity to the contemplation of the glory of God.

The two witnesses resemble and help each other. Hengs-   The contents. tenberg remarks that the *law* is from the same source as the *sun and firmament,* and has, accordingly, many features of resemblance. In all probability, the special description of the *sun* going forth as a *bridegroom* and warrior (ver. 5), with all the images of cheerfulness and joy it is fitted to suggest, was designed to hint to us a counterpart in the firmament of the spiritual heavens, which are reflected in the law. Christ is the Sun, the Bridegroom, the Warrior, whose words ("line"† ver. 4), and going forth shall yet be from one end of the world to

---

* The words פֶּשַׁע רָב may be taken in the same sense of we find מְזִמָּה רָב, Deut. iii. 19, or Proverbs xxviii. 20, רַב בְּרָכוֹת, "*abounding* in blessings." Is not this the sense of Psa. xxv. 11, רַב הוּא ?

† "Line ;" compass of their territory ; (Isaiah xxiv. 17), (Hengstenberg). Paul seems to do no more than refer by way of allusion to this verse in Romans x. 18.

the other, and nothing be hid from His heat. Then shall Romans x. 18 be more thoroughly accomplished. But even if the two witnesses did not resemble each other, they do at least help each other, and point to the same object; and happy is the man who is led thereby to the glory of God. For verily there is a " GREAT REWARD" (ver. 11), both *in the* act of keeping His Revelation, and as the Lord's mark of approval *for our having kept it*; a present and a future " *recompence of reward*," such as Heb. x. 35 holds up before our view. Happy they who are found " upright and innocent" (ver. 13), because " found in Christ," found " without spot and blameless" (2 Pet. iii. 14), even in those last days when iniquity abounds. O, Jehovah, accept this meditation, fulfil these prayers ! Thou art-

> " *My rock*," never shifting from Thy promise ;
> " *My Deliverer*," from every evil work (ver. 14).

Thus sings this worshipper, perhaps at early dawn. But now the sun is up—gone forth on his fiery race; the altar's smoke is ascending—busy men are abroad, each pursuing his own calling, and he must join them. We seem to see him rise up from his place of calm contemplation, and return to his active duties for a season, quickened by what these two witnesses for God have presented to his soul, leaving us to ponder and apply,

The Righteous One's meditations on the twofold witness to Jehovah's glory

Psalm 20

To the chief Musician, A Psalm of David

1 THE Lord hear thee in the day of trouble ; the name of the God of Jacob defend thee.
2 Send thee help from the sanctuary, and strengthen thee out of Zion.
3 Remember all thy offerings, and accept thy burnt sacrifice. Selah.
4 Grant thee according to thine own heart, and fulfil all thy counsel.
5 We will rejoice in thy salvation, and in the name of our God we will set up our banners :
   The Lord fulfil all thy petitions.
6 Now know I that the Lord saveth his anointed ;
   He will hear him from his holy heaven with the saving strength of his right hand.

7 Some trust in chariots, and some in horses :
   But we will remember the name of the Lord our God.
8 They are brought down and fallen : but we are risen, and stand upright.
9 Save, Lord : let the king hear us when we call.

WHAT typical occurrence, or what event in Israel's history, may have given the groundwork of this Psalm ? *Luther* calls it a "battle-cry;" while others have imagined it appropriate to such an occasion as that of the high priest going in to the Holiest on the Day of Atonement, and reappearing to the joy of all who waited without in anxious prayer. We think the truth may be reached by finding some scene that may combine the *"battle-cry"* and the *priestly* function, such as was once presented in Numbers xxxi. 1–6, when the zealous priest Phinehas was sent forth at the head of the armies of Israel to battle. David may have been led to recal some such scene, as he sang. The drapery of the Psalm.

Full of zeal for his God, Phinehas, in his priestly attire, and with priestly solemnity,--with " Holiness to the Lord" on his mitre,—prepares for the conflict with Jehovah's and Israel's most subtle foes. We may suppose him at the altar ere he goes, presenting his offerings (ver. 3), and supplicating the Holy One of Israel (ver. 4), amid a vast assemblage of the camp, small and great, all sympathizing in his enterprise. This done, he takes the holy instruments and the silver trumpets in his hand, and sets forth. There is now an interval of suspense,—but soon tidings of victory come, and the priestly leader reappears, crowned with victory, leading captivity captive. The confidence expressed in ver. 5 is not vain, for victory, or " salvation," has been given.

Perhaps there were times when David was in such circumstance as these, and there are still times when any member of the Church may be, in some sense, so situated ; while "all weep" with the one member that weeps, and then " all rejoice" in the joy of the one. But still the chief reference is to *David's* Son, our Lord. He is the Leader and the Priest, the true Phinehas, going out against Midian. It is " the *Anointed*" (ver. 5) that is principally the theme. Christ's members Christ.

This Psalm is the prayer which the Church might be sup- The contents.

posed offering up, had all the redeemed stood by the cross, or in Gethsemane, in full consciousness of what was doing there. Messiah, in reading these words, would know that He had elsewhere the sympathy he longed for, when he said to the three disciples, "Tarry ye here, and watch with me," (Matt. xxvi. 38). It is thus a pleasant song of the sacred singer of Israel, to set forth the feelings of the redeemed in their Head, whether in his sufferings or in the glory that was to follow. In ver. 1–4, they pray:

" *Jehovah hear thee in the day of trouble,*
" *The name of* (i. e., He who manifests himself by deeds to be) *the God of Jacob defend thee.*
" *Send thee help from the sanctuary,*" where his well-pleasedness is seen.
" *And bless thee out of Zion,*"—not from Sinai, but from the place of peaceful acceptance, Zion.

The solemn " Selah"-pause comes in when " *sacrifice*" has been spoken of, and then in verse 5, they exult at the success which has crowned his undertaking ; and, observe, reader, they speak now of Him as one that makes petitions—" *The Lord fulfil all thy petitions.*" Is not this recognising Him as now specially employed in interceding ? applying His finished work by pleading it for us ? It may, at the same time, remind us of that other request, which the *Intercessor* is yet to make, and to make which, speedily, the Church is often urging him, verse 15, "Ask of me, and I will give thee the heathen for thine inheritance."—(Psa. ii. 8.) In ver. 6–8, they exult again, " *knowing* whom they have believed" (2 Tim. i. 12), both as to what the Father *has* done for Him, and what the Father *will* do. They reject all grounds of hope not found in King Messiah ; express their souls' desire for *complete deliverance,* when He shall appear at last, and answer, by complete salvation (Heb. ix. 28), the continual cry of His Church, " Come ! Lord Jesus !" Verse 9 teaches us to expect both present and future victories, by the arm of our King ; and in hope of these further exploits, we look often upward to the right hand of the Father, and cry, "*Hosanna !*"

" *Save, Lord !*" or, Give victory, הוֹשִׁיעָה
" *Let the King (who sitteth there) hear us when we call.*"

It is a Psalm differing in its aspects from most others, for it presents to us,

Messiah prayed for, and prayed to, by his waiting people.

Psalm 21

To the chief Musician, a Psalm of David

1 THE king shall joy in thy strength, O Lord ;
   And in thy salvation how greatly shall he rejoice !

2 Thou hast given him his heart's desire,
   And hast not withholden the request of his lips.   Selah.

3 For thou preventest him with the blessings of goodness :
   Thou settest a crown of pure gold on his head.

4 He asked life of thee, and thou gavest it him, even length of days for
   ever and ever.

5 His glory is great in thy salvation : honour and majesty hast thou laid
   upon him.

6 For thou hast made him most blessed for ever :
   Thou hast made him exceeding glad with thy countenance.

7 For the king trusteth in the Lord,
   And through the mercy of the Most High he shall not be moved.

8 Thine hand shall find out all thine enemies :
   Thy right hand shall find out those that hate thee.

9 Thou shalt make them as a fiery oven in the time of thine anger :
   The Lord shall swallow them up in his wrath, and the fire shall devour
   them.

10 Their fruit shalt thou destroy from the earth,
   And their seed from among the children of men.

11 For they intended evil against thee :
   They imagined a mischievous device, which they are not able to perform.

12 Therefore shalt thou make them turn their back :
   When thou shalt make ready thine arrows upon thy strings against the
   face of them.

13 Be thou exalted, Lord, in thine own strength ; so will we sing and praise
   thy power.

WE have entered on a series of Psalms that more directly fix the eye on Messiah alone as their theme. This is the second of the series. It takes up the theme of the former Psalm. We are at once shewn the King Messiah, already triumphant at the Father's right hand ; and yet, as King, to triumph more ere all be done.

A series of Psalms pointing to Messiah.

David, now on the throne at Hebron, and soon to be on a loftier throne at Jerusalem, might be the original of the typical scene ; but certainly he was not more than this. It is of our King that the Holy Spirit speaks.

The plan is very simple. From ver. 1–7, we have *Messiah's* exaltation after his suffering : then ver. 8–12, His future acts when He rises up to sweep away his foes ; and ver. 13, the cry of His own for that day, as their day of realised bliss :

> " *Be exalted, Lord, in thy strength !*
> *So will we sing and praise thy power.*" *

He who was the "man of sorrows," and " whose flesh was weak," now (ver. 1), "*joys in thy strength, greatly rejoices.*" And how sweet to us to hear verse 2, " *Thou hast given Him His heart's desire,*" remembering, in connection with it, John xi. 42, " I know that thou hearest me always ;" for it assures us that He did not mistake the depth of the Father's love, or err in His faith in the Father's kindness of purpose towards Him. He knew what was in man, but he knew what was in God also, and declares it to us, sealing it with the " *Selah*"-pause of solemn thought. The Father "came before Him with," or rather, *anticipated, outran,* His desires ; for that is the meaning of

> " *For thou* preventest *Him with the blessings of thy goodness.*"

And in the " *crown of pure gold,*" already set on His head, we see this verified, inasmuch as it is not the crown which he is to get at his appearing. The Father has at present given Him the crown, mentioned in Heb. ii. 9, " Glory and honour," but it is as an assurance and pledge of something more and better, the "*many crowns,*" (Rev. xix. 12).

Let us often stay to rejoice that the man of sorrows is happy now—"*most blessed for ever !*" He feeds among the lilies. Shall we not rejoice in the refreshment of our Head—in the ointment poured on him—in the glory resting on his brow—

---

* One who paraphrases the Psalms (Barclay) has given this as the essence of the one before us :

> "The battle fought, the victory won,—
> The Church rejoicing in the spoil,
> Gives glory to her Lord alone,
> And hails Him home from all His toil."

in the smile of the Father which his eye ever seeth ! Shall the members not be glad when their Head is thus gladdened and lifted up ? Shall such verses as ver. 5, 6, not form our frequent themes of praise ?

In ver. 4, his prayers are referred to—those prayers that He offered during the lonely nights, when He made the desert places of Galilee echo to his moans and the voice of His cry— such prayers as Heb. v. 7 tells of, and such as Psalm lxxxviii. 10, 11, gives a sample of. He asked deliverance from death and the grave—and, lo ! He has now "Endless life" (Heb. vii. 16) in all its power. Verse 6 resembles in construction verse 9, and so presents the contrast of meaning more forcibly. The one is, " *Thou hast set him blessings*;" the other is, "*Thou hast set them like a furnace.*"

And here we see that "He is the author and finisher of faith ;" for if his prayers and cries prove him to have had truly our very humanity in sinless weakness, no less does ver. 7 shew that his holy human soul fixed itself for support, like ivy twin- ing round the tower, on the Father by *faith.* In this He was our pattern.

" The King trusted in the Lord." (Ver. 7.)

He is the true example of faith, surpassing all the "elders who have obtained a good report ;" he is "captain and perfecter of faith ;" he leads the van and he brings up the rear, in the ex- amples of faith given on this world's theatre. (Heb. xii. 3.) And the Father's love rests on Him for ever ; that love ("ten- der mercy," ver. 7) of which he prayed in John xvii. 26, that the same might ever be on us.

And now the scene changes ; for, lo ! he has risen up !

" <i>Thy hand finds out all thine enemies ;</i>
" <i>Yea, thy hand finds out all that hate thee !</i>
" <i>Thou puttest them in a furnace of fire,</i>" &c. (Ver. 8, 9.)

It is his rising up to judgment ! His foes hide in the caves and rocks of earth, but he finds them out. It is the day which burns as an oven (Malachi iv. 1) that has come at length. It is the עֵתְּפָנֶיךָ ; the time of his *presence;* the day of his appear- ing ; " the day of his *face*"—that face before which heaven and earth flee. His enemies flee, and they perish in their impotence, his arrows striking them through, (Ver. 12).

" They formed a design which they could not effect,"

is truly the history of man's attempts to thwart God, from the day of Babel tower down to the day when Babylon and Antichrist perish together. And who would not have it so? Who will not join the Church in her song, "Rise high, O Lord, in thy strength ?"—the song of

Messiah's present joy and future victory.

Psalm 22

To the chief Musician upon Aijeleth Shahar, A Psalm of David

1 My God, my God, why hast thou forsaken me?
Why art thou so far from helping me, and from the words of my roaring?
2 O my God, I cry in the daytime, but thou hearest not ;
And in the night season, and am not silent.
3 But thou art holy, O thou that inhabitest the praises of Israel !
4 Our fathers trusted in thee : they trusted, and thou didst deliver them.
5 They cried unto thee, and were delivered : they trusted in thee, and were not confounded.
6 But I am a worm, and no man ; a reproach of men, and despised of the people.
7 All they that see me laugh me to scorn :
They shoot out the lip, they shake the head, saying,
8 He trusted on the Lord that he would deliver him :
Let him deliver him, seeing he delighted in him.
9 But thou art he that took me out of the womb :
Thou didst make me hope when I was upon my mother's breasts.
10 I was cast upon thee from the womb : thou art my God from my mother's belly.
11 Be not far from me ; for trouble is near ; for there is none to help.
12 Many bulls have compassed me : strong bulls of Bashan have beset me round.
13 They gaped upon me with their mouths, as a ravening and a roaring lion.
14 I am poured out like water, and all my bones are out of joint :
My heart is like wax ; it is melted in the midst of my bowels.
15 My strength is dried up like a potsherd ; and my tongue cleaveth to my jaws ;
And thou hast brought me into the dust of death.
16 For dogs have compassed me : the assembly of the wicked have inclosed me :
They pierced my hands and my feet.

17 I may tell all my bones : they look and stare upon me.

18 They part my garments among them, and cast lots upon my vesture.

19 But be not thou far from me, O Lord : O my strength, haste thee to help me.

20 Deliver my soul from the sword ; my darling from the power of the dog.

21 Save me from the lion's mouth : for thou hast heard me from the horns of the unicorns.

22 I will declare thy name unto my brethren :
In the midst of the congregation will I praise thee.

23 Ye that fear the Lord, praise him ;
All ye the seed of Jacob, glorify him ; and fear him, all ye the seed of Israel.

24 For he hath not despised nor abhorred the affliction of the afflicted ;
Neither hath he hid his face from him ; but when he cried unto him, he heard.

25 My praise shall be of thee in the great congregation :
I will pay my vows before them that fear him.

26 The meek shall eat and be satisfied :
They shall praise the Lord that seek him : your heart shall live for ever.

27 All the ends of the world shall remember and turn unto the Lord :
And all the kindreds of the nations shall worship before thee.

28 For the kingdom is the Lord's : and he is the governor among the nations.

29 All they that be fat upon earth shall eat and worship :
All they that go down to the dust shall bow before him:
And none can keep alive his own soul.

30 A seed shall serve him ; it shall be accounted to the Lord for a generation.

31 They shall come, and shall declare his righteousness
Unto a people that shall be born, that he hath done this.

WHAT a change ! Instead of the songs of victory, we hear the moaning of one in anguish. It is not the voice of those that shout for the mastery, as were the preceding songs of Zion, but the voice of one that cries in weakness. And yet this abrupt transition is quite a natural one. We saw the warrior—we saw the fruits for his victory—we saw the prospects of yet farther glorious results from that victory. Now then we are brought to the *battle-field* and shewn the battle itself—that battle which virtually ended the conflict with Satan and all his allies. We hear the din of that awful onset. Our David in " the irresistible might of weakness" is before us, crying in the crisis of conflict,

" Eli, Eli, lama sabacthani !"

the words uttered on Calvary, and preserved in every syllable as they were used by the Saviour then.

Some have sought to mingle the believer's confidence with

[margin note: The position of this Psalm.]

[margin note: Christ here alone.]

Christ's in this Psalm. But it is too awful in its strain to admit of this application, though we may learn from Christ's example, as well as words, on the cross ; as Peter is fond of shewing us in his first epistle. The words of verse 1st may indicate that such cries were uttered more than once during the Redeemer's days of anguish. There were other seasons besides the cross when the Father was near to lay on Him the weight of the burden of guilt, and when, for a time, he left Him, forsaken. These were seasons of the hottest trial ever known in warfare, for it was warfare wherein nothing could exhaust the resources brought up against the champion, while also there were divine supplies on his side.

The plan. The scheme of this Psalm is evident at a glance. There are two parts in it ; the one from verse 1 to middle of verse 21 ; the other from the middle of verse 21 to the end. The first part is Messiah's sufferings ; the second is his entering into his glory. His first coming is the theme of the one ; his glorious kingdom, established fully at his second coming, is the theme of the other ; and this is so very obvious, that we shall be very brief in our remarks, leaving the reader to meditate for himself, with the history of the Lord in the Evangelists* before him for the first part, and his eye glancing through the Apocalyptic visions for the second.

The title. The title is strange : " *On Aijeleth Shahar,*"—literally, " The hind of the morning." This was probably some instrument used for compositions of a peculiar cast, wherein joy gave

---

* This Psalm is quoted in Hebrews ii. 11, where verse 23 is the passage referred to. The "*piercing of hands and feet,*" verse 17, may be considered as referred to in such passages as Luke xxiv. 39, John xx. 27, when he carefully shewed his hands and his feet. The attempt of the modern Jews to translate כָּאֲרִי "like a lion," admits of a very complete and satisfactory refutation. Whether we adopt the Keri כָּאֲרוּ, or retain the Ketibh כָּאֲרִי, the sense is the same, only in the former case the literal rendering is, " *They have pierced,*" in the latter, it is to be understood participially, " *They are piercing.*" See an article in No. IV. of Bibliotheca Sacra and Biblical Repository, 1852 (combined series), where it is shewn that the Masora on Numbers xxiv. 9, plainly states that the text read, " They pierced," and Jacob bon Haiim says it was so " In many copies." All the ancient versions, *e.g.*, Septuagint and Syriac, and such critics as De Wette, Winer, Bahr (in Tholuck's Lit. Anzeig. 1853), agree in this rendering.

place to anguish, and then anguish to joy. The hind leaps from height to depth, from valley to hill-top, rising up from its quiet lair, where it had reposed till morning, when met by the hunters' cry. That there was such an instrument used we cannot tell—it is a mere conjecture ; at the same time it is interesting to notice how truly the scene of the hind, roused at morning from its rest (not to bound at liberty like Naphtali in Gen. xlix. 21, but) to be chased by the hunters, corresponds to the tale of persecution related here, when "dogs encompass him about."

Without attempting to explore the riches, the unsearchable riches, of these mournful cries, let us listen to a few of their sad echoes. In verse 3, "*But thou art holy, O thou who inhabitest the praises of Israel*," we have a declaration that Israel's Holy One shall be praised more than ever for his holiness, because of his impartial treatment of Him who cries, " Why hast thou forsaken me?" Strange as it may seem, it shall turn out to be an illustration of his holy character ; and if before this He inhabited Israel's praises, much more hereafter. In verse 4, that note, "OUR fathers," (as in Psalm xl. 5) from such lips may well touch our hearts. He is not ashamed, reader, to call you and me *his brethren !* He identifies himself with us ! *Our* fathers are *His* fathers, that His Father may be ours. How like Him who afterwards (ver. 22), calls us "*my brethren ;*" and who on earth did say, after resurrection, " Go and tell *my brethren*," (Matt. xxviii. 10).

We do not dwell on the ample field of remark opened to us from verses 6–22. "The people," in verse 6, is specially " *His own*" Israel. The taunt, ver. 8, is equivalent to He was fond of saying " *Roll on the Lord !*" what Psalm xxxvii. 5 expresses more fully. In verse 20, " My *only one*" is understood to be the soul described as dear like an only son.* How appropriate is the lips of Him who asked the memorable question, in Matt. xvi. 26.

* The word is the fem. of יָחִיד, used in Gen. xxii. 2 and elsewhere, for a thing that is precious because the only one of its kind. Is there any thing of this idea in Homer's φίλον ἦτορ (Iliad iii. 31, &c.), *his own dear heart ?*

It is in verse 21 that the tide turns. The clause

> " *Thou hast heard me*"

ought to be taken by itself. It is a cry of delight. It is like Luke xxii. 43. The lamentation of ver. 2 is over now—He is heard now ! And his being now heard is not a blessing to Him alone ; he runs to bring his disciples word :

> " *I will declare thy name to my brethren,*" (ver. 22) ;

words characteristic to the full of Him who spoke, John xvii. 26, and whose first resurrection-act was to send word to his disciples, by the name " *my brethren,*" and then to send them to all the earth. His special love to *Israel*, too, is apparent, as when He said, " to all nations, *beginning at Jerusalem*"—"Both in Jerusalem and in all Judea." Here he calls to them,

> " *Ye seed of Jacob, glorify Him—*
> *For He has not abhorred the affliction of the poor.*" (V. 23, 24.)

He has not treated the poor sinner as an unclean thing to be shrunk from (Levit. xi. 11), passing by on the other side. (Luke x. 31.) All shall yet praise Him who makes their heart live for ever by feeding them on this sacrifice (verse 26). Verse 28 shews us the *Kingdom* come, and Christ the *Governor* among the nations ; at which time we find a *feast partaken of by all nations*, and observed by sinners that were ready to perish :—

> " *All they that be fat* (the rich) *on the earth shall eat and worship.* (V. 29.)
> *Before Him shall bow all that go down to dust*, (the poor)
> *And he who could not keep alive his soul*," (the most destitute of the poor).

The essence of the *feast* is indicated at verse 26, as consisting in knowing and feeding upon Him who is our Paschal Lamb ; even as in Isaiah xxv. 8, the feast of fat things is Christ Himself, seen and known, eye to eye. The people of that millennial time are " *the seed*" of ver. 30. If men do not at present serve Him, yet their *seed* shall—there is a generation to rise who shall so do. (" *Hoc semen illi serviet,*" says Buchanan.)

> " *Posterity shalt serve Him,*
> *It shall be related of the Lord to the generation to come.*
> *These shall go forth* (on the theatre of the world) *and declare his righteousness*
> *To a people then to be born.* (Ps. cii. 18.)
> *For He has done it !*"

The Hebrew is very elliptical. It seems as if עָשָׂה were here intentionally used in an absolute and indefinite way in order to fix our thoughts on the thing being done. A finger points to the scene, and a voice says עָשָׂה ! *q. d. "He has performed !"* Here is *deed*, not word only. Here is *fulfilment, not promise only.* The meek may eat and be filled ! For lo ! there is the thing done ! performance of all that this Psalm describes, of all that Jesus meant when he cried, "*It is finished.*" In that hour He saw his sufferings ended and his glory begun, and could proclaim victory through suffering. What a song of Zion is this ! Messiah at every step ! beginning with " Eli, Eli," and ending with Τετελεσται, " It is finished."

Messiah bearing the cross, and wearing the crown.

Psalm 23

A Psalm of David

1. The Lord is my shepherd; I shall not want.
2. He maketh me to lie down in green pastures: he leadeth me beside the still waters.
3. He restoreth my soul: he leadeth me in the paths of righteousness for his name's sake.
4. Yea, though I walk through the valley of the shadow of death, I will fear no evil:
For thou art with me; thy rod and thy staff they comfort me.
5. Thou preparest a table before me in the presence of mine enemies: Thou anointest my head with oil; my cup runneth over.
6. Surely goodness and mercy shall follow me all the days of my life: And I will dwell in the house of the Lord for ever.

AFTER the conflict of the preceding Psalm, and its bright glimpse of triumph, we might have thought that such an ode as we afterwards find in Psalm xxiv. would have immediately followed, leading us to survey the scenes of victory anticipated by the sufferer. But, instead of this, we suddenly find ourselves in the quiet peace of the quietest valley that imagination could paint ; where is seen One walking by his shepherd's side singing,

The position of the Psalm.

> *" Jehovah is my shepherd !*
> *I shall not want."**

The arrangement seems intentional ; the soothing after the exciting, the stillness of the still waters after the fury of the tempest, the calm of rural peace before the engrossing and enrapturing scene of the Mighty One's dominion.   It is like the pause of Milton's angel,

> "As one who in his journey bates at noon,
>   Though bent on speed, so here the Archangel paused,
>   Between the world destroyed and world restored."

And, besides, it is most suitable that between the conflict finished successfully in man's behalf and the glorious issues of that conflict, as seen from the throne of dominion, there should interpose a view of that state of soul toward the Father in which the Head and his members pass through their wilderness.

Christ and His members

The Church has so exclusively (we might say) applied this Psalm to herself, as almost to forget that her shepherd ("that Great Shepherd !") once needed it and was glad to use it. *The Lamb* (now in the midst of the throne ready to lead us to living fountains of water) was once led along by his Father. He said to his disciples, " And yet I am not alone, for the Father is with me," (John xvi. 32).   Was not the burden of his song :—" The Lord is my shepherd ; I shall not lack," (Ver. 1) ?   When he said, on another occasion, (John x. 14, 15,) " I know my sheep, and am known of mine, as the Father knoweth me," was he not saying, " I lead you as my Father leads me ?"   But try every clause, and every syllable will be found applicable not to David alone, but to David's Son, to the

---

* Perhaps these **verses** were never more poetically rendered into **another** **tongue** than by Buchanan in his Latin version :

> —— "Sicut Pastor ovem, me Dominus regit;
>   Nil deerit penitus mihi.

> " Per campi viridis mitia pabula,
>   Quæ veris teneri pingit amœnitas,
>   Nunc pascor placide, nunc saturum latus
>   Fessus molliter explico.

> "Parcæ rivus aquæ leniter adstrepens
>   Membris restituit robora languidis;
>   Et blando recreat fomite spiritus,
>   Solis sub face torridâ."

Church and to the Church's Head. If verse 1 sings, " *I shall not want*," it is just a continuance of the testimony of Moses, Deut. ii. 7, " The Lord thy God—knoweth thy walking through this great wilderness : these forty years the Lord thy God has been with thee ; *thou hast lacked nothing.*" Christ and his Church together review their wilderness-days and praise the Lord. The song of the Lamb is not less complete than that of Moses.

The occasional retreat to the Sea of Galilee, and desert places, and the Mount of Olives, furnished Christ with many such seasons as verse 2 celebrates. " *He maketh me to lie down on pastures of tender grass.*" His saints know so well that it is his wont to do this in their case, that the Song of Songs asks not, " *Dost* thou make thy flock rest at noon ?" but only, " *Where ?*" And as the Lord of the Ark of the covenant (Numb. x. 33) sought out for Israel a place to rest, so did the Father for his true Israel,—that Prince with God,—giving him refreshing hours amid his sorrow ; as it is written, " He is at my right hand, that I should not be moved : therefore did my heart rejoice," (Acts ii. 25).

In temptation seasons, or after sore conflicts with man's unbelief, the Lord " *restored* his soul" (ver. 3) ; that is, re-vived it with cordials, even as he does his people after such seasons, and after times of battle with their own unbelief. And when in the hour of trouble and darkness he cried, " What shall I say ?" the Father "led *him in paths of righteousness, for his name's sake,*" glorifying his own name in his Son, as we read, John xii. 27.

It was not once only, (though it was specially as the Garden and the Cross drew near,) that his soul was in " the valley of death-shade," (ver. 4). But he passed all in safety ; even when he came to that thick gloom of Calvary. And He who led *Him* through will never leave one of his disciples to faint there. The *rod* and *staff** that slew the bear and the lion, made David confident against Goliath ; so do we obtain confidence

* 1 Sam. xvii. 40 and 43, Micah vii. 14, These were for defence ; also for beat-ing bushes when the sheep went astray, for killing serpents, and the like.

from knowing how our Shepherd has already found a safe way through wolves and perils.

In verse 5, the *table*, the *oil*, and the *cup*, might be illustrated in Christ's case by the day of his baptism, by the shining forth of his glory, by such a miracle as that of Lazarus' resurrection, and by the light of the Transfiguration scene, as well by the "meat to eat which the world knew not of," and the "rejoicing in spirit" as he thought upon the Father's will—in all which blessings the sheep still share from time to time, getting occasional exaltations, and moments of "joy unspeakable and full of glory."

Even those scenes of woe, the essence of whose anguish is expressed by "*Eli, Eli, lama sabacthani,*" did not make the Master doubt that "goodness and mercy would follow him," till he reached his home, his Father's house, with its many mansions. And shall any member doubt of his persevering to the end? loved to the end with the love that first loved him, till he becomes a guest for ever in his Father's house?

"House of the Lord."

What is the "House of the Lord," the true *Bethel*, where the ladder is set between earth and heaven? The Tabernacle was such in type. And of the antitype Christ spoke when, leaving his few sheep in the wilderness and amid wolves, he said, "In my *Father's house are many mansions,*" (John xiv. 1, 2). It is New *Jerusalem;* and He is gone to the right hand of the Father to gather in his elect, and then at length to raise up their bodies in glory, that they may enter into the full enjoyment of that House in the "kingdom prepared for the blessed of his Father." Fear not, then, little flock, it is your Father's good pleasure to give you the kingdom—and if so, you must be kept for it; goodness and mercy must follow you all the days of your life, bringing up the rear of the camp, and leaving not a straggler to perish. It will be then that every sheep of his pasture will fully know and use the words of this Psalm, which sets forth with inimitable simplicity,

The Righteous One's experience of the leadings of the Shepherd.

Psalm 24

A Psalm of David

1 THE earth is the Lord's, and the fulness thereof: the world, and they
   that dwell therein.
2 For he hath founded it upon the seas, and established it upon the floods.
3 Who shall ascend into the hill of the Lord? or who shall stand in his
   holy place?
4 He that hath clean hands, and a pure heart ;
   Who hath not lifted up his soul unto vanity, nor sworn deceitfully.
5 He shall receive the blessing from the Lord,
   And righteousness from the God of his salvation.
6 This is the generation of them that seek him,
   That seek thy face, O Jacob. Selah.
7 Lift up your heads, O ye gates ; and be ye lifted up, ye everlasting doors ;
   And the King of glory shall come in.
8 Who is this King of glory ?
   The Lord strong and mighty, the Lord mighty in battle.
9 Lift up your heads, O ye gates ; even lift them up, ye everlasting doors ;
   And the King of glory shall come in.
10 Who is this King of glory ?   The Lord of hosts, he is the King of glory.
   Selah.

THIS may have been written by David when the ark was
brought up to Zion. Every eye in the universe is looking on, *The tone of the Psalm.*
and every ear listening in heaven, earth, and under the earth.
The strain of this Psalm brings up to our thoughts, Revelation v. 2, 3 ; for it is as if a voice proclaimed

" *The earth is the Lord's !*"

And then, " *It is He, and no one else, who founded it above the surrounding seas.*"

The claim of the Lord's dominion is made in hearing of the
universe ; and the proclamation challenges a denial. This is
done in verses 1, 2, and no one in heaven, or earth, or hell, is
found, who does not acquiesce in this declaration of Jehovah's
sovereignty.

Amid the universal attention of all beings, a voice asks the
question,

" *Who shall ascend into the hill of the Lord ?
And who shall stand in his holy place ?*"   (Ver. 3.)

The import of the question is this. There is in that world a
tabernacle on Zion, typical of God's prepared mansion for his   *Christ.*

redeemed. Who shall enter and "*stand*" (that is, keep his place) there, claiming as his proper home both that Tabernacle and the better things of which it is the type?

The voice states the character of the accepted one in verse 4,- "*He that hath clean hands;*" that is, he that washes in the water of the laver after being at the altar. This, O men of Israel, has been shewn to you. Is not that every day exhibited in your tabernacle? No priest enters the holy *place* until he has washed at the laver after being at the altar, (Exod. xxx. 19). Or, to express it without a type,

> "*He that has a pure heart,*
> *Who has not lifted up his soul to vanity,*
> *Nor sworn deceitfully.*" (Ver. 4.)

He must be pure, free from charge of sin against God and man. This is the man that receives " the blessing,".(Gen. xxvii. 36); this is the man that receives it, not as Jacob by stealth, but as the award of " righteousness," being treated as righteous by the "*God of salvation.*" Messiah is this man.

But Israel knew the way to obtain this purity. His " holy place" presented to him in type the provision that the "God of salvation" had revealed for a sinner. And so the voice pronounces, (referring to a company who resemble The Man described),

> "*This is the generation of them that seek him :*
> *That seek thy face, O Jacob.*" (Ver. 6).

The generation of those who seek Jehovah are such. And this further praise is given them, viz., "The diligent seekers of thy face are *Jacob,*" *i.e.*, persons who have a claim to the name of the peculiar people—if we adopt the rendering of Hengstenberg. But, retaining the common version, we understand the words in the following way :—These whose hands are clean are the true seekers of Jehovah : and they are taking the true way to get Jacob's *birthright* and Jacob's *blessing,*—" *They seek thy face,* *O Jacob :* they do not seek Esau, with the fatness of earth, but thee, Jacob, who hast got the *blessing from the Lord.*"*

---

* In Prov. vii. 15, and xxix. 26, we have, " *seeking the face of*" in the sense of seeking the favour of, or shewing delight in. Their delight is not in Esau, who got " the fatness of earth" (Gen. xxvii. 39) as his portion. And those writers may be right who consider *Jacob* as a name for Messiah, to whom belong the true birthright and blessing.

If we understand it in reference to the possession of the *birth-right* and the *blessing*, that is, to the promise of Messiah and the pre-eminence involved herein, we see a reason for introducing the name "*Jacob.*" Properly and directly it is Christ only who can advance the claim to be regarded as "pure," and in all respects unspotted. It is Christ who in his own person is accepted as such, and is proclaimed righteous. But all He does and receives is in behalf of his people ; and hence the words, "*This is the generation of them that seek Him,*" *q. d.,* Lo ! here is a generation of such men.

There is a pause, intimated by "*Selah*" (ver. 6), not unlike that in Prov. i., between verses 23 and 24 ; and the voice, having before declared who may hope to enter the Lord's presence, suddenly announces that their *King* is at hand ! The accepted pure and righteous One is the King !

> "*Lift up your heads, O ye gates ;*
> *And be ye lifted up, ye everlasting doors ;*
> *And the* KING OF GLORY *shall come in.*" (Ver. 7.)

That name, "KING OF GLORY,"* from whence is it derived? Is it not from the cloud of *glory* in the Holy of Holiest ? Is He not thus designated as being the Antitype of that symbol of the Divine presence ? And the *doors* are called "*Everlasting,*" because he who enters in at them is to keep for ever and in everlasting freshness this palace and sanctuary which he makes for himself in our Earth. "The beams of his house are to be cedar, and the rafters fir," (Song i. 17) because the upholder of all is come. *Earth* is now to be his sanctuary and palace—Earth full of his glory —Earth with New Jerusalem come down from heaven.

It is the Lord himself, perhaps, who asks at the wondering universe (just as the Elder asked at wondering John, Rev. vii. 13) concerning his Well-beloved, now brought into the world in honour, and glory, and majesty, not as at his first coming, in humiliation,

> "*Who is this King of Glory ?*" (Ver. 8.)

* Dr Allix remarks, "If some Christians have applied it to Christ's ascension, it was for want of considering that it gives to Christ the title of Jehovah, *King of Glory* (1 Cor. ii. 8), and of being powerful in battle. These titles suppose his enemies destroyed." (Rev. xix. 6.)

It is like Jeremiah xxx. 21, מִי זֶה, " Who is this that has engaged his heart to approach to me? saith the Lord." And the reply also is the Father's, who tells of his Son that he has gained victories and overcome in battles, and so won the Kingdom. But when the proclamation is repeated, and wondering onlookers half incredulous again put the question, "*Who is this* King?" the Father's reply is,

" The Lord of Hosts, He is the King of Glory."

thus proclaiming the oneness of *our King* with *Jehovah*, before all creation.

"*Selah*" ends the Psalm—a solemn pause ere the people depart from the spot where they heard this lofty song.

The Church.   It is a glorious hymn for the Church in all ages. Paul writing to Corinth (1 Cor. x. 26), claims *a believer's right* to the things of earth, on the ground that this Psalm claims *for God* a right to it : " *The earth is the Lord's and the fulness thereof.*" Evidently Paul associated himself and his fellow-saints with " *The King of Glory,*" in whose train we also expect to enter through the everlasting gates. The Psalm describes our mode of joining the royal procession, and so passing on to glory with the King. There is no Psalm which, with such sublime and simple grandeur, describes-

The path of the Righteous to the throne of glory.

Psalm 25

A Psalm of David

1, 2. Unto thee, O Lord, do I lift up my soul. O my God, I trust in thee !
Let me not be ashamed, let not mine enemies triumph over me.

3 Yea, let none that wait on thee be ashamed :
Let them be ashamed which transgress without cause.

4 Shew me thy ways, O Lord ; teach me thy paths.

5 Lead me in thy truth, and teach me :
For thou art the God of my salvation ; on thee do I wait all the day.

6 Remember, O Lord, thy tender mercies and thy lovingkindnesses ;
For they have been ever of old.

7 Remember not the sins of my youth, nor my transgressions :
According to thy mercy remember thou me, for thy goodness sake, O Lord

8 Good and upright is the Lord: therefore will he teach sinners in the way.

9 The meek will he guide in judgment: and the meek will he teach his **way.**

10 All the paths of the Lord are mercy and truth
Unto such as keep his covenant and his testimonies.

11 For thy name's sake, O Lord, pardon mine iniquity; for it is great.

12 What man is he that feareth the Lord? Him shall he teach in the way that
he shall choose.

13 His soul shall dwell at ease; and his seed shall inherit the earth.

14 The secret of the Lord is with them that fear him; and he will shew them
his covenant.

15 Mine eyes are ever toward the Lord; for he shall pluck my feet out of the
net.

16 Turn thee unto me, and have mercy upon me; for I am desolate and
afflicted,

17 The troubles of my heart are enlarged: O bring thou me out of my distresses.

18 Look upon mine affliction and my pain; and forgive all my sins.

19 Consider mine enemies; for they are many; and they hate me with cruel
hatred.

20 O keep my soul, and deliver me! let me not be ashamed; for I put my trust
in thee.

21 Let integrity and uprightness preserve me; for I wait on thee.

22 Redeem Israel, O God, out of all his troubles.

THE inquiry may have crossed the reader's mind, Why was this Psalm placed next such a one as the 24th? We almost think we can answer that question; and if our answer is right, it gives us a key to the structure of the Psalm. We suppose that the resemblance of verse 12 to the style of the closing verses of Psalm xxiv. may account for the juxtaposition. The resemblance is much closer than appears at first sight. *The position of the Psalm.*

As in Psalm xxiv. 8 (like Jer. xxx. 21) we had Messiah in- *Messiah in it.* troduced to our notice by the question, מִי זֶה מֶלֶךְ, so in ver. 12 of this Psalm we find suddenly the question put,

מִי זֶה הָאִישׁ יְרֵא יְהוָֹה

" Who is this man who feareth the Lord ?"

Up to that verse, we may suppose the Psalmist speaks in the name of a member of the Church, such as himself, amid snares (ver. 15) and troubles (ver. 17) at a time when Israel, too, was tried (ver. 22)—times when David was as a partridge on the mountains. This member of the Church prays for deliver-ance and guidance, appealing to the Lord's compassions. He feels sure that the Lord "*will guide the meek,*" (*i.e.*, those who give up their will to His) "*in judgment,*" *i e.*, on the the highway where all is lawful and right. At verse 11 he utters the appeal, "Pardon mine iniquity *for thy name's sake,*" throwing his burden down as too heavy for him to bear; "*For it is great.*" At this point the scene changes. An answer is coming to the petitioner. His eyes fix on the Perfect One, who seems suddenly to come in sight.

> " WHO IS THIS MAN *that feareth the Lord,*
> *Whom he teacheth the way that he shall choose?*
> *His soul lodgeth at ease,*
> *And His seed shall inherit the earth.*"

What a blessed vision! What a sweet sketch of Messiah and his blessings! Himself in his glorious rest, and his seed filling the earth! Instantly, in verse 14th, it is added that a share in this bliss belongs to all who fear the Lord:

> "*The secret of the Lord is with them that fear him,*
> *And he will shew them his covenant.*"

All the blessings of the covenant are yours; the hidden treasures of the Lord's friendship ("*secret*") are yours, O fearer of Jehovah. Having seen and heard all this, the Psalmist exclaims,

> " MINE EYES ARE EVER TOWARDS THE LORD,"

who provides such blessings, present and future, and thus makes my soul dwell at ease, while I behold Him. And so he prays again in full hope and confidence. When he reaches verse 20, "*Let me not be ashamed, for I put my trust in thee,*" we are reminded of Coriolanus betaking himself to the hall of Attius Tullus, and sitting as a helpless stranger there, claiming the king's hospitality, though aware of his having deserved to die at his hands. The Psalmist throws himself on the compassions of an injured God with similar feelings; "*I trust in Thee!*"

Appeal to mercy. It is to be noticed, that throughout the appeals of this Psalm are far more to the *compassion* and *mercy* of the Lord than to any other attribute. Only let his pity awake, and he has a righteous channel down which to pour it. In Psalm xxvi., as we shall see, it is different. But here the general strain of all the appeals is that of verses 5–8, 10, 11.

It is the first fully *Alphabetic* Psalm ;* that is, the first in- An Alphabetic Psalm.
stance we have met with where every verse begins with a letter
of the Hebrew alphabet in succession. There seems nothing
peculiar in this sort of composition ; and as if to guard us against
the idea of any mystery in it, the regularity is twice broken in
upon in this Psalm, as in most of the others of the same structure. Nor are these irregularities the effect of careless tran-
scription ; for every MS. agrees in the readings, and the ancient versions shew that the text existed in its present state
from the earliest times. The only lesson which the use of the
Alphabetic form may teach is this : that the Holy Spirit was
willing to throw his words into all the moulds of human
thought and speech ; and whatever ingenuity man may exhibit
in intellectual efforts, he should consecrate these to his Lord,
making him the "*Alpha and Omega*" of his pursuits.†

It is a Psalm, then, wherein the letters of the Hebrew alphabet are made use of to help the memory and to vary the structure—all with the view of enabling the Church in every age
to do as the Psalmist does here, viz., confess and pray for pardon,
help, guidance, deliverance, with the eye on Him who is set
before us in verse 12, "*This Man*," the true pattern of the
fear of God, and the bestower of blessing from himself on all
that fear the Lord. And who would not say with the Church
in every land, and with the souls under the altar, as well as
with David here,

"*Redeem Israel, O God, from all his troubles !*" (Ver. 22.)

If the day when that prayer was first answered by David
being raised to tho throne was glorious, what will be the day
when the true *David* ascends his throne and dwells at ease,
and his seed inherit the earth ? Let us learn to use the Psalm
if we would fully enter into

The confidence of the Righteous in the Lord's mercies.

* We met with partially alphabetic Psalms in Psalms ix. and x.

† Psalms xxv., xxxiv., xxxvii., cxi., cxii., cxix., and cxlv., are all written in
this manner,—so that there are seven Alphabetic Psalms, thus exhibiting a full
specimen of this form of writing. Fry, Horsley, and others insist on trying to
rectify the omitted letters in those cases where there is a deficiency, quite un-
warrantably.

Psalm 26

A Psalm of David

1 JUDGE me, O Lord; for I have walked in mine integrity:
I have trusted also in the Lord; therefore I shall not slide.

2 Examine me, O Lord, and prove me; try my reins and my heart.

3 For thy lovingkindness is before mine eyes: and I have walked in thy truth.

4 I have not sat with vain persons, neither will I go in with dissemblers.

5 I have hated the congregation of evil doers; and will not sit with the wicked.

6 I will wash mine hands in innocency: so will I compass thine altar, O Lord:

7 That I may publish with the voice of thanksgiving, and tell of all thy wondrous works.

8 Lord, I have loved the habitation of thy house, and the place where thine honour dwelleth.

9 Gather not my soul with sinners, nor my life with bloody men:

10 In whose hands is mischief, and their right hand is full of bribes.

11 But as for me, I will walk in mine integrity: redeem me, and be merciful unto me.

12 My foot standeth in an even place: in the congregations will I bless the Lord.

The tone.

THE distinguishing peculiarity of this Psalm, in the tone of its appeals, is, that it dwells so much on the *righteousness* of Jehovah's character. Having in the preceding one dealt much with his mercies, it was fitting in this one to trace the channel down which these mercies flow to sinners.

Christ in it as well as his Members.

Our Head himself speaks here as well as his members. We may consider Him as teaching his members to take up his words, and address them to the Father in his name.

"*Judge me, O Lord,*" &c., (Ver. 1). Who could so well speak thus, as He who prayed that prayer and held that converse in John xvii.

" *Examine me, O Lord, and prove me ;*
" *My heart and reins have been tried*"—as gold is tried, (Ver. 2). John xvii. 4.

And who could so well say as Jesus, in verse 3,

" *Thy lovingkindness is before mine eyes ;*—(as Deut. vi. 8, frontlets.)
And I have walked in thy truth."

He fears not to invite this searching of heart and reins, for he knows the "*lovingkindness*" of the Lord; and he fears not to be driven from any favourite path he is upon, for his desire is to "walk habitually in his truth." "*I love the Father*," said Jesus, (John xiv 31). "I come to bear witness to *the truth*," (John xviii. 37). And we might thus go through the Psalm, and shew its application to Him. But more particularly observe verses 6, 7,

"*I will wash my hands in innocency* (*i.e.*, I will touch no unclean thing, like Gen. xx. 5, Deut. xxi. 6) :
I will compass thine altar, O Lord; (as Jericho was compassed, Josh. vi. 3)
That I may publish with the voice of thanksgiving ;
And tell all thy wondrously accomplished works."

The meaning is, that he will go round and round the altar, looking at it, looking at the blood on its base, and the blood on each of the four horns, towards north, south, east, and west, and beholding the smoke of the fire, and thinking of the sacrificial victim that has died there,—all in the way of joyful thanks, for salvation provided for men ! It is a survey of redemption-work, taken by the Redeemer ; such a survey, as every member of his body often takes after having felt the power of free forgiveness, and while aiming at "innocency." For the "*compassing*" of the altar takes place after pardon : it is made in order to view it leisurely.

Jesus loved the types, and that typical Temple, because they shewed forth his work ;

"*Lord, I have loved the habitation of thy house,*
And the place where thine honour dwelleth"—(Ver. 8),

where his Glory dwelt, and where God was shewn as just, while gracious. He hated the thought of sin ; and though "numbered with transgressors," abhorred their company as hell. (Ver. 9, 10.) And is not this the feeling of every member of his mystical body ? And do not all join in the resolution and prayer of verse 11 ?

We consider verse 12 as anticipating the future. "*The even place*," seems to be the place of security, where no farther danger of falling shall occur ; though it may express also the present sure standing of the soul in God's love. At all events,

"*In the congregations will I bless the Lord*" (ver. 12),

points farther than to the assemblies of God's people on earth. However pleasant these may be, they are but types of better. They are but shadows of those multitudes, "numbers without number" in the kingdom, and their voice of praise but the prelude to the anthems that shall arise from "blessed· voices uttering joy," when the Lord shall have gathered his great multitude that no man can number. Till that day dawns, let us use this Psalm, in order to enter fully into sympathy with the appeals of the Righteous One and his members. It is, throughout, a breathing forth of-

The confidence of the Righteous in the Lord's righteousness.

Psalm 27

A Psalm of David

1 Thᴇ Lord is my light and my salvation; whom shall I fear?
The Lord is the strength of my life; of whom shall I be afraid?

2 When the wicked, even mine enemies and my foes, came upon me to eat up my flesh,
They stumbled and fell.

3 Though an host should encamp against me, my heart shall not fear:
Though war should rise against me, in this will I be confident.

4 One thing have I desired of the Lord, that will I seek after;
That I may dwell in the house of the Lord all the days of my life,
To behold the beauty of the Lord, and to inquire in his temple.

5 For in the time of trouble he shall hide me in his pavilion:
In the secret of his tabernacle shall he hide me;
He shall set me upon a rock.

6 And now shall mine head be lifted up above mine enemies round about me:
Therefore will I offer in his tabernacle sacrifices of joy;
I will sing, yea, I will sing praises unto the Lord.

7 Hear, O Lord, when I cry with my voice: have mercy also upon me, and answer me.

8 When thou saidst, Seek ye my face; my heart said unto thee, Thy face, Lord, will I seek.

9 Hide not thy face far from me; put not thy servant away in anger:
Thou hast been my help; leave me not, neither forsake me, O God of my salvation.

10 When my father and my mother forsake, then the Lord will take me up.

11 Teach me thy way, O Lord, and lead me in a plain path, because of mine enemies.

12 Deliver me not over unto the will of mine enemies:
For false witnesses are risen up against me, and such as breathe out cruelty.

13 I had fainted, unless I had believed to see the goodness of the Lord in the
land of the living.

14 Wait on the Lord: be of good courage,
And he shall strengthen thine heart. Wait, I say, on the Lord.

THE Righteous One does not walk without opposition. We
are led here to a field of conflict ; or rather to the height,
whence the Righteous One surveys the legions of foes that are
embattled against him ; and standing by his side, we hear his
song of confidence, and cry of dependence, as he looks up to
the Lord as his " light and salvation." Is it Christ that we
hear thus expressing what his soul felt ? or is it one of his own
who encounters the same foes ? It is both ; for David was
taught by the Spirit to write the blessed experience of the
Church and its Head. The Church's experience here is obvious.
Let us dwell a little on her Lord's.

Christ and his people.

Is this, then, " the light of the world" walking through
darkness, and staying himself on his Father ? What an illustration of his own words, in John xvi. 32, 33, " The hour cometh
when ye shall be scattered, every man to his own, and shall
leave me alone ; and yet I am not alone, for the Father is with
me. In the world ye shall have tribulation : but be of good
cheer, I have overcome the world." And then, soon after, his
enemies " stumbled and fell," (Ver. 2). The band, with Judas
at their head, " went backwards and fell to the ground" (John
xviii. 6), as if in token of the future falling of all that come out
against him ; while Judas, their leader, stumbled over the cor-
ner-stone to his eternal ruin. So sure is this, that in verse 3
he appropriates to his own use, and the use of all the righteous,
the protecting hosts that Elisha saw round Dothan. (2 Kings
vi. 15.) Our Lord's words, " Thinkest thou not that I cannot
pray to my Father, and He will presently give more than
twelve legions of angels?" were at once a reference to the
guard of Elisha, and a breathing forth of the strong confidence
of this Psalm.

Christ.

The words, " IN THIS *will I be confident,*" refer us back to
the faith of verse 1, " I will be confident, that Jehovah is my
light, salvation, strength."

The contents.

We have our Lord's style, so to speak, in verse 4,—" *One*
thing." He, who on earth pointed out the " one thing lack-

Christ.

ing," to the Ruler : and " the one thing needful," to Martha,
declares what himself felt regarding that " one thing." To see
the Lord, in his temple where everything spoke of redemption,
—there to see the Father's "*beauty*," was the essence of his
soul's desire. This "*beauty*," נֹעַם is the Lord's well-pleased
look ; such a look as the Father gave, when his voice proclaimed, "This is my beloved Son, in whom I am well-pleased."
It also means, all that makes God an object of affection and delight to a soul.* Nothing could be more desirable to Christ,
than this approving look of his Father, telling, as it did, his
love to the uttermost. And nothing to us sinners, can equal
this look of love ; it is the essence of heaven now, and heaven
for ever. It is the "*one thing ;*" for from this holy love pro-
ceed all other blessings. To catch glimpses of this " beauty "
in the temple was our Lord's aim ; he engaged in no other
pursuit on earth. Neither did David, this true disciple, amid
the glory of a kingdom. In the light of this Divine smile, the
soul is sure of deliverances manifold, deliverance from every
evil, and eternal gladness ; and can sing (ver. 7) even now,
as if full deliverance were come already. Real assurance of
salvation depends in our seeing the Father's " beauty,"—
his reconciled countenance, his heart of love ; in seeing which,
the soul feels certain beyond measure, that his future state will
be well, for that love is too deep to change ; and so it " sings and
makes music to Jehovah."

But verse 8 has a tinge of sadness again. It is, in our Lord's
case, like John xii. 17, " Now is my soul troubled," after a season of peaceful rest. Never was there an experience so varied
and full as our Lord's in his human nature ; and never an experience which his saints so often turn to as their own. The
cry for help ascends ; and perhaps the broken words of verse 9
are intentional, being the difficult utterance of one in trouble
quoting words of hope,

> " My heart says to thee, *Seek ye my face.*"

My soul repeats to thee thine own call and encouragement.

---

* Luther understood it. " The beautiful services of the Lord " in the Tabernacle (Tholuck) ; the spiritual truths reflected in the mirror of that symbolic
worship.

How often hast thou bidden us, "Seek my face?" My heart reminds thee of thine own words; I will not let thee go. To me, and to the sons of men, thou hast sent forth an invitation to this effect, "Seek ye my face;" therefore, my heart in all its distress holds up to thee this call of thine. *I will seek thy face*, and I will urge thee, "Hide not *thy face*," (ver. 9).

In verse 10, the harp sings of a lonely, friendless, orphan state. "*My father and mother have left me!*" But forthwith faith responds, "*The Lord will take me in.*" (Josh. xx. 4, Judges xix. 5.) Our Lord, no doubt, felt *as man* the desire for a father's and a mother's sympathy and help. But in want of that sympathy and help, he turns to what he finds in Jehovah ; for the Lord has a *father's* "heart," " Like as a father pitieth his children, so the Lord pitieth them that fear him," (Ps. ciii. 13); and the *mother's* affections, too, " As one whom his mother comforteth, so the Lord will comfort you," (Isa. lxvi. 13). Our Lord uses what is equivalent to "*take me in,*" in Matt. xxv. 43. (Hengstenberg.)

A shrill note of the harp touches upon reproach and calumny, in verses 13, 14, "*false witnesses are risen up.*" In Matt. xxvi. 62, 63, these *false witnesses* come in against our Lord, before the high priest ; and on that occasion, our Lord bursts forth after long silence, with the declaration, " Hereafter ye shall see the Son of man sitting on the right hand of power, and coming in *the clouds of heaven.*" Is this the train of thought on this Psalm ? For verse 15 sets forth the hope of seeing what Zechariah ix. 17 speaks of as yet future in a great measure, " His goodness."

" *The goodness of the Lord in the land of the living.*"

Our Lord was content, as real man, to sustain his soul by faith and hope ; resting on what He knew of his Father, and animating it in suffering and trouble, by the " hope set before Him," (Heb. xii. 2). Is not this his testimony (and the testimony of all his saints who have used this Psalm) to the advantages and blessedness of *hope ?* The words in the Hebrew run thus-

" *Unless I had believed to see the goodness of the Lord.*" (Ver. 15.)

There is no "*I had fainted.*" It is an imperfect sentence.

There is something to be supplied ; it is like our Lord's own words in Luke xix. 42, " IF *thou hadst known !*"—a sentence never ended, and all the more emphatic and awfully significant for this very reason. Here, also, there is the same significance. It is "Who can tell, what heart of man can conceive, what might have come on me,—*unless I had believed to see the goodness of the Lord !*" Faith, and the "*hope set before Him,*" carried Him through his darkest hour. And hence, in verse 16, He leaves for the Church in all ages the counsel of one who has tried it himself,—" *Wait on the Lord.*" Keep your eye ever on the Lord, expecting the light to break and help to come.

The Church, and the Church's head, can lay claim to every clause of this blessed Psalm. That pledge of its truth in verse 5 has already in all ages been found faithfully performed. The Lord has ever hid his own in evil days, finding an Obadiah to feed his prophets, or sending them to a Cherith, whither his ravens shall carry provision. So that Augustine's confidence is that of all saints, " Qui tantum pignus dedit peregrinanti, non deseret pervenientem." We may call it then,—

The Righteous One's confident assertion of safety when lonely amid surrounding foes.

Psalm 28

A Psalm of David

1 UNTO thee will I cry, O Lord my rock ; be not silent to me :
  Lest if thou be silent to me, I become like them that go down into the pit.
2 Hear the voice of my supplications, when I cry unto thee,
  When I lift up my hands toward thy Holy Oracle.
3 Draw me not away with the wicked, and with the workers of iniquity,
  Which speak peace to their neighbours, but mischief is in their hearts.
4 Give them according to their deeds, and according to the wickedness of
    their endeavours :
  Give them after the work of their hands ; render to them their desert.
5 Because they regard not the works of the Lord, nor the operation of his
    hands,
  He shall destroy them, and not build them up.
6 Blessed be the Lord, because he hath heard the voice of my supplications.

7 The Lord is my strength and my shield; my heart trusted in him, and I
   am helped:
   Therefore my heart greatly rejoiceth; and with my song will I praise him.
8 The Lord is their strength, and he is the saving strength of his anointed.
9 Save thy people, and bless thine inheritance: feed them also, and lift them
   up for ever.

THE cry at the commencement is the appeal heavenward of *The speaker.*
one who anticipates, in the future (ver. 9), full salvation to
the Lord's people, and a time when their Shepherd shall feed
them in green pastures, and lift them up as his heritage to
their place of dignity and dominion. The secret persuasion
of this final issue pervades his song. If the preceding Psalm
took us up to a field of Zophim, whence we might espy the en-
camped legions, this Psalm shows us from the same height
these hosts of the ungodly shattered and dissipated, in answer
to the prayer of Him who makes intercession against them.
We may imagine the Psalmist,—whether David or David's
Son,* the Church's head, or any member of the Church—ascending an eminence, overlooking the tents of the ungodly, and
there listening to their mirth and witnessing their revelry! He
is a Moses, crying to heaven against Amalek. It may be David,
who is the original *"Anointed"* of verse 8; but he is so as
uttering what *the Lord* and all his own might use in other days.

What intensity of earnest vehemence in verse 1! Not to be *The contents.*
heard, will be death! it will be the black despair of those who
go down to the pit! But his reasons for being heard are
powerful,—*"I lift up my hand toward thy Holy Oracle,"* (ver.
2). This is the Holy of Holies, where the Mercy-seat stood: for
the "oracle" is, in Hebrew, "דְּבִיר," the spot where *Jehovah
spoke* to men, referring probably to his promise in Exodus xxv.
22, "There will I meet thee, and commune (דִּבַּרְתִּי) with thee."
The supplicant refers God, in this brief way, to his own provision for sinful men, and his own promise of blessing whenever that provision should be used. If we take the words as
uttered by Christ, how interesting to find him pleading with
reference to the types of his own person and work, presenting
them to the Father for us! If we use them as the words of

---

* "Ipsius Mediatoris vox est, manu fortis, conflictu passionis."—*Augustine.*

David, or any saint, they still convey the same truth, namely, that the strongest plea which can rise from earth to heaven is drawn from the person and work of Jesus. No doubt, when Daniel prayed " with his windows open in his chamber toward Jerusalem" (Dan. vi. 10), he had his eye on "the Holy Oracle," —on the person and work of Him who was set forth in Jerusalem in the significant types that were to be found in the Holy of Holies.

In verse 3, the sympathy of the Righteous One in God's love of holiness appears ; and in verse 4, his sympathy in God's justice, even when his burning wrath descends. It is full acquiescence that is expressed—nay, almost positive desire. But it is only as the redeemed in Rev. xix. 1, 3, are enabled to shout "Alleluia" over the lost ; or as the Redeemer (Luke xiii. 9), in the parable of the Fig-tree, promised to cease at last from intercession, and bid the axe take its swing.

Verse 5 is the answer whispered to the conscious heart of those who pray ; which causes thanksgiving and rapturous triumph in the Lord, reviving faith bestowing strength, (in verses 6, 7, 8)* and raising the anticipation of bright days approaching, when full "salvation" comes out of Zion (verse 9), and there shall be no more casting down. Every stream seems to flow onward to the future day when joy shall no more be pent up within narrow banks, but have unlimited scope—the people "saved" —the "blessing" come—there being no more curse—the heirs arrived at their inheritance, joint-heirs of Him who is "Heir of all things"—the shepherd leading them to living fountains —and reproach all fled away!

We express the tone and substance of the Psalm if we describe it as-

The appeal and thanksgiving of the righteous as they view the tents of the ungodly.

* In verse 7 it is literally, "*I will give praise to him from out of my song*,"— as if it were a fountain. In verse 8, "The Lord is *their* strength." This mode of expression seems to be equivalent to "The strength of *yonder ones*," or, of such as possess the character just described. So in Psalm cxv. 9-11. Isa. xxxiii. 2. So also Psalm ix. 6 is to be explained, where, after addressing the foe directly, the Psalmist turns to those who stand by and sings, "*Their* memorial is perished ;" *i. e.*, the memorial of *such men as these.*

Psalm 29

A Psalm of David

1 GIVE unto the Lord, O ye mighty, give unto the Lord glory and strength.
2 Give unto the Lord the glory due unto his name;
Worship the Lord in the beauty of holiness.
3 The voice of the Lord is upon the waters:
The God of glory thundereth: the Lord is upon many waters.
4 The voice of the Lord is powerful; the voice of the Lord is full of majesty.
5 The voice of the Lord breaketh the cedars; yea, the Lord breaketh the cedars of Lebanon.
6 He maketh them also to skip like a calf: Lebanon and Sirion like a young unicorn.
7 The voice of the Lord divideth the flames of fire.
8 The voice of the Lord shaketh the wilderness;
The Lord shaketh the wilderness of Kadesh.
9 The voice of the Lord maketh the hinds to calve, and discovereth the forests:
And in his temple doth every one speak of his glory.
10 The Lord sitteth upon the flood; yea, the Lord sitteth King for ever.
11 The Lord will give strength unto his people; the Lord will bless his people with peace.

OUR attention is called seven times to the "voice of Jehovah," uttering majesty. The psalm presents such adoration as the Lord Jesus (himself "mighty God") could present to the Father, in the days of his flesh, when listening amid the hills round Nazareth, or at the foot of Lebanon by the sources of double-founted Jordan, to the voice of his Father's awful thunder. The redeemed, too, feel that such scenes furnish occasion for adoring the majesty and omnipotence of Godhead. At the same time, this seems to be more especially a Psalm of adoration for that great and notable Day of the Lord, when the Lamb's song shall be sung. "Great and marvellous are thy works, Lord God Almighty—for all nations shall come and worship before thee; for thy judgments are made manifest," (Psalm xv. 9). It is, in this view, a Psalm *to*, rather than *for*, our King. Dr Allix at once concludes, "This Psalm containeth an exhortation to all the princes of the world to submit themselves to the Messiah's empire, after he shall have re-established his people, and given as great proof of his vengeance on

Christ using it, as well as his people.

The time.

his enemies as He did in the time of the Flood." In this last clause He alludes to verse 10, and to the true rendering of it, (Hengstenberg, &c.)

> " *The Lord at theDeluge sat,* (יָשֵׁב לַמַּבּוּל)
> " *The Lord for ever sits, as King.*"

We might, no doubt, apply every clause of it to the Lord's display of his majesty in any tremendous thunder-storm. An awe-struck spectator cries as the lightnings play and the thunder rolls ; "The *God of Glory* thundereth !" (ver. 5). " *The voice of Jehovah is breaking the cedars !*" and as the crash is heard, " *The Lord has broken the cedars of Lebanon!*" Travellers tell us of the solemnity and terrific force of storms in the East. But the thunders of the Great Day shall most of all call forth these strains to the Lord the King. Earth at large, and the heavens, too, shall shake on that day, when "the Lord roars from Zion, and utters his voice from Jerusalem," (Joel iii. 16) ; while Israel's land, from Lebanon on the north to Kadesh on the south, shall be in the vortex of that storm. Meanwhile, secure as Noah in his ark, He and his redeemed witness the storm sweep along, beating down the wicked ; and they burst into this song, (See Isaiah xxx. 32) :

> " *Give unto the Lord, O ye sons of the mighty,* (*i.e.,* ye mighty ones in heaven and earth),
> " *Give unto the Lord glory and strength.*"
> " *Give unto the Lord the glory due unto his name.*" (Ver. 1, 2.)

Like the voice of much people in heaven heard by John (Rev. xix. 1), saying,

> " Alleluiah !
> " Salvation and glory !
> " And honour and power !
> " Unto the Lord our God ! "

followed up by the call " Praise our God—small and great," while the multitude who sing appear in their " fine linen, clean and white," corresponding to the description here (verse 2),

> " *Worship the Lord in the beauties of Holiness*"

in holy attire, in sanctuary array, in the beautiful robes of the priesthood. And then, again, verse 9 seems to tell of Earth filled with his glory.

" *In his temple everything saith* ' *Glory!* ' " (בְּלוֹ its all—the all of the temple.)

Happy they on whose side this Jehovah stands! (ver. 11). He can say to the soul as Jesus said to the sea in Mark iv. 39, " Peace." That this is the full reference of the Psalm, we may fully believe ; and yet this reference by no means forbids our using it as an appropriate song to the Lord when celebrating the majesty of his voice heard in the storms that sweep over the land, from Lebanon on the north to Kadesh on the south ; or that voice heard *in the hearts of men,* when He stirs their conscience and speaks his message of grace.

It is the same Lord, and the same majesty. that is shewn forth in scenes of *nature,* in the doings of *grace,* and in the full outburst of *glory.* Our Lord, in the days of his flesh, might use it in that threefold way, and we still do the same. We celebrate his present bestowal of "strength" and of " peace," in verse 11, while still we wait for the completeness of both in the day when we shall get the " grace that shall be brought us at the Appearing of Jesus Christ." The Psalm is thus fitted for manifold occasions, though most specially for the day of the Lord, being throughout

Threefold application.

" *The Righteous One's adoration of the God of Glory, in the Day of His storm.* *

* Barclay's Paraphrase will give the reader some help in filling up the pregnant brevity of these magnificent verses. We give a part of it wherein he refers to the events of the Cross, as much as to the events of the " Great Day," making the idea of *a storm* only the colouring of the style.

Ver. 3. " Messiah's voice is in the cloud,
The God of glory thunders loud,
Messiah rides along the floods,
He treads upon the flying clouds.

Ver. 4. Messiah's voice is full of power,
His lightnings play when tempests lower.

Ver. 5. Messiah's voice the cedars breaks,
While Lebanon's foundation quakes:
Messiah's voice removes the hills,
And all the plains with rivers fills.

Ver. 6. The voice of their expiring God
Shall make the rocks to start abroad;

Psalm 30

A Psalm and Song at the dedication of the house of David

1 I WILL extol thee, O Lord ; for thou hast lifted me up,
And hast not made my foes to rejoice over me.
2 O Lord my God, I cried unto thee, and thou hast healed me.
3 O Lord, thou hast brought up my soul from the grave :
Thou hast kept me alive, that I should not go down to the pit.
4 Sing unto the Lord, O ye saints of his,
And give thanks at the remembrance of his holiness.
5 For his anger endureth but a moment: in his favour is life :
Weeping may endure for a night, but joy cometh in the morning.
6 And in my prosperity I said, I shall never be moved.
7 Lord, by thy favour thou hast made my mountain to stand strong:
Thou didst hide thy face, and I was troubled.
8 I cried to thee, O Lord; and unto the Lord I made supplication.
9 What profit is there in my blood, when I go down to the pit ?
Shall the dust praise thee ? shall it declare thy truth ?
10 Hear, O Lord, and have mercy upon me ! Lord, be thou my helper !
11 Thou hast turned for me my mourning into dancing :
Thou hast put off my sackcloth, and girded me with gladness ;
12 To the end that my glory may sing praise to thee, and not be silent.
O Lord my God, I will give thanks unto thee for ever.

The title. *"A Psalm, a Song of the Dedication of the House; by David."* Such is the title in the Hebrew, referring to the occasion whereon the writer of it was moved by the Holy Ghost to take up his harp, and touch its plaintively-pleasant The occasion. strings. It is supposed that *"The house of David"* means that house,* or temple, which David wished to have built to the Lord—an "house of cedar—an house for my name" (2

Mount Zion and Mount Sirion
Shall bound along with Lebanon.
Ver. 7.   The flames of fire shall round him wreathe,
When He shall on the ether breathe.
Ver. 8, 9. Messiah's voice shall shake the earth,
And, lo ! the graves shall groan in birth
Ten thousand thousand living sons
Shall be the issue of their groans.
Ver. 11.   The peace of God, the Gospel sounds;
The peace of God, the earth rebounds,
The Gospel everlasting shines
A light from God that ne'er declines.
This is the light Jehovah sends,
To bless the world's remotest ends."

* Hengstenberg, Tholuck, Alexander, &c.

Sam. vii. 7–13.) This house David was not allowed to build; but he was permitted to fix upon the place where it was afterwards to be reared, and to *dedicate* that spot—doing which might be called undoubtedly, "The dedication of the house." The spot was Ornan's threshing-floor on Mount Moriah. The case is recorded in 1 Chron. xxi. 26, the Lord answering him by fire from heaven, so that David exclaimed, "This is the house of the Lord God!" (1 Chron. xxi. 1.) The circumstances are altogether such as to furnish a fit occasion for a psalm, whose strains are melancholy intermixed with the gladsome and the bright. The plague that followed the sin of numbering the people had brought the Psalmist low, to the very gates of death, for the sword was suspended over his head; but the voice that uttered, "*It is enough!*" lifted him and his up again. The morning of that day rose in clouds and portentous gloom, but its setting sun shed its sweetest rays on Jerusalem from a sapphire sky, and left a forgiven people and a forgiven king reposing in the restored favour of Jehovah.

Our David could take up these strains, and adopt them as his own. There was a time when his sacrifice was offered, and the *temple of his body* accepted by the Father. He, too, had been low, and had been lifted up (ver. 1); had cried, and been healed (ver. 2); had been brought up from among the dead (ver. 3). Who could call on men so well as He to sing to Jehovah (ver. 4), and "*celebrate the memorial of his holiness*"—that is, to celebrate whatever called that holiness to mind, and kept it before men. Was it not *holiness* that shone forth most brightly in all his suffering? Was it not *holiness* that shone through the darkness of Calvary? "But thou art *holy!*" was not that the comforting thought that upheld him on the cross? If the Lord's sore judgment on Israel, when 70,000 were cut off for one sin, shewed David how holy the Lord was, surely infinitely more did the outpoured fierceness of wrath manifest it to our David, and to all who are his saints. Yet, even as that wrath was not eternal, for the angel put up his sword in its sheath, so that anger poured out on the true David, "endured but a moment," and his resurrection morning

Christ using this Psalm.

was all joy (ver. 5). And once past, it never returns. Established on the Rock that never changes, He was able to say,

> " *In my prosperity, I shall never be moved.*"
> " *Thou, Lord, hast imparted strength to my mountain by thy love,*" (vers. 6, 7).

Once " Thou didst hide thy face, and I was troubled," and my prayer then was the prayer of one who sought thy glory even under gloom, and who pleaded that " *thy truth* " was pledged to deliver me. And thou didst deliver, with such a deliverance as calls for everlasting praise, and for praise which never has a break in it from this time and for evermore.

The members of Christ. At the resurrection morning (we have said) Christ began to enter into this joy, for it was then that the Father distinctly said, " It is enough ! Stay now thy hand "—fulfilling the type given in the angel's sword put up into its scabbard at the spot where " *The House* " was dedicated. But no one of his members, all of whom have been (ver. 2) healed, can fail to find in this Psalm very much that suits their own experience.* They have had their " *moment of anger ;* " when the Lord awoke them, and made them know their guilt, and dropped on their conscience a drop of wrath that might make them cry vehemently for deliverance, though He meant soon to wipe it off. Each of " his holy ones" has known this "moment of anger," followed by " *life in his favour,*" from the hour when his anger was turned away. From that time forth they have had their "*night of weeping* " oftentimes, but never any more of anger. They have had their sorrows, weeping has " *lodged* " in their dwellings oftentimes, and they have walked through many a howling wilderness ; but it was always followed by a " *morning of joy,*" some sweet beams of love and favour making them feel night turning into day. And they are expecting very soon *their Resurrection-morning*, when unmingled joy cometh, joy like that of their Lord's at his resurrection. It is then that they will, in the highest sense, sit on their Rock of Ages

---

* David was "healed " at his restoration to health and strength, and in being saved from the pestilence ; the Son of David at his resurrection. The soul is healed at its repentance and conversion : the body will hereafter be healed when it is repaired, beautified, and glorified.

and have their " *shouting for joy* " at morning, singing such
a song as this :

" *I* [even I] *am in peace ! I shall never be moved !*
" *O Lord, thou hast imparted strength to my mountain by thy love !* [alluding to Zion, the seat of royalty.]
" *Once thou didst hide thy face, and I was troubled ;*
" *And I called unto thee, O Lord,*
" *And I made supplication* [in words like these] :
" *What profit is there in my blood ?*
" *Shall the dust praise thee ?*
" *Would not thy faithfulness be honoured in saving the chief of sinners ?*
" *And now thou hast turned for me my mourning into dancing ;*
" *Thou hast put off my sackcloth and girded me with gladness,*
" *In order that my glory* may sing praise unto thee, and not be silent.*"

And with one accord all the " holy ones " join in the concluding burst of rapturous gratitude, the true David himself
leading the song—

" *O Lord, my God, I will give thanks unto thee for ever !*"

And thus comes to a blessed close this song of the righteous,
which we may call, perhaps not improperly,

*The Song of the Righteous concerning the Night of Weeping
and the Morning of Joy.*

Psalm 31

To the Chief Musician, A Psalm of David

1 In thee, O Lord, do I put my trust !
Let me never be ashamed : deliver me in thy righteousness.
2 Bow down thine ear to me ; deliver me speedily :
Be thou my strong rock, for an house of defence to save me.
3 For thou art my rock and my fortress ;
Therefore for thy name's sake lead me, and guide me.
4 Pull me out of the net that they have laid privily for me : for thou art my
strength.
5 Into thine hand I commit my spirit : thou hast redeemed me, O Lord
God of truth.
6 I have hated them that regard lying vanities : but I trust in the Lord.
7 I will be glad and rejoice in thy mercy :
For thou hast considered my trouble. Thou hast known my soul in adversities ;

* Tholuck, and many others, understand " my *soul*" by " my glory."

8 And hast not shut me up into the hand of the enemy : thou hast set my
feet in a large room.

9 Have mercy upon me, O Lord, for I am in trouble :
Mine eye is consumed with grief, yea, my soul and my belly.

10 For my life is spent with grief, and my years with sighing :
My strength faileth because of mine iniquity, and my bones are consumed.

11 I was a reproach among all mine enemies, but especially among my
neighbours,
And a fear to mine acquaintance : they that did see me without fled
from me.

12 I am forgotten as a dead man out of mind : I am like a broken vessel.

13 For I have heard the slander of many : fear was on every side :
While they took counsel together against me, they devised to take away
my life.

14 But I trusted in thee, O Lord : I said, Thou art my God.

15 My times are in thy hand !
Deliver me from the hand of mine enemies, and from them that persecute
me.

16 Make thy face to shine upon thy servant : save me for thy mercies' sake.

17 Let me not be ashamed, O Lord ; for I have called upon thee :
Let the wicked be ashamed, and let them be silent in the grave.

18 Let the lying lips be put to silence ;
Which speak grievous things proudly and contemptuously against the
righteous.

19 Oh how great is thy goodness, which thou hast laid up for them that
fear thee ;
Which thou hast wrought for them that trust in thee before the sons of
men !

20 Thou shalt hide them in the secret of thy presence from the pride of man :
Thou shalt keep them secretly in a pavilion from the strife of tongues.

21 Blessed be the Lord ! for he hath shewed me his marvellous kindness in
a strong city.

22 For I said in my haste, I am cut off from before thine eyes !
Nevertheless thou heardest the voice of my supplications when 1 cried
unto thee.

23 O love the Lord, all ye his saints :
For the Lord preserveth the faithful, and plentifully rewardeth the proud
doer.

24 Be of good courage, and he shall strengthen your heart, all ye that hope
in the Lord.

**Christ and his
members.**

THE Head and his members are here. The Head said (ver. 8),
in the hour when He gave up the ghost, "Into thy hands I
commit my spirit !" And how often have his members taken
up his words, from the days of Stephen to Huss, and from the
days of Huss to this hour.

Safety in the hands of the living God, and only there, is the The theme. theme of this plaintive Psalm ; safety in life as well as in death ; safety from the enemies' snares, and from all adversity, from grief and reproach, from calumny and contempt, from personal despondency as well as from the pressure of outward adversity. David needed his theme, the true David needed it yet more, and his followers will not cease to need it till verse nineteenth be realised in all its vastness.

> " *O how great is thy goodness, which thou hast laid up for them that fear thee!* "

They get at present (like Joseph's brethren) their ass-loads of the fine wheat from this granary ; but they shall yet stand amidst it, and "fear" (Isa. lx. 8) because of the very immensity of it.

In verse 6, there is an emphatic pronoun, אֲנִי, *q. d.* unlike Special clauses. those who regard lying vanities, *I*, for my part, trust in the Lord. In verse 8, the "*large room*" seems to be God's unbounded love, wide like a plain that stretches far beyond our ken. The complaint in verse 11 resembles Lament. iv. 15, where the people are represented as treating exiled Israel as a leper, "Depart ye, unclean ; depart, depart ; touch not !" and forcing them to flee away ;* and verse 12 reminds us of Job on his dunghill, inasmuch as the "broken vessel" is just a potsherd, like what he took to scrape himself withal. But verse 22 contains an expression which is worth dwelling upon, as it occurs Passover-haste. again in Psalm cxvi. 11. It is the expression, "In my haste, בְחָפְזִי. The words, בְּהָפְזָהּ occur in 2 Sam iv. 4, used of Mephibosheth's nurse *making haste to flee* when she heard the evil tidings of Jonathan slain on Gilboa. In Psalm xlviii. 6, the verb is used of the gathered kings *making haste* to flee away ; and in 1 Sam. xxiii. 26, of David making haste to get out of Saul's way. It is never used of *impatience*, or *heat of spirit*, or *irritation*, or *excited temper ;*† it always refers to speedy

---

* Here Augustine has a note applicable to this hour : "Dico vobis, fratres moi ; incipe, quicunque me audit, vivere quomodo Christianus, et vide si non tibi objiciatur *et a Christianis, sed nomine, non vitâ, non moribus.*"

† Fry goes far wrong here, speaking of "Hurry of mind, and confusion ; and a moment of despair ;" Hengstenberg gives it the sense of "rapid flight ;" Alexander, "terror ;" Horsley, "consternation ;" Street, "affright."

movement from one locality to another. But specially it is to be noticed, the cognate word חִפָּזוֹן is used regarding the *haste* in which they were to eat the passover : thus Exod. xii. 11, "Ye shall eat it *in haste ;"* Deut. xvi. 3, "Thou camest out of the land *in haste ;"* and Isa. lii. 12, foretelling the reverse of this, "Ye shall not go forth *in haste."* From all this, we infer that in the passage before us, the reference of the Psalmist is not to anything else than *passover-haste.* His words are to this effect : "I said when I was like a passover-man, hastening out of Egypt, *i. e.,* when I felt my condition to be that of one who must make haste to leave a people that had cast him out." Left in this condition, I was ready to say, "*I am cut off"* (ver. 22), even as Israel at the Red Sea. We come to the same conclusion, if we suppose the Psalmist refer to such circumstances of danger, and almost of despair, as are referred to when the radical word is used in 1 Sam. xxiii. 26.

Prophetic allusions.

In verses 17, 18, we hear the prayer of the Head and his members for the overthrow of the ungodly, the language of which, as well as the reference to the same in verse 20, reminds us irresistibly of words that occur in the prophecy of Enoch. In this Psalm (as Horsley suggests), the voice from the oracle declares their doom to be,

> " *They shall be motionless in hell !*
> *Let lying lips be put to silence,*
> *Which speak grievous things,*
> *Proudly and contemptuously,*
> *Against the righteous."*

Enoch's prophecy.

In Enoch's prophecy we find the foundation of his cry ; and inasmuch as Enoch's prophecy was known in the Church in David's time, would it not comfort the Lord's saints then, and the Lord himself when He came ?

> "Behold, the Lord cometh with ten thousand of his saints,
>   To execute judgment upon all, and to convince all that are ungodly among them,
>   Of all their ungodly deeds, which they have ungodly committed,
>   *And of all their hard speeches*
>   *Which ungodly sinners have spoken against Him."* (Jude 14.)

To this expected interposition, the response given is in verses 19, 20, "*Oh how great is thy goodness !"* wherein we are reminded of the Lord's granary of goodness, or love, and receive a promise of being hid *"from the strife of* tongues." **Verses** 21, 22, contain the grateful acknowledgment-

" Blessed be the Lord ! for he has shewn me marvellous love !
" In a strong city ;" (i.e., bringing me into his fortress).

This "strong city" is a contrast to the "hasty flight" of verse 22, when he thought he must surely perish.

But again, in verse 23, the delivered one speaks ; *" The Lord keeps the* אֱמוּנִים *faithfulnesses," i.e.,* his promises ; and then makes reference to the *"plentiful reward"* of wrath on the wicked at the Lord's Coming, even as verse 19 told of the abundant reward of His own yet to come. In prospect of that day, his saints are exhorted to persevere (ver. 24) ; and it is in some measure with a reference to the glory coming that they are called by the name, *" Ye that hope in* the Lord." Both now, however in a present evil world, and in the hour of death, and in the end when glory is revealed, the saints are safe, even as was their Head. This is the burden of this song of Zion—

The Righteous, though forlorn, safe and blest in the hand of the living God.

Psalm 32

A Psalm of David, Maschil

1 BLESSED is he whose transgression is forgiven, whose sin is **covered.**
2 Blessed is the man unto whom the Lord imputeth not iniquity,
And in whose spirit there is no guile.
3 When I kept silence, my bones waxed old through my roaring all **the day** long.
4 For day and night thy hand was heavy upon me :
My moisture is turned into the drought of summer.   Selah.
5 I acknowledge my sin unto thee, and mine iniquity have I **not hid.**
I said, I will confess my transgressions unto the Lord ;
And thou forgavest the iniquity of my sin.   Selah.
6 For this shall every one that is godly pray unto thee in a time when **thou** mayest be found.
Surely in the floods of great waters they shall not come nigh unto **him.**
7 Thou art my hiding place ; thou shalt preserve me from trouble ;
Thou shalt compass me about with songs of deliverance.   Selah.

8 I will instruct thee and teach thee in the way which thou shalt go :
I will guide thee with mine eye.

9 Be ye not as the horse, or as the mule, which have no understanding :
Whose mouth must be held in with bit and bridle, lest they come near
unto thee.

10 Many sorrows shall be to the wicked :
But he that trusteth in the Lord, mercy shall compass him about

11 Be glad in the Lord, and rejoice, ye righteous :
And shout for joy, all ye that are upright in heart.

The title:
Maschil.

WE cannot but agree with Ewald in thinking that the word in
the title, " *Maschil*," does not refer to any instrument, nor yet
is it used in the sense of " Didactic," but has reference to something *artistic in the melody*, something peculiarly calling for
the skill of the singer or player on the harp.   It is undoubtedly
used in some such sense in Psalm xlvii. 8, זַמְּרוּ מַשְׂכִּיל.*   Perhaps a Psalm of pardoning mercy was set to some special
music, which it required forgiven ones to appreciate, like some
of our hymn tunes.

References.

The mention of " transgression," " iniquity," " sin," recals
the name of the Lord proclaimed to Moses in the cleft of the
rock, " forgiving iniquity, transgression, and sin," (Exod. xxxiv.
7).   The " *imputing*" and " *non-imputing*" was well understood in David's day ; for we read (2 Sam. xix. 19), Shemei
confessing sin, and yet asking, " Let not my lord *impute it*."

Christ in it.

We generally take up this Psalm as if it was for the *members* of Christ alone ; but we should not forget that the Head
himself traversed the way of forgiveness.   He stood for us, in
our room, in our very place.   He stood as substitute, and all
the sins of all " that great multitude which no man can number" were upon him, laid upon him by imputation.   So
dreadful was his position, so truly awful did it seem to him
to be *reckoned* a sinner, that even this, apart from the wrath
and curse, would have been sufficient to make him cry, " O,
blessed the man to whom the Lord doth not impute sin."   He
was dumb for our sakes ; his bones wasted away ; he groaned

* See also in the Hebrew 2 Chron. xxx. 22, applied to the Levitical music.
If the word meant " A Didactic Poem," it is strange to find it omitted in the
case of such as Psa. cxix. and l., and inserted in the title to such a poetic ode
as Psa. xlv., wherein there is nothing didactic.

from day to day, and during the lonesome hours of midnight was kept awake by our woe. His moisture (ver. 4), or vigour of vitality, was changed, "*through means of* (see Hengstenberg) *the drought of summer, i.e.*, from the excessive heat of wrath, resembling the most parching heats of summer's hottest days, when the sun is fiercely shedding down his intolerable rays on the arid earth. In this state He acknowledged our sin ; it was only ours he had to acknowledge ; he spread it out before God on the cross ; he continued to do so till it was forgiven to him as our substitute.

Our head could use these words only in that one way. But in a *personal* sense, from *personal* experience of wrath, from a *personal* consciousness of our own sin, every member of His cannot but use the Psalm as expressing what they have passed through. Yes, they have each felt the silence, the waxing old, the roaring, the drying up of moisture, and the spreading out before the Lord of the whole sin and misery of their case ; and each has also found the forgiveness. (Ver. 5.)

> "*Thou forgavest the iniquity of my sin.*"   The plan.

Here is a pause. Here is "*Selah.*" Stay and ponder.

"*On this account*"—(עַל זֹאת), because Thou forgivest sin,—

"*On this account shall every godly one pray unto thee.*"

Forgiveness is so great a blessing that all else may follow. If the Lord *forgive our sin*, what next may we not ask ? On this account, then, His people pray. Our Head intercedes, because his offering of himself was accepted ; we pray, because through Him we have already got pardon, and may get any other real blessing. Yes, we may get such blessing, that "*at the time of* (לְ *) *the floods of great waters*," whensoever that be—whether calamities personal and national, or the waves of the fiery flood, parallel to that of Noah, that shall yet sweep away the ungodly,—even then we shall be altogether safe. The forgiven man is hidden, instructed, taught, guided by God's tender care. (Ver. 7, 8.) A *Selah* occurs at verse 7. Solemn truth has been spoken, which the worshipper may muse upon till it

---

* The לְ here is like the לְ in Psalm xxix. 10.

sink into his heart; and then a voice from heaven tells that *His eye* is ever on them.—" And (says Horne) next to the protecting power of God's being, is the securing prospect of his eye." The forgiven man is sanctified, yielding up his own will to the Lord's, not like the " *horse and mule that have no understanding, whose ornament is bit and bridle, because they will not come near unless by force."* Unhappy they who know not pardon ! " *Many sorrows"* are their portion ; while mercy compasses the forgiven, so that " *they are glad, they rejoice, they shout for joy !"* Already they anticipate the joy of the kingdom, " *glad and rejoice ;"* though it is when the kingdom comes that they shall say emphatically to one another, feeling mercy compassing them about, and no flood, nor drop of flood touching one of them, " Alleluia ! the Lord God Omnipotent reigneth. *Let us be glad and rejoice,* and give honour to Him !" (Rev. xix. 7.) And even then they may use this song of Zion ; for the Head and his members will often review, as is done here,

The way of forgiveness traversed by the Righteous.

Psalm 33

1 REJOICE in the Lord, O ye righteous : for praise is comely for the upright.
2 Praise the Lord with harp : sing unto him with the psaltery and an instrument of ten strings.
3 Sing unto him a new song; play skilfully with a loud noise.
4 For the word of the Lord is right : and all his works are done in truth.
5 He loveth righteousness and judgment : the earth is full of the goodness of the Lord.
6 By the word of the Lord were the heavens made :
And all the host of them by the breath of his mouth.
7 He gathered the waters of the sea together as an heap :
He layeth up the depth in storehouses.
8 Let all the earth fear the Lord : let all the inhabitants of the world stand in awe of him.
9 For he spake, and it was done; he commanded, and it stood fast.
18 The Lord bringeth the counsel of the heathen to nought;
He maketh the devices of the people of none effect.
11 The counsel of the Lord standeth for ever, the thoughts of his heart to all generations.
12 Blessed is the nation whose God is the Lord ;
And the people whom he hath chosen for his own inheritance.

13 The Lord looketh from heaven ; he beholdeth all the sons of men :
14 From the place of his habitation he looketh upon all the inhabitants of
the earth.
15 He fashioneth their hearts alike ; he considereth all their works.
16 There is no king saved by the multitude of an host :
A mighty man is not delivered by much strength.
17 An horse is a vain thing for safety : neither shall he deliver any by his
great strength.
18 Behold the eye of the Lord is upon them that fear him, upon them that
hope in his mercy ;
19 To deliver their soul from death, and to keep them alive in famine.
20 Our soul waiteth for the Lord : he is our help and our shield.
21 For our heart shall rejoice in him, because we have trusted in his holy
name.
22 Let thy mercy, O Lord, be upon us, according as we hope in thee.

THE last note of the former is the first note of this Psalm, *Connection.*
" *Rejoice in the Lord, ye righteous !* " The last Psalm had
much in it of the tone of confession and prayer : this is full of
praise ; for now the forgiven one is taking up his harp in
thankfulness :

> " *Give thanks to Jehovah with the harp,*
> *Make music to Him with an* instrument *of ten strings.*"

It is a very simple Psalm, yet full of the feelings which a
forgiven soul teems with. Never did any heart so abound in
those feelings as the heart of the Lord Jesus ; and his saints
learn from him. It is He who is to lead the praise in the great
congregation. (Psalm xxii. 22.) Let us see the topics taken *The contents.*
up in turn.

Verses 1–3 prepare us for song, shaking the strings of our
heart. And the call is for a " *new* song "—a redemption
melody.

Verses 4, 5, praise the Lord for his *character.*

Verses 6–9 praise the Lord for his *creation-work,* which
his providence still continues.

Verses 10, 11, praise the Lord for his *counsels.*

Verses 12–19 praise the Lord for his *care of his Church,*
his chosen ones, who are saved by grace alone (ver. 16, 17),
and kept by grace (ver. 18, 19).

Verses 20–22 contains the response. As exhorted, " Rejoice
in the Lord," (ver. 1),—so we reply, " Our heart rejoiceth in

Him." This will be the eternal response of the saints when the salvation yet in reserve comes. Then their *"waiting"* (ver. 20), their Jacob-like waiting, is ended (Gen. xlix. 18); then (as ver. 10, 11, as well as Psalm ii. 1, sing) the nations have *raged in vain ;* and then, in the fullest sense, " *Earth is full of the goodness of the Lord,"* as Hosea ii. 21, 22, described in part, and as the seraphim celebrate in Isaiah vi. 3. Then shall it be full of the Lord's glory, when love, redeeming love, the love of the God of Love, shall be felt by all the earth, the Gift of Love himself being in the midst. It is thus a Psalm wherein

Forgiven ones adore the Lord in his counsels and ways.

Psalm 34

A Psalm of David, when he changed his behaviour before Abimelech; who drove him away, and he departed

1 I will bless the Lord at all times : his praise shall continually be in my mouth.

2 My soul shall make her boast in the Lord : the humble shall hear hereof, and be glad.

3 O magnify the Lord with me, and let us exalt his name together.

4 I sought the Lord, and he heard me, and delivered me from all my fears.

5 They looked unto him, and were lightened : and their faces were not ashamed.

6 This poor man cried, and the Lord heard him, and saved him out of all his troubles.

7 The angel of the Lord encampeth round about them that fear him, and delivereth them.

8 O taste and see that the Lord is good : blessed is the man that trusteth in him.

9 O fear the Lord, ye his saints : for there is no want to them that fear him.

10 The young lions do lack, and suffer hunger :
But they that seek the Lord shall not want any good thing.

11 Come, ye children, hearken unto me : I will teach you the fear of the Lord.

12 What man is he that desireth life,
And loveth many days, that he may see good ?

13 Keep thy tongue from evil, and thy lips from speaking guile.

14 Depart from evil, and do good ; seek peace, and pursue it.

15 The eyes of the Lord are upon the righteous, and his ears are open unto their cry.

16 The face of the Lord is against them that do evil,
To cut off the remembrance of them from the earth.

17 The righteous cry, and the Lord heareth, and delivereth him out of all their troubles.

18 The Lord is nigh unto them that are of a broken heart;
And saveth such as be of a contrite spirit..

19 Many are the afflictions of the righteous : but the Lord delivereth him out of them all.

20 He keepeth all his bones: not one of them is broken.

21 Evil shall slay the wicked ; and they that hate the righteous shall be desolate.

22 The Lord redeemeth the soul of his servants ;
And none of them that trust in him shall be desolate.

THE primitive Christians used to sing this Psalm at the cele- Title. bration of the Lord's Supper—most suitably. An able writer on this Psalm has allowed himself to say rather rashly, " The title given by the Jewish editors, like most of the other titles they have thought proper to affix to the Psalms, has evidently no connection whatever with the subject." Now, we are not aware of a single case wherein there is no connection to be traced between the title and the contents of the Psalms ; and the fact that occasionally this connection is not very obvious at first view, seems to us to speak rather in favour of its genuineness than against it. A mere inventor would have taken pains to pin on to the composition something that would suggest itself easily to the reader as a probable occasion. Here, at all events, there is in the title just that combination of obscurity and probability that inclines us to assent at once to its genuineness— even apart from the fact that we have no authority for reject- ing it. It has frequently been observed, as a most beautiful David. and appropriate circumstance in the life and experience of David, the man of God, that the first notes of his harp should give forth praises at the very time " when he changed his behaviour (i.e., *concealed his intellect*, or disguised his reason) before Abimelech,* who sent him away, and he departed." Cast out again, homeless, friendless, helpless, David trudges

* Abimelech is the general title given to Philistine kings, like Pharaoh to the Egyptian. *Achish* was the special name of the prince. In Archbishop Parker's translation (1567), the title and argument are thus given-

" When David fled to Achish king,
The door of death he was full near ;
When saved, he this psalm did sing,
With all his friends in godly quire,
To God his Lord, to him so dear—
Give thanks I will, give thanks I will,
For aye to God most gracious," &c.

along the highway of Philistia, with the world all before him, where to choose his place of rest ; and though he knows not where to lay his head, he journeys on, singing, " I will bless the Lord ! I will bless Him at all times : His praise shall continually be in my mouth." Is he not recalling past experience as a source of encouragement, when he says, " I sought the Lord, and He heard me, and delivered me from all my fears ? " (Ver. 4.) The word for " *They looked*" (הִבִּיטוּ) in verse 5 is that used in Num. xxi. 9, when Israel looked to the serpent of brass ; and in Zech. xii. 11, when they look on Him whom they pierced.* And in verse 6, " This poor man cried," is no other than himself ;—I who am thus using my harp to celebrate Him,—I who am an outcast,—this poor man whom you see before you. In the same happy strain of faith the whole psalm flows on, till verse 20 rises to the height of confidence,—" He keepeth all his bones, not one of them is broken,"†—while the ruin of all his foes is foreseen as sure, " Evil shall slay the wicked." Could any circumstances afford a more suitable occasion for such a psalm being given to the Church ? Taking advantage of David's peculiar state and feelings, the Holy Ghost gives to the Church a song that might suit her *Head,* the true David when He came, and might equally suit every member. Augustine writes : " *Dicit Christus ; dicat et Christianus ;* " because the Head and members agree so truly in feeling and experience.

Alphabetic.   It is one of the alphabetic psalms, carefully arranged for the memory easily to grasp ; and yet not so invariably regular as to cause us to think there is any mystery in that form of composition. It is interesting to note that the name of *Jehovah* occurs in each of the verses except three.

Christ.   Our Lord might use it all. He could as truly say, " This poor man cried," as David ; for He could point to Gethsemane, and to many a night of " strong crying and tears," (Heb. v. 7). Who more than He could tell of the ministering *angel* (ver. 7),

---

* In Isa. xlv. 22, the word is פְּנוּ " Turn from other objects and fix your eye on me," as Ps. lxix. 16, and Exod. xvi. 10.

† Some think this verse is referred to in John xiv. 36, and so infer that John understood the whole psalm of Christ throughout.

since, after The Temptation, and at the season of the Garden agony, He obtained such help? And it was He who could say, " Thinkest thou that I cannot pray to my Father, and He will presently give me more than twelve legions of angels?" Even (in ver. 11) the expression, " *Ye children,*" comes from his lips more naturally than from any other, for He it is that has spoken of all God's family as " *My little children.*"

The speaker would fain draw us to the Lord by telling us his own experience. We ought to connect verses 10, 11, together. " O fear the Lord ; for with him is all that can satisfy your soul. Come unto me, and I will teach you the fear of the Lord." Christ is he that utters to us the words of eternal life by revealing the Father ; and his disciples follow in his steps. Having taught us this "*fear of Jehovah,*"—*i. e.,* to cry " *Abba,* Father," and yet also to realise him as *Jehovah*— taught us, also, thereby what real life is,—he next points out the results. He shews us, in verses 12, 13, 14, the holy issues or effects of the fear of the Lord,—the lips, the life, the pursuit of the heart, all tending in a holy direction. After this all is safety to them (ver. 15–21), while " *the Lord's face is with evil doers,*" as the Pillar Cloud was with Pharaoh, to destroy them.

The prophetic reference of this Psalm is in the close. There the anointed eye of David, and the Son of David, and all the seed of David, beholds the final end of these trials. The righteous arrive in the kingdom, not one bone broken,—even as Christ came down from the cross, not a bone of him broken, to shew the inability of his foes really to injure him. They see the wicked slain, and the haters of the Righteous One " pronounced guilty" and made desolate. Is not this leading us up to the throne whence the sentence goes forth, " Those mine enemies bring hither and slay them before me ! Depart, ye cursed ! "

Prophetic reference.

The harp of David thus celebrates,

*The Righteous One's experience of the Lord's love under the cross.**

---

* Dr Allix :—" This Psalm containeth the praises which the Messias gives to his Father for having delivered him out of all his sufferings." Horsley : " Messiah exhorts to holiness and trust in God, by the example of his own deliverance."

Psalm 35

A Psalm of David

1 PLEAD my cause, O Lord, with them that strive with me:
Fight against them that fight against me.

2 Take hold of shield and buckler, and stand up for mine help.

3 Draw out also the spear, and stop the way against them that persecute me:
Say unto my soul, I am thy salvation.

4 Let them be confounded and put to shame that seek after my soul:
Let them be turned back and brought to confusion that devise my hurt.

5 Let them be as chaff before the wind: and let the angel of the Lord chase them.

6 Let their way be dark and slippery: and let the angel of the Lord persecute them.

7 For without cause have they hid for me their net in a pit,
Which without cause they have digged for my soul.

8 Let destruction come upon him at unawares;
And let his net that he hath hid catch himself: into that very destruction let him fall.

9 And my soul shall be joyful in the Lord: it shall rejoice in his salvation.

10 All my bones shall say, Lord, who is like unto thee?
Which deliverest the poor from him that is too strong for him,
Yea, the poor and the needy from him that spoileth him?

11 False witnesses did rise up; they laid to my charge things that I knew not.

12 They rewarded me evil for good, to the spoiling of my soul.

13 But as for me, when they were sick, my clothing was sackcloth:
I humbled my soul with fasting;
And my prayer returned into mine own bosom.

14 I behaved myself as though he had been my friend or brother:
I bowed down heavily, as one that mourneth for his mother.

15 But in mine adversity they rejoiced, and gathered themselves together:
Yea, the abjects gathered themselves together against me, and I knew it not.
They did tear me, and ceased not:

16 With hypocritical mockers in feasts, they gnashed upon me with their teeth.

17 Lord, how long wilt thou look on?
Rescue my soul from their destructions, my darling from the lions.

18 I will give thee thanks in the great congregation: I will praise thee among much people.

19 Let not them that are mine enemies wrongfully rejoice over me:
Neither let them wink with the eye that hate me without a cause.

20 For they speak not peace:
But they devise deceitful matters against them that are quiet in the land.

21 Yea, they opened their mouth wide against me,
And said, Aha! aha! our eye hath seen it.

22 This thou hast seen, O Lord: keep not silence: O Lord, be not far from me

23 Stir up thyself, and awake to my judgment! even unto my cause, **my** God and my Lord!

24 Judge me, O Lord my God, according to thy righteousness ; And let them not rejoice over me.

25 Let them not say in their hearts, Ah! so would we have it : Let them not say, We have swallowed him up.

26 Let them be ashamed and brought to confusion together that rejoice **at** mine hurt : Let them be clothed with shame and dishonour that magnify **themselves** against me.

27 Let them shout for joy, and be glad, that favour my righteous cause : Yea, let them say continually, Let the Lord be magnified, Which hath pleasure in the prosperity of his servant

28 And my tongue shall speak of thy righteousness and of thy praise all **the** day long.

THERE is this link of connection between this Psalm and the Connection. preceding, that in both we find " *the bones*" referred to ; in the former as "not broken" (ver. 20), in the latter as " rejoicing" (ver. 16). In both, too, we find *the angel of the Lord* acting as the Lord's instrument. In the former the angel acts to protect and preserve (ver. 6), because the whole song is one of the Lord's care ; but in the latter the angel acts in the way of vengeance, as an instrument in inflicting the Lord's wrath (ver. 5, 6), because the burden of the Psalm is an awful intercession against those who hate the righteous without cause.

Throughout this is an awful Psalm. Let us read it as the Christ in it. words of the Lord Jesus, and what do we find ? We find Him praying to the Father for help, and then consenting to the doom of his relentless, impenitent foes ; yea, rather pronouncing the doom with his own lips, even as when He shall say to the barren fig-tree, " Cut it down," and to those on the left The plan. hand, "Depart." It is in that spirit He says :

> " *Let them be confounded.*
> *Let them be turned back.*
> *Let them be as chaff,*
> *Let the angel of the Lord smite them down.*
> *Let their way be dark.*
> *Let the angel of the Lord chase them.*" (Ver. 4, 5, 6.)

This is their sentence, uttered by the lips of the Judge. It is not the wish of one who is revengeful ; it is the utterance of justice, compelled by the state of the parties to speak in stern severity. Our Lord himself quotes verse 19, " *they hate me*

120 / Bonar on the Psalms

without a cause," in John xv. 25, on the last evening he spent with his disciples before he suffered. For then he found himself in the very situation so strikingly described in verses 11, 12 ;—false witnesses rising up,—men rewarding his whole career of kindness by spoiling his soul.

What a deeply affecting picture do verses 13, 14, 15, give of the Saviour's life for us. It may have been literally realised at Nazareth ; Christ may have put on sackcloth when he heard of some one in sickness, fasting for the dying man whose soul he longed to save—none the less that the man was a foe. Jesus acted as if the man had been " friend or brother ;" yea, he felt such grief as men usually feel only when a beloved " mother" dies. And so he felt for all this miserable world. But now, says he, when the day of my calamity has come, they do not sympathise with me :

> *" They rejoice and gather together.*
> *They gather against me, the abjects !*
> *Even those whom I knew not, tear me, and cease not.*
> *The vile, who mock for a cake* (parasites), *gnash their teeth at me."*
>   (Ver. 15, 16.)

His cry ascends ; his pleadings up go before the righteous Father, " Lord, bring back my soul from desolations caused by their ruinous plots. The vehement appeal (ver. 23), " *My God, and my Lord !"* may have been in Thomas's thoughts on that memorable occasion, John xx. 28. We have the answer in verses 26, 27 :

> *" They are ashamed ; they are clothed with shame."*

This answer carries us forward to the day when they who rejected Him shall have as their portion " shame and everlasting contempt ;" while they that favour his righteous cause-

> *" Shout for joy, and are glad ;*
> *They cry continually, Let the Lord be magnified !*
> *Whose pleasure is the prosperity of his servants."*

Prophetic reference.

Is not this the " Hallelujah" of the glorified redeemed ? Is not this their shout of joy, when sorrow and sighing flee away ? And, once more, is not this the sound of the Lamb's harp and voice we hear, when amid this jubilee of bliss he says,

> *" And my tongue shall speak of thy righteousness,*
> *Of thy praise, all the day long."*

Throughout the endless day of eternity the Lord Jesus shall himself speak the Father's "praise," and shall put marked emphasis on his "*righteousness*"—that righteousness which shall have been exhibited both in the doom of those who hated the offered Redeemer, and in the salvation of those who received him. There is nothing in all this wherein his own may not fully join, especially on that day when their views of justice shall be far clearer and fuller than now. On that day we shall be able to understand how Samuel could hew Agag in pieces, and the godly hosts of Israel slay utterly in Canaan man and woman and child, at God's command. We shall be able, not only fully to agree in the doom, " Let them be confounded," &c., but even to sing, " Amen, Hallelujah," over the smoke of torment. (Rev. xix. 1, 2.) We should in some measure now be able to use every verse of this Psalm in the spirit in which *the Judge* spake it, we feeling ourselves his assessors in judging the world. (1 Cor. vi. 2.) We shall, at all events, be able to use it on that day when what is written here shall be all accomplished :

The awful utterance of the Righteous One regarding those that hate Him without a cause.

Psalm 36

To the chief Musician, A Psalm of David the servant of the Lord

1 THE transgression of the wicked saith within my heart,
That there is no fear of God before his eyes.
2 For he flattereth himself in his own eyes, until his iniquity be found to be hateful.
3 The words of his mouth are iniquity and deceit : he hath left off to be wise, and to do good.
4 He deviseth mischief upon his bed ;
He setteth himself in a way that is not good ; he abhorreth not evil.
5 Thy mercy, O Lord, is in the heavens ; and thy faithfulness reacheth unto the clouds.
6 Thy righteousness is like the great mountains ; thy judgments are a great deep.
O Lord, thou preservest man and beast.
7 How excellent is thy loving-kindness, O God !
Therefore the children of men put their trust under the shadow of thy wings.

8 They shall be abundantly satisfied with the fatness of thy house :
And thou shalt make them drink of the river of thy pleasures.

9 For with thee is the fountain of life : in thy light shall we see light.

10 O continue thy loving-kindness unto them that know thee ;
And thy righteousness to the upright in heart.

11 Let not the foot of pride come against me, and let not the hand of the
wicked remove me.

12 There are the workers of iniquity fallen ! They are cast down, and shall
not be able to rise.

The title. HE whom the Holy Ghost employs to write in these strains of
elevated thought and intense feeling, is one not ashamed of his
God.   It is David ; and as in Psalm xviii. 1, so here he describes himself as "*Servant of Jehovah.*"   Perhaps it was
specially appropriate to use this designation in a Psalm that
shews us so fully the apostasy of men and a world in rebellion.
David glories in being "Servant" to Him whom men desert
and despise.

The plan. Like Balaam (Numb. xxiv. 3 נְאֻם) speaking in the Lord's
name to Balak, so the Psalmist, in a kind of irony, represents
"transgression" as uttering its oracle to the wicked.   The first
verse reads thus :

"*Transgression utters its oracle to the wicked in my heart !* (*i.e.*, my
heart thus apprehends their meaning,)
There is no fear of God before his eyes ! "—(*Hengstenberg.**)

And then he states seven features of the man who has no fear of
God.   All this prepares the way for the contrast, *Jehovah's
character and thoughts towards us,* verses 5–9.   Nor is he done
till he has shewn us the Fountain of life, surrounded by the redeemed, and then pointed to the ruin of the lost, "*Yonder
are they fallen !*" (ver. 12),—scenes that carry us forward to the
Great Day and its issues.

What a Psalm is this !   David, and David's Son, and every
member of the household of faith, must always have found it
congenial ; it is such a picture of earth, and such a glimpse
of Godhead-glory and grace.   It suggests the deliverance of
all creation, "man and beast," and streams of bliss in reserve

---

* Tholuck renders it, "A divine oracle says from the depth of my heart,
concerning the wickedness of the ungodly"—adopting in substance the version
of Symmachus and Luther.   All agree that נְאֻם is very peculiar.

for us. It abounds in allusions to Old Testament history—allusions that make it more fragrant and savoury ; as when verse 7th sings of Jehovah's care of "*man and beast*," thereby calling up before us the ark of Noah, and the rainbow that spanned it after the flood ; or when verse 8 sings of " *the river*," as if to remind us of the streams that watered Paradise ("a river of thy *pleasures*" עֵדֶן) ; or when "*the fountain*" is spoken of, as if to send our thoughts to Deut. xxx. 20, Israel's fountain. It is such a song of Zion as can be appreciated only by meditation deep and frequent —such solemn meditation as will try to gaze up to those heavens (verse 5), wherein mercy dwells ; penetrate those clouds in which faithfulness is hid ; climb and explore the massy mountain-heights of justice (*hills of God*, worthy of his greatness, glorious and immense) ; cast the line into the fathomless deep of his judgments, (*i.e.*, his providential dealings) ; and feel drawn by that grace that leads men to the shade of the Almighty wings, and then to the rivers of pleasure which flow from the fountain of life. If asked to describe what we see in this Psalm, we would say, We see here

*The Righteous One looking up to the God of grace from amid
a world lying in wickedness.*

Psalm 37

A Psalm of David

1 FRET not thyself because of evildoers,
Neither be thou envious against the workers of iniquity.
2 For they shall soon be cut down like the grass, and wither as the green herb.
3 Trust in the Lord, and do good ;
So shalt thou dwell in the land, and verily thou shalt be fed.
4 Delight thyself also in the Lord ; and he shall give thee the desires of thine heart.
5 Commit thy way unto the Lord ; trust also in him ;
And he shall bring it to pass.
6 And he shall bring forth thy righteousness as the light, and thy judgment as the noonday.
7 Rest in the Lord, and wait patiently for him :
Fret not thyself because of him who prospereth in his way,
Because of the man who bringeth wicked devices to pass.

8 Cease from anger, and forsake wrath : fret not thyself in any wise to do evil.

9 For evildoers shall be cut off : but those that wait upon the Lord, they shall inherit the earth.

10 For yet a little while, and the wicked shall not be :
Yea, thou shalt diligently consider his place, and it shall not be.

11 But the meek shall inherit the earth ;
And shall delight themselves in the abundance of peace.

12 The wicked plotteth against the just, and gnasheth upon him with his teeth.

13 The Lord shall laugh at him : for he seeth that his day is coming.

14 The wicked have drawn out the sword, and have bent their bow,
To cast down the poor and needy, and to slay such as be of upright conversation.

15 Their sword shall enter into their own heart, and their bows shall be broken.

16 A little that a righteous man hath, is better than the riches of many wicked.

17 For the arms of the wicked shall be broken : but the Lord upholdeth the righteous.

18 The Lord knoweth the days of the upright : and their inheritance shall be for ever.

19 They shall not be ashamed in the evil time : and in the days of famine they shall be satisfied.

20 But the wicked shall perish,
And the enemies of the Lord shall be as the fat of lambs :
They shall consume ; into smoke shall they consume away.

21 The wicked borroweth, and payeth not again : but the righteous sheweth mercy, and giveth.

22 For such as be blessed of him shall inherit the earth ;
And they that be cursed of him shall be cut off.

23 The steps of a good man are ordered by the Lord : and he delighteth in his way.

24 Though he fall, he shall not be utterly cast down :
For the Lord upholdeth him with his hand.

25 I have been young, and now am old ;
Yet have I not seen the righteous forsaken, nor his seed begging bread.

26 He is ever merciful, and lendeth ; and his seed is blessed.

27 Depart from evil, and do good ; and dwell for evermore.

28 For the lord loveth judgment, and forsaketh not his saints.
They are preserved for ever : but the seed of the wicked shall be cut off.

29 The righteous shall inherit the land, and dwell therein for ever.

30 The mouth of the righteous speaketh wisdom, and his tongue talketh of judgment.

31 The law of his God is in his heart ; none of his steps shall slide.

32 The wicked watcheth the righteous, and seeketh to slay him.

33 The Lord will not leave him in his hand, nor condemn him when he is judged.

34 Wait on the Lord, and keep his way, and he shall exalt thee to inherit
the land.
When the wicked are cut off, thou shalt see it.

35 I have seen the wicked in great power, and spreading himself like a green
bay tree.

36 Yet he passed away, and, lo, he was not! yea, I sought him, but he could
not be found.

37 Mark the perfect man, and behold the upright! for the end of that man is
peace.

38 But the transgressors shall be destroyed together: the end of the wicked
shall be cut off.

39 But the salvation of the righteous is of the Lord: he is their strength in
the time of trouble.

40 And the Lord shall help them, and deliver them:
He shall deliver them from the wicked, and save them, because they trust
in him.

THERE are *seven* alphabetic Psalms, and this is one of them. It is a song of Zion, in which precious truths are stored up in the memory by the aid of the alphabetic beginnings of each verse. But, as usual, there occurs one irregularity (viz. **ע** is omitted), to prevent us, perhaps, attaching too great importance to this form of structure. *Alphabetic structure.*

The two-edged sword gleams bright here ; justice and mercy ride together over the field of earth. It is a song suitable for the Church and the Church's Head alike, and for every age of the Church's history. And yet how exactly some verses suit special scenes. Thus, verses 31, 32, is a full-length portrait of the Just One—word, thought, deed ; while Antichrist might be said to have sat for his picture in verses 35, 36. " I saw the wicked," &c. *Christ and his Church.*

Our Lord seems to quote this Psalm in Matt. v. 2 : " Blessed are *the meek—they shall inherit the earth.*" And in this Psalm " *the little while*" is spoken of, that " little while" of the Church's patient waiting, now so well known to us : *The future.*

" *Yet a little while and the wicked shall not be.*"
" *And the meek shall inherit the earth.*" (Ver. 10, 11.)

Verses 37, 38, describe the final reward, "The End," of the perfect man, and the final doom, "the end," of transgressors, on the Great Day, when He comes who has " His reward with him." And so it closes with ascribing all victory to the Lord alone. (Ver. 39, 40.)

The title is simply, " *of David*," and this much we may re-mark regarding the penman's style in it, that in very many portions his own history supplied striking exemplifications of his doctrinal statements.

In verses 1–6 we have *the Lord's treatment of His own*. He lets them be proved and tried, while the wicked prosper. David's adversity in the day of Saul's authority, and Nabal's history, might be referred to as illustrating these verses. " *Dwell in the Land*" may send us to Gen. xxvi. 34, or to 1 Sam. xxvii. 1, 2, by contrast. Notice how it is *faith* and *hope* together that are recommended in verses 5, 6, and remark that " *judgment*" may well be rendered " *The decision of thy cause in favour of the right*," just as in Isaiah xlii. 3, 4 ; John xii. 31, and xvi. 11, it signifies the decision of the controversy pending between God and us, against the great Accuser.

In verses 7–15 we have *The Lord's treatment of his foes*. Instead of complaining of our burdens, and anxieties, and cares, and fears, and instead of throwing them off in stoical indifference, let us " *roll them on the Lord*" (as ver. 5), and then " Wait—be *silent*"—*q.d.*, standing still at the Red Sea, till God opens the way. " *The meek*" are they who bow to God's will ; they shall as surely " *inherit the earth*," as ever Israel entered into possession of Canaan. This is a promise repeated in verses 11, 22, 29, 34, as if to reiterate, " that though you have little of earth and earth's good things now, all shall yet be yours, and the ungodly be gone for ever."

From verses 16–22 we have *God's blessing on the substance of the godly, and his curse on what belongs to the wicked*. This is seen in the godly enjoying sufficiency at all times, and in their being able (ver. 21) to give to others also ; whereas the ungodly are blighted, yea so reduced (ver. 21) as to be found " borrowing," and unable to repay. All this is a fore-taste of the future day described in Matt. xxv. 34, 41, and to which reference is made in these words,

> " *For the Lord's blessed ones shall inherit the earth,*
> *And his cursed ones shall be cut off.*"

In verses 23–26 we have *contrasts that even now distin-guish the lot of these two classes of men*. The godly are directed ; lifted up when calamity has overtaken them (ver. 24) ; never forsaken (ver. 25).

> " *I have never seen the righteous forsaken* (of God),
> *Nor* (have I seen) *his seed* (forsaken) *even when in greatest poverty.*"

Nay, so far from this, the righteous is enabled to shew kindness to others (ver. 26), and leaves blessing to his seed. " For (says one) so far is charity from impoverishing, that what is given away, like vapours emitted by the earth, returns in showers of blessing."

From verses 27–33 we have *an implied invitation to join the godly, whom the Lord so cares for, in cherishing all that is holy.* Things are said which in their full sense are realised only in the person of the Righteous One.

In verses 34–40 we arrive *at the final issues of things.* Wait—that " wicked one" who is so " *terrible*" (עָרִיץ), shall soon disappear—that Saul, that foe of yours, that Antichrist, the Church's foe ! And fail not to mark the perfect, " *For to the perfect there is an end,*" an אַחֲרִית. This " אַחֲרִית" is what Balaam speaks of in Numb. xxiii. 10, the end in the latter day, the resurrection time.

And now let us revert to several expressions, in which we find a marked likeness to our Lord's mode of speaking when on earth. We noticed at verse 22, the resemblance to Matt. xxv. 34, 41, the " blessed" and the " cursed ;" but not less remarkable is the five times repeated " *inherit the earth,*" for our Lord quotes it in Matt. v. 5, when promising still future blessing. Add to these the " *little while*" of verse 10, as used by the Lord in John xvi. 16–19, and also " *the end*" as parallel to our Lord's " *end of the age*" in Matt. xiii. 19. With all these expressions before us, may we not say that *the Master himself* is the chief speaker of this Psalm ? It is as properly the lips of David's Son that utter it, as it is the pen of David that writes it. And this is the theme of it—

The Righteous One quieting our heart by teaching us to discern between the godly and the wicked.

Christ the speaker.

Psalm 38

A Psalm of David, to bring to remembrance

1 O LORD, rebuke me not in thy wrath: neither chasten me in thy hot displeasure.

2 For thine arrows stick fast in me, and thy hand presseth me sore.

3 There is no soundness in my flesh because of thine anger;
Neither is there any rest in my bones because of my sin.

4 For mine iniquities are gone over mine head: as an heavy burden, they are too heavy for me.

5 My wounds stink and are corrupt, because of my foolishness.

6 I am troubled; I am bowed down greatly; I go mourning all the day long.

7 For my loins are filled with a loathsome disease: and there is no soundness in my flesh.

8 I am feeble and sore broken: I have roared by reason of the disquietness of my heart.

9 Lord, all my desire is before thee; and my groaning is not hid from thee.

10 My heart panteth, my strength faileth me:
As for the light of mine eyes, it also is gone from me.

11 My lovers and my friends stand aloof from my sore; and my kinsmen stand afar off.

12 They also that seek after my life lay snares for me:
And they that seek my heart speak mischievous things,
And imagine deceits all the day long.

13 But I, as a deaf man, heard not; and I was as a dumb man that openeth not his mouth.

14 Thus I was as a man that heareth not, and in whose mouth are no reproofs.

15 For in thee, O Lord, do I hope: thou wilt hear, O Lord my God.

16 For I said, Hear me, lest otherwise they should rejoice over me:
When my foot slippeth, they magnify themselves against me.

17 For I am ready to halt, and my sorrow is continually before me.

18 For I will declare mine iniquity; I will be sorry for my sin.

19 But mine enemies are lively, and they are strong:
And they that hate me wrongfully are multiplied.

20 They also that render evil for good are mine adversaries;
Because I follow the thing that good is.

21 Forsake me not, O Lord: O my God, be not far from me.

22 Make haste to help me, O Lord my salvation.

Christ in it. HERE is "The inhabitant saying, I am sick"—David, and every believer with him, and the Head of all believers, David's Son, when he took his place in our world as The Inhabitant who was to heal the sicknesses of others. One writer vehemently asserts, "It is a prophetic prayer of Christ; it has no personal refe-

ence whatever to David" (Tucker) ; while one of the ancient
fathers is content with saying, " It would be hard not to apply
to Christ a Psalm that as graphically describes his passion as
if we were reading it out of the gospels. (Valde durum et
contrarium est, ut ille Psalmus non pertineat ad Christum ubi
habemus tam apertam passionem ejus tanquam ex Evan-
gelio recitetur."—Aug). We are content to notice that the
tone of the voice of him that speaks is none other than
that of the speaker in Psalm vi., as verse 1 in both is sufficient to prove. Nor is it unlike Psalm xxii., as verses 21 and
22 will at once suggest (Psa. xxii. 29). The difficulty in the
way of supposing it used by the Lord Jesus, as descriptive of
his feelings and state, when he took on *our guilt by imputation*, is not at all greater than in some passages of Psalms
xl. and lxix., which almost no one doubts to be his utterances.
There is some light cast on our Lord's feelings under the
imputation of our sins, if we consider verse 5 to be a statement
of his abhorrence of the sin he bears : " *My wounds stink
and are corrupt*"—*i. e.*, there is inexpressible loathsomeness
in my festering wounds, those wounds which I have been
subjected to " *because of my foolishness,*" viz., the folly imputed to me (as in Psa. lxix. 5), the foolishness, the infatuation
and sins of my people. He was weary of wearing that poisoned
garment of our sins ; he was weary of having our leprosy appearing on his spotless person ; he was weary and woe-begone,
and longed for the time when he should " *appear without sin,*"
(Heb. ix. 28).

It is thus that we can understand it to have been used by   The title.
Christ, and yet to be suitable at the same time, though in a
different manner, to Christ's redeemed ones, who feel their
personal corruption and guilt. And in either case the title is
appropriate, " *To bring to remembrance*"—just as in Psalm lxx.
It speaks of God *apparently* forgetting the sufferer, so that
a cry ascends, equivalent to, " Lord, remember David and all
his afflictions."

What a cry is verse 1, " *Lord, rebuke me not,*" &c., in the   The content.
lips of the Head, or of the members. It conveys a foreboding
apprehension of another wave of the wrath to come, ready to

break over the already bruised soul. "If it be possible, let this cup pass !" What a groan is verse 2, " *For thine arrows stick fast in*, or, *sink into me*"—one of which arrows we saw on the bow in Psalm vii. 12—arrows that drink up the life-blood. What an overwhelming sight verse 4 presents, " *Mine iniquities are gone over my head*,"—like the tide rising while he is within tide-mark. What convulsive agony is depicted in verse 6, " *I am racked with pain, I am bowed down greatly. Day by day do I go in sadness.*"

How terrible in their very calmness are verses 9 and 10 :

> " *Lord, all my desire is before thee,*
> *And my groaning is not hid from thee.*
> *My heart panteth, my strength faileth,*
> *The light of mine eyes—even that no longer remains to me ;*"

for weeping and sorrow have dimmed the eye : a state to which His members have been at times reduced, as when that remark-able disciple in the Highlands of Scotland *wept herself blind*, through sorrow for sin, after her awakening. And then the gloomy cloud closes round Him, verse 11, " *Lovers and friends stand aloof*,—sympathy there is none. Nor does his gloom soon pass ; for verse 17 renews the sad complaint,

> " *I am ready to halt,*" *i.e.*, to fall and be broken,

for the keeper of Israel has to appearance forgotten me, and does not " keep my feet from sliding," (Psa. cxxi. 3).

The deliverance is foreseen in verse 21, " *Haste to my help ;*" to save me from those who are to me like Satan (ver. 20) ; and the fulness of it at last is implied and wrapt up in " *O ! Jehovah, my salvation.*" If *Jehovah* is my salvation, then is He to me what he was to Moses at the Red Sea (Exod. xv. 2), and my triumph is sure and full. The Head and his members have a *salvation* from Jehovah of wondrous extent—beginning in the resurrection of the Head, and to be completed at the resurrection of all the members.

Read, then, in either application, this Psalm describes

The Leprosy of sin abhorred by the righteous.

Psalm 39

To the chief Musician, even to Jeduthun, A Psalm of David

1 I SAID, I will take heed to my ways, that I sin not with my tongue:
I will keep my mouth with a bridle, while the wicked is before me.
2 I was dumb with silence, I held my peace, even from good;
And my sorrow was stirred.
3 My heart was hot within me, while I was musing the fire burned:
Then spake I with my tongue.
4 Lord, make me to know mine end, and the measure of my days, what it is;
That I may know how frail I am.
5 Behold, thou hast made my days as an handbreath;
And mine age is as nothing before thee:
Verily every man at his best state is altogether vanity. Selah.
6 Surely every man walketh in a vain show! surely they are disquieted in vain!
He heapeth up riches, and knoweth not who shall gather them.
7 And now, Lord, what wait I for? my hope is in thee.
8 Deliver me from all my transgressions: make me not the reproach of the foolish.
9 I was dumb, I opened not my mouth; because thou didst it.
10 Remove thy stroke away from me: I am consumed by the blow of thine hand.
11 When thou with rebukes dost correct man for iniquity,
Thou makest his beauty to consume away like a moth:
Surely every man is vanity. Selah.
12 Hear my prayer, O Lord, and give ear unto my cry; hold not thy peace at my tears:
For I am a stranger with thee, and a sojourner, as all my fathers were.
13 O spare me, that I may recover strength, before I go hence, and be no more.

IN last Psalm, verses 13, 14, resemble the first verse here, *The position.* and on this account the two Psalms have been put side by side. But besides, here is one whom we might call "*Gershom,*" for he is a stranger in a strange land, and he is the same speaker (whoever that was) as in the previous Psalm. For, if the one Psalm spoke thus, "*I said, I am ready to halt*" (ver. 16), this begins with, "*I said, I will take heed to my ways;*" and if the one spoke of being "*dumb with silence*" (ver. 14), not less does this in verse 2; and if the one said, verse 15, "In thee do *I hope,*" this also says, verse 7, "*My hope* is in thee."

The title does not tell us more than that there was a musical *The title.* chorus, in which, perhaps, "*Jeduthun*" may have been the name

of the presiding singer, to whose care it was committed. But
a glance at the contents shews a pilgrim-spirit, one journeying
through a world of vanity, and praying at every step to be
taught and kept in the will of God. Christ, when "learning
obedience" and identifying himself with us (as in ver. 12), could
use it, supplicating his Father in verse 4 ; sympathising with
our feeble frame in verse 5, "Thou hast given me some hand-
breadths as the length of my days : and my life is as non-
existence before thee ;" pronouncing the sentence of "Vanity
and Vexation" on all that this world presents, however good
and fair to the eye (ver. 6), and in verse 7 turning towards
Jehovah, as the only source of bliss. In verses 9, 10, not only
can every believer find his own experience, or what should be
his experience under trial, but the Lord Jesus also could have
used these words. On earth, he said, "Even so, Father, for so
it seemeth good in thy sight," praying at the same time, "If it
be possible, let this cup pass." The marred countenance of
the Son of Man, in which nothing of the "King in his beauty"
could be seen, may be described in the words of verse 11. Like
verse 5, this verse is followed by a "*Selah*," calling for silent
thought. But intermixed with all the pilgrim's melancholy
laments, do we not recognise his hope and expectation of
something better to come? Is not "*the vanity*" of verse 6,
like that of Romans viii. 20, for it is followed up by verse 7,
"*My hope is in thee.*" There is "*Hope*" for this world ! its
"*vanity*" may give place to reality of bliss. An Israelite, amid
Canaan's plenty, could feel this, as 1 Chron. xxix. 15 shews,
and as Levit. xxv. 33 had taught them to feel. And is not
verse 13 a Samson-like cry (Judges xvi. 28) to be carried
through the crisis of a final struggle ! The believer and his
Lord could find here a most suitable petition. Alexander
notices also how full of references to Job is this verse : thus
chap. vii. 19, xiv. 6, and x. 20, 21. But "*Spare me that I
may be refreshed*," is a prayer that all in him which sin
withered may be renovated, and his sad soul be refreshed with
Divine grace. The Psalmist thus describes Christ when on
earth, and at the same time every one of his family while
passing through this earth to the kingdom. It is,

The Righteous One a Pilgrim and a Stranger.

Psalm 40

To the chief Musician, A Psalm of David

1 I WAITED patiently for the Lord; and he inclined unto me, and heard my cry.

2 He brought me up also out of an horrible pit, out of the miry clay, And set my feet upon a rock, and established my goings.

3 And he hath put a new song in my mouth, even praise unto our God: Many shall see it, and fear, and shall trust in the Lord.

4 Blessed is that man that maketh the Lord his trust, And respecteth not the proud, nor such as turn aside to lies.

5 Many, O Lord my God, are thy wonderful works which thou hast done, And thy thoughts which are to us-ward : They cannot be reckoned up in order unto thee ! If I would declare and speak of them, they are more than can be numbered.

6 Sacrifice and offering thou didst not desire ; mine ears hast thou opened. Burnt offering and sin offering hast thou not required :

7 Then said I, Lo, I come : in the volume of the book it is written of me,

8 I delight to do thy will, O my God : yea thy law is within my heart.

9 I have preached righteousness in the great congregation : Lo, I have not refrained my lips, O Lord, thou knowest.

10 I have not hid thy righteousness within my heart; I have declared thy faithfulness and thy salvation : I have not concealed thy lovingkindness and thy truth from the great congregation.

11 Withhold not thou thy tender mercies from me, O Lord : Let thy lovingkindness and thy truth continually preserve me.

12 For innumerable evils have compassed me about: mine iniquities have taken hold upon me, So that I am not able to look up; they are more than the hairs of mine head : Therefore my heart faileth me.

13 Be pleased, O Lord, to deliver me: O Lord, make haste to help me.

14 Let them be ashamed and confounded together, that seek after my soul to destroy it; Let them be driven backward and put to shame, that wish me evil.

15 Let them be desolate, for a reward of their shame, that say unto me, Aha! aha!

16 Let all those that seek thee rejoice and be glad in thee. Let such as love thy salvation say continually, The Lord be magnified.

17 But I am poor and needy; yet the Lord thinketh upon me: Thou art my help and my deliverer ; make no tarrying, O my God.

"*I waited, I waited for Jehovah,*" I did nothing but wait, Christ in it. (Alexander). Here is one who cries, " Lo ! I come to do thy will, O God." We cannot fail to recognise Messiah here, even if we had not had the aid of the writer of Hebrews x. 5–10. The iniquities he speaks of in verse 12 are *all ours** imputed to him. He might say, "And I am a sinner in thy sight, although I never sinned." *Christ* speaks throughout, so exclusively indeed, that the believer must here take up the words not as his own experience (except where he can follow Christ to gather the spoil), but as the experience of the Captain of Salvation, in fighting that battle which has ended in everlasting triumph. It is only by accommodation that even verses 1–3 can be used by the believer in describing his own case. Christ is the Joseph and Jeremiah of this pit.

The theme. Read verse 4, and meditate on what He who is the Word suggests—" *God's thoughts toward us !*" The unnumbered multitude of his thoughts of love to us ! The forests with their countless leaves, the grass on every plain and mountain of earth with its numberless blades, the sands on every shore of every river and ocean, the waves of every sea and the drops of every wave of every sea, the stars of heaven—none of these, nor all combined, could afford an adequate idea of " *His thoughts toward us !*"—" *there is no comparison to thee*"—nothing wherewith to help out a statement. And the *depth of love* in every one of these thoughts ! Who can sit down and meditate on Redemption's wonders ? Who would not be confounded ?

The plan. Now the whole Psalm has this as its theme. From verses 1 to 3, a summary of God's dealings toward the Saviour, ending in the gathering of multitudes to Him *as the Shiloh.* Verses 4 and 5, adoration of the purposes of God ; and from verse 9 to the end, we are made to witness something of the style in which these glorious purposes were carried on to fulfilment, in the actual coming and suffering of the Saviour. See him *obeying ;* see him proclaiming Jehovah's name in its breadth and fulness, wherever he came, in the villages, towns, cities, the synagogues, the temple, the open air assemblies, " I have proclaimed righteousness, and I will not at any future time restrain my lips." Hear in verse 12 his unutterable groanings, when " *sorrowful* unto death." Then hear him in

---

* " Noluit enim loqui separatus, qui noluit esse separatus."—August.

verse 15 foretelling Israel's desolation, and that of others like them, because of their rejection of Him ; while verse 16 pictures to us present "joy and peace in believing," with the ultimate result in the ages to come, in the joy of The Kingdom. It would be endless were we to dwell on the rich and copious suggestions afforded by almost every verse.* It is a manual of the History of Redemption. It is

Messiah exhibited as our once-for-all Sacrifice, and all our Salvation.

Psalm 41

To the chief Musician, A Psalm of David.

1 BLESSED is he that considereth the poor :
   The Lord will deliver him in the time of trouble.
2 The Lord will preserve him, and keep him alive ; and he shall be blessed upon the earth:
   And thou wilt not deliver him unto the will of his enemies.
3 The Lord will strengthen him upon the bed of languishing :
   Thou wilt make all his bed in his sickness.
4 I said, Lord, be merciful unto me : heal my soul ; for I have sinned against thee.
5 Mine enemies speak evil of me, when shall he die and his name perish ?
6 And if he come to see me, he speaketh vanity ;
   His heart gathereth iniquity to itself ; when he goeth abroad he telleth it.
7 All that hate me whisper together against me : against me do they devise my hurt.
8 An evil disease, say they, cleaveth fast unto him :
   And now that he lieth he shall rise up no more.
9 Yea, mine own familiar friend, in whom I trusted, which did eat of my bread,
   Hath lifted up his heel against me.
10 But thou, O Lord, be merciful unto me, and raise me up, that I may requite them.

* The much-disputed passage, verse 6, " *Thou hast dug through my ears*," or " *Thou hast prepared ears for me*," is rendered from the Septuagint, " A body hast thou prepared for me," in Heb. x. 5 ; because his taking our human nature was the first and most direct step to his being made servant, like the man *whose ears were bored* to the door-post. Possibly, too, there is reference to his being a Priest prepared for his office, by having his ears tipt with blood, as Lev. xiv. 14 ; Exod. xxix. 20. For the Hebrew is scarcely " *bored*," it is rather " *prepared*." Alexander says, " The Septuagint version may have been retained as suggesting that the *Incarnation* of the Son was a pre-requisite to his *obedience*.

11 By this I know that thou favourest me, because mine enemy doth not triumph over me.

12 And as for me, thou upholdest me in mine integrity, and settest me before thy face for ever.

13 Blessed be the Lord God of Israel from everlasting, and to everlasting. Amen, and Amen.

Quoted by Christ.

THE melancholy interest attached to this Psalm has made it well-known in Zion. Our Lord quoted it as his own, on the night when he was betrayed (see John xiii. 18, compared with ver. 9), when he saw the traitor take his seat at the Passover table with him, and sit down on his left hand, so near that he could hand him the sop, and dip with him in the dish. The strain, however, is such as suits his family as well as himself; they may use it in Him.

The contents.

It is the Lord who says, " *Blessed is he that acts wisely toward the poor,*" ver. 1 ; the same who said " *Blessed are the merciful !*" and the same who on the day of his coming shall say, " Come, ye blessed ; I was sick, and ye visited me." He encourages us to do good works in his Name, especially to those of the household of faith. What is written from verse 1 to 3 is a promise which *Barzillai* could have claimed ; and *Ebed-melech*, who drew Jeremiah from the pit; and *Onesiphorus*, who oft refreshed Paul ; and the women of Galilee, Susannah and others, who ministered to Christ of their substance ; and the *daughters of Jerusalem*, who gave him sympathy as he bore the cross, pitying his marred countenance.

Perhaps in verse 4 Christ may be understood as saying, " I, even I, myself, did that to others, and do, therefore, claim the blessing. But how differently my foes act toward me ! All my miracles of kindness are forgotten, the memory of all my thousand benefits is drowned in their malice ; they wish my death, " When shall He die ;" and " his name perish ?" (Ver. 5.) " If he comes to *see* me," (*i.e*, to play the spy on me), he goes away, saying,

" *Some cursed thing cleaves to him.*" (Ver. 8, literally, "*is soldered into him.*")

But the issue shall disappoint them ; I shall not even once **err,** and I shall soon stand at thy right hand;

" Mine enemy is not to triumph over me :
And as for me, thou upholdest me in my integrity,
And settest me before thy face for ever." (Ver. 12.)

In this he anticipates the reward of his obedience unto death, and *" the glory that should follow,"* as we too may do.

In this prospect it is interesting to hear him say, " Blessed   Israel in it. be *Jehovah, God of Israel,"* (ver. 13). The rejected and despised One has not forgotten or given up the people who rejected him. He will be their King, *" King of the Jews,"* though they crucify him; he intends grace and glory for them in the latter day. " Rabbi, thou art the Son of God ; thou art *the King of Israel."* And that *" Amen and Amen,"* how sweetly it dropped from the lips of the Faithful Witness, who delighted to preface his weighty sayings with " Verily," verily, Αμην, Αμην, and who fixes his mark to this blessed Psalm (resembling what Paul does in some of his Epistles), as if to say, " The signature of me, the Faithful Witness, with mine own hand."

The Righteous One unpitied in his time of need.

Psalm 42

To the chief Musician, Maschil, for the sons of Korah

1 As the hart panteth after the water brooks, so panteth my soul after thee, O God.

2 My soul thirsteth for God, for the living God!   When shall I come and appear before God?

3 My tears have been my meat day and night, While they continually say unto me, Where is thy God?

4 When I remember these things, I pour out my soul in me : For I had gone with the multitude, I went with them to the house of God, With the voice of joy and praise, with a multitude that kept holyday.

5 Why art thou cast down, O my soul? and why art thou disquieted in me? Hope thou in God : for I shall yet praise him For the help of his countenance.

6 O my God, my soul is cast down within me! Therefore will I remember thee from the land of Jordan and of the Hermonites, From the hill Mizar.

7 Deep calleth unto deep at the noise of thy waterspouts; All thy waves and thy billows are gone over me.

8 Yet the Lord will command his lovingkindness in the daytime,
And in the night his song shall be with me,
And my prayer unto the God of my life.

9 I will say unto God my rock, Why hast thou forgotten me ?
Why go I mourning because of the oppression of the enemy ?

10 As with a sword in my bones, mine enemies reproach me ;
While they say daily unto me, Where is thy God ?

11 Why art thou cast down, O my soul ? and why art thou disquieted within
me ?
Hope thou in God : for I shall yet praise him,
Who is the health of my countenance, and my God.

THE Jews begin *Book* II. with this Psalm. There is little
doubt that their fourfold division of the Book of Psalms is arbi-
trary, and was suggested by the single circumstance that
"*Amen*" happens to occur at the close of Ps. xl., lxxii., lxxxix.,
and cvi., which are the closing Psalms of the different divisions.

The title.

The *Maschil* has reference to the music. As for the *sons of
Korah,* descendants of the rebel Korah whose children, spared
by grace, took a conspicuous part in the Temple worship of
song, they were only the *receivers*, not the writers of the Psalm.
Probably the Levites who were with David (2 Sam. xv. 24) include the sons of Korah.

Christ.

Here is the *hart in the wilderness panting for the water
brooks* which it had not got at. It stands on some bank that
hangs over (עַל), the brook,—the water is not reached. Such
is the Psalmist's state of soul. "O that I might see the face
of God !" is the force of verse 2 ; and verse 4 is the soul responding to itself, saying, in remembrance of past joys now
withheld, "Thereon will I think, and pour out my soul within
myself."

The Septuagint has translated this very nearly in the words
used in Matt. xxvi. 38, and John xii. 27.

" *Why art thou* ('περίλυπος' Septuagint) *very sorrowful, O my soul ?
And why art thou* (ταρασσεις με) *troubled within me ?*"

Our Lord, as well as every troubled and sorrowful one of
his people, could use this Psalm, when, as the true David, he
was driven out, not by a son, but by his Father for our sakes
—driven farther from heaven than Hermon or Jordan, or "the
Little Hill," are from Zion and the Tabernacle, hearing deeper

floods calling to one another, and mustering their waters, as at the deluge the cataracts dashed upon the ark from above, while bursting fountains heaved it up from below.* Still, He knew the issue : " For the joy set before Him he endured the cross." He could sing in the gloom, "*I shall y.t praise him*, the salvation of my countenance, and my God !" The marginal reading is, " His presence is salvation ;" but verse 11 is against this. The meaning is, I shall praise Him as He who shall change my marred form, and give me beauty ; who shall change my humiliation into exaltation ; who shall in my case, and then in the case of all my people, exchange the wilderness and its parched sands for the kingdom and its rivers of pleasure.

The sorest pang of Christ, arising from reproach and scorn, was that which he felt when they cast suspicion on the love and faithfulness of his Father (ver. 10), "*Where is thy God ?*" In proportion as sanctification advances, his members feel this, too, forgetting their own glory, and intent upon his. In the primary use of the Psalm, this taunt would be felt by David when his enemies insinuated that though God had anointed him king, yet He could not bring him to his kingdom : or even if " the *sons of Korah* "† wrote this Psalm, (as Hengstenberg thinks), there would be the same feeling in them in regard to this taunt flung at that devoted leader, whose cause they espoused, coming to him at Ziklag. (1 Chron. xii. 6.) But the Holy Ghost founded on these circumstances a song of Zion, which was meant for Zion's King, and all his princes in their passage to the throne and kingdom. The Lord Jesus might specially call it to mind, and sing it with his disciples on that remarkable day when, at *Cæsarea Philippi* (Matt. xvi. 13), he asked what men were saying of him ? On that day,

The speaker.

All believers.

Christ.

---

* The various cataracts of Jordan (see Lynch's Narrative of Expedition to Jordan) might give origin to the figures of " deep unto deep—noise of thy waterspouts."

† " *The sons of Korah* " have their name prefixed to fourteen Psalms. Herein is free sovereign grace! The descendants of the rebel are spared (Numb. xxvi. 11), and honoured. We find them "porters" and " over the host of the Lord," 1 Chron. ix. 19, for they were Levites of the family of Kohath. Some of them came to David at Ziklag, 1 Chron. xii. 6, and these may be specially the "sons of Korah" mentioned here, viz., Elkanah, Jesiah, Jaser, Joshobeam, and Azareel. Their after history, too, is interesting, grace still shining in it throughout, in the days of the later kings.

Hermon was in sight, and Jordan's double-fountain close beside him, and some *"Little Hill"* near them, some *"Mizar,"** that, by contrast, called up to mind the *Hills of Zion.* On that day, it may be, the Head of the Church made special use of this Psalm, and embalmed it in the hearts of his disciples, who would never afterwards fail to sing it (even as we do), with double refreshment in the thought that it had comforted the Master, expressing, as it does,

The Righteous One in his weariness looking up to the Father
for refreshment.

Psalm 43

1 JUDGE me, O God, and plead my cause against an ungodly nation!
  O deliver me from the deceitful and unjust man !
2 For thou art the God of my strength : why dost thou cast me off ?
  Why go I mourning because of the oppression of the enemy ?
3 O send out thy light and thy truth : let them lead me
  Let them bring me unto thy holy hill and to thy tabernacles.
4 Then will I go unto the altar of God, unto God my exceeding joy :
  Yea, upon the harp will I praise thee, O God, my God.
5 Why art thou cast down, O my soul ? and why art thou disquieted within me ?
  Hope in God : for I shall yet praise him, who is the health of my countenance, and my God.

The tone.

MANY ancient and modern writers make this Psalm a part of the former. They have failed to see that the strain is now more gladsome and hopeful. *The hart is now bounding on to the water brooks.* The psalmist is claiming his right to refreshment, and anticipating it as at his very lips. The gloom of "night" (xlii. 8) and of "mourning" (ver. 2) is to be exchanged for favour or *"light"* (ver. 3), and *"truth,"* i.e., the fulfilment of the promises made to him (Aben-Ezra) shall

---

* Tucker has made an interesting suggestion, though it will not bear examination : "I will remember thee *concerning* the land" (ב). God's past mercies displayed there, at the miraculous passage of the river *Jordan*, and the getting possession of the land even to *Hermon ;* and then "The Little Hill" would be *Zion* itself, only great because the Tabernacle is there. The construction of the Hebrew refuses to yield this sense.

soon shew that he has not been "forgotten" (xlii. 9) ; and soon his God shall be his jubilee-song, "*joy of his joy,*" and the harp shall celebrate the well pleased countenance of "Eloi, Eloi," my God, who once seemed to stand afar of.

To Christ and to his members, the highest gladness (spoken of verse 4) comes from *The altar, with its accepted sacrifice.* Christ risen, and Christ ascended, are pointed out therein ; and it is in his resurrection and ascension that we see the sacrifice accepted, and our hearts learn true joy. No doubt this same source of joy is to be opened up to us more fully still when He appears the second time "without sin" unto salvation, and all enemies are put under him. He, too, shall rejoice afresh in that day, drinking of the coolest of the longed-for water brooks. Let us, meanwhile, read and sing this Psalm in happy confidence, as *The Righteous One's claiming his right to full refreshment.*

Christ and his members.

Psalm 44

To the chief Musician, for the sons of Korah. Maschil

1 WE have heard with our ears, O God, our fathers have told us,
What work thou didst in their days, in the times of old.
2 How thou didst drive out the heathen with thy hand, and plantedst them;
How thou didst afflict the people, and cast them out.
3 For they got not the land in possession by their own sword,
Neither did their own arm save them :
But thy right hand, and thine arm, and the light of thy countenance,
Because thou hadst a favour unto them.
4 Thou art my King, O God ! command deliverance for Jacob.
5 Through thee will we push down our enemies :
Through thy name will we tread them under that rise up against us.
6 For I will not trust in my bow, neither shall my sword save me.
7 But thou hast saved us from our enemies, and hast put them to shame that hated us.
8 In God we boast all the day long, and praise thy name for ever. Selah.
9 But thou hast cast off, and put us to shame ; and goest not forth with our armies !
10 Thou makest us to turn back from the enemy ; and they which hate spoil for themselves.
11 Thou hast given us like sheep appointed for meat ;
And hast scattered us among the heathen.
12 Thou sellest thy people for nought, and dost not increase thy wealth by their price.

13 Thou makest us a reproach to our neighbours,
    A scorn and derision to them that are round about us.

14 Thou makest us a byword among the heathen, a shaking of the head
    among the people.

15 My confusion is continually before me, and the shame of my face hath
    covered me;

16 For the voice of him that reproacheth and blasphemeth; by reason of the
    enemy and avenger.

17 All this is come upon us; yet have we not forgotten thee,
    Neither have we dealt falsely in thy covenant.

18 Our heart is not turned back, neither have ur steps declined from thy
    way;

19 Though thou hast sore broken us in the place of dragons,
    And covered us with the shadow of death.

20 If we have forgotten the name of our God, or stretched out our hands to a
    strange God,

21 Shall not God search this out? for he knoweth the secrets of the heart.

22 Yea, for thy sake are we killed all the day long; we are counted as sheep
    for the slaughter.

23 Awake! why sleepest thou, O Lord? Arise! cast us not off for ever.

24 Wherefore hidest thou thy face, and forgettest our affliction and our op-
    pression?

25 For our soul is bowed down to the dust: our belly cleaveth unto the earth.

26 Arise for our help, and redeem us for thy mercies' sake.

A series. THERE is apparently a series commencing here and extending to Psalm l., wherein *the Head is addressed,* and the various phenomena of his actings described, *by the members of his body.* *The title.* This Psalm, committed to "the Sons of Korah," is the cry of David and any other true followers of the Lord, in times of trial, when the witnesses prophesy in sackcloth. It is not so much a national Psalm, as one for the Church Universal, inasmuch as verses 17–22, humbly protest (what Israel as a nation could not) firm, unfaltering adherence to his name; and in Rom. viii. 36, are applied by Paul as expressive of the believer's state in a persecuting world. The *Maschil* is a musical reference.

The contents. It is the cry, or appeal, of the slaughtered sheep to their Shepherd. They begin by recalling to mind his great deeds in behalf of his people coming out of Egypt. They lay all the stress of that deliverance on Himself, on his holy arm alone. (Ver. 2.)

"THOU (אַתָּה) *didst drive out the heathen,*" &c.

This "*Thou*" is emphatic, quite similar to the use of the

pronoun in Ezekiel xxxvii. 3, "Thou (אַתָּ), and none else,
knowest;" and then verse 5, "I (אֲנִי), and none else, will cause
the Spirit of life to enter into you." Or like the pronoun (Rev.
iv. 11), "For *thou* (σύ), and none else, hast created all things."
Then in verse 5, there is an emphatic הוּא, "*O God, thou art
he, my King.*"

Not less significant is that other monosyllable (ver. 9),

"But (אַף) *thou hast cast off.*"

A *Selah*-pause (ver. 8) had for a moment brought the harp
to silence; and when its strings are touched again, it is to
breathe forth lamentation. It seems to reverse the case stated
in Leviticus xxvi. 44, where, after long tribulation, there is
hope of the removing of the calamity introduced by וְאַף, which
the Jews have marked on this account as "a golden אַף,"
speaking as it does of a change to prosperity. All different
here! The tide has ebbed, and no prospect of its coming in
appears! We are sold for the most trifling sum, as if the
master were only anxious to get his sheep off his hand. (Ver.
12.) We are a by-word (ver. 14), and are put to shame by
"the enemy and the avenger," whom thou couldest so easily
still. (Psa. viii. 2.)

And yet the sheep own no Shepherd but Jehovah. Their
protest is without reserve.

> "*Thou hast broken us,* (and laid us helpless,) *in the place of dragons,*
> *And covered us with the shadow of death,*
> *If we have forgotten the name of our God*
> *Or (if) we have stretched out our hands to a strange God*"

We are cut off from the society of our fellow-men, we are
thrust out into dens and caves, we flee to where serpents are
the only inhabitants, we are lingering on the brink of the grave.
Yet we can appeal "If we have forgotten!" This "If" is a
form of strong asseveration. It is the same form as our Lord
employs in Luke xix. 42, "If thou hadst known"—then would
blessing have come. It is like Exod. xxxii. 32, "Yet now, *if*
thou wilt forgive their sin." It is like Psa. xcv. 7, "To-day,
if ye will hear his voice"—then ye shall enter into rest.

Having made this protestation, they add, "*Shall not God
search this out?*" He knoweth all things; He knoweth that

we love Him ; He knoweth that *"our belly is grovelling on the earth,"* like the serpent.

" Awake, why sleepest thou, O Lord ?" (Ver. 23.)

Hope dawns. Their God shall hear. He allows them to awaken Him, and they in a manner cry through the curtains of his Pavilion, *" Up ! why sleepest thou ?"* (Prayer Book version.) The Banner of the Deliverer appears through the gloom. The sleeping Saviour awakes at the cry of his disciples, and is about to arise and still the storm " For his mercies' sake" (ver. 26), —for the sake of the tender love he bears to them. In the Latter Day we shall see, what is meant by this arising, in its full glory.

Such is this Psalm-

The cry of the slaughtered sheep to the Shepherd.

Psalm 45

To the chief Musician upon Shoshannim, for the sons of Korah   Maschil   A Song of loves

1 My heart is inditing a good matter :
   I speak of the things which I have made touching The King !
   My tongue is the pen of a ready writer.
2 Thou art fairer than the children of men ! grace is poured into thy lips !
   Therefore God hath blessed thee for ever.
3 Gird thy sword upon thy thigh, O Most Mighty, with thy glory and thy
   majesty.
4 And in thy majesty ride prosperously—because of truth and meekness and
   righteousness ;
   And thy right hand shall teach thee terrible things.
5 Thine arrows are sharp in the heart of the king's enemies :
   Whereby the people fall under thee.
6 Thy throne, O God, is for ever and ever ! The sceptre of thy kingdom is a
   right sceptre.
7 Thou lovest righteousness, and hatest wickedness :
   Therefore God, thy God, hath anointed thee with the oil of gladness above
   thy fellows.
8 All thy garments smell of myrrh, and aloes, and cassia,
   Out of the ivory palaces, whereby they have made thee glad.
9 Kings' daughters were among thy honourable women :
   Upon thy right hand did stand the queen in gold of Ophir.
10 Hearken, O daughter, and consider, and incline thine ear ;
   Forget also thine own people, and thy father's house ;

11 So shall the king greatly desire thy beauty :
  For he is thy Lord ; and worship thou him.

12 And the daughter of Tyre shall be there with a gift ;
  Even the rich among the people shall intreat thy favour.

13 The king's daughter is all glorious within : her clothing is of wrought gold :

14 She shall be brought unto the king in raiment of needlework.
  The virgins her companions that follow her shall be brought unto thee.

15 With gladness and rejoicing shall they be brought : they shall enter into
  the king's palace.

16 Instead of thy fathers shall be thy children, whom thou mayest make
  princes in all the earth.

17 I will make thy name to be remembered in all generations :
  Therefore shall the people praise thee for ever and ever.

THE appeal made to the Shepherd, by the sheep led to the *Connection.* slaughter, is heard. Here is what Hengstenberg would call a " matter-of-fact reply." The Shepherd at the bleating of his flock appears in glory to help them ; but appears in the character of a Mighty Conqueror. The Lamb is the Lion of Judah.

The title given to this Psalm corresponds to its glowing *The title.* words and theme. " *Upon S'toshannim,*" the lily-instrument, some Temple instrument of music, peculiarly adapted for the celebration of themes that were fresh and bright and beautiful. "*For the sons of Korah,*" and "*To the Chief Musician*"— the services of the Chief Singer, and the help of the whole choir of singers are put in requisition. It is also " *Maschil,*" what calls for skill in the musician as being the product of great skill in the Singer of Israel who writes it, whether he were David or Solomon, and whether or not the *occasion of its composition* were the marriage-festivities of the royal Court. And once more ; it is "*A song of loves ;*" or rather "*of the Beloved,*" viz., the Bride. At least the word "ידידות" may mean this. It is used in Jeremiah xii. **7,** as a term for Israel while Israel was *God's Beloved* (God's Spouse), and He the Husband ; and so it corresponds to *Jedidiah,* " Beloved of Jehovah," just as *Shulamite* does to *Solomon.* If so, it is a Song concerning *The contents.* *The Bride,* as well as concerning *The King,* the Bridegroom.

> " *My heart boils with goodly words.*
> *My work is for the King !*
> *My tongue is the pen of a ready writer !* " (Ver. 1).

Abrupt and fervent surely—the Holy Spirit thus using the

faculties and feelings of the human instrument to indicate the exciting nature of the subject.

" Thou art beautified with beauty among the sons of men ! "

The verb employed has an unusual form, and might be rendered " Beautiful, beautiful art thou," (Alexander).

" Grace is poured upon thy lips."

Everything that is attractive, everything that is *graceful* in character and form, in feature and expression, is meant by *" grace."* It is not what we usually call by that name ; it is a term for what fits with the person and draws the eyes of others to him. It is thus used (Prov. iv. 9), "She shall give to thy head an ornament of *grace*, a crown of *glory* shall she deliver to thee"—wisdom so clothing the person with moral beauty. It is thus, too, in Psalm lxxxiv. 11—"The Lord will give *grace* and *glory*"—the ornament of beauty, the crown of glory. All this, in full perfection, is found in Messiah's person ; all that is fitted to attract and fix the soul's gaze ; all that is beautiful in excellence ; all that is drawing in holiness and majestic worth.

Now comes verse 3,

" Warrior ! gird thy sword upon thy thigh, (Horsley).

This is *"The Mighty One"* whom Isaiah (ix. 5) calls "The Mighty God." He is the גִּבּוֹר who goes forth to victory, and yet acts in behalf of " meekness and truth and righteousness " (see Rev. xix. 15), or more literally, " *in behalf of meekness and truth ;"* the doing which in such a cause is " *righteousness."* " *On his thigh,"* we find a name in Rev. xix. 16 in perfect keeping with the גִּבּוֹר here, " King of kings, Lord or lords."

> *" Thine arrows are sharpened !*
> *The nations fall under thee !*
> *They* (thy arrows) *are in the hearts of the King's enemies ! "*

He reaches the Throne, and sits down, his enemies made his footstool. Messiah, thus seated on the throne in visible majesty, is addressed in verses 6, **7**, by the name *" God ;"*

> *" Thy Throne, O God, is for ever and ever."*
> *" Thy God hath anointed thee, O God !"* (Comp. Heb. i. 8, 9, in the Greek, and undoubtedly the true rendering of the Hebrew.)

Everything is ready for the Marriage : "myrrh and aloes and
cassia"(Song iii. 6) have been prepared for this day of Espousals,
brought out of "palaces of ivory" to help the joy, or in other
words, to complete the mirthful arrangements of this day of
heavenly gladness.

"*Out of the ivory palace, the sound of the harp (מִנִּי) maketh thee glad,*"
(taking מִנִּי to mean "stringed instruments."—Tholuck.)

The "*King's daughters*" who are in attendance "*precious
ones,*" *i.e.*, of high value, seem to be like the "*daughter of
Jerusalem*" in The Song ; and especially does this portion of
the Psalm remind us of Song vi. 8, 9, " The threescore queens,
fourscore concubines, and *virgins* without number." We suspect that both in that Song and here also, these represent *the
Angelic hosts*. They are natives of that heavenly country-—not,
like *The Bride*, brought into it from a far foreign land. *The
Bride*, or *Queen*, is the redeemed Church, made up of Jew and
Gentile saints, the one Body of the redeemed who are referred
to in Hebrews xi. 39, 40.

In this view we find no difficulties left. " Be it," sings the
sweet singer, " Be it that thy princesses who fill thy court are
of highest rank, such as are Kings' daughters, yet pre-eminent
stands *The Queen* in gold of Ophir ! No rival to her ! She is
honoured, and worthy of honour, above all !"

A pause follows. The Bride is addressed in *prospect of this
day*. It is, *q.d.*, " Wilt thou not, since this is thy glorious
destiny, be willing to leave all former relationships ? Wilt
thou not, O daughter, be as Rebecca going to Isaac ? This
Mighty One is thy *Lord ;* be thou as Sarah to Abraham."
(Gen. xviii. 12 ; 1 Pet. iii. 5, 6.)

But the scene is not yet sufficiently set before us. The sweet
singer touches his harp again to a lofty strain, to describe the
splendour of dominion possessed by·the *Bride* in right of the
Bridegroom.

"*The daughter of Tyre shall be there with a gift.
The rich among* THE PEOPLE (עַם) *shall entreat thy favour.*" (Ver. 12.)

This tells of the Glorified Church, the Lamb's Wife, ruling over
a subdued world, in the millennial days. "*Tyre*" is taken as a
sample of *Gentile* nations, and is elsewhere referred to as acting

a part in these happy times (see Isa. xxiii. 18) ; while "the rich among *the People*" are *the Jews* in their restored prosperity.   The glorified Church reigns with Christ over the nations upon earth.   The glorified Church is with Christ on his throne, wherever that may be, while he rules the people and nations under the whole heaven, Gentile and Jew, Tyre and The People.

" *The virgins her companions*" are, we think, the same as verse 9 and as Song vi. 8, " virgins without number," namely, the angelic hosts.   These participate in the joy of this scene, even as they sympathized with the birth of the Bridegroom at Bethlehem.   As for her she is all *splendour*, and "*gold embroidery*" is her vesture, *i. e.*, the richest and the rarest fabric of creation.

And (not to dwell too long on verses that tempt us to linger at every step), at last comes the final strain.   *The Queen*, or Bride, is addressed in verse 16.   It is, like Genesis xxiv. 60 and Ruth iv. 11, the expression of a wish for the after fruitfulness of the *Bride*.   The Glorified Church, reigning with Christ, is to see her prayers answered and her labours crowned, in the blessings which shall be poured on Earth in those glad millennial days.

" *Instead of thy fathers*," those who filled earth in thy former days " *shall be thy children*."   Earth shall have its new generations, generations of holy men,—"*whom thou mayest make princes in all the earth*"—every one fit to be a prince, the weakest among them as David, and the House of David as the Angel of the Lord.

> " *So shall the nations praise thee for ever and ever !* "

This ends the loftiest Epithalamium ever sung.   It is what Milton would call

> " The unexpressive nuptial song,
> In the blest kingdom meek of joy and love."

It is Earth taught by Heaven to sing heaven's infinite love to man.   It is a prelude to the New Song.   Every clause in it is melody, and every thought in it is sublimity ; but it is just such as we might expect to be breathed forth when the theme on hand was-

Messiah the Mighty One appearing as King and Bridegroom.

Psalm 46

To the chief Musician. For the sons of Korah. A Song upon Alamoth

1 Gᴏᴅ is our refuge and strength, a very present help in trouble.
2 Therefore will not we fear, though the earth be removed,
   And though the mountains be carried into the midst of the sea;
3 Though the waters thereof roar and be troubled,
   Though the mountains shake with the swelling thereof. Selah.
4 There is a river, the streams whereof shall make glad the city of God,
   The holy place of the tabernacles of the Most High.
5 God is in the midst of her; she shall not be moved:
   God shall help her, and that right early.
6 The heathen raged, the kingdoms were moved: he uttered his voice, the
   earth melted.
7 The Lord of hosts is with us; the God of Jacob is our refuge. Selah.
8 Come, behold the works of the Lord, what desolations he hath made in the
   earth.
9 He maketh wars to cease unto the end of the earth ;
   He breaketh the bow, and cutteth the spear in sunder; he burneth the
   chariot in the fire.
10 Be still, and know that I am God :
   I will be exalted among the heathen, I will be exalted in the earth.
11 The Lord of hosts is with us; the God of Jacob is our refuge. Selah

Bᴇꜰᴏʀᴇ the dawn of that day of the Bridegroom and the Bride, **Connection**
the Marriage-feast, earth shall shake with commotions ; wars,
rumours of wars, earthquakes, famines, pestilence, all combin-
ing to make men perplexed. But here we find the same
Mighty One giving strength to his own in these perilous times.

The title is peculiar, " *on Alamoth*," suggesting " a choir of **Title.**
virgins," as if this Virgin-choir were selected to sing a Psalm
that tells of perils and fears and alarms abounding, in order to
shew that even the feeble virgins may in that day sing without
dread because of " *The Mighty One*" on their side. They
and the " Sons of Korah" join in this lofty strain of confidence. We all know how Luther used to sing this Psalm
in times of peril and alarm, and many have done the like in
all ages.

They sing of Jehovah " *a very present help*," or more lite- **The plan.**
rally, " *He is found a help most truly*," נִמְצָא, being the same
word here as in 1 Sam. xiii. 16, " *present* with Saul ;" 2 Chron.
xxxv. 18, " Judah and Israel *present*," or found at their post ;

and 1 Sam. xxi. 3, "whatever is *present*"—is at hand. He has proved himself to be a help at hand.

The river in verse 4 alludes to the Euphrates of Babylon, and the Tigris of Assyria. Jerusalem has not such mighty floods to boast of. Yet Jerusalem has a river too. She has her "*waters of Siloah,*" flowing softly from her Temple (Isa. viii. 6–8), which may be despised by men of might, yet are Jerusalem's glory. Her glory is, that Jehovah is in her Temple, from beneath whose rock flows out Siloah ; and thus " A river is there, that gladdens this city of God." Or, if this be not the primary reference, the allusion is to this same *Siloah* when it shall flow from the Temple (see Joel iii. 18 ; Isa. xxxiii. 21 ; Ezek. xlvii. 1–16), and shall heal whatever it laves ; far excelling the mighty waters of Euphrates and Hiddekel, which bear the proud gallies of tyrants.

Victory shall come as soon as the Lord's set time arrives ; "*when morning appears,*" as at the Red Sea. (Exod. xiv. 27). The Lord himself shall invite men to see his victory : "*Come and see !*" (ver. 8), and to hear Him proclaim his own right to exaltation. At this announcement, his people shout in reply, verses 7 and 11, each marked (like ver. 5) by the "*Selah.*"

> " *The Lord of hosts is with us !*
> *The God of Jacob is our refuge !*"
> (*Our* מִשְׂגָּב, more than מַחְסֶה of verse 1.)

Thus setting forth

The Mighty One on the side of the righteous, amid earth's sorest throes.

Psalm 47

To the chief Musician. A Psalm for the sons of Korah

1 O CLAP your hands, all ye people ! shout unto God with the voice of triumph !

2 For the Lord most high is terrible : he is a great King over all the earth.

3 He shall subdue the people under us, and the nations under our feet.

4 He shall choose our inheritance for us, the excellency of Jacob, whom he loved. Selah.

5 God is gone up with a shout, the Lord with the sound of a trumpet !

6 Sing praises to God, sing praises : sing praises unto our King, sing praises.
7 For God is the King of all the earth : sing ye praises with understanding.
8 God reigneth over the heathen : God sitteth upon the throne of his holiness.
9 The princes of the people are gathered together, even the people of the
God of Abraham :
For the shields of the earth belong unto God : he is greatly exalted.

SOME have applied this Psalm to Christ's ascension ; but it speaks of his Second Coming. The Mighty One is seated peacefully on his throne. We are referred back to Psalm xlv. 9. His happy people stand around, exulting in his coronation, *The tone.* as Israel (to use a feeble emblem) rejoiced till earth rang again, when *Athaliah*, the usurper, was deposed, and the King of David's line was manifested after his long concealment. Then they clapt their hands (2 Kings xi. 12) to shew their rapturous joy, as here all earth is invited to do ; for even woods and trees and rivers are elsewhere represented as joining in this ecstacy of bliss (Isa. lv. 12) ; Psa. xcviii. 9), when our King sets the New Earth in its regenerated order.

Verses 2, 3, 4, shew what the King has come to do, viz., to *The plan.* choose the "*excellency*," or the excellent Land, "*of Jacob*." Resting over this blissful scene, the Psalmist inserts his "*Selah*" —a pause of meditation. But verse 5 breaks the thoughtful silence with a shout to our Immanuel—for he it is who is celebrated as "God"

> "*Sing praises to God !*
> *Sing praises !*
> *Sing praises to our King !*
> *Sing praises !*
> *For God is King over all the earth !*
> *Sing praises with understanding.*
> *God reigneth over the nations !*
> *God sitteth upon the throne of his holiness !*"

Around our Incarnate God and King are gathered Israel's princes—" princes of the *God of Abraham*"—Abraham's seed now receiving in full the blessings promised to their father, and all earth blest in him. Everywhere, "*the shields of earth*," earth's princes, who once, like "the shields" mentioned in Hosea iv. 18, instead of defending their people, robbed and preyed on them, now gather round our God to receive authority

from him and use it for him. He is King of kings. He is
Lord of lords. And this is the enthusiastic celebration of
The Mighty One on the throne of earth.

Psalm 48

A Song and Psalm for the sons of Korah.

1 GREAT is the Lord, and greatly to be praised
In the city of our God, in the mountain of his holiness.
2 Beautiful for situation, the joy of the whole earth, is mount Zion,
On the sides of the north, the city of the great King.
3 God is known in her palaces for a refuge.
4 For, lo, the kings were assembled, they passed by together.
5 They saw it, and so they marvelled; they were troubled, and hasted away.
6 Fear took hold upon them there, and pain, as of a woman in travail.
7 Thou breakest the ships of Tarshish, with an east wind.
8 As we have heard so have we seen, in the city of the Lord of hosts, in the
city of our God:
God will establish it for ever. Selah.
9 We have thought of thy lovingkindness, O God, in the midst of thy temple.
10 According to thy name, O God, so is thy praise unto the ends of the earth:
Thy right hand is full of righteousness.
11 Let mount Zion rejoice,
Let the daughters of Judah be glad, because of thy judgments.
12 Walk about Zion, and go round about her: tell the towers thereof:
13 Mark ye well her bulwarks, consider her palaces;
That ye may tell it to the generation following.
14 For this God is our God for ever and ever: he will be our guide even unto
death.

Connection. THE subject of the Mighty One's history is still continued.
The Mighty One is king, has entered on his dominion, is seated
on his throne, is ruling in righteousness. But where is his
The plan. capital? It is at *Jerusalem.* Here He manifests himself; and
by the glory of his presence being shed over that "City of the
Great King," brighter than the light of seven days, yet far
more mellow and tranquillising than the sweetest hues of evening, *Jerusalem* becomes

'" *The joy of the whole earth.*
(The joy) *of the sides* of the north.*" (Jer. vi. 22.)

* " SIDES," יַרְכְּתֵי utmost extremes. See especially Isa. xiv. 9, where the
proud tyrant says, "I will sit on the mount of the congregation," *i. e.*, Zion,

She has become the joy of earth, far and near, the source of joy to earth's remotest bounds. Now is fulfilled Isaiah xxiv. 23. Now is Jerusalem made " beautiful for situation," or, set aloft on its hills in beauty, in another sense than formerly. Now is Zion exalted above the mountains, and obtains established pre-eminence above the hills.

And if associations are needed to make any place completely interesting, these are not wanting here. Such deeds have been done here, that Sennacherib's overthrow is, in a manner, cast into the shade. The gathered kings of earth came up, " they passed" in all the pomp of battle, and the Lord scattered them ; and writes here his " *Veni, vidi, vici*," to all nations.

> " *They saw !*
> *They marvelled !*
> *They were troubled !*
> *They hasted away !*" (Ver. 5.)

It was as when an east wind hurls the ships of Tarshish on the rocks. (Ver. 7.) It comprised in it all that is recorded as wonderful in the achievements of former days ; present events now come fully up to the measure of former good deeds,

> " *As we have heard, so have we seen,*
> *In the city of the Lord of hosts.*" (Ver. 8.)

The solemn *Selah-pause* occurs here; and then we look out on a peaceful scene, God known in all the earth. (Ver. 10.) " *Thou art praised wherever thy name is known,*" or rather, now at last thou art getting praise worthy of thy glorious name. Zion is glad, Judah's tears are wiped away, while a voice invites all men to come and survey the bulwarks of the city of the Great King, that they may tell it from age to age. The bulwarks are strong, for the Lord's presence, *Jehovah Shammah*, is the wall of fire, on whose battlements the happy citizens walk in security, singing,

and then, " on the *sides of the north*," earth's widest bounds. Hengstenberg objects to this construction of the verse, that we do not find in Hebrew this resumption of a status constr. But Isa. xiv. 19 is a clear case, " the raiment of the slain, of the pierced with the sword." So Job xxvi. 10, according to Ewald; and Prov. xv. 26. Tholuck renders it, " A joy of the earth to the remotest north." There is another explanation that makes, " Sides of the north, the city of the Great King," to be descriptive of the town (afterwards Acra) built on he ground north of Mount Zion.

" This God is our God for ever and ever ;
He is our guide even over death." (Tholuck, " even beyond death.")

The last clause is much misunderstood, It is not, " Our guide *unto* death," for the words are יְנַהֲגֵנוּ עַל מוּת, " shall lead us *over death.*" Surely it means, " It is He who leads over *death* to *resurrection*"—over Jordan into Canaan. The עַל is used in Levit. xv. 25 for " BEYOND," in regard to time, and is not this the sense here ? " *Beyond* the time of death ?" Till death is to us over ? Till we have *stood upon the grave of death ?* Yes : He it is who leads us on to this last victory ; he swallows up death in victory, and leads us to *trample on death.* And so viewed, we easily discern the beautiful link of thought that joins this Psalm to that which follows.

Such is the celebration of

The Mighty One become the glory of Jerusalem.

Psalm 49

To the chief Musician. A Psalm for the sons of Korah

1 HEAR this, all ye people ; give ear, all ye inhabitants of the world :

2 Both low and high, rich and poor, together.

3 My mouth shall speak of wisdom ; and the meditation of my heart s' all be of understanding.

4 I will incline mine ear to a parable : I will open my dark saying upon the harp.

5 Wherefore should I fear in the days of evil,
When the iniquity of my heels shall compass me about ?

6 They that trust in their wealth, and boast themselves in the multitude of their riches ;

7 None of them can by any means redeem his brother, nor give to God a ransom for him :

8 (For the redemption of their soul is precious, and it ceaseth for ever :)

9 That he should still live for ever, and not see corruption.

10 For he seeth that wise men die, likewise the fool and the brutish person perish,
And leave their wealth to others.

11 Their inward thought is, that their houses shall continue for ever,
And their dwelling places to all generations ;
They call their lands after their own names.

12 Nevertheless man being in honour abideth not : he is like the beasts that perish.

13 This their way is their folly : yet their posterity approve their sayings.
Selah.

14 Like sheep they are laid in the grave ; death shall feed on them ;
And the upright shall have dominion over them in the morning :
And their beauty shall consume in the grave from their dwelling.

15 But God will redeem my soul from the power of the grave :
For he shall receive me. Selah.

16 Be not thou afraid when one is made rich, when the glory of his house is
increased ;

17 For when he dieth he shall carry nothing away : his glory shall not descend after him.

18 Though while he lived he blessed his soul :
And men will praise thee, when thou doest well to thyself.

19 He shall go to the generation of his fathers ; they shall never see light.

20 Man that is in honour, and understandeth not, is like the beasts that
perish.

THE mighty one never rests till he has " *led us over death*"   Connection.
(xlviii. 14), to Resurrection-fulness of bliss in the kingdom.
Thrice happy they who shall enjoy it ! But who shall tell the
misery of those who are excluded from that bliss? It is this
misery that is the theme of this Psalm. As sure as the eternal
felicity of the redeemed is the miserable doom of the unredeemed ; and this Psalm is the dirge over them.

The Redeemer himself speaks this " *parable*," this weighty   The speaker.
discourse, which in its topics is to the world no better than an
unintelligible enigma—" *a dark saying.*" But nevertheless,
" these things which have been kept secret from the beginning"
(Matt. xiii. 38), are here laid open in their solemn grandeur,
in their awful importance, in their truth and certainty. Messiah here speaks " *wisdom*" (חָכְמוֹת) and " *understanding*," as
in Prov. i. 20, revealing the deep things of God to man. It is
Messiah who says (ver. 5), " *Wherefore should I fear in the
days of evil, when iniquity at my heals doth compass me
about ?*" Messiah in our world of evil, *pursued by* sons of
Belial, who would fain trample on him, surrounded by the
troops of hell, breathing the atmosphere of this polluted world,
walking amid its snares, is able to break through all unscathed,
and foretell impending ruin to every foe.

Man has no means of paying to God his ransom-money   The plan.
(Exod. xxi. 30), although he bring the most costly price earth

can furnish. He "must *let that alone for ever*" (*Prayer Book Version*) ; he cannot come up to the amount demanded ; he cannot give even what might be sufficient to redeem *the life* from the grave. See how generations die, disappear, give place to other generations, all equally the prey of corruption ; and yet fools continue to hope for immortality for themselves. Think of this infatuation ; pause, meditate ; the harp will be silent for a time that you may ponder it—" *Selah !*"

But lift the veil ! Where are these sons of folly ? In the grave ; "*Death leads them into his pastures,*" as his sheep (Hengstenberg) ; and

> " *The righteous have dominion over them in the morning.*
> . *Their beauty consumes away ;*
> *The grave is the dwelling for every one of them.*" (Ver. 14.)

The *First Resurrection* is described in these few strokes, the Resurrection of the Just. They live and *reign*—have dominion—while " *the rest of the dead live not again until the thousand years* are finished." (Rev. xx. 5.) And to stifle all doubts in their birth, the Redeemer declares himself sure of resurrection ; and if he, then they also, for he is the first fruits, the pledge of theirs.

> " *Surely, (*אַךְ*) God shall redeem my soul from the hand of the grave ;*
> *For He shall redeem me.*" (Ver. 15.)

He shall receive me as Enoch was received, receive me up to glorious rest. (See Gen. v. 24, the same word, לָקַח.) Hear, therefore, the sum of the whole matter. The ungodly shall never see "*the light*" of that "*morning*" (ver. 14) ; yea, (ver. 20), "*man in prosperity,*" even Antichrist in the flush of his power, " is like the beasts ; *he is to be rooted* out," (Hengstenberg)—he has no lot or portion with the blessed.

In such strains the Redeemer himself utters this melancholy
Dirge of the Righteous over the unredeemed.

Psalm 50

A Psalm of Asaph

1 THE mighty God, even the Lord, hath spoken,
And called the earth from the rising of the sun unto the going down thereof.

2 Out of Zion, the perfection of beauty, God hath shined.

3 Our God shall come, and shall not keep silence:
A fire shall devour before him, and it shall be very tempestuous round about him.

4 He shall call to the heavens from above, and to the earth, that he may judge his people.

5 Gather my saints together unto me; those that have made a covenant with me by sacrifice.

6 And the heavens shall declare his righteousness: for God is judge himself. Selah.

7 Hear, O my people, and I will speak; O Israel, and I will testify against thee.
I am God, even thy God.

8 I will not reprove thee for thy sacrifices,
Or thy burnt offerings, to have been continually before me.

9 I will take no bullock out of thy house, nor he-goats out of thy folds.

10 For every beast of the forest is mine, and the cattle upon a thousand hills.

11 I know all the fowls of the mountains: and the wild beasts of the field are mine.

12 If I were hungry, I would not tell thee: for the world is mine, and the fulness thereof.

13 Will I eat the flesh of bulls, or drink the blood of goats?

14 Offer unto God thanksgiving; and pay thy vows unto the Most High!

15 And call upon me in the day of trouble: I will deliver thee, and thou shalt glorify me.

16 But unto the wicked God saith,
What hast thou to do to declare my statutes,
Or that thou shouldest take my covenant in thy mouth?

17 Seeing thou hatest instruction, and castest my words behind thee.

18 When thou sawest a thief, then thou consentedst with him,
And hast been partaker with adulterers.

19 Thou givest thy mouth to evil, and thy tongue frameth deceit.

20 Thou sittest and speakest against thy brother; thou slanderest thine own mother's son.

21 These things hast thou done, and I kept silence;
Thou thoughtest that I was always such an one as thyself:
But I will reprove thee, and set them in order before thine eyes.

22 Now consider this, ye that forget God,
Lest I tear you in pieces, and there be none to deliver.

23 Whoso offereth praise glorifieth me:
And to him that ordereth his conversation aright will I shew the salvation of God.

Connection.

"*El, Elohim, Jehovah, has spoken!*"* So reads the Hebrew. Arrived at the end—having sung of the elect's cry, the response to their cry in the Mighty One's appearing, the Mighty One's protection, the throne on which he sits, the city where his glory abides, and himself in the glory—having also sung that melancholy dirge over those who have no portion in this lot of

Theme and plan.

the righteous—the Psalmist is led by the Spirit to strike his harp to one other strain of a kindred nature. He here sets forth the *principles of judgment* that guide the decision of *the King* "who sits on the throne of his holiness," and reigns from "*out of Zion.*"

It is the day of Rom. i. 18. The heavens are not silent now; angels come with the God of heaven. The glory of the Lord, and the gathering of the saints around him (see 2 Thess. ii. 4), those who *over the sacrifice* have entered into covenant with him, being celebrated in ver. 1–6, and the solemn *Selah*-pause having given us time to fix our eye upon the scene, *the Lord* suddenly speaks, reasoning with men as to their wrong ideas of the way of salvation (ver. 7–15). Then follows their sinful practice (ver. 16–22). In ver. 22d the word אנ is emphatic—"*Consider this, I beseech* you, ye who forget God." Man treats God as if he were a being to be ministered unto, instead of a gracious, sovereign benefactor. Man acts in the view of God as if the holy God were such a one as himself. But the end comes. None shall enter into glory, none be shewn "*the salvation of God,*" *i. e.*, his glorious completed redemption (such as Paul spoke of, Rom. xiii. 11, and Peter, 1 Pet. i. 5) at the Lord's Appearing, excepting the man who "*orders his conversation aright;*" that is, who regulates his life by such rule as ver. 5; in other words, by gospel-rule —who prepares his way according to the preparation revealed to him by the Lord. The man who would so do must begin

* Coming to judge, he appears as in Rev. xix. with all his names. "*El,*" the Mighty God; "*Elohim,*" God, the object of worship and fear; "JEHOVAH," he who has made himself known to Israel and his people, as *having all being and perfection.*

at the altar (ver. 5), and there "*sacrifice*," or, "*offer praise*," even as ver. 14 also declared. He must begin by owning Jehovah's benefits to us sinners, responding to the song of the angels at Bethlehem over a Saviour born, and answering to the Saviour's cry, "*It is finished,*" by his soul's glad acceptance of that finished work. This is the "*ordering of the conversation*"—and to declare this is the object of this Psalm. It sets forth, at the lips of the Righteous Judge himself,

The principles that shall guide the judgment of the Righteous One at the gathering of the Saints.

Psalm 51

To the chief Musician. A Psalm of David, when Nathan the prophet came unto him, after he had gone in to Bath-sheba.

1 HAVE mercy upon me, O God, according to thy lovingkindnesses:
According unto the multitude of thy tender mercies blot out my transgressions.

2 Wash me throughly from mine iniquity, and cleanse me from my sin.

3 For I acknowledge my transgressions: and my sin is ever before me.

4 Against thee, thee only have I sinned, and done this evil in thy sight:
That thou mightest be justified when thou speakest, and be clear when thou judgest.

5 Behold, I was shapen in iniquity; and in sin did my mother conceive me.

6 Behold, thou desirest truth in the inward parts:
And in the hidden parts thou shalt make me to know wisdom.

7 Purge me with hyssop, and I shall be clean: wash me, and I shall be whiter than snow.

8 Make me to hear joy and gladness; that the bones which thou hast broken may rejoice.

9 Hide thy face from my sins, and blot out all mine iniquities.

10 Create in me a clean heart, O God; and renew a right spirit within me.

11 Cast me not away from thy presence; and take not thy Holy Spirit from me.

12 Restore unto me the joy of thy salvation; and uphold me with thy Free Spirit.

13 Then will I teach transgressors thy ways; and sinners shall be converted unto thee.

14 Deliver me from bloodguiltiness, O God, thou God of my salvation:
And my tongue shall sing aloud of my righteousness.

15 O Lord, open thou my lips; and my mouth shall shew forth thy praise.

16 For thou desirest not sacrifice; else would I give it: thou delightest not in burnt offering.

17 The sacrifices of God are a broken spirit:
A broken and a contrite heart, O God, thou wilt not despise.

18 Do good in thy good pleasure unto Zion : build thou the walls of Jerusalem.

19 Then shalt thou be pleased with the sacrifices of righteousness,
With burnt offering and whole burnt offering:
Then shall they offer bullocks upon thine altar.

The position of this Psalm, and subject of it.

"THE riches, the power," (says a well-known writer), the glory of a kingdom, could neither present nor remove the torrent of sin, which puts the monarch and the beggar upon a level." No one has more keenly scrutinized his own backslidings, and more bitterly lamented them, "laying bare the iron ribs of misery," than David, in this Psalm. We saw a series of considerable length concluded in Psalm l. The Psalm before us stands in an isolated position. It is not part of any series. It has a peculiarity that no previous Psalm has exhibited, for it is written (and the Hebrew title authenticates the fact) on occasion of David's adultery, and his detestable attempts to hide his adultery by murder of the basest kind. Now, no such circumstances as these could ever have in them aught that corresponded in the remotest manner to any circumstances in the life of the Surety, David's Son. On the contrary, so far is this Psalm from being fitted to express the work of the Surety, that it seems introduced at this point in order to lead us to look back on the former songs of David, and to say of what was set forth therein, " Surely *this* David, who here appears as a leper all over, with a heart as vile as the worst action of his life, cannot be *the* David of whom such glorious things were formerly spoken ?" Viewed in this light, the Psalm before us is fitted, both by its title and its contents, to direct us in the other Psalms to the true David, as He of whom the lofty things of preceding Psalms were sung.

The plan.

Coming, as this Psalm does, close upon one which set the *principles of judgment* before us, it is not uninteresting to observe that it falls into its place very appropriately. For here we find a sinner—an individual sinner—realizing his position at that bar, and consenting to the decisions of a tribunal whereat nothing but justice has free course. The sinner acknowledges in verse 4 that his sin is all his own, and done in direct opposition to the Holy One ; and he owns his folly before all the universe.

" That thou mayest be justified, in the matter of the law proclaimed by thee,
And be clear, in regard to the judgment pronounced by thee on the law-breaker."

He finds nothing in the terms of the law too strict, nor aught in the penalty annexed too severe. The use of דְּבָרֶךָ may be a reference to Exod. xx. 1, where the Ten Commandments are called הַדְּבָרִים.

It is as if God had printed the diary of David, and, in order to humble him, handed it to the " *Chief musician*," that all Israel might know his bitter repentance, and might say, in substance, what Augustine writes, (" *Non ergo cadendi exemplum propositum est, sed si cecideris resurgendi. Tu hoc amas in David, quod in se odit David ?*") " It is not an example of falling into sin that is set before thee, but of rising if thou hast fallen. Dost thou love in David that which David hated in himself ?"

1. Deep groans for pardoning mercy, from the pit of pollution. (Ver. 1, 2.)
2. Confession of sin, and acknowledgment of the Lord's righteous law. (Ver. 3, 4.)
3. An awful gaze upon the source of all actual sin. (Ver. 5.)
4. Deliverance from falsehood, folly, and guilt, must come from God alone. (Ver. 6, 7.) " *Purge me from sin with hyssop,*" as the leper is purged.
5. The voice of a reconciled God heard again. (Ver. 8.) Perhaps it was the idea of *Resurrection* that suggested " *bones rejoicing.*"
6. On the foundation of thorough forgiveness, prayer is made for thorough and constant holiness. (Ver. 9, 10.) " *Renew to me the gift of a fixed* (נָכוֹן) *spirit.*"
7. He seeks permanent holiness, as well as permanent fellowship. (Ver. 11.)
8. The joy of full salvation (i.e., *of both pardon and holiness*) is sought, and the presence of the Holy Spirit, the true and natural equipment for future usefulness. (Ver. 12.) " *Uphold me with the Spirit, who is generous,*"—*princely.*

9. Efforts are to be made for the good of others. (Ver. 13.)
10. Sorrow for having, in days past, injured others is expressed. (Ver. 14, first clause.)
11. Closing strain of adoring gratitude. (The last clause of verse 14, and 15, 16, 17.)
12. A closing prayer for the glory of God in the land and in the earth. (Ver. 18, 19.)

This desire for God's glory, the unfailing mark of a soul in communion with God, is expressed in terms that indicate hope as well as faith. " Be favourable to Zion *for thine own sake*, as a fruit of thy free-will," בִּרְצוֹנֶךָ. This is the sense ; as if he said, " I have given thee cause to forsake my kingdom and people, and even to abandon Zion, where thine ark stands ; but wilt thou not rather shew free grace ?"

" Build the walls of Jerusalem !"

Make thy people in Jerusalem strong against their foes ; *build up** this city which I took from the Jebusites and am seeking to beautify, though my sin might provoke thee to give it back to the Canaanite again. Make Zion and Jerusalem strong in their bulwarks as thou wilt yet do in the latter day. (Psalm xlviii. 11.)

" Then shalt thou be pleased with sacrifices of righteousness."

In that spot where thy name has been blasphemed by me thou shalt yet again be honoured, if instead of judgment thou sendest us victory and peace. We shall testify of thee to all lands by the " *sacrifices* according to just rule and measure" (Levit. xix. 36), and by " *bullocks*," as our פָּרִים " *calves of thank-offering*." (Hosea xiv. 3.) This city Jerusalem shall be a place wherein *atonement* is proclaimed, and thy praises sung by thy forgiven ones, whose *contrite, broken hearts shall be a daily thankoffering*. (Ver. 17.)

This last result was specially attained under *Solomon*. But in addition to what we have stated as the primary meaning, is there not a look into the future ? Is not the strain to this effect :—Hasten Zion's final glory, and then shall there be no

---

* " Build " signifies here as in Micah iii. 10; Prov. xxiv. 3; Josh. vi. 26; 2 Chron. viii. 2, *fortifying and ornamenting*.

more scandals to give the enemy cause to blaspheme, no more
backslidings, no more falls ; then shalt thou be fully honoured
as the God of atonement and fully praised with the calves of
our lips. Hasten the day of Jerusalem's glory under the true
Solomon.

Such is this Psalm of David—

The broken-hearted sinner's cry to the God of grace.

Psalm 52

To the chief Musician. Maschil. A Psalm of David, when Doeg the Edomite came and told
Saul, and said unto him, David is come to the house of Ahimelech

1 WHY boastest thou thyself in mischief, O mighty man?
  The goodness of God endureth continually.
2 Thy tongue deviseth mischief; like a sharp razor, working deceitfully.
3 Thou lovest evil more than good, and lying rather than to speak righteousness. Selah.
4 Thou lovest all devouring words, O thou deceitful tongue.
5 God shall likewise destroy thee for ever,
  He shall take thee away, and pluck thee out of thy dwelling place,
  And root thee out of the land of the living. Selah.
6 The righteous also shall see, and fear, and shall laugh at him—
7 Lo, this is the man that made not God his strength!
  But trusted in the abundance of his riches, and strengthened himself in
  his wickedness.
8 But I am like a green olive tree in the house of God:
  I trust in the mercy of God for ever and ever.
9 I will praise thee for ever, because thou hast done it :
  And I will wait on thy name ; for it is good before thy saints.

THIS Psalm was originally written when Doeg informed Saul   *The position.*
against David. In arranging the Psalms it was natural to
place it after the last, inasmuch as the assaults which it describes would no doubt be repeated in some shape on the occasion of David's fall, and even after his restoration to the full
sunshine of divine fellowship. The enemy of the Woman's
Seed has never in any age been at a loss for matter of calumny
and reproach, nor will he cease till the Lord come and he be
finally cast out.

In verse 1, *"the mighty man"* is גִּבּוֹר, even as *Nimrod* is   *The contents.*

called in Gen. x. 9, the very antithesis in character to "אֵל־גִּבּוֹר,"
"*the mighty God*," (Isaiah ix. 6,) who is to destroy him.

In verse 5, closed by the significant Selah, the true rendering
of the middle clause is, "He will pluck thee out of *The Tabernacle;*" not only referring us back to such cases as Korah, or
any rebels whom the Lord thrust out of the holy camp of Israel,
but pointing us onward to the time when "*the Tabernacle of
God shall be with men.*" On that day thou shalt have no place
among the blessed ones; they shall see thee uprooted with
ease, and shall enjoy the "*laugh*" of Him who sitteth in the
heavens (Psalm ii. 4), and of Wisdom whom thou didst despise
(Prov. i. 26), but who then mocks at thy calamity. Men will
not then say of the Son of God (as they could say in the day
of his humiliation), but shall say of his ruined foes,

"*Behold the man!*" (Ver. 7.)

All along their history true Israelites could adopt and appropriate the words of verse 8, but they shall sing it better
still on the day of Antichrist's final ruin, when they become
"*The Olive tree*" again. (Rom. xi. 17.) At the same time it

Christ in it. is *David's Son*, Christ himself, who best of all could sing this
Psalm, and best of all could appropriate these words:

"*I am a green olive tree in the house of God.*" (Ver. 8.)

He being indeed the true Israelite who "continued in God's
goodness" (Rom. xi. 17, 22), the tender love of his God ever being
as dew on his branches. He will, on the Day of his Appearing, give the key-note of praise over foes overthrown for ever,
raising the "Hallelujah" of Rev. xix. 2,—"*Because thou hast
done it.*" Nothing less than this result is what we look for and
expect; and Christ along with us is looking for that display
of the Divine character, "*waiting for thy name,*" (as in Psalm
lxxv. 1) when it shall be discovered in judgment acts. Thus
viewed, this Psalm may be entitled,

*The hope of the Righteous One when everywhere spoken
against.*

Psalm 53

To the chief Musician. Upon Mahalath. Maschil. A Psalm of David

1 THE fool hath said in his heart, There is no God.
Corrupt are they, and have done abominable iniquity : there is none that
doeth good.

2 God looked down from heaven upon the children of men,
To see if there were any that did understand, that did seek God.

3 Every one of them is gone back ; they are altogether become filthy ;
There is none that doeth good, no, not one.

4 Have the workers of iniquity no knowledge,
Who eat up my people as they eat bread ? They have not called upon God.

5 There were they in great fear, where no fear was :
For God has scattered the bones of him that encampeth against thee :
Thou hast put them to shame, because God hath despised them.

6 Oh that the salvation of Israel were come out of Zion !
When God bringeth back the captivity of his people,
Jacob shall rejoice, and Israel shall be glad.

THE unknown instrument " *Mahalath*" (derived from the $\quad$ The title.
Ethiopic root " to sing"), is here fixed on as the one to be used
by " the *chief Musician*." And the music is to be selected
with care, for this Psalm is, like some others, one that has the
mark " *Maschil*."

The state of earth ought to be deeply felt by us. The world $\quad$ This Psalm a
lying in wickedness should occupy much of our thoughts. The $\quad$ repetition;
$\quad$ why?
enormous guilt, the inconceivable pollution, the ineffably provoking atheism of this fallen province of God's dominion,
might be a theme for our ceaseless meditation and mourning.
To impress it the more on us, therefore, this Psalm repeats
what has been already sung in Psalm xiv. It is the same
Psalm, with only a few words varied; it is "line upon line, precept
upon precept;" the harp's most melancholy, most dismal notes
again sounded in our ear. Not that the Lord would detain us
always or disproportionably long amid scenes of sadness, for
elsewhere he repeats in like manner that most triumphant melody, Psalm lx. 6–12 ; cviii. 6–13 ; but it is good to return
now and then to the open field on which we all were found,
cast out in loathsome degradation.

There is one variation of some interest. It is in verse 5. $\quad$ Compared with
The words of Psalm xiv. 5 are referred to, but altered to ex- $\quad$ Psalm 14.

press much more of triumph and victory on the part of God's despised ones ; for the two passages run thus :

Psalm 53.

" *There were they in great fear where no fear was,*
For God has scattered the bones of the encamper against thee.
Thou hast put them to shame !
For God has despised them !"

Psalm 14.

" *There were they in great fear,*
For God is in the generation of the righteous.
You shamed the counsel of the poor,
Because the Lord is his refuge."

Besides substituting " *Elohim*" for Jehovah throughout, the changes in the Psalm before us seems made on purpose to declare emphatically the complete overthrow of the ungodly. "*Thou*" is emphatic in verse 5, and like Isa. xxxvii. 22, the verse expresses victory over the ungodly. The term employed in verse 6 is to be noticed. In Psalm xiv. 6 it was, " O that the *salvation*, יְשׁוּעַת, were come ;" in this Psalm it is " *salvations*," " יְשׁוּעוֹת," full, entire deliverance. On these grounds they may be right who suggest that Psalm xiv. (which see), may be read as the report of the Son of man regarding earth at his *First Coming*, and Psalm liii. as his description of its state and prospects at his *Second*.* There is here certainly more said of the full victory ; so that while we gave Psalm xiv. the title of " The Righteous One's view of earth and its prospects," we are inclined to state as the contents of this-

The Righteous One's view of earth, and the victory of God's people.

---

* Ryland says, " Psalm xiv. refers chiefly to God's enemies and their alarm ; this Psalm to God's people and their interests. The former contemplates judgments, the latter, deliverances.

Psalm 54

To the chief Musician. On Neginoth. Maschil. A Psalm of David, when the Ziphims came and said unto Saul, Doth not David hide himself with us?

1 SAVE me, O God, by thy name, and judge me by thy strength.
2 Hear my prayer, O God; give ear to the words of my mouth.
3 For strangers are risen up against me, and oppressors seek after my soul: They have not set God before them. Selah.
4 Behold, God is mine helper: the Lord is with them that uphold my soul.
5 He shall reward evil unto mine enemies: cut them off in thy truth.
6 I will freely sacrifice unto thee: I will praise thy name, O Lord, for it is good.
7 For he hath delivered me out of all trouble:
And mine eye hath seen his desire upon mine enemies.

THE title is such as we have already met with, " *On Neginoth*" and " *Maschil;*" and the occasion when it was first written is mentioned as the time when the men of Ziph informed against David. *The title.*

The burden of this Psalm is simply—to what quarter should one look for help in the time of trouble? Wholly to the Lord. " Save me by *thy name*" (ver. 1), reminds us of John xvii. 11. We are kept by the putting forth of God's *perfections* in our behalf, truth, mercy, love, power, wisdom, holiness. Our Lord was so kept by the Father, when he prayed in the words of verse 1, using them as his own, and giving his Church an instance in himself of that safe keeping. The *Selah*-pause of thoughtfulness in verse 3 is beautifully followed by " *Behold*" of verse 4. It is *q. d.*, silent prayer followed by confidence of an answer. *The contents.*

It is in verses 6 and 7 that the *future* dawns on our view. David, David's Son, and all who follow David's Son, may exult in the prospect of that sacrifice of thankfulness to be offered. When delivered out of all distress, we shall look with triumph on our enemies; for as Calvin remarks (quoted by Hengstenberg), " Only let the eye be pure, and we can piously and holily refresh ourselves with the manifestations of God's justice." That will be the time of the hallelujah in Rev. xix. 1–4, all resulting from his *name* glorified, his name manifested as " good." (Ver. 6.)

We have therefore in this short Psalm,

The Righteous One's help found in the Lord's name.

Psalm 55

To the chief Musician. On Neginoth, Maschil. A Psalm of David

1 GIVE ear to my prayer, O God ; and hide not thyself from my supplication.

2 Attend unto me, and hear me : I mourn in my complaint, and make a noise ;

3 Because of the voice of the enemy, because of the oppression of the wicked : For they cast iniquity upon me, and in wrath they hate me.

4 My heart is sore pained within me : and the terrors of death are fallen upon me.

5 Fearfulness and trembling are come upon me, and horror hath overwhelmed me.

6 And I said, Oh that I had wings like a dove! for then would I fly away, and be at rest.

7 Lo, then would I wander far off, and remain in the wilderness. Selah.

8 I would hasten my escape from the windy storm and tempest.

9 Destroy, O Lord, and divide their tongues: for I have seen violence and strife in the city.

10 Day and night they go about it upon the walls thereof: Mischief also and sorrow are in the midst of it.

11 Wickedness is in the midst thereof : deceit and guile depart not from her streets.

12 For it was not an enemy that reproached me ; then I could have borne it : Neither was it he that hated me that did magnify himself against me; Then I would have hid myself from him :

13 But it was thou, a man mine equal, my guide, and mine acquaintance!

14 We took sweet counsel together, and walked into the house of God in company.

15 Let death seize upon them, and let them go down quick into hell : For wickedness is in their dwellings, and among them.

16 As for me, I will call upon God; and the Lord shall save me.

17 Evening, and morning, and at noon, will I pray, and cry aloud : And he shall hear my voice.

18 He hath delivered my soul in peace from the battle that was against me : For there were many with me.

19 God shall hear, and afflict them, even he that abideth of old. Selah. Because they have no changes, therefore they fear not God.

20 He hath put forth his hands against such as be at peace with him : He hath broken his covenant.

21 The words of his mouth were smoother than butter, but war was in his heart. His words were softer than oil, yet were they drawn swords.

12 Cast thy burden upon the Lord, and he shall sustain thee : He shall never suffer the righteous to be moved.

23 But thou, O God, shall bring them down into the pit of destruction : Bloody and deceitful men shall not live out half their days. But I will trust in thee.

THE title is the same as that of some former Psalms, " on Neginoth," " Maschil," and then " of *David.*" We may read
these strains as expressing David's feelings in some peculiar
seasons of distress, and as the experience of Christ's Church in
every age ; for we find much, very much, that accords altogether with humanity in a state of intensely stirred emotion,
and affection wounded to the quick. Yet still it is in Jesus,
the Man of Sorrows, that the Psalm finds its fullest illustration.
His was the soul that was stirred to its lowest depth by scenes
such as are described here. The quotation of Psa. xli. 9 by our
Lord, is almost equivalent to a quotation of verse 13, they are
so similar as to words.

It is the wickedness of the wicked that raises this mournful
cry, and makes him say,

" *I mourn in my complaint ;*" or, " give free course to my sorrow." (Ver. 2.)

It is not unlikely that our Lord, possessed as he was of true
humanity, might often give utterance to this expressive wish
(verse 6), " *O that I had wings as a dove,*" when seeing the
turtle-dove fly out from the olives of the Mount of Olives over
guilty Jerusalem, the city wherein He saw " violence and
strife"—" wickedness, deceit, and guile, never absent from her
streets." Either there, or standing on some of the hills around
Nazareth, He might witness the home-loving dove's swift
flight,* and hear its peace-suggesting note, and be led to this
utterance of strong feeling, not at all unfit for Him who so rejoiced in the thought, " And now I am no more in the world !
Now I come to thee, Holy Father," (John xvii. 11). He to
whom he was thought to bear so close a resemblance (Matt.
xvi. 14), the weeping prophet Jeremiah, gave utterance to his
wounded feeling in strains that naturally took a similar form,
" Oh that I had in the wilderness a lodging-place," though
only that of the *wayfaring* man ! (ix. 2). But the melancholy
Psalmist here rises a degree beyond this-

" *I would remain in the desert.*" (Ver. 7.)

And then there is the *Selah*-pause, as there is in the middle of

---

* Paxton says, the dove, when flying to its resort, never rests on trees or the
like, as other birds, but uses one wing till the other rests.

verse 19, indicating the calm, solemn state of soul in which these things were uttered.

The judgment pronounced. The prayer in verse 9 reminds us of Babel, where the language of earth was divided that pride might be humbled for ever, and its aims irretrievably baffled ; while verse 15, " *go quick to hell*," at once recalls the doom of Korah and his company, who rejected the true High *Priest*, and the Lord's *King* in Jeshurun. Our Lord describes Israel in verse 13, " *his own*" nation (John i. 11), though, especially, Judas, one of his trusted ones who owned him as Master ; and " *mine equal*" signifies, " Thou who wert by my side on terms of equality, as if on a level with me." He permits them to perish in unbelief, they having rejected the true Priest and King. He no longer acts the Intercessor's part towards such, but stands over them as a Judge, pronouncing their doom. And then in verses 16, 17, **The deliverance.** we hear him express his confidence of full deliverance. " The twelve legions of angels," whom He might at any time have called to his help, have arrived, or rather He sees them on their way.

" *For there are many with me.*
God heareth and answereth,
Yea, He sits enthroned for ever !" *Selah.* (Ver. 19.)

The invitation to share in It is a glance at future redress for every wrong, in the Day of Vengance and the Year of the Redeemed. In prospect of this, verse 22 invites us to cast our burden upon the Lord, whatever that burden be, even if it be the crushing weight of persecution, and reproach, and treachery. The Lord will " provide" as Joseph did, Gen. xlv. 11, and as 1 Kings iv. 7. " *The godly shall not be tossed about for ever ;*" the Lord shall arise to hurl the foe into " the pit of destruction" (" the lake of fire" of Rev. xx. 15), in which Antichrist sinks for ever.

In the last verse there is something of an enthymeme ; for while the clause, " *The bloody and deceitful men shall not live half their days*" predicts and pourtrays their doom, as cut off by untimely judgment, the responsive clause, " *And I will trust in thee,*" tells of no proper converse, no judgment in favour of the godly. But it nevertheless contains in it the equivalent to a declaration that his lot shall be the reverse of the bloody and deceitful. It is equivalent to saying, We go different ways—they on the broad road, where ruin overtakes them speedily, and I on the safe road of faith in thee, where I shall soon meet with Him whom unseen I loved, and in whom I believed, though as yet I saw him not. Does not, then, this Psalm depict-

The Righteous One's weary soul resting in the certainty of what the Lord will do.

Psalm 56

To the chief Musician. Upon Jonath-elem-rechokim. Michtam of David, when the Philistines took him in Gath

1 Be merciful unto me, O God: for man would swallow me up!
He fighting daily oppresseth me.
2 Mine enemies would daily swallow me up:
For they be many that fight against me, O thou Most High.
3 What time I am afraid, I will trust in thee.
4 In God I will praise his word.
In God I have put my trust; I will not fear what flesh can do unto me.
5 Every day they wrest my words: all their thoughts are against me for evil.
6 They gather themselves together, they hide themselves,
They mark my steps, when they wait for my soul.
7 Shall they escape by iniquity? In thine anger cast down the people, O God.
8 Thou tellest my wanderings:
Put thou my tears into thy bottle: are they not in thy book?
9 When I cry unto thee, then shall mine enemies turn back: this I know, for God is for me.
10 In God will I praise his word: in the Lord will I praise his word.
11 In God have I put my trust: I will not be afraid what man can do unto me.
12 Thy vows are upon me, O God: I will render praise unto thee.
13 For thou hast delivered my soul from death: wilt not thou deliver my feet from falling,
That I may walk before God in the light of the living?

THE reason why fear gains ascendancy in a believing soul on occasions of danger and trouble is sententiously expressed by Augustine, "*Magnitudinem mali vides, potestatem medici*

The tone and the contents

non vides." " Thou seest the magnitude of the evil; the power of the physician thou dost not see." The faith which penetrates the unseen reaches the case. This Psalm, in verses 1, 2, sets forth perils and evils in their magnitude, every day felt, every day repeating their vigorous assaults; but verses 3, 4, declare the remedy.

> " *In the day of my fear, I will trust in thee.*" (Ver. 3.)

This is nothing less than the voice of the Master, of him who said in John xiv. 1, 27, " Let not your heart be troubled, believe in God;" " Peace I give unto you; not as the world giveth, give I unto you. Let not your heart be troubled, neither let it be afraid."

> " *God I will extol—his Word.*" (Ver. 4.)

I will rest my heart in God; I will praise God (אֲהַלֵּל בּ, as in Psalm xliv. 9, and as in verse 10 again); I will praise God with a special reverence to "*his Word*"—his promises, which are not like those of the world.* *David* might refer to the Lord's special promise to him of the *seed* that was to come,—a promise that of course implied his preservation in order to its accomplishment. The *Son of David* had his eye on that same promise in another of its aspects, its implied engagement to supply strength and give victory. Every believing one, in hours of darkness, reverts to that promise, saying to his soul, " He that spared not his own Son, how shall he not with him also freely give us all things ?" It is thus that the Lord " *magnifies his Word,*" making it felt to be the prominent and most attractive to sinful men of all his ways of revealing himself. (Psalm cxxxviii. 2.)

The world goes on, adding sin to sin. The world goes on, seeking daily to overthrow God by overthrowing his people; even as it sought to overthrow God by overthrowing his Son. (Verses 5, 6.) But

> " *Shall they escape by* (עַל) *iniquity ?* " (Ver. 7.)

They have made a covenant with death and hell; shall it

---

* Some give this force to the בּ, " I, in union with, or as one with God, will praise;" in which latter case it is like Paul's, " *In the Lord.*"

stand? No; if they were to escape by their iniquity, by their boldness in defying God, this would be a result wholly unlike the past dealings of God.

"*God, in anger, has brought down the nations*" (ver. 7);

and will do so again on that day when their anger is hot against him. (Rev. xi. 18.)

On the other hand, He has never failed to take account of the wanderings and tears of his own. Their נוֹד, " wandering," and his נֹאד, " bottle" (something far more expressive than the Roman Lacrymatory urn), correspond so far, that every tear shed by them in their *wanderings* is in that *bottle* of his; as if he had travelled along with them through their wilderness, and never suffered one drop to reach the ground. His bottle and his book of remembrance have preserved these precious tears; and if so, what good reason have we for exultation (verses 9–11), and for reiterating

"*God I will extol—the Word!*" *

I will praise Jehovah, and why? that " *Word*," already referred to, verse 4, explains all. He has spoken, he has promised; all shall go on well, and then shall come the glorious issue—

"*I shall walk before God in the light of the living.*" (Ver. 13.)

Which, while not necessarily confined to the future, yet surely carries us forward to New Jerusalem days, when he who is " *Life*," and who by being so, is " the *Light*" of man, shall walk with his redeemed in the kingdom. He himself is the grand example of this. His every tear was precious, his every step was marked; the book of remembrance has a record of these so vast, and ample and full, that, were it published here, " I suppose the world itself could not contain the volumes that could be written." He arose on the third day, " walking in the light of the living;" no more a prisoner in the darkness of the grave; no more subjected to the gloom of his Father's wrath; no more walking through the dark valley where love

Christ in it.

---

* Fry suggests, " God shall be the theme of my praise; *He hath spoken;*" דָּבַר.

was withheld; entering on the endless brightness of divine favour at the right hand. A believer's course resembles His, ending, too, in this unclouded noon of resurrection glory. "O come that glorious morning (says Horne), when the redeemed shall sing eternal praise to the God of salvation, for having delivered their souls from death, and feet from falling, that they might walk before him in the land of the living."

The title.

One point we have not noticed. The title of this Psalm is peculiar. It is " *Michtam,*" in common with Psalm xvi. (which see) and many others; but also it is " Upon *Jonath-elem-recho kim.*" Hengstenberg renders this " *The silent dove among strangers;*" which certainly well expresses the substance of the Psalm, as being the breathing of One who returned not reviling for reviling, but moaned his sorrows in the ear of his God. Still, since we have reason to believe that these titles all refer to something in the music to which the Psalms were set, especially when עַל, "Upon," is prefixed, we incline to think that these words indicate somewhat of the instrument and the tune; no doubt, however, a tune and an instrument suited to the subject, and used on occasions of melancholy interest, such as "Dove among strangers" may suggest. In either view the title corresponds to what we gather up as the substance of the Psalm, written by inspiration, when David had put himself into the hands of the Philistines, and was "sore afraid" (1 Sam. xxi. 12), namely,

God's word enabling the Righteous One, amid his wanderings, to anticipate final rest.

Psalm 57

To the chief Musician. Al-taschith. Michtam of David, when he fled from Saul in the cave

1 Be merciful unto me, O God, be merciful unto me: for my soul trusteth in thee.

Yea, in the shadow of thy wings will I make my refuge, until these calamities be overpast.

2 I will cry unto God most high; unto God that performeth all things for me.

3 He shall send from heaven, and save me
 From the reproach of him that would swallow me up. Selah.
 God shall send forth his mercy and his truth.

4 My soul is among lions: and I lie even among them that are set on fire,
 Even the sons of men, whose teeth are spears and arrows, and their
 tongue a sharp sword.

5 Be thou exalted, O God, above the heavens; let thy glory be above all
 the earth.

6 They have prepared a net for my steps; my soul is bowed down:
 They have digged a pit before me,
 Into the midst whereof they are fallen themselves. Selah.

7 My heart is fixed, O God, my heart is fixed: I will sing and give praise.

8 Awake up, my glory; awake, psaltery and harp: I myself will awake early.

9 I will praise thee, O Lord, among the people: I will sing unto thee among
 the nations.

10 For thy mercy is great unto the heavens, and thy truth unto the clouds.

11 Be thou exalted, O God, above the heavens: let thy glory be above all
 the earth.

WE spoke of the title of last Psalm as peculiar, and as suitable _The title._
to the theme handled. We may say the same of the title of
this Psalm, "_Al-taschith,_" _i. e._, destroy not; for it is suitable,
whether taken as a musical term or as indicating the spirit
breathed throughout. We do not, however, think that it is
taken from Deut. ix. 26, nor yet from 1 Sam. xxvi. 9,* where
the sentiment occurs, addressed in the one case to God, in the
other to man. We suspect it is a musical term of some sort,
perhaps connected with the lofty ideas entertained regarding
the harp and its accompaniments,—the "_Ære perennius,_" the
"indestructible," common to all nations as an epithet of poetic
and musical compositions.

 Christ is the chief Speaker, entering into his own difficulties _Christ and his_
and those of his Church. The tone is such as we find in _Church._
John xii. 27, 28, "Father, save me! Father, glorify thy
name!" But his people can use every word of it also. Perhaps the publican's prayer was drawn from the 1st verse, "_O_
God, be merciful to me." (John v. 1.) The calamities, or
rather the "mischiefs" (הַוּוֹת) of a malicious world and a malicious hell are spoken of, but spoken of in order to fix our attention on the means of victory. The means of victory is (verse 2)
"God _Most High,_" God "who _accomplishes all things,_" in spite

 * This is the view of several writers, and they suggest that it is an abbreviation similar to "De profundis," or "Miserere!"

of foes ;* it is God, too, doing this with *"mercy and truth,"*—the attributes that are prominent in redemption, kindness to the guilty in consistency with his adherence to everything his mouth has uttered. *" Selah,"* verse 3, gives peculiar force to the words, *" The devourer snorts at me! Selah."* Stop, my soul, and ponder ; for, lo ! God sends help. As for men, they are as lions, in violence ; or if you refer to their secret ways, they are equally to be distrusted; for their tongue scoffs at all that is holy. (Verses 4, 6.) They have fallen into their own pit—and another *" Selah"* calls us to ponder. But God, God in his glory, let me ever be in his hands (verses 5, 7)! My heart is fixed, my glory (i.e., *my soul*) bursts into song, " I awake the morning dawn" to sing his praises. For full is He of tender mercy that reaches above the heavens, as well as of truth that stretches unto the clouds,—*such mercy and truth* as was prayed for in verse 3, and which shine bright in all his redemption-acts. The issue must be glory to himself, infinite glory, glory above the heavens, glory above all the earth. A flood of glory is to cover this earth above its highest mountains, nay, to cover heaven, too, above its loftiest pinnacles. The eye of the Psalmist is gazing on the ages to come in the New Heavens and New Earth, wherein dwelleth righteousness. David " in the cave," in the very presence of Saul, was taught by the Holy Spirit thus to sing for his own use, and the use ot the Church, and the use of the Son of Man in the days of his flesh.

The Righteous One connecting his deliverance with Jehovah's glory.

Psalm 58

To the chief Musician, Al-taschith. Michtam of David

1 Do ye indeed speak righteousness, O congregation ? do ye judge uprightly, O ye sons of men ?

2 Yea in heart ye work wickedness ; ye weigh the violence of your hands in the earth.

* The Targum curiously paraphrases this clause ; " Who ordered the spider that wrought the web on my account at the mouth of the cave ; " applying a later historical fact, which, however, may have had its prototype in David's history.

3 The wicked are estranged from the womb :
They go astray as soon as they be born, speaking lies.
4 Their poison is like the poison of a serpent :
They are like the deaf adder that stoppeth her ear ;
5 Which will not hearken to the voice of charmers, charming never so
wisely.
6 Break their teeth, O God, in their mouth:
Break out the teeth of the young lions, O Lord.
7 Let them melt away as waters which run continually :
When he bendeth his bow to shoot his arrows, let them be as cut in pieces.
8 As a snail which melteth, let every one of them pass away :
Like the untimely birth of a woman, that they may not see the sun.
9 Before your pots can feel the thorns,
He shall take them away as with a whirlwind, both living and in his
wrath.
10 The righteous shall rejoice when he seeth the vengeance :
He shall wash his feet in the blood of the wicked.
11 So that a man shall say, Verily there is a reward for the righteous:
Verily he is a God that judgeth in the earth

THOLUCK supposes that David was led to write this on occasion of Joab murdering Abner. At any rate, it might suit that event. The Righteous One reasons with the ungodly in prospect of their doom. It is another " *Al-taschith*" and " *Michtam*," as to its musical accompaniments. The title.

A difficulty meets us in verse 1, some rendering the Hebrew by a change in one letter, (viz., אֵלִים foɪ אֵלֶם,) " Ye mighty ones, do ye speak righteousness ?" others retaining אֵלֶם as a verb, " Is justice then silent?" (Deut. i. 16), or, " Are ye, then, indeed dumb, so that ye will not speak what is right ?" Horsley puts it thus, " *Are ye in earnest reflection when ye talk of righteousness ?*"

It is addressed to " *the sons of men*" (ver. 1), not to rulers only, though to rulers also, as being among the sons of men. (See Psalm lxxxii. 6.) The contents.

> " *The wicked are alienated* (from God) *from the womb ;*
> *The speakers of falsehood have gone astray as soon as they are born.*"
> (Ver. 3.)

They are of the " seed of *the serpent;*" and, like the adder, they hide their ears in the dust, in order not to be charmed, let the charmer chant however sweet and long. Men bury their conscience in the things of earth, and shut out the alluring sound of the tidings of love to the guilty. Hence, judgment comes. " Woe to thee, Chorazin"—Wóe to thee, O earth, that hast heard the offers of love as well as the demands of law. In verses 6–9 the wrath is shewn under which the mighty melt away " *as a snail*," suggesting (it has been thought) the idea of the filthy trail or mark which their beastly pollutions used to leave behind them. Their glory is no more than " *an abortion*." It is at the coming of the Son of man that it overtakes them. They are devising much and planning great schemes, but " ere their pots can feel the blazing thorn," ere their designs of ambition are reached, " he carries them away with a tempest,"—the green and the dry, the sodden and the raw (כְּמוֹ־חָי כְּמוֹ־חָרוֹן), their finished and their unfinished works, and themselves, too, with all their gratified and all their as yet ungratified desires. There are seven similitudes : the lion's teeth broken ; the torrents running off ; the bow snapping asunder ; the snail wasting away ; the abortion that scarcely can be said to have had existence ; the pots that never get time to feel the heat ; the whirlwind that makes them its victim.

No doubt, at the sight of Sodom, Gomorrha Admah, and Zeboim, destroyed, angels saw cause to rejoice and sing, " Hallelujah." Wickedness was swept away ; earth was lightened of a burden ; justice, the justice of God, was highly exalted ; love to his other creatures was displayed in freeing them from the neighbourhood of such hellish contaminations. On the same principles, (entering, however, yet deeper into the mind of the Father, and sympathizing to the full in his justice,) the Lord Jesus himself and each one of his members shall cry " Hallelujah" over Antichrist's ruined hosts. (Rev. xix. 3).

> " *The righteous shall rejoice when He seeth the vengeance,*
> *He shall wash his feet in the blood of the wicked.*" (Ver. 10.)

He shall be refreshed at the end of his journey (John xiii. 5 ; Luke vii. 44 ; Gen. xviii. 4), He shall wipe off all the dust of the way, and end its weariness by entering into that strange, that divine joy over sin destroyed, justice honoured, the law magnified, vengeance taken for the insult done to Godhead. the triumph of the Holy One over the unholy. It is not merely *the time when* that joy begins,—it is also the occasion and cause of that day's rapturous delight.

But what follows now ? It is said, verse 11, וְיֹאמַר אָדָם, " And *man* shall say." Is not this the effect upon the world at large in turning them to know their God, his law, his justice, his hatred of sin, his love to his own ? Now shall John xvii. 23 be fulfilled. Seeing Christ and his bride, the Church, triumphant and glorified, "The world shall know that the Father sent him, and that the Father loved them as he loved Christ." As they gaze on his and their enthroned glory, they shall confess, " *Verily there is a reward for the righteous !*" and shall bend their knee and say of Him who sitteth on the throne of his glory, with his princes who truly decree justice (Isa. xxxii. 1), " *Verily, God judgeth the earth !*" Its government has come into the hands of the Just One and his saints ; there is a God, there is a God who judges !

O that the sons of men would hear in this their day ! O that every ear were opened to these words of

The Righteous One reasoning with the ungodly in prospect of the day of vengeance.

Psalm 59

To the chief Musician. Al-taschith. Michtam of David; when Saul sent, and they watched the house to kill him

1 DELIVER me from mine enemies, O my God !
Defend me from them that rise up against me.
2 Deliver me from the workers of iniquity, and save me from bloody men.
3 For, lo, they lie in wait for my soul : the mighty are gathered against me ;
Not for my transgression, nor for my sin, O Lord.
4 They run and prepare themselves without my fault : awake to help me, and behold !
5 Thou therefore, O Lord God of hosts, the God of Israel, awake to visit all the heathen :
Be not merciful to any wicked transgressors. Selah.
6 They return at evening : they make a noise like a dog, and go round about the city.
7 Behold, they belch out with their mouth : swords are in their lips :
For who, say they, doth hear ?
8 But thou, O Lord, shall laugh at them ; thou shalt have all the heathen in derision.
9 Because of his strength will I wait upon thee : for God is my defence.

10 The God of my mercy shall prevent me :
   God shall let me see my desire upon mine enemies.

11 Slay them not, lest my people forget : scatter them by thy power,
   And bring them down, O Lord our shield.

12 For the sin of their mouth and the words of their lips let them even be
   taken in their pride :
   And for cursing and lying which they speak.

13 Consume them in wrath, consume them, that they may not be :
   And let them know that God ruleth in Jacob, unto the ends of the earth.
   Selah.

14 And at evening let them return ;
   And let them make a noise like a dog, and go round about the city.

15 Let them wander up and down for meat, and grudge if they be not
   satisfied.

16 But I will sing of thy power ; yea, I will sing aloud of thy mercy in the
   morning :
   For thou hast been my defence and refuge in the day of my trouble.

17 Unto thee, O my strength, will I sing : for God is my defence, and the
   God of my mercy.

The title. *"His own received Him not."* The Sweet Singer of Israel knew what it is to be cast off by those who should have been his bosom friends ; and it was on one of those occasions, when his father-in-law sent a band to take him, dead or alive, from his own house (1 Sam. xix. 14), that David was taught by the Holy Ghost to pour out his soul in these strains of strong appeal to justice and to mercy. Perhaps it was at Ramah, when resting in Samuel's dwelling for a time, that this Psalm was written—a Psalm for David himself—a Psalm for *David's Son*, when he too should be rejected of his own—a Psalm for all his followers when they should, in after ages, feel that the disciple is not greater than the Master. It is another *"Al-tasc'ith"* and *"Michtam,"* such as we have seen,

Christ and his members. If a disciple, persecuted *"for righteousness' sake,"* can confidently use the language of verse 4, saying, *" not for any particular crime in me, nor yet for general unholiness*, but because I am thine ; without being able to fix on anything to justify their hostility"—if a disciple can use this language, much more the Master. And in this consciousness of being hated solely for "righteousness' sake," the Head and his members claim the help of Jehovah as being

The contents. 1. *" God of hosts,"* and therefore *able ;* 2. *" God of Israel,"* and therefore *willing.* (Ver. 5.)

It seems to be apostate Israel (Tholuck says, "heathenish-minded Israel") that is primarily described in verse 5 as "the heathen," *q. d.*, these children of Abraham who are now children of the devil—Israelites become *Goim !* (Comp. Isa. i. 10.) They are in character and conduct like city dogs, prowling for prey, feeding on the filth of the town, scouring its streets as if to clear them of the godly. But Jehovah—he who in Psalm ii. 4 was seen on the throne of his glory deriding the kings of earth in their vain attempts—laughs at these impotent apostates. In verse 7, the Psalmist complainingly utters, "For who is there that hears ?" And then (verse 8) as one confident in God, he exclaims,

> "*His strength !*" (Yes, this is our stronghold—the idea flashes hope through the soul—
> "*Jehovah's strength !*")—"*I will wait on thee.*" (Ver. 9.)

The "*sin of their mouth*" may be specially their declared rejection of Messiah's grace. Then, an intercession ascends, like that of Elijah *against* Israel—a prayer that these blinded apostates may be scattered, though not destroyed from the earth.* The prayer of verse 13-

> "*Consume them, in wrath consume them till they be no more*"—

reminds us of 2 Thess. ii. 16, "Wrath has come on them to the uttermost" (εἰς τελος). As a nation, as a kingdom, they are "*consumed*," but as a people they are "*scattered*," and men to earth's end are taught of Jacob's God by their doom. It is a doom of retribution for their treatment of the righteous. A solemn "*Selah*" follows, like that which in verse 5 closed the prayer for divine interposition, that we may ponder the awful judgment, *Jacob driven to the ends of the earth !* (ver. 13.) Now they are as hungry dogs in another sense than when they snarled at the godly—they prowl about the world for food. (Verses 14, 15.) In spite of them, the Just One flourishes, singing of Jehovah, mighty and merciful, and looks forward to a time when he shall sing louder still—*a morning* after a

---

* Not destroyed—that they may be a whetstone to others' faith—as the Spartans (mentioned in Plutarch's Apothegms) refused to allow the destruction of a neighbouring city which had often called forth their armies, saying, "Destroy not the whetstone of our young men!"

dark night, viz., the resurrection-morning, " *Mane*, transactis tentationibus ; *mane* cum nox hujus sæculi transierit ; *mane* quando jam latronum insidias, et Diaboli et angelorum ejus, non expavescimus ; *mane* quando jam non ad lucernam Prophetiæ ambulamus, sed ipsum Dei Verbum, tanquam Solem, contemplamur," (Augustine).

In verse 11, the Righteous One seems to see the sword hanging over apostate Israel, as when it was suspended over Jerusalem in the days of that pestilence that cut off 73,000 men of Israel. Seeing this exterminating sword, he cries, " *Slay them not!*" He asks a mitigation of their doom, even that which has been granted—their dispersion instead of their extirpation. Let them be as Cain, Gen. iv. 12 ; "make them wander." Still, he fully agrees with the Lord as to their deserving wrath to the uttermost, and expresses this entire agreement in the closing verses. It is therefore a Psalm wherein the Head and members present an appeal against apostate Israel, and then consent to their long-enduring desolation, in prospect of mercy breaking out of the gloom at last, " *in the Morning.*" It is

The Righteous One's appeal against apostate Israel, to the Lord's might and mercy.

Psalm 60

To the chief Musician. Upon Shushan-eduth Michtam of David, to teach : when he strove with Aram-naharaim and with Aram-zobah when Joab returned, and smote of Edom in the valley of salt twelve thousand

1 O GOD, thou hast cast us off, thou hast scattered us,
Thou hast been displeased ; O turn thyself to us again.
2 Thou hast made the earth to tremble ; thou hast broken it:
Heal the breaches thereof ; for it shaketh.
3 Thou hast shewed thy people hard things :
Thou hast made us to drink the wine of astonishment.
4 Thou hast given a banner to them that feared thee,
That it may be displayed because of the truth. Selah.
5 That thy beloved may be delivered ; save with thy right hand, and hear me.
6 God hath spoken in his holiness;
I will rejoice, I will divide Shechem, and mete out the valley of Succoth.
7 Gilead is mine, and Manasseh is mine ;
Ephraim also is the strength of mine head ; Judah is my lawgiver;

8 Moab is my washpot; over Edom will I cast out my shoe:
   Philistia, triumph thou because of me.
9 Who will bring me into the strong city? who will lead me into **Edom**?
10 Wilt not thou, O God, which hadst cast us off?
   And thou, O God, which didst not go out with our armies?
11 Give us help from trouble: for vain is the help of man.
12 Through God we shall do valiantly: for he it is that shall tread down **our**
   enemies.

THE Sweet Singer outlived the dismal days of Saul. Seated The time.
firmly on his throne, he saw his armies go forth and return
crowned with victory. One of his victories, gained by Joab,
was over the king of Zobah, who, it appears, had engaged the
men of Mesopotamia (Aram-naharaim) to take his side. When
the trophies of victory from the river Euphrates (2 Sam. viii. 3)
were brought in, David's harp awoke, touched by the Spirit of
God. It sang of a happier day to come—happier than that
triumphant day of Israel in the birth-land of their father Abraham—a day when Israel's breaches shall be for ever healed, and
Israel's strongest foes for ever subdued.

Sometimes it is the nation, sometimes it is the leader of the The speaker
nation, that sings. (See ver. 1, 5, 9.) It may be used by Is- and the title.
rael, or by Israel's Lord as one of themselves. But what is
"*upon Shushan-eduth?*" It must be connected with "joy,"
or with "lilies," (שׁוּשַׁן), and may speak of some instrument such
as Psalm xlv. and Psalm lxxx. refer to. But no writer has
come nearer certainty in regard to "*Eduth*" than that it may
allude to *Israel* as the nation that had the "*Testimony*" (עֵדוּת),
or the Ark of Testimony. "*To teach*"—as if pointing back to
Moses' song, Deut. xxxi. 19, and indicating that this also is
such a national song as that.

The Psalm may be said to take up the preceding one's hope The plan.
expressed at the close. The dispersion of Israel does not last
for ever. Though they have been broken, and though God has
put into their hand a cup of wrath that stuns them (Isa. li. 22),
yet they shall arise. Their's is not the malefactor's cup of
myrrh that deadens pain just as a prelude to death and utter
extinction. Though Israel be broken, and his land cleft
asunder a thousandfold more terribly than David's wars or

any of the desolations of his time ever threatened, yet that desolation ends. (See verse 4.)

> " *Thou hast given a Banner to them that fear thee.*"

Here is the voice of Israel owning Jehovah's gift of Messiah to them. Messiah is the ensign or banner, Isaiah xi. 10.

> " *To be lifted up as an ensign, because of truth.*"

Holding up this banner*—in other words, owning God's truth, or the fulfilment of his ancient promise to Adam, to Abraham, to all the fathers—Israel may expect favour ; and they find it. For suddenly, verse 5, Messiah appears, himself urging their request, and at verse 6 he gets a favourable answer ; " God speaks in holiness," (or, as Israel's Holy One,) and grants the desire of him who asks. *Shechem*, on the west side of Jordan, where Jacob's first altar was raised, and where he bought the first parcel of ground (Gen. xxxiii. 18), and where afterwards destruction threatened the whole feeble family because of Levi and Simeon's enormity, is now re-possessed in peace. *Succoth*, on the east side of Jordan, where Jacob first erected a dwelling (Gen. xxxiii. 17), and booths for cattle, as one intending to remain, is next claimed permanently. The country eastward beyond Jordan, under the name *Gilead*, where stood the mountain famed for *healing balm*, emblematic of healing to Israel, and which was one of the first districts settled and peopled by Israel, comes next, as well as westward *Manasseh*, on the opposite side ; thus shewing us the stretching of the wing over the breadth of the land. *Ephraim*, full of power, comes in as being to push the foe with his horns (Deut. xxxiii. 17), while *Judah* appears as " *Lawgiver*," or " Ruler," the tribe of Messiah. The nations round submit ; *Moab* stands as a slave at his master's foot ; *Edom* picks up the sandal cast down at his feet by his lord (Hengst.) ;† and *Philistia* is compelled to receive the king with triumphant shouts.

> " *Philistia, shout to me The conqueror !*"

And whose power is it that accomplished all this ? Who is it that leads the conquering nation and its king to the

---

* Harmer says, that delivering a banner into the hands of a supplicant, was a sure pledge of protection in the East.

† Tholuck says, that the casting of the shoe is still an emblem of subjugation in India and Abyssinia.

strong city? even to Edom's strongholds, and to the battle-field of Edom in the latter day? (Isaiah lxiii. 1.) It is the very God who once cast them off—the very God that scattered them. Glory to the Lord of hosts, and to Him only! Israel and Israel's Leader rest on him, and so do valiantly—as Balaam, pointing to Moab and Edom, long since foretold (Num. xxiv. 18, 19). And thus the scene of Psalm lix. is happily reversed at length.

The Righteous One asks, and rejoices in, Israel's restoration.

Psalm 61

To the chief Musician. Upon Neginah. A Psalm of David

1 HEAR my cry, O God; attend unto my prayer.
2 From the end of the earth will I cry unto thee, when my heart is **overwhelmed**:
  Lead me to the rock that is higher than I.
3 For thou hast been a shelter for me, and a strong tower from the enemy.
4 I will abide in thy tabernacle for ever: I will trust in the covert of thy wings. Selah.
5 For thou, O God, hast heard my vows:
  Thou hast given me the heritage of those that fear thy name.
6 Thou wilt prolong the king's life: and his years as many generations.
7 He shall abide before God for ever: O prepare mercy and truth, which **may** preserve him.
8 So will I sing praise unto thy name for ever, that I may daily perform **my** vows.

" ON *Neginah*," (like *Neginoth*, unknown), and " by *David*," and perhaps sung at Mahanaim, (Tholuck). In this life, every member of the Church has a varied lot—now at rest, then troubled; now hopeful, then fearful; now a conqueror, then a combatant. Seated as he is on the Rock of Ages, immoveably seated, he sees at one time a fair sky and a bright sun; then, the thick cloud spreads gloom over nature; soon, the beam struggles through again, but soon all is mist once more. Such being the sure complexion of our sojourning here, we rejoice to find sympathy therewith evinced by our God who knoweth our frame, and evinced by the fact that he so often turns in the Songs of Zion from one state of mind to another, and from one aspect of our case to another.

The tone.

Here is the Head and his members in a state of loneliness. As if suggested by the case of dispersed Israel, language (in verse 2) is adopted such as we find in Deut. xxx. 41 and Neh. i. 9. Our Lord could use such a Psalm in the days of his humiliation, looking to the Father, as in John xiv. 28, " the Rock higher than I," higher than the *man* Christ Jesus, higher than all his members. This Rock casts its shadow over those beneath it. The *"Selah"* at verse 4 gives us time to look upon the believing one's quiet repose under the wings of God, and then we hear the calm acknowledgment of verse 5, which may remind us of Psalm xxii. 25. The tone of the Song changes; all thereafter is hope, sure anticipation, a future of bliss realised as already at hand. *" He shall sit* (on the throne) *before God for ever,* (ver. 7).

Two things let us specially notice. *" Mercy and truth"* (ver. 7) are the attributives which preserve him. Now, *" mercy and truth"* are the prominent features of *Redemption-blessing;* God able to say, *" Live,"* and yet to do this without retracting the sentence, *" Thou shalt die."* Christ's pillar-cloud was " mercy and truth;" the Christian's pillar-cloud is the same. Christ, by harmonising, magnified these perfections of Godhead; the Christian magnifies them by pointing the Father to them as harmonised. Thus this prayer is answered,

> " O prepare mercy and truth ;
> Let them preserve him !"

Perhaps the unusual word מן, "appoint," "prepare," may have been chosen as suggesting a reference to *manna*, the wilderness-provision. Give a manna-like provision of mercy and truth. This be our everlasting food while we dwell before God !

Another thing worthy of brief notice is verse 6, *"The King."* *David's* title was, *" King,"* though a wanderer in Judah's deserts ; *David's Son*, too, had the same name and title ; and in the right of their Head, disciples of Christ claim kingship under him, and look forward with hope and expectation to the days of his visible manifestation as *King* in the kingdom that has no end. Here, then, we have

The Righteous One, when an outcast, looking for the day of his Restoration.

Psalm 62

To the chief Musician, to Jeduthun. A Psalm of David

1 TRULY my soul waiteth upon God : from him cometh my salvation.
2 He only is my rock and my salvation ; he is my defence ; I shall not be
greatly moved.
3 How long will ye imagine mischief against a man ?
Ye shall be slain all of you: as a bowing wall shall ye be, and as a totter-
ing fence.
4 They only consult to cast him down from his excellency :
They delight in lies : they bless with their mouth, but they curse inwardly.
Selah.
5 My soul, wait thou only upon God ; for my expectation is from him.
6 He only is my rock and my salvation : he is my defence ; I shall not be
moved.
7 In God is my salvation and my glory : the rock of my strength, and my refuge, is in God.
8 Trust in him at all times ; ye people, pour out your heart before him :
God is a refuge for us. Selah.
9 Surely men of low degree are vanity, and men of high degree are a lie :
To be laid in the balance, they are altogether lighter than vanity.
10 Trust not in oppression, and become not vain in robbery :
If riches increase, set not your heart upon them.
11 God hath spoken once ; twice have I heard this ;
That power belongeth unto God.
12 Also unto thee, O Lord, belongeth mercy :
For thou renderest to every man according to his work.

THIS Psalm has three parts, each beginning with אַךְ, "truly ; "   The connection.
verses 1, 4, 9.   There was a "*Rock*" spoken of in Psalm lxi. 2.
The God of Israel had long been known under that name, ever
since Jacob, and Moses, and Hannah, had appropriated the
Rock, with its many properties of shade, shelter, strength, so-
lidity, dignity, to give a people accustomed to level deserts and
sands an emblem of the Unchanging One to whom the helpless
may resort.   This Rock is prominent throughout this Psalm.
At the commencement, the soul of the speaker is seen under
it as his shelter—he reposes in its shade, and on its strength.

"*Only upon God my soul reposeth !*" (Horsley.)   He is a   The plan.
rock, while enemies are as an "*inclining wall and a fence
that has had a shove*"—on the verge of ruin.   Thus he can
sing,

"*Truly in God
My soul takes rest.*" (Verses 1 and 6.)

Foes and bitter persecutors are around him, and this keeps him very near the Refuge at all times. We have here the soul of the Righteous One—Christ and his members—resorting to Jehovah while iniquity surrounds them, and persecution tries them. We hear them calling on Him, and stirring up one another to do the like (ver. 8.), affixing the solemn, " *Selah.*"

" *Trust in him at all times, ye people,*" (עָם, true Israel of God !)

" Our estimate of man (it has been said) depends on our estimate of God ;" and here God is felt to be most gloriously great. The sons of·men (ver 9) are a mere vapour ; their greatness, even when it shall flush up to the splendour of Antichrist's dominion, is a mere mirage. The sentence against it is on the way. Already you may hear God speaking ; it is no fancy. Two things have been declared by our God, viz., that he will bring down the proud, and that he has mercy for his own. As out of Sinai, so out of the Rock, we hear a voice telling that Jehovah is *God Almighty,* and yet *merciful* too.

> " *One thing God has spoken,*
> *Two things there are which I have heard—*
> **viz.**, *That might is God's ;*
> *And that mercy also is Jehovah's !*"   (Verses 11, 12.)

In this certainty we look for the Great Day of the Lord—the day when a mismanaged world shall be set in order—a day sure to come, and sure to satisfy us when it has come,

" *For thou renderest to every man according to his work.*"

When the choir of singers, at whose head was Jeduthun, sang this Psalm together, the godly in Israel would feel their souls raised to the very heights of confidence, sympathising with

The Righteous One, when threatened, looking to the Rock
for help.

Psalm 63

A Psalm of David, when he was in the wilderness of Judah

1 O GOD, thou art my God ; early will I seek thee !
My soul thirsteth for thee, my flesh longeth for thee
In a dry and thirsty land, where no water is:

2 To see thy power and thy glory, so as I have seen thee in the sanctuary.

3 Because thy loving-kindness is better than life, my lips shall praise thee.

4 Thus will I bless thee while I live : I will lift up my hands in thy name.

5 My soul shall be satisfied as with marrow and fatness ;
  And my mouth shall praise thee with joyful lips :

6 When I remember thee upon my bed, and meditate on thee in the night watches.

7 Because thou hast been my help, therefore in the shadow of thy wings will I rejoice.

8 My soul followeth hard after thee : thy right hand upholdeth me.

9 But those that seek my soul, to destroy it, shall go into the lower parts of the earth.

10 They shall fall by the sword : they shall be a portion for foxes.

11 But the king shall rejoice in God ; every one that sweareth by him shall glory :
  But the mouth of them that speak lies shall be stopped.

IT may have been near the Dead Sea, on his way to the ford of Jordan, that the Psalmist first sung this song. It is a Psalm first heard by David's faithful ones in the wilderness of Judah ; but truly a Psalm for every godly man who in the dry world-wilderness can sing—" All my springs are in thee"—a Psalm for David—a Psalm for David's Son—a Psalm for the Church in every age—a Psalm for every member of the Church in the weary land ! What assurance, what vehement desire, what soul-filling delight in God, in God alone—in God the only fountain of living water amid a boundless wilderness ! Hope, too, has its visions here ; for it sees the ungodly perish (verses 8, 9, 10), and *the King* on the throne surrounded by a company who swear allegiance to Jehovah. Hope sees for itself what Isaiah lxiv. 16 describes—every mouth " swearing by the God of truth ;" and what Rev. xxi. 27 has foretold, the mouth of "*liars*"closed for ever—all who sought other gods, and trusted to other saviours, gone for ever. And when we read all this as spoken of Christ, how much does every verse become enhanced. *His* thirst for God ! *His* vision of God ! *His* estimate of God's loving-kindness ! *His* soul satisfied ! *His* mouth full of praise ! *His* soul following hard after God !

" *O God, thou art my El*," mighty one. Thou art my omnipotence. It is this God he still seeks. The בְּ of verse 2 and of verse 4 is interesting. In verse 2 the force of it is this— " No wonder that I so thirst for thee ; no wonder that my first

The title.

The theme and plan.

thoughts at morning are toward thee ; no wonder that my very flesh longeth for thee ! Who would not, that has seen what I have seen ? *So* have I gazed on thee in the sanctuary, seeing thy power* and glory !" The " so" is like 2 Peter i. 17, "*Such* a voice !" And then, if the past has been thus exquisitely blessed, my prospects for the future are not less so. I see illimitable bliss coming in as a tide ; " *so* will I bless Thee while I have being !" (ver. 4.) Yes ; in ages to come, as well as in many a happy moment on earth, my soul shall be satiated as with marrow and fatness ! And when verse 7 shews us the soul under the shadow of God's wings, rejoicing, we may say, it is not only like as "the bird sheltered from the heat of the sun amid the rich foliage sings its merry note," but it is the soul reposing there as if entering the cloud of glory, like Moses and Elias.

O world ! come and see

The Righteous One finding water-springs in God.

Psalm 64

To the chief Musician. A Psalm of David

1 HEAR my voice, O God, in my prayer : preserve my life from fear of the enemy.

2 Hide me from the secret counsel of the wicked ;
From the insurrection of the workers of iniquity.

3 Who whet their tongue like a sword,
And bend their bows to shoot their arrows, even bitter words :

4 That they may shoot in secret at the perfect :
Suddenly they do shoot at him, and fear not.

5 They encourage themselves in an evil matter :
They commune of laying snares privily ; they say, Who shall see them ?

6 They search out iniquities ; they accomplish a diligent search :
Both the inward thought of every one of them, and the heart, is deep.

7 But God shall shoot at them with an arrow ; suddenly shall they be wounded.

8 So they shall make their own tongue to fall upon themselves :
All that see them shall flee away.

9 And all men shall fear, and shall declare the work of God ;
For they shall wisely consider of his doing.

10 The righteous shall be glad in the Lord, and shall trust in him ;
And all the upright in heart shall glory.

* "*Thy power*"—with special reference to the "Ark of his Strength" (2 Chron. vi. 41). So in Psalm lxxviii. 61—"*his glory*," is his Ark.

IT is a probable conjecture that David may have been led to write this Psalm while still a youth at Saul's court, when there discerning the arts and deceits of courtiers. We may illustrate it by referring to the case of Joseph and his many foes. Here is the Righteous One, or "*the Perfect*" (ver. 4), set before us—a name applicable to Christ in its fullest significancy, but applied also to his members, as being "Perfect" in purpose and in prospects, impartially aiming at the whole will of their God in heart and life. But the world hates such, as his brethren hated Joseph ; the world lays snares, and levels arrows of malignity at them. "The archers have shot at them"—at our Joseph and his seed. He says, verse 5, "*They will tell about hiding snares,*" and they think no eye is on them.

"*They search deep into iniquity,*" (to find out the most deadly device).
"*We have got it ready ! Here is a well-matured plan !*" (This is their shout over their deep-laid plot.)
"*And close is each one,*
And deep of heart." (Ver. 6.)

But there is another that is an Archer : "*God has shot at them.*" God has his bow, and his time is coming, (ver. 7). "*All their hard speeches,*" are to be brought into judgment at the Lord's coming (Jude 15) ; and if they wounded others sorely, sorely shall they in turn be wounded. Theirs shall be a doom like Korah's (ver. 8), when all Israel fled at the cry (Num. xvi. 34).

"*He has cast them down ! Their tongues come on themselves.*" (Ver. 8.)

All earth shall then discern the righteous ways of God. That is the day of his Redeemed so often spoken of, so long expected —the day when the Righteous shall "enter into the joy of their Lord," and utter aloud their rejoicings and their glorying in Him.

"*The Righteous One shall be glad in the Lord,*
And flee for refuge to none but to him;
And all the upright in heart shall boast themselves." (Ver. 6.)

May we not, then, describe this song of Zion as one in which we find

Our Joseph and his seed foreseeing the doom of the archers
that have shot at them.

Psalm 65

To the chief Musician. A Psalm and Song of David.

1 PRAISE waiteth for thee, O God, in Sion: and unto thee shall the vow
   be performed.

2 O thou that hearest prayer, unto thee shall all flesh come.

3 Iniquities prevail against me : as for our transgressions, thou shalt purge
   them away.

4 Blessed is the man that thou choosest,
   And causest to approach unto thee, that he may dwell in thy courts:
   We shall be satisfied with the goodness of thy house, even of thy holy
   temple.

5 By terrible things in righteousness wilt thou answer us, O God of our
   salvation,
   Who art the confidence of all the ends of the earth,
   And of them that are afar off upon the sea :

6 Which by his strength setteth fast the mountains; being girded with
   power:

7 Which stilleth the noise of the seas, the noise of their waves, and the
   tumult of the people.

8 They also that dwell in the uttermost parts are afraid at thy tokens:
   Thou makest the outgoings of the morning and evening to rejoice.

9 Thou visitest the earth, and waterest it :
   Thou greatly enriches it with the river of God, which is full of water:
   Thou preparest them corn, when thou hast so provided for it.

10 Thou waterest the ridges thereof abundantly : thou settlest the furrow
    thereof:
    Thou makest it soft with showers: thou blessest the springing thereof.

11 Thou crownest the year with thy goodness; and thy paths drop fatness.

12 They drop upon the pastures of the wilderness : and the little hills rejoice
    on every side.

13 The pastures are clothed with flocks ; the valleys also are covered over with
    corn :
    They shout for joy, they also sing.

The title.

" *A psalm of David ; a true song,*" is the import of the title,
thus describing the tone that prevails throughout.   Possibly
(as some think) it was composed at Passover time, when the
sheaf of first fruits of barley harvest used to be offered.

The contents.

Every note in this song tells the feeling of a happy soul reviewing the past, and seeing mercy abounding then and now.
Messiah and his redeemed ones—the Lamb and his 144,000—
might sing it on their Mount Zion, and we may sing it now.
The Head leads the choir, and this is the substance of the
song-

" O God, praise is thine!" such praise as leaves the worshipper "*silent*," because the theme is too great for his harp to
handle.* Now is the vow performed to thee! " O Hearer of
Prayer, to thee (yes, even as far as to Thee, עַד). the Holiest
of all, all flesh are coming now." Our iniquities (iniquities
which have been imputed to our Head) once prevailed against
us (as Gen. vii. 24, גָּבַר) like the waters of the deluge, sur-
mounting the highest hills; but thou purgest them away, and
we sing, " Blessed is the man whom thou causest to approach
unto thee as a priest" (Num. xvi. 8). Aye, blessed, indeed,
for he shall dwell in thy courts, and there be satisfied with
good; thy house, thy holy place, yielding him its heavenly
stores. When we cried to thee, terrible things (things of such
surpassing glory and majesty as spread awe around) were thine
answer. Thou wert God of salvation, displaying thy grace
in such a way as to draw the confidence of all ends of earth.
Creator, too, setting fast the mountains! and God of providence, stilling the raging waves of the most tumultuous sea,
and by thy wonderful signs ("*tokens*," אוֹתֹת) causing distant
lands, the lands of the setting and rising sun, the east and the
west, to fear and to rejoice.

And now let us sing together of the crowning act of all, displaying grace, creation, and providence in one—thy dealings
with this Earth, which thou wilt renew into paradise. Once
we sang, " What is man that thou *visitest him?*" and now we
sing, " *Thou visitest his dwelling-place*, and makest it teem
with plenty!" Yes, " Thou hast the earth under thy care,
and waterest it."

> " *The fountain of God has plenty of waters.* (Heng.)
> *Thou preparest* (Horsley, makest sure)*their corn, for lo*! *thus
> hast thou prepared!*" (V. 9.)

What a table spread with abundance is that once barren earth!

* " To *thee belongeth silence-praise;*" praise without any tumult (Alexander). It has been said, " The most intense feeling is the most calm, being con-
densed by repression." And Hooker says of prayer, " The very silence which
our unworthiness putteth us unto doth itself make request for us, and that in
the confidence of his grace. Looking inward, we are stricken dumb; looking
upward, we speak and prevail" (v. 48, 4). Horsley renders it, " Upon thee is
the repose of prayer."

It is " *thus* (כן as in Ps. lxiii. 3) thou dealest as God, with infinite liberality." The soaking rain descends on her furrowed fields.

> " *Thou layest down its ploughed fields ;*
> *Thou dost moisten it with showers ;*
> *Thou blesseth the springing thereof.*
> *Thou hast crowned the year, so as to make it a* year *of goodness ;*
> *Thy chariot-wheels drop fatness.*
> *They drop on the wilderness which has pastures now* (meadow-lands);
> *The hills are girded with gladness.*"

What a changed world! And every season we see something of this exhibited. But the yearly return of spring and summer after winter is an emblem of Earth's summer day, when it shall be renewed. Then, even more than now, it shall be sung,

Scenes in the New Earth.

> " *The pastures are clad with flocks ;*
> *The valleys are covered over with corn !*
> *They shout for joy ! they break out into song !*

Who does not seem, in reading this majestic Psalm, to hear the very melody that issues from the happy people of that New Earth? Originally it may have been sung as a "*Psalm of David, a lively song,*" at a Feast of Tabernacles, when Israel's happy land and prosperous tribes furnished a scene that naturally suggested the future days of a renewed earth—earth's golden age returned. It is, however, on a much higher key than this; it is a Song of the Lamb, while he leads his glorified ones to fountains of living water, and shews them their old world presenting at length a counterpart to heaven—all paradise again, and better than paradise. Is it not then

Prayers exchanged for praises because of blessings
showered on Earth ?

Psalm 66

To the chief Musician. A Song or Psalm

1 MAKE a joyful noise unto God, all ye lands :

2 Sing forth the honour of his name : make his praise glorious.

3 Say unto God, How terrible art thou in thy works !
Through the greatness of thy power shall thine enemies submit themselves unto thee

4 All the earth shall worship thee,
And shall sing unto thee; they shall sing to thy name. Selah.
5 Come and see the works of God: he is terrible in his doing toward the children of men.
6 He turned the sea into dry land: they went through the flood on foot: There did we rejoice in him.
7 He ruleth by his power for ever; his eyes behold the nations: Let not the rebellious exalt themselves. Selah.
8 O bless our God, ye people, and make the voice of his praise to be heard,
9 Which holdeth our soul in life, and suffereth not our feet to be moved.
10 For thou, O God, has proved us: thou has tried us, as silver is tried.
11 Thou broughtest us into the net; thou laidst affliction upon our loins.
12 Thou hast caused men to ride over our heads; we went through fire and through water:
But thou broughtest us out into a wealthy place.
13 I will go into thy house with burnt offerings: I will pay thee my vows,
14 Which my lips have uttered, and my mouth hath spoken, when I was in trouble.
15 I will offer unto thee burnt sacrifices of fatlings, with the incense of rams; I will offer bullocks with goats. Selah.
16 Come and hear, all ye that fear God, and I will declare what he hath done for my soul.
17 I cried unto him with my mouth, and he was extolled with my tongue.
18 If I regard iniquity in my heart, the Lord will not hear me:
19 But verily God hath heard me; he hath attended to the voice of my prayer.
20 Blessed be God, which hath not turned away my prayer, nor his mercy from me.

Another שִׁיר מִזְמוֹר (as lxv. 1), at once a solemn *Psalm*, and a lively Temple *song*. It is specially the song of Messiah and the *Church of Israel*—a kind of Red Sea song, sung, however, in Canaan. *The title. The plan.*

> " *Raise the shout of joy !*
> *All the earth to God !*
> *Shew forth the glory of his name !*
> *Give glory* (to him) *as his praise.*"

Then, leading us to such scenes as were spoken of in Psalm lxv. 5—

> " *Say unto God, How awful these works of thine !*"

There is a Bethel-solemnity in these scenes, though they bring us to the very gate of heaven—

> " *All the earth shall worship Thee.*
> *They sing ! they sing thy name !*" Selah.

This *Selah*-pause divides the Psalm into portions at suitable times, and intimates a change of scene or tone. Here, as usual, it gives time for solemn thought ; and then an invitatation is given to men to " Come and see." As John i. 26, 27, at Christ's First Coming, and Rev. vi. 3, 5, 7, in events leading on to his Second-

> " *Come and see the works of God !*
> *Awful in his dealings to the sons of men.*" (Ver. 5.)

And when we have cast our eye back to Red Sea and Jordan wonders, and have seen Him to be the same for ever, still subduing the nations, another " *Selah*" gives us time to pause and adore. But the harp is soon struck again (ver. 8),

> " *Bless our God, ye nations*" (עַמִּים, not as Psa. lxii. 8.)*

The Jews are now inviting the Gentiles ; for the Jews are life from the dead to the world. They tell how their God refined them ; how He " *laid pressure on their loins,*" the seat of strength ; yet made their trials act as a furnace to take away the dross. Even אֱנוֹשׁ " frail men" were made strong against them ; yet Israel passed through desert and flood ; and, at length, reached

> " *The wealthy place*" (ver. 12)—affluence—refreshing. (רְוָיָה).

Each of their number, as well as their Leader, thus invites the Gentile nations ; and they do it by example, and not by word only-

> " *I will go into thine house with offerings ;*
> *I will perform my vows unto thee.*
> *I will offer fat victims as burnt-offerings,*
> *Along with rams that have incense-savour.* Selah. (Ver. 13, 14.)

Another pause—like Wisdom's in Prov. i. 23. And then once more, voice and instrument together sound forth a cheerful summons to draw near and listen to *Messiah and the Church of Israel*-

> " *Come, hear, and I will tell,*
> *All ye that fear God,*
> *What he has done for me.*" (Ver. 16.)

He was (ver. 17) " Hearer of prayer" to me (Isa. lxv. 2) ; for

---

* It may remind us of Isa. xxiv. 13, " There shall be among the עַמִּים, *the nations*, the shaking of an olive-tree,"—the Gentiles taking up what Israel lets fall.

no sooner did I call upon Him than he answered—turning my prayer into praise. Had I sought to "lying vanities," or had tried crooked paths, I should have failed in finding this blessed result. But the God of Israel, the Holy One, was honoured.

> " *Verily God hath heard,*
> *He hath hearkened to the voice of my prayer."* (Ver. 19.)

But the way to this blessedness is by a holy path, verse 18 Messiah magnified the law ; and in Him, we who come to God through his blood and righteousness do the same, and so shall sing the same song, and bless the same God.

> " *He has not turned away my prayer !*
> *He has not turned away his mercy from me !"*

A close equivalent to Rev. v. 8, where the golden vials, full of saints' prayers, are held up by the saints, and owned by the Hearer of Prayer on that day. Far from turning away my prayer, lo ! he has done exceeding abundantly beyond all I asked. Instead of turning away his mercy from me, lo ! He has brought me to *the Wealthy Place !* Such is the Song of

Messiah and his ransomed Israel praising the prayer-
hearing God.

Psalm 67

To the chief Musician. On Neginoth. **A** Psalm or Song

1 GOD be merciful unto us, and bless us ; and cause his face to shine upon us. Selah.
2 That thy way may be known upon earth, thy saving health among all nations.
3 Let the people praise thee, O God ; let all the people praise thee.
4 O let the nations be glad and sing for joy !
  For thou shalt judge the people righteously, and govern the nations upon earth. Selah.
5 Let the people praise thee, O God ; let all the people praise thee.
6 Then shall the earth yield her increase ; and God, even our own God, shall bless us.
7 God shall bless us ; and all the ends of the earth shall fear him.

ONCE more the Jewish Church is prominent in this solemn The title. " *Psalm,*" which is sung as a lively " *Song,*" on Neginoth.

The contents. They pray for the outpouring of the full blessing which their High Priest, Jesus, is to bestow by their means on all the earth.

The language of verse 1 refers us to Num. vi. 24, 25, and very appropriately ; for the time is the Lord's Second Coming, when, as true High Priest, he comes forth from the Holiest to bless the people. The "*Selah*" at the end of verse 1 and verse 4 is, in both cases, very expressive, indicating, as it does, pauses in the sense and feeling, as well as the music.

> " *God be merciful to us*
> *And bless us !*
> *And cast the light of his countenance*
> (So as that it may be) *with us.*" (אִתָּנוּ. See Hengst.)

Bless us and guide us in thy way, (thy mode of dealing with thy people), that by us thy way may be known on the earth, as fore-told in Gen. xii. 3, and since those days, in Amos viii. 14 ; Isa. lx. 1, 2 ; Acts xv. 15–17 ; Rom. xi. 15, and many other places.

> " *The nations* (עַמִּים) *shall praise thee, O God ;*
> *The nations shall praise thee !*" (Ver. 3.)

The peculiar people, הָעָם, here anticipate with joy the time when the עַמִּים, the whole Gentile people, shall praise their God and Saviour, and that through their means.

> "*Let the tribes* (of earth, the לְאֻמִּים who once raged against thee, Psa.
> ii. 1) *rejoice and sing,*
> *For thou judgest* (*i. e.,* rulest) *the* (עַמִּים) *nations righteously,*
> *And as for the tribes of earth* (לְאֻמִּים) *thou guidest them.*" (Isa. lviii.
> 11, Hengst.)

And again at the happy prospect they cry, " Hallelujah !" for they repeat their song-

> " *The nations* (עַמִּים) *shall praise thee, O God,*
> *The nations shall praise thee ! every one of them !*" (Ver. 5.)

And now Earth, as well as Palestine, giveth its increase, for the curse is away, and the blessing rests on it (Lev. xxvi. 4). Israel rejoices in this communication of their blessing to all men-

> " *Earth giveth its increase !*
> *God, our God, blesseth us !*
> *God blesseth us !*
> *And they fear Him !*
> *All ends of the earth !*"

Horsley says, this is " A hymn for the Feast of Tabernacles, prophetic of a general conversion of the world to the worship of God." Dr Allix entitles this Psalm, " A Prayer of the Synagogue for the Second Coming of the Messias, when her empire is to be extended over all nations, and the temporal blessings which are promised to the Jews in several oracles shall be conferred on them." But it is simpler, and perhaps more correct to describe it thus-

The Prayer of Israel for the blessing which Messiah is to bestow on them, for the sake of earth at large.

Psalm 68

To the chief Musician. A Psalm or Song of David

1 LET God arise, let his enemies be scattered : let them also that hate him flee before him.

2 As smoke is driven away, so drive them away :
As wax melteth before the fire, so let the wicked perish at the presence of God.

3 But let the righteous be glad ; let them rejoice before God :
Yea, let them exceedingly rejoice.

4 Sing unto God, sing praises to his name :
Extol him that rideth upon the heavens by his name JAH, and rejoice before him.

5 A father of the fatherless, and a judge of the widows, is God in his holy habitation.

6 God setteth the solitary in families : he bringeth out those which are bound with chains :
But the rebellious dwell in a dry land.

7 O God, when thou wentest forth before thy people,
When thou didst march through the wilderness. Selah.

8 The earth shook, the heavens also dropped at the presence of God :
Even Sinai itself was moved at the presence of God, the God of Israel.

9 Thou, O God, didst send a plentiful rain,
Whereby thou didst confirm thine inheritance, when it was weary.

10 Thy congregation hath dwelt therein :
Thou, O God, hast prepared of thy goodness for the poor.

11 The Lord gave the word : great was the company of those that published it.

12 Kings of armies did flee apace : and she that tarried at home divided the spoil.

13 Though ye have lien among the the pots,
Yet shall ye be as the wings of a dove covered with silver, and her feathers with yellow gold.

14 When the Almighty scattered kings in it, it was white as snow in Salmon.
15 The hill of God is as the hill of Bashan ; an high hill, as the hill of Bashan.
16 Why leap ye, ye high hills ?
This is the hill which God desireth to dwell in ;
Yea, the Lord will dwell in it for ever.
17 The chariots of God are twenty thousand, even thousands of angels :
The Lord is among them, as in Sinai, in the holy place.
18 Thou hast ascended on high, thou hast led captivity captive :
Thou hast received gifts for men ;
Yea, for the rebellious also, that the Lord God might dwell among them.
19 Blessed be the Lord, who daily loadeth us with benefits,
Even the God of our salvation.   Selah.
20 He that is our God is the God of salvation ;
And unto God the Lord belong the issues from death.
21 But God shall wound the head of his enemies,
And the hairy scalp of such a one as goeth on still in his trespasses.
22 The Lord said, I will bring again from Bashan,
I will bring my people again from the depths of the sea :
23 That thy foot may be dipped in the blood of thine enemies,
And the tongue of thy dogs in the same.
24 They have seen thy goings, O God : even the goings of my God, my King,
in the sanctuary.
25 The singers went before, the players on instruments followed after ;
Among them were the damsels playing the timbrels.
26 Bless ye God in the congregations, even the Lord, from the fountain of
Israel.
27 There is little Benjamin with their ruler, the princes of Judah and their
council ;
The princes of Zebulun, and the princes of Naphtali.
28 Thy God hath commanded thy strength :
Strengthen, O God, that which thou hast wrought for us.
29 Because of thy temple at Jerusalem shall kings bring presents unto thee.
30 Rebuke the company of spearmen,
The multitude of the bulls, with the calves of the people.
Till every one submit himself with pieces of silver.
Scatter thou the people that delight in war.
31 Princes shall come out of Egypt ; Ethiopia shall soon stretch out her hands
unto God.
32 Sing unto God, ye kingdoms of the earth ; O sing praise unto the Lord.
Selah.
33 To him that rideth upon the heavens of heavens, which were of old !
Lo, he doth send out his voice, and that a mighty voice.
34 Ascribe ye strength unto God :
His excellency is over Israel, and his strength is in the clouds.
35 O God, thou art terrible out of thy holy places !
The God of Israel is he that giveth strength and power unto his people.
Blessed be God.

ANOTHER " Psalm and Song," by David, the sweet singer of
Israel. As David's days of adversity furnished many occasions
for appropriate Psalms, which the Son of David and his Church
were afterwards to use in their times of trial, so the more prosperous season, when the Ark which had been removed in procession by David to Mount Zion, was and afterwards by Solomon
carried up to Moriah, seems to have provided a fit occasion for
this triumphant song. It has been called "The magnificent
march." Certainly it is throughout a tracing of the stately
steps of the Lord in his goings forth for His Church, from the
Wilderness onward to final rest.

The plan is as follows :—

Ver. 1–3. Prefatory strains, celebrating Jehovah as almighty
to scatter foes, almighty to make friends exult with joy.

Ver. 4–6. General characteristics of his ways—grace to the
helpless—to all that do not reject his help.

Ver. 7–9. His ways, with Israel in the Wilderness—glorious
majesty and gracious bounty.

Ver. 10–14. His ways, in bringing Israel into Canaan—the
irresistible might of a King in behalf of his own.

Ver. 15–17. His ways, in fixing his seat on Zion, the ark
being carried up thither—sovereignty.

Ver. 18–23. His ways, in the typical setting forth on Zion
of an ascended Saviour, the savour of life to his own,
though the savour of death to his rejecters.

Ver. 24–31. His ways, in the Ark removed afterwards to the
temple on Moriah —Israel gathered round it (ver. 26, 27),
and the Gentiles flocking to Shiloh there (ver. 29, 31).
All this typical of the Lord's advent, as true Solomon.

Ver. 32–35. The closing doxology to the King of kings on
reviewing the whole, and seeing "the Kingdom Come."

Such seems to be the plan. It would carry us beyond our
limits to go into full details, since almost every verse is rich and
laden with meaning. A few hints may be of use, however, on
some of the more difficult clauses. Some render verse 1 "God
shall arise," q. d., it shall always be thus, as they sang Num.
x. 35, and Judges v. 31.

In verse 4 the justified ones, singing before their justifier,
cry, " Make a way for him that rideth through the wilder-

ness" (עֲרָבוֹת) or *plain ;* the Angel of the Covenant that redeemed them from all evil. It is *their King* whom they thus
honour, and so they raise the cry, " *Prepare the way !"* as in
Isa. xl. 3, and as the Baptist did when he saw the King of the
kingdom at hand. His name " *Jah,"* יָהּ expresses the fulness
of *being* and perfection·; and Horsley would fain add *beauty*
too.

Verse 5

In verse 5, Israel's helpless case in Egypt, Earth's helpless
case since the Fall, the sinner's state, " without strength," may
all be found here. The " widow's *judge,"* implies his *manag-
ing and ruling* the affairs of such as have no other to interpose, like as Gideon, or any judge of Israel, put in order
a disordered county, and bore the burden of its cares. And
does not Jas. i. 21 refer to this verse, for we have ·" the *fatherless,"* " the *widow,"* and then the " *holiness,"* of the God
we serve ?

Verse 8.

In verse 8 the ratifying of the covenant at Sinai, in circumstances of awful grandeur, is the theme ; and verse 9 speaks
of the " *rain of gifts"* (Hengst.) that attended Israel all
through the Desert—manna, quails, water from the rock—
when God's heritage pitched their tents on the flinty and
scorched soil of that weary wilderness.

Verse 10.

Then, in verse 10, the host of Israel " settle down on *It,"*
i. e., the well-known, ever-in-view Land of Promise. The Lord
" gave the word"—(as in Psa. cv. 19)—as if at every step there
had been repeated, like Joshua vi. 16, " Shout, for the Lord has
given you the land !" and responding multitudes, even of the
women of Israel, proclaim the victory, and sing, as did Miriam
at the Red Sea,

> " *Kings of armies flee ! they flee !*
> *And she that tarries at home divides the spoil."* (Ver. 12.)

Verse 14.

So easily does Jehovah conquer ! And now, " *Ye lie down
amid the borders, and are as doves ;"* or rather, they who were
" *lying among the pots"* are now like the dove that has washed
itself in the streams, and is basking in the sun whose bright
beams glance on its feathers with the sheen of silver and gold.
Yes, it was easy for Jehovah to scatter kings. " *There was
snow on Zalmon."* They fell before him as snow disappears

among the thick-wooded heights of Zalmon (Judg. ix. 48) in the day of tempest.*

Israel now at rest, where is the *Ark of the Covenant?* Not on Bashan, *i. e.*, the range of Antilibanus, though that was a "hill of God," such a hill as reminded one of the power of Him who setteth fast the hills by his might (Hengst.)—nor yet on other lofty hills such as Tabor, Lebanon, or Carmel. The more lowly Zion is selected, and thither the sovereign Lord comes with all his hosts. There he resides, as in a pavilion—in that Holy of Holies which combines the manifestation of justice and mercy at the mercy-seat—for "*Sinai is in the sanctuary*" (סִינַי בַּקֹּדֶשׁ). He is as much present here as when the law was given on Sinai. There, though unseen except by the eye of faith, he reigns, more mighty in his angelic heavenly hosts than ever was king with his chariots, so that Israel need no more fear a Jabin with his nine hundred chariots of iron (Judg. iv. 2). An anointed eye, (like his in 2 Kings vi. 27,) might see these hosts in Israel's land at any moment, under the rule of Israel's king.

Ascended to Zion, no more wandering from place to place, *the Ark* is the centre of blessing to Israel—there worshippers get gifts ; there daily benefits are dispensed. And in this was typified the Saviour, no more a wanderer on earth from place to place, seated at the Father's right hand, and showering down his gifts on man—the antitype infinitely greater than the type, and his gifts infinitely more spiritual and plentiful (Eph. iii. 8). Here is (ver. 7) a "*Selah,*" the mark of solemn thought ; for herein is a great mystery of love (ver. 19). The words are literally rendered, "*Thou hast received gifts among men.*" Here is a constr. prægn. for "*received, and given out among men* (Eph. iv. 18), *even among the rebels.*" And then follows, "*At the tabernacling of Jah Elohim*" (as ver. 16), that is, at the time when he pitched his tabernacle. But, there is refe-

Verse 16.

Verse 18.

---

* *Zalmon* is mentioned rather than Hermon, or any other of that northern range, because it is so nearly in the heart of the Land, and near Shechem (Josh. xxiv. 1), where some of the earliest gatherings of Israel took place. *Tholuck* thinks the allusion to the snow is to its flakes falling on the ground. So fell the ranks of the foe, and their silver ornaments glittered white as they fell.

rence 1. To the type on Zion; 2. To the days of his First
Coming; 3. To the still future Tabernacling, Rev. xxi. 3.

But again let the harp sing of Him who is thus exalted,
Verses 21, 22. mighty to save, and mighty to overcome his enemies.   Jehovah
is "*God of our salvation,*" and "*Selah*" calls on us to ponder.
Then it is repeated,

> "*The God* (of Israel) *is God to us,* as to salvations. (לְמוֹשָׁעוֹת)
>
> *And to Jehovah belong the issues,* as to the death" (לְמָוֶת). (Ver. 21.)

He dashes his foes in pieces, cleaving their hairy scalp from
the head from which the helmet has been struck off.   Yes,
says the Lord,

> "*I will turn him* (the foe) *back from Bashan,*
> *I will turn him back from the depths of the sea.*" (Ver. 22.)

Though they were to make lofty Bashan their fortress, or hide
in the caverns of the deep.   (See Amos vii. 3 ; Obad. 4.)

But all is not yet over.   The Ark moves again !   It moves
to Moriah—to Solomon's temple.   Then see the royal procession (ver. 24), and hear the songs of happy thousands under
Verse 24. the reign of that Prince of Peace-

> "*Bless ye God in the congregations,*
> *The Lord* (in the congregations that are), *from the fountain of Israel.*"

There the gathered tribes are seen ; the south sends Benjamin,
once "*their ruler,*" (as it sent Saul, 1 Sam. xiv. 7, and so became the conquering tribe) and Judah, their prince, or perhaps
"*their bulwark.*"*   The north is represented by Zebulon and
Naphtali.   Thus God has provided strength to them.   And
Gentiles, too, are there (ver. 29).   What a type of the latter
Verse 29. days, when the true Solomon, Prince of Peace, has come from
the Father's right hand to his own throne—from Zion to Moriah !
Then, more fully than in the first Solomon's days, it will be
sung-

> "*He has rebuked the Beast of the Reed,*
> (The hippopotamus, who, like leviathan, is the type of Antichrist.)
Verse 30. > *The assembly of mighty ones* (bulls, Psa. xxii. 12),
> *With calves of the nations.*" (Ver. 30.)

These mighty kings and their subjects—bulls and calves—
with their leader, are rebuked and destroyed ; and along with

* Parkhurst refers to Homer's " ἕρκος Ἀχαιῶν," as parallel.

these, the mammon-worshipper, "who crouches with pieces
of silver ;" or rather,

"*He that prostrates himself on pieces of silver.*"

The nations that delight in war are scattered, for it is the reign
of the *Prince of Peace.* Egypt sends princes to Zion, and
Ethiopia hastens to submit to God. And thus we are led on
to the closing strain—the shout of joy over earth now delivered and put under Jehovah's sway-

> "*Ye kingdoms of earth, sing ye to God !*   Verse 32.
> *Chant ye to the Lord !*
> *Who rideth in the heaven of ancient heaven*" (שְׁמֵי קֶדֶם),

(*i. e.,* Who claims as his domain the inmost recess of the eternal heaven.)
"*Lo ! he uttereth a mighty voice when he speaketh.*" (Ver. 33.)

He calls on the universe for praise in verse 34. But even in   Verse 34.
that universal hallelujah there is prominence given to Israel—
"*His majesty is over Israel*" (ver. 34), as if Israel's land were
the spot of the universe where his manifested glory is to be
seen in its peculiar radiance-

"*God of Israel ! thou are a terrible God from thy holy places !*"
(Ver. 36.)
"*Giving strength and might to the* (peculiar) *people ! Blessed be God !*"

Let every soul cry, "Blessed be God !" Let that be the heart-
cry of earth for evermore. And let it not fail to be ours, while
we trace in such a record as this,

Messiah's leadings of Israel and the Church from the Wil-
derness into final Rest.

Psalm 69

To the chief Musician. Upon Shoshannim. A Psalm of David

1 SAVE me, O God ! for the waters are come in unto my soul.
2 I sink in deep mire, where there is no standing :
   I am come into deep waters, where the floods overflow me.
3 I am weary of my crying : my throat is dried : mine eyes fail while I wait
   for my God.
4 They that hate me without a cause are more than the hairs of mine head :
   They that would destroy me, being mine enemies wrongfully, are mighty :
   Then I restored that which I took not away.
5 O God, thou knowest my foolishness ; and my sins are not hid from thee.
6 Let not them that wait on thee, O Lord God of hosts, be ashamed for my sake :
   Let not those that seek thee be confounded for my sake, O God of Israel.

7 Because for thy sake I have borne reproach: shame hath covered my face.

8 I am become a stranger unto my brethren, and an alien unto my mother's children.

9 For the zeal of thine house hath eaten me up ;
And the reproaches of them that reproached thee are fallen upon me.

10 When I wept, and chastened my soul with fasting, that was to my reproach.

11 I made sackcloth also my garment; and I became a proverb to them.

12 They that sit in the gate speak against me ; and I was the song of the drunkards.

13 But as for me, my prayer is unto thee, O Lord, in an acceptable time :
O God, in the multitude of thy mercy hear me, in the truth of thy salvation.

14 Deliver me out of the mire, and let me not sink :
Let me be delivered from them that hate me, and out of the deep waters.

15 Let not the waterflood overflow me, neither let the deep swallow me up.
And let not the pit shut her mouth upon me.

16 Hear me, O Lord ; for thy lovingkindness is good :
Turn unto me according to the multitude of thy tender mercies.

17 And hide not thy face from thy servant; for I am in trouble : hear me speedily.

18 Draw nigh unto my soul, and redeem it : deliver me because of mine enemies.

19 Thou hast known my reproach, and my shame, and my dishonour:
Mine adversaries are all before thee.

20 Reproach hath broken my heart ; and I am full of heaviness:
And I looked for some to take pity, but there was none ;
And for comforters, but I found none.

21 They gave me also gall for my meat; and in my thirst they gave me vinegar to drink.

22 Let their table become a snare before them :
And that which should have been for their welfare, let it become a trap.

23 Let their eyes be darkened, that they see not ; and make their loins continually to shake.

24 Pour out thine indignation upon them, and let thy wrathful anger take hold of them.

25 Let their habitation be desolate ; and let none dwell in their tents.

26 For they persecute him whom thou hast smitten ;
And they talk to the grief of those whom thou hast wounded.

27 Add iniquity unto their iniquity :
And let them not come into thy righteousness.

28 Let them be blotted out of the book of the living, and not be written with the righteous.

29 But I am poor and sorrowful: let thy salvation, O God, set me up on high.

30 I will praise the name of God with a song, and will magnify him with thanksgiving.

31 This also shall please the Lord better than an ox, or bullock that hath horns and hoofs.

32 The humble shall see this, and be glad: and your heart shall live that seek God.

33 For the Lord heareth the poor, and despiseth not his prisoners.
34 Let the heaven and earth praise him, the seas, and every thing that
   moveth therein.
35 For God will save Zion, and will build the cities of Judah:
   That they may dwell there, and have it in possession.
36 The seed also of his servants shall inherit it:
   And they that love his name shall dwell therein.

A deeply plaintive song. It is seven times quoted (and no The title. other Psalm is so often quoted) in the New Testament as the utterance of Messiah. Why it is said to be *"On Shoshannim,"* we cannot tell, till we know more of what that instrument was. It seems to speak of joy ; and if so, it suits this Psalm so far that in it *sorrow ends in joy.*

The plan of it is very simple. There are three parts.

I. From verse 1–21, Messiah's sufferings are related by him- The contents. self. What an embodiment of " prodigious passion" in the cry " *Save me"* (ver. 1), from the lips of the Saviour ! Under the sea of wrath, sinking in the slime at the very bottom of this prisoner's dungeon (see Jer. xxxviii. 6), Messiah's voice is heard ascending to the Father. The " slime and mire" represent the loathing he felt toward sin. He is weary with crying, for in his true, real humanity he has all the experience of one in pain, who, during the slow, heavy hours of darkness and suffering, feels as if it were never to end. He is spent with calling on his God ; he is unsympathised with, for foes are on every side, and all this at the very time when he is not taking from them, but restoring the blessings which they had forfeited. (Ver. 4.) As to the *folly* and the *trespass* imputed to him, he lays it before God-

" Lord, thou knowest as to my folly" (לְאִוַּלְתִּי)

Thou knowest the history of the folly and sin laid to my charge, and why I stand charged therewith. He appeals to him as *able* to help, for he is " God of *hosts,"* and proved to be *willing,* for he is " God of *Israel"* (ver. 6). While it is out of love to man that he suffers, it is also to glorify God (ver. 7), "for *thy* sake." He " *weeps away his soul with fasting"* (ver. 10), for the good of men, and yet they mock at him. He pours his sorrows into the bosom of his God (ver. 13), at a time when (perhaps in Nazareth) he was " *the song of the drunkard," i. e.,* the נְגִינוֹת *satire* (Ges.), as Job xxx. 9, Lam. iii. 14.

> *" They who sat in the gate talk at me ;*
>   *And the songs of drunkards* (do the same)."
> *" As for me, I pray to thee, O Jehovah."*

And then he adds (though the punctuation in our version gives
the sense differently), in a passage which Isaiah xlix. 8 seems
to refer to—

> *" O God, in an acceptable time (i. e.,* a time when thou art favourable),
>   *In the multitude of thy mercy, in the truth of thy salvation,*
>   *Answer me ! "*

Hear and answer me when thou seest fit, when thou art well-
pleased. Let there be a time of acceptance. Jehovah, in Isa.
xlix. 8, replies to this cry—" In *an acceptable time I have
heard thee"*—well pleased with thy work, I give thee all thy
desire. The cry at verses 14–16 is parallel to Heb. v. 7, and
the complaint of want of sympathy (ver. 20) reminds us how
even his three favoured disciples fell asleep during his agony ;
for here he seeks comforters with the cross in view (ver. 21).
True, his whole life might be said to be a life in which he fed
on gall, and drank vinegar, grief and bitterness being the everyday portion of the Man of Sorrows—still, the chief reference
is to his life's closing scene, the scene of Calvary. And hence,
immediately after this, the strain changes, and we find ourselves in another scene. He has finished his work ; and they
who crucified Him have gone away unmoved.

II. From ver. 22–28, the theme is, how these sufferings of
Messiah become the *" savour of death"* to the unbelieving.
It resembles Prov. i. 22, 23. He gives them up, saying, *" Let
their table become a snare to them,"* since they give the Beloved Son only gall and vinegar, *" and for a recompence and
for a trap."*—(So *Mendelssohn* apud *Phillips*, and many others;
and so Rom. xi. 9). Ruin overtakes them at unthought-of
moments, like 1 Kings xiii. 20, in the case of the disobedient
prophet ; and their *" habitation is desolate,"* as Matt. xxiii. 38
emphatically threatens.* The cup of iniquity is filling up, drop
by drop, and Messiah does not interfere, but on the contrary,
says to Him who records it in his book, " Add iniquity to

---

* It has been proposed to understand " their *Table* " as *the altar* (Mal. i. 7),
and then the sentence is, " Let the letter kill them, since they refuse the spirit
let their ceremonial institutions become a trap to them ! " Their " *habitation*"
is the word in 2 Chron. vi. 54, for the enclosures fenced off for the sons of Aaron.

iniquity, and let them never be justified." Such is the " *savour of death.*" Instead of " *Come* to me !" it is now, " Let them *not* come !"

III. From ver. 29–36, the theme is, " *the savour of life*" from Messiah's sufferings. Himself is delivered and glorified, accepted of Jehovah as full type of, or fulfiller of every sacrifice of clean animals, " ox, and horned bullock with cloven hoof," (ver. 31). The sinner who ceases from self, " *the humble,*" finds herein his source of joy, his acceptance with God. Men everywhere over all the earth may thus be blessed in him ; and heaven and earth rejoice over the consummation. Israel, who once rejected him, shall then be his, proving that he can soften the most hardened, and pardon the most guilty. Such, then, is this Psalm-

Messiah's manifold sufferings a savour of death to the Unbelieving, and of life to the Believing.

Psalm 70

To the chief Musician. A Psalm of David, to bring to remembrance

1 Make haste, O God, to deliver me ; make haste to help me, O Lord.
2 Let them be ashamed and confounded that seek after my soul :
  Let them be turned backward, and put to confusion, that desire my hurt.
3 Let them be turned back for a reward of their shame that say, Aha! aha!
4 Let all those that seek thee rejoice and be glad in thee :
  And let such as love thy salvation say continually, Let God be magnified.
5 But I am poor and needy : make haste unto me, O God :
  Thou art my help and my deliverer ; O Lord, make no tarrying.

It has been said by some that this Psalm is a prayer upon the 69th. It may be so taken. The title seems to mean, a Psalm " *to put God in mind*"—Messiah himself being the chief of God's *Remembrancers.* Compare this לְהַזְכִּיר with Isa. lxii. 6, where they who pray unceasingly are called הַמַּזְכִּרִים אֶת יְהֹוָה. The words are adopted from Psalm xl. 13.

The title.

We have in verse 1, the cry ; in verses 2, 3, a reason for the cry being heard, viz. the guilt of his foes ; in verse 4, another reason for the same, viz. the benefit of those that love the Lord ; in verse 5, a third reason, viz. his own claims on God for deliver-

The contents.

ance from this state of humiliation and sorrow. And thus the cry rises up to heaven on the wings of three strong arguments certain to be answered in *" The Glory that was to follow,"* implied in the *" help."*

Christ and
his members.It is such a Psalm as every member of the Church has often had occasion to use, in sympathy with David, and in which he is sympathised with by the Son of David, whether asking present help or hastening to the day of his Coming, which brings full help and deliverance—" Tarry not !" But still, it is most of all Messiah whose voice is heard here. It might be called, in reference to Heb. v. **7,**

One of the Righteous One's strong cries for speedy help.

Psalm 71

1 In thee, O Lord, do I put my trust: let me never be put to confusion.
2 Deliver me in thy righteousness, and cause me to escape:
Incline thine ear unto me, and save me.
3 Be thou my strong habitation, whereunto I may continually resort:
Thou hast given commandment to save me; for thou art my rock and my fortress.
4 Deliver me, O my God, out of the hand of the wicked,
Out of the hand of the unrighteous and cruel man.
5 For thou art my hope, O Lord God: thou art my trust from my youth.
6 By thee have I been holden up from the womb:
Thou art he that took me out of my mother's bowels:
My praise shall be continually of thee.

7 I am as a wonder unto many; but thou art my strong refuge.
8 Let my mouth be filled with thy praise, and with thy honour all the day.
9 Cast me not off in the time of old age; forsake me not when my strength faileth.
10 For mine enemies speak against me;
And they that lay wait for my soul take counsel together,
11 Saying, God hath forsaken him: persecute and take him; for there is none to deliver him.
12 O God, be not far from me! O my God, make haste for my help.
13 Let them be confounded and consumed that are adversaries to my soul;
Let them be covered with reproach and dishonour that seek my hurt.

14 But I will hope continually, and will yet praise thee more and more.
15 My mouth shall shew forth thy righteousness
And thy salvation all the day;
For I know not the numbers thereof.

16 I will go in the strength of the Lord God:
   I will make mention of thy righteousness, even of thine only.
17 O God, thou hast taught me from my youth:
   And hitherto have I declared thy wondrous works.
18 Now also when I am old and greyheaded, O God, forsake me not;
   Until I have shewed thy strength unto this generation,
   And thy power to every one that is to come.
19 Thy righteousness also, O God, is very high,
   Who hast done great things. O God, who is like unto thee!
20 Thou, which hast shewed me great and sore troubles, shalt quicken me
   again,
   And shalt bring me up again from the depths of the earth.
21 Thou shalt increase my greatness, and comfort me on every side.
22 I will also praise thee with the psaltery, even thy truth, O my God:
   Unto thee will I sing with the harp, O thou Holy One of Israel.
23 My lips shall greatly rejoice when I sing unto thee;
   And my soul, which thou hast redeemed.
24 My tongue also shall talk of thy righteousness all the day long:
   For they are confounded, for they are brought unto shame, that seek my
   hurt.

The Third Part of the Book of Psalms (according to the Jewish division) begins, not inappropriately, with a plaintive yet pleasant song for the time of our sojourning here, embracing both prospect and retrospect. Our Head could sing it too, when in all our affliction he was afflicted. It will be asked, however, how Christ could use such verses as verses 9 and 18, since these look forward apparently to the frailty of age. The reply to this felt difficulty is, that these expressions are used by him in sympathy with his members, and in his own case denote the state equivalent to age. *His* old age was ere he reached three-and-thirty years, as John viii. 57 is supposed to imply; for "worn-out men live fast." Barclay seems to give the right sense in the following lines: The tone and the singer. References to old age.

> "Grown old and weak with pain and grief
> Before his years were half complete.*

Besides, the words signify, "Forsake me not from this time

---

* Parkhurst (*apud* Fry), remarks, that זָקֵן, "old age," rather expresses the effect that age has on the body, than the time of life. Gesenius gives "decrepit, the chin hanging down," as the radical meaning, and compares it with the Latin "*senex*," which is said to be an abbreviation of "*seminex*," half-dead. In verse 18, also, שֵׂיבָה is the head grown white.

onward, even were I to live to grey hairs." This is a view that conveys precious consolation to aged ones, who might be ready to say that Christ could not altogether enter into their feelings, having never experienced the failing weakness of age, the debility, the decay, the bodily infirmities so trying to the spirit. But this Psalm shews us that in effect he did pass through that stage of our sojourning, worn out and wasted in bodily frame and feeling, by living so much in so short a time. The aged members of his Church may find his sweet sympathy breathed out in Isaiah xlvi. 3, 4 ; and here they may almost see him learning the lesson in a human way, as he bends under the weight of our frailties. For this reason, among others, this psalm was specially prized by Robert Blair, one of our godly forefathers. He used to call it "*His psalm.*"

Such expressions as verse 6, "continually," verse 8, "all the day," verse 15, "all the day," may be illustrated by Augustine's comment :- "In prosperis, quia consolaris ; in adversis, quia corrigis ; antequam essem, quia fecisti ; quum essem, quia salutem dedisti : quum peccâssem, quia ignovisti, quum conversus essem, quia adjuvisti : quum perseverâssem, quia coronâsti."

The plan.

The plan of the Psalm is interesting. We have, from verses 1–4, prayer ; verses 5–8, motives for confidence ; verses 9–13, prayer ; verses 14–17, confidence expressed ; verse 18, prayer ; verse 19 to end, confidence largely declared.

Verse 7.

In verse 7, "*wonder*" is *q. d.*, a monster, a prodigious sight.

Verse 16.

We are to understand verse 16 a little differently from our version. It may read thus (as lxvi. 13)

> "*I will go forward* (thinking) *upon the mighty deeds of the Lord Jehovah.*
>
> *I will celebrate thy righteousness* (in working these mighty deeds); *Thee alone!*"

Giving no glory to human skill and valour (Psalm xliv. 3), and finding in Jehovah himself alone a sufficient theme for praise, the Head and every member journeys on. His trust and theirs look to the power, and wisdom, and love of him who guides the vessel, not boasting of the frail vessel's strength to buffet the billows of a tempest-lashed ocean.

There are precious glimpses given us of Messiah's childhood *Messiah.* in verses 5, 6, 17, when we listen to this Psalm as sung by his lips. And then in the close, from verse 20 to 24, *resurrection-deliverance* is the theme. The Head has enjoyed all that he anticipated ; the members as surely will. Do we not see *Messiah and* (verses 22–24) the ransomed company—the hundred and forty- *his company.* four thousand with the Lamb—on Mount Zion, and hear the harpers harping with their harps in that day's unclouded bliss ?

" *I, too* (as well as angels), *praise thee with the psaltery,*
 Thy truth, O God !
I chant thee with the harp,
 O Holy One of Israel !
My lips rejoice when I sing of thee,
 And my soul which thou hast redeemed.
Yea, my tongue (as well as that of angels) *all the day speaketh of thy righteousness* (see verse 16):
For put to shame, sunk in confusion, are they who sought my hurt ! "

Antichrist and all foes are for ever ruined ; Christ and his Church triumph and reign. This is the anticipation that leads to these closing strains of rapturous exultation.

We may refer to Hebrews iii. 6, as suggesting the substance of the whole Psalm ; for what else is it than

The Righteous One's confidence of hope to the end ?

Psalm 72

A Psalm for Solomon

1 Give the king thy judgments, O God, and thy righteousness unto the king's son.
2 He shall judge thy people with righteousness, and thy poor with judg-ment.
3 The mountains shall bring peace to the people, and the little hills, by righteousness.
4 He shall judge the poor of the people, he shall save the children of the needy,
And shall break in pieces the oppressor.
5 They shall fear thee as long as the sun and moon endure, throughout all generations.
6 He shall come down like rain upon the mown grass: as showers that water the earth.

7 In his days shall the righteous flourish ;
And abundance of peace so long as the moon endureth.
8 He shall have dominion also from sea to sea, and from the river unto the ends of the earth.
9 They that dwell in the wilderness shall bow before him, and his enemies shall lick the dust.
10 The kings of Tarshish and of the isles shall bring presents :
The kings of Sheba and Seba shall offer gifts.
11 Yea, all kings shall fall down before him, all nations shall serve him.
12 For he shall deliver the needy when he crieth ; the poor also, and him that hath no helper.
13 He shall spare the poor and needy, and shall save the souls of the needy.
14 He shall redeem their soul from deceit and violence :
And precious shall their blood be in his sight.
15 And he shall live, and to him shall be given of the gold of Sheba :
Prayer also shall be made for him continually ; and daily shall he be praised.
16 There shall be an handful of corn in the earth upon the top of the mountains ;
The fruit thereof shall shake like Lebanon :
And they of the city shall flourish like grass of the earth.
17 His name shall endure for ever ! his name shall be continued as long as the sun :
And men shall be blessed in him : all nations shall call him blessed.
19 Blessed be the Lord God, the God of Israel, who only doeth wondrous things.
19 And blessed be his glorious name for ever :
And let the whole earth be filled with his glory. **Amen, and Amen.**
20 The prayers of David the son of Jesse are ended.

The title. As ל in all the other titles expresses the order, the title, לִשְׁלֹמֹה is by many (such as Rosenmuller, Tholuck, Hengstenberg) rendered, " A Psalm of Solomon." But what then of verse 20 ? It seems to leave just one alternative ;—the Psalm is not David's *directly* (uttered, as some think, in connection with 2 Sam. xxiii. 1–5), but it must be David's *indirectly ;* dictated *to Solomon,* and given forth *by Solomon,* who received it at David's lips for this end, and who says in the end, that his father's prayer will all be completely answered when this scene is realised. It would not ill suit the events of 1 Kings i., and it may be that the Holy Spirit gave this song to David's harp, as he resigned it to Solomon along with his crown, on occasion of his coronation in the *valley of Gihon,* so near the *Upper Pool* where Isaiah afterwards stood foretelling the birth of Immanuel, the true Solomon.

In verse 1 the subjects pray for their King, the Church for her Head, as in Psa. xx. They ask that their anointed King, who is the Son of the King of kings,* may be sent forth to govern them. They ask this by requesting that all regal authority may be entrusted to him, and all regal qualifications imparted. They are referring, in this request, to the Lord's revealed will, to his decree given forth in Psa. ii. 6, **7**, 8. It is as if they said, `The plan.`

> " *Put thy statute-book into the hands of Him who is our King ;*
> *Clothe Him, thine own Son, with righteousness, that royal robe !*"

At the same time, it may be the Psalmist himself praying— David for Solomon, Messiah for himself. And then follows the glowing picture of anticipated blessedness, when this king begins his reign of righteousness. Israel's poets and prophets know of no golden age of which the very centre and life is not Messiah, God incarnate. Restored paradise has streams ; Messiah is their fountain-head. Restored paradise must have an Adam that cannot fall, that its scenes may never suffer blight, nor its bowers be invaded by the old serpent the devil. Dr Allix rightly speaks of this Psalm being that of " The Church and synagogue concerning the glorious kingdom of Messiah at his Second Coming." How intensely tranquil, and yet intensely glowing, are all the scenes ! If it be true that the mediæval hymn, " Dies iræ, dies illa," (a hymn of man's composition), has exerted a solemnising and overawing influence upon thousands in whose ears it has been sung, sh uld not this glorious burst of song leave its never-effaced impressions of noon-bright hope, soon to be realised, on every saint who has a heart to feel ?

The hills and mountains (ver. 3) prominent in Israel's land, the hills and mountains, too, of earth at large, generally so barren, hills and mountains on which the feet of other messengers have often stood (Isa. xl. 9), but never any messengers so blest as those that visit them now—these hills and mountains display the signs of peace, viz., abundant produce, " *because of righteousness*"—because the Righteous One has come to dwell in this New Earth. Antichrist and all oppressors are

* On Turkish coins, says Philipps, we find, " Sultan, son of the Sultan."

overthrown (ver. 4) ; earth's thick-peopled regions fear Him, and shall go on fearing him in peace, so long as sun and moon remain, that sun and moon which at creation's dawn were appointed to light up earth and guide men to keep holy festivals to the Lord, (Gen. i. 14). The Lord Jesus is there. Like " plenty-dropping showers" that reach the very roots of the mown grass (ver. 6), so is He to the earth after it has been shorn by the scythe of war, and every form of ruin and wrath. He revives it, as summer's genial rains cause grass to spring up in new vigour, clothing the soil with a richer and thicker mantle of verdure than before—as Layard* tells us how in the season of spring the dusty soil of Mesopotamia will change its aspect, in one night the tame plains turning to a bright scarlet, or to deepest blue through the burst of flowers, while the meadows put on the emerald green of the most luxuriant pastures, causing even the wild Bedouin, as he riots in the rich herbage and scented air, to exclaim, " What delight has God given us equal to this!"

The wealth of opposite nations, Sheba and Seba (Meroe and Arabia), is consecrated to Him, as they bring ." gifts" (ver. 10), or tribute, 2 Kings iii. 4.

> " *The swart Sabeans and Panchaia's king*
> *Shall cassia, myrrh, and sacred incense bring ;*
> *All kings shall homage to The King afford ;*
> *All nations shall receive him for their Lord.*" (Sandys.)

He is the true Job (see xxix. 12) who delivers the poor (ver. 12) ; " he looks with pity upon" (Fry), or " *sympathises with*" (Horsley), the poor and needy (ver. 13). He redeems them from Satan's *craft* and *cruelty*, from Satan as the serpent, and Satan as the lion, " from deceit and from violence."

We agree with Keble's hint in his metrical version of this book, that verse 15 refers to the well-known salutation offered to kings, " O king, live for ever." It runs thus-

> " *Yes, let him live !*
> *And the gold of Sheba be given him !*
> *And let him pray for* every one *continually.*"

The pronoun of the third person ו is used to express " every one," viz., every one of his subjects. They adore him and worship ; he intercedes and acts as mediator to them for ever.

* *Discoveries in Nineveh and Babylon*, pp. 273 and 301.

And what sights of strange fertility and beauty shall be seen, as indicated by verse 16 ! corn to the summit of the hills rustling like cedar boughs on Lebanon ; while *The City*, the metropolis (Psa. lxxxvii.), flourishes in population like the numberless blades of grass, all holy, all praising their King, presenting the spectacle of a *model-city* to the world.

And now is fulfilled to the utmost the promise made to Abraham, " in thy seed shall all nations of the earth be blessed" (Gen. xxii. 18), so oft repeated ; for Messiah's name (ver. **17**) "*produces posterity,*" *i. e.*, renovates itself, acquiring fresh vigour, "*for ever*" (Hengst.). All nations are blessed in him, and all call him blessed.

Sing, then, as verses 18, 19, sing with heart and voice **for** evermore-

> " *Blessed be Jehovah !*
> *God* (without a rival), *God of Israel !*
> *Who alone* (needing no help of any) *doeth wondrous works.*
> *And blessed be his glorious name for ever and ever !*
> *Yea, let the whole earth be filled with his glory !*
> *Amen, and amen !*"

The prospect of this consummation fills the heart of the **Sweet** Singer of Israel ; it leaves him nothing more to wish for. **He** has reached the height and summit of desire and hope. **Per-** haps the last words of verse 19 should be joined to verse **20,** and run thus-

וְאָמֵן כָּלוּ תְפִלּוֹת

דָּוִד בֶּן־יִשָׁי

The "*Amen*" of the whole Psalm falls on his ear from his own harp strings, and he catches it up and repeats it thus—" **Yea,** amen ! the prayers are ended of David the son of Jesse."

> " So let it be ! Thy will on earth now done,
> No more to seek has David, Jesse's son."

And thus it is that an individual's own peculiar desires shall all be satisfied in that kingdom, satisfied because absorbed in the flood of bliss. Who is there that ever takes up the for- mer Psalm or the next, wearied, faint-hearted, and despond- ing ? Look forward and see here

The Righteous One's hopes realised in the glory of the kingdom.

Psalm 73

A Psalm of Asaph

1 TRULY God is good to Israel, even to such as are of a clean heart.

2 But as for me, my feet were almost gone ; my steps had well nigh slipped ;

3 For I was envious at the foolish, when I saw the prosperity of the wicked

4 For there are no bands in their death : but their strength is firm.

5 They are not in trouble as other men; neither are they plagued like other men.

6 Therefore pride compasseth them about as a chain ; violence covereth them as a garment.

7 Their eyes stand out with fatness : they have more than heart could wish.

8 They are corrupt, and speak wickedly concerning oppression : they speak loftily.

9 They set their mouth against the heavens, and their tongue walketh through the earth.

10 Therefore his people return hither : and waters of a full cup are wrung out to them :

11 And they say, How doth God know ? and is there knowledge in the Most High ?

12 Behold, these are the ungodly, who prosper in the world ! they increase in riches.

13 Verily I have cleansed my heart in vain, and washed my hands in innocency.

14 For all the day long have I been plagued, and chastened every morning.

15 If I say, I will speak thus ; behold, I should offend against the generation of thy children.

16 When I thought to know this, it was too painful for me ;

17 Until I went into the sanctuary of God ; then understood I their end.

18 Surely thou didst set them in slippery places : thou castedst them down into destruction.

19 How are they brought into desolation, as in a moment!
They are utterly consumed with terrors.

20 As a dream when one awaketh ;
So, O Lord, when thou awakest, thou shalt despise their image.

21 Thus my heart was grieved, and I was pricked in my reins.

22 So foolish was I, and ignorant : I was as a beast before thee.

23 Nevertheless I am continually with thee : thou hast holden me by my right hand.

24 Thou shalt guide me with thy counsel, and afterward receive me to glory.

25 Whom have I in heaven but thee ? and there is none upon earth that I desire beside thee.

26 My flesh and my heart faileth :
But God is the strength of my heart, and my portion for ever.

27 For, lo, they that are far from thee shall perish:
Thou hast destroyed all them that go a whoring from thee.
28 But it is good for me to draw near to God:
I have put my trust in the Lord God, that I may declare all thy works.

A SORT of historical series begins here, relating to Israel's posi- *A new series.*
tion in the world (lxxiii.), to their temple (lxxiv.), their land
(lxxv.), God's deeds therein (lxxvi., lxxvii.), God's dealings in
days past (lxxviii.), Israel's desolation (lxxix.), and prayer regarding the same (lxxx.).

"*A Psalm of Asaph;*" perhaps one of those specially sung *The title.*
by Hezekiah's appointment at the altar (2 Chron. xxix. 30);
and what more fit to be sung there when the ascending smoke
and poured-out blood declared in type Jehovah's unspeakable
gift, and so seemed to say, "*Yes, God is good to Israel!*" (2
Chron. v. 13.)

How well it follows the last Psalm! As if Asaph had been *Connection*
singing it, and thereupon had felt all his surmises and faithless *and subject.*
fears dissipated by the triumphant prospects held out there to
the people of Messiah. It is a Psalm, not about Messiah himself, but about "*his people*" (ver. 10), about "*Israel*" (ver. 1);
about the members, not the Head. It is uttered in the presence of the Head; but it tells how its members have often
been nearly "offended in Him" (Luke vii. 23). Had Asaph
lived in Herod's day, such suspicious surmises as are expressed
in verses 3–9 might have been raised in his soul, by seeing
the Baptist first in the dungeon, and then in the tomb, while
Herod ruled and rioted in luxury. Horsley remarks on the
first word אַךְ, "It expresses the state of mind of a person
meditating a difficult question, in which he is much interested
and can hardly come to a conclusion."

Verse 4 should be rendered—"There *are no death-bands* *Verse 4.*
to them" (Horsley); "they are never fettered with death"
(Hengst.), *i. e.*, there are no death-bringing circumstances in
their lot. They escape the annoyances and reproaches which
God's people meet with (see 1 Cor. x. 13); their "*pride*" is
their "*ornamental* chain" (ver. 6), and, (ver. 7) "the imagination of their hearts overflows"—that is, speaks out, or vents
itself;

"*They speak of oppression from on high*" (ver. 9) (Hengst.); *Verses 6-9.*

as if they were out of reach of danger, aloft on their rock ; or as old Sandys renders the line, " They speak like thunder from the troubled sky." Hence,

" His people return hither" (ver. 10) ;

i. e., God's people return to the state of mind described in verse 2, or to this sight which causes the unbelieving surmises. To quote Sandys again, as giving the right sense—

" The good not seldom, through their scandal, stray."

How like a desponding man's words is verse 12, " Yet they prosper *for ever,"* or more literally, " *They are everlasting prosperers !"* But now, the likelihood of giving occasion to others to stumble crosses his mind ; and forthwith the same Spirit who suggested that consideration, leads Asaph *in his thoughts* (as some understand the words of verse 17) to the sanctuary. Standing there, the very thought of the Holy One on his Throne is enough to remind him of what must be the end of these ungodly ones ; but more especially is the remembrance that there is a *resurrection day*—a day when God will arise

and scatter these dreams of earthly felicity (ver. 20).

> *" O Lord, when thou awakest,* (see Psa, xvii. 15) *thou wilt despise*
> *their splendid show,*
> *As one does a dream, when he awakes out of it ! "*

Telling his grief and shame because of such unbelief, confessing himself a beast* or brute, he yet returns to sing that, notwithstanding all this, God has not forsaken him, and never will-

> *" And I continually am with thee !*
> *And thou holdest me fast by my right hand."*† (Ver. 23.)

I am in the wilderness, and thou art my guide, and wilt " *receive* me," as thou didst Enoch (Gen. v. 22, same word). The Hebrew words are rather obscure, but this may be because of

---

* Barclay, in his zeal to prove that every Psalm is Christ's words directly, falls into the strange error here of rendering בְּהֵמוֹת " *a lamb,"* as if parallel to Isaiah liii. 7. Hengstenberg has remarked, that בְּהֵמוֹת implies, (like other such plural forms) the *essence* of the *brute* character.

† Might it not be rendered (neglecting the accents), " *And with the hand thou dost hold my right hand ?"*

the ideas rushing through the mind of the Psalmist, so various and so fast. They are literally rendered thus-

> " *Thou wilt lead me by thy counsel.*
> *And afterwards, glory ! Thou wilt receive me ! "*

Not unlike Psa. xlix. 16—" God shall redeem my soul from the grave" (equivalent to "afterwards glory !") " for he shall *receive* me."

Thus God is "*the rock of my heart ;*" my heart rests on him as on a solid basis. All foes, and all prosperous wicked men, are from this point seen as ruined. No wonder. For has *glory* come ? has the *glory of the kingdom* dawned on us ? has the Lord himself welcomed us in ? has he given us a place beside himself ? Then, from this height we look down and see the impotency and ruin of Antichrist and all such opposers of God, "who *go a-whoring* from thee." (Comp. Rev. xvii. 5, "mother of harlots.") Meanwhile we *draw near* to God, re-enter paradise, enjoy our lost fellowship ; and our great employment is to praise Him, all clouds of providence being now cleared away, and no more unbelief to hinder our "*telling of all his works.*"

The glory.

The tone of this Psalm, especially of the latter part, is that of James v. 7, 8—" Be patient, brethren, unto the coming of the Lord." The prevailing topic may be said to be,

> " *Messiah's people almost offended in Him.*"

Psalm 74

Maschil of Asaph

1 O God, why hast thou cast us off for ever ?
  Why doth thine anger smoke against the sheep of thy pasture ?
2 Remember thy congregation, which thou hast purchased of old;
  The rod of thine inheritance, which thou hast redeemed ;
  This Mount Zion, wherein thou hast dwelt !
3 Lift up thy feet into the perpetual desolations;
  Even all that the enemy hath done wickedly in the sanctuary.
4 Thine enemies roar in the midst of thy congregations;
  They set up their ensigns for signs.
5 A man was famous according as he had lifted up axes upon the thick trees.

6 But now they break down the carved work thereof at once with axes and hammers.

7 They have cast fire into thy sanctuary,
They have defiled by casting down the dwelling-place of thy name to the ground.

8 They said in their hearts, Let us destroy them together:
They have burned up all the synagogues of God in the land.

9 We see not our signs: there is no more any prophet:
Neither is there among us any that knoweth how long.

10 O God, how long shall the adversary reproach?
Shall the enemy blaspheme thy name for ever?

11 Why withdrawest thou thy hand, even thy right hand? Pluck it out of thy bosom!

12 For God is my King of old, working salvation in the midst of the earth.

13 Thou didst divide the sea by thy strength:
Thou brakest the heads of the dragons in the waters.

14 Thou breakest the heads of leviathan in pieces,
And gavest him to be meat to the people inhabiting the wilderness.

15 Thou didst cleave the fountain and the flood: thou driedst up mighty rivers.

16 The day is thine, the night also is thine: thou hast prepared the light and the sun.

17 Thou hast set all the borders of the earth: thou hast made summer and winter.

18 Remember this, that the enemy hath reproached, O Lord,
And that the foolish people have blasphemed thy name.

19 O deliver not the soul of thy turtle dove unto the multitude of the wicked:
Forget not the congregation of thy poor for ever.

20 Have respect unto the covenant:
For the dark places of the earth are full of the habitations of cruelty.

21 O let not the oppressed return ashamed: let the poor and needy praise thy name.

22 Arise, O God, plead thine own cause:
Remember how the foolish man reproacheth thee daily.

23 Forget not the voice of thine enemies:
The tumult of those that rise up against thee increaseth continually.

The title. "*Maschil*" refers us to something (as elsewhere remarked) in the mode of setting the Psalm to music, or playing it on the harp, of which we know nothing. As in the last Psalm, so in this, *Asaph's* name appears. Some, however, suppose this *Asaph* to be a later individual of the same godly family. Patrick adopts the idea that he may have been the Asaph who was "*the keeper of the king's forest*" (Neh. ii. 8), and hence some of the allusions to the cedar-trees and the like. It is arresting

to the fancy to set before us *Asaph* led to compose this melancholy hymn amid some of the lonely woods of his now desolate
Land ! But all we can say is, that it certainly is the composition of an Asaph long after the days of David, who perhaps
was one of the family mentioned in Ezra iii. 10 (for 2 Chron.
xx. 14 is too early), and so *possibly* the very " *keeper of the
king's forests.*"

The desolation of Israel's land and people are spread before   The tone
the Lord. The Head of the Church, who wept over Jerusalem   and plan.
on the Mount of Olives, and lamented their too sure ruin,
could use these strains, and pour them into the Father's ear.
Every Israelite's heart would thrill in singing such a solemn
melody. Every believer's soul should fully enter into the sorrow for ancient Israel which is taught us here.

" *The signs*" of verse 4 and verse 9, are the holy emblems.
The significant pillars, " Boaz and Jachin," the brazen sea, the
altar, the lavers, mercy-seat with cherubims, candlestick, and
the like, all had disappeared. The standards of the enemy
appear in the sanctuary instead ! Oh how unlike (in significance as in form) the *vail* that hid the ark because Jehovah
was there, and the *ensigns* of *Babylon* that too surely proved
that Jehovah had forsaken his heritage ! The "synagogues"
may mean places where the elders met to exhort and pray
with the people. (Tholuck.)

In verse 5 some render the line to this effect :- " The enemy
makes himself look like, and known as, one who lifts up the
axe on the trees," applying it to the same subject as verse 6.
But our version gives the better meaning. When the temple
was building, every man that cut down a cedar on Lebanon to
help in the glorious erection was reckoned famous ; whereas
now, men have become renowned by using " chisel and club" in
destroying the carved work and tracery of the sanctuary walls.*

In verse 9, the " *no prophet*" is like Lament. ii. 9. In verse
11 we have " *Pluck* (it) *out of thy bosom* "—literally, כַּלֵּה,
" finish—destroy." It is meant to express something far more

---

* Barclay expresses the idea in another form :

" In former days of *Jerubbaal,*
An high renown was truly won,
By hewing down the groves so tall,
Where foul idolatry was shewn." (Judg. vii. 28.)

terrible than "*plucking the hand out of the bosom ;*" it is a cry for "*destruction on foes ;*" and, as Hengstenberg says, "the annihilation *proceeds from* the bosom of God, when his right hand is at the moment reposing." May we not add, "from *that bosom* whence came his Son !" just as the fire on Sodom was "out of heaven, from God." This appeal represents to our imagination the suppliant gazing upward on the bosom of his King, to see if that right hand begins to be plucked forth ! Thereafter, reasons of confidence are rehearsed. No less than *seven times* is the emphatic "אַתָּה" used, "the sevenfold *thou*" (Hengst.), while his deeds are set forth ; dividing the Red Sea, drying up the "ever flowing river" (ver. 18), and the like ; and forthwith the suppliant, as if thus anew invigorated to hope, urges his plea—

"*Give not up thy turtle dove to the greedy host,*" (Phillips). (Ver. 19.)

Applicable to other times.

If this Psalm was written by a later Asaph, the verse 20, which speaks of the *covenant* in connection with earth's dark *places*, might tacitly refer to such predictions as Isaiah lx. 1–3. The nations are said, in Rev. xi. 18, to be in the very condition spoken of here at the close, when the Lord arises to judge the earth, and to make the kingdoms become "*The Kingdom* of our God, and of his Christ." Israel's case will be attended to that day ; Israel's wrongs will be avenged ; Israel's sins forgiven ; Israel's sorrows relieved. That will be the day when this wailing appeal shall find at the hands of Him who hears the voice both of his own Son, our Head, and of the members of his Son, a full acknowledgment of this

The appeal of the scattered heritage to the mighty God of Israel.

Psalm 75

To the chief Musician. Al-taschith. A Psalm or Song of Asaph

1 UNTO thee, O God, do we give thanks, unto thee do we give thanks :
   For that thy name is near thy wondrous works declare.

2 When I shall receive the congregation, I will judge uprightly.

3 The earth and all the inhabitants thereof are dissolved : I bear up the pillars of it.   Selah.

4 I said unto the fools, Deal not foolishly! and to the wicked, Lift not up the horn !

5 Lift not up your horn on high : speak not with a stiff neck.

6 For promotion cometh neither from the east, nor from the west, nor from the south.

7 But God is the judge : he putteth down one, and setteth up another.

8 For in the hand of the Lord there is a cup, and the wine is red ;
It is full of mixture, and he poureth out of the same :
But the dregs thereof, all the wicked of the earth shall wring them out, and drink them.

9 But I will declare for ever ; I will sing praises to the God of Jacob.

10 All the horns of the wicked also will I cut off ;
But the horns of the righteous shall be exalted.

THE same Asaph takes the harp again, at the bidding of *The title.* the Holy Ghost, to write an ode that, like many of David's (see Psa. lvii.), has been marked " *Al-taschith*," and called, " *A Song*," lively in theme, and with life in every line.

" *We have praised thee, O God ! we have praised thee !*
And (now at length) *thy name is near,*
Thy wondrous works are telling it."

This is the delighted cry of Messiah's people, who see Him *The plan.* near at hand, and could join with Isaiah xxv. 9, " Lo ! this is our God !" Their hosannahs are becoming hallelujahs. And Messiah himself responds, as in Isaiah lxiii. 1, 2, explaining his ways. He refers to their words regarding " *his name being now near*," his long-hid discovery of his person and promised deeds, " *I will take a set time*" (Heng.), or rather thus :

" (It is so) *for I now get the appointed day !* (Acts i. 7.)
I (אֲנִי, unlike earth's usurpers), *judge uprightly.*
Earth and its inhabitants have melted away.
I am he who (אָנֹכִי) *have poised its pillars. Selah.*" (Ver. 2, 3.)

He has weighed the pillars and so knows, and has power to order earth. After a pause, Messiah opens his lips to utter the sentences of doom. He addresses the apostate nations, with Antichrist at their head (ver. 4)

" *I say* (אָמַרְתִּי, the word has passed my lips) *to the boastful,*
Boast no more," &c.

No help will come to you from *east or west, i. e.*, from land or sea ; nay, nor from the *wilderness* (מִמִּדְבָּר) shall any caravan bring you ought to lift up your head ;

> " *For God is judging now !*" (ver. 7).   (As Psa. lvii. 11,
>
> (כִּי אֱלֹהִים שֹׁפֵט.

And the processes of judgment are commenced, the rever al of unrighteous sentences, and the pouring out of that terrible " Cup" (ver. 8).   John (Rev. xiv. 10) saw this cup, full of " wine *without mixture*," *i. e.*, without one drop of water to alleviate its fierce poison ; but here it is "*full of mixture*," *i. e.*, of all strong ingredients, that make its taste more bitter, and its wrathful poison more sure.   This blood-red wine of vengeance is the measured-out portion of all earth's wicked, great or small.

At verse 9, Messiah seems to wind up the proceedings by indicating the general result.   As in Psa. ii. 7, a full announcement is made of these sentences in their hearing-

> "*And I* (אֲנִי, who am entitled so to do), *declare this a thing eternally fixed ;*"

and then turning towards his blessed ones, inviting them to join him in praise, he may be said to cry, " *Hallelujah !*"

> " *Let me sing* (אֲזַמְּרָה) *to the God of Jacob !*
>
> *And I will cut off all the horns of the wicked*" (while my song ascends).

As the final issue of the whole, lo !

> " *The horns of the Righteous One are exalted !*"

prophecy is fulfilled ; what Hannah sang of in 1 Sam. ii. 10, and so many others besides, is now come to pass ; for his " *name is near*," his kingdom is come.   And thus, referring all the while to the beseeching prayer of Psalm lxxiv., Asaph has sung

> *Messiah's response to his people who are expecting His Coming.*

Psalm 76

To the chief Musician. On Neginoth. A Psalm or Song of Asaph

1 In Judah is God known: his name is great in Israel.
2 In Salem also is his tabernacle, and his dwelling place in Zion.
3 There brake he the arrows of the bow, the shield, and the sword, and the battle. Selah.
4 Thou art more glorious and excellent than the mountains of prey.
5 The stout-hearted are spoiled, they have slept their sleep:
And none of the men of might have found their hands.
6 At thy rebuke, O God of Jacob, both the chariot and horse are cast into a dead sleep.
7 Thou, even thou, art to be feared:
And who may stand in thy sight when once thou art angry?
8 Thou didst cause judgment to be heard from heaven; the earth feared, and was still,
9 When God arose to judgment, to save all the meek of the earth. Selah.
10 Surely the wrath of man shall praise thee: the remainder of wrath shalt thou restrain.
11 Vow, and pay unto the Lord your God:
Let all that be round about him bring presents unto him that ought to be feared.
12 He shall cut off the spirit of princes: he is terrible to the kings of the earth.

MILTON celebrates "the inviolable saints," the holy hosts that guard the throne of God. But the family of saints on earth may claim that title equally with them, being invincible and inviolable in their King. Asaph sings of these "on Neginoth" (see Psalm iv.), and uses the lively "song" for his triumphant strains. *The title.*

He looks back upon the past, when God made himself renowned as Israel's God, dwelling on Zion, breaking there (שׁמּה, thitherward, like Ezekiel's "Jehovah-Shammah," xlviii. 35, q. d., his eye and heart ever toward them) the "flashing arrows of the bow," giving fame to Zion beyond all other hills and kingdoms. All was done by the God of Jacob for his people. The "Selah" (ver. 3) bids us pause to consider this, as it does again verse 9. By him "the stout-hearted were made a prey; they slept deep their sleep;" by him who could give foes the same "rebuke" that he gave to the swelling waters (Psalm civ. 7), causing the warrior and his war-chariot *The plan.*

to be alike motionless and dead in the silent camp. Ah, it is
" *Thou*" (אַתָּה) who art to be feared, *Thou* (אַתָּה) *alone!* And
we might have noticed also, there is significance in using the
name " Salem," (ver. 2). It reminds us of the reign of *Mel-
chizedeck*, and hints at the slaughter of the kings, whom God's
Abrahams overcome.

And ever shall it be thus. Ever shall it be an unanswer-
able question, " *Who shall stand before thee when thou art
angry?*" (verse 7), down to that great and terrible day when
all earth, at the sight of thy throne, shall ask, " Who shall be
able to stand?" (Rev. vi. 17). And then shall verses 8, 9, be
fulfilled most emphatically-

" *Out of heaven thou hast proclaimed judgment* (דִּין, see Dan. vii. 10,
דִּינָא יְתֵב).
Earth fears, and is at rest! (שָׁקְטָה, like Josh. xiv. 15, and Isa.
xiv. 7.)
*When God arises to judgment,
Saving all the meek of earth.* Selah."

Is not this the day when the Saviour comes to reign ?—the
day when the results of things shall best be seen—the day
when every saint with anointed eye shall see that events all
tended to the glory of their God—the day when they shall
sing better far than now,

" *Surely the wrath of man praiseth thee.
Thou girdest thyself with the remnant of wrath;* "

turning it to use, even every particle of it ?

Vow, then, and perform the vow, O Israel! a people near
to Him (Num. ii. 2). Bring a gift to him that is the true
object of fear, to him who has cut off, as in a time of vintage
(בָצַר, as Rev. xiv. 18), the breath, the life, of princes; to him
who is terrible to earth's kings. If this Jehovah be for us,
who can be against us ? Let us even now sing this

*Song to the Mighty One, who is the fear of Israel and of
Earth.*

Psalm 77

To the chief Musician. To Jeduthun. A Psalm of Asaph

1 I CRIED unto God with my voice,
Even unto God with my voice; and he gave ear unto me.
2 In the day of my trouble I sought the Lord:
My sore ran in the night, and ceased not: my soul refused to be comforted.
3 I remembered God, and was troubled:
I complained, and my spirit was overwhelmed. Selah.
4 Thou holdest mine eyes waking: I am so troubled that I cannot speak.
5 I have considered the days of old, the years of ancient times.
6 I call to remembrance my song in the night:
I commune with mine own heart: and my spirit made diligent search.
7 Will the Lord cast off for ever? and will he be favourable no more?
8 Is his mercy clean gone for ever? doth his promise fail for evermore?
9 Hath God forgotten to be gracious? hath he in anger shut up his tender mercies? Selah.
10 And I said, This is my infirmity.
But I will remember the years of the right hand of the Most High.
11 I will remember the works of the Lord: surely I will remember thy wonders of old.
12 I will meditate also of all thy work, and talk of thy doings.
13 Thy way, O God, is in the sanctuary! Who is so great a God as our God?
14 Thou art the God that doest wonders: thou hast declared thy strength among the people.
15 Thou hast with thine arm redeemed thy people, the sons of Jacob and Joseph. Selah.
16 The waters saw thee, O God, the waters saw thee: they were afraid:
The depths also were troubled.
17 The clouds poured out water: the skies sent out a sound:
Thine arrows also went abroad.
18 The voice of thy thunder was in the heaven: the lightnings lightened the world:
The earth trembled and shook.
19 Thy way is in the sea, and thy path in the great waters.
And thy footsteps are not known.
20 Thou leddest thy people like a flock, by the hand of Moses and Aaron.

"*For Jeduthun,*" the choir over which Jeduthun and Heman presided (1 Chron. xvi. 42). They are to sing now a plaintive psalm. Asaph's harp's strings are moaning to the chill night-wind. Instead of triumphing in the Mighty One, whom all must fear, Asaph is full of unkindly fears, fears arising from clouds around his soul. Our Lord on earth had such changes in his soul as we find in this Psalm. One day, under the   *The title.*   *The tone.*

opened heavens at Jordan ; another, in the gloom of the howling wilderness ; one evening, ascending the Transfiguration-
hill ; another, entering Gethsemane. And so with every member of his body. Not that the love of their God varies toward
them, and not that they themselves feel that love exhausted ;
but providences and trials of strange sort, and temptations
buffeting the soul, hide the sun by their dark mists.

The contents. We find, verses 1–4, *The time of darkness* pictured to us
most pensively and plaintively. " In the night my hand was
stretched out, and grew not numb, " (Alexander). And the
" Selah " in the midst of it, verse 3, seems to give us time to
observe the dismal plight of the soul.

In verses 5–9 we have *remembrance of former days*, leading
to the profoundly melancholy question—" *Has El* (the Mighty
God) *forgotten to be gracious.*"

> " Hath he in anger shut the spring
> Of his eternal love ?

And another " *Selah*" leaves us to pause and ponder.

At verse 10, *The cause of this darkness.* " This is my sickness," (Jer. x. 19). My present circumstances of body, and
the oppressive providences around, have averted mine eye
from God's love. Tholuck renders it, " This affliction of mine
is a change of the right hand of the Most High ;" but we prefer
another view, viz., after having mournfully admitted " This is
my infirmity," the thought flashes in, " *The years of the right
hand of the Most High !*" Yes, let me recall what he has done !

At verse 11, *The light breaks*—God is seen, still mighty to
save. Asaph is taught by " the years of the right hand of the
Most High," seeing " *his way in the sanctuary ;*" and in such
past "*wonders*" as Exod. xv. 11. *He sees God redeeming "the
sons of Jacob*" from their Egypt exile, and doing it so as to remind us of "*Joseph,*" once separated from his brethren, but afterwards the head of them all, (11–15). A " *Selah*" again bids
us ponder, and the Psalm closes by recounting some of his
wonders in providence. " God's *way in the sanctuary*" (ver.
13) suggests composing thoughts regarding his " *Way in the
Sea.*" (Ver. 19.)

There is a day coming when we shall, with Christ our Head,
sing of the Church's safe guidance to her rest, in such strains

as these, remembering how often by the way we were ready to ask, " Has God forgotten to be gracious ?" We are taught by the harp of Asaph, in moments of despondency, to " *remember the days of old,*" and assure ourselves that the God of Israel liveth—the God of the Passover-night, the God of the Red Sea, the God of the Pillar-cloud, the God of Sinai, the God of the wilderness, the God of Jordan,—the God, too, we may add, of Calvary, and the God of Bethany, who shall lead us as he led Israel, even when earth shakes again, till that day when he comes to cast some light on " his way that was in the sea, and his paths that were in the great waters, and his footsteps " that were a mystery. Asaph has been the instrument of the Holy Ghost to cheer us here, by bidding us look on this picture of

The Righteous One under the cloud recalling to mind the Lord's former doings.

Psalm 78

Maschil of Asaph

1 GIVE ear, O my people, to my law : incline your ears to the words of my mouth.

2 I will open my mouth in a parable : I will utter dark sayings of old :

3 Which we have heard and known, and our fathers have told us.

4 We will not hide them from their children,
Shewing to the generation to come the praises of the Lord,
And his strength, and his wonderful works that he hath done.

5 For he established a testimony in Jacob, and appointed a law in Israel,
When he commanded our fathers, that they should make them known to their children :

6 That the generation to come might know them, even the children which should be born ;
Who should arise and declare them to their children :

7 That they might set their hope in God,
And not forget the works of God, but keep his commandments :

8 And might not be as their fathers, a stubborn and rebellious generation,
A generation that set not their heart aright, and whose spirit was not stedfast with God.

9 The children of Ephraim, being armed, and carrying bows,
Turned back in the day of battle.

10 They kept not the covenant of God, and refused to walk in his law ;

11 And forgat his works, and his wonders that he had shewed them.

12 Marvellous things did he in the sight of their fathers,
In the land of Egypt, in the field of Zoan.

13 He divided the sea, and caused them to pass through ;
   And he made the waters to stand as an heap.

14 In the daytime also he led them with a cloud, and all the night with a light of fire.

15 He clave the rocks in the wilderness, and gave them drink as out of the great depths.

16 He brought streams also out of the rock, and caused waters to run down like rivers.

17 And they sinned yet more against him, by provoking the Most High in the wilderness.

18 And they tempted God in their heart, by asking meat for their lust.

19 Yea, they spake against God ; they said, Can God furnish a table in the wilderness ?

20 Behold, he smote the rock, that the waters gushed out, and the streams overflowed ;
   Can he give bread also ? can he provide flesh for his people?

21 Therefore the Lord heard this, and was wroth :
   So a fire was kindled against Jacob, and anger also came up against Israel ;

22 Because they believed not in God, and trusted not in his salvation,

23 Though he had commanded the clouds from above, and opened the doors of heaven,

24 And had rained down manna upon them to eat, and had given them of the corn of heaven.

24 Man did eat angels' food : he sent them meat to the full.

26 He caused an east wind to blow in the heaven :
   And by his power he brought in the north wind.

27 He rained flesh upon them as dust, and feathered fowls like as the sand of the sea :

28 And he let it fall in the midst of their camp, round about their habitations

29 So they did eat, and were well filled : for he gave them their own desire.

30 They were not estranged from their lust.   But while their meat was yet in their mouths,

31 The wrath of God came upon them, and slew the fattest of them,
   And smote down the chosen men of Israel.

32 For all this they sinned still, and believed not for his wondrous works.

33 Therefore their days did he consume in vanity, and their years in trouble

34 When he slew them, then they sought him :
   And they returned and inquired early after God.

35 And they remembered that God was their rock, and the high God their redeemer.

36 Nevertheless they did flatter with their mouth,
   And they lied unto him with their tongues.

37 For their heart was not right with him, neither were they stedfast in his covenant.

38 But he, being full of compassion, forgave their iniquity, and destroyed them not :
   Yea, many a time turned he his anger away, and did not stir up all his wrath.

39 For he remembered that they were but flesh;
A wind that passeth away, and cometh not again.

40 How oft did they provoke him in the wilderness, and grieve him in the desert!

41 Yea, they turned back and tempted God, and limited the Holy One of Israel.

42 They remembered not his hand, nor the day when he delivered them from the enemy.

43 How he had wrought his signs in Egypt, and his wonders in the field of Zoan:

44 And had turned their rivers into blood; and their floods, that they could not drink.

45 He sent divers sorts of flies among them, which devoured them;
And frogs, which destroyed them.

46 He gave also their increase unto the caterpillar, and their labour unto the locust.

47 He destroyed their vines with hail, and their sycamore-trees with frost.

48 He gave up their cattle also to the hail, and their flocks to hot thunderbolts.

49 He cast upon them the fierceness of his anger, wrath, and indignation, and trouble,
By sending evil angels among them.

50 He made a way to his anger; he spared not their soul from death,
But gave their life over to the pestilence:

51 And smote all the firstborn in Egypt;
The chief of their strength in the tabernacles of Ham:

52 But made his own people to go forth like sheep,
And guided them in the wilderness like a flock.

53 And he led them on safely, so that they feared not:
But the sea overwhelmed their enemies.

54 And he brought them to the border of his sanctuary,
Even to this mountain, which his right hand had purchased.

55 He cast out the heathen also before them, and divided them an inheritance by line,
And made the tribes of Israel to dwell in their tents.

56 Yet they tempted and provoked the most high God, and kept not his testimonies:

57 But turned back, and dealt unfaithfully like their fathers:
They were turned aside like a deceitful bow.

58 For they provoked him to anger with their high places,
And moved him to jealousy with their graven images.

59 When God heard this he was wroth, and greatly abhorred Israel:

60 So that he forsook the Tabernacle of Shiloh, the tent which he placed among men;

61 And delivered his Strength into captivity, and his Glory into the enemy's hand.

62 He gave his people over also unto the sword; and was wroth with his inheritance.

63 The fire consumed their young men : and their maidens were not given
  to marriage.

64 Their priests fell by the sword ; and their widows made no lamentation.

65 Then the Lord awaked as one out of sleep,
  And like a mighty man that shouteth by reason of wine.

66 And he smote his enemies in the hinder part : he put them to a perpetual
  reproach.

67 Moreover, he refused the tabernacle of Joseph, and chose not the tribe of
  Ephraim :

68 But chose the tribe of Judah, the mount Zion which he loved.

69 And he built his sanctuary like high palaces,
  Like the earth which he hath established for ever.

70 He chose David also his servant, and took him from the sheepfolds :

71 From following the ewes great with young
  He brought him to feed Jacob his people, and Israel his inheritance.

72 So he fed them according to the integrity of his heart ;
  And guided them by the skilfulness of his hands.

The title. *Maschil,"* referring to the music. " By *Asaph,"* who wrote
Psalm lxxiv.

Christ here. See Jesus in the ship, teaching parables. Compare him
that day by the sea-side with the Singer here, whose words,
though neither new nor dark, are yet meant to convey hidden meanings. From verse 2, compared with Matt. xiii. 34,
35, we are led to conclude that Asaph here was directed
to foreshadow Messiah, *the Prophet,* disclosing the mind and
ways of God, where these were hidden from the gaze of the
common eye. There is throughout this Psalm a " concealed
background of instruction" (Hengst.), intimated at verse 2, just
as Jesus, in speaking very obvious and plain things about the
seed and the sower, the leaven and the mustard-tree, meant all
the while to lead disciples to a " concealed background of instruction"—God's ways toward man, and man's toward God.

We can easily believe that our Master, in using this Psalm,
would not hesitate to say, verse 3, " *We* have heard," identifying himself with us ; for he does so in Psalm xxii. 4, " *Our*
fathers," yours and mine ; and he does so in the Prayer he
taught us, " *Our* Father in heaven," mine and yours. On the
other hand, in saying, verse 4, " *We will not hide them from
their children,"* is he not assuming the tone of Godhead ? for
it is the very same voice we hear in Gen. xviii. 19, " Shall I
hide from Abraham the thing that I do ?"

The contents He brings before us most affectingly God's ways in contrast

to man's ! Thus, verse 5, *God's mercies to the infant nation.*
Prophets, priests, Levites, Moses, the Tabernacle, all are implied
in " He set up a testimony in Israel ;" and all was meant to
make permanent among them the knowledge and love of the
glorious Jehovah. This was an act of grace; for verse 8 recalls
the perverseness of their fathers, "stubborn, rebellious, not
right, not stedfast with God." Truly, *His* ways are not our
ways ; and soon that after generation shewed their fathers' corruption, refusing to face Anak (ver. 9 ; see Num. xiii. 33, and
xiv. 1–4), and to go whither God would.

But, again, *His guiding mercies from Egypt onward* (ver.
17). How numerous ! every one how marvellous ! all so unde-
served, all so constant ! The Red Sea divided, the cloud, the
smitten rock ! Yet they provoked the Most High !

Again, *His un-upbraiding mercies* (ver. 18–29). The history
of the manna shews this—instinct with wonders of Grace ! for
see how the everyday shower comes to a people most ungrateful, and forgetful, and unbelieving ! " *Each man* did eat," as
Exodus xvi. 16 ; each had his omer every day.

Again, *His chastising mercies* (ver. 30–33). He tries them
with fatherly chastenings, and for a time the wayward children
feel. But these, too, avail not. Shall he then leave them ?
No, he has more kindness in reserve for them.

Again, he sings of *His long-suffering mercies* (ver. 34–41).
Amid frowardness, how very pitiful ! how tender ! how sympathising !

> " *For he remembered that they were but flesh,*
> *A wind that passeth away, and cometh not again.*
> *And all this while they insulted him.*" (" Set a mark on Israel's Holy
> One."—Hengst.)

But to deepen the contrast, he sings of *his judgments on
their foes* (ver. 42–53) ; and then of *Canaan-mercies* to themselves, (ver. 54- 58) ; and of *Canaan-chastisements*, (ver. 58–
64). What a God ! What a people ! How glorious in grace
the One ! How low sunk in sin the other ! How low must
mercy condescend in helping such a people !

But he has still another note to the praise of grace. *His
mercies in the days of David* (ver. 65 to the end), when the

Lord arose, resolved to throw down every barrier to his love, smiting foes, and erecting his tabernacle on its fixed seat at Jerusalem, and giving to his people David, the type of a better David yet to come-

> " *And he built his sanctuary, like lofty palaces ;*
> *Like the earth, he has established it for ever.*" (Ver. 69.)

This is ever to be a renowned spot, "morally gigantic" (Hengst.), and not to be as *Shiloh*, forsaken for ever. There are great things to come, awaiting that very spot. The type of the scene in David's days is not yet realised in full. At verse 70, the Singer has his eye on what Ezekiel (xxxiv. 23) has foretold,—the David and the Tabernacle of that coming day, when our "Beloved," led up from the Bethlehem manger to the throne, shall feed Israel and Jacob, with upright heart and skilful hand—dealing prudently, exalted, extolled, and very high. Grace shall reach its zenith then. Our earth shall bask under the hot noonday sun of grace, grace no more thwarted and slighted, no more forgotten and denied, no more disbelieved and hated. Come quickly, Faithful and True Witness ! Come quickly, and be again among us, not King only, not Priest only, but

Messiah, the Prophet, shewing us that God's ways are not our ways.

Psalm 79

A Psalm of Asaph

1 O GOD, the heathen are come into thine inheritance !
Thy holy temple have they defiled ; they have laid Jerusalem on heaps.

2 The dead bodies of thy servants have they given to be meat unto the fowls of the heaven,
The flesh of thy saints unto the beasts of the earth.

3 Their blood have they shed like water round about Jerusalem ;
And there was none to bury them.

4 We are become a reproach to our neighbours,
A scorn and derision to them that are round about us.

5 How long, Lord ? wilt thou be angry for ever ? shall thy jealousy burn like fire ?

6 Pour out thy wrath upon the heathen that have not known thee,
And upon the kingdoms that have not called upon thy name.
7 For they have devoured Jacob, and laid waste his dwelling place.

8 O remember not against us former iniquities :
Let thy tender mercies speedily prevent us : for we are brought very low.
9 Help us, O God of our salvation, for the glory of thy name:
And deliver us, and purge away our sins, for thy name's sake.
10 Wherefore should the heathen say, Where is their God?
Let him be known among the heathen in our sight,
By the revenging of the blood of thy servants which is shed.

11 Let the sighing of the prisoner come before thee!
According to the greatness of thy power, preserve thou those that are
appointed to die ;
12 And render unto our neighbours sevenfold into their bosom
Their reproach, wherewith they have reproached thee, O Lord.
13 So we thy people and sheep of thy pasture will give thee thanks for ever:
We will shew forth thy praise to all generations.

ANOTHER of the " Asaph-Psalms"—the cry, evidently, of *The title.*
widowed Zion in the ear of the righteous Judge ; such a cry
as our Head (Luke xviii. 7) describes the Church at large as
raising in the Latter Days. It suits alike the Church in Israel
in Asaph's time, and the Church scattered over earth in these
Last Days, and not less will it suit Israel in the days of their
final tribulation, (Zech. xiv. 1, &c.).

It tells of martyrdom (1–3), with a remnant left behind, *The contents.*
appealing to the Lord with somewhat of the awful power we
feel to be in the cry of the souls under the altar (Rev. vi. 9)—
q. d., " Pour out thy wrath on Antichrist (see 2 Thess. i. 8),
and on the nations that know thee not and that persecute thy
people,

" *Even as they poured out the blood of thy servants.*" (Ver. 3.)

When they confess (ver. 8) "*former iniquities,*" is not this in
the lips of Israel an acknowledgment of their forefathers' unbelief, when Jerusalem rang with—" His blood be upon us and
upon our children ?" It includes this, no doubt, and their
idolatry, too, presenting the long-expected cry spoken of in
Lev. xxvi. 45, on hearing which the Lord shall arise, and as
" *they are brought very low,*" shall fulfil Deut. xxxiii. 16,when
he seeth that their power is gone. " *Let the avenging of thy
servant's blood be known,*" (ver. 10).

When (ver. 11) we hear them plead, "*Let the sighing of the prisoner come before thee,*" we call to mind Manasseh in his Assyrian dungeon. We seem to see Israel taking Manasseh's position, and obtaining Manasseh's wondrous pardon. Nor are they like Manasseh only, but are, besides, "*children of death,*" בְּנֵי תְמוּתָה, that is, exposed to a *continuing death;* for תְמוּתָה is more than מוּת just as "*νεκρωσις*" is more than "*θανατος*" (see Beza on 2 Cor. iv. 10). And then there is "*the reproach*" that lay upon them, the essence of which (like the "reproach of Egypt," Josh. v. 9, Num. xiv. 13) had been, "Is God able to accomplish his promises? *Where is their God?*" (Ver. 16.)

Melody from freed souls bursts on our ear at verse 13. The old pastures, Sharon, Carmel, Bashan, are repossessed by the long-lost sheep; and this is the burden of the praise of these ransomed of the Lord, returning to Zion with songs and everlasting joy:

> "*And we are thy people, and sheep of thy pasture!*
> *We will give thee praise for evermore!*
> *We will record thy praise to all generations!*"

We, too, belonging to the Church at large, shall join in this hallelujah, and take part in this eternal song to the faithful Jehovah—that same incarnate Jehovah who once wept on the Mount of Olives, over Jerusalem ready to become heaps. With them, therefore, let us join in raising this

Cry of widowed Zion to the Righteous Judge.

Psalm 80

To the chief Musician. Upon Shoshannim-Eduth. A Psalm of Asaph

1 GIVE ear, O Shepherd of Israel, thou that leadest Joseph like a flock!
Thou that dwellest between the cherubim, shine forth!

2 Before Ephraim and Benjamin and Manasseh,
Stir up thy strength and come and save us.

3 Turn us again, O God, and cause thy face to shine; and we shall be saved.

4 O Lord God of hosts, how long wilt thou be angry against the prayer of thy people?

5 Thou feedest them with the bread of tears: and givest them tears to drink great in measure.

6 Thou makest us a strife unto our neighbours: and our enemies laugh among themselves.

7 Turn us again, O God of hosts, and cause thy face to shine; and we shall be saved.

8 Thou hast brought a vine out of Egypt: thou hast cast out the heathen, and planted it.

9 Thou preparedst room before it,
And didst cause it to take deep root, and it filled the land.

10 The hills were covered with the shadow of it,
And the boughs thereof were like the goodly cedars.

11 She sent out her boughs unto The Sea, and her branches unto The River.

12 Why hast thou then broken down her hedges,
So that all they which pass by the way do pluck her?

13 The boar out of the wood doth waste it, and the wild beast of the field doth devour it.

14 Return, we beseech thee, O God of hosts!
Look down from heaven, and behold, and visit this vine:

15 And the vineyard which thy right hand hath planted,
And the branch that thou madest strong for thyself.

16 It is burned with fire, it is cut down: they perish at the rebuke of thy countenance.

17 Let thy hand be upon the Man of thy right hand.
Upon the Son of man whom thou madest strong for thyself.

18 So will we not go back from thee: quicken us, and we will call upon thy name.

19 Turn us again, O Lord God of hosts, cause thy face to shine! and we shall be saved.

THE sun in the firmament shone cloudless on the field of Aus- The title.
terlitz, where a conqueror of earth was gaining his renown;
and that bright sun was recognised by the victors as a fit accompaniment of what they reckoned a day so glorious in its
triumphs. It may have been on this principle of suiting the
external symbol to the nature of the theme on hand, that the
temple musicians selected for this Psalm an instrument called
" Shoshannim-eduth." In Psalm xlv. we have mention of
" Shoshannim," and in Psalm lx. we have the " Shushan-
eduth," referring, as some fancy, to the joy or the lily-bloom
that shall overspread the land, when the nation that alone possessed God's " Testimony" should receive the answer of these
prayers. But more than this we cannot say.*

---

* It is a conceit of the Jews to mark the ע in verse 13, מִיַּעַר as the middle letter of the Psalter, by suspending it above the line of the other letters.

It is an Asaph-prayer again, full of pleas in Israel's behalf.
It is as if they had before them Isa. lxiii. 11, "Then he remembered the days of old." They call to his mind the days
of Joseph, when (Gen. xlix. 24) the Lord miraculously fed them
in Egypt. And then the *tabernacle-days,* when first, since the
days of Eden, the Lord was known to dwell between the cherubim, on the mercy-seat. They call to his mind *wilderness-
times* (ver. 2), when their march was gladdened by his presence,
" Ephraim, Benjamin, and Manasseh" looking on the Pillar of
Glory as it rose before them, the guide and partner of their
way (see Num. x. 22–24). " O God, bring us back again !
Cause thy face to shine ! and all shall be well again ! "

They appeal to his power, verse 4, " *O God of Hosts*" (ver.
4 and 7), and to his love for his people (ver. 4). Why smokes
thine anger, rejecting the smoke of incense that speaks of
favour ? Instead of joyful feasts (ver. 5), we weep sore, and
foes divide our substance for spoil, instead of the safety our
fathers enjoyed in serving thee (Exodus xxxiv. 24). " O God
of Hosts, bring us back again ! Cause thy face to shine ! and
all shall be well !"

Again the harp sounds to a melancholy reminiscence of the
past. Memory recalls the time when Israel was the *Lord's
Vine*—an emblem of him who is the True Vine. Taken out
of Egypt, and made to spread (Isa. v. 2), it filled the land.
The hills of Judah on the south, the cedar region of Lebanon
on the north (ver. 11), the great Mediterranean sea on the west,
and the Euphrates on the far eastern border, were all witnesses of the Vine's luxuriance. How desolate now ! " O
God of Hosts, come back, we pray ! Look down from heaven,
and see ! Visit this vine."

Some think that in verse 17 they are acknowledging *Messiah,* calling him by the name, " Man of thy right hand,"
" Branch made strong for thyself." The Chaldee Targum says,
this is " King Messiah." Others claim these names for Israel ;
for Israel is God's *Benjamin,* and God's strong rod wherewith
to rule the nations. The words are in the original such as
surely point to Messiah ; for they are not, " son of thy right
hand," but אִישׁ יְמִינֶךָ, " *Man* of thy right hand," and "*son of*

man whom thou hast made strong for thyself," בֶּן אָדָם ; in
this resembling Psalm viii. 6. Even if the terms were appropriate to Israel as God's favoured people, still there would be
here simply an allusion to that fact, while the real possessor of
the name is Messiah, God's true Israel. And if so, then verse
17 is Israel, in the Latter Day, crying "Hosanna !" to Christ,
and so entitled to what his words implicitly promised in Matt.
xx. 39—" Thou shalt not see me henceforth TILL thou shalt
say, Blessed is he that cometh in the name of the Lord." They
pray, " *Appoint Him* our captain—*let thy hand be upon him,*
designating him to his office, as Moses did Joshua," (Num.
xxvii. 23). And so they may claim to be gathered and blest
with a fuller blessing than their fathers, who, *by the hand of
God* upon them, were led up by Ezra (vii. 9), and Nehemiah
(ii. 18) ; for they claim as their leader Messiah, the true Ezra,
" Helper," and true Nehemiah, " the Lord's consolation." Is
not Psalm cx. 1 of itself sufficient to justify the name, "The
man of *thy Right Hand ?"*

> " *Jehovah, God of Hosts, bring us back !*
> *Cause thy countenance to shine on us !*
> *And we shall be saved,"* (נִוָּשֵׁעָה the response to " *Hosanna !"*
> הוֹשִׁיעָה נָא).

May we not sympathise in these appeals ? May we not put The Church.
in our own case with theirs ? Appoint, Lord, Messiah to be
our captain, our soul's leader, and we individually shall be
saved ! We cry, " Hosanna !" הוֹשִׁיעָה נָא, and thou wilt give a
response that shall make us shout back נִוָּשֵׁעָה. Yes, thy Church
in all the earth, Lord God of Hosts, with one consent joins in
presenting to thee,

Israel's pleas for full restoration.

Psalm 81

To the chief Musician. Upon Gittith. A Psalm of Asaph

1 Sing loud unto God our strength: make a joyful noise unto the God of
Jacob.
2 Take a psalm, and bring hither the timbrel, the pleasant harp with the
psaltery.

3 Blow up the trumpet in the new moon,
    In the time appointed, on our solemn feast-day.

4 For this was a statute for Israel, and a law of the God of Jacob.

5 This he ordained in Joseph for a testimony, when he went out through the
    land of Egypt:
    Where I heard a language that I understood not.

6 I removed his shoulder from the burden:
    His hands were delivered from the pots.

7 Thou calledst in trouble, and I delivered thee;
    I answered thee in the secret place of thunder;
    I proved thee at the waters of Meribah.   Selah.

8 Hear, O my people, and I will testify unto thee: O Israel, if thou wilt
    hearken unto me!

9 There shall no strange god be in thee: neither shalt thou worship any
    strange god.

10 I am the Lord thy God, which brought thee out of the land of Egypt:
    Open thy mouth wide, and I will fill it.

11 But my people would not hearken to my voice: and Israel would none
    of me.

12 So I gave them up unto their own hearts' lust: and they walked in their
    own counsels.

13 Oh that my people had hearkened unto me, and Israel had walked in
    my ways!

14 I should soon have subdued their enemies, and turned my hand against
    their adversaries.

15 The haters of the Lord should have submitted themselves unto him :
    But their time should have endured for ever.

16 He should have fed them also with the finest of the wheat:
    And with honey out of the rock should I have satisfied thee.

The title.   ASAPH is the writer of this Psalm. Whether or not it was written (as some suppose) for Hezekiah's passover, we need not stay to inquire (2 Chron. xxx. 2). It does not affect our view of the mind of God—the heart, the bowels of compassion, displayed in every line,—the breathing of tender love. The Lord is ever well pleased with such a cry as the two preceding Psalms sent up; for his heart is toward his people; and he here tells how he has longed over them, even in their back-slidings. It is " *on Gittith,*" like Psalm viii.

The contents.   In the first verses (1–3), is it the voice of Israel we hear? Is it not rather the voice of the Church's Head and Israel's, identifying himself with us and them ? Is it not Messiah, the lawgiver and redeemer of Israel ? To understand the speaker throughout to be He, gives beautiful unity and force to the

whole. It is He, we suppose, who summons them in these
lively, inviting strains :

> " *Sing loud unto God our strength !*
> *Raise the shout of joy unto the God of Jacob !*
> *Take music (מְרֵדָה voice and instrument), and bring the timbrel,*
> *The pleasant harp aad the psaltery !*
> *Blow the horn in the month* (*i. e.,* Abib., Exodus xii. 1.)
> *On the full moon, on the day of our feast* (*i. e.,* the Passover),
> *For this is a statute for Israel,*
> *A law in reference to* (לְ for the worship of.—Hengst.) *the God of*
> *Jacob.*" (1–4.)

Then mention is made of " *Joseph,*" because the Passover-
reference calls back to mind the days of Egypt, when Joseph
was Israel's shepherd in Goshen ; and it is said that this feast
was ordained for a " *testimony,*" viz., to the Lord's goodness
and sparing mercy.

> " *When he went out against the land of Egypt ;*" (to destroy it by
> plagues.)
> " *When I heard a language that I knew not ;*" (not the tongue of Israel,
> which is so well known to me, as one knows his friend.)

And having thus identified himself with Israel—the shepherd
with the flock—he speaks in his own name of what he wrought
for them. He took them from bondage,* at their going forth ;
and often did he reason with them, as at Sinai, when the
thunder's roar was heard from thick clouds that were the
curtains of his pavilion, and from the pillar-cloud-

> " *Oh ! hadst thou heard my voice alone !*
> *When thunders rolled above thy head,*
> *And lightnings flashed before thine eyes,*
> *When I of thee a trial made,*
> *Where, Meribah, thy waters rise !*" (Barclay.)

There is " *Selah,*" the pause for solemn thought, here. And
then the expostulation begins, tender, but earnest and searching (8–12), till, after saying verse 12, " *Let them go on in their*
own counsels," as Deut. xxix. 18, He seems to recall his words,
giving vent to that burst of impassioned feeling, verse 13-

* The burden and " the pots," or *clay-basket,* are remarkably illustrated
(says Tholuck) by the Egyptian sculptures, which still shew *Israelites carrying*
the clay and the tiles.

> *" Oh, if my people would hearken to me !*
> *Would Israel walk in my ways !"*

Revealing the very same Jesus whose words and tears, as he beheld Jerusalem, are reorded in Luke xix. 43. It is the same speaker that continues thus to tell what they have lost by their waywardness-

> *" I would soon have subdued their enemies,*
> *" The haters of Jehovah should have submitted unto him."*

And, on the other hand, *He* (Jehovah) *would have fed them with " kernelled wheat,"*—alluding to the rich old covenant promises, Deut. xxxii. 14, xxxiii. 14. All this (says Messiah), Jehovah was ready to do. Yes, these covenant promises, every one, even to the honey from the rock (Deut. xxxii. 13), I would have given thee in all abundance, till thou hadst not a want remaining.*

Thus from beginning to end, in this Psalm, we hear

The Redeemer of Israel's tender lamentation over his people's rejection of His grace.

Psalm 82

A Psalm of Asaph

1 God standeth in the congregation of the mighty ; he judgeth among the gods.
2 How long will ye judge unjustly, and accept the persons of the wicked? Selah.
3 Defend the poor and fatherless : do justice to the afflicted and needy.
4 Deliver the poor and needy : rid them out of the hand of the wicked.
5 They know not, neither will they understand ! they walk on in darkness ! All the foundations of the earth are out of course.
6 I have said, Ye are gods ; and all of you are children of the Most High.
7 But ye shall die like men, and fall like one of the princes.
8 Arise, O God, judge the earth ! for thou shalt inherit all nations.

The title.   ASAPH'S name is at Psalm l., in which the solemn scenes and expostulations of the Great Day are given ; and here, too, is

---

* The change of persons, "He" and "I," is quite natural, if Messiah is the speaker throughout. But, besides, we find such changes from the indirect to the direct frequently, *e. g.*, Exodus xxiii. 25, and Isa. x. 12.

his name, prefixed to this awfully authoritative rebuke and warning-

We see, verse 1, the Judge surveying earth's rulers.

> " *God hath placed himself in the assembly of the mighty.*" (Isa. iii. 13.)
> " *He judges in the midst of the gods,*" (*i. e.*, earth's judges, Exodus xxii. 28, John x. 34.)

We hear his voice (ver. 2), and we recognise in it him who speaks to us, " How long, ye simple ones," in Proverbs i. 26. The "*Selah*" completes it, giving a solemn seal to the words.

We listen again (verses 3, 4) ; he is declaring the rules that should guide them—rules on which the Judge himself has ever acted—defending the poor ; interposing where no help of man was on the side of the oppressed ; maintaining equity ; doing acts of disinterested grace and favour.

We are told of the contempt poured upon Him (ver. 5), for it is said, " *They take no notice*" (they disregard God and his Christ), &c. ; and as a consequence, " *The foundations of earth begin to totter,*" (comp. Isa. xxiv. 20) ; and we hear the voice of the Great Judge (ver. 6)

> " *I have said !* (אָנִי, *i. e.*, This is now your doom—I solemnly pro-claim it)
> *Ye are judges* (bearing the name of God, as verse 2) ;
> *All of you are sons of the Most High !*"

This is your great name, in which you rest secure. **But**

> " *Surely ye shall die, as other men have died ;*
> *Ye shall fall, as other men of rank have fallen.*"*

Your day is coming ! The saints are raising the loud cry of verse 8, inviting Messiah, the true God, the Son of the Most High (John x. 34), the Mighty One, the Judge and Ruler, to arise and take his *inheritance*, for he is the "*heir of all things;*" and to be the true Othniel, Ehud, Shamgar, Barak, Gideon, Tola, Jair, Jephthah, Samson, and Samuel, who will *judge*, or govern and rule, a mismanaged earth. We sing this song of Zion in his ears, urging him to come quickly ; and we sing it to one another in joyful hope, while the foundations of earth seem out of course, because here we find

Messiah the true Judge of a misgoverned world.

* " As *other* men," see note on Psalm lxxxvii.

Psalm 83

A Song or Psalm of Asaph

1 KEEP not thou silence, O God: hold not thy peace, and be not still, O God.

2 For, lo, thine enemies make a tumult: and they that hate thee have lifted up the head.

3 They have taken crafty counsel against thy people, and consulted against thy hidden ones.

4 They have said, Come, and let us cut them off from being a nation; That the name of Israel may be no more in remembrance.

5 For they have consulted together with one consent: they are confederate against thee:

6 The tabernacles of Edom, and the Ishmaelites; of Moab and the Hagarenes;

7 Gebal, and Ammon, and Amalek; the Philistines with the inhabitants of Tyre;

8 Assur also is joined with them: they have holpen the children of Lot. Selah.

9 Do unto them as to the Midianites; as to Sisera, as to Jabin, at the brook of Kison,

10 Which perished at En-dor: they became as dung for the earth.

11 Make their nobles like Oreb, and like Zeeb: · Yea, all their princes as Zebah, and as Zalmunna:

12 Who said, Let us take to ourselves the houses of God in possession.

13 O my God, make them like a wheel! as the stubble before the wind!

14 As the fire burneth a wood, and as the flame setteth the mountains on fire;

15 So persecute them with thy tempest, and make them afraid with thy storm.

16 Fill their faces with shame; that they may seek thy name, O Lord.

17 Let them be confounded and troubled for ever; yea, let them be put to shame, and perish:

18 That men may know that thou, whose name alone is JEHOVAH, Art the Most High over all the earth.

The title and the time. A *song* and *psalm* by Asaph; lively, yet solemn; for there is in it both victory and vengeance. The appeal of last Psalm to the Judge, by Asaph in the name of Messiah and his people, is of the same spirit with this more lengthened and full prayer by the same Asaph. The times are the same. Whatever were the circumstances of the Psalmist that furnished an appropriate season in the view of the Spirit of God for giving it to the Church—whether such as those of Jehoshaphat's reign

(2 Chron. xx. 14) or not—it seems probable that He who knew men's hearts saw more than once this same hatred to Israel taking the form of a combined conspiracy of all the nations round. Even thus has it been more than once in regard to Britain, the retreat of God's hidden ones ; and even thus, were the vail lifted up, might it be found to be true at this hour of the foes of Protestant truth. And yet more shall the Latter Day bring to view a combination of kings and people against the Lamb and his faithful few—a combination which shall meet with extinction on the plains of Megiddo, most fully realising the prayer and anticipations of this Psalm, verses 9, 10, 11. What a song for days when Antichrist shall be wondered at by all the earth ! It is pervaded by a tone of astonishment at the Lord's long-suffering.

From verses 1 to 8, where " Selah " introduces the pause, the The plan. prayer ascends, spreading before the Lord like (Acts iv. 29) the threatening aspect of his foes, who direct their malice against " his *hidden ones*" (ver. 3)—that is, his people, not unknown or obscure, but hid as his treasure. (See Psa. xxvii. 5.) They who were all jealous of each other, like Pilate and Herod, are friends now

> " *They consult from the heart with one accord* " (ver. 5).
> *They make a covenant against Thee !* "

A circle seems drawn round Israel's land ; the hunters have inclosed their prey—Edom and Ishmael on the *south ;* Moab and the Hagarenes who dwelt near Gilead (1 Chron. iv. 18), to the *east,* along with Gebal (i. e., *Gebalene,* which means the mountainous region, from the Arabic *Djebel,* the district whose capital was Petra, or Sela), and Ammon, and old Amalek ; and on the *west* Philistia and Tyre—all these call *Assyria* to their aid, to pour down from the *north* his resistless bands ! " *The children of Lot,*" the nations who, because of the relationship of their ancestors, might have been expected to befriend Israel, take the lead against Israel in this unbrotherly covenant.

But faith sees this armada scattered, as surely as was that of Spain on our shores.

> " *Treat them as Midian !*
> *As Sisera ! as Jabin !*
> *At the torrent of Kishon !*
> *At Endor they have perished !*
> *They have become dung for the soil !* (Ver. 9, 10.)

All this, at the very time when they are saying, " *We will take possession of these habitations of God*" (ver. 15), the cities of Israel, protected by their God.* The Lord answers their prayers—" *Make them like a wheel*" that threshes the corn and beats the straw to pieces (Phillips), or like the *thistle-down* in the whirl of the storm.

The end is like the issue of judgment so often declared by Ezekiel, *e. g.* xxx. 26, xxxv. 15, xxxviii. 23, xxxix. 28.

> " *Men seek thy name, O Jehovah !* (Ver. 16.)

And again-

> " *And they know that Thou—thy name alone is Jehovah !*
> *Most high over all the earth !*"

The Armageddon of the Last Days, ended by the Lord's appearing, when his feet stand on the Mount of Olives, and he recapitulates (so to speak) all the victories of ancient days in that one, shall result in the fame of the Lord being spread over earth, and his one name acknowledged. What a glorious answer to

The prayer of the Hidden Ones against the crafty **counsel** *of Messiah's foes.*

Psalm 84

To the chief Musician. Upon Gittith. A Psalm for the sons of Korah.

1 How amiable are thy tabernacles, O Lord of hosts!
2 My soul longeth, yea, even fainteth for the courts of the Lord:
   My heart and my flesh crieth out for the living God.
3 Yea, the sparrow hath found an house,
   And the swallow a nest for herself, where she may lay her young,
   Even thine altars, O Lord of hosts, my King and my God.
4 Blessed are they that dwell in thy house! they will be still praising thee!
   Selah.
5 Blessed is the man whose strength is in thee ; in whose heart are the ways
   of them.

---

* Stanley (Palestine and Sinai, p. 336), " pastures of God," or pasture-grounds.

6 Who passing through the valley of Baca make it a well; the rain also filleth the pools.

7 They go from strength to strength, every one of them in Zion appeareth before God.

8 O Lord God of hosts, hear my prayer: Give ear, O God of Jacob. Selah.

9 Behold, O God our shield, and look upon the face of thine anointed.

10 For a day in thy courts is better than a thousand.
I had rather be a doorkeeper in the house of my God, than to dwell in the tents of wickedness.

11 For the Lord God is a sun and shield: the Lord will give grace and glory. No good thing will he withhold, from them that walk uprightly.

12 O Lord of hosts, blessed is the man that trusteth in thee.

THOLUCK has suggested that this Psalm may have been sung at Mahanaim, during David's flight. But, at any rate, it is for all times. We are now with the Lord's "hidden ones" in their quiet land, where they wait on their God. We see here their joys, their earthly heaven. They may see at a distance *"the tents of the wicked,"* as Balaam from his rocks saw Israel's; but they feel no envy, they desire nothing of the luxuries there, they seek not the fame of being one of these "men of renown." Like the first Psalm *"on Gittith"* that we met with (Psa. viii.), this *" Psalm of, or for, the sons of Korah,"* * celebrates the excellencies of the Lord's name, for it presents us with the pleasant sight of a company of worshippers going up to the house of the Lord. *(The title.)*

That pilgrimage of Israel, to the place where the Lord had put his name, was significant of more than met the eye. It told of other pilgrims who should in after ages travel through the world with their heart toward the Lord, and their hope fixed on seeing him revealed at the end of their pilgrimage in another manner than they knew him by the way. It included, too, the journey of him who, as Chief of Pilgrims, was to take the same road, share the same hardships, feel the same longings, hope for the same resting-place, and enter on the same full enjoyment of the Father's grace and glory. *(The speakers.)*

It is, then, the *Just One and his members on their way to Zion, " the city of the living God,"* that forms the essence of the Psalm.

* The sons of Korah kept the gates of the tabernacle, 1 Chron. ix. 19. Hence verse 10 is peculiarly natural in their lips.

We have *their setting forth,* verse 1, 2. "*How beloved*
(יְדִידוֹת) *are thy tabernacles,*" they say to the "*Lord of Hosts,*"
in deeper feeling than Num. xxiv. 5, for they love the place
because they love the person. They speak to one another in
verse 2, "*Longing, yea, even fainting has my soul felt for
the courts of the Lord.*"

> "*My heart and my flesh sing for joy
> Toward God, the Living One!*"

We next find *objects on the way* attracting a moment's attention, and furnishing help to their thoughts, verse 3.

> "*Truly* the sparrow reaches her home,
> And the swallow her nest,
> Where she has placed her young!*"

And who is this sparrow? Is it not as Psalm xi. 2, a name for
the feeble homeless one? Who is this swallow, a wanderer to
another clime, though here for a time? It is the pilgrim himself (Hengst.). The pilgrim identifies himself with these birds
of the air, and perhaps thinks of his family while he sings of
the nest—

> "*Thy altars, O Lord of Hosts* (see Num. iv. 31, altar of sacrifice and
> altar of incense.)
> *My King and my God!*"

The pilgrim-sparrow has found *thine altars, O Lord of Hosts!*
The stranger-swallow has found *thine altars!* They could not
be a home for the birds, but they are so to him. There is the
home and the nest! That atoning altar of sacrifice speaks
peace! That golden altar of incense holds out acceptance
through the infinite merits of the sacrifice offered ; here is my
home, my nest ;† for here is God, my God and my king, who
will care for me, defend me, be all in all to me.

The pilgrim (verse 4, which is followed by the "*Selah*"-pause),
seems to *rest by the way*—he is under some fig-tree, at some

---

* This is a common use of נֵם, Job xviii. 5. "Yea (נֵם), the light of the
wicked shall be put out." So Ps. xxv. 3, and elsewhere.

† Our English version misleads the reader. The Hebrew does not mean to
imply that birds built their nests at the altars : the thing was a moral impossi-
bility. The French is good—"*Et moi quand verrai-je tes autels ?*"

well. He thinks of those who are never away from the Lord, and covets their bliss. But he rises up, verses 5, 6, *and journeys on,* comforted and strengthened by the thought that they are already blessed whose *" strength is in Thee"*—and

" In whose hearts are ways,"

pilgrim-ways, the roads that are cast up for travelling. Blessed it is to have the resolution to traverse these ways, instead of slothfully abiding at home (Jer. xxxi. 21). They are willing to endure hardship and inconvenience, taking what they find, less or more.

" Passing through the valley of Baca,*
They make it a well—
Yea, the pools which the rain has filled."

Little as there may be of water, that little suffices them on their way. It is a well to them. They find only *"pools* (which) *the early rain has* (barely) *covered"*—but are content with the supply by the way. It is as good and sufficient to them as if showers of the heavy autumnal rains had filled the well. Pilgrims forget the scanty supply at an Inn, when they have abundance in view at the end. Israelites going up to the Passover made light of deficient water, for their hearts were set on reaching Jerusalem. Our Elder Brother, the leader of the pilgrim-band, endured such hardships for the joy set before him —aye, even endured to be *"thirsty"* on the cross under infinite wrath—and in this he set us an example, as well as wrought out salvation.

In verse 7 we see the *arrival* of the pilgrims at the city.

In verses 8, 9, we hear their *prayer when* arrived-

" O God, see our shield ! (the position of מָגֵן is peculiar)
Behold the face of thine Anointed !"

Israel's *Priest* was *" shield and anointed"* to the worshippers ; *Christ* is all this in antitype. Christ himself could use this prayer. Identifying himself with the pilgrim-band, they might be supposed pointing to him and saying, *" Our shield look*

---

* Valley of tear-shrubs (Hengst.), or mulberries. Valley of lamentation, *Jammerthal,* (Gesen.)—some sterile, gloomy spot, on the way to Jerusalem, like that near the barren knoll of Scopos, where *Nob* once stood. Others suppose the spot where the mulberry-trees grew, 1 Chron. xiv. 15.

upon, O God !"   While he himself might be supposed second-
ing the plea by calling the Lord's attention to himself—"*Behold the face of thine Anointed One.*"

And now, verses 10, 12, you are made to hear the report of
the place given by those who reach it.   *Israelites* would thus
commend God's holy place to their fellows ; but they who reach
the kingdom, of which all this was the shadow, what would
they not say of the glory, and beauty, and bliss, and peace ?
If a day in the Lord's typical courts was so satisfying, what
would be a day in the kingdom ?   And if *one* day, what the
Eternal Day,—"*dies sempiternus, cui non cedit hesternus,
quem non urget crastinus ?*"   (August.)

> " *For the Lord is a sun and shield;*
> *God giveth grace and glory ;*
> *The Lord withholds no good*
> *From them that walk uprightly.*"

The Lord is all brightness and no gloom, and all safety.   He
gives " honour and glory," (see Prov. iv. 9, &c.).   He leaves not
one unsatisfied wish.   Not one in that kingdom but ever sings
(and O that all on earth heard it now !)

> " *O Lord of Hosts, blessed is the man that trusteth in Thee !*"

This is the heartfelt utterance of each one that has travelled
thither ; the testimony, ungrudging and unqualified, of

The Righteous One on his way to the city of the Living God.

Psalm 85

To the chief Musician.   A Psalm for the sons of Korah

1 LORD, thou hast been favourable unto thy land:
  Thou hast brought back the captivity of Jacob.
2 Thou hast forgiven the iniquity of thy people, thou hast covered all their
  sin. Selah.
3 Thou hast taken away all thy wrath:
  Thou hast turned thyself from the fierceness of thine anger.
4 Turn us, O God of our salvation, and cause thine anger toward us to cease.
5 Wilt thou be angry with us for ever? wilt thou draw out thine anger to
  all generations?
6 Wilt thou not revive us again! that thy people may rejoice in thee?

7 Shew us thy mercy, O Lord, and grant us thy salvation.

8 I will hear what God the Lord will speak:
For he will speak peace unto his people, and to his saints:
But let them not turn again to folly.

9 Surely his salvation is nigh them that fear him ; that glory may dwell in our land.

10 Mercy and truth are met together; righteousness and peace have kissed each other.

11 Truth shall spring out of the earth; and righteousness shall look down from heaven.

12 Yea, the Lord shall give that which is good ; and our land shall yield her increase.

13 Righteousness shall go before him, and shall set us in the way of his steps.

WHEN Israel ceased to be pilgrims to the city of God, the Lord *The title.* made them in another sense pilgrims and strangers, "tribes of the wandering foot and weary breast." The captivity of Babylon was only a foretaste of centuries of exile and oppression. But, on the other hand, the restoration under Ezra and Nehemiah is, after all, but a foretaste of the final restoration of that people, still beloved for their fathers' sakes. " *The sons of Korah*" sang this song, perhaps first by Babel's streams, and then at Jerusalem when the few thousands returned.

They pray for full deliverance, from verse 1 to 7. The *The contents.* burden of it is ; " Lord, thou hast in other times been gracious, thou didst in former days turn back Jacob's captivity ; thou didst forgive his sins"—pausing in the midst of the review, " *Selah*"—and then returning to their plea.

" *Wilt thou not quicken us again ?* (give us life again.)
And thy people (no more scattered) *shall rejoice in thee.*" **(Ver. 6.)**

And that " *life*" to them as a nation (תְּחַיֵּינוּ) is what Paul refers to as " *life* from the dead to the world," (Rom. ix. 15).

They get an answer, verse 8. The people as one body (Hengst.) suddenly hear a voice from the Holy One. "*Let me hear what God the Lord speaketh !*" It may be their *priest*, as representative of the nation, that says, אֶשְׁמְעָה " *Let me hear*," in which case we might see Christ, their long-rejected Priest, becoming their Intercessor, and bringing them the Lord's message from the true Holy of Holies. The nation is waiting, and their representative says, "*Let me hear*"—for it is worth hearing, it is glorious news,

> "*For he speaks peace to his people !*"

words like those of Jeremiah—"Thoughts of peace and not of evil !" But, besides, he seems to tell of their being instrumental, as "life from the dead," in blessing the nations ; for while he speaks peace, it is to Israel, but not to them only, it is to

> "*His people, and to his saints.*
> *And they shall turn no more to folly !*"

The time of millennial blessedness has come. The time for displaying grace to the full has come. Jew and Gentile shall meet, like David and Araunah, at the altar on Moriah.

> "*Surely,* (אַךְ *as Psa. lxxiii. 1*) *his salvation is near them that fear him,*
> *So that glory tabernacles in our Land.*"

The salvation of Israel has come out of Zion. The Saviour has come, the Redeemer, "*the glory*," in its fullest sense, antitype of the cloud of glory. And what a full display of divine perfections now in the salvation of Jerusalem-sinners, Mannasseh-sinners, unbelieving souls ! * The Redeemer is there, and hence "*grace and truth*" have met, for "*mercy* and truth" here, are the "*grace and truth*" of John i. 17, of which Messiah is the full vessel, the living fountain. "*Righteousness and peace*" also—for here is the true Melchizedec, who is "*first* king of righteousness, and *then* king of peace." The harmonised perfections of the Holy One shine bright over Israel restored ; these, guiltiest once of all unbelieving ones, illustrate in their conversion every attribute which the cross has magnified. They are received on principles of righteousness and truth, as well as love and mercy, because received through Christ's atoning sacrifice ; and then they reflect these attributes (as the sea does the sky above it) in their life. " What were joined as attributes in Christ, ought not as virtues to be separated in a Christian who may learn to resemble his blessed Lord and Master by

---

* It is said in Romans xi. 31—" *At present they have not believed your mercy* (ἠπείθησαν τῷ ὑμετέρῳ ἐλέει) *in order that they may be objects of mercy*" —monuments of what that very mercy can do.

observing that short but complete rule of life, *Shew mercy and speak truth ; do righteousness and follow peace."* (Horne.) Restored and converted Israel walk in a singular land ! for their heaven over them is *righteousness*, and the soil under their feet yields *truth*. God's unbroken word is illustrated by them in manifold ways, so that it is as if *" Truth sprang up like the flowers of their land"* when the rains are over and gone ; and then, all is done in righteousness, their sins being forgiven through atoning blood ; so that, *"righteousness"* is their canopy, *" looking down from heaven."** " A carpet of truth ! a canopy of righteousness !"

> *" Truly Jehovah giveth what is good ; (Exod. xxxiii. 19)*
> *And our land yieldeth its increase."*

In verse 13 our attention is turned again to the magnifying of his *" righteousness ;"* for now more than ever his character is manifested as *" righteous,"* since it is the work of a law-fulfilling Redeemer no longer rejected by Israel, but heartily embraced, that has brought about these glorious changes on the nation.

> *" Righteousness goeth before Him,*
> *And sets His steps on the way."* (Ver. 13.)

His steps are not straitened as he walks through Israel's land ; righteousness itself, as a " royal harbinger," makes a way for his footsteps. Such is

> *The bringing back of Israel's captivity expected by the righteous.*

---

* This " looking down," נִשְׁקָף rendered generally by παρακυπτω in the Greek, implies such a look as in 1 Pet. i. 12 angels give into the things of salvation, and such a look as the disciples gave into the sepulchre. It is really the *Righteous One* who is resting over them in complacent love, **not as** in Psa. xiv. 2, and liii. 3, but fulfilling Psa. cii. 20.

Psalm 86

A Prayer of David

1 Bow down thine ear, O Lord, hear me! for I am poor and needy.
2 Preserve my soul; for I am holy:
   O thou my God, save thy servant that trusteth in thee.
3 Be merciful unto me, O Lord: for I cry unto thee daily.
4 Rejoice the soul of thy servant: for unto thee, O Lord, do I lift up my soul.
5 For thou, Lord, art good, and ready to forgive,
   And plenteous in mercy unto all them that call upon thee.
6 Give ear, O Lord, unto my prayer; and attend unto the voice of my supplications.
7 In the day of trouble I will call upon the: for thou wilt answer me.
8 Among the gods there is none like unto thee, O Lord;
   Neither are there any works like unto thy works.
9 All nations whom thou hast made shall come
   And worship before thee, O Lord;
   And shall glorify thy name.
10 For thou art great, and doest wondrous things: thou art God alone.
11 Teach me thy way, O Lord; I will walk in thy truth!
   Unite my heart to fear thy name.
12 I will praise thee, O Lord my God, with all my heart:
   And I will glorify thy name for evermore.
13 For great is thy mercy toward me: and thou has delivered my soul from
   the lowest hell.
14 O God, the proud are risen against me,
   And the assemblies of violent men have sought after my soul;
   And have not set thee before them.
15 But thou, O Lord, art a God full of compassion, and gracious,
   Long-suffering, and plenteous in mercy and truth.
16 O turn unto me, and have mercy upon me;
   Give thy strength unto thy servant, and save the son of thine handmaid.
17 Shew me a token for good; that they which hate me may see it, and be
   ashamed:
   Because thou, Lord, hast holpen me, and comforted me.

The title.   THERE was much, very much, of God's peculiar character, his glorious name, brought to view in the close of the last Psalm. This may account for its being followed by another, "*A prayer of David,*" almost equally full of the character of Jehovah. The key-note of this Psalm is Jehovah's name.

The contents.   From verse 1 to 4, the worshipper states his case; "poor, needy," affording an argument in our approach to Him of whom we can say, "Though he was rich, yet for our sakes he became poor" (such was his grace !), "that we through his poverty might become rich," (2 Cor. viii. 9). There is emphasis in verse 4 in the words, "for to THEE"—to no other, "do I lift up my soul." But what, then, is the plea, verse 2, "Preserve my soul, for *I am holy*?" It is חָסִיד, and we can refer at once to Psalm iv. 3,- "Know that the Lord has set apart him that is חָסִיד for himself." Is it a poor and needy member of Christ that prays still? that poor member is חָסִיד ; he is a saint, he is devoted to the Lord, and beloved by the Lord, and has that of which Psa. iv. 3 has spoken. He is set apart for the Lord ; he is a temple-vessel ; the Lord will own the plea, "Keep the temple-vessel from being profaned or broken." And when the Lord Jesus so prayed, Jesus the true הָסִיד, what force was in the cry !

At verse 5 the worshipper begins to tell us what he sees in God—the God of love and grace-

> "*Thou, Lord, art good* (love), *and one whose very nature is forgiving, Abundant in mercy* (as Exod. xxxiv. 6) *to all that call on thee.*"

It is this sight that draws forth the requests of verses 6, 7, and then another look is directed to the Lord.

At verse 8 the Lord is seen as unparalleled in heart and hand; and the full heart of the Psalmist feels (ver. 9) that there is enough there to encourage, not him alone, but whole nations, to draw near and adore. It is a note from the song of Moses, Exod. xv. 11.

Then at verse 10 he looks again towards the throne and Him that sitteth thereon, and sees his greatness in Himself and his great deeds, which leads to the prayer of verse 11, for guidance in his way. It is surely a matter of spiritual skill thus to look first at the Lord, and then, with our soul bathed in his perfections, to pour forth our desires. "*Keep my heart to the one thing, to fear thy name!*" (Tholuck.)

But at verses 12, 13, he recalls the past kindness of his God, what he has done in his behalf already ; and thus he is encouraged to ask for what he needs now, surrounded as he is by proud foes, (ver. 14).

Once more, at verse 15, he gazes on the blaze of divine love ;

and forthwith utters his request for his special needs, in verse
16. He quotes Exod. xxxiv. 7, and expects such favour as
Moses found. And then, gathering strong confidence from the
many views he has had of his God, the words of verses 16, 17,
are a closing petition, in which he refers to Exod. xxiii. 12,
"the son of thine handmaid" ("verna"), thy home-born slave,
and asks a sign (an אוֹת), a rainbow-like sign of wrath for ever
past (Gen. ix. 12), and mercy bending over him like a canopy.

Christ here.   Let us think of Jesus uttering verse 8 to his Father ; and
Jesus amid such foes as verse 14 speaks of ; of Jesus, " truly thy
servant," verse 16, and of Jesus asking a " sign for good." In His
case, the *sign* would be resurrection-victory; this would be the
true "*helping and comforting*" for all other " Ebenezers" led on
to that final triumph. The הוֹשִׁיעָה of verse 16, is the "*hosan-
nah*" of Psa. cxviii. 25, both alike answered by the king Messiah riding forth in glorious triumph. And this shall be the
full " help and comfort," as well as the overflowing cup of
" salvation :" bestowed on each member, too ! In verse 9
there may be a glimpse, a passing glance, at the time of this
—when all nations shall come and worship. There was a time
when Israel sang verse 8 at the Red Sea ; there has been a
time when the Church has sung it in view of the cross ; there
is a time at hand when Christ and every member of his shall
sing it before the throne, when all kingdoms troop together to
acknowledge and adore Jehovah's name, revealed in his acts of
redemption-grace. Here, then, is the theme of this Psalm—
*The Righteous One, in his day of distress, resting his faith
and hope on the character of Jehovah.*

Psalm 87

A Psalm or Song for the sons of Korah

1 His foundation is in the holy mountains.
2 The Lord loveth the gates of Zion more than all the dwellings of Jacob
3 Glorious things are spoken of thee, O city of God.   Selah.
4 I will make mention of Rahab and Babylon to them that know me :
   Behold Philistia, and Tyre, and Ethiopia; this man was born there.

5 And of Zion it shall be said, This and that man was born in her ;
And the highest himself shall establish her.
6 The Lord shall count, when he writeth up the people, that this man was
born there. Selah.
7 As well the singers as the players on instruments shall be there.
All my springs are in thee !

"A Psalm, a song, for the sons of Korah" —a title similar   *The title and
to many former Psalms. "Repletus Spiritu Sancto" (says   tone.*
Augustine), " civis iste, et multa de amore et desiderio civi-
tatis hujus volvens secum, tanquam plura intus se meditans
erupit in hoc. Multa secum in silentio de illa civitate par-
turiens, clamans ad Dominum erupit etiam in aures hominum,
' Fundamenta ejus,' " &c. He supposes this citizen of Zion,
who sings of Zion, to be so rapt in soul, and filled with the
Spirit, that he abruptly exclaims, as if giving unwitting utterance to his overflowing feelings-

" His foundations are on the holy hills !"

or as more exactly rendered-

" His founded city is upon the holy hills !"

We consider it a Psalm in which Jerusalem is celebrated as   *The theme.*
"*the city of the Great King*," and this in reference in some
measure to the past, but in still fuller measure to the future,
when Isa. xxxiii. 20-24 shall be fulfilled. " Look upon Zion,"
says Isaiah—and here is one looking on—like John, gazing on
New Jerusalem and examining its splendour. These mountains, Moriah, Zion, Olivet, long famous in Israel, they are
adorned now with a city of which

" Glorious things are spoken."

or as some render it-

" Glorious things in thee have been spoken."

The Lord loves it above all the other* dwellings of Jacob, or all
his other cities, even as was announced of old, Deut. xii. 5.
It is here he is to be for ever known as "*Jehovah Shammah,*" Ezek. xlviii. 35. And this is "*a psalm, a song*" of that
glorious time.

* Though " other " is omitted, this is the sense, as in Psa. cxxxviii. 2,
" Magnified thy word above all thy name," *i. e.,* thine other manifestations of
thyself; so Psa. lxxxii. 6.

Let us keep "*Jehovah Shammah*" before us as the key-note of the Psalm. The Psalmist says—

> "*I will bring Rahab and Babel to the remembrance of all my*
> *acquaintance.*
> *Behold Philistia, and Tyre, with Ethiopia !*"

Having said this, the wondering narrator of Jerusalem's glory abruptly breaks off, as if to intimate to us that it is mere absurdity to speak of these in the same breath with Zion. As the Persian poet (see Dr Clark) introduces one saying, " What celebrity can Egypt or Syria, or any thing on earth or in the sea, pretend to, when compared to *Shiraz ?* These are but villages ; this alone is a city." So the Psalmist here. Speak of Egypt, proud Egypt (רָהָב), speak of Babylon, speak of Philistia, speak of Tyre ! Speak of the far-off Ethiopia ! Speak of these in comparison—no, never ! This is my boast to those that know me—

> "*I was born there*" (שָׁם) in yonder city, on the holy hills !

For "*this man*" means no other than the speaker himself.[*] He goes on in his rapturous excitement, to tell more of the city's renown, in such a strain as this : Well may I glory in being a citizen of Zion, for many shall be proud of their relation to it when the cities of the nations have long been forgotten. I boast of my connection therewith, and many shall take up my boast.

> " *Of Zion it shall be said,*
> *This man and that man was born in her.* (אִישׁ וְאִישׁ).
> *And the Most High shall establish her.*" (Ver. 5.)

Yes, says the Psalmist, it shall be thus ; and happy am I who belong to that happy city ; for the Lord himself, and not men alone, shall proclaim its pre-eminence, and give me my place as one of its citizens.

> " *The Lord shall record, when he enrolls the nations,*[†]
> *This man* (that is, I who sing) *was born there.*" (שָׁם).

[*] That " *This man*" may be the speaker himself, see Psalm xxxiv. 6. It is, *q. d.*, I who am speaking thus,—as John ii. 19.

[†] In Num. i. 18, יְתְיַלְדוּ, " *declared themselves to be born,*" is an expression to be noted in connection with this Psalm. For here, as in Numbers i., the Lord is represented as taking the census of his Israel.

Happy me ! who am to dwell in that city. Thrice happy me!
Then, still speaking with all the abruptness of deep excitement—

> " And also singers, as well as players on instruments,"

shall be there, filling the city with praise and holy joy ; and
this shall be the burden of our everlasting song—

> " All my springs (fountains) are in Thee ! "

In thee, O Zion, where Jehovah Shammah for ever dwells ! in
thee I have found my rest. I have traced the streams of bliss
up to their fountain-head ! Such shall be Jerusalem redeemed,
restored, made the metropolis of a redeemed and restored
world, and the pattern or model of a holy capital to the nations.
It may be taken as sung by the Lord Jesus himself, who said,
" Salvation is of the Jews" (John iv. 22), not ashamed to call
himself one of us, and glorying in the city built by God his
Father—not in the world's glory which Satan shewed him on
the high mountain of temptation. In that case his " being
born there" refers to his, " This day I have begotten thee"
his resurrection and glory. Or it may be taken up in the lips
of any pilgrim and stranger who is looking for the " City that
has foundations ;" the city which God has prepared and thinks
worthy of himself, to give to his weary ones for everlasting
rest, and which they on their part receive with grateful wonder,
conscious that even if it had been a Cabul (1 Kings ix. 13),
they could not speak of having merited more. For the earthly
Jerusalem restored, and become the place of the manifestation of the Lord on his throne, will be to the " new Jerusalem" as the outer courts leading to the inner shrine. Sing,
then, pilgrims,—sing, O Church of God,

> *The glory of the place where the Righteous One shall be
> manifested.*

Psalm 88

A Song or Psalm for the sons of Korah. To the chief Musician. Upon Mahalath Leannoth.
Maschil of Heman the Ezrahite

1 O LORD GOD of my salvation, I have cried day and night before thee.
2 Let my prayer come before thee : incline thine ear unto my cry ;

3 For my soul is full of troubles: and my life draweth nigh unto the grave.

4 I am counted with them that go down into the pit: I am as a man that hath no strength:

5 Free, among the dead, like the slain that lie in the grave,
Whom thou rememberest no more: and they are cut off from thy hand.

6 Thou hast laid me in the lowest pit, in darkness, in the deeps.

7 Thy wrath lieth hard upon me,
And thou hast afflicted me with all thy waves. Selah.

8 Thou hast put away mine acquaintance far from me;
Thou hast made me an abomination unto them:
I am shut up, and I cannot come forth.

9 Mine eye mourneth by reason of affliction:
Lord, I have called daily upon thee, I have stretched out my hands unto thee.

10 Wilt thou shew wonders to the dead?
Shall the dead arise and praise thee? Selah.

11 Shall thy lovingkindness be declared in the grave?
Or thy faithfulness in destruction?

12 Shall thy wonders be known in the dark?
And thy righteousness in the land of forgetfulness?

13 But unto thee have I cried, O Lord; and in the morning shall my prayer prevent thee.

14 Lord, why castest thou off my soul? why hidest thou thy face from me?

15 I am afflicted and ready to die from my youth up!
While I suffer thy terrors I am distracted.

16 Thy fierce wrath goeth over me; thy terrors have cut me off.

17 They came round about me daily like water; they compassed me about together.

18 Lover and friend hast thou put far from me, and mine acquaintance into darkness.

The tone. IT has been said of some of our poets, that their living utterance threw more feeling into particular phrases than those phrases conveyed in themselves, and that consequently they who knew the men saw far more meaning in their language than strangers could. In reference to the same fact, it has been said, " Who would part with a ring that contained a dead friend's hair? and yet a jeweller will give for it only the value of the gold." In many compositions of our deep-feeling poets, there is " the hair of the dead friend in the gold." Their verses are not to be weighed in the scale, and judged of, by mere style and expression. To read them right, we should be able to call up the person himself who wrote, and make the verse glow with his impassioned feeling.

If this can be said of mere human compositions, how much more of such a Psalm as this before us? The language is strangely and awfully saddening ; and yet, evidently he who speaks is far more deeply sad than his words express, and filled with submissive calmness, while he bends his soul under the storm. *Heman*, the grandchild of Samuel, was the instrument of delivering it to the Church, perhaps on some occasion when very singularly tried—nigh overwhelmed—but still, his case was but the shadow of one who sank

— — " Beneath a rougher sea,
And whelmed in deeper gulfs than he."

Heman is the person who, in 1 Chron. xv. 17, stands side by side with Asaph, and with the *Ethan*, who writes the Psalm that follows. *Heman* selected the most suitable instrument, no doubt, for a piece so profoundly melancholy ; and this may be meant by " *Mahalath*," if derived from the root that signifies "to sing," (see Gesenius). Hengstenberg translates it as the noun that means " *sickness, or distress*," as in the title of Psalm liii. We agree, however, with most interpreters in supposing it an instrument of music, that same instrument used in singing Psalm liii., where the world's disease and sore sickness are sung of in strains so sad. That same instrument is to be used in singing the sorrows of Him who bore the world's sickness. And then "*Leannoth*" means, " in *reference to affliction*," such *affliction* as is described by that very term in verse 7 and verse 9. Some, indeed, join the term " *Leannoth* " to " *Mahalath*," as if it had formed one compound name for the instrument used by Heman. But even if this be so, the etymology would still point to something melancholy, something of affliction, in the occasions on which it was to be used.

" We have in this Psalm the voice of our suffering Redeemer," says Horne ; and the contents may be thus briefly stated-

1. *The plaintive wailing* of the suffering one, verses 1, 2. It strongly resembles Psa. xxii. 1, 2.

2. *His soul exceeding sorrowful, even unto death*, verses 3, 4, 5. The word "*free*," in our version, is חָפְשִׁי, properly denoting separation from others, and here rendered by Junius

The title.

Christ the speaker.

and Tremellius, " set aside from all intercourse and communication with men, having nothing in common with them, like
those who are afflicted with leprosy, and are sent away to separate dwellings." They quote 2 Chron. xxvi. 21.

3. *His feelings of hell*, verses 6, 7. For he feels God's prison, and the gloom of God's darkest wrath. And " *Selah*"
gives time to ponder.

4. *His feelings of shame and helplessness*, verse 8. " His
own receive him not."

5. *The effects of soul-agony upon his body*, verse 9.

6 *His submission to the Lord*, verse 9. It is the very tone
of Gethsemane, " Nevertheless, *not my will !*"

7. *The sustaining hope of resurrection*, verses 10 (with a solemn pause, "*Selah*"), 11, 12. The "*land of forgetfulness*," and
"*the dark*," express the unseen world, which, to those on this
side of the vail, is so unknown, and where those who enter it
are to us as if they had for ever been forgotten by those they
left behind. God's wonders shall be made known there. There
shall be victory gained over death and the grave : God's " *loving-kindness*" to man, and his "*faithfulness*," pledge him to
do this new thing in the universe. Messiah must return
from the abodes of the invisible state ; and in due time, Heman, as well as all other members of the Messiah's body, must
return also. Yes, God's *wonders* shall be known at the grave's
mouth. God's *righteousness*, in giving what satisfied justice
in behalf of Messiah's members, has been manifested gloriously,
so that resurrection must follow, and the land of forgetfulness
must give up its dead. O morning of surpassing bliss, hasten
on ! Messiah has risen ; when shall all that are his arise ? Till
that day dawn, they must take up their Head's plaintive
expostulations, and remind their God in Heman's strains of
what he has yet to accomplish.

" *Wilt thou shew wonders to the dead,*" &c.

8. *His perseverance in vehement prayer*, verses 13, 14.

9. *His long-continued and manifold woes*, verses 15, 16, 17.

10. *His loneliness of soul*, verse 18. Hengstenberg renders
the last clause of this verse more literally—" The dark kingdom of the dead is instead of all my companions." What un-

utterable gloom ! completed by this last dark shade—all sympathy from every quarter totally withdrawn ! Forlorn indeed ! Sinking from gloom to gloom, from one deep to another, and every billow sweeping over him, and wrath, like a tremendous mountain, "*leaning*" or resting its weight on the crushed worm! Not even Psalm xxii. is more awfully solemnising, there being in this deeply melancholy Psalm only one cheering glimpse through the intense gloom, namely, that of resurrection hoped for, but still at a distance. At such a price was salvation purchased by Him who is the resurrection and the life. He himself wrestled for life and resurrection in our name—and that price so paid is the reason why to us salvation is free. And so we hear in solemn joy the harp of Judah struck by Heman, to overawe our souls not with his own sorrows,* but with what **Horsley** calls "The lamentation of Messiah," or yet more fully,

The sorrowful days and nights of the Man of Sorrows.

Psalm 89

Maschil of Ethan the Ezrahite

1 I **WILL** sing of the mercies of the Lord for ever !
  With my mouth will I make known thy faithfulness to all generations,
2 For I have said, Mercy shall be built up for ever :
  Thy faithfulness shalt thou establish in the very heavens.
3 I have made a covenant with my chosen, I have sworn unto David my
  servant,
4 Thy seed will I establish for ever, and build up thy throne to all generations. Selah.
5 And the heavens shall praise thy wonders, O Lord!
  Thy faithfulness also in the congregation of the saints.
6 For who in the heaven can be compared unto the Lord ?
  Who among the sons of the mighty can be likened unto the Lord!
7 God is greatly to be feared in the assembly of the saints,
  And to be had in reverence of all them that are about him.
8 O Lord God of hosts, who is a strong Lord like unto thee?
  Or to thy faithfulness round about thee ?

  * " Thy suffering Lord, believer, see,
     And praise the heart that bled for **thee.**
     The horrors of his hell-touched soul
     From wounds of death hath made thee whole."—**BARCLAY.**

9 Thou rulest the raging of the sea: when the waves thereof arise, thou stillest them.

10 Thou hast broken Rahab in pieces, as one that is slain;
Thou hast scattered thine enemies with thy strong arm.

11 The heavens are thine, the earth also is thine:
As for the world and the fulness thereof, thou hast founded them.

12 The north and the south thou hast created them:
Tabor and Hermon shall rejoice in thy name.

13 Thou hast a mighty arm: strong is thy hand, and high is thy right hand

14 Justice and judgment are the habitation of thy throne:
Mercy and truth shall go before thy face.

15 Blessed is the people that know the joyful sound:
They shall walk, O Lord, in the light of thy countenance.

16 In thy name shall they rejoice all the day, and in thy righteousness shall they be exalted.

17 For thou art the glory of their strength: and in thy favour our horn shall be exalted.

18 For the Lord is our defence; and the Holy One of Israel is our king.

19 Then thou spakest in vision to thy holy one,
And saidst, I have laid help upon one that is mighty;
I have exalted one chosen out of the people.

20 I have found David my servant; with my holy oil have I anointed him:

21 With whom my hand shall be established: mine arm also shall strengthen him.

22 The enemy shall not exact upon him; nor the son of wickedness afflict him.

23 And I will beat down his foes before his face, and plague them that hate him.

24 But my faithfulness and my mercy shall be with Him:
And in my name shall His horn be exalted.

25 I will set his hand also in the sea, and his right hand in the rivers.

26 He shall cry unto me, Thou art my father, my God, and the rock of my salvation.

27 Also I will make him my firstborn, higher than the kings of the earth.

28 My mercy will I keep for him for evermore, and my covenant shall stand fast with him.

29 His seed also will I make to endure for ever, and his throne as the days of heaven.

30 If his children forsake my law, and walk not in my judgments;

31 If they break my statutes, and keep not my commandments;

32 Then will I visit their transgression with the rod, and their iniquity with stripes.

33 Nevertheless my lovingkindness will I not utterly take from Him,
Nor suffer my faithfulness to fail.

34 My covenant will I not break, not alter the thing that is gone out of my lips.

35 Once have I sworn by my holiness that I will not lie unto David.

36 His seed shall endure for ever, and his throne as the sun before me.

37 It shall be established for ever as the moon,
And as a faithful witness in heaven. Selah.
38 But thou hast cast off and abhorred, thou hast been wroth with thine
anointed.
39 Thou hast made void the covenant of thy servant :
Thou hast profaned his crown by casting it to the ground.
40 Thou hast broken down all his hedges ; thou hast brought his strongholds
to ruin.
41 All that pass by the way spoil him : he is a reproach to his neighbours.
42 Thou hast set up the right hand of his adversaries ; thou hast made all his
enemies to rejoice.
43 Thou hast also turned the edge of his sword, and hast not made him to
stand in the battle.
44 Thou hast made his glory to cease, and cast his throne down to the ground.
45 The days of his youth hast thou shortened : thou hast covered him with
shame. Selah.
46 How long, Lord ? wilt thou hide thyself for ever ?
Shall thy wrath burn like fire ?
47 Remember how short my time is :
Wherefore hast thou made all men in vain ?
48 What man is he that liveth, and shall not see death ?
Shall he deliver his soul from the hand of the grave ? Selah.
49 Lord, where are thy former lovingkindnesses, which thou swearest unto
David in thy truth ?
50 Remember, Lord, the reproach of thy servants ;
How I do bear in my bosom the reproach of all the mighty people ;
51 Wherewith thine enemies have reproached, O Lord,
Wherewith they have reproached the footsteps of thine anointed.
52 Blessed be the Lord for evermore. Amen, and Amen.

THE title assigns this Psalm to " *Ethan the Ezrahite*," as the *The title.*
last was by " *Heman the Ezrahite*." These were probably
called " *Ezrahites*," *i. e.*, sons of Zerah, as a name of honour,
because of their skill in music. For, in 1 Chron. ii. 6, we find
the grandchildren of Judah bear these names, and in 1 Kings
iv. 31, they are spoken of as renowned for skill in song, being
" *sons of Mahol, i.e.*, sons of the choir." Hence, in after times,
Levitical singers who were conspicuous in this department
were called " *Ezrahites*," *q. d.*, Handels or Mozarts. And this
is a " *Maschil*."

The subject here is followed out in progressive development. *The plan.*
He is to sing, verse 1, of the Lord's mercies and faithfulness ;
in other words, of " the sure mercies of David," spoken of by
Isaiah lv. 4. He seems to be revolving in his thoughts the

Lord's words to David, 2 Sam. vii. 14. Impressed with that solemn covenant, he sings, verse 2-

> " *I have said, Mercy shall be built up for ever !*"

Not as the tower of Babel, to be left unfinished, and then destroyed, but built up heaven-ward, a grateful sight to God and man-

> " *The heavens! thy faithfulness thou wilt establish therein !* "

The Lord himself replies to this expression of faith in verses 3, 4, clearly referring to his word pledged to David in 2 Sam. vii. When his voice has uttered its sealing testimony, there is a solemn pause—" *Selah !*" The Lord has spoken ! And then silence is broken by rapturous praise, verse 5-

> " *The heavens shall praise thy wonderful doing ;*
> *Thy faithfulness, also, in the congregation of the saints.*"

Unfallen angels, and the great congregation of redeemed men, shall yet unite in praise to the God whose mercies have been promised to David. Messiah's Second Coming will be the special season for that praise, when his gathered elect, " *the congregation of the saints,*" survey the foundation of their blessedness, and review the way by which he led them on. Every time an assembly of saints now, in this time of ingathering, unites in so celebrating the Lord, we have a type of that coming day ; especially when they so unite on the *Sabbath* of rest, itself a type. And the strains that follow are a specimen to us of what may be the topics of the Song of the Lamb.

Here are his praises. From verse 6 to verse 18, Ethan sings of the Lord's incomparable glory and greatness, felt by saints, as well as by angels, the sons of the mighty. He is " God of Hosts," irresistible in might, and yet never once unloosening the girdle of *faithfulness* to his covenant. " *Faithfulness is round about thee !*" (ver. 8). It is God in Christ whom Ethan praises ; it is he who at his coming again bears the name, " *Faithful and true*" (Rev. xix. 11), and who has " faithfulness as the girdle of his reins," (Isa. xi. 5). He is the ruler of the stormy sea, and of proud Egypt ; the Creator of the glorious heavens, and of the earth with its fulness ; the founder

of Israel's land, who appointed Tabor and Hermon* to stand
in the midst of that land as witnesses of the Lord's doings.
This is Jehovah ; and he is at once righteous and loving-

> " *Righteousness and judgment are the platform on which thy throne*
> *stands,*
> *Mercy and truth stand before thy presence.*" (Ver. 14.)

Happy they who know him ! who have heard and joined in
the " *joyful sound,*" *i. e.*, the shout of joy raised by Israel to
this king (Num. xxiii. 21), when they worship him at their
solemn feasts (Lev. xxv. 9). Happy people ! They walk in
his light ! They anticipate the day when the shout of joy
shall be raised at his Coming, and when they shall have no
other light to walk in than what beams from God and the
Lamb. So they go on from day to day-

> " *For our shield, it belongs to the Lord* (ל) ;
> *And our king he belongs to the Holy One of Israel.*"
> (Our protector is himself protected by the Lord.) (Ver. 18.)

A fuller and plainer declaration, however, is given at verse 19
and onwards, of the source of all this rejoicing. Israel's shield
and king was the type of another whom Jehovah gives to Israel and to earth-

> " *Thou spakest in vision to thy holy ones,*" *i. e.*, thy people. (Ver. 18.)

Thou revealedst to thy saints, by Nathan and others, thy purpose to send Messiah in David's line ; and from 19 to 28, this
is sung of in lofty strains. He has made him the depositary
of help ; and he tells how he will uphold him, honour him, extend his kingdom, exalt his name to the highest. Nay (29–34),
he shall not be disappointed of his glory and promised bliss
even by his children's unfaithfulness ; for they even (35–37),
when unfaithful, must be brought back to him, that he may
want no joy. His truth is pledged to this, as surely as when
he made the rainbow " *his witness in the heavens*" to Noah.

A " *Selah*"-pause follows. O that this scene were realised !
O that all were come !

But, alas, as yet these things are not arrived. We must

---

* This is surely better than to suppose the allusion to either side of Jorda
Tabor on the west and Hermon on the north-east.

hang on his.*faithfulness*. For at present (vers. 38–45) desolation and ominous disaster abound. Another "*Selah*"-pause follows ; the worshipper is mournfully pondering the scene, and wondering what he shall do ; and soon the Lord's remembered *faithfulness* draws forth prayer from his lips, the cry (ver. 46)—

> " *How long, Lord* "

accompanied by the plea that days are passing away, and that the millions of earth are ever disappearing from the scene, none able to resist the stroke—

> " *What mighty man liveth and seeth not death ?*
> *Shall he deliver his soul from the hand of the grave ?* Selah !"
> *(*Ver. 48.*)*

Messiah. It may be that this verse (with its מִי גֶבֶר) points to the longed-for Messiah, as if saying-

> " *Where is He that shall live and not die?*
> *That shall deliver his soul from the hand of the grave ?* Selah !"

Another burst of impassioned desire follows this pensive pause, verses 49–51,—an appeal to the Lord's love in former days, enforced by the consideration that his name is reproached in his servants, and by a touching reference to Moses, in Num. xi. 12, and the gracious answer he got when bidden " *carry in his bosom*" that stiff-necked people-

> " *I bear the many nations in my bosom,*
> *For thy foes, O Lord, have reproached,*
> *They have reproached the footsteps of thy Messiah !*"

They have been told of his Coming ; but he tarries, and they scoff at this delay ; they cast it up to me. " *The footsteps*" are explained by the Targum, and by Kinchi, to mean " the tardiness of his steps,"[*] but by others as equivalent to the whole movements or ways of Messiah. In either case the taunt of the scoffers, 2 Peter iii. 4, and Malachi ii. 17, is included—" Where is the promise of his coming ? Where is the God of judgment ?"

---

[*] M. Anton. Flaminius says, that it is by some understood of scoffers who derided the Jews—" Quod ii Christum liberatorem expectarent, cujus vestigia et pedes venientes nunquam visuri essent."

But faith holds out, nay, realises the happy issue, (ver. 32)—

> *" Blessed be the Lord for ever !*
> *Amen, and amen !"*

Let it come, let it come ? (γενοιτο, γενοιτο ! Sept.) or rather, testifying its assurance that all this shall come, not one thing failing ; for the theme from beginning to end has been-

The faithful covenant with Messiah and his Seed.

Psalm 90

A Prayer of Moses, the man of God

1 LORD, thou hast been our dwelling-place in all generations.
2 Before the mountains were brought forth, or ever thou hadst formed the earth and the world,
  Even from everlasting to everlasting, thou art God.
3 Thou turnest man to destruction ; and sayest, Return, ye children of men
4 For a thousand years in thy sight are but as yesterday when it is past,
  And as a watch in the night.
5 Thou carriest them away as with a flood; they are as a sleep:
  In the morning they are like grass which groweth up.
6 In the morning it flourisheth, and groweth up ;
  In the evening it is cut down, and withereth.
7 For we are consumed by thine anger, and by thy wrath are we troubled.
8 Thou hast set our iniquities before thee,
  Our secret sins in the light of thy countenance.
9 For all our days are passed away in thy wrath : we spend our years as a tale that is told.
10 The days of our years are threescore years and ten ;
  And if by reason of strength they be fourscore years,
  Yet is their strength labour and sorrow;
  For it is soon cut off, and we fly away.
11 Who knoweth the power of thine anger? even according to thy fear, so is thy wrath.
12 So teach us to number our days, that we may apply our hearts unto wisdom.
13 Return, O Lord ! how long? and let it repent thee concerning thy servants.
14 O satisfy us early with thy mercy; that we may rejoice and be glad all our days.
15 Make us glad according to the days wherein thou hast afflicted us,
  And the years wherein we have seen evil.
16 Let thy work appear unto thy servants, and thy glory unto their children.
17 And let the beauty of the Lord our God be upon us:
  And establish thou the work of our hands upon us ;
  Yea, the work of our hands establish thou it.

272 / Bonar on the Psalms

The position of the Psalm.

Part IV. of the Book of Psalms, according to the Jewish division, begins here. It is, however, unsuitable in this way to separate the 90th from the 89th, inasmuch as the latter sets forth the abiding faithfulness of God the Lord, while the former shews the need of that faithful covenant, because of man's sin and frailty. Perhaps the reference in the close of Psa. lxxxix. to the words of Moses, in Num. xi. 12, may have in part led to the position of this Psalm next to it.

The title.

The title, " *The prayer of Moses, the man of God,*" is a title, the genuineness of which we have no grounds for disputing, as all manuscripts have it. Some diminish the interest of this title by giving it a figurative turn, as if all that was meant was that the Psalm is a proper prayer for one who, like Moses, is a pilgrim in the world's wilderness. But it is far better to take it as it stands—a real prayer and psalm of Moses, perhaps written about the time of that awful event, Num. xi., or, in the 38th year of the desert-journey, when himself had so sinned as to be forbidden to enter the land. Some even fix on Pisgah as the spot where he sang so pensively.

The contents.

Moses, bemoaning the sentence gone forth on Israel, and already in prospect seeing the sands of the desert covering the whitening bones of the thousands that had followed him, sings of these three themes-

(a) From 1–10, *Nothing found stable but Jehovah.* He is מָעוֹן, not a tent in the desert, but a fixed abode (ver. 1); and shall be so more gloriously still, (Horne).

> " *Thou turnest them even to brokenness,* (*i. e.,* crumbling down the mass of dust) ;
>
> *And sayest, Return, ye children of men,*" (*q. d.,* let the sentence recorded in Gen. iii. 19, take its course).

Man fades though his sentence of death be deferred, and even if he were, like those before the flood, to live onward to a thousand years. All this because of sin,—sin which God's holy eye cannot overlook, for his countenance is spoken of (ver. 8) as מָאוֹר, a *luminary.* And then the shortened period of seventy years ever tells of the limit to man. Our days pass away as " a tale," or " ejaculation," or " sigh," or " thought ;"

and if there be fourscore years, yet רָהְבָּם, that in which they prided themselves (their Rahab), becomes toil and suffering. (Hengst.)

(b) In verses 11, 12, he sings, *Nothing able to stand before the wrath of the Lord-*

> " *Who knows the power of thine anger,* (Ezra viii. 22)
> *And thy wrath, up to the measure of thy fear ?*

Who knows, or cares for, thy wrath in a manner suitable to what is demanded by thy perfection. O to know it so as to be led thereby to *wisdom-*

> " *Cause us to know* (it), *numbering our days !*
> *That we may bring our heart to wisdom.*"

(c) But in verses 13–17, he sings of *The days of the Restitution of all things*—days when " *the Lord returns,*" that is, " turns back from his wrath,'' and comforts his servants—days, when the dark night is past, and when " *at morning*" (בַּבֹּקֶר, ver. 14) the Lord satiates his own, so that they are evermore rejoicing—days like what Jesus speaks of, John xvi. 20–22, that make anguish no more remembered—days when the Lord's work appears in power, and his glory is unveiled—days, when the " *beauty* (נֹעַם, see Psa. xxvii. 4,*) *of the Lord,*" his well-pleased look, rests on all his people, and on earth at large. Of such days the times of David and Solomon were a type, and the times of Immanuel on earth and his apostles were so far a specimen. But the fulness is still a thing hoped for, to be brought us at the Lord's appearing.

The meeker than Moses, Christ on earth, could use this Psalm in sympathy with us. As in Psa. cii. 3, 10, 11, he mourns over sin, and the results of sin, which he by imputation was made to share, so here he might speak as one of us throughout. *Used by our Head.*

This very ancient Psalm, " The prayer of Moses, the man of God," has for its burden

Man's sin and frailty leading to the cry for the better days.

---

* The Targum has here—" Let the sweetness of the garden of Eden be upon us."

Psalm 91

1 HE that dwelleth in the secret place of the Most High
  Shall abide under the shadow of the Almighty.

2 I will say of the Lord, He is my refuge and my fortress:
  My God; in him will I trust.

3 Surely he shall deliver thee from the snare of the fowler, and from the
  noisome pestilence.

4 He shall cover thee with his feathers, and under his wings shalt thou trust:
  His truth shall be thy shield and buckler.

5 Thou shalt not be afraid for the terror by night;
  Nor for the arrow that flieth by day;

6 Nor for the pestilence that walketh in darkness:
  Nor for the destruction that wasteth at noonday.

7 A thousand shall fall at thy side, and ten thousand at thy right hand;
  But it shall not come nigh thee.

8 Only with thine eyes shalt thou behold, and see the reward of the wicked.

9 Because thou hast made the Lord which is my refuge, even the Most High,
  thy habitation;

10 There shall no evil befall thee, neither shall any plague come nigh thy
   dwelling.

11 For he shall give his angels charge over thee, to keep thee in all thy
   ways.

12 They shall bear thee up in their hands, lest thou dash thy foot against a
   stone.

13 Thou shalt tread upon the lion and adder:
   The young lion and the dragon shalt thou trample under feet.

14 Because he hath set his love upon me, therefore will I deliver him
   I will set him on high, because he hath known my name.

15 He shall call upon me, and I will answer him:
   I will be with him in trouble; I will deliver him, and honour him.

16 With long life will I satisfy him, and shew him my salvation.

This is the
scheme.

> "Incarnate God! the soul that knows
> Thy name's mysterious power,
> Shall dwell in undisturbed repose
> And fear the trying hour."

Christ the
chief speaker.

THE Messiah, of whom former Psalms have sung, and to whom every sweet singer of Israel had regard, is here prominently before us. In contrast to the utter failure of man in himself, here is Messiah's safety in his God. Besides (in the wonted manner of all these holy songs for the Church in all ages), Messiah's seed are included, who, though as reeds in themselves, are as the cedars of God in their Head

The imagery is taken from Israel's history. Thus, verse 1 speaks of "*the Almighty*," the "*Shaddai*" who spoke to Abraham, Gen. xvii. 1; verse 5, the *Passover night*, and David's *escape from the pestilence*; and the same again, in another aspect, in verses 6, 7, 8. Not to speak of the reference in verse 2 to the *Tabernacle* and its *Holy of Holies*, verses 3, 4, allusion is made to Jehovah as *the eagle* (Deut. xxxiii. 12) who bore up Israel. Not less so verses 11–13, where the scorpions of the desert, and the beasts of "the waste, howling wilderness" are in view, as well as the flints and the pit-falls of the desert, needing an angel-hand to do the service done by the angel of the covenant in the Cloudy Pillar. Even verse 15 abounds in such references; the "*calling*" and "*trouble*" resemble Psa. lxxxi. 7, where Israel's distresses are the theme; the "*delivering*," too, and then the "*glorifying*" remind us of Israel made glorious in the eyes of the nations; while the "*length of days*" sends us back to such promises as Deut. xi. 21.

Allusions to Israel's history.

The Psalm, then, may be viewed as gathering round *Messiah and his seed* all the Lord's gracious and glorious interpositions in behalf of his own from the beginning; and all the Lord's promises. It is Christ who realises verse 1 to the full, (as Satan seems to have known when he used this Psalm in the temptation, Luke iv. 10, 11)

Christ and his members.

> "*He who sits in the covert of the Most High*
> *Shall spend the night (i. e., his darkest hours) under the shade of the Almighty;*
> *Saying to Jehovah, 'He is my Refuge,' &c.*"

Let us simply notice that אָמַר may very naturally be rendered as the present part, "*He sits, saying to Jehovah.*" Christ's people, in their measure, may be thus described; for does not faith confidingly "*sit in the covert of the Most High*," going in by the rent vail? And in the measure they so do, in the same measure they claim and they enjoy the blessings afterwards set forth. It is interesting to notice in verse 6 the דֶּבֶר and the קֶטֶב which Hosea xiii. 14 alludes to, when telling that at the resurrection morn he will be plague and destruction to death. The putrid plague-fever often comes on in the night while the patient is asleep; the solstitial disease seizes in heat of harvest upon a man in open air, and cuts him off, per-

haps ere evening. It is safety from perils like these that is
spoken of. All these blessings are derived from and rest on
verse 1, the position of Him that claims them "*under the
covert of the Most High.*" Hence, verse 9 brings this prominently into view again, and in the Hebrew the form of it is
peculiar. The speaker says,

> "*Because thou, Lord, art my confidence!*"

and forthwith a voice from heaven* seems to reply, "Yes,

> "*Thou hast made the Most High thy habitation.*" (Psa. xc. 1.)

And that same voice utters the blessing onward to the end. It
is the Lord's own voice, for verse 14 has the words of Deut.
vii. 7-

> "*Because he has set his love on me,
> Therefore will I deliver him.
> I will set him on high
> Because he has known my name.*"

Referred to in
John 17.
The tenor of the Psalm reminds us of John xvii., when the
Lord prays down his own privileges and blessings on his disciples. How like is this last clause to John xvii. 6–25, where
the Incarnate Son describes his disciples (ver. 14) by that
same feature, "They have known thee." The "*length of
days,*" in verse 15, corresponds to Isa. liii. 10, "He shall
prolong his days," but tells here of resurrection and eternal life
to Messiah's seed as well as to himself.

One thing still let us notice-

> "*I will shew him my salvation.*"

The salvation.
This salvation is the full redemption—all the glory purchased
by the Saviour as well as all the grace. "*Salvation*" is here
used as in Psa. l. 23, in Rom. xiii. 11, 1 Thess. v. 8, Heb. ix.
18, 1 Peter i. 5, and many other passages. It tells of the day
that is yet to come, when Rev. xii. 10 shall be sung, and all
the unknown glory of the New Jerusalem and its King shall
burst on our view. "All these promises," says Bishop Horner,
" have already been made good to our gracious Head and Representative. Swift fly the intermediate years, and rise that
long-expected morning, when He who is gone to prepare a

---

* "A voice from heaven," remarks Tholuck, "seems to accompany the promise of God."

place for us shall come again and take us to himself, that where he is we may be also !"

Augustine speaks of this Psalm as, "*Psalmus iste* de quo Dominum nostrum Jesus Christum tentator tentare ausus est." And we may say of it, that it exhibits

More than Israel's blessings resting on Messiah and his seed.

Psalm 92

A Psalm or Song for the sabbath-day

1 It is a good thing to give thanks unto the Lord,
   And to sing praises unto thy name, O Most High :
2 To shew forth thy lovingkindness in the morning, and thy faithfulness
   every night,
3 Upon an instrument of ten strings, and upon the psaltery,
   Upon the harp, with a solemn sound.
4 For thou, Lord, hast made me glad through thy work:
   I will triumph in the works of thy hands.
5 O Lord, how great are thy works ! and thy thoughts are very deep.
6 A brutish man knoweth not, neither doth a fool understand this.
7 When the wicked spring as the grass, and when all the workers of iniquity
   do flourish ;
   It is that they shall be destroyed for ever.
8 But thou, Lord, art Most High for evermore.
9 For, lo, thine enemies, O Lord, for, lo, thine enemies shall perish ;
   All the workers of iniquity shall be scattered.
10 But my horn shalt thou exalt like the horn of an unicorn :
   I shall be anointed with fresh oil.
11 Mine eye also shall see my desire on mine enemies,
   And mine ears shall hear my desire of the wicked that rise up against me.
12 The righteous shall flourish like the palm-tree : he shall grow like a cedar
   in Lebanon.
13 Those that be planted in the house of the Lord shall flourish in the courts
   of our God.
14 They shall still bring forth fruit in old age ; they shall be fat and flourishing ;
15 To shew that the Lord is upright. He is my rock, and there is no unrighteousness in him.

WHEN we have arrived at the *eternal Sabbath,* this " Song or *The title.* Psalm *for the Sabbath-day* " shall be enjoyed in full. In other words, when the last words of Psalm xci. are accomplished, " *I will shew him my salvation,*" then shall this Psalm have its most fitting place, sung, as it shall be, in the stillness and calm of the eternal day, when works are over—works of creation, works of redemption, aye, and works of providence, too—when Pharaohs are sunk in the deep, and when no sound but of psaltery and harp breaks upon Sabbatic quiet—sung, too, by the *Lord of the Sabbath,* not only at the beginning of his " glorious rest," but oftentimes, as the ages to come roll on—sung in memory of the past! Glorious, glorious anthem! taken up by every member of Christ, by every harper present in that congregation of the saved, by every sweet singer of the new song! The Chaldee paraphrast ascribes the original to " *the first man Adam,*" forgetting that he could not refer to " ten-stringed instruments," nor to " Lebanon." Jewish writers generally refer it to *Moses,* in whose lips certainly the reference to the " palm-tree," such as he might see at Elim, and to the " cedar on Lebanon," and that goodly mountain he longed to see, would be quite appropriate. It is handed down for the Church in all time, whatever may have been the circumstances in which it was first given, and whoever may have been the penman.

The theme of the Psalm.   It is tuned, we noticed, to the strains of the eternal Sabbath.* But still, it is no less suitable for *every Sabbath* now, inasmuch as every Sabbath speaks in type of the " rest remaining for the people of God." A redeemed soul will sing it gladly as he awakes on the Lord's day; our day of rest on which Jesus finished his work of resurrection, and which he seems, by his own act, to have set apart as " The Lord's day." The dawn of day, after dark night, the dawn of day without toil before him, cannot but seem a sweet type, or emblem of the Lord's " *lovingkindness*" appearing in salvation after a night of sin; while the bright day that follows, with its hours of enjoyment and peace, presents as true an emblem and specimen of the everlasting " *faithfulness*" that upholds his lot, fulfilling all the promises that mercy gave. And hence, at morning (perhaps over the morning lamb on the altar), " *He shews forth God's loving-kindness,*" and at evenings, (Heb. בַּלֵּילוֹת) (it may be, over the evening lamb,) he praises the Lord for realising all his expectations, proving himself a " *faithful*" God. He uses every instrument of praise that tabernacle or temple could

---

* The Talmud is quoted by some writers as entitling it, " For the future age, all of which shall be Sabbath."

furnish, aye, adding one to all the other instruments, namely, הִגָּיוֹן, "*solemn heart-musing,*" to accompany the harp. For this seems the only plain sense of עֲלֵי הִגָּיוֹן. It is upon the *heart*-strings, so to speak, as well as *harp*-strings.

But what thoughts are these that call forth such emotions? Verses 4, 5, 6, are the answer. The *Most High's* פְּעָלִים, מַעֲשִׂים, מַחְשְׁבֹת, "works, deeds, thoughts"—his plans, and his plans accomplished, in creation, redemption, providence. The "*brutish man,*" the carnal man, "*a man-brute*" (Alex.), understands not these ; but the Lord's spiritual ones do, beholding his glory in every act, and perceiving height, depth, length, and breadth of love, as well as holiness. in them all.

One of these mysterious plans and mysterious works of God has ever been his dealings with his foes. He lets them prosper long. But the Sabbath (every Sabbath that leads us to the sanctuary where we consider their latter end, and see persecutors buried in their Red Sea), and especially the great Sabbath that fulfils all, comes to remove the veil from this part of the Lord's ways. The Lord is seen in the end all the more illustriously exalted ;

"*But thou, Lord, art* HEIGHT (מָרוֹם) *for evermore !*" (Ver. 8.)

Thou art found exceedingly exalted, nay, placed on the pinnacle of exaltation—*height*, or *exaltation* in the abstract !

Another of God's wondrous ways has been the trials of his own. But the *Sabbath* clears up these too. Indeed, every Sabbath gives a specimen of this, when the godly worshipper goes forth to the sanctuary, anticipating the refreshments of the final rest, and saying as the day advances-

"*But my horn shalt thou exalt as the unicorn* (or reem) ;
I am anointed with fresh oil." (Ver. 10.)

These anticipations, no doubt, are only foretastes of the enjoyments and revelations of the *eternal Sabbath;* but they are tokens of its bliss. That clause, "*anointed with fresh oil,*" is peculiar, the word being בַּלֹּתִי, a term used in Numbers and Leviticus (*e. g.*, ii. 4, 5), for "*soaked in oil,*" copiously drenched in oil. And this abundance of refreshment, this overflowing of anointing oil, leads on the singer to other refreshings, as plentiful and as desirable-

" The righteous shall flourish as the palm-tree,*
He shall grow like a cedar on Lebanon," (his *root* fixed).

Is this the *Lord Jesus?* Is He the Righteous One? It may be, he is referred to as the model Righteous One, the only true full specimen of God's palms and cedars, though his members in him come in for their share. Indeed, is not He the true Adam, who takes up this Sabbath-song with all his heart and soul? On His resurrection morning, and on the morning of the resurrection of his own, it suits him more than any other.

If Sabbaths now are days of grace to men, what shall that *great Sabbath* be? O what shall saints be then! If now it be said,

" They are planted in the house of the Lord !
They flourish in the courts of our God !" (Ver. 13.)

how much more when the "*house of God*" is the "*palace*" of the Great King !—when the earthly courts are superseded by the heavenly, even as Israel's typical courts were supplanted by the spiritual.

In " *old age*" we expect such fearers of the Lord to be found like Simeon and Anna ; but what shall be their growth after ages on ages spent in the *eternal Sabbath* in the kingdom ! "*Fat and flourishing !*" fertile and vigorous, as those described by Isaiah lxv. 20. (Fry.)

All this—ruin to the enemies of God, everlasting blessedness and increase to his own—shall prove the truth of what in all ages had been sung, in confidence of faith, Ps. xxv. 8. It shall

" Shew that the Lord is upright." (Ver. 15.)

It shall prove that Jehovah's ways, as well as his words, are all on the side of holiness. It shall be permitted to each individual soul in the kingdom to appropriate Him as his own—

---

* *Jarchi* says, " bearing abundant fruit," as the palm yields its precious dates. *Tholuck* quotes from Schubert's Journey—" The open country wears a sad aspect now ; the soil is rent and dissolves at every break of wind ; the green of the meadows is almost entirely gone. The palm-tree alone preserves its verdant roof of leaves in the drought and heat." Nor are we to forget the *growth* of the tall palm, a growth that can be marked. In the case of the cedar, its roots and its age, as well as its strength, **are** all to be considered.

"*He is my rock*" (as the Head said in Psa. lxxxix. 26), "*and no unrighteousness is in Him.*"

Such is the close of this Sabbath-song, which has been entitled by Dr Allix, "A prophecy of the happiness of the Jews in the great Sabbath of which Paul speaks in Hebrews iv.," but which might better still be described as

The Righteous One's Sabbath-song, anticipating final rest and prosperity.

Psalm 93

1 THE Lord reigneth! He is clothed with majesty!
  The Lord is clothed with strength, wherewith he hath girded himself:
  The world also is established, that it cannot be moved.
2 Thy throne is established of old : thou art from everlasting.
3 The floods have lifted up, O Lord, the floods have lifted up their voice;
  The floods lift up their waves.
4 The Lord on high is mightier than the noise of many waters,
  Yea, than the mighty waves of the sea.
5 Thy testimonies are very sure : holiness becometh thine house, O Lord,
  for ever.

FROM the lips of unfallen Adam might have come the joyful exclamation, "The Lord is King!" It was true then, yet true no less when he looked on creation fallen, and himself and his posterity ruined. "God reigneth!" was the rainbow of hope. So, also, in every age, God's people have called this truth to remembrance, and have been of good cheer amid frowning providences. But still, their King was invisible, and his plan of government involved in obscurity. Our Psalm refers to all this, but to more besides.

The theme.

We have heard the Sabbath-song of the redeemed in the day of "The Rest that remaineth." Now, the Eternal Sabbath is contemporaneous with the Kingdom. The saints glorified shall enter on the enjoyment of the former in all its manifold phases of positive rest ; the saints still on earth shall have their share in the latter when it comes, reigned over by the reigning saints, and by the King to whom these are kings (Rev. i. 6). This is the theme of the Psalm before us.

When the Lord by a prophet anointed Jehu king, we are told how those around him blew the trumpet, saying, "*Jehu reigneth !*" (2 Kings ix. 13, מָלַךְ as here.) So the Lord's anointed Messiah is proclaimed king by every voice and heart in his dominions—

> "*The Lord is King !*"

His robes are not mere show, nor is his strength merely the power of armies attending him.

> "*He is clothed with majesty !*
> *The Lord is clothed !*
> *He hath girded himself with might !*"

Nor is this all that is to furnish matter of wonder and delight and praise.   This enthronization of Jehovah in our nature has intimate connection with our world's felicity.

> "*The world also is established ;*
> *It does not totter.*"   (See Psalm lxxxiii. 5.)

That is, if we may be allowed to give a paraphrase of the words,

> "*It is made stedfast now, after all its shakings ;*
> *It rests from all its commotions, and totters no more.*"

The throne of Jehovah (once seen in Exod. xxiv. 10 for a few hours), is now stretched over earth, according to God's ancient purpose, and as they look up to it, they sing,

> "*Thy throne was established of old,*
> *Thou thyself art from eternity.*"

From the height of that immovable throne, the saints, in company with their King, look down on enemies made their footstool.   They sing of the past—how these foes gathered together —"*The floods, O Lord, lifted up their voice ;*" but in a moment the universe was witness of their impotency-

> "*The Lord is glorious in the height* (ἐν ὑψίστοις, Luke ii. 14,
>   xix. 38),
> *More than the voice of majestic waters,*
> *Than billows of the sea.*"

The Kingdom has come, the Kingdom so often prayed for, so ardently desired, so long expected ; and its coming has realised every hope.

" Thy testimonies are most true." (Ver. 5).

Our Joshua (Josh. xxiii. 14), can call all to witness that not one thing hath failed of all the good things which the Lord God spoke, (compare Rev. xxi. 5, and xxii 6). All the glorious things spoken, and all his promises, have been verified, himself being "faithful and true," (Rev. xix. 11). And the characteristics of his happy government are unlike those that marked all former dominions on earth. His palace, or "house," (see Psa, xcii. 15), is not like the gay, loose courts of earthly kings —*holiness* is there ; it is holiness only that would be suitable there. And, it is added,

" O Lord (all this shall remain) *to eternity."*

The Septuagint translators felt there was such a real connection between this and the foregoing Psalm, that they entitle it, " Εἰς τῆν ἡμεραν τοῦ σαββατου ὁτε κατῳκισται ἡ γῆ," " For the Sabbath-day, when the earth has been settled"—referring, evidently, to the title of Psa. xcii., "A song for the Sabbath-day." But we prefer describing it with a reference to Rev. xi. 15, as being *Messiah's kingdom stilling the uproar of the nations.*

Connection with the preceding Psalm.

Psalm 94

1 O LORD God, to whom vengeance belongeth,
  O God, to whom vengeance belongeth, shew thyself!
2 Lift up thyself, thou judge of the earth! render a reward to the proud.
3 Lord, how long shall the wicked, how long shall the wicked triumph?
4 How long shall they utter and speak hard things?
  And all the workers of iniquity boast themselves?
5 They break in pieces thy people, O Lord, and afflict thine heritage.
6 They slay the widow and the stranger, and murder the fatherless.
7 Yet they say, The Lord shall not see, neither shall the God of Jacob regard it.
8 Understand, ye brutish among the people : and ye fools, when will ye be wise?
9 He that planted the ear, shall he not hear? he that formed the eye, shall he not see?
10 He that chastiseth the heathen, shall not he correct?
  He that teacheth man knowledge, shall not he know?
11 The Lord knoweth the thoughts of man, that they are vanity.

12 Blessed is the man whom thou chastenest, O Lord, and teachest him out of thy law;

13 That thou mayest give him rest from the days of adversity, Until the pit be digged for the wicked.

14 For the Lord will not cast off his people, neither will he forsake his inheritance.

15 But judgment shall return unto righteousness: and all the upright in heart shall follow it.

16 Who will rise up for me against the evildoers? Or who will stand up for me against the workers of iniquity?

17 Unless the Lord had been my help, my soul had almost dwelt in silence.

18 When I said, My foot slippeth! thy mercy, O Lord, held me up.

19 In the multitude of my thoughts, within me thy comforts delight my soul.

20 Shall the throne of iniquity have fellowship with thee, which frameth mischief by a law?

21 They gather themselves together against the soul of the righteous, And condemn the innocent blood.

22 But the Lord is my defence; and my God is the rock of my refuge.

23 And he shall bring upon them their own iniquity, And shall cut them off in their own wickedness; yea, the Lord our God shall cut them off.

The connection with the preceding. THE Kingdom, then, and its King, have been anticipated, or rather realised as if already come. With this prospect before them, the oppressed Church and its Head cry for vengeance —joining the cry of Rev. vi. 10, from under the altar; pointing the Judge to "The Day vengeance," Isa. lxiii. 4; recalling to his mind the words of the song of Moses, Deut. xxxii. 41.

The plan. The appeal is made in pointed heaven-penetrating cries, verses 1, 2. Reasons for the appeal, strong and vehement, are alleged, verses 3–7. The world is warned that the appeal is lodged, verses 8–11.* This done, the Church and her Head bless the Lord for those very dealings that call for vengeance, these being instructive and sanctifying chastenings to his own, though their enemies did not mean to help them to their crown. They also bless the Lord for revealing the final issues, "*teaching them out of his law*," *i. e.*, advertising them in the pages of his revealed Word of what is coming on, so that they have peace amid the storm (ver. 12–14). "*Judgment shall*

* Bagster has a curious remark on the phrase " He that *planted* the ear." The mechanism of the ear, *like a root planted in the earth*, is sunk deep into the head, and concealed from view.

return to righteousness !" they exclaim : long has it seemed otherwise; judgment seemed to lodge in the streets, or stand afar off. But in God's due time, the Judge comes (ver. 3), and judgment goes home to the righteous—justice vindicates their cause.

From verse 16 to the end, we hear the same parties encouraging themselves to wait on for a season. When my soul is bewildered by endless thoughts, when every human scheme of relief seems vanity, my resort is to thyself, the God of all consolation ! What streams for the thirsty are in thee. The past, if it brought anxiety, has never failed to bring help, while the future presents the prospect of the entire overthrow of ungodliness-

> " *Is the throne of iniquity confederate with thee ?* (Is it become **thy**
> friend ? Ewald.)
> *Framing wickedness* (or, misery, Hengst.) *by right of law !* "
> (Ver. 20.)

The question contains in itself its own answer ; and even meanwhile there is a refuge-

> " *Jehovah shall be my high place,*
> *And my God* (shall be) *my rock of shelter,*"

till he arises in the day of his wrath to cut them off for ever. Thus, beginning with prayer,* the Psalm ends with prophecy ; beginning with an earnest call, it ends with faith's confidence of an answer, and sounds in our ear

The cry of the oppressed Church and her Head for the day
of vengeance.

Psalm 95

1 O come, let us sing unto the Lord! Let us make a joyful noise **to the rock** of our salvation !

2 Let us come before his presence with thanksgiving,
And make a joyful noise unto him with psalms.

3, For the Lord is a great God, and a great King above all gods.

4 In his hand are the deep places of the earth : the strength of **the hills is** his also.

* Augustine says, on verses 1, 2—" Prophetia est prædicentis, non audacia jubentis."

5 The sea is his, and he made it: and his hands formed the dry land.

6 O come, let us worship and bow down: let us kneel before the Lord our maker.

7 For he is our God, and we are the people of his pasture, and the sheep of his hand.

8 To-day if ye will hear his voice! harden not your heart, as in the provocation,

And as in the day of temptation in the wilderness:

9 When your fathers tempted me, proved me, and saw my work.

10 Forty years long was I grieved with this generation,

And said, It is a people that do err in their heart, and they have not known my ways:

11 Unto whom I sware in my wrath that they should not enter into my rest.

The connection with the preceding Psalm. " HOLY joy in God, not discord nor dejection, appear in the old covenant as the fundamental sentiment of adoration." Thus truly spoke Tholuck in regard to the gladsome calls that begin so many of these Psalms.

The King and Kingdom, the Judge and the Judge's vengeance, are within sight, hastening on, almost at the door.* With these solemn prospects influencing them, the flock and the shepherd are now heard inviting men to enter the fold while it is the day of grace. Augustine felt this connexion when he wrote—" Venturus est! præveniamus faciem ejus in confessione."

The contents.
" *O come, let us sing cheerfully to Jehovah* (Deut. xxviii. 47),
Let us raise the peal of melody to the rock of our salvation!
Let us come early before him (q.d., ere ever he calls), *with praise;*
We will raise the peal of melody in psalms to him." (Ver. 1, 2.)

He is great, and he is Sovereign over all (ver. 3); the deeps and the heights are his (ver. 4); the sea and the land (ver. 5); he is our *Maker*—and "MAKER" is equivalent to God *who made us all that we are in grace*, as a nation and as individuals. Deut. xxxii. 6 illustrates it. So in Psa. c. 2, and many other places. Our God is a shepherd to us who glory in the blessedness of being pastured by him, and defended as well as guided by him (ver. 6, 7)—

" *To-day, O that ye would hear his voice!*"

---

* Horsley connects Psa. xcv., xcvi., xcvii., xcviii., xcix., c., as an entire prophetic poem, and calls it, " *The introduction of the First-begotten into the world.*"

This is the force of verse 7, אִם תִּשְׁמָעוּ, like Exod. xxxii. 32, "And now, O that thou wouldst forgive their sin!" and like Luke xix. 42, "O that thou hadst known!" It is an intensely earnest call on those addressed to hearken to that voice, viz., to the call of God ; while verse 8, in the same breath, entreats them not to be as Israel at Meribah and Massah—"like *Meribah*, like the day of *Massah* in the wilderness." Only let us not fail to notice, that while it is *the flock* who speak in verses 1–7, it is *the Shepherd* who takes up their expostulating words, and urges them home himself at verse 8 to the end, using the argument which by the Holy Ghost is addressed to us also in Hebrews iii.

The voice of Christ.

There is something very powerful in this expostulation, when connected with the circumstances that give rise to it. In themselves, the burst of adoring love, and the full outpouring of affection in verses 1–7 are irresistibly persuasive ; but when the voice of the Lord himself is heard (such a voice, using terms of vehement entreaty !) we cannot imagine expostulation carried further.   Unbelief alone could resist this voice ; blind, malignant unbelief alone could repel

The flock and the Shepherd together inviting men now to enter the fold.

Psalm 96

1 O sing unto the Lord a new song! Sing unto the Lord, all the earth!

2 Sing unto the Lord, bless his name ; shew forth his salvation from day to day.

3 Declare his glory among the heathen, his wonders among all people.

4 For the Lord is great, and greatly to be praised : he is to be feared above all gods.

5 For all the gods of the nations are idols : but the Lord made the heavens.

6 Honour and majesty are before him : strength and beauty are in his sanctuary.

7 Give unto the Lord, O ye kindreds of the people, give unto the Lord glory and strength.

8 Give unto the Lord the glory due unto his name : bring an offering, and come into his courts.

9 O worship the Lord in the beauty of holiness : fear before him, all the earth.

10 Say among the heathen that the Lord reigneth:
   The world also shall be established that it shall not be moved:
   He shall judge the people righteously.
11 Let the heavens rejoice, and let the earth be glad;
   Let the sea roar, and the fulness thereof.
12 Let the field be joyful, and all that is therein:
13 Then shall all the trees of the wood rejoice before the Lord:
   For He cometh! for He cometh to judge the earth!
   He shall judge the world with righteousness, and the people with his
   truth.

The position of the Psalm. SOME say that wherever "*new* song" occurs, it is a song to Messiah directly, At any rate, He is always prominent, for the manifestation of Godhead is in all such Psalms a prominent theme.

The call of last Psalm came at a critical moment, namely, in the interval between the cry for vengeance in Psa. xciv., and the answer to that cry in Psa. xcvi. For it is with the Kingdom and the Coming King just at hand, that Psa. xcvi. is sung.

Its origin. The first draught of this song appears in 1 Chron. xvi. That scene was a type. There was joy because of rest to the land, and rest to the ark of God in the midst of the land. And " If creation (says Horne) be represented as rejoicing at the establishment of the kingdom of grace, how much greater will be the joy at the approach of the kingdom of glory, when, at the resurrection of all things, man, new-made, shall return to the days of his youth, to begin an immortal spring, and be for ever young."

The theme. It is in harmony with Rev. xiv. 7, and xix. 1–11. *Creation at its first birth* had its joyful songs from the morning stars, the sons of God (Job xxxviii. 7); shall not *creation renewed* have its songs (Isa. lxii. 10)? and shall not Earth itself sing its own bliss? It is not angels that are invited to sing, though no doubt they will join ; it is a redeemed world—and the men of that redeemed world are to be telling of the salvation not for a few moments only, but from " day to day." In telling the salvation, they are to tell chiefly the glory of Him who has wrought it out (ver. 1–10)—his wonderful doings, his greatness, his praise-worthiness, his fear, the nullity of all other gods, the creator-skill of our God who made the heavens-

> *" Glory and majesty are his inseparable attendants :*

(Not mere transient displays, such as Esther i. 4 records.)

> *" Power and splendour are in his sanctuary."* (Ver. 6.)

(The originals of all kingly magnificence are in his palace.)

> *" Give unto Jehovah, ye families of the nations ;*
> *Give unto Jehovah glory and power.*
> *Give unto Jehovah the glory of his name !*
> *Bring a present,* and come into his courts !*
> *Worship Jehovah in* (real sanctuary splendour) *the beauty*
> *of holiness.*
> *Tremble at his presence, all earth !*
> *Tell among the nations, Jehovah is king ! "*

As a consequence, there is the reverse of Psa. lxxxiii. 5. Yes, tell this also to men,

> *" The world stands firm ; it totters no more!*
> *He judges the people with uprightness ! "*

On this announcement, there is a shout that makes the welkin ring—a shout like that at Corinth, when " Soter, Soter !" rang through the air, and astonished birds as they flew, reeled, and dropt their wings. It is earth rejoicing (Rev. xix. 5) that now what was foretold in Rom. viii. 19–21 about the deliverance of the whole creation is at last accomplished-

> *" For He cometh ! for He cometh !*
> *To judge the earth ! "*

That is, to put earth in order,† to be its Gideon and Samson, to be its *ruler*, to fulfil all that the Book of Judges delineates of a judge's office. It is, as Hengstenberg says, " a gracious judging," not a time of mere adjudication of causes or pronouncing sentences—it is a day of jubilee. It is the happiest day our world has ever seen, Who would not long for it ? Who is there that does not pray for it ? It is the day of the Judge's glory, as well as of our world's freedom—the day when

---

* See 1 Sam. ix. 7, 1 Kings xiv. 3. Allusion is made to the customary forms of approach to the great.

† The Septuagint has given this title to this Psalm—" ὅτε ὁ οἶκος ᾠκοδομεῖτο μετα την αἰχμαλωσιαν." We may suppose they meant their title to be figurative.

" *the judgment of this world*" (John xii. 31, and xvi. 11), which his cross began and made sure, is completed by the total suppression of Satan's reign, and the removal of the curse. All this is anticipated here ; and so we entitle this Psalm

The glory due to Him who Cometh to judge the earth.

Psalm 97

1 THE Lord reigneth; let the earth rejoice ;
Let the multitude of isles be glad thereof.

2 Clouds and darkness are round about him :
Righteousness and judgment are the habitation of his throne.

3 A fire goeth before him, and burneth up his enemies round about.

4 His lightnings enlightened the world : the earth saw, and trembled.

5 The hills melted like wax at the presence of the Lord,
At the presence of the Lord of the whole earth.

6 The heavens declare his righteousness, and all the people see his glory.

7 Confounded be all they that serve graven images, that boast themselves
of idols.
Worship him, all ye gods !

8 Zion heard, and was glad ;
And the daughters of Judah rejoiced because of thy judgments, O Lord.

9 For thou, Lord, art high above all the earth :
Thou art exalted far above all gods.

10 Ye that love the Lord, hate evil :
He preserveth the souls of his saints ; he delivereth them out of the hand
of the wicked.

11 Light is sown for the righteous, and gladness for the upright in heart.

12 Rejoice in the Lord, ye righteous ; and give thanks at the remembrance
of his holiness.

The time referred to.

WE advance a step further. In this Psalm, Messiah *has* come in glory—he is not merely expected and anticipated. And here the effects of his Coming, in the ruin of his foes and their idols, are sung of. In Heb. i. 6 there is a quotation of verse 7, —" Worship Him all ye אֱלֹהִים" gods, or *angels*, as in Psalm viii. 5. In making that quotation, the sacred writer prefaces it with a definite mark of time—" *When he bringeth his first-begotten again into the world*"—the time of his Second Advent—

" Jehovah reigneth ! Let the earth* dance for joy ! (Horsley, תָּגֵל.)
   Let the multitude of its regions rejoice."

The *"basis of his throne"* (comp. Psa. lxxxix. 15) is formed   The theme.
by "Righteousness and judgment," while "clouds" are its
curtains. And then is described the judgment upon idols, in
language borrowed from the Sinai-appearing of the Lord, (ver.
3, 4). When in verse 6 it is said,

      " The heavens declare his righteousness,"

the sense corresponds to Romans i. 18 ; it is equivalent to saying that now the Lord from heaven, from his opened heavens,
rises up in favour of righteousness. From age to age the
heavens seemed silently to hear, as if almost indifferent to the
cry of sin ; but not so any longer. At verse 7 *Angels* are called
upon, "Ye gods,"(Heb. i. 6); and called upon to worship " Him"
who now appears, viz., Christ who now comes into the world
again, (Heb. i. 6). Angels who were present, and who adored
him at Bethlehem, at his first Coming, are again adoring. Israel and earth at large rejoice, witnessing his *"judgments," i e.*,
his providential dealings. But specially his saints, who have
long prayed and waited, now find that they waited not in vain ;
and hence the exhortation in verse 10, and the promise in verse
11, a verse illustrated by Esther viii. 16 in one view of it-

      " Light is sown for the righteous."

Into the furrows made by the plough of affliction and temp-   Christ and his
tation, God casts the seeds of after-joy. Christ, " the Right-   members.
eous One," is first partaker of this harvest of joy, as abundant as were his tears, his woes, his sorrows—and joy is syno-
nymous with *"light,"* because of light's cheerfulness, and because the rich flood of rays from the sun may be emblematic
of the gifts and blessings to be poured on the Righteous One
and his members. It is interesting to notice that an apparent
reference to the Head and members is contained in the change
of numbers in the clauses of verse 11-

    " Light is sown for the Righteous One, צַדִּיק

      And gladness for those who are upright in heart," (who keep to his
      rule).

      * Dathe makes הָאָרֶץ, " the land," Palestine.

All this blessedness, at the very hour judgment comes on idols and idolaters, may well call forth the rejoicing with which our Psalm begins and ends. And the *"holiness"* of verse 12 may remind us that all this joy is the result of Jehovah having at length introduced his own holiness into a fallen world. It is a blessed song concerning

The Advent of Messiah, and its results to earth.

Psalm 98

A Psalm

1 O sing unto the Lord a new song! for he hath done marvellous things:
His right hand, and his holy arm, hath gotten him the victory.
2 The Lord hath made known his salvation:
His righteousness hath he openly shewed in the sight of the heathen.
3 He hath remembered his mercy and his truth toward the house of Israel:
All the ends of the earth have seen the salvation of our God.
4 Make a joyful noise unto the Lord, all the earth:
Make a loud noise, and rejoice, and sing praise.
5 Sing unto Lord with the harp; with the harp, and the voice of a psalm.
6 With trumpets and sound of cornet, make a joyful noise before the Lord, the King.
7 Let the sea roar, and the fulness thereof; the world, and they that dwell therein.
8 Let the floods clap their hands:
Let the hills be joyful together before the Lord;
9 For he cometh to judge the earth:
With righteousness shall he judge the world, and the people with equity.

The time.　RYLAND (in " Psalms restored to Messiah,") thinks that as the Jews held that Moses wrote Psalm xc. and onward to the xcviii., it may be to this Psalm that Rev. xv. alludes, as " The Song of Moses and the Lamb." This is improbable; but the Psalm suits that time. The kingdom and the King have arrived; the blessedness of that happy day has been celebrated. But the harp cannot be silent yet! Another song on the same

The theme.　key! Another sweet and solemn melody on the same theme; but with this special addition, the *Lord's faithfulness to Israel.*

　Hengstenberg remarks that this Psalm is full of allusion to Isaiah. At any rate, this Psalm and Isaiah, whichever was the earlier, answer to one another, as seraph to seraph, celebrating " wonders," " salvation with his right hand," " his holy arm," " his righteousness revealed." And may not the clause in verse 2,

> " *He hath remembered his mercy and truth*,"

be considered as equivalent to " full of *grace and truth*" in John i. 17? That *grace and truth* is now to be revealed to Israel in particular, for he who is the fountain of it is to dwell among them—his throne stretched over Jerusalem as a rainbow spans the plain beneath, and his sceptre swayed over earth to its utmost ends.

> " *Sing to Jehovah with the harp!*
> *With the harp and voice of psaltery!*
> *With cornets and sound of trumpet* (as at the bringing up of the ark to Zion, and as in 1 Kings i. 34, when Solomon was crowned).
> *Raise the peal of melody*
> *Before* THE KING, *Jehovah!*"

And as at the commencement of a reign in Israel, we read of the shout, " Let the king live!" (2 Kings xi. 12, and ix. 13,) " Jehu is king!" and as they clapped the hand (2 Kings xi. 12), as well as shouted and blew the trumpet (2 Kings ix. 13), so we find all these recognitions of The King in this Psalm— " The rivers clap their hands," and " the hills shout for joy," for the king foretold in David's last words has at length come (2 Sam. xxiii. 3), to rule over men in the fear of the Lord.

It is the only Psalm called simply מִזְמוֹר, "*Psalm*," without addition. Some say that the reason is, there are so many verses that have some form of the root זָמַר, verses 1-8, &c. Hengstenberg accounts for it by supposing it the lyrical accompaniment of the more directly prophetical preceding Psalm, and the lyrical echo of the second part of Isaiah. It is at least interesting to notice, that a song of Zion which so exults in the king's arrival should be called pre-eminently, מִזְמוֹר; as if the Psalm of Psalms were that which celebrates

Israel, and Earth at large, blessed in Messiah's Advent.

The title peculiar.

Psalm 99

1 THE Lord reigneth, let the people tremble :
He sitteth between the cherubim, let the earth be moved.
2 The Lord is great in Zion ; and he is high above all the people.
3 Let them praise thy great and terrible name ; for it is holy.
4 The king's strength also loveth judgment ; thou dost establish equity,
Thou executest judgment and righteousness in Jacob.
5 Exalt ye the Lord our God, and worship at his footstool;
For he is holy.
6 Moses and Aaron among his priests, and Samuel among them that call
upon his name ;
They called upon the Lord, and he answered them.
7 He spake unto them in the cloudy pillar :
They kept his testimonies, and the ordinance that he gave them.
8 Thou answeredst them, O Lord our God : thou wast a God that forgavest
them,
Though thou tookest vengeance of their inventions.
9 Exalt the Lord our God, and worship at his holy hill ;
For the Lord our God is holy.

The theme. THE King and kingdom having come and been established, the
Psalmist sings of the principles of government. Holiness is
the rule. Jehovah is as holy as when he manifested himself
to Israel dwelling between the cherubim. Or rather, the idea
seems to be that Jehovah, *while fulfilling the type exhibited
in his dwelling between the cherubim* by dwelling with men in
Zion, is nevertheless so holy that earth bows prostrate before
him, and the nations quake.

The contents.
" *They praise thy name !*
Great and terrible, holy is He !
And * *royal strength loveth judgment !*"

This is their song, because he has established judgment in
Jacob. They call on others to join (ver. 5), bidding them fall
before " *His footstool*," *i.e.*, his ark, where he gave his manifestation of himself to men who approach to worship.

" *He is holy* " (ver. 5),

* Like " the *might of Gabriel* fought " (Milton, P. L. vi. 355), " *Crispi fa-
cunda senectus.*" (Juven. iv. 31). Others refer back to verse 3, " *Let them
praise the strength of the King* (who) loveth judgment.*"

This is one of their arguments; another is, Moses and Aaron, Israel's leaders in the wilderness, are there ; and Samuel, the first of the judges in the land, is there. These men, and such as these, used to call upon the Lord and get answers, during their days of trial, he speaking from the pillar-cloud.

" They kept his testimonies "

this is an abridged description of the obedient life of all these saints—even as John xvii. 6, " They have kept My word," is the Master's delineation of his disciples.

" He gave them a code of statutes,"

refers to such a passage as Deut. xxxiii. 4, where *the law* is reckoned among the prime blessings of Israel. Yes, it was always thus ; Jehovah answered them, and forgave them, yet was

" An avenging God because of their iniquities."

He is the same for ever. Just, sin-hating, righteous! And then a third time, as if to cause earth to respond to the song of heaven (Isa. vi. 3, Rev. iv. 8), the Psalmist extols Jehovah's holiness-

" Worship at the hill of his holiness,
For Jehovah our God is holy !"

It is throughout a Psalm proclaiming the untarnished **perfections** of the King,

Messiah ruling in holiness.

Psalm 100

A Psalm of praise

1 MAKE a joyful noise unto the Lord, all ye lands.
2 Serve the Lord with gladness : come before his presence **with singing.**
3 Know ye that the Lord he is God: it is he that hath made us, and **not we** ourselves ;
  We are his people, and the sheep of his pasture.
4 Enter into his gates with thanksgiving, and into his courts with praise :
  Be thankful unto him, and bless his name.
5 For the Lord is good; his mercy is everlasting ; and his truth endureth to all generations.

THE King and kingdom come. and holiness now swaying the

sceptre of a happy world, behold the whole earth as one great congregation uttering praise, and blessing, and thanksgiving, led by Messiah, the Chief Musician !

The title. Its title is, "*A psalm for thanksgiving.*" The word תּוֹדָה, the word used in Lev. vii. 12 for sacrifices of thanksgiving, when thankful men brought to the Lord fine flour, and oil, and wine, in token of their deep sense of blessings bestowed. Here, then, is Earth's thankoffering day arrived—

> "*Raise the peal of melody to Jehovah !*
> *All the earth !*"

The contents. They sing, in verse 2, of his redemption, not of creation-work. They say, " He *made us*," *i. e.*, made us what we are, a people to himself; as in Psa. xcv. 5, 1 Sam. xii. 6, and Deut. xxxii. 6. It was not we that made ourselves his (comp. Ezek. xxix. 3).

> " *He* (and not ourselves) *made us*
> *His people, and the flock whom he feeds.*" (Ver. 3.)

And of this psalm for all nations, this thanksgiving for redemption, this utterance of every heart and lip on earth and in heaven, this song of the whole family of God, of the glorified from their place, and the saved nations on earth in theirs, the burden is that old and well-known ascription to Jehovah—

> " *Jehovah is good*—(1 John iv. 8, ' God is love).*'*
> *His mercy endureth for ever,*"

sung at the altar long ago, 2 Chron. v. 13, and vii. 3, and 1 Chron. xvi. 34, Ezra iii. 11, and Jer. xxxiii. 11. To this they add—

> " *And his truth is from generation to generation.*"

He has fulfilled all he ever spoke ! He will continue for ever fulfilling all he has begun to fulfil ! He who is " full of grace and truth," is no doubt the leader of this song (Psa. xxii. 22), though He be not mentioned specially ; and it is just such a burst of rapturous delight and gratitude as will respond to the invitation from the throne, Rev. xix. 5–7. We therefore call it—

The heartfelt thanksgiving of the Great Congregation led by Messiah.

Psalm 101

A Psalm of David

1 I WILL sing of mercy and judgment : unto thee, O Lord, will I sing.
2 I will behave myself wisely in a perfect way. O when wilt thou come
   unto me ?
   I will walk within my house with a perfect heart.
3 I will set no wicked thing before mine eyes :
   I hate the work of them that turn aside ; it shall not cleave to me.
4 A froward heart shall depart from me : I will not know a wicked person.
5 Whoso privily slandereth his neighbour, him will I cut off.
   Him that hath an high look and a proud heart will not I suffer.
6 Mine eyes shall be upon the faithful of the land,
   That they may dwell with me :
   He that walketh in a perfect way, he shall serve me.
7 He that worketh deceit shall not dwell within my house :
   He that telleth lies shall not tarry in my sight.
8 I will early destroy all the wicked of the land ;
   That I may cut off all wicked doers from the city of the Lord.

WE descend into the valley again. The Righteous One is before *A new series.*
us, proposing to himself the rules of rectitude that shall be exhibited in his kingdom. We may suppose him pacing the valley
of Jehoshaphat, while still only on his way to the kingdom. The
Psalm that follows (cii.) lets us hear his complaints, and shews
us his comforts ; and the series proceeds, till we reach the end
of the cviii., where we rest under the banner of victory.

The first note of the Psalm guides us to Jehovah's true character, the *grace* and yet the *holiness* of his blessed name.

   " Mercy and judgment I will sing !"

This is Israel's " Arma virumque cano." Israel's theme of *The title.*
praise is never man, but always Jehovah. It is " *A Psalm of
David ;*" and therefore let us take it as David's utterance
when anticipating the establishment of his throne in Jerusalem—but as typical of David's Son, when he shall receive that
kingdom foretold in Isa. ix. 7, as well as now while he presides
over the Church, which is " *His house,*" (Heb. iii. 6).

The whole Psalm may be used by a believer. When he re- *David and*
calls " that night to be remembered" in his history, his time *believers.*
of escape from bondage, he will sing of " mercy and judgment,"
and not less when he reviews the way God has led him since,

mingling chastisements with forbearance. And, then, his desires and his resolutions as to the way he is to follow, resemble what is here breathed out by his Head. Still, it is of Christ that every clause speaks most fully. David could use it only in the measure in which a believer can.

The contents.   *" The perfect way,"* in verse 2, reminds us of faithful Abraham (Gen. xv. 1), whose seed, Christ, obeys what was then enjoined ; nor less are we reminded by אַשְׂכִּילָה, *" I will deal prudently,"* or *" walk wisely,"* of David, in 1 Sam. xviii. 14, 15, exhibiting a type which was more than fulfilled by him of whom Isaiah (liii. 13) has sung in lofty strains. If he asks, like one wearying for a friend that seems to tarry, *" When wilt thou come unto me ?"* it is no more than the language which David would be inclined to use in his wanderings, and even at Hebron, when still the kingdom was only half his own—" When wilt thou give me my promised kingdom ? when wilt thou *come to me* with that glory wherewith I am to come to my own ?"

He sees that day as if already come, and tells how he shall rule, from verses 3–7. May we not say that the germs of the *Book*

Proverbs.   *of Proverbs* are here—germs unfolded in the sunshine of Solomon's reign ? There can be no doubt of the similarity in many characteristic expressions (even such as using the word מְלָשְׁנִי, ver. 5, occurring nowhere else again but Prov. xxx. 10) ; and, indeed, these verses sketched what that great book of practical wisdom expands, the rules of holy living, by which every subject of Christ's kingdom shall be guided—the principles of Divine jurisprudence that shall be applied to the details of government in every province and in every house. With truth to which Absalom was a stranger, he could say, " Oh that I were made judge in the land, that any man that hath any suit or cause might come to me, and I would do him justice," (2 Sam. xv. 4). Rising early and standing beside the way of the gate, Absalom feigned to be eager for the interests of justice and of his fellow-men, even as Antichrist can still pretend ; but Christ shall sit on the throne of judgment for ever, the true antitype of every faithful judge who, at morning, sat at the gate-

From morning to morning will I destroy all the wicked of the land,
Cutting off from the city of the Lord all the workers of iniquity.

Terrible words ! the words of that same Jesus who, in expounding on the Mount of Beatitudes the law which he came to obey, declared his purpose to cast off all unholy pretenders to his favour, " *Ye that work iniquity*, depart from me," (Matt. vii. 23). And thus shall he sit on " the throne of David" (Isa. ix. 7), to order it and to settle it, and to rule earth at large. Then shall it be well known, that to " *sing of mercy and judgment*" (ver. 1), was to sing of Christ ruling " his own house." And thus the Psalm presents us with

The Righteous One's rules of holy government.

Psalm 102

A Prayer of the afflicted, when he is overwhelmed, and poureth out his complaint before the Lord

1 HEAR my prayer, O Lord, and let my cry come unto thee.

2 Hide not thy face from me in the day when I am in trouble ;
Incline thine ear unto me : in the day when I call answer me speedily.

3 For my days are consumed like smoke, and my bones are burned as an hearth.

4 My heart is smitten, and withered like grass : so that I forget to eat my bread.

5 By reason of the voice of my groaning my bones cleave to my skin.

6 I am like a pelican of the wilderness : I am like an owl of the desert.

7 I watch, and am as a sparrow alone upon the house top.

8 Mine enemies reproach me all the day ;
And they that are mad against me are sworn against me.

9 For I have eaten ashes like bread, and mingled my drink with weeping,

10 Because of thine indignation and thy wrath : for thou hast lifted me up, and cast me down.

11 My days are like a shadow that declineth ; and I am withered like grass.

12 But thou, O Lord, shalt endure for ever ;
And thy remembrance unto all generations.

13 Thou shalt arise, and have mercy upon Zion,
For the time to favour her, yea, the set time, is come.

14 For thy servants take pleasure in her stones, and favour the dust thereof.

15 So the heathen shall fear the name of the Lord,
And all the kings of the earth thy glory.

16 When the Lord shall build up Zion, he shall appear in his glory.

17 He will regard the prayer of the destitute, and not despise their prayer.

18 This shall be written for the generation to come :
And the people which shall be created shall praise the Lord.

19 For he hath looked down from the height of his sanctuary ;
From heaven did the Lord behold the earth ;

20 To hear the groaning of the prisoner; to loose those that are appointed to death;

21 To declare the name of the Lord in Zion, and his praise in Jerusalem;

22 When the people are gathered together, and the kingdoms, to serve the Lord.

23 He weakened my strength in the way; he shortened my days.

24 I said, O my God, take me not away in the midst of my days!
Thy years are throughout all generations:

25 Of old hast thou laid the foundation of the earth: and the heavens are the work of thy hands.

26 They shall perish, but thou shalt endure: yea, all of them shall wax old like a garment;
As a vesture shalt thou change them, and they shall be changed:

27 But thou art the same, and thy years shall have no end.

28 The children of thy servants shall continue, and their seed shall be established before thee.

The connection with the preceding. THE Greek lawgiver, Zaleucus, exemplified his own laws, even in their sorest penalties, by bearing half of his son's justly-deserved doom; and men read of the deed, and praise it. But our Lawgiver, God over all, has cast into the shade every such act of homage to law by the infinitude of suffering he in our nature endured, to honour the law of heaven and save the doomed transgressors. The twinkle of a taper bears more proportion to the blaze of the ever-burning sun, than this one act of Zaleucus, dictated by partiality for his own family, does to the honour rendered to law and justice by our Divine Redeemer. out of love to that holy law. In this Psalm we may see him, of whom Psa. ci. sang, giving honour to those rules of rectitude which there he proclaimed. For here we see the Righteous One, the Lord Jesus, laying the foundation of his kingdom of redeemed ones, by fully satisfying the demands of justice in their room.

The title. It is Christ, in the days of his humiliation, that is before us. The title has been thus versified,

" *This is the mourner's prayer when he is faint,*
And to the Eternal Father breathes his plaint," (Keble).

The simplicity of the Hebrew is most expressive—" *The prayer of the needy one when he is overwhelmed, and poureth out his complaint before the Lord.*" The " needy one" is Christ, who, " though he was rich, yet for our sakes became poor, that we through his poverty might become rich." A believer, also, can take it up, for much of it expresses what the members may often feel while taking the same view of the Father's face that Christ sought.

His doleful complaint occupies from 1 to 11 verses, resem- The contents. bling closely the deep pathos of Psa. xxii. Many of the allusions add depth to the words, conveying the idea, that all that was ever sorrowful in other men is to be found in this one " Man of Sorrows." Hannah's and David's sorrow, that took away all appetite for food (1 Sam. i. 7 ;* 2 Sam xii. 17), and even Saul's blank horror (1 Sam. xxviii. 20), are to be found in him—

> " *My heart is smitten, and withered like grass,*
> *So that I have forgotten to eat my bread.*" (Ver. 4.)

At such cost He purchased for believers on his name the privilege of "eating their meat with gladness and singleness of heart, praising God," as exemplified in the men of Pentecost (Acts ii. 46). He is like "*the pelican of the wilderness*" (sometimes seen at the Lake of Galilee, or by the shore of the Waters of Merom,) when it has left its companions in their desert resorts, and lingers alone, drooping and dying ; or like " *the owl in desolate places*," sometimes haunting ruins, sometimes sitting on some hollow tree forlorn, even at noon-day, as travellers have observed in Palestine (see *Narrative of Mission to the Jews,* chap. v.) ; or, like some solitary sparrow, separated from the happy company of its fellows, mournful on the house-top.† He is like Job in the ashes, tears mingling with his drink, cast away, or cast down low now, and yet once lifted high (vers. 9, 10), his days like the shadow.

But, as an angel strengthened him in Gethsemane, so the thought of his Father's purposes supports him here. At verse 12 he looks upward, as if he said, " But, O Father ! I do not

---

* Daniel's, too, chap. x. 3. Some have supposed *Daniel* the writer of this Psalm, the Holy Spirit using him in the days of the captivity, as a fit penman for a subject that touched upon many circumstances like his own.

† Waterston, the naturalist, however, fixes on the " *Passer solitarius,*" which is known in Egypt and Syria, and in the south of Italy. This bird is like a thrush in size, shape, habits, and has a sweet plaintive note ; but never associates with others of its species, not even with its own mate, except in breeding time. It is seen sitting solitary on house-tops, warbling, it may be, its plaintive song.

distrust thee (comp. Psa. xxii. 3) ; thou art to me the same as from all eternity ; thou art Jehovah ;

> "*Thy memorial is from generation to generation.*" (Ver. 13.)

That is, thy name manifested by deeds of love, and left on record for after ages, never changes.

> "*It is thou that shalt arise* (אַתָּה תָקוּם), *and have mercy on Zion ;*
> *For the time to favour her, the appointed time, cometh on*" (כִּי בָא,
> comp. Psa. xcvi. 13).

At that time, "Thy servants have mercy upon (יְחֹנְנוּ) the very dust of Zion ;" they feel sorrow for it.   At that time shall instruments be found not less efficient than Nehemiah in his day (see Neh. iii. 34, and iv. 4) to repair her wastes ; and at that time the nations shall not hinder but help on the work, seeing the glory of the Lord.   "*For*"—as if already beholding it accomplished, the vision is so clear (vers. 17, 18)—

> "*For the Lord has builded Zion !*
> *And His Glory has been seen !*
> *He has regarded the prayer of the destitute,*
> *And has not despised their prayer.*" (Comp. Psa. xxii. 24.)

He has heard the prayer of Zion's helpers, as well as the prayer of Him who was emphatically "The *Destitute* One"— the הָעַרְעָר, naked of all things, nowhere to lay his head ; like (as the word means) the heath in the wilderness (Jer. xvii. 6), like a bare solitary tree.   This humiliation ends in exaltation ; a future generation shall see it ; for the Lord's character is known as helper of the miserable, manifesting his grace in their deliverance ; and he has ever "*looked down*" (Deut. xxvi. 15) on Israel with such feelings, delivering (as he did Peter in after days) at times when men expected to see the captive's end.   He will look down (ver 20),

> "*To hear the groaning of the Prisoner* (Christ),
> *To set at large the children of death.*"   (Compare Isa. lxi. 1 ; Christ's
> members, and Israel among the rest.)

And this delivered company shall shew forth his praise on that day when Messiah appears in his glory among the nations, the Shiloh to whom, at length, all kindreds and people gather.

Such is the bright prospect, the glorious vision! From the garden of Gethsemane, with the cup at his lips, Christ sees the throne—glory, for a moment, bursting through the gloom. But it passes away; he feels himself still in the valley, and his sense of weakness and woe returns. "Sorrowful unto death," his soul cries-

> " *He has weakened my strength* in the way ;*
> *He has shortened my days.*
> *I say, O my God !*
> *Take me not away in midst of my days.*" (Ver. 23, 24.)
> Take me not away, let me not sink, ere my Mediatorial
> work is accomplished.

It is here (compare Heb. i. 10–12) that the voice from the Father addresses him. It is at this cry that the silence above is broken. The Father speaks words of strength and hope.

> " *Thy years are to all generations !* (בְּדוֹר דּוֹרִים, *q.d.*, in the depth
> of ages past, "generation of generations." Not as verse 12,
> לְדֹר וָדֹר.)
> *Of old thou hast laid the foundations of earth,*
> *And the heavens were the work of thy hands,*" &c. (Ver. 24, 25.)

The Eternal Son cannot faint or fail. He must be conqueror. He must pass safely up from this humiliation to the throne whence he descended. Yes, it is his to create these heavens and earth anew.

> " *These shall perish, but thou remainest-*
> *These shall wear out as a garment.*"

And when they have been worn out,

> " *Thou shalt change them as a vesture* (splendid attire, Gesen.),
> *And they shall be changed*" (יַחֲלִיפוּ).

The word for "change" implies in it (see Schultens on Prov.   Resurrection
time.
xxxi. 8) something *succeeding* to another, חָלַף, (the root of
"Caliph,") having in it the radical idea of *substitution*. It is
used in Arabic in regard to plants, when they are changed, by a
new effloresence, at spring-time; it is used by Job (xiv. 14) regarding his Resurrection change; it is used in Isa. ix. 9—" We

---

* "*His* strength," כֹּחוֹ is the true reading, (Hengst). Is it, "God has withdrawn the help which he used to make me feel?"

will put cedars in the room of sycamores." If so, we see very clearly the assurance contained in these words, that Christ must not only suffer, but enter into his glory too. As certainly as in the beginning he was the glorious Creator of all things, but was pleased to stoop to our world as a man of sorrows, so certainly he must once again create these fallen heavens and earth anew—no more the Man of Sorrows, but manifested as the Eternal Son.

Christ's members. In that glory his children shall share—in that unchanging bliss they "receive a kingdom that cannot be moved," (Heb. xii. 28). They at present often drink of his cup; they have some of his sorrows; for many an age their lot on earth has been like his—sorrowful. But, at length, the day of his glory dawns, and the "*children* of *his servants*" shall no more be strangers and wanderers; but (יִשְׁכֹּנוּ) "*shall continue,*" or pitch their tents and be fixed. The children of Abraham, Isaac, and Jacob, "*his servants,*" may be specially intended; at least, they are not forgotten. For now his saints enter on the possession of Earth, and the millennial race of Israelites inherit their Land, reigned over by the Lord and his glorified saints. And thus we understand this Psalm, beginning in woe, ending in gladness. It is

Messiah's complaint and comforts in the days of his humiliation.

Psalm 103

A Psalm of David

1 Bless the Lord, O my soul! and all that is within me, bless his holy name!

2 Bless the Lord, O my soul, and forget not all his benefits:

3 Who forgiveth all thine iniquities; who healeth all thy diseases;

4 Who redeemeth thy life from destruction;
Who crowneth thee with lovingkindness and tender mercies;

5 Who satisfieth thy mouth with good things; so that thy youth is renewed like the eagle's.

6 The Lord executeth righteousness and judgment for all that are oppressed.

7 He made known his ways unto Moses, his acts unto the children of Israel.

8 The Lord is merciful and gracious, slow to anger, and plenteous in mercy.

9 He will not always chide : neither will he keep his anger for ever.

10 He hath not dealt with us after our sins; nor rewarded us according to our iniquities.

11 For as the heaven is high above the earth, so great is his mercy toward them that fear him.

12 As far as the east is from the west, so far hath he removed our transgressions from us.

13 Like as a father pitieth his children, so the Lord pitieth them that fear him.

14 For he knoweth our frame ; he remembereth that we are dust.

15 As for man, his days are as grass : as a flower of the field, so he flourisheth.

16 For the wind passeth over it, and it is gone ; and the place thereof shall know it no more.

17 But the mercy of the Lord is from everlasting to everlasting upon them that fear him,

And his righteousness unto children's children ;

18 To such as keep his covenant, and to those that remember his commandments to do them.

19 The Lord hath prepared his throne in the heavens ; and his kingdom ruleth over all.

20 Bless the Lord, ye his angels, that excel in strength,

That do his commandments, hearkening unto the voice of his word.

21 Bless ye the Lord, all ye his hosts; ye ministers of his, that do his pleasure.

22 Bless the Lord, all his works, in all places of his dominion.

Bless the Lord, O my soul.

How often have saints in Scotland sung this Psalm in days when they celebrated the *Lord's Supper !* It is thereby specially known in our land. It is connected also with a remarkable case in the days of John Knox. Elizabeth Adamson, a woman who attended on his preaching " because he more fully opened the fountain of God's mercies than others did," was led to Christ and to rest, in hearing this Psalm, after enduring such agony of soul that she said, concerning racking pains of body, " A thousand years of this torment, and ten times more joined, are not to be compared to a quarter of an hour of my soul's trouble." She asked for this Psalm again before departing : " It was in receiving it that my troubled soul first tasted God's mercy, which is now sweeter to me than if all the kingdoms of the earth were given me to possess."

Of this Psalm, when viewed as following the preceding, we Connection. may say, Fruits of Messiah's work appear—glory to God, goodwill to man. We might exclaim, Behold the Redeemer and his gifts! for it is the song of a redeemed one by the Redeemer's side. *Forgiveness* is the chief and foremost of the mercies celebrated. In tone it might be compared with Mark ii. 5, 9.

The plan. 1. *The Gifts received* (ver. 1–5) are celebrated, not only with the lips, but with the whole soul. God's Israel do not now forget him when he has blessed them (Deut. vi. 12 ; viii. 11, 12), for the blessings are more than temporal, and the diseases healed are more than bodily (Exod. xv. 26 ; Deut. xxix. 23). The strength imparted, that makes them like the soaring eagle, and to be imparted when the resurrection body is bestowed, is a removal of the evils of sin. An usual word is employed in verse 5, " *Who hath satisfied* עֶדְיֵךְ *with good;*" rendered by some, " thy *mouth ;*" by Hengstenberg, " thy. *beauty,*" or ornament, *i. e.*, thy soul ; by Gesenius and others, "thine *age ;*" and by some, simply, " *even thee.*" This full, rich, overflowing burst of song has led to the use of a term as rare as the tone of the song. The term " *crowning*" expresses the bestowal of dignity as well as favour, and the reference to the eagle is, *q. d.*, makest me grow young again, and so to soar like an eagle.

2. *The Receivers of the Gifts* (ver. 6, 7).—The oppressed, the helpless, have been the receivers of his mercy. It is the manner of Jehovah to give thus graciously. He is the Jehovah who made known " his *ways*" to Moses (his principles of action), and shewed his " *works*" to Israel, in the days of their bondage.

3. *The Giver*, the fountain-head of these blessings (ver. 8–18).—He is that Jehovah whose name Moses heard (Exod. xxxiv. 6) at the rock of Horeb—a name more plentiful in streams for the thirsty souls, than the smitten rock of Horeb for thirsty Israel. Here is the *Fountain-head*—" Merciful, gracious, slow to anger, plenteous in mercy." Here are seven *streams* from that fountain-head :—*a*, Love *unupbraiding* (ver. 9) ; then, *b*, Love that blesses *the undeserving* (ver. 10) ; *c*, Love *infinite in extent* (ver. 11) ; *d*, Love *thoroughgoing* in its nature (ver. 12) ; *e*, Love very *tender* (ver. 13) ; *f*, Love that

sympathizes with us (ver. 14, 15, 16); Love that is *undecaying* (ver. 17, 18).

4. *The Kingdom of the Giver.*—In verse 19 we see that these many streams bear us on to the ocean—for we are led first to the Throne in the heavens, then to the Kingdom that ruleth over all the earth.

5. *The closing burst of Praise to the Giver.*—The morning stars sang together, and the sons of God shouted for joy, at the sight of creation issuing from the Creator's hands. Much more cause is there now for such another song ; ay, and a song so much nobler as the theme is loftier. Angels must bear a part, bringing all their strength to the work—this work of praise. All Jehovah's hosts, all Jehovah's servants, all Jehovah's creatures, inanimate as well as animate (Psa. civ. 4), in all places of his dominion, must take up the thanksgiving, and praise, and blessing. It is Rev. v. 13 anticipated. The man that hears that song, shall he not be counted a blessed man ? a thousand times blessed ? But the man himself shall cast his crown of bliss at the feet of his Lord—" *Bless the Lord,* O my soul !" ending as he began this

Song of a redeemed one by the Redeemer's side.

Psalm 104

1 BLESS the Lord, O my soul !
   O Lord my God, thou art very great; thou art clothed with honour and majesty.
2 Who coverest thyself with light as with a garment :
   Who stretchest out the heavens like a curtain :
3 Who layeth the beams of his chambers in the waters :
   Who maketh the clouds his chariots: who walketh upon the wings of the wind :
4 Who maketh his angels spirits; his ministers a flaming fire :
5 Who laid the foundations of the earth, that it should not be removed for ever.
6 Thou coveredst it with the deep as with a garment : the waters stood above the mountains.
7 At thy rebuke they fled ; at the voice of thy thunder they hasted away.
8 They go by to the mountains; they go down by the valleys.
   Unto the place which thou hast founded for them.

9 Thou hast set a bound that they may not pass over;
   That they turn not again to cover the earth.
10 He sendeth the springs into the valleys, which run among the hills.
11 They give drink to every beast of the field : the wild asses quench their
    thirst.
12 By them shall the fowls of the heaven have their habitation, which sing
    among the branches.
13 He watereth the hills from his chambers : the earth is satisfied with the
    fruit of thy works.
14 He causeth the grass to grow for the cattle, and herb for the service of
    man,
    That he may bring forth food out of the earth,
15 And wine that maketh glad the heart of man, and oil to make his face to
    shine,
    And bread which strengtheneth man's heart.
16 The trees of the Lord are full of sap, the cedars of Lebanon which he
    hath planted ;
17 Where the birds make their nests : as for the stork, the fir-trees are her
    house.
18 The high hills are a refuge for the wild goats ; and the rocks for the
    conies.
19 He appointed the moon for seasons : the sun knoweth his going down.
20 Thou makest darkness, and it is night, wherein all the beasts of the forest
    do creep forth.
21 The young lions roar after their prey, and seek their meat from God.
22 The sun ariseth, they gather themselves together, and lay them down in
    their dens.
23 Man goeth forth unto his work and to his labour until the evening.
24 O Lord, how manifold are thy works!
    In wisdom hast thou made them all : the earth is full of thy riches.
25 So is this great and wide sea,
    Wherein are things creeping innumerable, both small and great beasts.
26 There go the ships : there is that leviathan, whom thou hast made to play
    therein.
27 These wait all upon thee, that thou mayest give them their meat in due
    season.
28 That thou givest them they gather : thou openest thine hand, they are
    filled with good.
29 Thou hidest thy face, they are troubled :
    Thou takest away their breath, they die, and return to their dust.
30 Thou sendest forth thy spirit, they are created : and thou renewest the
    face of the earth.
31 The glory of the Lord shall endure for ever : the Lord shall rejoice in
    his works.
32 He looketh on the earth, and it trembleth : he toucheth the hills, and
    they smoke.
33 I will sing unto the Lord as long as I live : I will sing praise to my God
    while I have my being.

34 My meditation ot him shall be sweet: I will be glad in the Lord.

35 Let the sinners be consumed out of the earth, and let the wicked be no more.

Bless thou the Lord, O my soul. Praise ye the Lord.

ONE of our poets has said-

> " — — *The song of woe*
> *Is, after all, an earthly song.*"

The theme distinguished from the preceding.

It is not perpetuated in heaven, nor in the glorious kingdom; for there praise, " from blest voices uttering joy," fills the many mansions. Last Psalm shewed us this coming joy, arising from spiritual sources—the soul enjoying God, bathing in his holy love, knowing him, obeying him, serving him, blessing him, seeing him as he is, and for ever with him. This Psalm calls our attention to the glory of our God *displayed in the material world* already, and *yet to be d sp ayed* in it more fully.

The key-note, " *Bless the Lord, O my soul!* " is that on which it is raised. The same redeemed soul that, with anointed eyes, saw Jehovah in Redemption works, beholds him here in Creation scenes—in the scenes of the old and new earth. With the Book of Genesis (chap i.) in his hand, he surveys the *first day's* handiwork (ver. 1, 2),* God's mantle of light, and some folds of it thrown over the new-made earth. Unlike the array of earthly monarchs, " *glory and majesty*" (symbolised by *light*,) are his robe, the skirts of which adorn the earth, which is his footstool.† Then the *second day's* work (ver. 3-5)—" *He maketh his upper chambers with waters;*" that is, the very waters in the clouds are the beams on which the floor of the upper chamber of his palace is laid.—He makes *winds* to act for him as angels, and *lightnings* to do the office of *servants.*‡

The contents.

---

* Not that the writer keeps close to historical arrangement; for, as Augustine says, on Psa. cv.—" Libera est laudatio a lege narrantis et texentis historiam."

† The eastern upper chamber was for retirement and refreshment; God is spoken of as having such an *Aliah*, built up in bright æther on the slender foundation of rainy clouds. (Tholuck.)

‡ In Heb. i. 7, the argument is, that angels are truly no more than the mere handiwork of the Creator; for he says that he uses winds for angels, flames of fire for ministering ones, and *vice versâ*. Thus angels are classed with other common material agencies employed by God, and no higher.

The *third day's* work, wherein the platform of our earth was cleared, is celebrated from verses 6 to 18—"*As for the deep, thou coverest it* (ל) *as with a garment*" (see Hengstenberg). Does not this mean that, on the third day, the Lord *first* shone on the waters that covered earth, and stood above the hills, *then,* the voice from The Glory commanded these waters to their beds? And thus it was that springs began to flow among the hills, and have flowed ever since, wild asses coming to drink, birds among leafy trees, overhanging the brooks (עֲלֵיהֶם, verse 12), uttering their cheerful notes, "living their life of music" —the Lord condescending to care for every creature, yes, and for every blade of grass, and for the olive that yields oil for man, and for the vine, and the corn ; for the cedars, too, and the pines or cypresses on Lebanon, where little birds and stately storks alike find nestling ; while goats and jerboas sport among the rocks below. Over this scene, the *fourth day's creation* casts its beams (ver. 19–24). Sun and moon go forth to regulate man and beast, by interchange of day and night. And the *fifth day's* creation scene is not forgotten (vers. 25, 26)—the wonders of the sea ; the living creatures of the immense ocean. If man has found use for that ocean, and has floated his ships upon it, in so doing he has discovered some of the uses to which the Lord's treasures hid there for him may be applied ; at the same time, how feeble man's work appears, when you observe that the Lord has constituted these mighty waters the home and native abode of such monsters as "*Leviathan whom thou hast made to take his pastime therein.*" As for the *sixth day's* work, it was introduced at verses 21–23—man and beast. As the Psalm is not historical, but a review of creation by one of the created ones who inhabit that earth, hence it may be that *man and beast* were introduced when singing of the uses of *sun and moon* to us— all the rather, because man's workmanship, "the *ships,*" could not be spoken of without previously introducing man himself.

Providence is creation continued from hour to hour, from age to age ; and of this, verses 27, 28, 29 sing, casting in the thought of "*creation subject to vanity*" (ver. 29).

Every spring we have a specimen of the Creator's power, to

renew the earth. It may be, in part, to this annual renewal, when winter is over and gone, that verse 30 refers. Even if it be so, however, it contains, besides, the promise and prospect of earth's final renewal at the "Times of Restitution of all things ;" for then only shall we know the meaning lodged in the words,

" Thou makest new the face of the earth."

If, at verse 24, the adoring exclamation spontaneously broke from the beholder's lips, " O Lord ! how manifold are thy works ! in wisdom thou hast made them all !" it shall yet again burst from admiring witnesses of that New Creation. And then shall that chorus be heard from heaven and earth together ;

" The glory of the Lord shall endure for ever !
The Lord shall rejoice in his works !" (Ver. 31.)

They shall say of him in their songs—

" It is He who looked (הַמַּבִּיט) on earth and it trembled !
He toucheth the mountains, and they smoke."

One shall cry to the other—

" While I live, I will sing to the Lord ;
During the whole period of my existence (eternity) *I will praise my God.*
Sweet, as it rests on him, shall my meditation be !
I (אָנֹכִי though no one else should) will rejoice in the Lord."

At last has come that " New Earth, wherein dwelleth righteousness ;" for " *sinners are consumed* (as in Num. xiv. 35), the wicked are no more." Even in anticipation now we cannot but join in the " Bless the Lord, O my soul !" and the " *Hallelujah*" that closes this celebration of the Lord's glory—

The glory of the Lord revealed in Earth created and Earth renewed.

Psalm 105

1 O GIVE thanks unto the Lord ; call upon his name :
Make known his deeds among the people.

2 Sing unto him, sing psalms unto him : talk ye of all his wondrous works.

3 Glory ye in his holy name : let the heart of them rejoice that seek the Lord.

4 Seek the Lord, and his strength : seek his face evermore.

5 Remember his marvellous works that he hath done;
His wonders, and the judgments of his mouth ;

6 O ye seed of Abraham his servant, ye children of Jacob his chosen

7 He is the Lord our God : his judgments are in all the earth.

8 He hath remembered his covenant for ever,
The word which he commanded to a thousand generations.

9 Which covenant he made with Abraham, and his oath unto Isaac,

10 And confirmed the same unto Jacob for a law, and to Israel for an everlasting covenant,

11 Saying, Unto thee will I give the land of Canaan, the lot of your inheritance.

12 When there were but a few men in number ; yea, very few, and strangers in it.

13 When they went from one nation to another, from one kingdom to another people;

14 He suffered no man to do them wrong: yea, he reproved kings for their sakes,

15 Saying, Touch not mine anointed, and do my prophets no harm.

16 Moreover he called for a famine upon the land : he brake the whole staff of bread.

17 He sent a man before them, even Joseph, who was sold for a servant :

18 Whose feet they hurt with fetters: he was laid in iron :

19 Until the time that his word came, the word of the Lord tried him.

20 The king sent and loosed him ; even the ruler of the people, and let him go free.

21 He made him lord of his house, and ruler of all his substance:

22 To bind his princes at his pleasure ; and teach his senators wisdom.

23 Israel also came into Egypt; and Jacob sojourned in the land of Ham.

24 And he increased his people greatly ; and he made them stronger than their enemies.

25 He turned their heart to hate his people, to deal subtilely with his servants.

26 He sent Moses his servant; and Aaron whom he had chosen.

27 They shewed his signs among them, and wonders in the land of Ham.

28 He sent darkness, and made it dark ; and they rebelled not against his word.

29 He turned their waters into blood, and slew their fish.

30 Their land brought forth frogs in abundance, in the chambers of their kings.

31 He spake, and there came divers sorts of flies, and lice in all their coasts.

32 He gave them hail for rain, and flaming fire in their land.

33 He smote their vines also and their fig-trees ; and brake the trees of their coasts.

34 He spake, and the locusts came, and caterpillars, and that without number.

35 And did eat up all the herbs in their land, and devoured the fruit of their ground.

36 He smote also all the firstborn in their land, the chief of all their strength.

37 He brought them forth also with silver and gold :
And there was not one feeble person among their tribes.
38 Egypt was glad when they departed : for the fear of them fell upon them.
39 He spread a cloud for a covering ; and fire to give light in the night.
40 The people asked, and he brought quaïls, and satisfied them with the bread of heaven.
41 He opened the rock, and the waters gushed out ; they ran in the dry places like a river.
42 For he remembered his holy promise, and Abraham his servant.
43 And he brought forth his people with joy, and his chosen with gladness :
44 And gave them the lands of the heathen : and they inherited the labour of the people ;
45 That they might observe his statutes, and keep his laws.
Praise ye the Lord.

THE first fifteen verses were written at the bringing up of the Ark, 1 Chron. xvi. They tell that it is sovereign grace that ruleth over all—it is a sovereign God. Out of a fallen world he takes whom he pleases—individuals, families, nations. He chose *Israel* long ago, that they might be the objects of grace, and their land the theatre of its display. He will yet again return to Israel, when the days of his Kingdom of Glory draw near ; and Israel shall have a full share—the very fullest and richest—in his blessings, temporal and spiritual. In these days shall this song be sung again- God's sovereignty.

> " *O give thanks unto the Lord, call upon his name !*
> *Make known among the Gentiles his workings,*" &c.

Inviting, in such strains (ver. 1–8), all Israel to tell of their redeeming God among the nations ; " He, the Lord, is our God" (ver. 7). They recount his benefits, from the days of Abraham onward to their entering in peace upon possession of Canaan—the type of the more blessed rest remaining for them and us under the true Joshua. The *Covenant* (ver. 8, 9) was the sure foundation of this favour manifested toward them ; and that same *Covenant* (ver. 42) was the Lord's reason for putting the cope-stone on the work. It is " grace, grace," from beginning to end. And the repeated call on saints to "make God's deeds known" breathe a missionary spirit, and should be so felt by us who know the great deeds of Calvary and Pentecost. Horne, also, well remarks on verse 2, "*Sing —talk,*—music and conversation are two things by which the mind of man receiveth great good or a great deal of harm. The contents.

They who make Jehovah the subject of both will enjoy a heaven on earth."

1. The Psalm, then, selects incidents that may best touch the heart. Thus *Israel's insignificance*, even after becoming a nation, and their weakness, and wanderings (vers. 12–15). They went " from *the* kingdom," a land promised to them, (מִמַּמְלָכָה) " to a foreign people."

> " *From kingdom unto kingdom,*
> *Sojourned a little band :*
> *From place to place compelled to stray—*
> *Strangers in a strange land.*" (Barclay.)

Yet they are " *anointed ;*" the oil of him who set them apart is on their head ; and therefore they are safe (ver. 15). He has separated them for himself, and made them " *his prophets*" —teachers of his will to other nations of earth.

2. *Joseph's History* is next selected as a theme ; for there Jehovah is seen casting down and lifting up ; using, too, a despised instrument to be a glorious deliverer. There is something graphic in the language of verse 16, " *He called for famine,*" representing it as his waiting servant, (Horne). Scarcely less so is the literal rendering of verse 17, " He sent a man before them"—but how ? To man's eye there appeared no sending ; but it was to emerge from this, " *Joseph was sold for a servant.*" Here again is grace—grace flowing in unthought-of channels (vers. 16–24).

3. *Egyptian bondage* follows, but only as introducing *redemption*—redemption by power, and redemption that proclaimed Jehovah's wrath on the rebellious (vers. 25, 26). We see Jehovah removing from the rebellious resisters of his will the blessing of light, the blessing of water for their thirst, the blessing of domestic comfort, the blessing of fertilising rain, the blessing of the increase yielded by the vine and fig, the grass and grain, nay, the blessing of health and of life (27–36). On the other hand, his blessing rests, in sovereign grace, on his redeemed (vers. 37–43)—the blessing that is the reverse of these inflictions on Egypt, besides strength, security from foes, guidance, providential supply of food and water.

> " *He brought forth his people with rejoicing,*
> *His elect with the song of joy.*"

But all this—not for their sakes—only because of his holy covenant. " Grace, grace," pervades his ways ; and grace leads them into possession of their inheritance (ver. 44) ; but leads them thither to glorify their redeeming God, even as shall be the case at their final return–

> " *For the sake of having his statutes observed,*
> *And his laws preserved.*
> *Hallelujah !"*

Whether we consider the sweet singer here to be David, or David's Son, who sat in the pillar-cloud over Israel's tents, the theme is the same.

The singers.

The Lord glorified in his redeeming acts toward Israel.

Psalm 106

1 Praise ye the Lord.   O give thanks unto the Lord.
For he is good : for his mercy endureth for ever.
2 Who can utter the mighty acts of the Lord ? who can shew forth all his praise ?
3 Blessed are they that keep judgment, and he that doeth righteousness at all times.
4 Remember me, O Lord, with the favour that thou bearest unto thy people : O visit me with thy salvation !
5 That I may see the good of thy chosen, that I may rejoice in the gladness of thy nation,
That I may glory with thine inheritance.
6 We have sinned with our fathers, we have committed iniquity, we have done wickedly.
7 Our fathers understood not thy wonders in Egypt;
They remembered not the multitude of thy mercies;
But provoked him at the sea, even at the Red Sea.
8 Nevertheless he saved them for his name's sake,
That he might make his mighty power to be known.
9 He rebuked the Red Sea also, and it was dried up :
So he led them through the depths, as through the wilderness.
10 And he saved them from the hand of him that hated them,
And redeemed them from the hand of the enemy.
11 And the waters covered their enemies: there was not one of them left.
12 Then believed they his words ; they sang his praise.
13 They soon forgat his works; they waited not for his counsel:
14 But lusted exceedingly in the wilderness, and tempted God in the desert.
15 And he gave them their request ; but sent leanness into their soul.

16 They envied Moses also in the camp, and Aaron the saint of the Lord.

17 The earth opened and swallowed up Dathan, and covered the company of Abiram ;

18 And a fire was kindled in their company; the flame burned up the wicked.

19 They made a calf in Horeb, and worshipped the molten image.

20 Thus they changed their glory into the similitude of an ox that eateth grass.

21 They forgat God their Saviour, which had done great things in Egypt,

22 Wondrous works in the land of Ham, and terrible things by the Red Sea.

23 Therefore he said that he would destroy them,
Had not Moses his chosen stood before him in the breach,
To turn away his wrath, lest he should destroy them.

24 Yea, they despised the pleasant land, they believed not his word :

25 But murmured in their tents, and hearkened not unto the voice of the Lord.

26 Therefore he lifted up his hand against them,
To overthrow them in the wilderness :

27 To overthrow their seed also among the nations,
And to scatter them in the lands.

28 They joined themselves also unto Baal-peor, and ate the sacrifices of the dead.

29 Thus they provoked him to anger with their inventions : and the plague brake in upon them.

30 Then stood up Phinehas, and executed judgment : and so the plague was stayed.

31 And that was counted unto him for righteousness unto all generations for evermore.

32 They angered him also at the waters of strife, so that it went ill with Moses for their sakes :

33 Because they provoked his spirit, so that he spake unadvisedly with his lips.

34 They did not destroy the nations, concerning whom the Lord commanded them :

35 But were mingled among the heathen, and learned their works.

36 And they served their idols : which were a snare unto them.

37 Yea, they sacrificed their sons and their daughters unto devils,

38 And shed innocent blood, even the blood of their sons and of their daughters,
Whom they sacrificed unto the idols of Canaan :
And the land was polluted with blood.

39 Thus were they defiled with their own works,
And went a whoring with their own inventions.

40 Therefore was the wrath of the Lord kindled against his people,
Insomuch that he abhorred his own inheritance.

41 And he gave them into the hand of the heathen ; and they that hated them ruled over them.

42 Their enemies also oppressed them, and they were brought into subjection under their hand.

43 Many times did he deliver them; but they provoked him with their counsel,

And were brought low for their iniquity.

44 Nevertheless he regarded their affliction, when he heard their cry:

45 And he remembered for them his covenant,

And repented according to the multitude of his mercies.

46 He made them also to be pitied of all those that carried them captives.

47 Save us, O Lord our God, and gather us from among the heathen,

To give thanks unto thy holy name, and to triumph in thy praise.

48 Blessed be the Lord God of Israel from everlasting to everlasting:

And let all the people say, Amen. Praise ye the Lord.

WE are still traversing the same field   We are still listening   The theme.
to the gracious acts of the Lord toward one nation of his ransomed—namely, Israel. It is another portion of their history
that is reviewed, but there is as much of grace, sovereign grace,
in this portion as in the first.   And hence it opens, like the
former, with praise and adoring wonder-

> " Hallelujah ! praise ye the Lord !
> For he is good ! for his mercy is for ever.
> Who can tell the mighty deeds of the Lord ?
> Who can shew forth all his praise ?"

The only mode in which the creature can even attempt aright   The plan.
to shew forth his praise is, by continued and ever increasing
service—" Blessed are they that keep judgment, and they that
do righteousness at all times." So great has the Lord's favour
to his Israel been, that the sweet singer, whoever he be-
David, as in 1 Chron. xvi., or David's Lord, in his day—while
remembering that favour and singular love, exclaims (ver.
4, 5),

> " Remember me, Lord, with the favour of (shewn to) thy people !
> Visit me with thy salvation ! (such as was wrought for them.)
> That I may see the good of thy chosen ones,
> And may rejoice in the joy of thy nation,*
> And glory with thine inheritance."

If the type afforded such matter for praise, what shall the an-

* Here the term גּוֹי is applied to Israel. It is only so used when עַם has
preceded it, says Hengstenberg. It may also, in such cases, imply that God's
people (עַם) are, in themselves, no better than גּוֹיִם. But גּוֹי though they
be by nature, they are thine.

titype ? If that kingdom of Israel furnished such proofs of Jehovah's love, what shall The Kingdom that is yet to come ?

To magnify the Lord's grace, confession is made of Israel's sin—forgetfulness, ingratitude, selfishness (vers. 6–15) ; and then of rebellion, idolatry, murmuring unbelief, lust, and lewdness ; persevering unbelief, neglect of duty, conformity to the heathen world (vers. 16–39). Scene upon scene is brought before us in which Israel is seen defiled, polluted, stained to the core with sin. Yet the Lord saved them, when they returned from their ways (vers. 40–46), fulfilling the promise in Lev. xxvi. 12, and answering the prayer (1 Kings viii. 47), left for all ages.

Yes ; these scenes of grace toward the basest, most ungrateful, most perverse, are for all ages, to lead them to the cry in verse 47,

> " *Save us, O Lord, our God !*
> *And gather us from the Gentiles.*"

The amen. Israel must raise that cry in these latter days. Israel will raise it soon. Ere long, they shall take up the harp of David, and Solomon, and Asaph, and Heman, and the sons of Korah, and use all these songs ; and this among the rest—this among the first. On that day, instead of " *Amen*" to the solemn curse, as in Deut. xxvii. 15–26, the people shall, with one accord, say " *Amen*" to the song of thanksgiving raised to Jehovah, who has gathered them from the Gentiles.

> " *Blessed be Jehovah, God of Israel,*
> *From everlasting and unto everlasting !*
> *And let all the people* (הָעָם) *say, Amen !*
> *Hallelujah !*"

Thus setting forth

The Lord glorified in his long-suffering to Israel, and in their final gathering.

Psalm 107

1 O GIVE thanks unto the Lord, for he is good : for his mercy endureth for
ever.
2 Let the redeemed of the Lord say so, whom he hath redeemed from the
hand of the enemy ;
3 And gathered them out of the lands,
From the east, and from the west, from the north, and from the south.
4 They wandered in the wilderness in a solitary way ; they found no city to
dwell in.
5 Hungry and thirsty, their soul fainted in them.
6 Then they cried unto the Lord in their trouble, and he delivered them out
of their distresses ;
7 And he led them forth by the right way, that they might go to a city of
habitation.
8 Oh that men would praise the Lord for his goodness,
And for his wonderful works to the children of men!
9 For he satisfieth the longing soul, and filleth the hungry soul with goodness.
10 Such as sit in darkness and in shadow of death, being bound in affliction
and iron,
11 Because they rebelled against the words of God,
And contemned the counsel of the Most High :
12 Therefore he brought down their heart with labour;
They fell down, and there was none to help.
13 Then they cried unto the Lord in their trouble, and he saved them out
of their distresses.
14 He brought them out of darkness and the shadow of death, and brake
their bands in sunder.
15 Oh that men would praise the Lord for his goodness,
And for his wonderful works to the children of men !
16 For he hath broken the gates of brass, and cut the bars of iron in sunder.
17 Fools because of their transgression, and because of their iniquities, are
afflicted.
18 Their soul abhorreth all manner of meat ; and they draw near unto the
gates of death.
19 Then they cry unto the Lord in their trouble, and he saveth them out of
their distresses.
20 He sent his word, and healed them, and delivered them from their destruction.
21 Oh that men would praise the Lord for his goodness,
And for his wonderful works to the children of men !
22 And let them sacrifice the sacrifices of thanksgiving, and declare his works
with rejoicing.
23 They that go down to the sea in ships, that do business in great waters ;
24 These see the works of the Lord, and his wonders in the deep.

25 For he commandeth, and raiseth the stormy wind, which lifteth up the
waves thereof.

26 They mount up to the heaven, they go down again to the depths:
Their soul is melted because of trouble.

27 They reel to and fro, and stagger like a drunken man, and are at their
wit's end.

28 Then they cry unto the Lord in their trouble, and he bringeth them out
of their distresses.

29 He maketh the storm a calm, so that the waves thereof are still.

30 Then are they glad because they be quiet ; so he bringeth them into their
desired haven.

31 Oh that men would praise the Lord for his goodness,
And for his wonderful works to the children of men!

32 Let them exalt him also in the congregation of the people,
And praise him in the assembly of the elders.

33 He turneth rivers into a wilderness, and the watersprings into dry ground ;

34 A fruitful land into barrenness, for the wickedness of them that dwell
therein.

35 He turneth the wilderness into a standing water, and dry ground into
watersprings.

36 And there he maketh the hungry to dwell, that they may prepare a city
for habitation ;

37 And sow the fields, and plant vineyards, which may yield fruits of increase.

38 He blesseth them also, so that they are multiplied greatly ;
And suffereth not their cattle to decrease.

39 Again, they are minished and brought low through oppression, affliction,
and sorrow.

40 He poureth contempt upon princes,
And causeth them to wander in the wilderness, where there is no way.

41 Yet setteth he the poor on high from affliction, and maketh him families
like a flock.

42 The righteous shall see it, and rejoice : and all iniquity shall stop her
mouth.

43 Whoso is wise, and will observe these things,
Even they shall understand the lovingkindness of the Lord.

The connection. SCARCELY has the ascending cry of the preceding Psalm ceased,
when the answer* comes. For here is *all Israel gathered.*
We say, *all Israel ;* for it is Israel peculiarly who form the
subject of it. At the same time, on the same principle that

---

* The Jewish *Fifth division of the Psalms* begins here, apparently for no
other reason than because Psa. cvi. ended with an *Amen.* Properly there is a
close connection between Psa. cv., cvi., and cvii., equivalent to Part I., Part II.,
Part III., of one and the same narrative.

leads us to admit every member of Christ's body to share in David's hopes and faith, and in the Son of David's confidence and victory, we find this a Psalm which every one of God's redeemed, in any age, can sympathise in, and can sing with reference to themselves.

Hengstenberg thinks it suited peculiarly to a joyful, national service of thanksgiving, such as that Feast of Tabernacles in Ezra's day (chap. iii.), after the few bands of the dispersed of Israel had returned to their land. If it would be appropriate in such circumstances, much more will it be so when all Israel, from all lands of their dispersion, have returned home. And thus it is that Dr Allix describes it—"*A Hymn of the Synagogue, gathered from its last dispersion*"—applicable to that day foretold by Isa. xi. 11, when the Lord recovers the remnant of his people, the second time, "from Assyria, and from Egypt, and from Pathros, and from Cush, and from Elam, and from Shinar, and from Hamath, and from the isles of the sea." Some have experience of their forefathers' trials in the desert (ver. 4–7) ; some have come from the prison-house (ver. 10–14) ; some have been emaciated by sickness (ver. 17–20); others have been all but swallowed up by the sea (ver. 23–30) ; —all have been witnesses of the Lord's curse on their own land and nation for sin, and now have become witnesses of the blessing when sin is removed. A nation that has had, and is to have, such experience is the fittest of all to form a type, or be the pattern, of God's discovery of his ways in grace, to men of every nation, and kindred, and tongue, whom he redeems. It is such manifestations as these that make "*the righteous see and rejoice ;*" it is such views of God's ways that cause "*all iniquity to stop her mouth*" (ver. 42) ; and it is thus that men discover Jehovah's thoughts that are higher than our thoughts.

> "*Whoso is wise will consider these things,*
> *And will understand the mercies* (חַסְדֵי) *of the Lord.*"

The kingdom will be the time and place for a thorough and searching inquiry into the Lord's past ways. We try this inquiry now, and what we do succeed in discerning is most profitable. But our eyes are dim. O for the time when Israel,

(margin note: Its typical and emblematic scenes.)

and we beside them, shall look back on the Lord's ways, such ways as are described here, and understand the Lord's character and the Lord's lovingkindness! From the heights of glory we shall be able to look far down into the depths of grace.

The contents. But no wonder it closes thus, when we dwell upon its many subjects of praise and thanksgiving. Its first words are abundant in thought concerning Jehovah—"*For he is good.*" Is not this (as we saw in Psa. c.) the Old Testament version of "*God is love?*" (1 John iv. 8.) And then, "*For his mercy endureth for ever.*" Is not this the gushing stream from the fountain of Love?—the never-failing stream, on whose banks "the *redeemed of the Lord*" walk, "*those whom he has redeemed from the hand of the enemy*" (Hengstenberg, "*hand of trouble,*" צָר). Nor is the rich significance of these clauses diminished by our knowing that they were, from time to time, the burden of the *altar-song.* When the ark came to its resting-place (1 Chron. xvi. 34), they sang to the Lord—"*For he is good; for his mercy endureth for ever!*" In Solomon's temple, the singers and players on instruments were making the resplendent walls of the newly-risen temple resound with these very words, when the glory descended (2 Chron. v. 13); and these were the words that burst from the lips of the awe-struck and delighted worshippers, who saw the fire descend on the altar (2 Chron. vii. 3). And in Ezra's days (iii. 11), again, as soon as the altar rose, they sang to the Lord—"*Because he is good; for his mercy to Israel endureth for ever.*" Our God is known to be "Love," by the side of the atoning sacrifice. Jeremiah, (xxxiii. 11) too, shews how restored Israel shall exult in this name.

Dwell next on the experience of his redeemed, "*from east and west,*" so far separate from each other; and from "*north,*" the most obscure quarter of earth, and from "*the sea*" (יָם), the tempest-tossed region. They have witnessed strange scenes, and the love of God in them all. Think of the *wanderers in the desert* (ver. 4) realising their fathers' history, and joining to it Hagar and Ishmael's thirst and despondency—how they were delivered after all, and led to *the city*, to Jerusalem (Targum and Hengstenberg)—the city where they found the habitation of God, and where they were made to dwell.

" Let these praise the Lord for his goodness,
And for his wonderful doings to the sons of men ;
For he satisfieth the longing soul (שֹׁקֵקָה, going hither and thither
in vain),
' And filleth the hungry soul with good " (טוֹב ; his own name, ver. 1.)

Think of another scene. Yonder is a prison-house (ver. 10),
and there you find transgressors, such as Manasseh or Zede-
kiah, brought low, because they despised the words of (אֵל)
the Mighty God, and left in the dungeon to consider their
ways. Their cry goes up to the mercy-seat—they are delivered ; they are blessed.

" Let them praise the Lord for his goodness," &c.

Think of another scene—the bed of sickness, " Fools afflicted
because of their course of transgression," (ver. 17). Hear the
groan, look on the languid eye, observe the sore anguish of these
death-stricken ones. But, like the man described in Job xxxiii.
19–23, to whom the Interpreter comes, these cry to the Lord
and find mercy.

And so is it with those tempest-tossed ones (ver. 22), who
for a time were like Jonah and the mariners that were with
him.* The Lord commandeth, and the stormy wind ariseth,
(ver. 25).

" Which lifteth up His waves;" (*i. e.,* Jehovah's waves Psa. xliii. 7 ;
Jonah ii. 3).

But what a calm when Jehovah hears their cry !—like the sea
of Galilee that morning when The Master arose and rebuked
winds and waves with his " Peace ; be still." Was there need
then to exhort men to adore and praise ? Did they not cry
one to another, " What manner of man is this?" Even so
here ; when *"their* waves" (ver. 29)—*i. e.,* the waves that tossed
them, sent out by God (ver. 25), and made terrible to them—
are lulled by him who hears their cry.

* " Me miserum ! quanti montes volvuntur aquarum !
Jamjam tacturos sidera summa putes.
Quantæ diducto subsidunt æquore valles !
Jamjam tacturos Tartara regna putes.
Rector in incerto est, nec quod fugiatve, petatve
Invenit ! ambiguis ars stupet ipsa malis."
—Ovid, *Eleg.* I., ver. 28.

" Let them praise the Lord for his goodness," &c.

Let them praise Him in the place where the Elders sit together—
deliberating on the ways of God.

But now Israel, from all lands, meet on their proper soil—
Palestine. They see it had become waste and desolate, like
Sodom (Deut. xxix. 23), though once as the garden of Eden ;
and they own it is for *" the wickedness of those that dwelt
there,"* (ver. 34). They remember how, when their fathers
emerged from the wilderness, they found it a land flowing with
milk and honey ; and how to them it was exchanging a desert
for water-springs—there they dwelt, built their cities, reared
Jerusalem, and there they multiplied (ver. 35–38). It was sin
that " diminished them," and " poured contempt on their
princes," (ver. 39, 40). God is good ; God is Love. God would
have blessed them for ever, nor ever once have broken a link
of the chain, but for sin. And now He has returned in free
love to them.

" He setteth the poor on high,
And maketh families to him, like a flock of sheep." (Ver. 41.)

Shall not gathered Israel bless the Lord ? and shall not all the
earth hear, and see, and learn ?

" The righteous shall see and rejoice,
And all iniquity stop her mouth.
Whoso is wise will consider these things,
And will understand the mercies of the Lord."

By such closing words are all men invited to come and join
the Lord's redeemed, in their blessings and in their joyful song,
helping them to raise to the Lord this

Song of thanks from gathered Israel and the redeemed.

Psalm 108

A Song or Psalm of David

1 O God, my heart is fixed ;
I will sing and give praise, even with my glory.
2 Awake, psaltery and harp : I myself will awake **early.**
3 I will praise thee, O Lord, among the people :
And I will sing praises unto thee among the nations.
4 For thy mercy is great above the heavens : and thy **truth reacheth unto**
the clouds.

5 Be thou exalted, O God, above the heavens: and thy glory above all the·
earth.

6 That thy beloved may be delivered : save with thy right ʰand, and answer me.

7 God hath spoken in his holiness! I will rejoice ;
I will divide Shechem, and mete out the valley of Succoth.

8 Gilead is mine ; Manasseh is mine ;
Ephraim also is the strength of mine head ; Judah is my lawgiver ;

9 Moab is my washpot ; over Edom will I cast out my shoe;
Over Philistia will I triumph.

10 Who will bring me into the strong city ? who will lead me into Edom ?

11 Wilt not thou, O God, who hast cast us off ? and wilt not thou, O God,
go forth with our hosts ?

12 Give us help from trouble : for vain is the help of man.

13 Through God we shall do valiantly : for he it is that shall tread down our
enemies.

HE has brought them to their desired haven !   The tone.

> " O God ! my heart is fixed—
> My heart is fixed."

No more tossed, no more wandering.

> " I will sing and give praise ;
> Awake, my glory, awake ! "

A call to celebrate a greater victory than Deborah's (Judges
v. 12)—" Awake, my glory"—i. e., my tongue, the best member
I have for the purpose ; or, my heart (Hengstenberg), fitted to
be a harp that may sound thy name.

> " Awake, psaltery and harp !
> I will awake the morning ! "

For his mercy is great—that mercy sung of lately (Psa. cvii.
1, and ver. 43). It is "from above the heavens" (מֵעַל שָׁמָיִם) ;
i. e., coming down on us, as do drops of a fertilizing shower.
Even as the " Peace on earth," of Luke ii. 14, was first " Peace
in heaven" (Luke xix. 38).

We have already had the words of this Psalm in two others   Title and form.
—viz., the lvii. and lx. But here the joyful and the triumphant portions of these two are joined in one, to form a lofty
melody (" A song, a psalm," like Psa. xxx. in the title), cele-   Messiah, Israel
brating Israel's return and Messiah's triumph.* Messiah, and   and saints.

---

* Ryland says, that in Psalm lvii. and lx. the words were prophetic and
consolatory ; here they are rather eucharistic, and descriptive of what God
has prepared for his own.

all Israel along with him, and every saint " rejoicing with Jerusalem" (Isa. lxv. 18), utter this Psalm. Messiah, as Leader, speaks, in verse 9, in his own name (an intentional variation from Psalm lx. 8)

> " *Moab I will use as a vessel in which to wash my feet* (when the journey is over),
> *Over Edom I will cast my shoe* (as one does to his servant),
> *Over Philistia I will raise the shout of joy.*"

Both in this Psalm and Psalm lx., the words in verse 10— " Who *shall* lead me ?"—are in the present participle, מִי יֹבֵל —" Who is my leader ?"—thus admitting of application to the past, while they may be prospective also ; like the expression in Heb. xiii. 7, " Remember Τῶν ἡγουμένων ὑμῶν," your rulers. The speaker asks-

> " *Who is he that leadeth me to the strong city ?*
> *Who hath led me into Edom ?*
> *Is it not thou, O God, who hadst rejected us,*
> *And didst not go forth with our armies ?*"

Then, going forward in the Lord's name, and renouncing man's strength, He and His enter on possession, saying-

> " *Through God we shall do valiantly ;*
> *He it is that treads down our enemies.*"

" It is he that bruises Satan under our feet," may every saint reply ; and, when Israel's day has come, every saint shall find himself blessed in their blessing. And so shall the Church join

Messiah, in behalf of restored Israel, raising the shout of victory.

Psalm 109

To the chief Musician. A Psalm of David

1 HOLD not thy peace, O God of my praise!
2 For the mouth of the wicked and the mouth of the deceitful are opened against me :
They have spoken against me with a lying tongue.
3 They have compassed me about with words of hatred ;
And fought against me without a cause.

4 For my love they are my adversaries : but I give myself unto prayer.

5 And they have rewarded me evil for good, and hated for my love.

6 Set thou a wicked man over him : and let Satan stand at his right hand.

7 When he shall be judged, let him be condemned : and let his prayer become sin.

8 Let his days be few; and let another take his office.

9 Let his children be fatherless, and his wife a widow.

10 Let his children be continually vagabonds, and beg:
Let them seek their bread also out of their desolate places.

11 Let the extortioner catch all that he hath ; and let the stranger spoil his
labour.

12 Let there be none to extend mercy unto him :
Neither let there be any to favour his fatherless children.

13 Let his posterity be cut off;
And in the generation following let their name be blotted out.

14 Let the iniquity of his fathers be remembered with the Lord ;
And let not the sin of his mother be blotted out.

15 Let them be before the Lord continually,
That he may cut off the memory of them from the earth.

16 Because that he remembered not to shew mercy,
But persecuted the poor and needy man, that he might even slay the
broken in heart.

17 As he loved cursing, so let it come unto him :
As he delighted not in blessing, so let it be far from him.

18 As he clothed himself with cursing like as with a garment,
So let it come into his bowels like water, and like oil into his bones.

19 Let it be unto him as a garment which covereth him,
And for a girdle wherewith he is girded continually.

20 Let this be a reward of mine adversaries from the Lord,
And of them that speak evil against my soul.

21 But do thou for me, O God the Lord, for thy name's sake:
Because thy mercy is good, deliver thou me.

22 For I am poor and needy, and my heart is wounded within me.

23 I am gone like the shadow when it declineth : I am tossed up and down
as the locust.

24 My knees are weak through fasting; and my flesh faileth of fatness.

25 I became also a reproach unto them: when they looked upon me they
shaked their heads.

26 Help me, O Lord my God : O save me according to thy mercy :

27 That they may know that this is thy hand ; that thou, Lord, hast done it.

28 Let them curse, but bless thou :
When they arise, let them be ashamed ; but let thy servant rejoice.

29 Let mine adversaries be clothed with shame,
And let them cover themselves with their own confusion, as with a mantle.

30 I will greatly praise the Lord with my mouth ;
Yea, I will praise him among the multitude.

31 For he shall stand at the right hand of the poor,
To save him from those that condemn his soul.

A SERIES of four connected Psalms commences here, beginning with Messiah in his low estate.   It is an observation as old as the days of the Fathers, that this Psalm presents to us " *The sufferings of Christ,*" and the Psalm that succeeds celebrates " *The glory that should follow.*"   We here descend into the Valley of *Humiliation,* that we may look up from thence to the height of *Exaltation.*   Christ is here enduring the contradiction of sinners, and at last meeting with the traitor.   " *Et tu, Brute !*" is the tone of the complaint.   The Fathers called it

" the Iscariotic Psalm," because so specially applied by Peter (Acts i. 16–20) to Judas.   We may consider Judas, at the same time, as the virtual head of the Jewish nation in their daring attempt to dethrone the Son of God.   The doom pro-

nounced, and the reasons for it, apply to the Jews as a nation, as well as to the leader of the band who took Jesus.   In the words of verse 1,

> "Hold not thy peace, *O God of my praise,*"

we hear the Saviour taking up Israel's manner of addressing Jehovah ; for Moses uses it (Deut. x. 21) when expressing the feeling that during all his wilderness journey he had proved Jehovah sufficient for him under sorrow, fear, perplexity, suffering, temptation, and so had ever found reason to praise him. Jeremiah, the weeping Jeremiah, broken in spirit, and meeting with treachery in the house of his friends, could call on Jehovah by the same name (xvii. 14), " *Thou art my praise !*" The Lord Jesus identifies himself with his saints—" in all points tempted like as we are."   Yes, and if at one time he looks up to the Father and says, " *Thou art my praise !*" thinking of blessings already received, no less does he at another time, as one of us would do when needing more help, speak thus of himself, " *I am prayer,*" (ver. 4).

Christ speaks from verses 1–5 as one surrounded by foes, like Shammah amid the Philistines in the field of lentils (2 Sam. xxiii. 12) ; then suddenly his eye falls on the leader of the troop, the tallest and most prominent sinner of the many thousands whom he guides to the prey.   May we not say that verse 6, so abruptly isolating some one enemy, pointing the finger at him, and bidding the divine thunderbolt fall on his head, is like the Evangelist's "While he yet spake, lo ! Judas, one of the twelve !" Even as Judas said to those he led on, "That same is he, hold him fast ;" so the Son of man says to the Father, "There is *he!* let him die !"

We consider the terrific utterance of doom, from verse 6 to verse 20, as no other than a copy (if we may so speak) of the Father's sentence upon the traitor who sold the Beloved Son for thirty pieces of silver. Christ declares it, and consents to it—"Let it be even so !"

> " *Let the wicked one be set over him ;*
> *And let Satan stand at his right hand.*" (Ver. 6.)

Again,

> " *Let his children wandering, wander on,*
> *Let them beg, and seek* (food) *from among the ruins of their own homes.*"

And then he says,

> " *Let their sins be before the Lord continually, that he may cut off the*
> *memory of the sinner from the earth ;*
> *Because he remembered not to shew mercy* (worse than Gen. xl. 23),
> *But persecuted the poor and needy One ;*
> *The One that was broken-hearted even unto death !*" (Ver. 16.)

Our Master had this verse in substance on his lips at the very hour when Judas was on his way to Gethsemane to betray him; for Matt. xxvi. 38 tells us that Jesus spake of being " *sorrowful* UNTO DEATH ;" which is the form of the expression here, " *broken in heart unto death*" נִכְאֶה לֵבָב לְמוּתָה. (See on Psa. lxxix. 11, for the force of מוּתָה.)

We must not pass verse 18 without remarking that there is an allusion in its tone to Num. v. 21, 22, 24—the unfaithful wife. Her curse was to penetrate into her bowels; " the water that causeth the curse shall enter into her ;" and such a curse comes on unfaithful Judas, who violates his engagement to the Lord, and upon Israel at large also, who have departed from him as a "wife treacherously departeth from her husband," and have committed adultery against the Bridegroom.

After this manifestation of Jehovah's abhorrence of all Messiah's foes, from Judas downward, the Saviour looks again to the Father, committing all to him.

"And thou, Jehovah, art my Lord !" (Ver. 21.)

To us it is sweet consolation to be able to say, " My Beloved is mine, and I am his !" Was it less so to the Son of man ?

"Act for me, for thy name's sake !"

Father, glorify thy name ! Glorify thyself even in my continued suffering (ver. 22–25). For again he cries,

> *" For poor and needy am I* (אֶבְיוֹן, even I whom thou hast already
>> helped),
>> *And my heart is wounded within me.*
>> *Like the declining shadow I go away* (night is near),
>> *I am tossed to and fro as the locust"* (the storm has begun).

Blasts from hell, and from earth, drive me about, as brisk winds do the locusts, seeking to sweep me into the deep.

Once more (vers. 26–28) *prayer* arises from him who said in verse 4, " *I am prayer ;*" and after this, *praise.* For he sees deliverance on its way, and ends with praise to the " *God of his praise"* (ver. 1) as he began, adoring the grace of Jehovah, who rescues the helpless one, standing at his right hand. And in this " *Salvation"* is included glory and blessedness, the glory and the blessedness of the kingdom. The harp is soon to sing of this theme in louder notes ; and, therefore, it is no more than indicated at the close. What a Psalm !

Messiah's prayers and praises for judgment on Judas and Judas-like men.

Psalm 110

A Psalm of David

1 THE Lord said unto my Lord,
  Sit thou at my right hand, until I make thine enemies thy footstool.

2 The Lord shall send the rod of thy strength out of Zion :
  Rule thou in the midst of thine enemies.

3 Thy people shall be willing in the day of thy power ;
  In the beauties of holiness, from the womb of the morning,
  Thou hast the dew of thy youth.

4 The Lord hath sworn, and will not repent,
  Thou art a priest for ever after the order of Melchizedec.

5 The Lord at thy right hand shall strike through kings in the day of his wrath.

6 He shall judge among the heathen, he shall fill the places with the dead bodies;

He shall wound the heads over many countries.

7 He shall drink of the brook in the way : therefore shall he lift up the head.

"*The right hand of the poor !*" was heard in the closing lines of the last song—"*the right hand of the Poor One,*" viz., the Messiah on earth in his humiliation. But look up now ; this " poor and needy One is exalted ! The Lord has " *saved* him." We see no Judas now ; but we see Him whom Judas betrayed, and whom Israel agreed in rejecting, exalted to the right hand of God. Link of connection.

> " *Jehovah said to my Lord,* (אֲדֹנִי)
> *Sit at my right hand.*"

An oft-quoted passage—because it contains a memorable truth.* We find it quoted by Messiah himself to lead Israel to own him as greater than David, Matt. xxii. 41. It is quoted in Heb. i. 13, to prove him higher far than angels. It is brought forward by Peter, Acts ii. 34, to shew him Lord as well as Christ. It is referred to in Heb. x. 12, 13, as declaring that Jesus has satisfactorily finished what he undertook to accomplish on earth, " The one sacrifice for ever," and is henceforth on that seat of divine honour " expecting till his enemies be made his footstool"—the day of his Second Coming. Quotations.

In verse 1, We have the personal glory of the exalted Messiah declared by the Father. He sits in highest honour (see 1 Kings ii. 19 ; Psa. xlv. 9) till the day arrive for still farther honour, viz., the utter prostration of his foes, who shall be made his footstool alluding (Josh. x. 24) to the five kings. Then the land shall have rest. The plan.

In verse 2, The Father's promise to him of the subjugation of all his foes. The " rod" is מַטֶּה, not a sceptre, but a rod of chastisement, like that of Moses, used in bringing judgment on Egypt.

* Luther, in his " Familiar Sermons," uses the Hebrew words as a summary of abundant consolation and a fit watchword for Christians, " *Sheb limini,*" Sit at my right hand.

In verse 3, The promise of a people, loving, holy, spotless, and more than man can number.

In verse 4, His office as Royal Priest, specially exercised in bringing this innumerable people to himself and then blessing them. He is *Melchizedec,* but over a mighty kingdom, and he intercedes for and blesses his Abrahams.

In verses 5, 6, Details are given of his leaving the right hand. And verse 7 is a summary of his whole career.

But, we should notice, in verses 5, 6, how the prophetic telescope is shifted. Hitherto (ver. 1–4) our eye had been fixed on the Exalted *Son,* while David rehearsed in prophecy what the Father would do for him *" in the day of his power"*—that is, the day referred to, Rev. xi. 17, when he takes to himself his great power and reigns, the day of his Second Coming. But now, in verse 5, we are guided to *the Father ;* for it is he who " shall send Jesus," (Acts iii. 20 ; 1 Tim. vi. 15). And it is with our eye on the Father that we are to read verse 5.

" *The Lord* (אֲדֹנִי Chaldee, ' Shecinah') *at thy right hand,*" (O Jehovah). See verse 1.

Or, perhaps, more correctly still, in the manner of adoring joy and hope,

> " *The Lord* (Adonai) *is at thy right hand !*
> *He has smitten through kings in the days of his wrath !*
> *He will contend with the nations,*
> *He hath smitten The Head of earth in all its extent !* "

This last clause, which speaks of a usurper who claimed a right to our world, is the contrast to verse 7, wherein His own exaltation over earth is proclaimed by " lifting up *the head*" (see Gen. xl. 13, 20, &c.).

> " *Of the brook in the way he shall drink :*
> *Therefore shall he lift up the head.*"

We may now turn back to discuss some of the difficulties of this magnificent triumphal song. We shall notice two—one in the description of his army, verse 3 ; the other in the summary of his career, verse 7.

Difficulties.

We read in verse 3, " *Thy people shall be free-gifts to thee, in the day of thy power*"—themselves presenting themselves as living sacrifices. The allusion is probably to the many *free-will-offerings* brought to Israel's altar,—all of which, as well as their meat-offerings and drink-offerings, declared that God's people were a people who gave up themselves to him, soul, body, and spirit without reserve. And there was an old type in Judges v. 2, Barak's army—like this great assembly from all tribes, while those that were like Meroz perished with the foe. This army, this host of the Lord, may be specially meant of Israel as a nation, at Christ's Second Coming ; but if so, it is Israel as afterwards the centre-point of union to the converted nations of the whole earth. There may be reference, also, to that other part of the Lord's host on that day, his glorified saints " who attend upon him," and reign with him over these nations of earth, and over the twelve tribes of Israel. But the full reference is to all these multitudes together, gathered to Shiloh at his Coming. These shall be arrayed as *priests :* festively adorned ; for,

> " *In the beauties of holiness,*"

is an expression taken from Exodus xix. 6 and xxviii. 4 (compare Prov. xxxi. 25, הָדָר לְבֻשָׁהּ). It is used frequently, and always seems to refer us back to the dress of the priesthood, or Levites ;* so that we are to understand Messiah's host as then manifested to be " a nation of priests," to offer up earth's praise and service.

> " *Out of the womb of the morning*
> *Is the dew of thy youth.*"

Thy " youth-like soldiery are as dew for beauty" (Hengstenberg) ; some say also, in perpetual succession ; and we must add, for number too. But, is there not this other idea—they come suddenly as the dew appears, seen all at once under the light of the new-risen Sun of Righteousness ? And may we not adopt yet another from Hengstenberg, " all begotten from above"—as Job xxxviii. 28 might lead us to remember ? The metre version of Tate and Brady has thus expressed some of these views :

---

* 2 Chron. xx. 21 ought to be rendered, " He set singers . . . . according to the beauty of holiness;" *i. e.,* he set them in the beautiful robes worn by the tribe of Levi. (See Keil.)

> " *Shall all (redeemed from error's night)*
> *Appear as numberless and bright*
> *As crystal drops of morning dew.*"

But now let us briefly notice verse 7, " *He shall drink of the brook by the way.*" Ancients and moderns have all been at a loss how to decide the true meaning. The idea, so common among us, that the clause foretells *Christ's sufferings*, is very rarely found among old interpreters.* The words were understood by Junius and Tremellius long ago as meaning, " He shall steadily press on to victory, as generals of energy act, who, in pursuing routed foes, stay not to indulge themselves in meat or drink."† Hengstenberg and others substantially approve of this view. While a few hold that allusion may be made to Samson at Ramath-Lehi (as if the words spoke of Christ having a secret spring of refreshment when needful), most seem inclined to take *Gideon* as the type that best expresses the idea. Pressing on to victory, Messiah, like Gideon, " faint yet pursuing" as he passed over Jordan, shall not desist till all is won. " He shall not fail nor be discouraged till he has set judgment in the earth." Perhaps the full idea is this :—His career was irresistibly successful, like that of Gideon ; for he allowed nothing to detain him, nor did he shrink in the enterprise from any fatigue, nor did he stop to indulge the flesh. If we take it thus, there is both the Humiliation and the Exaltation of the Son of man contained in the words ; and Phil. ii. 8, 9 supplies a commentary.

---

* It was current, however ; for Antonius Flaminius, 1576, adopts it, and commenting on the *Latin*, not the *Hebrew* term, says that the Psalmist has used the word *torrent*, " ad significandum vim et magnitudinem ærumnarum." Some wished to understand it of " *drinking of the blood of the slain ;*" others, of his slaking his thirst as a poor pilgrim passing a brook. One saw in the words the *very brook Cedron*, and another was inclined to think it might be " the waters of truth and holiness." We think, nevertheless, that most readers will agree that the probable meaning lies in a view of the passage much less forced.

† See also the oldest version of the metre Psalms :—

> " Yea, he, *through haste for to pursue his foe,*
> Shall drink the brook that runneth by the way."

And Amyrald, " He shall not give his foes even a moment to recover breath. He himself shall just, as it were, lift his helmet and hastily drink of water from the running brook." Tholuck, " He shall combat without stoppage."

And thus the harp sings of David's Son and David's Lord.
May we not entitle the Psalm,

*Messiah, at the Right Hand, expecting till his enemies be made
his footstool ?*

Psalm 111

1 PRAISE ye the Lord.
I will praise the Lord with my whole heart,
In the assembly of the upright, and in the congregation.
2 The works of the Lord are great,
Sought out of all them that have pleasure therein.
3 His work is honourable and glorious:
And his righteousness endureth for ever.
4 He hath made his wonderful works to be remembered:
The Lord is gracious and full of compassion.
5 He hath given meat unto them that fear him.
He will ever be mindful of his covenant.
6 He hath shewed his people the power of his works,
That he may give them the heritage of the heathen.
7 The works of his hands are verity and judgment;
All his commandments are sure.
8 They stand fast for ever and ever, and are done in truth and uprightness.
9 He sent redemption unto his people:
He hath commanded his covenant for ever.
Holy and reverend is his name.
10 The fear of the Lord is the beginning of wisdom :
A good understanding have all they that do his commandments :
His praise endureth for ever.

AN Alphabetic Psalm. It may be sung now, in the same manner that it might be sung long ago in the temple ; but it is fit also for that day described in Rev. xix. 1, 3, 4, the day of many " Hallelujahs," such as this Psalm begins with and reiterates. Messiah might sing it on earth and in the kingdom, and so may each of his members. *The singers.*

The plan is simple. In verse 1 we hear of *" The assembly* (the confidential meeting) *of the upright,"* whether such assemblies as meet now, or that great multitude that shall meet at the Great Day in the kingdom, "The Congregation." In verse 2 we have the *theme of praise,* Jehovah's works, which engages the attention of all in these meetings, *" The works of Jehovah sought* *The contents.*

out according to all their wishes," (Hengst.). They find "majesty and glory" *therein*; they find (ver. 4) *"He has erected a memorial for his wonderful works,"* i. e., made them as certainly to be remembered as when men erect a memorial edifice. At verse 7 the *unchangeableness* of his ways is the leading thought, occurring in verses 8 and 9 again. And then this sweet song of Zion closes with (ver. 10) the solemn expression of *entire satisfaction* in the Lord and his ways.

It is worth noticing that verse 10 sings,

" The beginning of wisdom is Jehovah's fear."

Wisdom. Job had declared that truth to the sons of men in the earliest ages, xxviii. 28. In after days, Solomon (Prov. i. 7) declared it with all the authority of his unparalleled wisdom and greatness. But here, Messiah and his members may be regarded as singing it, not on earth only, but in the kingdom—in *" The assembly of the upright."* They shall tell for ever of all true wisdom being found in the Lord. Never till they knew Him did any of them know ought that could satisfy ; but in knowing Him, all found eternal life. Out of this Fountain of Wisdom they drink for evermore. *"Holy and fearful is his name !"* Herein lies wisdom—they that know that name (and Messiah came to reveal it all) are for ever blessed. Such shall be

The Hallelujah of Messiah and his members in reviewing the past.

Psalm 112

1 **PRAISE** ye the Lord.
　Blessed is the man that feareth the Lord,
　That delighteth greatly in his commandments.
2 His seed shall be mighty upon earth :
　The generation of the upright shall be blessed.
3 Wealth and riches shall be in his house :
　And his righteousness endureth for ever.
4 Unto the upright there ariseth light in the darkness :
　He is gracious, and full of compassion, and righteous.
5 A good man sheweth favour, and lendeth : he will guide his affairs with
　discretion.

6 Surely he shall not be moved for ever : the righteous shall be in everlasting remembrance.

7 He shall not be afraid of evil tidings: his heart is fixed, trusting in the Lord.

8 His heart is established, he shall not be afraid, until he see his desire upon his enemies.

9 He hath dispersed, he hath given to the poor ;
His righteousness endureth for ever ; his horn shall be exalted with honour.

10 The wicked shall see it, and be grieved ;
He shall gnash with his teeth, and melt away : the desire of the wicked shall perish,

ANOTHER Alphabetic Psalm. The 111th celebrated the character and ways of the Lord ; this song celebrates the blessings of those that are his, and speaks of the many points in which God's people are like God. Like the last, it is a " Hallelujah" song, fit to be sung by Messiah, and by each of his members, here on earth and hereafter in the kingdom. It tells of the reward of those that are the Lord's, while its description of their character prevents any mistake as to the persons meant. *The distinguishing theme.*

From verse 1 the features of character which mark the true fearer of God are noticed, carrying us back to verse 10 of Psalm cxi. It is Messiah who exhibits these in perfection ; he is " mighty," גִּבּוֹר, far above that conqueror mentioned in Gen. x. 8. *The contents.*

In verses 2, 3, the blessing, which follows this character as the shadow does the substance, is spread before us ; and as a crowning element of blessing, the clause, " *To the upright ariseth light in darkness*," intimates that all the *darkness* of the upright, his trials, sorrows, temptations, will end in *light*. It is a precious clause, applicable to Christ's day of sorrow, and applicable to each member's, telling us of present deliverances prepared for the righteous, and of the grand deliverance when " *the light*" of the Day of God appears (Mal. iv. 2).

In verses 4, 5, the features of likeness to God are spoken of. Of these, Messiah is the great exemplar ; *merciful* and *gracious* (Exod. xxxiv. 6), and *righteous.*

" *Happy the man !* (Isa. iii. 10.)
He sheweth favour and lendeth !"

Inverses 6–8, his sure, unchanging bliss is proclaimed. He

is "never moved;" he is remembered by God for ever, as the high priest had the names of Israel ever on his heart. No tidings can overwhelm him; he is fixed for ever.

In verse 9 his "*cups of cold water*" are spoken of. "*He gave to the poor;*" for as Christ did (Acts xx. 35), so each member has ever counted it more blessed to give than to receive. And this "*righteousness,*" *i. e.*, righteous conduct, is not forgotten; it is recorded in the book of remembrance, (see ver. 3, and 2 Cor. ix. 9).

In verses 10, 11, his *triumph* is proclaimed. He is exalted; the wicked is for ever fallen. This is the day of Glory—the time of rewards. How verily true of Christ the Head! "His horn exalted."

And thus every holy stream pours itself at last into the ocean of glory, meeting it on the day when Messiah and his members are glorified together. And this is the burden of this Psalm which the righteous might often sing in their dwellings in joyful anticipation-

The recompense of Messiah and his seed.

Psalm 113

1 PRAISE ye the Lord.
Praise, O ye servants of the Lord, praise the name of the Lord.
2 Blessed be the name of the Lord from this time forth and for evermore.
3 From the rising of the sun unto the going down of the same the Lord's name is to be praised.
4 The Lord is high above all nations, and his glory above the heavens.
5 Who is like unto the Lord our God, who dwelleth on high,
6 Who humbleth himself to behold the things that are in heaven, and in the earth!
7 He raiseth up the poor out of the dust, and lifteth the needy out of the dunghill,
8 That he may set him with princes, even with the princes of his people.
9 He maketh the barren woman to keep house, and to be a joyful mother of children.
Praise ye the Lord.

The Hallel.   THE Jews have handed down the tradition, that this Psalm, and those that follow on to the 118th, were all sung at the

Passover; and they are denominated "*The Great Hallel.*" This tradition shews, at all events, that the ancient Jews perceived in these six Psalms some link of close connection. They all sing of God the Redeemer, in some aspect of his redeeming character ; and this being so, while they suited the paschal feast, we can see how appropriate they would be in the lips of the Redeemer, in his Upper Room.* Thus-

In Psa. cxiii., he sang praise to Him who redeems from the lowest depth.

In Psa. cxiv., he sang praise to Him who once redeemed Israel, and shall redeem Israel again.

In Psa. cxv., he uttered a song—over earth's fallen idols—, to Him who blesses Israel and the world.

In Psa. cxvi., he sang his resurrection-song of thanksgiving by anticipation.

In Psa. cxvii., he led the song of praise for the great congregation.

In Psa. cxviii. (just before leaving the Upper Room to go to Gethsemane), he poured forth the story of his suffering, conflict, triumph, and glorification.

Our Psalm, then, begins with a twice-repeated invitation to all God's servants to join in praise. It is sometimes true, that for the soul, "solitude is best society ; " but in the matter of praise, the reverse may be oftenest held. The society of kindred souls is the best help to each individual soul ; every voice in the great multitude touches the heart-fibres of yonder sweet singer, as the wind does the Æolian harp. Hence it is that so many Psalms begin with "*Hallelujah !*" calling on others all around to praise—not that the "harper harping with his harp" means to delegate this blessed duty to others, but he seeks to tune his own soul by hearing their voices ascend. The warmth of their hearts fires his own.

The Psalm's commencement.

The persons invited (ver. 1), to praise, are "Jehovah's servants;" all those (as Nehemiah i. 10 expands the words) whom he has redeemed. The *time* (ver. 2) for praise is specially

---

* The term used in Matt. xxvi. 30, is ὑμνησαντες, the word used in Heb. ii. 12; and by the Sept. for הוֹדָה and הלּל occasionally.

"*henceforth*," from the date of this redemption. The *place* (ver. 3, 4) where it is to be celebrated is all the earth, not Israel's land alone ; for all nations are to hear what Jehovah has done on the theatre of that land. The *object* of praise (ver. 5) is Jehovah, he to whom they sang at the Red Sea, " *Who is like unto thee ?* " (Exod. xv. 11.)

> " *Who is like to Jehovah our God ?*
> *He who is exalted high, as to his dwelling* (ὁ ἐν ὑψηλοις κατοικῶν.—Sept.)
> *He who stoopeth low as to his beholding !* (τὰ ταπεινα ἐφορῶν.—Sept.)
> *In heaven, and in earth !* " (Ver 5, 6.)

Then follows the special subject of celebration (ver. 7, 8, 9) —what He does for the fallen. Hannah's song in 1 Sam. ii. 5, 6, 7, 8, seems kept in view, as well as God's own words to David, 2 Sam. vii. 8, 9, all to furnish suitable language to express redemption-acts. And the long " barren woman " of verse 9, while it reminds us of Sarah, Rebecca, Rachel, Manoah's wife, Elizabeth, who all in the end were filled with joy, may point to one and the same period of the world's history for its full and final illustration, as does Isaiah liv. 1. Isaiah seems expressly to allude to this Psalm as receiving its fulfilment to the full when Messiah's work of suffering (Isa. liii.) issues in illimitable blessing to Israel and the world. The redemption celebrated includes glory as well as grace ; for we have princes (ver. 8) spoken of, and these " *sit*" with them, becoming associates of the noble—thus highly exalted, though once fit for the lowest hell. It is an expression parallel to Hannah's "*throne of glory,*" (2 Sam. ii. 8). And lo ! the once barren one of the house "*sits a joyful mother of sons.*" Whether we look upon the speaker *as Christ* praising the Father, or as the *Church* of Christ, and every member of Christ praising the Father because of Christ, the theme cannot be mistaken. It is

Praise to Him who redeems from the lowest depth.

Psalm 114

1 When Israel went out of Egypt, the house of Jacob from a people of strange language;
2 Judah was his sanctuary, and Israel his dominion.
3 The sea saw it, and fled: Jordan was driven back.
4 The mountains skipped like rams, and the little hills like lambs.
5 What ailed thee, O thou sea, that thou fleddest? thou Jordan, that thou wast driven back?
6 Ye mountains, that ye skipped like rams; and ye little hills, like lambs?
7 Tremble, thou earth, at the presence of the Lord, at the presence of the God of Jacob;
8 Which turned the rock into a standing water, the flint into a fountain of waters.

EVERY tear dropt on the golden altar would appear golden, *The tone.* because the gold shone through ; and common things presented in sanctuary-vessels would become sacred. So it is with events of history referred to in these songs of Zion. Even if they were not wondrous in themselves, still they could not fail to be felt as unlike all other events, because so exquisitely celebrated on the harp of Israel.

This Psalm sings of the past, and of the future too. The *The contents.* *past* extends from verse 1 to verse 6, the time

" *When Israel, of the Lord beloved,*
Out of the land of bondage came."

When we find in verse 1, as in Psa. lxxxi. 5, Egypt spoken of as a land where the people were of a " *strange tongue,*" it seems likely that the reference is to their being a people who could not *speak of God,* as Israel could ; even as Zeph. iii. 9 tells of the " *pure lip,*" viz., the lip that calls on the name of the Lord. In verse 2, " Judah" (Sept. Ἰουδαία) is followed by a feminine verb, both to shew that it was not the land, but the people, and also to remind us of their helplessness at that time. It is, *q. d.,* the " *daughter* of my people." And in the same verse, we hear of " His sanctuary," as in Psa. lxxxvii. 1, without naming the person, because the heart is full of him. God dwelt in the camp, making the hearts of the people his " *Holy place,*" and taking the tribes as his *Kingdom ;* while the Red Sea and Sinai testified of his presence and power. What a privilege to have such a king! What a blessedness to be dwelt in by the Holy One.

There is a future time when the like shall occur again, and the question be again asked, " *What aileth thee, O sea, that thou fleest ?*" For (ver. 7, 8) the closing verses seem to be parallel to Haggai ii. 6, and Heb. xii. 26, when *all the earth* shall be moved at the presence of him whose presence so affected Sinai, and the Red Sea, and Jordan. Augustine also— " Illa quoque miracula, cum in illo populo fierent, præsentia quidem, sed non sine futurorum significatione, gerebantur." And Dr Allix says—" 'Tis a meditation upon the coming out of Egypt, and upon the several miracles which changed the order of nature ; from whence the sacred author lifted up the minds of his people to the thoughts of their redemption, when the Messiah, appearing for their deliverance, will cause the same changes in the world." See Micah vii. 15–17, Isa. xi. 15. And on that day they shall come forth from the crushing dominion of a power that has trod Jerusalem under foot, " whose tongue thou shalt not understand," (Deut. xxviii. 49).

Whether in the lips of Jesus at the passover table in the upper room, when using this as part of the great Hallel, or in the lips of any of his members, the song is one of

Praise to Him who has redeemed, and will again redeem,
his Israel.

Psalm 115

1 Not unto us, O Lord, not unto us,
 But unto thy name give glory, for thy mercy, and for thy truth's sake.
2 Wherefore should the heathen say, Where is now their God?
3 But our God is in the heavens : he hath done whatsoever he hath pleased.
4 Their idols are silver and gold, the work of men's hands.
5 They have mouths, but they speak not : eyes have they, but they see not :
6 They have ears, but they hear not : noses have they, but they smell not :
7 They have hands, but they handle not : feet have they, but they walk not :
 Neither speak they through their throat.
8 They that make them are like unto them ; so is every one that trusteth in them.

9 O Israel, trust thou in the Lord! He is their help and their shield.

10 O house of Aaron, trust in the Lord! He is their help and their shield.

11 Ye that fear the Lord, trust in the Lord! He is their help and their shield.

12 The Lord hath been mindful of us : he will bless us ;
   He will bless the house of Israel ; he will bless the house of Aaron.

13 He will bless them that fear the Lord, both small and great.

14 The Lord shall increase you more and more, you and your children.

15 Ye are blessed of the Lord which made heaven and earth.

16 The heaven, even the heavens, are the Lord's :
   But the earth hath he given to the children of men.

17 The dead praise not the Lord, neither any that go down into silence.

18 But we will bless the Lord, from this time forth and for evermore.
   Praise the Lord.

THE missionary, Adoniram Judson, was arrested in the midst *The theme.* of ambitious schemes, and led to lay himself at the feet of his Lord by the first verse of this Psalm, " *Not unto us.*"

This " *Not unto us* " has reference to the undeserving cha- racter of the recipients. Our God gives liberally ; and withal he gives as none other gives ; for (as Milton sings) he gives,

" With his good upbraiding none."

It is this divine peculiarity in his giving that ought more than all else to induce us to hasten to his throne with our thanks and adoring praise. His " *mercy and truth*" (ver. 1) are the Jachin and Boaz of the redemption-scheme ; his grace, or love, or *mercy*, prompting the gift of his Son, and his *truth*, or ad- herence to every word he ever spoke, to every law he ever gave, to every attribute of his character, are the reigning mani- festations of his name. In giving praise, therefore, should not his redeemed continually refer to " *mercy and truth*"—to " grace and truth that came by Jesus Christ ? " It is thus we give him " glory in the highest."

But contrast Jehovah with any other god. Why should the *The contrast.* heathen say, " Where, pray, (נָא) is your God ? " Take up Moses' brief description in Deut. iv. 28, and expand it as is done here. Idols of gold and silver have a *mouth*, but give no counsel to their worshippers ; *eyes*, but see not the de- votions nor the wants of those who serve them ; *ears*, but hear not their cries of distress or songs of praise ; *nostrils*, but smell not the fragrant incense presented to their images ; *hands*, but the thunderbolt which they seem to hold (as Jupiter Tonans in after days), is a *brutum fulmen*, they cannot launch it ; *feet*, but they cannot move to help the fallen. Ah ! they cannot so much as whisper one syllable of response, or even mutter in their throat ! And as man becomes like his god, (witness Hindoo idolaters whose cruelty is just the reflection of the cruelty of their gods), so these gods of the heathen being " soul-less, the worshippers become soul-less themselves," (Tholuck).

Happy Israel ! trust in Jehovah-

> " *For to all such an aid he is,*
> *A buckler and defence.*" (Oldest version.)

His people.   " *Their* help" means " the help of such as do so."* Some understand it as if a chorus uttered these words in reply. In either way the sense is clear. Israel at large ! house of Aaron ! all fearers of God ! trust him alone ; for all of you can say verse 12, 13.

In verses 14, 15, the latter-day blessing of Israel is referred to. Their God whom they praised pronounces blessing, a creation-like blessing (Gen. i. 28), upon them, by the mouth oi his High Priest, we may suppose ; and in that case, how appropriately uttered by the Lord Jesus on the night he was betrayed, while using these words at the passover table :

> " *May Jehovah add to you* (Deut. i. 11),
> *To you and to your children !*
> *May you be blessed of Jehovah,*
> *Maker of heaven and earth !*"

It is like Melchizedec blessing Abraham in the name of the Most High God, "possessor of heaven and earth." They who receive the blessing respond in the closing words-

> " *As to the heavens—the heavens belong to Jehovah !*
> *And it is he that giveth earth to the children of men !*"

Ay, and it is he who will give earth, in its renovated beauty, to the children of men. To him we owe all things. Should he not be praised—praised on his own earth ?

---

* See note on Psalm xxviii. 7.

" It is they that are not dead who will praise Jehovah,
And not those that go down to silence (Isa. xxvi. 14):
And as for us, let us bless Jehovah (וַאֲנַחְנוּ נְבָרֵךְ)
From henceforth and for ever ! Hallelujah !"

What a fervent act of praise !—a song, in defiance of idols.
Praise to Jehovah, the sovereign source of blessings
manifold to all that fear his name.

Psalm 116

1 I LOVE the Lord, because he hath heard my voice and my supplications,
2 Because he hath inclined his ear unto me, therefore will I call upon him
   as long as I live.
3 The sorrows of death compassed me, and the pains of hell gat hold upon
   me :
   I found trouble and sorrow.
4 Then called I upon the name of the Lord; O Lord, I beseech thee, deliver
   my soul !
5 Gracious is the Lord, and righteous; yea, our God is merciful.
6 The Lord preserveth the simple : I was brought low, and he helped me.
7 Return unto thy rest, O my soul; for the Lord hath dealt bountifully with
   thee.
8 For thou hast delivered my soul from death,
   Mine eyes from tears, and my feet from falling.
9 I will walk before the Lord in the land of the living.
10 I believed, therefore have I spoken : I was greatly afflicted :
11 I said in my haste, All men are liars.
12 What shall I render unto the Lord for all his benefits toward me ?
13 I will take the cup of salvation, and call upon the name of the Lord.
14 I will pay my vows unto the Lord now in the presence of all his people.
15 Precious in the sight of the Lord is the death of his saints.
16 O Lord, truly I am thy servant;
   I am thy servant, and the son of thine handmaid : thou hast loosed my
   bonds.
17 I will offer to thee the sacrifice of thanksgiving, and will call upon the
   name of the Lord.
18 I will pay my vows unto the Lord now in the presence of all his people,
19 In the courts of the Lord's house, in the midst of thee, O Jerusalem.
   Praise ye the Lord.

IF the greatest wonder that eye shall ever see, ear ever hear, The key-note
and the heart of man and angel ever conceive, is the sacrifice of the Psalm.
of God manifest in the flesh, *" Deity expended upon human*

weal !" it need not seem strange to us that the harp of Zion returns again and again and again to this theme. This is the theme before us here, for this Psalm is Christ's resurrection-song, sung by his own lips in the upper room at the passover, in anticipation of the darkness of Gethsemane and Calvary passing away into glory.

Paul, in 2 Cor. iv. 13, 14, furnishes the key-note—" We hav-ing the same spirit of faith, according as it is written, *I believed, and therefore have I spoken* (Psa. cxvi. 17), we also believe, and therefore speak." We, says Paul, go on with our testi-mony as Jesus did, believing, as he did, that the Father will raise us up at last in glory, though at present we "bear about with us the dying (την νεκρωσιν, the הַמָּוְתָה of Psalm cxvi. 15) of the Lord Jesus."

It has been noticed by Hengstenberg (who beautifully speaks of the speaker here as uttering "thanksgiving *with the tear in his eye*"), that there is a resemblance to the tone of this Psalm in Hezekiah's writing, when he had been sick, and was recovered of his sickness (Isa. xxxviii.). It may be that Hezekiah's case was meant to furnish a living type of the Saviour in some de-tails. It is also most true that in a certain sense and measure, every member of Christ can sing, " *I love the Lord,*" and say it, too, in the very style of the original writer. " I love ! because the Lord has heard "—so transported with joy and love, " as at first to express his affection without declaring its object, thinking all the world must know who is the person intended —like Mary Magdalene, John xx. 15," (Horne). Still it is the Master, rather than the disciples, who speaks here. The Lord Jesus is the true Hezekiah, who alone can appropriate all that is written here, having passed through sorer pangs, and gotten a more real resurrection, than Hezekiah could celebrate when he went up, on the third day, to the house of the Lord.

Christ the speaker.

It is Christ only who can say, in the full sense of the word, the very first syllable of the Psalm ; for the words run in the original thus, " *I love ! because the Lord has heard my voice, my supplications !*"

" *I love !*" (אָהַבְתִּי, like ἑστηκα, Rev. iii. 17. " I have so done, and do so still")

It is not, " I am well pleased that the Lord has heard ;" no, it is far more. It is as if he pointed to Deut. vi. 5, "Thou shalt love the Lord"—וְאָהַבְתָּ יְהֹוָה אֵת, exclaiming, " I have done so, and ever will !" And then, as the *proof* of this love (not as the *cause*, comp. Luke vii. 47), he adds, " For see, the Lord has testified to my love by hearing my prayers." Yes ; those tears and strong cries, to which reference is made, Heb. v. 7, were proofs of his love to the Father; and the Father's hearing and helping was proof of his love to the Son.

" And I will call so long as I live."

Literally, "during my days," בְּיָמַי, as in 2 Kings xx. 19, Isa. xxxix. 8 (Hengst.) Is there not an implied reference to his intercession ? and does not the phrase remind us of Rom. v. 18, " saved by his life," and of Heb. vii. 16 ?

Israel might use these words at their paschal table, reckoning Egyptian sorrows and bondage as a kind of tomb, and recalling the flight from Egypt, and the passage through the Red Sea, when all human help had failed. It was like a resurrection—a passage up from the grave. Still, all was but an imperfect shadow of God's Israel, his beloved Son. The world was his Egypt, his place of bondage, his scene of suffering ; and, on the night he left this Egypt's tasks and bricks for ever, all help of man failed him—not even a disciple offered him sympathy. It was he, therefore—it was he alone —who could so truly sing, as verse 11,

Christ and his members.

" *I said in my haste*" (*i. e.*, while hastening from Egypt, like Israel on the passover night),
" *All men are liars ;*"

for the term is altogether a passover-night one, חָפְזִי. It is not trepidation of mind, it is not irritation, it is not alarm, it is not tumult of soul, that the term indicates ; but it is *the flight* or *hasty escape* of Israel on that memorable night. See this discussed in Psa. xxxi. 22. The old metre version of Tate and Brady is right-

*" For in my flight all hopes of aid
From faithless man were lost."*

And so the Targum has בְּמֶעְרְקִי, "in my fleeing." Bishop
Patrick and some others have noticed this to be the true sense.*

These remarks help us to the scope and plan of the psalm.
The Saviour begins (ver. 1–4) with the Lord and his benefits ;
then (ver. 5, 6) celebrates some attractive features of his character, "*Gracious* is Jehovah," while still he is "*righteous*,"
"and our God sheweth mercy," (מְרַחֵם.) ; and this he does
by "Keeping *the simple*," *i. e.*, those whom Satan might easily
beguile. And now he gives a fuller history of his suffering
and deliverance (ver. 7), "I was brought low," and how the
Lord permitted not the enemy to triumph over him in the
awful hour of his tremendous woe ; "*He helped me*," (ver. 7, 8).
He seems to reveal to us some of the thoughts that upheld
him—some of "the joy set before him" that enabled him to
endure. They were such as these—paraphrasing the words a
little (verses 9, 10, 11)

> "*I shall yet walk before Jehovah*
> *In the lands* (בָּאַרְצוֹת) *of the living*," (*i. e.*, the regions of glory, not
>   the abodes of the dead).
> "*I have full confidence !* *That is the reason why I have so often declared*
>   *my resurrection.*"

Not that I had no temptations to the contrary. I was more
afflicted than other men.

> "*I* (אֲנִי) *was greatly afflicted.*"

Yes ; and forsaken too, so that

> "*I said, in my hastening away,*
> *All men are liars.*"

All that is *man* disappoints expectation (ver. 8) ; כֹּזֵב, as in
Jer. xv. 18. But now, taking up the *drink-offering* cup, and
pouring it on the altar as a thanksgiving-token† (ver. 12, to
the end), he looks up to the Lord, and expresses his entire

---

* Horsley gives "in ecstasy of despair," quite as far from the true meaning
as is Barclay's "agony to fulfil the law," and Bishop's Horne's "hurry and trepidation." But see Psa. xxxi. 22.

† Hengstenberg maintains that commentators have no ground at all for
saying that there was a *cup of thanksgiving* at the passover supper. Mede has
suggested the allusion to the drink-offering.

satisfaction in Him, uttering thanks, praise, blessing, vows, while looking forward to the results of all, in a people freed and gathered into glory; for this is contained in the oft-repeated words, (equivalent to " Our gathering together in him," 2 Thess. ii. 1),

" *In the presence of all his people.*"

This is twice declared (ver. 14 and 18), in peculiar language-

> " *I will pay my vows to the Lord,*
> *Yea, I will in presence of all his people ;* (or, in presence of—let me d
> it—all his people.)
> *Precious (are they) in the sight of the Lord ;*
> *Even the death which belongs to his saints.*" (.הַמָּוְתָה לַחֲסִידָיו)

This last line of the verse is quite peculiar. The word for death is peculiar, corresponding, as we noticed before, to the Greek νεκρωσις (like תְּמוּתָה in Psalm lxxix. 11), while it cannot be construed with יָקָר, " precious," because of the gender. We may, therefore, connect the " *precious*" with " *his people*" (as we find in Psa. lxxii. 14, Isa. xlii. 4), and may understand the next clause as a declaration that even such suffering, such death-like pangs, are no proof that Jehovah has forgotten his people—" *even in regard to their death-like suffering, they are precious in his eyes.*"* Everything that concerns his people is of interest to him, every hair of their head is numbered. With his eye on such a passage as this, well might Paul rapturously exclaim—" All things are yours, the world, life, *death !*" (1 Cor. iii. 22, 23.) Shall not all this bind me to thee? " I am thy servant." Who shall separate me from the love of God? Hallelujah. (Ver. 19.) Such is

The Redeemer's Resurrection-song of Thanksgiving.

---

* There is a simpler way of overcoming the difficulty. It is to take יָקָר as the noun (neglecting the masoretic pointing), and punctuate it יְקָר, " price, honour, glory," as in Job xxviii. 10, Dan. vii. 14. We might then render the verse,

> " *A precious thing in the sight of the Lord*
> *Is the death which befalls his saints.*"

Psalm 117

1 O PRAISE the Lord, all ye nations! Praise him, all ye people!
2 For his merciful kindness is great toward us : and the truth of the Lord
endureth for ever.
Praise ye the Lord.

Connection with the preceding. " THE presence of all his people !" Our gathering together in him ! This was heard in the close of the former Psalm. So now we seem to be introduced for one brief moment into that assembly where the Redeemer stands leading their praise. What a Hallel ! from " all nations" and " all tribes" (אֻמִּים), as in Rev. v. 9.

"Loud as the sound of seas,
Through multitudes that sing."

The plan. They celebrate, as in Psalm cxv. 1, and often at other times, the *mercy*, the tender love of God which to usward is גָּבַר, "*mighty*," prevailing as did the deluge-waters over the mountain-tops (Gen. vii. 24, יִגְבְּרוּ), and also his *truth*, going hand in hand with truth in man's redemption.

Paul quotes this short song in Rom. xv. 11 (this heavenly catch which seraph might cry to seraph, or one redeemed to his fellow), to remind us that the Ensign on Calvary was set up for all nations, Gentiles as well as Jews. Let us, then, from time to time, recall this song to mind, and therewith exhort one another to praise. In so doing, we are using words which the Master used in the upper room, and which he will use again when " he drinks the new wine with us in the Father's kingdom." For it is He specially who is the speaker in the

Call on the Great Congregation for praise,

Psalm 118

1 O GIVE thanks unto the Lord! for he is good : because his mercy endureth for ever.
2 Let Israel now say, that his mercy endureth for ever.
3 Let the house of Aaron now say, that his mercy endureth for ever.
4 Let them now that fear the Lord say, that his mercy endureth for ever.

5 I called upon the Lord in distress: the Lord answered me, and set me in a large place.

6 The Lord is on my side; I will not fear: what can man do unto me?

7 The Lord taketh my part with them that help me:
Therefore shall I see my desire upon them that hate me.

8 It is better to trust in the Lord than to put confidence in man.

9 It is better to trust in the Lord than to put confidence in princes.

10 All nations compassed me about: but in the name of the Lord will I destroy them.

11 They compassed me about; yea, they compassed me about:
But in the name of the Lord I will destroy them.

12 They compassed me about like bees; they are quenched as the fire of thorns:
For in the name of the Lord 1 will destroy them.

13 Thou hast thrust sore at me that I might fall: but the Lord helped me.

14 The Lord is my strength and song, and is become my salvation.

15 The voice of rejoicing and salvation is in the tabernacles of the righteous:
The right hand of the Lord doeth valiantly.

16 The right hand of the Lord is exalted: the right hand of the Lord doeth valiantly.

17 I shall not die, but live, and declare the works of the Lord.

18 The Lord hath chastened me sore: but he hath not given me over unto death.

19 Open to me the gates of righteousness: I will go into them, and I will praise the Lord:

20 This gate of the Lord, into which the righteous shall enter.

21 I will praise thee: for thou hast heard me, and art become my salvation.

22 The stone which the builders refused is become the head stone of the corner.

23 This is the Lord's doing; it is marvellous in our eyes.

24 This is the day which the Lord hath made; we will rejoice and be glad in it.

25 Save now, I beseech thee, O Lord: O Lord, I beseech thee, send now prosperity.

26 Blessed be he that cometh in the name of the Lord:
We have blessed you out of the house of the Lord.

27 God is the Lord, which has showed us light:
Bind the sacrifice with cords, even unto the horns of the altar.

28 Thou art my God, and I will praise thee: thou art my God, I will exalt thee.

29 O give thanks unto the Lord; for he is good: for his mercy endureth for ever.

LUTHER wrote on his study-wall, "The 118th Psalm is my Psalm, which I love. Without it, neither emperor nor king, though wise and prudent, nor saints, could helped me," Tholuck).

The tone.

Christ uses it.   Still remembering that there is reason to believe that our Lord used these Psalms, which formed the " Great Hallel," on the last night he sat with his disciples at the passover-supper, and now specially remembering that *this* was the hymn they must in that case have sung just before " *He went to the Mount of Olives*," every verse will appear lighted up with peculiar attractiveness.

           " What pleasing seemed, for Him now pleases more."

The plan.   The plan of it is as follows :—In verses 1–4, " Oh let Israel say," &c., the Saviour is calling upon others to help him in praise ; at verse 5 begins his thanksgiving narrative ; while

Christ in it. verses 6, 7, states a holy axiom, verified in his own case, and left for the use of all his own, to this effect-

> " *Let Jehovah be with me!*   *I fear not.*
> *What can man do to me ?*
> *Let Jehovah be with me, among my helpers !*
> *Then I will look in triumph on mine enemies.*"*****

Believers.   In all this, every member of Christ can join, even as in Rom. viii. 31 we find Paul, and those in whose name he speaks, using language equally bold.   Nor is there need of other help (vers. 8, 9), for " human dust and royal clay" cannot add to the Lord's strength.   Proceeding in his narrative, from verses 10 to 13, he tells the strength of his foes.   The term used for their destruction (ver 10), אֲמִילַם, may have been chosen because it calls up the idea that these foes are all מוּל, " uncircumcised" (Hengst.), and so he is the true David going forth against this Goliath (1 Sam. xvii. 36).

    " *In the name of the Lord* (I go forth) ! *for I will destroy them.*"

This seems the force of כִּי, though some insert, " *I swear that.*" The figure of bees (ver. 12) sends our thoughts to the Amorites, in Deut. i. 44 ; he chases and destroys them.   Then, the special foe (v. 13) that seems addressed, who is this ?   He speaks to some person, " *Thou didst sore thrust* :" is he speaking to the host as one ? the army of all nations ? or is he

---

   * *Wyckliffe's* spirited application of this verse to the monks who came to his bedside, hoping that his sickness would end in speedy dissolution, was an accommodation of the words ; but the incident may be used as emblematic.

singling out their chief? Were this last idea adopted, we might suppose we saw the *Serpent* combating the *Woman's Seed*, the " *sore thrust*" being the Serpent's bruising the heel of the Saviour.

See next the victory won by Jehovah's aid alone (vers. 14–16). As Moses, the leader of the host, sang in Exod. xv. 2, " The Lord is *my* strength, *my* salvation," so does Jesus ; but at the same time there are sharers in the victory. Hearken !

" *The voice of rejoicing and salvation in the tents of the righteous !*"

And what do they sing :

" *The right hand of the Lord hath done valiantly.*"

They sing this as at the Red Sea ; and three times they sing of that right hand that has won an infinitely greater victory.

But next he refers to death, and his triumph over it (ver. 17, 18). The curse, " *Thou shalt die,*" cannot now fall on me ; it is past and gone ; it is exhausted :

" *I shall not die ; for I shall live !*"

It is the voice of Jesus ; "I am the living one" (Rev. i. 18), " and I was dead, and, behold, I am alive for evermore !" And as he added then, "And I have the keys of Hades and of death," so here he adds (vers. 19, 20)

" *Open to me the gates of righteousness !*"

—the gates of the holy temple above that shut out iniquity, and admit only what is pure and righteous. The temple on earth was typical of the better temple above.

" *This is Jehovah's gate*" (this " righteousness-gate") ;
" *The righteous go in thereby.*"

He enters singing (ver. 21), " I will praise thee, for thou hast heard me, and art become my salvation." Upon which the shout of congratulation arises from " *the righteous*" who go in after him. They it is who sing from verses 22 to 26, rejoicing in " *the stone*" become the *head,* or main stone of the corner, the corner-piece foundation-stone, bearing the weight of two walls and uniting both—a beautiful figure of Christ reconciling God and man, as well uniting all the saved in one. It is they, too, who sing, " This is the day which the Lord *made,*" *i. e.,* set apart, consecrated (עָשָׂה as in Deut. v. 15, לַעֲשׂוֹת)—this day of the Saviour's victory. And then another shout arises from Israel, owning their King and Lord now risen and glorified—

"*Yea, Lord, hosanna!* (*i. e.*, give us a share in thy victory).
Yea, yea, Lord, send prosperity!"

Another shout from happy Israel!

"*Blessed is he that cometh! in the name of the Lord!*"

And looking, it would seem, on his attendants—"*the righteous,*" of verse 20—they shout again,

"*We pronounce you blessed* (it is plural רְכֶם),
You that are of the Lord's house."

In such strains are set forth the triumphs of the Saviour, when he had overcome death and the grave. When himself sung his Psalm, would not his eye look onward, not to Resurrection only, but to Ascension, too, when he entered "the gates of righteousness" above—but not least to his Second Coming and his passing in with his ransomed into the New Jerusalem, when they together "enter in through the gates into the city," (Rev. xxii. 14). The multitudes, who almost unwittingly (yet prophetically, in the sense wherein Caiaphas spoke prophetically, John xi. 51) applied to him verse 26, were, after all, presenting a type of the great and final triumph at which the innumerable ransomed shall raise the cry, "Hosanna!" In that day, *Israel*, looking on with opened eyes, shall join in blessing him, and blessing all that are his, though they so long were the builders who rejected that tried stone. And this last feature of the scene leads us to notice verse 27, where Israel specially look on Him and cry,

The time.

"*Jehovah is God* (אֵל mighty one); *and has shined upon us,*" (Exod. xiii. 21, Tit. ii. 11, ἐπεφάνη).

They see what had been hid from their eyes so long; they see Jesus of Nazareth to be the Saviour, their God, Jehovah. In transports of grateful wonder, they exhort one another to offer thanksgiving-offerings, hastening to the altar,

"*Bind the sacrifice*" (חַג as Isa. xxix. 1, &c.) "*with strong cords!*"
(בַּעֲבֹתִים).

"*Let us away to the horns of the altar!*"

The last line is peculiar ; for עַד קַרְנוֹת, " to the horns," can scarcely be connected with the verb to bind, in the sense of, Hold fast the victim till you reach the horns of the altar. The word עַד is rather a particle of locality. In Lament. iii. 40 it occurs thus : " Let us search and try our ways ; and let us return (let us go) to the Lord ! " And so we take it here. The restored and grateful people are hastening to bring their offerings of praise to their God and King, stimulating one another's zeal ; " *Sursum corda !* " to the altar ! to the altar ! whose horns hold up to view the blood of sacrifice.

It seems to be the Redeemer himself, now surrounded by this multitude of ransomed ones, in whom he sees of the travail of his soul and is satisfied, who closes the Psalm (in verses 28, 29) by a thanksgiving to his Father for these results, and by an invitation (as at ver. 1) to all the universe to join in praise to the God of love. In anticipation of these results, He, in the days of his First Coming, sang it as his hymn while rising from table to go to the garden of Gethsemane ; but at his Second Coming, he will sing it with the tone of the more than conqueror, having realized the whole. We may entitle a Psalm that contains such stirring incidents, past and prospective,

Christ with his people.

The Redeemer's Conflict, Triumph, and Glorification, shared in by his Redeemed.

Psalm 119

A PILGRIM AND STRANGER, GUIDED, DAY AND NIGHT, BY THE LAW OF
THE LORD, TILL HE REACHES THE CITY.

THE alphabetic peculiarities of this Psalm are well known, every part beginning with a new letter, and every line or verse of that part beginning with the same, till all the letters of the Hebrew alphabet have been exhausted. There may be something more than fancy in the remark, that Christ's name, " *the Alpha and Omega*"—equivalent to declaring Him all that which every letter of the alphabet could express—may have had a reference to this peculiarity of this Psalm,—a Psalm in

Alphabetic peculiarities.

which (with the exception of ver. 84 and 122, exceptions that make the rule more marked) every verse speaks of God's revelation of himself to man, under one or other of the twelve terms, 1. law, 2. testimony, 3. way, 4. commandment, 5. precept, 6. judgment, 7. word, 8. truth, 9. righteousness, 9. faithfulness, 11. statute, 12. name. If so, it gives additional meaning to that title of the Lord—he is not only first and last, but all between ; he is all that revelation can express.

The terms "Statutes" and "Precepts."

In Psalm xix. we tried to ascertain the different shades of meaning in " *Law*," " *Testimony*," &c. These hold good here ; only they are not to be considered as exclusive of one another. But our translators have unfortunately introduced some confusion into the terms employed in this Psalm, by rendering the Hebrew חֻקִּים, " *Statutes*," which term was not the one used in rendering פִּקּוּדִים, in Psalm xix. 8. In this Psalm, therefore, " *Statutes*" mean the *appointments* of the *ceremonial* law, q. d., the things prescribed to Israel by Jehovah's decree through their מְחֹקֵק " statute-giver."* On the other hand, our translators render פִּקּוּדִים by " PRECEPTS," invariably in this Psalm. This word (פִּקּוּד) we saw in Psa. xix. 8, signifies particular injunctions given in particular circumstances. Of course, the lessons taught by these special injunctions and appointments are included, as a chief part of the Psalmist's meditation and delight.

But it is remarkable that a Psalm, which we might suppose to belong to Christ, and to be his special utterance more than most others, has, in its language, some difficulties which have deterred many from applying it to the Lord Jesus at all. We think, however, the difficulties are such as admit of explanation. They are these, viz., verses 67, 71, 75, and 176. The 67th is the only really serious difficulty, for it seems to ascribe " *going astray*" to the speaker—שָׁגַג always meaning delinquency of some kind, it might be by inadvertency, yet still a deviation from the standard of law. Fry and some others try to dispute this, but have failed. How, then, are we to understand our Lord using such a verse as this ? We propose the following solu-

Difficulties in one portion.

---

* See Levit. xxvi. 46, " these are *the statutes*," הַחֻקִּים. The Prayer-book version translates the word " *ceremonies*," in the Psalms.

tion :—He had said in verse 66, " I have believed in thy commandments"—" I have kept faithful to what thou hast said."
Then follows the statement of still firmer adherence to the
Lord's word. He says, " I did not need the sorrow and shame
of experienced error to drive me into thy ways. Without this
teaching, which so often, by its bitter regrets, leads wilful ones
to Thee, I have been enabled to hold fast thy words—' Ere
ever I was afflicted, I kept thy word.'"

> " *I have not yet been afflicted, as one going astray,*
> *And still I have kept thy word.*"

The common rendering of אֲנִי שֹׁגֵג, " I WENT astray," or " I WAS
going," cannot be defended ; it ought to be " I *am* going astray."
Our proposed rendering is parallel to בְּטֶרֶם תָּבוֹא—וַיֵּלֵדְן, in
Exod. i. 19, in regard to the construction of טֶרֶם, and gives the
obvious and most natural sense of the whole clause. But then,
it may be asked, Is not the difficulty of verse 176 equally
great : " I have gone astray as a lost sheep ?" Not so; for
here the term is תָּעִיתִי, in the signification of wandering like
one who has no home. It is Abraham's word in Genesis xx.
13, " God caused me to wander (הִתְעוּ אֹתִי אֱלֹהִים) from my
father's house." It is most appropriate in the lips of him who
had left his heavenly home to be a stranger here, to be (as
Fry observes) " as a sheep whom no man taketh up" (Isa. xiii.
14). The word, indeed, seems to be the same as that which
has given the Arabic name *El Tyh* to part of the desert where
Israel wandered. And if this be so, then the difficulties of
verses 71, 75, are all that remain ; both of which are solved by
a reference to Hebrews v. 8, " Though he were a Son, yet learnt
he obedience by the things which he suffered."

We cannot but think that " the Songs of Degrees," all of which
have a pilgrim air about them, are appropriately prefaced by
this Psalm, breathing as it does the experience of a pilgrim,
with "a soft quiet melancholy" (Hengstenberg) in his tone,
met and comforted by the God of all consolation. If we adopt
the idea of the Psalm being a kind of manual for a pilgrim,
we are able to connect its different parts ; and we are able to

The position.

do so whether we read it as the utterance of the Lord of pilgrims, or of one of his band.

ALEPH

1 BLESSED are the undefiled in the way, who walk in the law of the Lord.
2 Blessed are they that keep his testimonies, and that seek him with the whole heart.
3 They also do no iniquity: they walk in his ways.
4 Thou hast commanded us to keep thy precepts diligently.
5 O that my ways were directed to keep thy statutes!
6 Then shall I not be ashamed, when I have respect unto all thy commandments.
7 I will praise thee with uprightness of heart,
When I shall have learned thy righteous judgments.
8 I will keep thy statutes: O forsake me not utterly.

Aleph.

(Ver. 1.) *The pilgrim setting out.* God's testimonies are his staff. The Lord of pilgrims might utter verse 1, as he uttered Matt. v. 3, 4, 5, "*Blessed are the merciful!*" Sin leads to misery; holiness leads to bliss, which is far more than joy. He looks along the way, revolving in his soul what he should be who would walk in paths of blessedness, till at verse 8 he lifts his staff for the journey, saying-

"*I will observe thy statutes!*
Thou wilt not forsake me utterly!" (See ver. 43, and comp·
1 Sam. xxvii. 1 with 2 Sam. vii. 15.)

BETH

9 Wherewithal shall a young man cleanse his way?
By taking heed thereto according to thy word.
10 With my whole heart have I sought thee: O let me not wander from thy commandments.
11 Thy word have I hid in mine heart, that I might not sin against thee.
12 Blessed art thou, O Lord: teach me thy statutes.
13 With my lips have I declared all the judgments of thy mouth.
14 I have rejoiced in the way of thy testimonies, as much as in all riches.
15 I will meditate in thy precepts, and have respect unto thy ways.
16 I will delight myself in thy statutes: I will not forget thy word.

Beth.

The pilgrim fairly on the way. God's testimonies smooth the journey. The Lord of pilgrims might be supposed arresting the attention of his followers by this question, verse 9, and by its answer, corresponding as it does to John xvii. 7, and xv. 3. He breathes a firm resolution to make the Word his guide—

" With my lips do I recount,*
All the judgments of thy mouth," (as in ver. 7, thy dealings in providence, and the principles that guide them as set forth by thee).

GIMEL

17 Deal bountifully with thy servant, that I may live, and keep thy word.
18 Open thou mine eyes, that I may behold wondrous things out of thy law.
19 I am a stranger in the earth: hide not thy commandments from me.
20 My soul breaketh for the longing that it hath unto thy judgments at all times.
21 Thou hast rebuked the proud that are cursed, which do err from thy commandments.
22 Remove from me reproach and contempt; for I have kept thy testimonies.
23 Princes also did sit and speak against me: but thy servant did meditate in thy statutes.
24 Thy testimonies also are my delight and my counsellors.

The pilgrim seeing the prospect open upon his view. He   Gimel.
seeks discoveries on his path, in spite of external difficulties,
and prays, " *Uncover mine eyes and I will look!*" Then, as if
dazzled, he exclaims, " *Wonders out of thy law!*" His plea is,–

" I am a stranger upon earth." (Ver. 19.)

This is not the country where I find my treasure and my home,
neither am I to be here long. He uses this as it is used in 1
Chron. xxix. 11, an argument which the Son of David, as well
as David in the name of any member of Christ, might use.
In seeking these discoveries, he looks backward to the days of
Pharaoh, verse 21. At verse 22, he remembers Israel's entrance into a large place when they crossed Jordan, " *Roll
off from me the reproach;*"—as Joshua (ver. 9) speaks of it
being rolled away at Gilgal, when the Lord shewed his faithfulness in bringing Israel into her land, thereby silencing the
taunts of Egypt. And verse 23, " For thy servant *meditates on thy statutes,*" reminds us of Joshua i. 6. " Let us
remember, (says Horne,) that he who alone, in the strict
and unlimited sense of the words, could say, ' *I have kept thy
testimonies,*' sustained the utmost degree of ' reproach and

* When we make the Scriptures the subject of our conversation, we glorify
God, we edify our neighbour, and we improve ourselves," (Horne). But this
recounting what God's mouth has appointed to be, is also a matter of private
meditation and prayer.

contempt' for our sakes, and was patient under all, till God *'removed'* it from him by a glorious resurrection. There remaineth likewise a resurrection for the mystical body of Christ, and then, Wisdom shall be justified of her children."

DALETH

25 My soul cleaveth unto the dust: quicken thou me according to thy word.
26 I have declared my ways, and thou heardest me: teach me thy statutes.
27 Make me to understand the way of thy precepts: so shall I talk of thy wondrous works.
28 My soul melteth for heaviness: strengthen thou me according unto thy word.
29 Remove from me the way of lying: and grant me thy law graciously.
30 I have chosen the way of truth: thy judgments have I laid before me.
31 I have stuck unto thy testimonies: O Lord, put me not to shame.
32 I will run the way of thy commandments, when thou shalt enlarge my heart.

Daleth.

The pilgrim weary. The Lord of pilgrims was often weary in spirit when he saw the world so cold, nay, so determinedly inimical, to his Father. "*My soul cleaveth to the dust,*" declares the feeling of degradation and feebleness, like Psa. xxii. 16; even as verse 28 expresses sorrow, "*My soul melteth away for grief.*" And still amid this weariness he cries, "Thy word," (ver. 25); "Thy statutes," (ver. 26); "Thy precepts," "Thy law," (ver. 29); "Thy testimonies," (ver. 31); these are my resort.

"*I run the way of thy commandments,* (Heb. xii. 1).
For thou enlargest my heart."

His frames and feelings may vary, because his circumstances vary, but his heart's desire and affection toward God and his truth remain unvarying.

HE

33 Teach me, O Lord, the way of thy statutes; and I shall keep it unto the end.
34 Give me understanding, and I shall keep thy law; yea, I shall observe it with my whole heart.
35 Make me to go in the path of thy commandments; for therein do I delight.
36 Incline my heart unto thy testimonies, and not to covetousness.
37 Turn away mine eyes from beholding vanity; and quicken thou me in thy way.
38 Stablish thy word unto thy servant, who is devoted to thy fear.
39 Turn away my reproach which I fear: for thy judgments are good.
40 Behold, I have longed after thy precepts; quicken me in thy righteousness.

The pilgrim stedfast in temptation. In spite of sights of He. vanity, yea, in spite of all he saw on the hill of Temptation, when the glory of the whole earth was shewn to him, the Master passed on unmoved ; and so it is in measure with his disciples. It may be, this very resistance of evil (as in Joseph's case) may bring them for a time into reproach ; or, it may be, their unlikeliness to the world may draw down on them its malignant assaults ; but the end shall be well. None lose by adhering to the Lord's testimony.

> " *Turn away my reproach which I fear,*
> *For thy judgments are good.*" (Ver. 39.)

VAU

41 Let thy mercies come also unto me, O Lord, even thy salvation, according to thy word.
42 So shall I have wherewith to answer him that reproacheth me : for I trust in thy word.
43 And take not the word of truth utterly out of my mouth ; for I have hoped in thy judgments.
44 So shall I keep thy law continually for ever and ever.
45 And I will walk at liberty : for I seek thy precepts.
46 I will speak of thy testimonies also before kings, and will not be ashamed.
47 And I will delight myself in thy commandments, which I have loved.
48 My hands also will I lift up unto thy commandments, which I have loved ; And I will meditate in thy statutes.

The pilgrim assailed. Outward foes and unsympathising Vau. men are not easily dealt with ; hence the prayer to be enabled to reply to assailing ones by words in season, getting courage and utterance to confess his name ;

> " *Take not the word of truth utterly out of my mouth,*
> *For I have trusted in thy word.*" (Ver. 43.)

" *Utterly,*" as in verse 8, and as in Isa. lxiv. 8, and elsewhere implies the belief, that it may seem right to the Lord to allow some humiliation to be felt ; only (says the suppliant) let him not wholly withdraw ! The father may teach some lesson by allowing the child to stumble, but surely will not let him so fall as to be injured. In verse 44 the Master alone could fully assert—

> " *I keep thy law*
> *Continually* (תָּמִיד) *for ever and ever.*"

That is, every day without interruption ; and this unbroken service prolonged to eternity.

" And I walk in a large place," (ver. 45)

—finding his service freedom and joy. Perhaps verse 46 may be illustrated by Matt. x. 18.

ZAIN

49 Remember the word unto thy servant, upon which thou hast caused me to hope.

50 This is my comfort in my affliction : for thy word hath quickened me.

51 The proud have had me greatly in derision : yet have I not declined from thy law.

52 I remembered thy judgments of old, O Lord, and have comforted myself.

53 Horror hath taken hold upon me, because of the wicked that forsake thy law.

54 Thy statutes have been my songs in the house of my pilgrimage.

55 I have remembered thy name, O Lord, in the night, and have kept thy law.

56 This I had, because I kept thy precepts.

Zain.   *The pilgrim under darkness, yet unmoved.* Manifold dark circumstances are the lot of Master and disciples here ; but the word of promise, in some of its many forms, sustains.

" Remember thy word to thy servant ;" or, for thy servant's benefit ;

" Because (עַל אֲשֶׁר, 2 Sam. iii. 30—Hengstenberg) *thou hast caused me to hope."*

God's pilgrims have a hope (Rom. v. 3, viii. 24, xii. 12, xv. 13), that shall never put them to shame ; having once spoken, he keeps his promise. As Newton sings-

" And can He have taught me to trust in His name,
And thus far have brought me to put me to shame ?"

In verse 52, the Lord of pilgrims might be supposed standing near Capernaum, and Bethsaida, and Chorazin, lifting up his eyes to heaven, thanking the Father who hides these things from the wise and prudent, and reveals them unto babes ; or amid his seventy, thanking the Father, and rejoicing because he had seen Satan as lightning fall from heaven. He sees the eternal purpose of the Lord. He sees the Lord himself, ruling all events, and bring about a glorious issue, even the glory of the kingdom.

" I remembered thy judgments from eternity ; (see ver. **13)**
(I remembered) *Jehovah, and comforted myself.*
Horror seized me,
Because of the wicked who forsake thy law ;
Thy statutes were my songs." (Ver. 52, 53.)

One thing, whatever else befalls, he is sure of, namely, that
happen what may, he has cleaved to the Lord.

" This I have,
That I have kept thy statutes." (Ver. 56. The **כִּי** is like ὅτι in
Rev. ii. 4.)

CHETH

57 Thou art my portion, O Lord : I have said that I would keep thy words.
58 I entreated thy favour with my whole heart : be merciful unto me according to thy word.
59 I thought on my ways, and turned my feet unto thy testimonies.
60 I made haste, and delayed not to keep thy commandments.
61 The bands of the wicked have robbed me : but I have not forgotten **thy**
law.
62 At midnight I will rise to give thanks unto thee, because of thy righteous judgments.
63 I am a companion of all them that fear thee, and of them that keep **thy**
precepts.
64 The earth, O Lord, is full of thy mercy : teach me thy statutes.

The pilgrim following on to know the Lord. He breathes Cheth.
the desire, " Da mihi *te,* Domine "-

" Keeping thy ways, I have said,
My portion is Jehovah." (Ver. 57.)

He values God's presence, (ver. 58) ; he compares his ways with
God's testimonies, (ver. 59) ; he never lingers in the performance, when he finds a commandment (ver. 60); amid the
bands of the wicked he adheres to the law, (ver. 61); at midnight (lit., *" half of the night,"* as Exod. xiii. 29, the time when
the Destroyer slew Egypt's first-born—Hengstenberg) he
awakes to praise (ver. 62) ; he shares (חָבֵר) with the fearers
of God, whatever be their lot, (ver. 63). And it seems as if
he saw the future glory awaiting those that follow the Lord ; or
rather, he delights in the future revelation of the Lord's riches
of Love ; for he sings, in a tone that reminds us of Isa. vi. 3-

" The earth is full of thy mercy !"

But the view is one that overwhelms the soul ; it cannot take in the vision but in part; and therefore he prays, "*Teach me thy statutes,*" that I may daily fathom more of the great deep.

TETH

65 Thou hast dealt well with thy servant, O Lord, according unto thy word.
66 Teach me good judgment and knowledge : for I have believed thy commandments.
67 Before I was afflicted I went astray : but now have I kept thy word.
68 Thou art good, and doest good ; teach me thy statutes.
69 The proud have forged a lie against me : but I will keep thy precepts with my whole heart.
70 Their heart is as fat as grease ; but I delight in thy law.
71 It is good for me that I have been afflicted ; that I might learn thy statutes.
72 The law of thy mouth is better unto me than thousands of gold and silver.

Teth.

The pilgrim is satisfied in the service of God, and with his dealings hitherto.

> " *Kindly hast thou dealt with thy servant,*
> *O Lord, according to thy word.*" (Ver. 65.)

The Lord of pilgrims had never ought but good to say of his Father ; neither have the followers of that Lord any fault to find. " He never wronged me nor mine," was the saying of a Scottish saint, even when the bloody head of his martyred son was held up to his view. So good, so infinitely satisfying to the soul are the Lord's ways and the Lord's revelations of himself, that the pilgrim says (ver. 67), "*I kept thy words, without being driven to them by affliction.*" (See above, in the introduction, p. 357.). He then (ver. 68) prays to be taught more still, as he prayed in verse 66 for " *discernment*" (טַעַם), the faculty to see spiritual things clearly. When in verse 71 he expresses satisfaction in having been afflicted, it is because by the hand of affliction these grapes were pressed for the refreshing of his thirst ; thereby he experienced somewhat more of the infinite adaptation of these statutes to a pilgrim's wants.

JOD

73 Thy hands have made me and fashioned me :
Give me understanding, that I may learn thy commandments.
74 They that fear thee will be glad when they see me ; because I have hoped in thy word.
75 I know, O Lord, that thy judgments are right,
And that thou in faithfulness hast afflicted me.

76 Let, I pray thee, thy merciful kindness be for my comfort,
According to thy word unto thy servant.
77 Let thy tender mercies come unto me, that I may live : for thy law is my
delight.
78 Let the proud be ashamed, for they dealt perversely with me without a
cause :
But I will meditate in thy precepts.
79 Let those that fear thee turn unto me, and those that have known thy
testimonies.
80 Let my heart be sound in thy statutes; that I be not ashamed.

The pilgrim speaks to the Lord about his future course. Jod.
He goes back to his creation—his being clay in the hands
of the potter. This is a reason for pleading to be led on
(ver. 73). Then, the joy it will give others is a reason,
verses 74 and 79. And complete soundness (ver. 80, תָמִים)
is the goal of his desires, that is, power to complete the work
given him to do, his heart impartial, sincere, thoroughly at one
with God. Every disciple breathes this desire—
" *et my heart be perfect in thy precepts,*
That I may not be ashamed." (Ver. 80.)
The desire is the same with that of the apostle in 1 John iv.
28, " Abide in Him, that we may have confidence, and not be
ashamed before Him at his coming," even as the assurance
breathed in the " *I know*" of verse 75 is like Rom. viii. 28,
and 1 John v. 18.

CAPH

81 My soul fainteth for thy salvation : but I hope in thy word.
82 Mine eyes fail for thy word, saying, When wilt thou comfort me ?
83 For I am become like a bottle in the smoke ; yet do I not forget thy
statutes.
84 How many are the days of thy servant ?
When wilt thou execute judgment on them that persecute me ?
85 The proud have digged pits for me, which are not after thy law.
86 All thy commandments are faithful : they persecute me wrongfully ; help
thou me.
87 They had almost consumed me upon earth ; but I forsook not thy precepts.
88 Quicken me after thy lovingkindness; so shall I keep the testimony of thy
mouth.

The pilgrim oppressed draws strength from the thought of Caph.
future glory. The " salvation " of verse 81 is like Jacob's in
Gen. xlix. 18, the deliverance in prospect for all the Lord's
children—the glory to come—the kingdom. Trials send for-

ward our hopes to that time of peace. Our Lord, "for the joy that was set before him, endured the cross" (Heb. xii. 3), having respect to the reward and the rest; and so his followers also, expecting the fulfilment of his promises.

> " *My soul fainteth for thy salvation.*
> *I wait for thy word.*" (Ver. 81.)

As the worshippers went up to Zion "*fainting*" (Psa. lxxxiv. 2) for the courts of the Lord, that is, thirsting even to faintness, even thus does the pilgrim for the Day of the Lord, "*waiting*" (as Rom. viii. 19) for the fulfilment of promises and hopes. There is here, too, an αποχαροδοχια, for

> " *Mine eyes faint* (כָּלוּ as ver. 81) *for thy word,*
> *Saying, When wilt thou comfort me ?*" (Ver. 82.)

On that day, "*the bottle in the smoke,*" the man of sorrows, the pilgrim who has been subjected to humiliation and dishonour, shall appear as a diadem in the hand of the Lord. No wonder, then, that again he cries-

> " *How many are the days of thy servants ?*
> *When wilt thou execute judgment on my persecutors ?*"

—the very prayer and appeal of the souls under the altar in Rev. vi. 9. And the force of verse 85 seems to lie in a reference of the same kind, *q. d.*, " The proud have digged pits for me, but shall find themselves disappointed ; these pits are not destined for me"—alluding to the Lord's judgment when his "Law" shall assign each his portion, the persecutor and the persecuted.* For his promises shall come to fulfilment ; they are faithfulness itself.

> " *All thy commandments are faithfulness.*" (Ver. 86.)

LAMED

89 For ever, O Lord, thy word is settled in heaven.

90 Thy faithfulness is unto all generations : thou hast established the earth, and it abideth.

91 They continue this day according to thine ordinances : for all are thy servants.

92 Unless thy law had been my delights, I should then have perished in mine affliction.

---

* Horne remarks, the *law* enacted punishment, Exod. xxi. 33, on the man who left open a pit into which a beast accidentally fell ; much more here.

93 I will never forget thy precepts: for with them thou hast quickened me.

94 I am thine, save me ; for I have sought thy precepts.

95 The wicked have waited for me to destroy me : but I will consider thy testimonies.

96 I have seen an end of all perfection ; but thy commandment is exceeding broad.

The pilgrim meditates on the unfailing certainty of the Lamed. *Law.* The revelation of God in his word and ordinances is just *Himself* presented to our view ; which being so, we find his word like himself, sure and unfailing amid all changes.

> " *For ever is Jehovah !*
> *Thy word is fixed in the heavens !*" (above reach of change) (Ver. 89.)

To this Law he ever resorts. In all else, he finds a limit ; other guides go only a certain length with you ; other supports are capable of bearing only a certain measure of burden ; but the Lord's revelation has no such limit ; "*it is exceeding broad*"—the contrast to mere human "*perfection,*" the completeness to which man may reach.

MEM

97 O how love I thy law ! It is my meditation all the day.

98 Thou through thy commandments hast made me wiser than mine enemies : For they are ever with me.

99 I have more understanding than all my teachers : for thy testimonies are my meditation.

00 I understand more than the ancients, because I keep thy precepts.

101 I have refrained my feet from every evil way, that I might keep thy word.

102 I have not departed for thy judgments : for thou hast taught me.

103 How sweet are thy words unto my taste ! yea, sweeter than honey to my mouth !

104 Through thy precepts I get understanding : therefore I hate every false way.

The pilgrim revels in the instructive properties of God's Mem. *law.* " *How I have loved thy law !*" (ver. 97). The *Law* (see Psa. xix.) is equivalent to God's revelation of himself, and his will to man. His foes have a sort of wisdom, much craft, much subtlety ; but as David, in 1 Sam. xviii. 30, was made wiser than all his foes in conduct and in war, even so shall it be here.

> " *Thy commandment shall make me wiser than mine enemies,*
> *For it is mine for ever*"—my possession and portion for ever. (Ver. 98.)

Glancing at the future, he glories in the law as making him wise, not only now, but for ever. " I have got (he says) what shall even in ages to come, in the kingdom, continue to teach me." No earthly teachers (ver. 99), not even the *elders** or the aged (ver. 100), afford anything that equals this revelation of God. No wonder ! for it is God's epistle to mankind offering reconciliation, peace, and union with himself in glory !

NUN

105 Thy word is a lamp unto my feet, and a light unto my path.
106 I have sworn, and I will perform it, that I will keep thy righteous judgments.
107 I am afflicted very much : quicken me, O Lord, according unto thy word.
108 Accept, I beseech thee, the freewill offerings of my mouth, O Lord,
    And teach me thy judgments.
109 My soul is continually in my hand : yet do I not forget thy law.
110 The wicked have laid a snare for me : yet I erred not from thy precepts.
111 Thy testimonies have I taken as an heritage for ever : for they are the rejoicing of my heart.
112 I have inclined mine heart to perform thy statutes alway, even unto the end.

The pilgrim proclaims God's law sufficient amid all difficulties. Yes, sufficient even in the darkest hour of the darkest night of earth. It shall shed its light, like the Pillar Cloud, on the pilgrim-path of those who travel in the Last Days, amid the shades of the world's evening ; it has shed its light on the gloomiest path ever trod by a saddened follower of the Lamb ; it does at this hour shed light, the purest, and the sweetest, into the souls of all who know the Lord.

Nun.

> *" Thy word is a lamp unto my feet,*
> *And a light unto my path."* (Ver. 105.)

It has all sorts of light in it ; it is like what is said in Rev. xxi. 23 ; it has sun light and temple-lamp light. It is a *"lamp"*—nay, the very *"light"* of day ! In this light, the Lord of pilgrims walked ; and in this light each of his band walks still, and purposes to walk, *"for ever, continually, unto the end,"* (ver. 112). The *" end"* contains in it a direct reference to the *reward ;* for the word is עֵקֶב, a word used elsewhere for wages or reward, *e. g.*, Psa. xix. 12, Prov. xxii. 14.

---

* Applying this passage to the Lord Jesus, Augustine says—" Agnosco eum plane, qui super docentes se intellexit, quando cum esset duodecim annorum remansit puer Jesus in Hierusalem."

The pilgrim has his eye on the blessed termination, and seems to speak abruptly as he gazes—"*For ever ! the end !*"—the rewarding close !

SAMECH

113 I hate vain thoughts : but thy law do I love.

114 Thou art my hiding-place and my shield : I hope in thy word.

115 Depart from me, ye evil-doers: for I will keep the commandments of my God.

116 Uphold me according unto thy word, that I may live :
And let me not be ashamed of my hope.

117 Hold thou me up, and I shall be safe ! and I will have respect unto thy statutes continually.

118 Thou hast trodden down all them that err from thy statutes : for their deceit is falsehood.

119 Thou puttest away all the wicked of the earth like dross : therefore I love thy testimonies.

120 My flesh trembleth for fear of thee ; and I am afraid of thy judgments.

The pilgrim, tempted to a compromise, cleaves to the Law. Samech. Water and oil cannot intermingle ; the word of God and the ways of fallen men are equally irreconcilable.

" I hate thoughts." (סְעַפִּים.)

I hate mere *opinions* on matters of duty, and on points of divine worship. I hate "*waverings,*" say some, implying the uncertainty of merely human thoughts on divine truth.

"*But thy law have I loved* "—(thy revelation of thyself and of thy will).

In verse 116, "ashamed of my hope" is, ashamed so as to abandon my hope as one disappointed. At verse 118, the end of all who adopt another rule than the law of God is hinted at ; and then dwelt upon in verses 119, 120. "*Their deceit (i. e.,* the lie they trust in) *leads to nothing*" (Hengst.), or ends in utter disappointment. It is a "*spem mentita seges.*" The wicked are put away as dross is flung out (ver. 119), and this with such accompaniments of terror, that the beholder, though safe in that day within the cloud, exclaims—

"*My flesh trembleth* (horripilavit caro mea, Jerome) *for fear of Thee ;*
And I am afraid at thy judgments ! "

AIN

121 I have done judgment and justice : leave me not to mine oppressors.

122 Be surety for thy servant for good : let not the proud oppress me.

123 Mine eyes fail for thy salvation, and for the word of thy righteousness.
124 Deal with thy servant according unto thy mercy, and teach me thy statutes.
125 I am thy servant; give me understanding, that I may know thy testimonies.
126 It is time for thee, Lord, to work : for they have made void thy law.
127 Therefore I love thy commandments above gold; yea, above fine gold.
128 Therefore I esteem all thy precepts concerning all things to be right;
And I hate every false way.

Ain. *The pilgrim seeks to endure to the end.* Do not leave me !
Be surety for thy servant that it may be well with him ! It
is time for thee to work ! These appeals indicate a pilgrim
feeling himself beset with much that makes him wish that the
journey were done, besides the 123d verse—

" *Mine eyes fail for thy salvation ;* (see ver. 81, 82)
And for the word which thou wilt perform." (Ver. 123.)

It might seem as if the "*therefore*" עַל כֵּן of verses 127, 128,
declared that the sight of the reckless course of the ungodly
has increased the pilgrim's love to the Lord's ways ; but we
incline to another view. The 126th verse is literally,

" *There is a time for the Lord to work.*" (Ver. 126.)

Vengeance is not speedily executed ; for God is long-suffering.
The effect of this delay is to tempt the ungodly to "make void
the law." But the effect of the Lord's *having a time,* a fixed
time, for the performance of his promises and threatenings, is
very different in regard to his servants ; they are thereby in-
duced to persevere in shewing love to him. "*Therefore,*" on
this account, " I have persevered till now in loving thy commandments, approving of every one of thy precepts, ('*all thy
precepts, even all*') and hating every false way." Yes, it is he
who says in his heart, " My Lord delayeth his coming," that
begins to beat his fellow-servants, and to eat and drink with
the drunken.

PE

129 Thy testimonies are wonderful : therefore doth my soul keep them.
130 The entrance of thy words giveth light : it giveth understanding unto
the simple.
131 I opened my mouth and panted : for I longed for thy commandments.
132 Look thou upon me, and be merciful unto me,
As thou usest to do unto those that love thy name.

133 Order my steps in thy word : and let not any iniquity have dominion over me.

134 Deliver me from the oppression of man : so will I keep thy precepts.

135 Make thy face to shine upon thy servant; and teach me thy statutes.

136 Rivers of waters run down mine eyes, because they keep not thy law.

The pilgrim manifests increasing, as well as intense, delight Pe. *in the Law.* It is a somewhat quaint, but at the same time faithful, view of his state of mind that is given by one who paraphrases verse 131 thus—

" *With open mouth I pant and run, like hart before the hounds,*
Until my lawful prize be won for which my spirit bounds.
Behold thou me, O Lord my God, the master of the race——."

The Lord Jesus, the Son of David, could utter these words ; and David, or any member of Christ, can find no better words to express their soul's desire when getting a glimpse of "the unsearchable riches." There is some difficulty, however, in verse 130, which is literally,

" *The door of thy words giveth light.*

Some say, " The opening up of the true sense of thy word ;" but this is not in the expression. The Lord's words are apparently represented as *the door* (פֶּתַח) *by which we enter into the chambers of his heart.* The idea is this. You cannot handle any saying of God in a true frame or spirit without finding yourself in so doing at a door which may lead you far in to the palace—to the innermost thoughts of God's heart toward us. A door is opened to you every time you apprehend one sentence or saying of the Lord's—"a door in heaven," shall we say ?—a door like that of which John (Rev. iv. 1) speaks, by which you are enabled, in the spirit, to pass farther in to the secrets of God ? Only this is not a revelation of things hidden from other saints—part of its blessedness is found in its being the common privilege of all saints ; just as verse 132 has expressed it, "*According to the manner** (Gen. xl. 13) *to-*

---

* כְּמִשְׁפָּט. The same expression occurs in verse 149, " Quicken me, O Lord כְּמִשְׁפָּטֶךָ, *according to thy manner.*" The sense would in this case be, " Quicken, in answer to my cry ; for thou art wont to hear such cries." Perhaps, also, verse 175 should be so understood.

ward those that love thy name"—toward Abel, toward Enoch, toward Abraham, toward Moses, toward us also who *love "thy name!"* We may be able to say nothing else of ourselves but this only, "We *love thy name!"* But this is enough. And how real, how intense, is this love, since it draws forth the heart in strains like verse 136–

> " *Mine eyes run down as brooks of water,*
> *Because of their not keeping thy laws!* "

Their present wickedness, and their final doom, are both referred to. It is, "If thou hadst known, even thou!" (Luke xx. 41.)

TZADDI

137 Righteous art thou, O Lord, and upright are thy judgments.

138 Thy testimonies that thou hast commanded are righteous and very faithful.

139 My zeal hath consumed me, because mine enemies have forgotten thy words.

140 Thy word is very pure : therefore thy servant loveth it.

141 I am small and despised : yet do not I forget thy precepts.

142 Thy righteousness is an everlasting righteousness, and thy law is the truth.

143 Trouble and anguish have taken hold on me : yet thy commandments are my delights.

144 The righteousness of thy testimonies is everlasting : give me understanding, and I shall live.

Tzaddi.

The pilgrim adopts the tone of adoration. Getting nearer his journey's end, it is natural for the man of God to praise more than at the outset. At the close of their warfare, saints are represented in Revelation (*e. g.*, chap. xv. 4) as discerning the Lord's *righteousness and faithfulness*, "Just and true have thy ways been, O King of saints!" They see this in his judgments on the ungodly ; for it is not with them as is told of the Emperor Mauritius, who uttered, in reference to his own sufferings and his family at the hand of Phocas, "*Righteous art thou, O Lord.*" And this is the utterance of verses 137, 138. The more that enemies forget the Lord's word, the more he remembers it. It is a word without dross, "pure," no defect in it.*

> " *Thy righteousness is righteousness for ever,*
> *And thy law is truth.*" (Ver. 142.)

---

* Pure gold (says Horne) is said to be so fixed that an ounce of it set in the eye of a glass-furnace, for two months, did not lose a single grain.

Joshua (xxiii. 14) testified to Israel, and they said Amen to the testimony, that not one good thing had failed of all that the Lord had spoken. His word of promise and of threatening cannot deceive, cannot disappoint, cannot come short of its declarations. And this is once more repeated, verse 144-

" Righteousness (צֶדֶק) *are thy testimonies for ever !*
Cause me to understand this and I shall live."

Life eternal !—the life of the redeemed in the everlasting kingdom, when the Righteous One has triumphed, and expelled ungodliness from earth !

KOPH

145 I cried with my whole heart ; hear me, O Lord ! I will keep thy statutes.
146 I cried unto thee ; save me, and I shall keep thy testimonies.
147 I prevented the dawning of the morning, and cried : I hoped in thy word.
148 Mine eyes prevent the night-watches, that I might meditate in thy word
149 Hear my voice according unto thy lovingkindness :
     O Lord, quicken me according to thy judgment.
150 They draw nigh that follow after mischief : they are far from thy law.
151 Thou art near, O Lord ; and thy commandments are truth.
152 Concerning thy testimonies, I have known of old that thou hast founded them for ever.

The pilgrim protests that all his expectation is from the **Koph**
Lord. Rising before daybreak, nay, even encroaching on the night-watches (like Mark i. 35, and Luke vi. 12), the Lord of pilgrims follows hard after God, going from strength to strength, instead of abating in his zeal, as men often do in other pursuits, through length of time.

" I came before thee in the morning twilight." (Ver. 147.)

And all his true followers may be expected to resemble the Lord in this hard pursuit, especially as they get nearer their journey's end, and approach the Lord's dwelling-place. What strength of comfort in verse 151-

" Thou art near, O Lord,
And all thy commandments are truth !" (cannot disappoint.)

There is an anomaly in verse 152, as to gender, if " Thou hast founded *them*" (ם), is to be referred to " *testimonies ;*" but probably it is meant to refer back to *all* the terms used in this context, *e. g.*, statutes (ver. 145), words (ver. 147), as well as commandments and testimonies. And this is the sense. *"Aforetime"* (קֶדֶם before experience had given me palpable proofs),

> *" Aforetime I knew from out of thy testimonies* (Hengstenberg)
> *That thou hast founded these for ever."* (Ver. 152.)

In the ages to come we shall still have God's words, and we shall then look back and see how truthful our God was. The Lord of pilgrims, who trod our path himself, will then lead us to review the dealings of Jehovah, talking with us as he talked with Moses and Elias about his own decease on the Transfiguration Hill.

RESH

153 Consider mine affliction, and deliver me : for I do not forget thy law.

154 Plead my cause, and deliver me : quicken me according to thy word.

155 Salvation is far from the wicked : for they seek not thy statutes.

156 Great are thy tender mercies, O Lord : quicken me according to thy judgments.

157 Many are my persecutors and mine enemies ; yet do I not decline from thy testimonies.

158 I beheld the transgressors, and was grieved ; because they kept not thy word.

159 Consider how I love thy precepts! quicken me, O Lord, according to thy lovingkindness.

160 Thy word is true from the beginning :
And every one of thy righteous judgments endureth for ever.

Resh.

Continued opposition causes the pilgrim to pray for continued quickening. The end of the journey has as many trials as the beginning ; we are to "hold fast the beginning of our confidence stedfast to the end." Three times to cry for *" quickening"* arises here, viz., in verses 154, 156, 159—an appeal for more life—which we now may specially urge, since we can hold up to the Lord his own words, " I am come that they might have life, and have it more abundantly," (John x. 10).

One like Paul, whose sympathy was so entirely with his Lord, might well use the words in 2 Tim. iv. 7, " I have fought a good fight ;" but all pilgrims, and he too among the rest, would gladly use to the last the appeal of verse 154, all the more after a life-time experience of the trials by the way.

> *" Fight my fight* (Psa. xliv. 1, Hengstenberg),
> *And redeem me."* (גְּאָלֵנִי.) (Ver. 154.)

Be a *Goel* to me ! Be to me what Job expected when he cried, "I know that my (גֹּאֵל) Redeemer liveth, and that he shall stand at the latter day upon the earth," (xix. 25). Meanwhile,

> "*Quicken me, according to thy word,*" (ver. 154. Thy promises to thy children who knock).
> "*Quicken me, according to thy judgments,*" (ver. 156. The principles of thy dealing with us).
> "*I beheld transgressors, and was sickened at those who kept not thy word.*" (Ver. 158.)
> "*Quicken me, according to thy lovingkindness,*" (ver. 159. The dictates of thine own free love).

Why should not all of us rest on the Lord's word with increasing confidence as our pilgrimage advances to its close, since experience adds to the evidence of his faithfulness,

> "*The beginnng of* (רֹאשׁ) *thy word is truth ;*
> *And to eternity is every appointment of thy righteousness.*"

There is nothing but truth and certainty in thy holy word. It may be rendered, "Truth is the sum of thy word," (Hengstenberg). At the same time, the Psalmist probably expresses far more by that peculiar form, " רֹאשׁ, *the head* of thy word." As רֹאשׁ פִּנָּה in Psa. cxviii. 22 is the "head, or chief, of the corner," may not this expression be intended to designate "that original promise which is the 'head, or chief promise, of the whole word of God'—the promise of the Woman's Seed ?" The faithful in Israel no doubt were ever reverting to it. To them could it be otherwise than "the רֹאשׁ, the head," the chief utterance of the Word ? It is, therefore, mainly to this that we suppose reference is made in this verse. The Lord Jesus could use it of himself when on earth ; and each one of his disciples could—but not less can we now, we who can point back to the Woman's Seed having come, to the fulfilment of that "*head of the word,*" and who may thus more than ever confidently look forward to the fulfilment of what remains, "*every appointment of his righteousness,*" in the ages to come, including the Day of the Lord, when all things shall be set in order.

161 Princes have persecuted me without a cause: but my heart standeth in awe of thy word.

162 I rejoice at thy word, as one that findeth great spoil.

163 I hate and abhor lying: but thy law do I love.

164 Seven times a day do I praise thee, because of thy righteous judgments.

165 Great peace have they which love thy law:
And nothing shall offend them.

166 Lord, I have hoped for thy salvation, and done thy commandments.

167 My soul hath kept thy testimonies; and I love them exceedingly.

168 I have kept thy precepts and thy testimonies: for all my ways are before thee.

Schin.

The pilgrim is full of peace and praise. It is now specially that *praise* seems to abound in the traveller; that is, it is now near his journey's end that it is poured forth, so as to be heard by others. His *Hosanna* is changing into the *Hallelujahs* of the heavenly citizens,

" *Seven times a day have I praised thee.*" (Ver. 164.)

The pilgrim is an Isaac, one who meditates at even-tide, and one who can call God his "*fear* ;" for verse 161 has פַּחַד, the very word used twice in Gen. xxxi. 42, 53 of Isaac's God, "the fear of Isaac." In this frame of solemn Bethel-like awe he approaches the end of his journey, and crosses the threshold of the King's palace. This reverent awe has deepened on him, the longer he has meditated on Jehovah's word. Very fitting it is, now that he is near the end, to tell, and to leave it for encouragement to those that come after, as a thing proved by experience,

" *Great peace is the portion of those that love thy law ;*
There is no stumbling-block to them." (Ver. 165.)

" At peace (says one) with God, at peace with themselves, at peace with all men; and the whole creation at peace with them." This peace enables them to wait patiently for the final glory—in the kingdom of peace.

" *I have waited for* (see Ruth i. 13, in the Hebrew the same word, שַׂבֵּר)
thy salvation, O Lord." Ver. 166.)

169 Let my cry come near before thee, O Lord : give me understanding according to thy word.

170 Let my supplication come before thee : deliver me according to thy word.

171 My lips shall utter praise, when thou hast taught me thy statutes.

172 My tongue shall speak of thy word : for all thy commandments are righteousness.

173 Let thine hand help me ; for I have chosen thy precepts.

174 I have longed for thy salvation, O Lord ; and thy law is my delight.

175 Let my soul live, and it shall praise thee ; and let thy judgments help me.

176 I have gone astray like a lost sheep ; seek thy servant;
For I do not forget thy commandments.

The pilgrim pours out prayer and praise, in a strong   Tau. *cry, at the close of his journey.* Praise is uttered in the midst of redoubled supplication ; repeated praise in the verses 171, 172.

> "*My lips shall stream forth with thy praise;* (gush forth, as Ps. xix. 1) *For thou wilt teach me thy statutes."*

> "*My tongue shall sing thy word,* (responsively תַעַן) ; *For all thy commandments are righteousness."*

Anticipating the employments, the discoveries, the enjoyments of the Coming Rest and Kingdom, the Psalmist tells of the hallelujahs that shall dwell upon his lips, gushing up from an ever full and ever filling soul—a soul full of the Lord's grace in the past, and ever filling with fresh manifestations ; for "*Thou wilt* teach me" still, and I shall see with increasing clearness that all thy commandments were holy, and just, and good.

Help me, then, to the end ; for (ver. 174)

> "*I have pined for thy salvation,*" (תָּאַבְתִּי).

This is (as we might expect at the close) the strongest expression of desire for Coming Glory that has yet been used. "Salvation," as we noticed above, is the final deliverance, with all the grace and glory that it brings. At verse 81, we find the soul "*thirsting,*" fainting in thirst for it ; at verse 123, the earnest expectation made "*the eye faint*" for it ; at verse 166, there was strong hope, and waiting ; but this verse rises to an almost impatient longing—a "*pining with desire*" for the arrival of the blessed day.

Again, verse 175, there is the anticipation of praise, because of a happy arrival ; and a burst of prayer such as might well sum up a lifetime's experience and desires.

"*I have been a wanderer,* (תָּעִיתִי) *like a lost sheep.**

I have all my life found nowhere to lay my head, and no rest to the sole of my foot. I have, like Hagar and Ishmael (תֵּתַע, Gen. xxi. 14), wandered in the wilderness where there was no water. I have, like Joseph (תֹּעֶה, Gen. xxxvii. 15), wandered in search of my brethren, without home or friends. I have, like Abraham, above all (הִתְעוּ, Gen. xx. 13), left my country and kindred, all my father's house, for the Lord's sake. My life has been a wandering, like sheep lost, when the shepherd is away, or when the shepherd chooses to send them away from his care (הִתְעוּ, Jer. l. 6), "turning them loose on the mountains, so that they go from mountain to hill, forgetting their resting-place."

(But in all my wanderings and weariness, and sorrow)
"*I have not forgotten thy commandments.*"

"*Seek, then, thy servant*"—*i. e.*, do the part of a shepherd who brings home his sheep to the fold ! It is a request that he would do as Ezekiel (xxxiv. 16) foretells the Lord shall do on the day when he gathers his scattered ones under the shade of the Plant of Renown ; for here the word is בַּקֵּשׁ, and there the word is אֲבַקֵּשׁ. "I will seek that which was lost, and bring again that which was driven away." Then shall Rev. vii. 15, 16, 17, be realised ; for the Lamb in the midst shall be Shepherd ever present ; himself once a wanderer in our world's wastes, and now feeding among the lilies, bringing home all his flock to where they thirst no more, nor hunger, neither does the sun light on them, nor any heat.

Amen ! Even so ! Come, Lord Jesus ! Surely this is the heart's feeling of the Singer of this Psalm,

A pilgrim and stranger guided day and night by the Law of the Lord.

* David Dickson says on this verse, "I have gone astray—driven out in the stormy and dark day; or by the hunting of the dogs chased out from the rest of the flock." Banished from his native country and the fellowship of the Church, as to bodily presence. Horne also notices that it may mean the misery of "wandering as an exile in foreign lands."

SONGS OF DEGREES.

It may be helpful to a right understanding of the Psalms we now approach, and may increase our interest in them, to begin with a synoptical view of the fifteen which are clustered together, and go by the name of "*Songs of Degrees.*" The progression of thought and subject thus becomes clear :

The Pilgrim Train and its Leader

Psalm 120.—*Weary with the strife of tongues.* (Comp. Psalm 81:6)

Psalm 121.—*Commit themselves to Jehovah alone, as they journey forth.*

Psalm 122.—*Sing of the City of Habitation, to which they journey.*

Psalm 123.—*Cast an upward look amid the contempt of those they meet with.*

At a stage in their way which we might call *Ebenezer-*

Psalm 124.—*Give praise for deliverance hitherto.*

Psalm 125.—*Express confidence of being kept faithful, through Jehovah's faithfulness, to the end.*

Psalm 126.—*Sing of the joys Jehovah has given, and will give, to his servants.*

Psalm 127.—*Cease from carefulness, and ascribe the success to Jehovah.*

Psalm 128.—*Pronounce blessing on all the fearers of God.*

Psalm 129.—*Review their past sufferings in hope.*

Psalm 130.—*Relate their earnest cry in trouble, and the rich result.*

Psalm 131.—*Express their contentment with Jehovah's will.*

Psalm 132.—*Remind Jehovah of pledges of favour to Zion, and are answered.*

Psalm 133.—*Admire and sing of the unity of those met in the Holy City, their habitation.*

Psalm 134.—*Call for unceasing praise from all Jehovah's servants.*

We adopt the idea of these fifteen Psalms being in some sense the *songs of those who went up to Jerusalem to worship.* They do not give us the inward experience of individuals only ; they bear reference to Israel at large ; for even when, as in the case of the 130th and 131st, the strain has a personal aspect, the closing verse sings of Israel.*

In the singular, מַעֲלָה frequently designates the going up to a higher spot, *e. g.*, the ascent of Bethhoron, the ascent of Luhith, and in Ezra vii. 9, the going up from Babylon. In the plural it is used for the *steps* of Solomon's throne, and in Ezekiel (xl. 26, 31, 34), for the *steps* of the temple-gates. The use of מַעֲלוֹת for the *degrees* or steps of a dial, has been fully illustrated by recent discoveries in Assyria, which prove that the sun-dial was a series of steps, or terraces, on which a pole cast its shadow. It would appear, therefore, that the name *"Song of the Steps"* is a poetical one, designating Psalms which specially suited the circumstances of those who *go up* to the Temple.

Hengstenberg remarks that they are grouped round the 127th, which is *Solomon's;* and we may add that that central " Song of Degrees," or steps, has special reference to *" The House,"* or Temple.

Psalm 120

A Song of degrees

1 In my distress I cried unto the Lord, and he heard me.

2 Deliver my soul, O Lord, from lying lips, and from a deceitful tongue.

3 What shall be given unto thee ? or what shall be done unto thee, thou false tongue ?

4 Sharp arrows of the mighty, with coals of juniper.

5 Woe is me, that I sojourn in Mesech, that I dwell in the tents of Kedar !

6 My soul hath long dwelt with him that hateth peace.

7 I am for peace : but when I speak, they are for war.

The theme. WE could have imagined Hannah, the mother of Samuel, taking up this song in her lips when going up to the Feast at

---

* This feature of these fifteen Psalms is itself sufficient to set aside the idea of a writer in the *Jewish Chronicle*, that they were specially for *domestic use*, and get their name from the steps, or ascent to the *house-top*, where devout Jews were wont to worship. Some have conjectured that the title "Degrees" may refer to the musical instruments used in chaunting them. The common idea that the name refers to the steps of the Temple, is that expressed in Parker's old translation—" These fifteen Psalms next following be songs benamed of steps and stairs, for that the choir on them did sing."

Shiloh. She carried her private sorrows to the Great Congre- *Hope in sorrow.* gation, that in the midst of the many worshippers she might find the special presence of Jehovah. The complaint, in her case, was her adversary's tongue ; so, here it is the tongue— *"the false tongue."* At the same time, it is *"sore distress,"* for the form צָרָת is emphatic (ver. 1), just as in Psa. iii. 3, יְשׁוּעָתָה is the emphatic form to signify complete deliverance.

We see a worshipper, who enjoys little peace in his own *The plan.* country, coming up to the City of Peace, *Salem*, there to realise peace at one of those feasts which exhibited such a spectacle of united devotion. In the sanctuary, the pilgrim is enabled to see the end of those who so hate the godly, that they make war upon them. He sees

> *" The arrows of the Mighty One sharpened ;"*

as if anticipating the day of God, when he, the Mighty One, sung of in Psa. xlv. 3, shall send forth his arrows—arrows of fire—*" glowing embers of genista-fuel"*—in other words, "The flaming fire that takes vengeance on his foes," (2 Thess. i. 8).

Meanwhile, it is a saddening thought that as yet the days of the Prince of peace have not come. But we may have his sympathy, for once the Prince of peace felt thus himself, taber-nacling among us,

> *" Woe's me ! for I tarry in Mesech !*
> *I pitch my tents with the tents of Kedar !"*

As Isaiah i. 10 brands the apostate people and rulers of Jeru-salem as " people of *Sodom* and rulers of *Gomorrha*," and as Ezek. xvi. 4 calls them " Amorites" and " Hittites," so does the Psalmist speak of his harassing foe, as like the barbarous men of Mesech in the obscure north (the Moschian mountains), or near the Caspian Sea (see Ezek. xxxviii. 2), and the ever-unsettled tribes of Kedar in the south. And so he sighs

> *" It is wearisome for my soul to dwell with the hater of peace !"* (Hengst.)

Literally, *" Enough* of this dwelling !" Is not this the very feeling of the Church at this hour, in these days of never-end-ing forms of lies and vanity that assail the truth ? They cry, " O when shall the Prince of peace arrive ! And so felt the Lord himself, when on earth, as we see in his teaching his followers the blessedness of being "peace-makers." Indeed, who would sing this pilgrim-song so truly from the heart as "The Master?" It is a song for

The servant of the Lord weary with the strife of tongues.

Psalm 121

A Song of degrees

1 I WILL lift up mine eyes unto the hills, from whence cometh my help.
2 My help cometh from the Lord, which made heaven and earth.
3 He will not suffer thy foot to be moved: he that keepeth thee will not slumber.
4 Behold, he that keepeth Israel shall neither slumber nor sleep.
5 The Lord is thy keeper: the Lord is thy shade upon thy right hand.
6 The sun shall not smite thee by day, nor the moon by night.
7 The Lord shall preserve thee from all evil: he shall preserve thy soul.
8 The Lord shall preserve thy going out and thy coming in
From this time forth, and even for evermore.

"A SONG FOR the goings up!" (לַמַּעֲלוֹת).* The pilgrim sings it as he leaves his home to meet the Lord in the Great Congregation at Jerusalem; and the believer (like the Master) sings it as he journeys through earth to the New Jerusalem.

The theme. Abraham (Gen. xxii. 4) "lifted up his eyes" and saw the hills of Moriah on the third day. The worshipper sets forth with the desire to fix his eyes at last on the hills where his trials are, not, like Abraham's, to reach their crisis, but to end.

Faith.   "*I will lift up mine eyes to the hills.*" (Ver. 1.)

This is his resolution; his motive for leaving home and kindred is to reach "the holy mountains," as they are called, Psa. lxxxvii. 1,—those hills that are the emblems of Jehovah's faithfulness, Psa. cxxv. 1, 2,—that spot where Jehovah is specially present because of the Propitiation being there, (1 Kings viii. 42; Dan. vi. 10).

---

   * This is the only time that this form of the expression occurs, and so it is probably meant to signify something different from " Song *of* Degrees." It may be, in poetical style, like ל in "Psalm לְדָוִד," Psalm *composed* by David, *q. d.*, a Psalm which the goings up to Jerusalem may be said to have composed.

This, then, is his resolution. But there are perils by the way, and so he asks-

"*Whence shall my help come?*" (מֵאַיִן, which Phillip and others remark, is always interrogative.)

What a full answer is at once returned to his soul : "*My help is from* (מֵעִם from with, coming out from that depository of help) *Jehovah, the Maker of heaven and earth.*" And then he speaks to his soul, as the singer of Psa. ciii. does—" He will not suffer my feet to totter ! Thy keeper is not one that slumbers !" He is not like Baal, (1 Kings xviii. 27).

> "*Behold, he never slumbers !*
> *He never falls asleep, the Keeper of Israel* (Num. vi. 24).
> *My keeper is Jehovah !*"—

that Jehovah in whom Israel is blessed (Num. vi. 24) by their High Priest—whose blessing awaits the pilgrim who reaches the city. He shall keep thee, making thy experience in thy journey to become oft-times a type of the rest where "the sun* shall not smite them nor any heat," (Rev. vii. 16)—the rest in the Kingdom, and the rest of which Israel shall partake in the latter day, (Isa xlix. 10). Thus shalt thou be kept till the glory comes, and thou " goest no more out," but art a pillar in the temple of God,

> "*From henceforth and for ever !*"

---

* The Psalmist speaks of "*the moon*" smiting. He may mean all the noxious influences of night, but still he refers most specially to the moon. The force of this allusion may be understood by the following quotation from Wallstedt's *City of the Caliphs* :—" The glare of the moon in the Persian Gulf is so baneful, and creates feelings so disagreeable, that at night a person may be seen sheltering himself from those rays with the same care as he would in the day from the heat of the sun. The effect of lunar rays in producing decomposition of fish, and other animal substances, is known, though not yet explained ; all in the East and West Indies are familiar with the fact." Moonlight specially injures the traveller's *sight*, as the *coup-de-soleil* endangers his very life. Prof. Piazzi Smyth, at Teneriffe, lately ascertained that there is *some heat* in moonbeams, for his thermometrical instruments were sensibly affected by the moon's rays. In these tropical climes, meat putrifies rapidly in moonlight, and negroes, who do not hesitate to expose themselves to the sun, muffle head and face from the moon, believing that it causes distortion of the face and swelling.

With such a song of faith, keeping in sight the faithfulness and love of Him in whose law he delights, whose feasts he keeps, in whose ways he walks, the Master and his disciples no doubt often left the peaceful shores of the Lake of Galilee to go up to Jerusalem to worship ; often realised, under some fig-tree's seasonable shade, or some convenient cloud bringing down the heat by its shadow the deliverance from the sun's intolerable rays ; and found in all an emblem of their journey through earth to the Kingdom whose capital is New Jerusalem, and whose congregation is the Assembly of the first-born. It is a song of

The Lord's servant, as he goes forth on his journey, committing himself to Jehovah alone.

Psalm 122

A Song of degrees of David

1 I WAS glad when they said unto me, Let us go into the house of the Lord.
2 Our feet shall stand within thy gates, O Jerusalem.
3 Jerusalem is builded as a city that is compact together :
4 Whither the tribes go up, the tribes of the Lord, unto the testimony of Israel,
   To give thanks unto the name of the Lord.
5 For there are set thrones of judgment, the thrones of the house of David.
6 Pray for the peace of Jerusalem ! they shall prosper that love thee.
7 Peace be within thy walls, and prosperity within thy palaces.
8 For my brethren and companions' sakes, I will now say, Peace be within thee.
9 Because of the house of the Lord our God I will seek thy good.

The theme. "A PSALM of David."

Love and joy. Hope was the prevailing feature of the first Song of Degrees ; faith characterised the second ; and surely love and joy abound in this one which we now take up. The first verse strikes the key-note-

> " O 'twas a joyful sound to hear
>   Our friends devoutly say,
> Up, Israel ! To your Temple haste !
>   And keep your festal day."—(*Tate and Brady.*)

"*I have rejoiced,*" says the worshipper, "*among* (or, over *those who say, Let us go to the house of the Lord!"* David, who wrote this song, had felt that joy fill his whole soul, because of the love he bore to the Lord of the place. And lo ! instantly the pilgrim-worshipper fancies himself arrived—he is already standing at the gate in the early morning, waiting to enter, along with those who said—*" Let us go."*

" Our feet are standing at thy gates, O Jerusalem !"

The gates are thrown open, and they enter ; the city on every side engaging their attention. They see in it a city, not ruined by war, but built in its place—not like the straggling dwellings of the villages, nor like the wide spaces of Babylon, with gardens between, but with firm-built streets of stately edifices.

" Jerusalem is builded as a city !
(A city) which is bound together." (Ver. 3.)

The very compactness of its streets suggesting the close union of its inhabitants in brotherly love.

" (A city) where are* the tribes who go up,
The tribes of Jehovah." (Jah, as Psa. lxviii. 4, &c.)

How pleasant to meet, not the Canaanite—not the uncircumcised—but the tribes who, with one accord, worship the Lord ; who go up to this city for that end.

" (A city where is) the testimony (given) to Israel,
That they might praise the name of the Lord."

" The Testimony" is by some considered to mean *"The Law;"* by others, more probably, *The Ark*, so often called " The Ark of the Testimony ;" as we also find " The *Tabernacle* of Testimony." We may perhaps best understand it as a reference to all these together—they together setting forth Jehovah's character, and will, and ways, to men. And there, in its gateways, sit those who explain and enforce these laws and testimonies, according to the ancient promise in Deut. xvii. 8, 9 ; and there, also, sit the king and his princes.

---

* The שׁ here, and in verse 3, is, according to Hengstenberg, the old *popular* dialect of common life, as found in Deborah's song. If it be the popular style, it is most suitably adopted in a song for the nation at large at its feasts.

" *For there* (שָׁמָּה) *are set* (Ezek. xlviii. 35).

Thrones for judgment, (לְ)

Thrones for the house of David." - (לְ)

In all this, we may easily trace a type of our Jerusalem and its privileges. With Christ our Head, as well as with David, we look for another city that " hath foundations"—surely built, and " that lieth foursquare," compactly built (Rev. xxi. 16)—a city where we shall meet none but friends, our own friends and friends of God,—a city where the Lord's testimony is fully opened out, and his name praised,—a city at whose gates judgment is fully given, and where " a King reigneth in righteousness, and princes decree judgment," (Isa. xxxii. 1).

And if Israel's devout people did so pray for their Jerusalem, verses 6, 7, 8, 9, how much more shall the pilgrims toward that New Jerusalem "seek the better, that is, the heavenly country." It is interesting to know that the expression, שַׁאֲלוּ שְׁלוֹם (ver. 6), generally means, " Salute ye,"—*q. d.*, Greet ye Jerusalem with your good wishes reminds us of some of the mediæval hymns,* *e. g.*

> " Urbs in portu satis tuto,
> De longinquo, *te saluto,*
> *Te saluto,* te suspiro,
> Te affecto, te requiro."

And these old hymns were borrowed from Augustine, who (in his *De Spirit. et Anim.*) exclaims, " O civitas sancta, civitas speciosa, de longinquo te saluto, ad te clamo, te requiro." All of us, who follow the Lord, surely join in this ardent panting for entrance into that city of which the other was but a type, and of which we can say-

---

* And of Tasso's famous passage (*Gierus.* lib. iii. 3)

> " Ecco apparir Gierusalem si vede,
> Ecco additar Gierusalem si scorge !
> Ecco da mille voci unitamente,
> Gierusalemme salutare si sente ! "

Horne mentions from De Thou, that Theodore Zuinger felt this Psalm so appropriate to one getting near glory, that he spent his last hours in versifying it in Latin : for he could sing—

> " Per *Christi meritum patet*
> *Vitæ porta beatæ.*"

> " *They that love thee shall prosper ;*
> *There shall be peace in thy bulwarks,*
> *Prosperity in thy palaces.*"

Or take it, as some render the words ; "*Peace within thy ram parts! Repose within thy palaces!*" Love to our brethren, whom we hope to meet there (ver. 8), and love to God who has so loved us (ver. 9), must lead us to this earnest desire—" because of my brethren, and because the house of my God is there." Thus, then, now concerning the Antitype, as hereafter of the type through which he looked to the Antitype,

The Lord's servant sings of the City of Habitation to which
he journeys.

Psalm 123

A Song of degrees

1 Unto thee lift I up mine eyes, O thou that dwellest in the heavens.
2 Behold, as the eyes of servants look unto the hand of their masters,
And as the eyes of a maiden unto the hand of her mistress ;
So our eyes wait upon the Lord our God,
Until that he have mercy upon us.
3 Have mercy upon us, O Lord, have mercy upon us :
For we are exceedingly filled with contempt.
4 Our soul is exceedingly filled with the scorning of those that are at ease,
And with the contempt of the proud.

If we have found hope, faith, joy, and love in these " Songs of Degrees" hitherto, we now find long-suffering patience. *David* is said to have been the writer. The worshipper, whether David, or David's greater Son, or any member of his body, " *lifts his eyes*" upward to the Lord in the heavens. The same Lord who, in Psa. cxxi. 1, is seen on Zion-hills, is here seen, " *in the heavens,*" because the contrast is intended to be made between the Earth that persecutes, and the Majesty, overcanopying earth, which protects. *(margin: The theme. Patient dependence.)*

Scorn is felt, such as Nehemiah's case illustrates (Neh. ii. 19), or Hezekiah's case, in 2 Chron. xxx. 10, when that godly king incited the tribes of Israel to join him in the passover feast. It is the scorn of those "*at ease,*" הַשַּׁאֲנַנִּים, persons on whom the world smiles, and who say in their hearts, " Where is the promise of his Coming?" like the nations of earth, in Zech i. 15, הַגּוֹיִם הַשַּׁאֲנַנִּים. It is the contempt of *" the proud"* גֵּאיֹנִים, that class of scorners who shall be found abounding on earth when " the day of the Lord" comes on " every one that is (גֵּאָה) proud,"—the " boasters, lovers of pleasure," of 2 Tim. iii. 2. The prayer for help has reference to the high priest's blessing, Num. vi. 24. In Psa. cxxi. 3, 4, he lifted up his eyes to the Lord, and sought that part of the blessing which consists in safe keeping ; here, he asks, חָנֵּנוּ, Be gracious ! Be gracious ! (Num. vi. 24.) The Lord makes his face shine upon the pilgrim ; and the grace that beams thence is the antidote to the contempt of men. Yes, even now it is so ; but if even now, what then when the lifted-up countenance shall be " the grace that shall be brought us at the appearing of Jesus Christ ?" Such is the reward of

The upward look of the Lord's servant amid contempt.

Psalm 124

A Song of degrees of David

1 If it had not been the Lord who was on our side, now may Israel say ;
2 If it had not been the Lord who was on our side, when men rose up against us :
3 Then they had swallowed us up quick, when their wrath was kindled against us :
4 Then the waters had overwhelmed us, the stream had gone over our soul :
5 Then the proud waters had gone over our soul.
6 Blessed be the Lord, who hath not given us as a prey to their teeth.
7 Our soul is escaped as a bird out of the snare of the fowlers :
The snare is broken, and we are escaped.
8 Our help is in the name of the Lord, who made heaven and earth.

The theme.

Thankful acknowledgment.

EBENEZER ! Hitherto the Lord hath helped ! This seems to be the tone of this song of David, sung at a stage of the way, or at a time, when the thought of past difficulties overcome, and dangers escaped, was active and lively. *Thankfulness* characterises it as much as hope, faith, joy, love, patience, characterised the previous Psalms.

In the year 1582, it was sung on a remarkable occasion in Edinburgh. An imprisoned minister, John Durie, had been set free, and was met and welcomed on entering the town by two hundred of his friends. The number increased till he found himself in the midst of a company of two thousand, who began to sing, as they moved up the long High Street, "*Now Israel may say,*" &c. They sang in four parts with deep solemnity, all joining in the well-known tune and Psalm. They were much moved themselves, and so were all who heard ; and one of the chief persecutors is said to have been more alarmed at this sight and song than at anything he had seen in Scotland.

" *Had it not been Jehovah ! He was for us, Oh* (נ) *let Israel say ;*
Had it not been Jehovah ! He who was for us, when men rose against us
They had at that time made one morsel of us (Patrick),
When their wrath burnt against us."

We should have been dealt with by them as Korah and his company were by the Lord, Num. xvi. 32. But the thunderbolt was not in our enemies' hand. We have got the help we sought (Psa. cxxi and cxxiii.), and have escaped every snare. Is not this a strain in which all saints can join by the way, at every palm-tree station, at every resting-stage, at every refreshing well,—a strain which the Lord of Pilgrims himself would often raise ? And Oh ! how he and his company shall sing it at the journey's end, when they who " were counted worthy *to escape all things,* and to stand before the Son of man" (Luke xxi. 36), lift up their voice in mighty thunderings-

" *The snare is broken, and we are escaped !*
Our help has been in the name of Jehovah ! "

that Jehovah to whom belongs earth, as well as heaven. Such is this Ebenezer song,

The song of the Lord's servant for deliverance vouchsafed at every step of the way.

Psalm 125

A Song of degrees

1 THEY that trust in thè Lord shall be as mount **Zion,**
Which cannot be removed, but abideth for ever.
2 As the mountains are round about Jerusalem,
So the Lord is round about his people from henceforth **even for ever.**
3 For the rod of the wicked shall not rest upon the lot of the righteous;
Lest the righteous put forth their hands unto iniquity.
4 Do good, O Lord, unto those that be good, and to them that are upright
in their hearts.
5 As for such as turn aside unto their crooked ways,
The Lord shall lead them forth with the workers of iniquity:
But peace shall be upon Israel.

Faithfulness.

The theme.

FAITHFULNESS under temptation is the grace that shines out in this song. It is sung amid enemies, when they environ the Lord's servant on every side. Two thoughts contribute mutually to strengthen and confirm the determined and decided adherence of the Psalmist to his Lord, viz., the thought of **J**ehovah's faithfulness to him, and the thought of the short-**lived** prosperity of foes.

> " *They that trust in Jehovah are like the hill of Zion,*
> *It moves not ;*
> *For ever it abides.*
> *Jerusalem, the hills are round about her ;*
> *And* (so) *Jehovah is round about his people,*
> *From henceforth, and unto eternity.*"

In verse 3 the "*lot* of the righteous" is *inheritance* or **possession.** The worshipper rejoices that never shall rod, or sceptre, of the wicked, extend its influence to that happy spot, the allotted portion, the Canaan-lot of the Lord's people ; and thus the old temptation to idolatry, and other evils, shall be for ever escaped. The language of verse 3 has a peculiarity in it ; it is literally, " *the rod of the Wicked One,*" thus fitting the Psalm for the circumstances of the saints even in the last days, when " *that Wicked,*" הָרָשָׁע shall be revealed and then destroyed.

In verse 5 the pilgrim seems to sing the unhappy end of **backsliders,** of those who once joined their company in going to the house of God. The Lord, it is said, " *will let them go* with the *workers of iniquity* (יְלִיכֵם, Hengstenberg), as if to suggest to us, who know now of the great day's awful scenes, the word of the Judge, " *Depart !*" and the description of the result—" These *shall go* away into everlasting punishment." He shall assign them their portion with the hypocrites, (Matt. xxiv. 51).

How calm, how sweet the contrast to which our eyes are suddenly and abruptly turned ! It is the high priest pronouncing what remained of his full blessing (Num. vi. 26). The Lord lifts up his countenance upon them, and gives the word— " *Peace upon Israel !*" Everything desirable is wrapt up in this peace. Thine eyes shall see Jerusalem a quiet habitation, a tabernacle that shall not be taken down, (Isa. xxxiii. 20). This will be the " *good*" which the Lord will do to his Israel, when he places him in his lot in the end of the days. And with his soul full of thoughts like these, we need but wonder at

The Lord's servant's faithful adherence to his faithful God.

Psalm 126

A Song of degrees

1 WHEN the Lord turned again the captivity of Zion, we were like them that dream.
2 Then was our mouth filled with laughter, and our tongue with singing. Then said they among the heathen, The Lord hath done great things for them.
3 The Lord hath done great things for us, whereof we are glad.
4 Turn again our captivity, O Lord, as the streams in the south.
5 They that sow in tears shall reap in joy.
6 He that goeth forth and weepeth, bearing precious seed, Shall doubtless come again with rejoicing, bringing his sheaves with him.

LORD, to whom shall we go for the joy of final victory, but to thee, who has been in all ages the source of Israel's joyful victories ? Jehovah has ever been the author of our blessings, of blessings almost too great to be believed, and He will give us " An autumn of joy for a seed-time of tears."

The theme.

Confidence.

" *We have been like those that dream.*"

On all such occasions, so great has been the blessing vouchsafed, that our *"mouth has been filled with laughter."* The word יְמָלֵא expresses the habit, or customary act, as does also יֹאמְרוּ, *q. d.*, at such times (אָז) our mouth was filled with laughter, and the old patriarch's words, Job viii. 21, were verified in us, and the Gentiles were wont to say,

> " *The Lord has wrought mightily*
> *In what he has done for them.*"

It was thus in the valley of Elah, where Goliath fell, and Philistia fled. It was thus at Baal-Perazim. It was thus when one morning, after many nights of gloom, Jerusalem arose at dawn of day, and found Sennacherib's thousands a camp of the dead. And it has all along been the manner of our God.

> " *The Lord has wrought mightily*
> *In what he has done for us ;*
> *And we have been made glad !*"

Ever do this till conflict is over ! Just as thou dost with the streams of the south, year by year, so do with us—with all, with each. And we are confident thou wilt ; we are sure that we make no vain boast when we sing this Psalm as descriptive of the experience of all thy pilgrims and worshippers. Horne beautifully says, " Thou sowest perhaps in tears, thou doest thy duty amidst persecution and affliction, sickness, pain, and sorrow ; thou labourest in the church, and no account is made of thy labours, no profit seems likely to accrue from thee. Nay, thou thyself must drop into the dust of death, and all the storms of that winter must pass over thee. Yet the day is coming when thou shalt reap in joy; and plentiful shall be thy harvest. For thus thy blessed Master 'went forth weeping,' a man of sorrows, bearing precious seed, and strewing it all around him, till at length his own body was buried, like a grain of wheat, in the furrow of the grave. But He arose and is now in heaven, whence he shall 'doubtless come again rejoicing,' with the voice of the archangel and the trump of God, 'bringing his sheaves with Him.' Then shall every man receive the fruit of his works, and have praise of God." Look, then, at this picture–

" He goes, and he goes weeping,
Bearing the basket of seed, (load of, Amos ix. 13) :
He comes, and he comes with singing,
Bearing his sheaves ! "

The worshipper, in all ages, has known the going forth to serve the Lord in tears—the following him with the cross—the scattering the se d in his field in sorrow and fear ; but as certainly shall he know the joy of harvest at his Lord's return. The disciple is in this merely tracing the Master's path—

" So came Messiah, friend of men,
(A man of sorrows he),
To fight with grief, and tears, and pain,
That we might conquerors be.
Behold, he comes the Second time
To wipe away our tears,
And takes us up along with him
For everlasting years."—BARCLAY.

Our Lord, in his parable of the Sower, seems to unfold the idea expressed here, so far as it bore on his service and labour here. The other part, referring to his Second Coming and glory, was not dwelt upon there. Nevertheless, it is well for us, in pondering the parable of the Sower, to revert to this Psalm, and see the reward of him who goeth forth like the master. We shall not serve less cheerfully by joining in this Psalm—

The Lord's servant thankfully recording past joys, and anticipating future.

Psalm 127

A Song of degrees for Solomon.

1 EXCEPT the Lord build the house, they labour in vain that build it:
Except the Lord keep the city, the watchman waketh but in vain.
2 It is vain for you to rise up early, to sit up late, to eat the bread of sorrows :
For so he giveth his beloved sleep.
3 Lo, children are an heritage of the Lord ! and the fruit of the womb is his reward.
4 As arrows are in the hands of a mighty man, so are children of the youth.
5 Happy is the man that hath his quiver full of them:
They shall not be ashamed, but they shall speak with the enemies in the gate.

The title. A SONG of the beloved!—of him who toiled himself till all was finished, and who now bids us enter into rest! A song of him who giveth his beloved ones sleep! Taking it as a song from the pen of *Solomon*, who was its author, Kimchi understands the "*Temple*" by the "House" of verse 1, as "the *City*" is Jerusalem. The connection in that case with the former is the thought of Jerusalem restored and rebuilt after the captivity —"Unless the Lord *build the city.*"

The theme. Here we find the worshippers exhibit that rare grace, *freedom from care*, arising from full confidence in Jehovah. Freedom from care. Solomon, who sang afterward of "vanity" (הֶבֶל emptiness) in all merely human pursuits, here sings of שָׁוְא, "nothingness," the uselessness of mere human anxiety and care—uselessness of it to the builders of the house, uselessness in the keeper of the city—uselessness in you who rise up early, who defer your resting till late, who eat bread of sorrows! How like the writer of *Ecclesiastes* is all this! And then the other side of the picture is presented, as in his "Song of Songs."

"*On this wise* (כֵּן) *giveth he to his beloved—sleep.*"

They may rest from care, and he will work; it is "the blessing of the Lord that maketh rich," says this same Solomon, "without the addition of צֶב —sorrow," such as verse 2 spoke of (Prov. x. 22). This is his manner with those who are יְדִיד like Solomon himself, who bore the name "Jedidiah" (2 Sam. xii. 25). "Sleep" is used for complete freedom from care, and peace of mind.

Having laid down this principle, those who inhabit the city and house are remembered, and the illustration follows in the style of the Greater than Solomon, who asked, "Which of you can add one cubit to his stature, one year to his life, by all his thought?" Who could, by care, secure a family like Jacob's twelve sons?

"*Behold, sons are a heritage of the Lord's giving.*" (Gen. xxxiii. 5.)
"*The fruit of the womb is the hire he gives.*" (Gen. xxx. 18.)

It is he that gives them, and it is he that makes them what they are—that makes "sons begotten in youth" (Gen. xlix. 3) to be like a warrior's arrows.

> " *Happy the man whose quiver he* (Jehovah) *has filled with these ;*
> *They shall not be confounded when they speak with their enemies in the*
> *gate.*"

They enjoy the blessing pronounced by Rebecca's friends,
(Gen. xxiv. 60). But it is the Lord that fills the quiver ; it is
not the forethought or anxiety of man.

Thus the pilgrim-band, and their Lord at the head of them
(Matt. vi. 25-34), cast their cares on Jehovah. Even when they
see a lack of men to defend the cause of God—even when ready
to ask, " When the Son of man cometh, shall he find faith on the
earth ?"—they still depend on Him whose part it is to give
sons of youth. And he will do it gloriously. Zion shall see
Isa. lxvi. 8 fulfilled—" a nation born at once ;" and earth shall
see the sons of Israel on the Lord's side, when " the weakest
of them shall be as David" (Zech. xii. 8). And thus, whether
as to The Temple, or as to Jerusalem, whether in regard to the
families of Israel, or as to who shall stand on the Lord's side in
evil days, he knows that the Lord, in the matter of salvation,
has " given his beloved sleep," and that this is his manner in
providence, too.

Christ's pilgrim band.

Horsley calls this Psalm, " A Psalm to be addressed by the
priest to the parents presenting the first-born ;" but though
that would no doubt be an appropriate time to use it, it is of
far wider significance. We see in it this sight, viz.-

The Lord's servant ceases from care, and expects prosperity
from the Lord.

Psalm 128

A Song of degrees

1 BLESSED is every one that feareth the Lord ; that walketh in his ways.
2 For thou shalt eat the labour of thine hands :
   Happy shalt thou be, and it shall be well with thee.
3 Thy wife shall be as a fruitful vine by the sides of thine house :
   Thy children like olive-plants round about thy table.
4 Behold, that thus shall the man be blessed that feareth the Lord !
5 The Lord shall bless thee out of Zion :
   And thou shalt see the good of Jerusalem all the days of thy life.
6 Yea, thou shalt see thy children's children, and peace upon Israel.

LUTHER calls this, " A wedding-song for Christians." It may be so used ; but it is more. Attention to every duty, and,

among the rest, attention to the Lord's ordinances and solemn feasts, is the means of prosperity. As in last Psalm the worshipper's words were to this effect, " Take no thought what ye shall eat ; for which of you by taking thought can add to his stature one cubit ?" (Matt. vi. 27), so in this Psalm the worshipper seems to sing, " *Seek first the kingdom of God and his righteousness, and all other things shall be added unto you,*" (Matt. vi. 33).

> " *Blessed is every fearer of the Lord !*
> *Every walker in his ways !* "

And then, to shew more personal sympathy with the man, the Psalmist looks in his face and says, " *For thou shalt eat the labour of thy hands.*" Instead of the frown spoken of in Lev. xxvi. 10, Deut. xxviii. 30–36, he shall surely eat what he laboured for ; his wife is like a vine by the house sides, yielding its clusters and its shade ; her children are not brambles, but like the useful olive-tree that served "God and man" (Judges ix. 9), also surround the family-table with cheerful faces.

> " *Behold !* (note it) *For thus is the man wont to be blest who feareth the Lord.*
> *Jehovah is wont to bless thee out of Zion.*" (Ver. 4, 5.)

Then follows the imperative אָמַר , as if it were the very words of the uttered benediction-

> " *And* (shall say), *See thou the good of Jerusalem all the days of thy life ; Yea, see thy children's children.*"

And then the benediction uttered before at the close of Psalm cxxv. closes all—" *Peace upon Israel !* " In such strains the well-satisfied worshipper encourages his fellows, rich or poor. In such strains the Lord Jesus used to admonish his band of pilgrim-like followers, telling them that not one of them that left father, or mother, or wife, or children, or lands, for his sake and the gospel, but would *receive a hundredfold even in this life,*" (Matt. xix. 29 ; Luke xviii. 30). And when he added, " *In the world to come* life everlasting," explained as it had been by his having just promised to the twelve a seat on the twelve thrones, in the day of The Regeneration, was it not the equivalent of the priestly benediction, " *Peace upon Israel ?* " That shall be the issue of service now ; for thus

The Lord's servant pronounces the present and future blessedness of the fearers of the Lord.

Psalm 129

A Song of degrees

1 MANY a time have they afflicted me from my youth, may Israel now say :
2 Many a time have they afflicted me from my youth : yet they have not prevailed against me.
3 The plowers plowed upon my back : they made long their furrows.
4 The Lord is righteous ! he hath cut asunder the cords of the wicked.
5 Let them all be confounded and turned back that hate Zion.
6 Let them be as the grass upon the house tops, which withereth afore it groweth up :
7 Wherewith the mower filleth not his hand ; nor he that bindeth sheaves his bosom.
8 Neither do they which go by say, The blessing of the Lord be upon you : We bless you in the name of the Lord.

PERSEVERANCE to the end is the burden of this song, inasmuch as in it we hear the pilgrim at another stage of the way recording deliverances and drawing from his past experience good hope of final deliverance. It is like 2 Cor. i. 10, " He *delivered* us from so great a death, and *doth deliver,* in whom we trust that he *will yet deliver.*

The theme Perseverance.

> " *Many a time have they afflicted me from my youth,*
> *Oh let Israel say !* " (א, I beseech you.)

Israel as a nation might refer to the time of their " youth ;" see Hosea xi. 1, Jer. ii. 1, and every man of Israel might do the like. Every worshipper, and not least the *Lord Jesus* in the days of his flesh, could take up this song. Abel, Enoch, Noah, and all the elders, and not less the Church in its latter days, when feeling the terrible blast of the enemy, might describe their experience by its verses ; all agreeing, too, in the expectation of final victory. The Lord cuts asunder " the cord" that fastens the oxen to the plough.

"Ashamed and turned back shall be all the haters of Zion. (Ver. 5.)
They shall be like the grass on the house tops,
That withereth ere it is plucked up."

Not as Job v. 26, the shock of corn in its season, but as 2 Kings xix. 26, Sennacherib's doom, which is the doom of all God's foes : "They are as the grass of the field, and as the green herb, *as the grass on the house tops, and as corn blasted before it is grown up !* " Antichrist, like all before him, shall thus perish. They are men working a vain work ; no Boaz shall ever bless them with a prayer, nor shall even a casual traveller. The Lord's foes perish unblest ; they perish with the curse upon them, on that day when the Lord comes forth to reward his own with the " *Come, ye blessed."* With expectations like these

The Lord's servant reviews past sufferings in assured hope.

Psalm 130

A Song of degrees

1 Out of the depths have I cried unto thee, O Lord.
2 Lord, hear my voice : let thine ears be attentive to the voice of my supplications.
3 If thou, Lord, shouldest mark iniquities, O Lord, who shall stand ?
4 But there is forgiveness with thee, that thou mayest be feared.
5 I wait for the Lord, my soul doth wait, and in his word do I hope.
6 My soul waiteth for the Lord more than they that watch for the morning : I say, more than they that watch for the morning.
7 Let Israel hope in the Lord :
For with the Lord there is mercy, and with him is plenteous redemption.
8 And he shall redeem Israel from all his iniquities.

The theme.
Pardon and peace.

A NEW series begins here. Though Horsley suggests the occasion of this Psalm to be " Upon bringing a sin-offering," there is nothing to fix it specially to this occasion. The costume of it is taken from a Levite, says the Targum, waiting for the first intimation of the hour of morning sacrifice ; but it may just as well be said to be taken from the case of any watchman on his watch-tower, wearying for the dawn of day. It reminds us of Hab. ii. 2.

The worshipper relates his former earnest cry (ver. 1, 2) from troubles and darkness that were to him like Jonah's *deep waters*, or the water-deeps of Psa. lxix. 14. The Lord of Pilgrims, as well as each of his, band, became familiar with such deeps. He cried the cry of verse 1, feeling intense agony all the while, under his load of imputed guilt,

"*If thou, Lord* (Jah), *wert to mark* (Job x. 14, 16) *iniquity, who, Lord, could stand?*" (Ver. 3.)

But he cried in expectation of being heard, being able to point to satisfaction given to the law for that guilt.

"*For with thee the forgiveness is*" (הַסְּלִיחָה) —*Sept., ὁ ἱλασμος ἐστι.*

The forgiveness spoken of in the law of sacrifice, such as Lev. iv. 20, 26, 31, verses 10, 13, and proclaimed at Horeb, Exod. xxxiv. 9, and in the Temple, 1 Kings viii. 34, 36, 39. This being so, the worshipper learns there "*the fear of the Lord,*" and goes on his way, waiting for further light and teaching, waiting for the opening out of the Lord's hid treasures from day to day, waiting for these discoveries with intenser interest than watchman wait for morning. With intense desire Israel waited for Christ's coming in the flesh, and for the offering up of the "one sacrifice for ever," that was to make the worshipper "perfect as pertaining to the conscience." Yet still he sees only a part ; he waits for more of "the Spirit of wisdom and revelation in the knowledge of Him." And if the Lord's Second Coming be the chief time for the unfolding of all that the worshipper desires, then the waiting for that day is not one of the least intense of his feelings. And so, "*O Israel, hope thou in the Lord ;*" for who knoweth the flood of mercies that shall yet burst on them and on earth, when Jacob's redeeming God (Gen. lxviii. 17) brings "plenteous redemption," or, as it is literally, "*shall multiply* to his people *redemptions,*" as he "*multiplied pardons*" (Isa. lv. 6), at their first return to him. To all of them he fulfils the name "*Jesus,*" saving from all transgressions. In such strains we find

The Lord's servant relating his earnest cry and its results.

Psalm 131

A Song of degrees of David

1 LORD, my heart is not haughty, nor mine eyes lofty:
Neither do I exercise myself in great matters,
Or in things too high for me.
2 Surely I have behaved and quieted myself,
As a child that is weaned of his mother:
My soul is even as a weaned child.
3 Let Israel hope in the Lord, from henceforth and for **ever.**

The theme.
Holiness.

THINK of the calm bosom of the Lake of Galilee that morning
after Christ had spoken peace to the tempest—think of that
glassy sea, resting in a morning without clouds under the rising sun. Was it not a fit and fair emblem of the soul of the
man whose name had once been " Legion," whom Jesus that
morning met, and whose spiritual storms Jesus calmed by a
word ? Is that man's soul now not as peaceful and at rest as
that lake ? It is such a picture of repose we have here. In
the case of the Master, no previous storm had vexed it ; in the
case of the disciple, the tempest has preceded the peace.

It is the Master who can in full measure look up to his
Father and say-

" *Lord, my heart is not haughty, neither are mine eyes lofty ;*
I walk not in great things, and matters too high for me."

He was willing on earth to be ignorant even of the day of his
own glory—his Second Coming—and, while grieving intensely
over Capernaum, and the other cities, was content to rest his
spirit in this one consideration, " Even so, Father ; for so it
seemed good in thy sight."

" *Surely* (אִם לֹא like Isa. v. 9, &c.) *I have smoothed and silenced my soul,*
As a child weaned from its mother. My soul in me is as a weaned child."

Others say,

" *As a weaned child leans upon his mother,*" (עֲלֵי אִמּוֹ,) without any desire to suck the breast as before.

Not of this world, loving the Father, Christ walked through
earth without a murmur, or suspicion, or doubt, as to his Father's will—" Not my will, but thine be done." And his heart

overflowed toward man also (ver. 3); he pressed men to partake of his joy in the Lord. Such was the Master.

His followers are only in some measure like him. It is when they shall " see him as he is," that they shall be able to take up the Psalm in all its breadth. True, they receive the kingdom of God "as a little child;" they are " not of the world, even as he is not of the world;" they have accepted the punishment of their iniquity, and their once uncircumcised hearts have been humbled. Still, they have only some measure of this " mind that was in Him;" but they are expecting the entire likeness, on that day when Israel realizes what is written in Lev. xxvi. 41, and hopes in the Lord, from henceforth and for ever." Thus the harp sings of

Christ's members.

The Lord's servant's contentment with Jehovah's will.

Psalm 132

A Song of degrees.

1 LORD, remember David, and all his afflictions:

2 How he sware unto the Lord, and vowed unto the **mighty God of** Jacob;

3 Surely I will not come into the tabernacle of my house, nor go up into my bed,

4 I will not give sleep to mine eyes, or slumber to mine eyelids,

5 Until I find out a place for the Lord, an habitation for the mighty God of Jacob.

6 Lo, we heard of it at Ephratah: we found it in the fields of the wood.

7 We will go into his tabernacles : we will worship at his footstool.

8 Arise, O Lord, into thy rest ; thou, and the ark of thy strength.

9 Let thy priests be clothed with righteousness; and let thy saints shout for joy.

10 For thy servant David's sake, turn not away the face of thine anointed.

11 The Lord hath sworn in truth unto David ; he will not turn from it ; Of the fruit of thy body will I set upon thy throne.

12 If thy children will keep my covenant and my testimony that I shall **teach** them, Their children shall also sit upon thy throne for evermore.

13 For the Lord hath chosen Zion ; he hath desired it for his habitation.

14 This is my rest for ever: here will I dwell ; for I have desired it.

15 I will abundantly bless her provision : I will satisfy her poor with bread.

16 I will also clothe her priests with salvation: and her saints shall shout aloud for joy.

17 There will I make the horn of David to bud : I have ordained a lamp for mine anointed.

18 His enemies will I clothe with shame : but upon himself shall his crown flourish.

The theme.
The glorifying
of God.

THE pilgrim-worshipper spreads before his God the pledges of his favour to Zion, reminds him of prayers presented, and gets a reply that leaves him in adoring silence. The anxiety David felt about the Ark, and the Lord's care in general, is meant in verse 1. "*Lord, remember* (לְ) *as to David all his trouble:*" all his efforts to establish thy sanctuary, and all he has undergone for thee, (or, in behalf of) even as 2 Chron. vi. 42, Solomon prays—" Remember the mercies of David thy servant." Remember David's solemn oath to the " *Mighty One of Jacob*" (see Gen. xlix. 25)—the Blesser of Joseph with all blessings of heaven, and earth, and the deep beneath. As the men of Israel so resolutely pursued the evil-doers of Gibeah that they swore (Judges xx. 8), " *We will not any of us go to his tent, neither will any of us turn into his house,*" so did he swear, in following hard after the Lord's glory, when desiring to build the Temple.

It seems as if the appeal altered its form at verse 6. The worshippers refer to the past history of the Ark, when dwelling at *Shiloh ;* for by " *Ephratah,*" we do not understand *Bethlehem,*[*] the place where David spent his youth, but *the district of Ephraim.*[†] As a man of Mount Ephraim is called אֶפְרָתִי, in 1 Sam. i. 1, so the district would be אֶפְרָתָה. The worshippers say, " We have heard the past history of the Ark at *Shiloh* in Ephraim ; how the Lord warned Israel by judgments there against all formality and all irreverence. We have found it at *Kirjath-jearim,* where the Lord blessed those who made it welcome ; and so we have learnt to honour it." For, "*fields of the wood,*" is agreed to be a name equivalent to " city of the woods," *i. e.,* Kirjath-jearim.

---

[*] It will not at all accord with the original, to find here an allusion to Christ's journeying through the land—born at *Ephratah,* sitting on Jacob's Well, &c. Nor, as Alexander would have it, " When in my youth I resided at Bethlehem, I heard of the Ark's movements."

[†] So, J. H. Michaelis' Bible, note on 1 Sam xvii. 12, " Regio, Ephrata dici videtur." And Tholuck says here that Shiloh in Ephraim is meant.

" Let us come to his tabernacles (the Holy and Most Holy),
Let us worship at his footstool (the Ark with its Mercy-seat, Lam. ii. 1).
Arise, O Lord, (to go) *to thy resting-place,*
Thou and thy mighty Ark." (2 Chron. vi. 41.)

Let us notice the prayer, verse 9, with the answer, verse **16.**
The prayer asks in behalf of the priests *" righteousness," i. e.,*
what shews forth God's *righteous character ;* the answer is,
" I will clothe her priests with *salvation," i. e.,* with what shews
forth God's *gracious character.* Caring for the interests of
God, the worshipper finds his own interests fully cared for.
And now, after spreading the Lord's pledged word (verses 11,
12), before him, the worshipper hears the Lord himself utter the
reply, *q. d.,* " I will do all that has been sought."

" For the Lord hath chosen Zion. (Ver. 13.)
There will I make a horn bud up to David (one full of power, Messiah).
I have prepared (עָרַכְתִּי *as Exod. xxvii. 20) a lamp for mine anointed One."*

In time of darkness, lo ! the lamp (like the burners on the
seven-branched lamp,) of mine Anointed shines ! Messiah
and his Church, the light of the world ! As yet this has been
fulfilled only in part ; the lamp is lighted ; the horn of David
has shot up ; but it is only in part that the last verse has been
accomplished. The Lord's Second Coming will accomplish all
to the full.

" His enemies will I clothe with shame,
But upon himself shall the crown flourish."

It is thus the pilgrim-worshippers going up to the feasts remind their Lord of the mercies he has given them reason to
expect. They imitate the heavenly worshippers in Rev. v. 8,
holding up their golden vials " full of incense," *i. e.,* of prayers
as yet unanswered. When the type of *the Ark* at rest in *Solomon's Temple* is fulfilled, all our prayers shall be answered.
Meanwhile let us often use such an appeal as this, an appeal in
which our Master could take part in the days of his flesh. It
is a Psalm wherein we hear,

The Lord's servant reminding Jehovah that he has pledged
himself to bless Zion.

Psalm 133

A Song of degrees. Of David

1 BEHOLD, how good and how pleasant it is for brethren to dwell together
in unity!
2 It is like the precious ointment upon the head,
That ran down upon the beard, even Aaron's beard :
That went down to the skirts of his garments.
3 As the dew of Hermon, and as the dew that descended upon the mountains of Zion :
For there the Lord commanded the blessing, even life for evermore.

The theme.

Unity.

" A JOYOUS and hearty Psalm (says one) on occasion of one of
the great feasts." A song for *David's* harp—one of the breathings of that sweet singer of Israel. How gladly would the *Son
of David* sing it, full as it is of the love of brethren—the very
spirit of his " new commandment," and fitted so well for the
use of even the Great Congregation at " our gathering together
in him." It is spoken by one looking on, and calling the attention of others to the pleasant spectacle—

> " *Behold ! how good and how pleasant*
> *The dwelling of brethren entirely as one !*"   (גַּם יָחַד)

But the last clause may mean as גַּם usually does, " *also*." How
pleasant to see them " *together also*," as well as in their tents or
separate abodes. Two comparisons are chosen to set forth the
excellency of such brotherly harmony ; one taken from the tabernacle, the other from the Promised Land. The holy oil, for
the priests, was made of four sorts of the best spices, mixed
into one (Exod. xxxiv. 22) ; and thus compounded, its fragrance was felt by all in the sanctuary, breathing from the
high priest Aaron's head and garments—an emblem of the
unity of many tribes, unity called forth by the presence of one
High Priest, and emblem also of all that gratifies the senses and
strengthens the heart. One and the same oil sheds its sweet
odour from the head, the beard, and the skirts of the priestly
robes—

> " *Like the precious oil on the head,*
> (Like oil) *which descended on the beard—Aaron's beard,*
> (Like oil) *which descended on the very border of his garments.*"

Or, changing the figure,

> " *Like the dew of Hermon,* (not the Hermon or Sirion of Deut. iii. 9, **for**
> it is crowned with perpetual snow—but that Hermon which **rises**
> from the plain of Jezreel)
> (Like the dew) *which descended on the hills of Zion.*"

The oil diffuses a like fragrance, whether it bê on head, beard,
or garment that you find it ; the dew is alike reviving and
refreshing, whether it fall on Hermon* or on the hills of Zion ;
and so it is with the harmonious congregations of Israel, one
spirit breathes in them all, though some come from the extreme
parts of the land, and some from the more distinguished portions ; some from the plain of Jezreel, others from the hills of
Jerusalem.

It is " *there*" where such brotherly love is seen, in such assemblies as these, that the Lord commands the blessing. It will
be in the assembly of the first-born, gathered together into one,
at his Second Coming, that the blessing shall descend in all its
richness, even " *life for evermore.*" And then shall the pilgrim
band, arrived at their holy city, with their Leader in the midst,
burst out into this wondering and delighted cry—" *Behold !*"
—a sight to which our eyes were strangers during all our pilgrimage—" *Behold ! men dwelling together as brethren !*"
without jar or discord, in entire love and unity ! In strains
like these shall we at last hear

*The Lord's servant admiring the unity of those who meet in
the Holy City.*

---

* Buchanan has Latinised this Psalm very happily. After beginning with

> " Nil oaritato mutuâ fratruш, ullиl
> Jucundius concordiâ."—

he says :

> " Non ros, tenella gemmulis argenteis
> Pingens Zionis gramina,
> Aut verna dulci inebrians uligine
> Hermonis intonsi juga."

Psalm 134

A Song of degrees

1 BEHOLD, bless ye the Lord!
   All ye servants of the Lord, which by night stand in the house of the
   Lord.
2 Lift up your hands in the sanctuary, and bless the Lord.
3 The Lord that made heaven and earth bless thee out of Zion.

The theme.

Praise without ceasing.

THIS is the last of the "*Songs of Degrees;*" consisting of praise and blessing, yea calling on us for never-ceasing praise. The shutting of the Temple gates at night is by some (*e. g.,* Horsley) supposed to indicate the appropriate time for singing this song. Hengstenberg assigns it to the time of the evening sacrifice, and compares Psa. xcii. 2, denying that there was any Levitical service during night. But 1 Chron. ix. 33 seems to assert, very clearly, that there was a service of song by night ; and other places hint the same.

There is animation at least in Barclay's paraphrase of this most lively Psalm-

> "O bless the Lord, his servants all,
>   Who watch within the Temple-wall,
>   And nightly praise him as ye stand
>   With lifted eye, and lifted hand!
>   Clap, clap your hands, exult and **sing,**
>   In holiness of Christ your King!
>   Behold he hath redeemed you
>   To bless and praise him as ye do."

Benediction was most appropriate in closing this series of "Psalms of Degrees." The worshipper calls upon those who inhabit the sanctuary to be ever praising (ver. 1), and lifting up their hands "*towards* his sanctuary," Psa. xxviii. 2 ; a call in which Paul most heartily joins, 2 Tim. ii. 8. And then, in verse 3, the priest pronounces a Melchizedec-blessing ; for it is in the very style of Melchizedec, Gen. xiv. 18, 19. And this is the final blessing reserved for the Lord's weary Abrahams, to be pronounced on them by the " Possessor of heaven and earth," on the day of Christ ; in prospect of which, and in enjoyment of all that cometh even now from the same Lord,

The Lord's servant calls for unceasing praise to Jehovah.

Psalm 135

1 PRAISE ye the Lord! Praise ye the name of the Lord!
Praise him, O ye servants of the Lord.

2 Ye that stand in the house of the Lord, in the courts of the house of our God.

3 Praise the Lord, for the Lord is good: sing praises unto his name, for it is pleasant.

4 For the Lord hath chosen Jacob unto himself, and Israel for his peculiar treasure.

5 For I know that the Lord is great, and that our Lord is above all gods.

6 Whatsoever the Lord pleased, that did he in heaven, and in earth,
In the seas, and all deep places.

7 He causeth the vapours to ascend from the ends of the earth;
He maketh the lightnings for the rain: he bringeth the wind out of his treasuries.

8 Who smote the first-born of Egypt, both of man and beast.

9 Who sent tokens and wonders into the midst of thee, O Egypt,
Upon Pharaoh, and upon all his servants.

10 Who smote great nations, and slew mighty kings;

11 Sihon king of the Amorites, and Og king of Bashan,
And all the kingdoms of Canaan:

12 And gave their land for an heritage, an heritage unto Israel his people.

13 Thy name, O Lord, endureth for ever;
And thy memorial, O Lord, throughout all generations.

14 For the Lord will judge his people, and he will repent himself concerning his servants.

15 The idols of the heathen are silver and gold, the work of men's hands.

16 They have mouths, but they speak not; eyes have they, but they see not;

17 They have ears, but they hear not; neither is there any breath in their mouths.

18 They that make them are like unto them: so is every one that trusteth in them.

19 Bless the Lord, O house of Israel: bless the Lord, O house of Aaron:

20 Bless the Lord, O house of Levi: ye that fear the Lord, bless the Lord.

21 Blessed be the Lord out of Zion, which dwelleth at Jerusalem.
Praise ye the Lord.

WE have been descending the river, finding its banks very varied, with sometimes shade, sometimes sunshine on its waters, yet all along the incessant murmur of praise. The river is now nearer its ocean, and hence the utterance of praise becomes louder, fuller, more distinct and direct than ever. In this Psalm and the next, we have two very lofty bursts of song, "Hallelujahs" from the lips of men on earth. The peculiar

The tone.

people, Israel, sing in the name of all God's people ; and no doubt the Lord Jesus, when on earth, took up the song as chief musician.

The contents. The first ground of praise is *what the Lord is* in himself.

> " *Praise ye Jah* (יָהּ),
> *Praise ye the name of Jehovah* (יְהֹוָה),
> *Praise ye, ye servants of Jehovah.*" (Ver. 1.)

Ye who " stand" in the Lord's house ; that is, wait there to serve him, as Deut. x. 8 ; Judges xx. 28.   Then verse 3-

> "*Praise ye Jah* (יָהּ),
> *For good is Jehovah* (יְהֹוָה) ;
> *Hymn ye to his name,*
> *For it is pleasant* (נָעִים))."   (Ver. 3.)

His name is *pleasant*, it is נָעִים ; it has in it נֹעַם (Psa. xxvii. 4 ; Psa. xc. 17).   It discovers to us the Lord's well-pleasedness ; it shews us the awful frown of the Judge changed into the sweet smile of favour.   *Israel* sees it thus—Israel, to whom the altar and all its significant accompaniments belong.

The next ground of praise is the *Lord's sovereignty,* (verses 4–6,) choosing a people, shewing himself above all gods, doing as pleaseth him ; and it is sweet for Israel to say as they sing, that this Jehovah is *theirs,* as they are his סְגֻלָּה, peculiar property, his valuable jewels.

> " *And our Lord is above all gods.*"   (Ver. 5.)

Then they praise him for *creation-works,* (ver. 7).   He does what he pleases.

> " *Bringing up vapours from the ends of earth ;*
> *Making lightnings for rain ;*
> *Bringing the wind from his treasure-chambers.*"

But chiefly is he praised for works of *providence and redemption,* (ver. 8–12) ; smiting Egypt and great kings.*   And all this contrasts so broadly with all other gods, that no name but Jehovah's shall be exalted, no one shall be named along

---

* " *In regard to Sihon and Og, he smote them.*"   The construction of verse 11 is peculiar, the verb הָרַג having had the accusative before, now employs a preposition לְ.

with him ; his *"memorial,"* *i. e.*, that by which he is known
and remembered, shall be for ever singular and peculiar. See
Exod. iii. 15.

> *"For Jehovah will act the part of a judge* (יָדִין) *to his people," i. e.*,
>   defend their rights. (Gen. xxx. 6 ; Jer. xxii. 16.)
>   *And will repent (i. e.,* change his procedure) *toward his servants ;"*

reminding us of Deut. xxxii. 26, the utterance of the Lord's
name in that song of Moses. But as for idols, they have a
"mouth," but speak not to give advice ; *"eyes,"* but see not
the circumstances, nor yet the gifts, of their devotees ; *"ears,"*
but hear neither their praise nor prayer ; and as they have no
"breath in their nostrils," they cannot inhale the sweet and
fragrant incense offered to them. Their worshippers become
equally helpless and vain. Oh, then, Israel, bless thou Jehovah ! House of Israel, house of Aaron, house of Levi, fearers
of Jehovah everywhere, bless ye Jehovah !

> *"From out of Zion let Jehovah be blessed (i. e.,* let the voice of praise
>   to him be heard from Zion),
> (Jehovah) *who dwells at Jerusalem.*
> *Hallelujah !"*

We may easily suppose Christ thus exhorting his own in the
days of his flesh, using this very Psalm ; aye, and at this closing verse, would he not feel peculiarly? for he was Jehovah,
come to fulfil all types and shadows, being himself the Incarnate God inhabiting Jerusalem. And then he would look forward to the future, when his throne shall be as a canopy over
Jerusalem, and when he shall in glory inhabit it as the city of
the Great King, while out from Zion issues forth such praise
as makes earth wonder—the joy of Jerusalem heard afar off.
We, too, may sing it with such thoughts, joining Israel and
Israel's King. It suits all the redeemed, inasmuch as it is

The peculiar people's song of praise, as they adore the excel-
lency of their sovereign God.

Psalm 136

1 O GIVE thanks unto the Lord; for he is good: for his mercy endureth for ever.

2 O give thanks unto the God of gods: for his mercy endureth for ever.

3 O give thanks to the Lord of lords: for his mercy endureth for ever.

4 To him who alone doeth great wonders: for his mercy endureth for ever.

5 To him that by wisdom made the heavens: for his mercy endureth for ever.

6 To him that stretched out the earth above the waters: for his mercy endureth for ever.

7 To him that made great lights: for his mercy endureth for ever:

8 The sun to rule by day: for his mercy endureth for ever:

9 The moon and stars to rule by night: for his mercy endureth for ever.

10 To him that smote Egypt in their first-born: for his mercy endureth for ever:

11 And brought out Israel from among them: for his mercy endureth for ever:

12 With a strong hand, and with a stretched-out arm: for his mercy endureth for ever.

13 To him which divided the Red Sea into parts: for his mercy endureth for ever:

14 And made Israel to pass through the midst of it: for his mercy endureth for ever:

15 But overthrew Pharaoh and his host in the Red Sea: for his mercy endureth for ever.

16 To him which led his people through the wilderness: for his mercy endureth for ever.

17 To him which smote great kings: for his mercy endureth for ever:

18 And slew famous kings: for his mercy endureth for ever:

19 Sihon king of the Amorites: for his mercy endureth for ever:

20 And Og the king of Bashan: for his mercy endureth for ever:

21 And gave their land for an heritage: for his mercy endureth for ever:

22 Even an heritage unto Israel his servant: for his mercy endureth for ever.

23 Who redeemed us in our low estate: for his mercy endureth for ever:

24 And hath redeemed us from our enemies: for his mercy endureth for ever.

25 Who giveth food to all flesh: for his mercy endureth for ever.

26 O give thanks unto the God of heaven! for his mercy endureth for ever.

The theme. THE theme of last Psalm is taken up again ; but whereas the *glory* of Jehovah was chiefly dwelt upon there, now it is his *love.* The same acts display more than one illustrious perfection, and may therefore call forth variety of praise.

That *"God is love"* is the pervading view; or, in other words, " God is good, and his mercy endureth for ever"—the fountain and the stream, the fountain sendeth forth its streams on our

scorched and blighted world, streams that shall never be withdrawn, and which are not like the brook Cedron, flowing only
now and then, but are perennial and perpetual. We refer back
to what was said on Psalm cvii. 1, in reference to this theme
and this view of Jehovah being taught at the *allur :* it was
taught there most specially, and is still taught by the blood of
Him who was the sacrifice. Indeed, we may say that it is
only when standing by His side that we can truly sing this
Psalm. He raises the tune ; he calls on us thus to sing–

" Praise ye (הוֹדוּ) *Jehovah ;"*

not as in Psa. cxxxv. 1, " Hallelujah," but varying the words,
" Be ye *Judahs* to the Lord ! "

Praise him for what he is, (ver 1–3). The contents.
Praise him for what he is able to do, (ver. 4).
Praise him for what he has done in creation, (ver. 5–9).
Praise him for what he did in redeeming Israel from bond-
age, (ver. 10–15).
Praise him for what he did in his providence toward them,
(ver. 16–22).
Praise him for his grace in times of calamity, (ver. 23, 24).
Praise him for his grace to the world at large, (ver. 25).
Praise him at the remembrance that this God is the God of
heaven, (ver. 26).

Is he *" God of gods ?"* (ver. 2.) Well may we praise him, and
be sure that the mercy which has issued forth from his throne,
like the crystal river of the Apocalypse, shall flow on for ever ;
for there is none higher than himself ; no rival to mar his
plans, or interfere with his schemes. Yes, he is as Moses described in Deut. x. 17,—so infinitely higher than any creature
that ever bore the name of " god," that they dared not be
named in his presence.

Is he *" Lord of lords ?"* (ver. 3) as Moses also said long ago
in Deut. x. 17. Then no principality in heaven, no power in
hell, no assumed lordship in earth, can at all resist him : his
mercy shall be impeded by none. It is the mercy of the " God
of gods and the Lord of lords !" What height, depth, length,
breadth, in his mercy ! And you may sing on the banks of

this river that fertilizes our desert world—"I am persuaded that neither death, nor life, nor angels, nor principalities, nor powers, nor things present, nor things to come, nor height, nor depth, nor any other created thing, shall be able to separate us from the love of God, which is in Christ Jesus our Lord," (Rom. viii. 38, 39).

Does he "*alone*" do great wonders? (ver. 4.) That means, he does so by himself, unaided, needing nothing from others, asking no help from his creatures. As the Nile from Nubia to the Mediterranean rolls on 1300 miles in solitary grandeur, receiving not one tributary, but itself alone dispensing fertility and fatness wherever it comes; so our God "alone" does wonders. (See Deut. xxxii. 12, Psa. lxxii. 18, &c.) No prompter, no helper; spontaneously he goes forth to work, and all he works is worthy of God. Then we have no need of any other; we are independent of all others; all our springs are in him.

Did he "*make the heavens by his understanding?*" (תְּבוּנָה) (ver. 5)—not only the firmament, but the third heavens, too, where all is felicity, where is the throne of glory. Then, I infer, that if the *mercy* which visits earth is from the same Jehovah who built that heaven and filled it with glory, there must be in this *mercy* something of the same "*understanding*," or wisdom. It is wise, prudent mercy; not rashly given forth; and it is the mercy of Him whose love has filled that heaven with bliss. The same architect—the same skill —the same love!

It is he who "*spread the earth above the waters*" (ver. 6), making a solid platform for man's abode. The Creator is he who sheweth mercy on us. He was preparing a theatre for the display of mercy. He was thinking thoughts of grace ere ever man appeared, so that his love has a deep source, and was issuing forth from its far back source all the time he was forming our earth.

It is he who "*made the great lights*," (ver. 7). Instead of causing the light that was shot out from his presence, on the three first days of creation, to serve our earth, He kindly prepared the "*Great Lights.*" That our comfort might be fully attended to, two great orbs were so placed, or our earth so placed towards them, as that our habitation might thus be full of cheerful light. Was he not remembering man ? O praise him ! And think as you praise, " His mercy endures for ever ! "

He made " *the sun to rule by day*," (ver. 8). Though he knew how our earth would abuse its mercies, and sinners employ the light in order to carry on schemes of wickedness, yet still he made it thus, and left it thus after the fall, to shine on the fields and dwellings even of the ungodly. Yea, and " *the moon and stars by night*" (ver. 9),*—the same that shone in Paradise and Eden. He has not withdrawn them. " His mercy endureth for ever ! "

But again ; this is he who " *smote Egypt's first-born*," (ver. 10). Remember his sovereign grace, when righteousness would shew itself upon the guilty. There was mercy even then to Israel—drops of that mercy that for ever endureth—at the very time when judgment fell on others. Should not this give emphasis to our praises ? The dark background makes the figures in the foreground more prominent.

He "*brought out Israel from among them*," (ver. 11). This was mercy, separating them from all the evil and all the misery there. Aye, and with " a *strong hand*" (ver. 12): for mercy prompted him to exercise power against the mighty. What a ground of encouragement in after ages to his own ! That same " *strong hand*" ready at *mercy's* call to do such acts, and that mercy enduring for ever !

" He *divided the Red Sea into parts*," (ver. 13). Obstacles are nothing to him whose " mercy endureth for ever." The divided Red Sea is a " pawn of his purpose and power to deliver his Church" in all ages. He " *made Israel pass through the midst of it*" (ver. 14), making the very bed of the sea their highway of safety ; as he has often done since then, when the very calamities of his own have become their blessings.

Did he " *shake off*" (נְעֵר) (ver. 15, as Exod. xiv. 27) Pharaoh

---

* In this verse the expression " to rule " is כֶּמְשְׁלוֹת in the plural ; whereas in Gen. i. 16 there is the repetition of כֶּמְשֶׁלֶת. It is, *q. d.*, their jurisdictions over night : for the term seems properly to mean the *post* of a ruler, the *office* he fills as a ruler.

and his host, as he did the locusts, into the Red Sea, and this when they would have hung on Israel's rear, and clung to his skirts ? This was mercy to his own, their foes overthrown ; such mercy as shall awake hallelujahs when Antichrist is destroyed, in the last days, (Rev. xix. 1, 2).

Did he *"make his people walk in the wilderness?"* (ver. 16.) Such a floor! such a pathway! Yet who has not heard of their safety and well-being there? Now, this mercy shall still act thus—for ever! All through the desert, and till it is done, his people shall be kept.*

Aye, but enemies again appear : "He *smote great kings*," (ver. 17). Great as they were, it availed nothing ; they lost their credit and prestige of greatness. And *" noble kings*," too (ver. 18), were shorn of their pomp when they touched his anointed. Such is his mercy—mercy that lasts still for us in these last days. Yea, *"Sihon, king of Amorites"* (ver. 19), like the goodly cedar (Amos ii. 9), and the first that opposed their entrance into their land—he fell ; an example to those who might afterwards dare to oppose the Lord's people. And when *"Og, the king of Bashan"* (ver. 20), took the field. a giant, a new and more terrific foe, he too fell. And the *mercy* that thus dealt with enemies so great, enemies so strong. one after another. *" endureth for ever."* When Antichrist raises up his hosts in the latter days, one after another—when the great, the famous, the mighty, the noble, the gigantic men, in succession assail the Church, they shall perish. *"* For *his mercy* endureth for ever."

But celebrate the Lord's praise again: for *" he gave their land for an inheritance,"* (ver. 21). His mercy to his own soon comforted them for all their toils and conflicts, in a land flow-

---

* The Arabic interpolates,

> *" And made the waters flow from the solid rock :*
> *For his mercy endureth for ever."*

This, however, is of no authority, and may have originally been the pious amplification of some reader who felt that these were but samples of God's many doings. Like that devout soul who said to a friend that we might, in the very spirit of this Psalm, give thanks for affliction, singing,

> *" To Him who withered our grounds ;*
> *For his mercy endureth for ever "*

ing with milk and honey—a type of that inheritance awaiting his saints now, after conflict is over. It was " *an inheritance to Israel, his servant,*" (ver. 22) ; to Israel who had served him, and who would yet serve him better. *Mercy* gave this reward ; it was not *merit* that won it ; and so it shall be to the end, even in the case of the Lord's servants who labour most for him. Israel and all the saints are debtors to mercy to the last.

He was the God " *who remembered us when we were brought low,*" (ver. 23). He did thus to Israel in times when sin brought on chastisement, as in Judges ii., iii., iv., &c., or 2 Kings xiii. 4, xiv. 26, 27. In backsliding times he still kept hold of us, not forgetting us when we forgot him. Oh what mercy ! Like the mercy of Him whose love changes not ! The river flowed on day and night, even when we came not to draw ! " *And redeemed us* (broke us off) *from our enemies,*" (ver. 24). Grace interposed for the helpless, the doubly helpless ; and redeemed the backsliding ones from the very adversaries whom their sins raised up to chastise them. And thus mercy will do in the latter day to Israel again ; and thus it is ever doing for saints at this present time.

We might fancy that they who have so much to sing of in regard to themselves, so much done for their own souls, would have little care for others. We might fear that they would be found selfish. But not so ; the love of God felt by a man makes the man feel as God does towards men ; and as God's love is ever going forth to others, so is the heart of the man of God. We see how it is even as to patriotism—a man's intensest patriotic feelings do not necessarily make him indifferent to the good of other countries, but rather make him wish all countries to be like his own ; so it is, much more certainly and truly, with the Lord's people in their enjoyment of blessing. Their heart expands toward others ; they would fain have all men share in what they enjoy. They therefore cannot close their song without having this other clause—Praise Him who is

" *The giver of bread to all flesh !*" (Ver. 25.)

Not to Israel only does he give blessing. Israel had their manna ; but, at the same time, the earth at large has its food. So in spiritual things. Israel's God is he who giveth himself as Bread of Life to the world. Perhaps at this point the Psalmist's eye may be supposed to see *Earth in its state of blessedness*, after Israel is for the last time redeemed from all enemies, and become " life from the dead" to the world—when Christ reigns and dispenses bread of life to the New Earth, as widely as he gave common food—" the feast of fat things to all nations," (Isa. xxv. 10) ; for his mercy will not rest till this is accomplished.

" *O give praise* (הוֹדוּ) *to the God of heaven !* " (Ver. 26.)

Whom having not seen we love, for his mercy endureth for ever ; whom seated in heaven, we see not, but from whom all these blessings come down to earth. It is *Heaven* that blesses *Earth*, and shall not Earth send up its praise to Heaven. Oh, that all men were *Judahs*—joining in this song to Jehovah—

Praise to Jehovah because of his mercy that has blessed, and will bless, for ever !

Psalm 137

1 **By** the rivers of Babylon, there we sat down ; yea, we wept, when we remembered Zion!

2 We hanged our harps upon the willows in the midst thereof.

3 For there they that carried us away captive required of us a song;
  And they that wasted us required of us mirth, saying, Sing us one of the songs of Zion.

4 How shall we sing the Lord's song in a strange land ?

5 If I forget thee, O Jerusalem, let my right hand forget her cunning.

6 If I do not remember thee, let my tongue cleave to the roof of my mouth ;
  If I prefer not Jerusalem above my chief joy.

7 Remember, O Lord, the children of Edom, in the day of Jerusalem ;
  Who said, Rase it, rase it, even to the foundation thereof.

8 O daughter of Babylon, who art to be destroyed ;
  Happy shall he be, that rewardeth thee as thou hast served us.

9 Happy shall he be, that taketh and dasheth thy little ones against the stones.

The tone.

WHEN a fitful gust of wind has blown aside for a time the sand that hid an ancient tomb or monument, the traveller, arrested by the sight, may muse beside it, and feel himself borne back into other days, sympathising with the mourning friends who

piled these monumental stones. But his deepest sympathy
can never equal, and scarcely can resemble with much near-
ness, that burst of grief with which the real mourners consecrated the spot. It is even thus with our Psalm. We feel it
to be a peculiar song of Zion, strangely beautiful, full of pathos,
and rising to sublimity ; but what would be the fresh emotions
of those who sang it first, and who dropped their tears into
these rivers of Babel ? No author's name is given ; but so
plaintive is it, that some have ascribed it to Jeremiah, the
weeping prophet, of whose Lamentations it has been said,
" Every word seems written with a tear, and every sound seems
the sob of a broken heart."

Tholuck says it is a Psalm by an exiled Levite, " A master The title.
of song." Perhaps we expected to find some notice prefixed
of the instrument used when it was set to music, such as,
" On Gittith,"—when first the sound of its commencing strain
broke on our ear—עַל־נַהֲרוֹת and עַל־עֲרָבִים,

" On the banks of the rivers—
On the willow-trees."

But the only instrument before the singer is the murmuring
streams of Babylon, with the wind moaning through the willows
on either bank. Whether wandering along by Euphrates, or
Tigris, or Ulai, or Chabor,* all of them *" rivers of Babylon,"*
the exiles of Israel felt the burden of Jehovah's anger in their
state of estrangement from the land given to their fathers. We
have a series of most moving scenes presented to our view :

1. The river's banks fringed with mourners, who sit there, The scene.
shaded by the willows. You see above their heads their harps
which they used in Judah, and perhaps in the temple of Jerusalem, some of those mentioned, 1 Chron. xv. 16 (Patrick),
carried with them as precious memorials of happier days.

2. You see some of their gay, heartless oppressors approaching the weeping band, asking a song. Q. Curtius, in his history of Alexander the Great (vi. 2), tells us of the captive

---

* " In the midst thereof," in the midst of *her* (בְּתוֹכָהּ), means in the midst
of the country. The four streams we have named, are four of these that Scripture speaks of in connection with the captives. Alas ! not four rivers of
Paradise to them !

woman from Persia being ordered to sing in the fashion of their country (*suo ritu canere*), when, in the midst of the scene, the king's eye caught the spectacle of a mourner on the ground, sadder than all the rest, the wife of Hystaspis ; for the lordly oppressors of Israel were then feeling the retribution of being summoned to do as they had done to their captives. The wife of Hystaspis, says the historian, struggled against those who would fain have led her forward to the king, foremost among the captive band with whose songs they sought to entertain themselves ; even as here Israel, though fallen, replied in princely dignity, to those who asked of them "words of the song," some stanza, at least, out of some song of Zion (מִשִּׁיר)—

> *" How shall we sing Jehovah's song*
> *On the soil of a stranger ? "* (Ver. 4.)

3. You see their oppressors retire, and the exiles are alone again, dropping their tears into the stream. They sing now, the one to the other, and this is the burden-

> *" If I lose my memory of thee, O Jerusalem,*
> *Let my right hand lose its memory !*
> *Let my tongue cleave to the roof of my* **mouth**
> *If I do not remember thee—*
> *If I do not lift up Jerusalem*
> *On the top of my joy ! "* (Ver. 5, 6.)

They remember the past ; and they know it is foretold (Isa. xxxv. 10) that one day they shall return to Zion with songs. But, till that day arrives, they will continue to hang up their harps.

4. You see them assume the attitude of appeal and prayer. They call upon Jehovah to visit their oppressors. *Edom* is first mentioned. Why is this? We find the explanation in Obad. 8–14, where Edom's unbrotherly exultation over Israel's day of calamity is described ; as it is also in Lam. iv. 21. *Babylon* is next. The awful cry against this foe, the Antichrist of that day, resembles Rev. xviii. 20, " Rejoice over her ! " The emphasis is to be put on " thee," and in verse 9, " thy children," in opposition to God's people and their children. Happy the man who, instead of being an oppressor of God's heritage, is the Lord's instrument in bringing low, even to the foundation, the city that has fought against him, thus requiting

her in her own way ; yes, happy is that man even though in executing the judgment he be sent to dash the children on the rocks (children being reckoned one with their parents, as in Achan's case, Josh. vii. 24), in pouring out the vial of wrath.

Could our Master sing this song? If he identified himself *Christ in it.* with his people in Egypt, as we find him doing in Psa. lxxxi. 5, why should he not sympathise in this strain also? He would use it when on earth. And his Church herself, a stranger in a strange land, can use it, not only in sympathising with Israel's ruin, but in thinking of what has endeared *Jerusalem* to us. *Calvary, Mount of Olives, Siloam,* how fragrant are ye with the Name that is above every name! " *If I forget thee, O Jerusalem !"* Can I forget where he walked so often, where he spoke such gracious words, where he died? Can I forget that his feet shall stand on that " Mount of Olives, which is before Jerusalem, on the east?" Can I forget that there stood the Upper Room, and there fell the showers of Pentecost? And can I not pray against Antichrist in using the names of Edom and Babylon, the old foes of the Lord and his people? Yes, I fully sympathise in every verse of this sacred song, for it is

Exiled Israel's tender zeal for Jerusalem and Jehovah.

Psalm 138

A Psalm of David

1 I WILL praise thee with my whole heart : before the gods will I sing praise unto thee.

2 I wi worship toward thy holy temple,
And praise thy name for thy lovingkindness and for thy truth :
For thou hast magnified thy word above all thy name.

3 In the day when I cried thou answeredst me,
And strengthenedst me with strength in my soul.

4 All the kings of the earth shall praise thee, O Lord, when they hear the words of thy mouth.

5 Yea, thy shall sing in the ways of the Lord : for great is the glory of the Lord.

6 Though the Lord be high, yet hath he respect unto the lowly :
But the proud he knoweth afar off.

7 Though I walk in the midst of trouble, thou wilt revive me:
Thou shalt stretch forth thine hand against the wrath of mine enemies,
And thy right hand shall save me.
8 The Lord will perfect that which concerneth me;
Thy mercy, O Lord, endureth for ever: forsake not the works of thine own
hands.

David. DAVID'S harp again sounds, from this Psalm onward to Psalm cxlv., where praises of every kind, and probably proceeding from various singers, close the Book.

The theme. The theme is the promise made to David (Psa. lxxxix. 26, and 2 Sam. vii. 28, which is in effect the same as Isa. lv. 3), "The sure mercies of David. It is the definite promise of a Saviour who is to descend from David's loins, that furnishes the subject. And is not this substantially the same as the *first promise*, the great promise of a Deliverer, the promise of the Seed of the woman? Let one read over the seventh chapter of 2 Samuel, as it came from David's full heart, and he has found the key-note of the Psalm; and then let us realise what was wrapt up in the promise of a Saviour in its fulness, and we will join in every clause of the Psalm. Our Master would feel all at home in every verse.

The contents. In verses 1–3 he sings to this effect—No god, no pretended god, in any country, or any age, ever gave utterance to such a thought as I am now to sing of—"*before the gods I will sing*," and I worship toward thy holy temple as I sing, praising thee for such a matchless display of mercy and truth! (Comp. John i. 14.)

"*For thou hast magnified, above all thy name, thy word,*
In the day when I called, and thou didst answer
(When) *thou didst make me brave in my soul with might!*" (Ver. 2, 3.)

In that day when the Lord brought to him *the word*, or promise, of which he speaks (the word concerning the future Son), he did an act of grace that might be said to cast into the shade even all the other displays of grace God had given. "*All thy name*" is used here as equivalent to "*all that hitherto has made thee known and famous in our eyes.*" This is the sense of "name" in such places as 2 Sam. vii. 9, and 23, a passage closely allied to this; as also viii. 13, xxiii. 18. In short, it is like as if one had said of Abishai (1 Chron. xi. 20), "You had a name among the three, but that last exploit of yours has raised you above all your previous name ;" or take Jer. xxxii. 20—" Thou hast made thee a name" by thy wonders in Egypt, but this promise to David is "above all that name of thine."

In verses 4, 5, he sings to this effect—No king ever heard news like this that thou art making known. When they hear it,

> " *They will sing in the ways of the Lord!* " (Ver. 5.)

They will sing **בְּ** " upon," as if to say they will enter on these ways (Hengst.) ; or rather, *at* or *over*, because of hearing such an account of Jehovah's dealings with men.

In verses 6, 7, he sings to this effect—Unparalleled grace ! The Lofty One has stooped down to shew mercy to one so low as I, to the family of Jesse—yea, to the fallen family of man-

> " *The Lord is exalted ; and* (yet) *he looks upon the mean !*
> *While the proud he knoweth afar off.*" (Comp. Luke i. 51, 52.)

This gracious Jehovah removes all my fears, whatever shall betide ; for he will help me. And in the person of our Master, he has given his saints a pledge of the fulfilment of verse 7, for the Master " *walked in the midst of trouble,*" as did the three youths in the fiery furnace, and yet was " *revived*"-brought back to the enjoyment of favour and peace ; brought back from the sepulchre to the " fulness of joy."

In verse 8 he sings to this effect—Lord, leave me not till thou hast brought me into glory. Confidence of getting leads him to ask boldly, as in 2 Sam. vii. 27, and what he asks is, that he may be kept till glory come. For by " *the works of thy hand*" is meant the undertaking God has commenced. Every saint has this same confidence, remembering that it is written, " He that hath begun a good work in you, will perform it until the day of Jesus Christ," (Phil. i. 6). Our Lord, the Son of David, as well as David's Lord, would often, in the days of his flesh, use this appeal, and sing in man's behalf this glorious Psalm ; and shall we not take it up, now that " *the Word*" has been fully developed, and developed in such astounding magnificence of grace ? It suits us as much as it did David, or any other ; for it is

Heartfelt praise for Jehovah's Great Promise.

Psalm 139

To the chief Musician. A Psalm of David

1 O LORD, thou hast searched me, and known me.

2 Thou knowest my downsitting and mine uprising, thou understandest my thought afar off.

3 Thou compassest my path and my lying down, and art acquainted with all my ways.

4 For there is not a word in my tongue, but, lo, O Lord, thou knowest it altogether.

5 Thou hast beset me behind and before, and laid thine hand upon me.

6 Such knowledge is too wonderful for me! it is high, I cannot attain unto it.

7 Whither shall I go from thy Spirit? or whither shall I flee from thy presence?

8 If I ascend up into heaven, thou art there: if I make my bed in hell, behold, thou art there.

9 If I take the wings of the morning, and dwell in the uttermost parts of the sea,

10 Even there shall thy hand lead me, and thy right hand shall hold me.

11 If I say, Surely the darkness shall cover me! even the night shall be light about me.

12 Yea, the darkness hideth not from thee; but the night shineth as the day:
The darkness and the light are both alike to thee.

13 For thou hast possessed my reins: thou hast covered me in my mother's womb.

14 I will praise thee; for I am fearfully and wonderfully made!
Marvellous are thy works; and that my soul knoweth right well.

15 My substance was not hid from thee,
When I was made in secret, and curiously wrought in the lowest parts of the earth.

16 Thine eyes did see my substance, yet being unperfect;
And in thy book all my members were written,
Which in continuance were fashioned, when as yet there was none of them.

17 How precious also are thy thoughts unto me, O God! how great is the sum of them!

18 If I should count them, they are more in number than the sand.
When I awake, I am still with thee.

19 Surely thou wilt slay the wicked, O God: depart from me therefore, ye bloody men.

20 For they speak against thee wickedly, and thine enemies take thy name in vain.

21 Do not I hate them, O Lord, that hate thee?
And am not I grieved with those that rise up against thee?

22 I hate them with perfect hatred: I count them mine enemies.

23 Search me, O God, and know my heart: try me, and know my thoughts:

24 And see if there be any wicked way in me, and lead me in the way everlasting.

" A PSALM of David," and no doubt often sung by the " Son of David." For, rightly understood, there is not in it any thought of desiring an escape from the Lord's happy presence in verses 7, 8 ; far from this, it is meant to express delight in the remembrance of Jehovah's omnipresence and omniscience. It is not the utterance of the First Adam, slinking from sight behind the trees of Eden ; but it is the utterance of the Second Adam, dwelling in the blissful fellowship with God, which fellowship he would not for all worlds ever lose. Think of it as sung by David, and by Christ, and by all the family of Christ.

The key-note, then, is delight in the Lord's presence. The structure is very simple, and there are no difficulties in any verses but 15, 16 ; to the understanding of which it is needful to know that *"lower parts of earth,"* is a proverbial expression for *secresy*—what is hidden from view of man—as the parallelism shews. The verses are to this purpose—" Thou hast at thy disposal *" my reins,"* the seat of my heart, thoughts, and feelings ; for-

> *" My substance was not hid from thee when I was made in secret,*
> *When I was curiously wrought, hid from the view of all men.*
> *Thine eyes saw when I was still unprepared* (*i. e.*, my unformed substance ; or, the unwound ball of the thread of life),
> *And in thy book all of them were written,* (viz.)
> *The days which were still to be, and of which none then was."* (Hengst.)

And because of this singular care of the Creating Hand, and the skill displayed in the rare workmanship, verse 14 sings-

> *" I praise thee on this account, that I am fearfully distinguished !*
> *Marvellous are thy works ! Yes, my soul perceives it well !"*

But now let us trace the thread of connection that runs through the whole Psalm. There is in verses 1-6, *adoration of Jehovah's omniscience.* The Lord Jesus could sing it all ; even verse 6, " too wonderful for me" (Prov. xxx. 18), was suitable to him as man, in his humiliation-days, when he knew not the day of his Second Coming, and when he stood on the shore and adored the awful depth of his Father's counsels. The expression, " *Laidst thy hand over me*" (עָלַי תָּשֶׁת), denotes a kind, friendly act ; not the act of one in anger, as when שָׁלַח יָד is used, in such passages as Exod. xxiv. 11. The Psalmist is rejoicing in the shadow of this Omniscient One. " Thou hast searched, and knowest me."

In verses 7–12, there is *adoration of Jehovah's omnipresence.* If I had cause to flee from thee, whither could I go ? " *If I scale heaven, or if I spread the grave*" (Alexander), or if (ver. 1) the thought occurs, " *I will raise the wing of morning,*" travelling swift as the light which travels 200,000 miles in a second, all would be vain. Whither, then ? Not to *Heaven,* for that is the very centre and seat of his manifested presence ; not to *Hell, i. e.,* sheol, or the grave, for the disembodied spirit is even more than before in his felt presence ; not to any part of creation, for his providence is at work there in every sparrow that lights on the ground. What a comforting thought to a believer ! If God's eye is on me, then I am blessed, though I be obscure, and though I suffer unheeded by man. He is with the prisoner in the Inquisition, with the soldier, the sailor, the miner ; yes, he is so truly with his saints, that wherever their dust may be laid, he will find it, and gathering every particle from the dark grave, will raise up therefrom a glorious body. And let us note that verse 10 expresses the gracious leading of a father and friend—" *Thy hand would lead me,*" like verse 5 ; while verse 11 is still more expressive of favour-

> " *If I should say, surely the darkness will crush me,* (יְשׁוּפֵנִי)
> *Then night would be light about me.*"

Were I apprehensive of danger, some appalling evil ready to *crush* me (שׁוּף, as Job ix. 17, and as Gen. iii. 15) during the darkness, the Omnipresent One would haste to my help. Is there any reference to Satan's " hour and power of darkness" involved in this use of the first word applied to his assaults on the woman's Seed (שׁוּף) ?

In verses 13–18, there is *adoration of Jehovah as owner and Creator of men.* " For thou (אַתָּה), and no other, possessest andhast the right to my most inmost parts ;" and then he sings of the wonderful work of the heavenly Father, forming the human frame, closing with that exclamation of amazed delight-

" How precious are thy thoughts to me, O God !
I will count them !—(but no)*—more than sand they are many !"*

In this there is a resemblance to Psa. xl. 5, where we find Christ identifying himself with his own, and wondering at his Father's thoughts " to usward." There, however, it is chiefly his thoughts, or plans, about our redemption, while here it is more specially about our creation. Unless, indeed, we suppose that the glowing description of verses 14, 15, 16, may refer, not to creation only, but also to the forming anew of the body after it has lain in the dust, when it is to arise in honour, in glory, in power, the very likeness of Christ's perfect human form.

In verses 19, 20, there is presented to us the omniscient and omnipresent Creator *as Judge.* It is literally, " *If thou wouldst slay the wicked !"*—an unfinished sentence, pointing at the terrible results. Though at present he bears long with the ungodly, he hates their sin, and will destroy the sinner. In this he glances at the great day when the Judge shall say, " *Depart."*

In verses 21, 22, there is a *protestation on the part of the Psalmist,* against all who are foes to Jehovah whom he has held up to our adoration. It reminds us of John xxi. 17.

In verses 23, 24, there is a prayer that this *omniscient and omnipresent Creator would keep his worshipper for ever* on his side. Some render " wicked way" (ver. 24), the way of an idol (so Gesenius) ; but Hengstenberg seems right in rendering it, " *the way of pain ;"* that leads to pain or trouble ; the contrast of the " *everlasting way,"* (the " *ancient paths"* of Jeremiah vi. 16), where a man finds rest to his soul. This is the way that ushers a man into the kingdom, into the bliss of the ages to come. It reminds us of Isaiah xxxv. 8, the holy way in which those walk who enjoy the bliss of the Restored Paradise.

Thus we see that this Psalm is one of joy and happy confidence in God, abounding in views that enlarge the heart and strengthen it. It expresses the worshipper's happy remembrance of the omniscient and omnipresent God ;

*Satisfaction in thinking upon the all-knowing Creator
and Judge.*

Psalm 140

To the chief Musician. A Psalm of David

1 DELIVER me, O Lord, from the evil man, preserve me from the violent man,
2 Which imagine mischiefs in their heart. Continually are they gathered
    together for war :
3 They have sharpened their tongues like a serpent ;
    Adders' poison is under their lips. Selah.
4 Keep me, O Lord, from the hands of the wicked ;
    Preserve me from the violent man ; who have purposed to overthrow my
    goings.
5 The proud have hid a snare for me, and cords ;
    They have spread a net by the wayside ; they have set gins for me. Selah.
6 I said unto the Lord, Thou art my God : hear the voice of my supplica-
    tions, O Lord.
7 O God the Lord, the strength of my salvation, thou hast covered my head
    in the day of battle.
8 Grant not, O Lord, the desires of the wicked :
    Further not his wicked device, lest they exalt themselves. Selah.
9 As for the head of those that compass me about, let the mischief of their
    own lips cover them.
10 Let burning coals fall upon them : let them be cast into the fire,
    Into deep pits, that they rise not up again.
11 Let not an evil speaker be established in the earth :
    Evil shall hunt the violent man to overthrow him.
12 I know that the Lord will maintain the cause of the afflicted, and the right
    of the poor.
13 Surely the righteous shall give thanks unto thy name :
    The upright shall dwell in thy presence.

The Psalmist. ANOTHER Psalm *"of David,"* to be sung by all saints, even as

The plan. it was used by their Head, David's Son. In it we have (ver. 1–3) the *picture of the wicked,* with a "Selah," that bids us pause over its dark colours. Then we have (ver. 4, 5) *a view of the snares spread by the wicked,* with another "*Selah-*" pause. Thereafter, we see a soul in *the attitude of faith* (ver. 6–8). They are laying their snares, but calm as Elisha beholding the Syrian host assembling (2 Kings vi. 15), the stayed soul sings-

"*I have said to the Lord, My God art thou ;*"

And then he prays, putting a "Selah"* at the close, that we may again pause and survey the scene.

    * We meet with *Selah* here for the first time since Psa. lxxxix. From Psa. xc. to Psa. cxl. no *Selah* occurs. Why omitted in these fifty, we cannot tell, any more than why so often occurring in others. However, there are only about forty Psalms in all in which it is used.

In ver. 9–11 we have the *certainty of the wicked's overthrow.* It is spoken of as a thing to be realised as a matter of course. It is a glance at the great day of the Lord, when he destroys the Man of Sin, and all such foes.

> " *Coals of fire shall be thrown upon them ;*
> *He will precipitate them into raging gulfs* (מְהֹרֹמוֹת);
> *They shall rise no more.*"

And then we have (ver. 12, 13) *the calm assurance of blessing to the righteous,* introduced by an expression that sends our thoughts away to Job's memorable utterance of his hope that the Redeemer would appear on the earth at the latter day, (xix. 25). " *I know,*" says the Psalmist-

> " *I know that Jehovah will execute*
> *The judgment of the poor, the right of the needy.*"

And then in verse 13 the expression אַךְ, like that in Psa. lxxiii. 1, intimates that these are inferences drawn from previous reflection. The issue shall be this, the righteous shall praise his name, and dwell before his face for ever. They shall inherit the promised kingdom, entering in with songs, and continuing their songs for ever. Such is this song of the sweet singer of Israel, under the inspiration of the Holy Ghost, setting forth *The Righteous One amid snares, confidently expecting the ruin of the ungodly, and his own reward.*

Psalm 141

A Psalm of David

1 LORD, I cry unto thee : make haste unto me ! give ear unto my voice when I cry unto thee.

2 Let my prayer be set forth before thee as incense ;
And the lifting up of my hands as the evening sacrifice.

3 Set a watch, O Lord, before my mouth : keep the door of my lips.

4 Incline not my heart to any evil thing, to practise wicked works with men that work iniquity :
And let me not eat of their dainties.

5 Let the righteous smite me, it shall be a kindness :
And let him reprove me, it shall be an excellent oil, which shall not break my head :
For yet my prayer also shall be in their calamities.

6 When their judges are overthrown in stony places,
They shall hear my words; for they are sweet.
Our bones are scattered at the grave's mouth,
As when one cutteth and cleaveth wood upon the earth.

8 But mine eyes are unto thee, O God the Lord!
In thee is my trust; leave not my soul destitute.

9 Keep me from the snares which they have laid for me, and the gins of the
workers of iniquity.

10 Let the wicked fall into their own nets, whilst that I withal escape.

The tone of the Psalm. A PSALM of David, for the Church's Head and the Church's members in every age. For may the members not cry, and might not the Head cry, with as much urgency as verses 1, 2, asking for as speedy an answer as that given to Daniel at the hour of the evening sacrifice (ix. 19–21)? And should not prayer and alms-giving go together, now as of old as in the days of Cornelius (Acts x. 3)? Here, the "*lifting up of hands,*" is, whatever our hands bring to God, by way of offering or service (see 2 Sam. xi. 8). The "*incense*" represented the sweet savour arising from the blood on the altar's horns, and from the atoning sacrifice in general.

The plan. In all ages, *help against temptation* has been needed, as in verses 3–5. Surely we need still to pray in this self-indulging age, as verse 4, Let me not be ensnared by their prosperity,

"*Let me not eat of their dainties.*"

Nay, rather, instead of this self-indulgence,

"*Let the righteous smite, it is mercy;
My head refuses not the oil for the head.*" (Hengst.)

This oil for the head is better to me than all that these guests find at their festive board. Yes, and if tempted to avenge myself (Matt. xxv. 51), I will pray instead. The force of the clause may be thus given—"*For still while it continues, my prayer shall ascend in the midst of their evil,*" (Hengst.). The Church has in every age needed the help of hope, when her persecutors were strong; and this we have in verses 6, 7—

"*Their judges are overthrown in* (precipitated on) *the sides of the rock,*"
(2 Chron. xxv. 12; 2 Kings ix. 33, Jezebel rock). Selah.

they who were leaders of the oppressing crew are fallen! crushed! dashed in pieces by the mighty hand of the Judge of all! And though now they refuse to listen to warning, yet it is their interest so to do; "*Let them hear my words;*" for there is no terror in them, no bitterness if listened to now (comp. Psa. ii. 12) ; "they are sweet."

In verse 7, "*Our bones are scattered, like one ploughing and clearing* (making furrows in) the earth," has been supposed to contain an allusion to *Resurrection*, as if the Psalmist said. These persecutions are the precursors of a time when the seed shall spring up. The Church never doubts, and never in any age has doubted, that soon shall come *her final escape from all snares*, "from the hands of the snare" (ver. 9) ; and this we have in the closing verses, verses 8–10. They remind us much of Paul's words in 2 Tim. iv. 18—" And the Lord shall preserve me from every evil work, and will preserve me to his heavenly kingdom." Like Jehoshaphat in 2 Chron. xix. 12, the Church fixes her eye on the Lord (ver. 8) whatever be her case, imitating her Lord in the days of his flesh, when he, too, used this Psalm, most emphatically praying, " Leave not my soul *bare*" (אַל־תְּעַר), when about to pour out his soul (הֶעֱרָה Isa. liii. 12. It is interesting to notice that the last words of the Psalm are literally,

" *Until that I pass over.*"

Go on overthrowing them till they are annihilated ; go on destroying them till thy people are safely in the kingdom— "*passed over*" into Canaan, as when the ark stood keeping back Jordan's waters for them ; or as when Israel passed the Red Sea and entered on the conquest of the land, for the expression is the same as occurs in Exod. xv. 16. Augustine was wrong in thinking the reference was to the *Passover ;* for that is expressed by a peculiar term, whereas this is the usual אֶעֱבוֹר. He has been followed by others, *e. g.*, one who paraphrases the clause thus-

Prophetic reference.

" *And let my saints escape with me ;*
My blood their passover shall be."

But the allusion is to the *passing into Canaan*, and so reminds us more directly of the glory. Christ and his host of ransomed ones march in triumph into possession of the kingdom, while his and their enemies are falling on every side, like snow falling on fire. The whole Psalm is

A prayer of the Head and his Members to be kept from every evil work and preserved to the kingdom.

Psalm 142

Maschil of David. A Prayer when he was in the cave.

I CRIED unto the Lord with my voice;
With my voice unto the Lord did I make my supplication.

2 I poured out my complaint before him; I shewed before him my trouble.
When my spirit was overwhelmed within me, then thou knewest my path.
In the way wherein I walked have they privily laid a snare for me.

4 I looked on my right hand, and beheld, but there was no man that would
    know me:
Refuge failed me; no man cared for my soul.

5 I cried unto thee, O Lord!
I said, Thou art my refuge and my portion in the land of the living.

6 Attend unto my cry; for I am brought very low:
Deliver me from my persecutors; for they are stronger than I.

7 Bring my soul out of prison, that I may praise thy name:
The righteous shall compass me about; for thou shalt deal bountifully
    with me.

The title.   *Maschil*—" *A prayer of David, when he was in the cave;*"
or, more closely adhering to the order of the original, " *Maschil,
(i. e.,* as in Psa. xxxii., which see) *of David, when he was in
the cave; a prayer.*" The cave of Adullam echoed these holy
strains; and David's men, "the distressed, the debtors, the
bitter of soul," (1 Sam. xxii. 2,) heard, as did the prisoners in
Philippi when Paul and Silas sung, and were not only soothed
but sanctified, when the Holy Ghost used the same harp that
had calmed Saul's spirit, to cast out the evil that wrought in
that strange band. But is it not written for all ages? David's
Son, and all that follow him, use it when "bitter in soul," or
in "distress."

The contents.   Let us see how beautifully it utters our Master's heart as
" A prayer."

Verse 1. The cry of the Son of David—" *I cry unto Jehovah, who has so often heard my voice; I supplicate Jehovah with my voice.*" Is not this suitable in the lips of
him who was ever calling on his Father, and whose agony
drew forth all the more that filial cry, " O my Father!"

Verse 2. " *I pour forth my complaint before him.*" Compare the title of Psa. cii., and remember the Lord's words
in the garden, " *Let this cup pass!*" when reading " *I
shewed before him my distress.*"

Verse 3. " *When my spirit is overwhelmed within me*" (compare again the title of Psa. cii.), *and thou knewest* (אַתָּה emphatic, as if to say, I did not know, but thou didst) *my path, or the way where I was going where they hid a trap for me.*" How suitable in the mouth of him who was " *sore amazed*" as he entered the garden !

Verse 4. " *Look on thy right hand, and behold*"—an abrupt, or broken cry ; look, and behold, and you will see only this—" *no one knoweth me ! refuge fails me ! no one concerns himself for my soul.*" Such language might actually be used by our Lord Jesus to the Father, when he saw even his disciples fleeing from him, as the band drew near to take him in their snare ; or when he saw them all asleep in that terrible hour.

Verse 5. " *I have cried* (and do still cry) *to thee, O Jehovah; Thou art my portion* (both now and hereafter) *in the land of the living.*" The Master returned to the Father for sympathy, finding it only there.

Verse 6. Another cry pointed with the appeal, " *For I am brought very low.*" He needed an angel to strengthen him, so low did he become—lower in every sense than angels. His flesh was weak.

Verse 7. But here, as in Psa. xxii., the scene begins to brighten. His disciples may sleep on and take their rest, for he has accomplished his sufferings. He sees in prospect the results, and prays,

> " *Bring my soul from being shut up ;*" (as Joseph was, Gen. xxxix. 20, as Isa. xxiv. 22.)
> *That men may praise thy name.* (Hengstenberg.)

And then in confidence of hope, seeing down the vista of ages, his eye resting on the millions of his saved ones,

> " *The righteous shall form a circle close round me;* (בִּי יַכְתִּרוּ press closely in upon me ; Hengst.)
> *For thou shalt deal bountifully with me.*"

Is not this His anticipation of the great multitude, whom no man can number, in his kingdom, round his throne, as in Rev. vii. 9, where the redeemed stand nearer than angels, as

Prophetic reference.

if pressing in ?   And, being one with our Head, each of us the
members may take up this song in our Adullam sojourn—for
the disciple is as the Master, in his degree.   Arrived at last at
the Throne, disciples shall feel solitude no more, nor complain
of sympathy withheld, amid the great congregation.

Horsley entitles this Psalm, " A prayer of Messiah, when he
was taken and deserted."   Let us call it,

*The cave-thoughts of David, and of David's Son, for all in
extremity.*

Psalm 143

A Psalm of David

1 HEAR my prayer, O Lord, give ear to my supplications:
In thy faithfulness answer me, and in thy righteousness.

2 And enter not into judgment with thy servant:
For in thy sight shall no man living be justified.

3 For the enemy hath persecuted my soul; he hath smitten my life down to
the ground :
He hath made me to dwell in darkness, as those that have been long dead.

4 Therefore is my spirit overwhelmed within me; my heart within me is
desolate.

5 I remember the days of old; I meditate on all thy works;
I muse on the work of thy hands.

6 I stretch forth my hands unto thee: my soul thirsteth after thee, as
thirsty land.   Selah.

7 Hear me, speedily, O Lord! my spirit faileth :
Hide not thy face from me, lest I be like unto them that go down into the pit.

8 Cause me to hear thy lovingkindness in the morning; for in thee do I trust !
Cause me to know the way wherein I should walk; for I lift up my soul
unto thee.

9 Deliver me, O Lord, from mine enemies : I flee unto thee to hide me.

10 Teach me to do thy will; for thou art my God:
Thy spirit is good; lead me into the land of uprightness.

11 Quicken me, O Lord, for thy name's sake :
For thy righteousness' sake bring my soul out of trouble.

12 And of thy mercy cut off mine enemies,
And destroy all them that afflict my soul: for I am thy servant.

The author
and tone of
the Psalm.

David is still the sweet singer here, his harp sounding in the
wilderness of Judah, or, as in Psa. xlii., from some still more
remote retreat.   Here, however, he alludes to no particular

external privation—it is his *soul's sadness* that is the burden
of his song.   Christ could use these utterances, feeling not his
bodily absence from heaven so much as the Father's hidden
face.   And it suits the believer at times, when he mourns most
of all for the absence of any tokens of the Lord's special presence, in himself or the church around.

From verses 1 to 4 we have the strong appeal of one who   *The plan.*
feels the darkness in which he is enveloped by the absence of
special tokens of God's love.   Our Lord uses the argument of
God's "*truth and righteousness*," in seeking an answer ; and
so we, his members, appeal to these same perfections, in our
expostulations with our God, warranted by 1 John i. 9, "He
is *faithful and just* to forgive us."   And then the deprecation
in verse 2,

> "*And enter not into judgment with thy servant,*"

is, in our Lord's lips, equivalent to "If it be possible, let this
cup pass from me !"   Do not argue the case with me (see Job
ix. 32, and xxii. 4, and xxxiv. 23), to shew me that there is
cause for all this darkness.   I know there is a cause ; the cause
is the sin which I have undertaken to bear, "*For before thee
shall no living one be justified*"—not one of all descended
from Adam.   (Compare כָּל־חָי here with Gen. iii. 20, when
Eve's posterity got that name after the Fall.)   But my appeal
is to thy "*truth and righteousness*," which are engaged to
carry me through ; and my need of help is great.

> "*For the foe is pursuing* (רָדַף) *my soul !*"   (Ver. 3.)

And then, as if overtaken in the pursuit, he cries, "*He has
smitten my life to the ground ! He has made me stand in
deep darkness, like one eternally dead* (Hengst) ; *and my
spirit is overwhelmed* (Psa. cii., title, and cxlii. 4) *within me ;
my heart in the midst of me is desolate.*"

At verse 5, there is a gleam of light through the "darkness ;" he recalls to mind God's love manifested to Israel in
former days.

At verse 6, there is a renewed appeal to the Lord's pity,
drawn from his state, resembling "a weary land"—(אֶרֶץ עֲיֵפָה
like Isa. xxxii. 2)—a land where a traveller's strength is ex-

hausted by the rough roads and crooked paths, and the oppressive heat of the sun's intolerable rays. It was thus our Surety
learned by experience to sympathise with us ; and thus it was
he became the "shadow of a great rock in a weary land." He
here calls the Father to notice his self-emptying and humiliation, while bearing wrath for our sins ;

> *" My soul is to thee* (see Hebr.) *as a weary land."*

At verses 7 and 9 he seeks speedy relief ; and the clause,
" Make me to know the path I should walk in," is similar to
the *" If it be possible"* in his prayer in the garden. In the
case of one of his members, the words have of course a different application, and yet one resembling his in the circumstance, that it is a petition for guidance under our personal
difficulties.

At verse 10 do we not hear, "Not my will, but thine be
done," mingled with the filial accents of confidence, "My God !"

But at verses 11, 12, the prospect opens out on future glory.
The Spirit, that same *" loving,"* or *" good Spirit"* who instructed Israel (Nehem. ix. 20), that same " eternal Spirit by
whom he offered himself without spot to God," shall lead him
forth from those scenes, and place him

> *" In the land of uprightness."*

The land of plainness (מִישׁוֹר), a land where no wickedness of
men, and malice of Satan, vex the soul from day to day ; a
land where no rough paths and crooked turns lengthen out
the traveller's weary journey, (see ver. 5) ; but where all is like
the smooth pasture lands of Reuben (Deut. iii. 10, Josh. xiii.
9), a fit place for flocks to lie down. *" Thy Spirit"* will do this
in his love, when *"my Spirit"* (ver. 7), my overwhelmed human
soul, seemed ready to fail. Thou wilt be to me what thou wert
to David, in " bringing his soul out of all distress" (1 Kings
i. 29), and establishing him on his throne. All foes shall be
extirpated, (תַּצְמִית). Is not this the kingdom come, and its
King exalted ! And is not this a song alike for the Head and
the members ?

A prayer of the Righteous One, when feeling the heat of the
weary land

Psalm 144

A Psalm of David

1 BLESSED be the Lord my strength,
Which teacheth my hands to war, and my fingers to fight:
2 My goodness and my fortress; my high tower, and my deliverer;
My shield, and he in whom I trust; who subdueth my people under me.
3 Lord, what is man, that thou takest knowledge of him!
Or the son of man, that thou makest account of him!
4 Man is like to vanity: his days are as a shadow that passeth away.
5 Bow thy heavens, O Lord, and come down: touch the mountains, and they
shall smoke.
6 Cast forth lightning, and scatter them: shoot out thine arrows, and destroy
them.
7 Send thine hand from above; rid me, and deliver me out of great waters,
From the hand of strange children;
8 Whose mouth speaketh vanity, and their right hand is a right hand of
falsehood.
9 I will sing a new song unto thee, O God:
Upon a psaltery and an instrument of ten strings will I sing praises unto
thee.
10 It is he that giveth salvation unto kings:
Who delivereth David his servant from the hurtful sword.
11 Rid me, and deliver me from the hand of strange children,
Whose mouth speaketh vanity, and their right hand is a right hand of
falsehood.
12 That our sons may be as plants grown up in their youth;
That our daughters may be as corner-stones, polished after the similitude
of a palace:
13 That our garners may be full, affording all manner of store:
That our sheep may bring forth thousands, and ten thousands in our
streets:
14 That our oxen may be strong to labour; that there be no breaking in, nor
going out;
That there be no complaining in our streets.
15 Happy is that people, that is in such a case!
Yea, happy is that people, whose God is the Lord.

THE Spirit of the Lord spake by David the words of this song, _The allusions._
when the king felt his need of the King of kings to subdue
the turbulent and proud spirits who were ambitious of distinc-
tion (ver. 2), as well as to conquer the nations of idolaters
who hated God's anointed, (ver. 7-11). The Spirit leads him
back to the day when he sang Psa. xviii. (see ver. 1, 2), the
day when he was delivered from Saul and other foes; and still

farther back to the quiet night when the strains of Psa. viii.
ascended to the ear of Jehovah, (see ver. 3); but he does not
fail also to lead him forward to a future day, when earth shall
witness its millennial scenes, among which not the least wonderful and refreshing shall be Israel in all the restored plenty
of his last times, with the favour of Jehovah over all. In all
this, David was the type of Christ.

The contents.   *Jehovah's grace to man* is the theme of verses 1, 2; that
expression, " *My goodness*," חַסְדִּי, may be understood as if declaring that all the *kindness* or *mercy* that is in God is made
over to his own people; *q. d.*, all in thee that is kind is my
property.

Man's unworthiness and littleness are the theme of verses
3, 4—the contrast to the preceding verse. The Hebrew of
verse 4, "*man* is a *vapour*," reads suggestively אָדָם לַהֶבֶל, recalling the disappointment of the first family on earth; *q. d.*,
all come of *Adam* are as sure to disappoint, and to be disappointed, in the fond hopes cherished concerning them, as *Abel*,
so short-lived, and untimely in his end.

God's strength laid hold upon by his own against foes is
the theme of verses 5–8. The God of Sinai is remembered in
verse 5; and the ease with which he can overwhelm his foes is
expressed, verse 6, " *Lighten with lightning*," and forthwith
they are scattered, (ἀστραψον ἀστραπην.—Sept.). The "*right hand
of falsehood*," verse 8, expresses the violation of solemn oaths
and engagements, in ratifying which the right hand was lifted
up to heaven, (Gen. xiv. 22). Hence Tholuck renders it,
" Their oaths are perjuries." With majesty and might, with
lightning and fire like this, shall the Lord appear, when he
arises at last to the final conflict.

Praise and prayer, in prospect of victory, form the matter
of verses 9–11. And here " The New Song" is mentioned,
which " *New Song*" is ever sung by one whose eye is on that
vail which was rent—looking either at the Saviour going in
with the sacrifice, or coming out the second time to bless.

*The happy scene to be witnessed, when these desires are re-
sponded to*, is the subject of verse 12, to the end. Do all this
for us, in answer to our prayer, so that, as a consequence of
this deliverance.

> " *Our sons may be as plants* (of the *palm-tree*, says the Targum),
> *Vigorously shooting up in their youth ;*
> *Our daughters like corner-columns,*
> *Polished like a palace.*"

Others take this last clause to contain an allusion to the costly stones so carefully prepared for the building of the Temple: " hewn *for the building* of the Temple." These are the choice of men ! each one full of life and beauty, walking before the Lord.

> " *Our granaries full, supplying one kind of food after another ;* "

like Egypt in Joseph's days. It is a scene of plenty, as if the curse were lifted off the soil.

> " *Our flocks increased to thousands,*
> *Increased to thousands in our fields.*" (חוצות, Job v. 10.)

Here are the pastures peopled with their appropriate tenants, and a scene of peaceful plenty is set before us. And then follow the yoked cattle, carrying their loads through the streets—a token of busy commerce.

> " *No breach*" in the tribes, like Judges xxi. 15 ; or in individuals, like
> Uzzah, 2 Sam vi. 8.
> " *No going forth*" to war.
> " *No cry*" like that in Isa. xxiv. 11, over disasters.

Happy days when these scenes are realised ! Happy people who shall enjoy them. Men shall in that day exclaim with Balaam, " How goodly are thy tents, O Jacob !"—or rather, all shall then unite in tracing the blessing to its fountain-head,

> " *Blessed are the people whose God is Jehovah.*"

Every member of Christ may take up this Psalm in behalf of his own country and people—yea, in behalf of our common humanity, praying for the day when all earth shall enjoy these blessings, by enjoying Jehovah as their God. It is a prospect that awaits the world when Christ returns ; and our expectation of such happiness in reserve for our world is kept alive by a song like this, ^{The speaker}

A prayerful song of David, and David's Lord, anticipating the prosperity which Jehovah brings to his own.

Psalm 145

David's Psalm of praise

1 I WILL extol thee, my God, O King! and I will bless thy name for ever and ever.

2 Every day will I bless thee; and I will praise thy name for ever and ever.

3 Great is the Lord, and greatly to be praised; and his greatness is unsearchable.

4 One generation shall praise thy works to another, and shall declare thy mighty acts.

5 I will speak of the glorious honour of thy majesty, and of thy wondrous works.

6 And men shall speak of the might of thy terrible acts: and I will declare thy greatness.

7 They shall abundantly utter the memory of thy great goodness,
And shall sing of thy righteousness.

8 The Lord is gracious, and full of compassion;
Slow to anger, and of great mercy.

9 The Lord is good to all: and his tender mercies are over all his works.

10 All thy works shall praise thee, O Lord; and thy saints shall bless thee.

11 They shall speak of the glory of thy kingdom, and talk of thy power;

12 To make known to the sons of men his mighty acts,
And the glorious majesty of his kingdom.

13 Thy kingdom is an everlasting kingdom,
And thy dominion endureth throughout all generations.

14 The Lord upholdeth all that fall, and raiseth up all those that be bowed down.

15 The eyes of all wait upon thee; and thou givest them their meat in due season.

16 Thou openest thine hand, and satisfiest the desire of every living thing.

17 The Lord is righteous in all his ways, and holy in all his works.

18 The Lord is nigh unto all them that call upon him, to all that call upon him in truth.

19 He will fulfil the desire of them that fear him:
He also will hear their cry, and will save them.

20 The Lord preserveth all them that love him:
But all the wicked will he destroy.

21 My mouth shall speak the praise of the Lord:
And let all flesh bless his holy name for ever and ever.

Alphabetic structure. THE well-known 45th Psalm sang of the King in his beauty: this 145th is a hymn of praise concerning the reign of Jehovah, and his kingdom. It is a Davidic and an alphabetic Psalm. In regard to its alphabetic structure, it has one peculiarity, viz., the "*nun*" is omitted; the reason of which may be, that

(as we have seen in some other Psalms of this structure) by
means of that, or some other such omission, we might be kept
from putting stress on the mere form of the composition.

It is peculiar, also, in its title ; indeed, quite unique—" *Of* The title.
David ; praise." The word is תְהִלָּה. Some render this " a
hymn ;" others, such as Hengstenberg, " a *praise-song*," differing in this from the תְּפִלָּה, the "*prayer-song.*" It is prayer
turned into praise. Patrick remarks, that the term seemed so
peculiar and excellent that it was given from this Psalm to the
whole book, which is entitled by the Jews, the book of תְהִלִּים.
Bythner has this note on the word—" So called because it is
throughout nothing but the celebration of God ; so that the
ancient Jews used to say, that the man was already enjoying
the felicity of the age to come who daily recited it three times
with the mouth and heart." We are getting now beyond the
region of former themes ; all in the remaining Psalms is praise,
praise ; and this title is an appropriate introduction to the
closing group of praise-psalms. Nor is its burden less appropriate ; for, being a song of the kingdom, it ushers us into the
region of eternal praise.

It is a song for all saints. But we may say also, What a The speaker.
song in the lips of Christ for the Father's ear ! What a song
to soothe his own soul, when still " man of sorrows !" For the
prospect is presented here of the kingdom made manifest, so
that all see the glory of the Lord. It is a Psalm that gathers The theme.
up much of the excellency of former Psalms ; and so truly is
the style of royalty and the manner of a kingdom in it, that
we find, in after days, the writer of the Book of Esther using
expressions regarding the king and kingdom of Media and
Persia, that bear a striking resemblance to the terms employed
by the Psalmist—only the one speaks of an earthly, and the
other of the heavenly throne.

1. The harp extols *Jehovah for what He is*, in verses 1–3, The plan.
" *My God, O King !*"—rather, " My God, who art THE KING."
It is much more emphatic than Psa. v. 3, " My God, and my
King ;" here he is sung of as the only King. We are reminded
at once of Psa. xlv. 2, " My words concern *the King.*" Of this
God and King the Psalmist sings, that he is unlike all idols.

He is self-existent, and infinite, and so the greatness of any of his perfections cannot be told. He is eternal and unchangeable ; for he must be celebrated " *For ever and ever.*" And all this he is in his very *being* or essence, for he is " Jehovah." All he does is so wisely done, that for all he is to be praised. And his deeds display such power !   Righteous too, is He, and yet abounding in love, kindness, and grace.

> " *Yes, let me bless* (וַאֲבָרְכָה) *thy name for ever and ever*," (comp. 1 Pet. i. 3, &c.).
>
> *Every day will I bless thee* (comp. Psa. **xix.** 2) ;
>
> *Yes, let me praise* (וַאֲהַלְלָה)—*q. d.*, let me Hallelujah) *thy name for ever and ever !*"
>
> *Great is Jehovah ; and* (מְהֻלָּל) *worthy to be praised !*" (ver. 1–3.)

How many terms of adoration and honour !   *Praise, praise,* is on his lips ; the harp-strings will utter nothing but praise ; for " *of his greatness there is no searching out,*" (comp. Job v. 9).

2. The harp extols *the deeds that shew Jehovah's name,* in verses 4–6, or *what He is.*

> " *Generation to generation shall commend his works.*
> *Yea, they shall declare his mighty acts.*"   (Ver. 4.)

Compare Psa. xix. 2, " day unto day" uttering the Lord's praise in creation.   But here it is both creation-works and redemption-wonders that are shewn ; for גְּבוּרֹת cannot fail to remind us of the acts of Him who overthrew Israel's foes, and of Him whose name is גִּבּוֹר, "Mighty One" (Psa. xlv. 3), and "Mighty God," (Isa. ix 6).   His mighty acts, in establishing his kingdom on earth upon the ruins of Antichrist's dominion, shall form part of the theme.   And that is the time when, in a special sense, the next clause shall be understood, though it may apply in some degree to his creation-works :

> " *Of the majesty of glory* (which is), *thy beauty,*
> *And of the chronicles of thy wondrous acts, let me speak.*"   (Ver. 5.)

O how his beauty shall burst forth when the King appears with his many crowns ! And if Herod, arrayed in royal apparel, amid gorgeous splendour, suggested to his people to cry, " A god, not a man ! " what shall creation feel at this sight ?   The Lord's *beauty,* הוֹד (a word applied to creature-beauty in Hos. xiv. 6, Zech. x. 3), is here emphatically exalted beyond comparison by the addition of "*the glory* of thy beauty;" aye, and "*the majesty of the glory.*" And then the "*Chronicles* (דִּבְרֵי) *of thy wondrous acts*" is a term applied in 1 Chron. xxvii. 24, 1 Kings xi. 41, to the acts of Solomon and David, the journals or records made of their deeds ; even as it is in Esther vi. 1, to the king of Persia. The terms all bear reference to royalty and government. Then he adds that in all these coming ages there will be a company of those who delight to record the manifestation of his name in his deeds.

> "*They shall speak of the overwhelming might* (עֱזוּז) *of thy terrible acts,*"
> (Ver. 6)

done in past days, such as Israel has delighted to tell to their children (Psa. lxxviii. 4), even such as He did at the Red Sea (Exod. xv. 11, נוֹרָא, as here), and upon the cities of the plain, as well as on the nations of Canaan.

> "*And thy greatness, I will recount it !*"

Leave me to declare, or recount, the manifestations of his "*Greatness.*" While other men are uttering praise, the Psalmist catches up the theme, as one which he must appropriate to himself—that "greatness" spoken of in 1 Chron. xvii. 19, when he sat before the Lord—that *royal greatness* which a Persian king's wealth and magnificence would faintly shadow forth (Esther i. 4, " excellency of his *greatness*") when taken as an emblem. But it is chiefly here the display of his *greatness* in acts of kindness that he is to shew.

3. The harp extols *Jehovah's past manifestation of His gracious character,* in verses 7–9. The first words in verse 7 are, " *They shall pour out* (as from a gushing spring, Psa xix. 2) *the memory of thy great goodness ;*" and perhaps we ought to understand the clause as asserting that the Lord's " *great goodness*" is itself the " זֵכֶר," the *thing to be remembered concerning Him*—His memorial, as in Exod. iii. 15, Psa. cii. 12. And then there is allusion to Exod. xxxiv. 6, Numb. xiv. 8, in verse 8.

> "*The Lord is gracious and merciful,*
> *Slow to anger and abundant in goodness* (חֶסֶד).*"

The very words of Exod. iii. 4, though unfortunately altered
in our version ; and the more to be noticed, as verse 4, " Thy
goodness," is טוּבְךָ corresponding so exactly to Exod. xxxiii. 19,
טוּבִי   The God who was thus gracious in the wilderness to his
people remains the same evermore.   And this is He who at
Calvary, in his incarnate Son, manifested his gracious name.
We, in our day, turn to the sacrifice of Calvary, as best displaying his great goodness, his memorial, and we sing of " his *righteousness*" as shining there.

> " The Lord is good to every one ;
>> And his yearning bowels are over all his works."   (Ver. 9.)

He attends to individual souls, and yet also bends, like the
blue sky, over all his universe in mercy.   His mercies, like the
rainbow, span the world.   We see this at the rock of Horeb
(Exod. xxxiv.) ; but we see it best of all at Calvary.   What
yearnings there !—what love !—what goodness !   And the
" *whole creation*" shall yet have a share in that mercy, when
the time spoken of in Rom. viii. 19–21 has arrived.

4. The harp *extols Jehovah's kingdom* in verses 10–13.   All
he has created, and all he has wrought in providence, has been
of such a character as to yield him a revenue of praise ; and
his saints act as his priests, presenting the praise.   But this
will be peculiarly the case when the kingdom is manifested.

> " They shall speak of the glory of thy kingdom,
>> And shall talk of (chronicle, as ver. 5) thy might (see ver. 4),
>> Making known to the sons of men thy mighty acts ;
>> And the glory of the majesty of thy kingdom."   (Ver. 11, 12.)

The writer of Esther i. 4 says, " While he shewed them the
riches of the glory of his kingdom"—a kingdom which was to
last only a season.   May we suppose that that writer, a man
of Israel, was led to use these terms, with this Psalm in his hand,
purposely in order to suggest by contrast the infinite difference
between that earthly monarch's splendour, and the glory of the
God of Israel ?   The Persian monarch's display lasted 180
days, and when its half-year was over, the splendour had
vanished ; whereas Jehovah's is (as Dan. iv. 31)

> " A kingdom of all eternities-
> " In every generation and generation."   (Ver. 13.)

5. The harp extols *the qualifications of Him who reigneth* in verses 14–19,

> " *The Lord is an upholder to all that are falling,*
> *And maketh all that are bowed down to stand upright.*" (Ver. 14.)

Those in distress and trouble are meant by the "*falling*," as in Prov. xiii. 16, 17 ; and who the "*bowed down*" are, we see by Psa. lvii. 7, where the Psalmist's soul is nearly overwhelmed by the thought of snares and foes shutting him in. Rejoice, O saints ! though ye are feeling disaster and calamity, and are sore distressed, your Lord is coming to put all things in order. He is the uplifter of a fallen World ; he will not break the bruised reed. The world shall soon hear no sigh, no murmur, no voice of weeping ; for his unsuffering kingdom is at hand ! He has provision for all (ver. 15, 16) ; he is more than was Joseph in Goshen, to his own and to all creation. And he acts on the holiest principles of administration (ver 17), while giving access and audience to his subjects who seek his presence, (ver. 18). Yes, he will satiate their weary souls, and leave not one wish ungratified—not one craving, not one longing—" *He will accomplish the desire of those that fear him,*" (ver. 19).

6. The harp sings the safe arrival in the kingdom (2 Tim. iv. 18) of his saints, and *the ruin of those who resist His kingdom*, in verse 20. There is a reference to the day of the Lord's Coming, when his Israel reach the safe shore, and see the Pharaohs that pursued them overwhelmed in the deep. When he is spoken of as preserving the souls that love him, while "*destroying the wicked ones,*" the word for "destroy" is the same (יַשְׁמִיד, the opposite of שׁוֹמֵר) as that in Deut. ii. 12, 21, 22, where we are told of the extirpation of various nations ; and the same used in Isa. xiv. 23, of Babylon's ruin ; and the same in Esther iii. 6, when Haman plotted to uproot Israel at one blow. *Antichrist* shall be consumed and " destroyed" by the brightness of the Lord's coming, and all that are on his side, in that day when the King establishes his holy kingdom. On the other hand, his saints shall be " *preserved*" (1 Tim. iv. 18), not only from succeeding dangers, but from the grasp of death itself, and brought by resurrection into his kingdom.

7. The harp invites *all to join the sweet singer in praise*

to the King, (ver. 21). We saw that the Psalm began by pre-fixing the peculiar title, " Praise," תְּהִלָּה, in order to excite at-tention, and tune our hearts for its lively, joyful, thrilling strains. And now it closes, uttering the same note-

" *My mouth shall speak the praise* (תְּהִלָּה) *of the Lord,"*

the praise of Him who at the Red Sea was known as " terrible in praises" (תְּהִלֹּת), and who is known by Calvary, and by scenes of judgment since then, and is to be known ere long in scenes that will never be forgotten. " *Let all flesh bless the name of his holiness for ever ;"* let them cry, in response to the seraphim, " Holy, holy, holy, is the Lord of Hosts ; the whole earth is full of his glory !" for we are borne onward to the millennial day by this Psalm, which is so plainly

A praise-hymn concerning the kingdom of the Lord, and the Lord the King.

Psalm 146

1 PRAISE ye the Lord. Praise ye the Lord, O my soul!

2 While I live I will praise the Lord : I will sing praises unto my God while I have any being.

3 Put not your trust in princes, nor in the son of man, in whom there is no help.

4 His breath goeth forth, he returneth to his earth; in that very day his thoughts perish.

5 Happy is he that hath the God of Jacob for his help, whose hope is in the Lord his God :

6 Which made heaven, and earth, the sea, and all that therein is:

7 Which keepeth truth for ever: which executeth judgment for the op-pressed :

Which giveth food to the hungry.

8 The Lord looseth the prisoners : the Lord openeth the eyes of the blind :

The Lord raiseth them that are bowed down : the Lord loveth the righteous:

9 The Lord preserveth the strangers: he relieveth the fatherless and widow :

But the way of the wicked he turneth upside down.

10 The Lord shall reign for ever,

Even thy God, O Zion, unto all generations.

Praise ye the Lord.

THIS is the beginning of that closing series of Psalms which has been called " *Hallelujah Psalms.*" The Septuagint ascribes this Psalm, and the three following, to the prophets Haggai and Zechariah, but on what ground we know not. It seems probable, however, that they are nearly right as to the time of their composition ; for it is likely that as the day of Christ's first coming approached nearer, the Holy Spirit did indite songs of Zion that were fuller of triumph and praise than any preceding ones, and so constructed them, too, that they might be used afterwards in prospect of the day of his Second Coming. In these latter Psalms, the tone is that of peace attained, and tribulation passed, for the most part. The Lord Jesus himself, as well as his followers, could take up this Psalm.

Jehovah's peculiar character, in contrast to all earthly princes, and benefactors, and friends, is the theme.

> " *I will praise Jehovah while I live ;*
> *I will play to my God so long as I am.*"

Confide not in earth's nobles, earth's princely ones, who are each of them but " a son of man" (אָדָם) returning to his אֲדָמָה, dust ;

> " *For salvation is not in any one of them ;*"

All their " *thoughts,*" their schemes for good or for evil, pass away. Blessed 'the man who has Jacob's *God* (אֵל, the strong one), " *amid his help*" (Psa. cxviii. 7, liv. 4) ; for he is Jehovah, maker of heaven, earth, and sea ; and this Maker of heaven, earth, and sea, is the same

> " *Who keepeth truth for ever !* "

Whatever he has promised to the sons of men, he will perform. Whatever he promised about " The Seed of the woman," he will perform it. Whatever he has spoken to David of the Son who was to sit on his throne, he will fulfil. Whatever he has declared by his prophets regarding Israel, he will accomplish—" the *truth* to Jacob, and the mercy to Abraham," (Mic. vii. 20). Yes, the *truth* shall assuredly be kept ; and there is *mercy* too, there is love, there is grace in this truth. For verses 7–9 describe the same Jehovah acting for men in accordance with his truth. We, in our day, read the words, and at every step we see their verification in the incarnate Son of God ; even as Jesus, in singing those words when on earth, would have reference to himself as the great illustration of each clause (Luke xviii: 75 ; Matt. ix. 27), and as he may have thought upon them when he gave that answer to John's disciples, Matt. xi. 4, 5, *q. d*, all that characterises *Jehovah* has been done by me. Did not Jesus relieve " all that were *oppressed* of the devil" (Acts x. 38), as a sample of verse 7 ; and did he not " *give food to the hungry*," (John vi.) ? Did Jesus not set free " *the prisoners*," when he beheld the Bethesda man, bound for thirty-eight years (John v.), and when he sent his angel to set Pete free, (Acts xii.) ? How often did he " *open the eyes of the blind !*" and the literally " *bowed down*" he made straight (Luke xiii. 16), as well as the spiritually laden (Matt. xi. 20) ; and, in spite of their low condition, "*he loved the righteous*"— for a fisherman of Galilee lay on his bosom ; his parables told of a diseased Lazarus ; and there was a Lazarus of Bethany, in whom he delighted. We know his care " *of the stranger ;*" for we read of his words to the Syrophenician, and to the Samaritan leper (Luke xvii. 16–19) ; while " *the widow*" of Nain, and his tender words in John xiv. 18, tell how he " *restored*" (יְעוֹדֵד) to cheerfulness the orphan and the widow. His Second Coming shall tell what his purging the temple intimated (John ii, 15, Matt. xxi. 12), namely, how

" He overturneth the way of the wicked."

This is he who is " King" for ever ! This is " *thy God, O Zion*," who shall be thine to all generations. The mention of such a King and God may well draw forth another " Hallelujah !" a " Hallelujah" such as we hear again in Rev. xix. 1–6, when " the Lord God omnipotent reigneth." For " that great voice of much people in heaven" fully accords in spirit, and may be joined with the Psalm before us, uttering, as it does,

Rapturous praise, in contrasting all Earth's great ones with Jehovah the King.

Psalm 147

1 PRAISE ye the Lord!
For it is good to sing psalms unto our God;
For it is pleasant and praise is comely.
2 The Lord doth build up Jerusalem : he gathereth together the outcasts of Israel.
3 He healeth the broken n heart, and bindeth up their wounds.
4 He telleth the number of the stars; he calleth them all by their names.
5 Great is our Lord, and of great power : his understanding is infinite.
6 The Lord lifteth up the meek : he casteth the wicked down to the ground.
7 Sing unto the Lord with thanksgiving; sing praise upon the harp unto our God :
8 Who covereth the heaven with clouds, who prepareth rain for the earth, Who maketh grass to grow upon the mountains.
9 He giveth to the beast his food, and to the young ravens which cry.
10 He delighteth not in the strength of the horse : he taketh not pleasure in the legs of a man.
11 The Lord taketh pleasure in them that fear him, in those that hope in his mercy
12 Praise the Lord, O Jerusalem! praise thy God, O Zion.
13 For he has strengthened the bars of thy gates; he hath blessed thy children within thee.
14 He maketh peace in thy borders, and filleth thee with the finest of the wheat,
15 He sendeth forth his commandment upon earth : his word runneth very swiftly.
16 He giveth snow like wool : he scattereth the hoarfrost like ashes.
17 He casteth forth his ice like morsels : who can stand before his cold?
18 He sendeth out his word, and melteth them :
He causeth his wind to blow, and the waters flow.
19 He sheweth his word unto Jacob, his statutes and his judgments unto Israel.
20 He hath not dealt so with any nation : and as for his judgments, they have not known them.
Praise ye the Lord.

THE God of Israel, what he has done, what he does, what he can do--this is the "*Hallelujah*" note of his song. So gladsome is the theme, that in verse 1 we find a contribution for it levied on Psa. xxxiii. 1, xcii. 1, and cxxxv. 3 ; each must furnish their quota of testimony to the desirableness of giving praise to such a God.

Another Hallelujah Psalm.

The theme is stated in verse 2, and then expatiated upon onwards to the end of verse 11, where the Septuagint finish

The theme.

the Psalm, casting the remaining verses into a Psalm by itself. It is probably one of those songs of Zion which the Holy Ghost gave to Israel under Nehemiah and Ezra, when the circumstances of that partial restoration furnished an appropriate occasion for celebrating the joy of the still greater restoration in the latter days, when Messiah should go up at the head of them.

Let us remark upon verse 4. It sets forth the true greatness and grandeur of Israel's God, who can attend at once to every wound of every broken-hearted one, and to the glorious host of stars. This power of attending so carefully to what is minute is peculiar to Jehovah. And he "counts" or determines the number of the stars, just as he does the dust of Jacob (Num xxiii. 10)—assigning each his " *name,*" according to his quality, as Adam did to the creation in Paradise on a limited scale, (Gen. ii. 20). His resources are inexhaustible, for " *His understanding is infinite,*" as well as his " power."

" *Sing to Jehovah a responsive song*" (עֲנוּ).

like what we find in Nehem. xii. 27–43. For he, the God of creation, feeds even the ravens (Luke xii. 24 may be Christ's quotation of these words), disagreeable as these ravens often seem to man ; and, judging not as man does, he delights in his children's reverend faith, not in displays of warlike pomp and military valour (ver. 10)—yes, in his children's godly fear, and in their hope also.

" *In the hopers for his mercy.*"

Prophetic reference.

Is not this equivalent to Jude 21, " who look for the mercy of the Lord Jesus" at his coming ; and in 1 Pet. i. 13, " who hope for the grace that is to be brought them at the appearing of Jesus Christ." And it is at that day when (ver. 12–14) shall be fully realised, Israel getting back again " *the fat* of wheat," as Moses sang, (Deut. xxxii. 14). On that day they will remember how, long ago, they had appealed to Jehovah as able to reverse their captivity, even as he changed night unto day, winter into summer, the floods into dry land, (Psa. lxxiv. 15–17). He who commands and forthwith snow appears, and who summons the frost to serve him and then dissolves it (see ver. 15–18), he it is who reverses Israel's desolation, sending his word, relaxing their bonds, and causing rivers of milk and honey to flow in their land, and themselves walk on the shady banks. This is the God of Israel, who selected his people as a peculiar people, in ages past, *"declaring his word to Jacob, his statutes and ordinances to Israel"*—the revealer of the way of salvation, and the appointer of the types that foreshadowed better things, all which Israel enjoyed. He has been sovereign from the first ; he will act in sovereignty to the last. In times past, *"He dealt not thus with any heathen nation;"* and to the end it will be seen that he has done for Israel, in sovereign grace, more than he has done for all other peoples. *"Hallelujah,"* then ! Let a sovereign God be praised on earth now, even as he shall be by the "voice of much people in heaven" (Psa. xix. 1), who see him glorified in his mysterious dealings and terrible judgments. Let us take up this calmly triumphant song of

Israel's praise to the sovereign Jehovah, who blesseth and rejoiceth over their nation restored to prosperity.

Psalm 148

1 PRAISE ye the Lord!
    Praise ye the Lord from the heavens : praise him in the heights.
2 Praise ye him, all his angels : praise ye him, all his hosts.
3 Praise ye him, sun and moon : praise him, all ye stars of light.
4 Praise him, ye heavens of heavens, and ye waters that be above the
    heavens.
5 Let them praise the name of the Lord !
    For he commanded, and they were created.
6 He hath also stablished them for ever and ever : he hath made a decree
    which shall not pass.
7 Praise the Lord from the earth, ye dragons, and all deeps :
8 Fire, and hail ; snow, and vapours ; stormy wind fulfilling his word :
9 Mountains, and all hills ; fruitful trees, and all cedars :
10 Beasts, and all cattle ; creeping things, and flying fowl :
11 Kings of the earth, and all people ; princes, and all judges of the earth :
12 Both young men, and maidens : old men and children :
13 Let them praise the name of the Lord !
    For his name alone is excellent ; his glory is above the earth and heaven.
14 He also exalteth the horn of his people, the praise of all his saints ;
    Even of the children of Israel, a people near unto him.
    Praise ye the Lord

THE Apocrypha has borrowed from this Psalm the supposed
song of the three Hebrew youths in the fiery furnace. It is
Israel's uncontrollable burst of praise at the thought of him
who makes them "a people near to him ;" a priestly people
(see Levit. x. 3 ; Ezek. lxii. 13 ; Deut. iv. 7 ; and Num. xvi.
5–9). How they rejoice before him in the latter day ; restored
from their wanderings ! One great deed of a benefactor excites
us to draw the attention of others to him, and inclines us to
dwell upon all that is in him; and so it is here with Israel in this
"*Hallelujah.*" They call for praise "*from the heavens ;*" they
bid those "*in the heights*" give praise ; "*all angels,*" of whatever rank, "*all his hosts,*" with one accord. *Sun* at noon,
moon at midnight, *stars* so bright (the *visible* host of the sky,
as the angels are the invisible), "*heaven of heavens,*" where
is the orbit of the planet and the path of the comet, and the
track of every star ; "*waters above the heaven,*" or firmament,*
the clouds of the sky—unite ye in one song of praise ! Do ye
wonder at this summons ? Why should ye ? (Gen. i 7.)

"*For he commanded and they were created,*"—

Yes, even angels ; for, as Augustine says, in Psa. lxxi. 19, "Ne
putes hominem solum pertinere ad gratiam Dei. Quid erat
Angelus antequam fieret? Quid est angelus, si deserat qui
creavit?" Again, then, he takes up the call—and now it is
as if one from heaven looked down to earth and summoned
it to praise, as before it was one on earth looking upward to
heaven. "Praise ye Jehovah *from the earth !*" *Ye* sea-mon-
sters, or *great whales* (Gen. i. 21), and ye *floods* wherein they
swim ; *heat* and *cold, white snow* and *dark smoke* (Gen. xix.
20 ; Psa. cxix. 83, Hengstenberg) ; *strong wind* that, amid
apparent anarchy, dost his will ; *mountains,* and more lowly
hills, diversifying the face of earth ; ye palms and pomegra-
nates, *fruit-trees,* ye firs and pines, "*cedars of every kind ;*"
wild beasts and tame ; *reptiles* and *fowls* of every wing, whether
small as the wren, or majestic as the eagle—unite in one song
of praise ! All the more because ye, too, shall be delivered

---

*⁻ This is the *first heavens,* the sky ; the *second* is that just mentioned ; the
third heavens was called upon in verses 1, 2.

from the bondage of corruption, and have your share in the millennial liberty of the sons of God, (Rom. viii. 21).

As in creation, so here, *man* appears on the scene last of all, just because chief of all.

> *" Kings of earth, and all ye tribes,*
> *Princes, and all earth's judges."*

Young men, who are in your strength ; *maidens* in your beauty ; *old men*, with lips of age dropping wisdom ; *children*, who can only lisp his name—all of you join, for there is no name exalted but his alone. " *His beauty is over earth and heaven*"—his beauty (הוֹד, Psa. cxlv. 5), his splendour, sheds its beams now over the earth as well as heaven. For the times of refreshing are come.

And of all men, none should so extol him as his peculiar people Israel. For,

> *" He hath raised up a horn for his people."*

He has fulfilled the words of Zechariah, (Luke i. 69). Messiah has come ; Messiah, with all the blessings purchased at his first coming, is now made known to Israel, and has pushed Israel's enemies off the field. And he who is this horn is *" the theme of praise"* to the peculiar people, and to all saints besides, wherever found, though none have more reason than Israel to adore and love him who saves the chief of sinners, and in sovereignty exalts the stiffnecked people to preeminence among the nations, making them a people קְרֹבוֹ " His intimate friend," as Psa. xxxviii. 12 ; lxxv. 2 ; Job xix. 14.

> *" The theme of praise* (as Deut. x. 21, הוּא תְהִלָּתְךָ) *to all his saints.*
> *To the children of Israel, a people near to him !"*
> *" Hallelujah !"*

Surely the " great voice of much people in heaven, saying, *Hallelujah !*" (Rev. xix. 1) will present an appropriate response to the call in verses 1–6. And not less does their summons to men on earth (Rev. xix. 5, 6) accord with the call in verses 7–13. Indeed, there is the very tone and energy of heaven in this glorious burst of praise—

Israel's rapturous burst of adoration to Him who makes them a people near to him.

Psalm 149

1 PRAISE ye the Lord !
Sing unto the Lord a new song, and his praise in the congregation of saints.
2 Let Israel rejoice in him that made him :
Let the children of Zion be joyful in their King.
3 Let them praise his name in the dance :
Let them sing praises unto him with the trimbrel and harp.
4 For the Lord taketh pleasure in his people : he will beautify the meek with salvation.
5 Let the saints be joyful in glory : let them sing aloud upon their beds.
6 Let the high praises of God be in their mouth, and a two-edged sword in their hand ;
7 To execute vengeance upon the heathen, and punishment upon the people ;
8 To bind their kings with chains, and their nobles with fetters of iron ;
9 To execute upon them the judgment written : this honour have all his saints.
Praise ye the Lord.

Another Hallelujah Psalm. THIS *Hallelujah* Psalm begins somewhat in the strain with which the preceding one closed. In Psa. cxlviii. 14, not Israel
The connection. only, but " all saints," were represented as giving honour to him who had in sovereign grace redeemed his people ; and so here, while Israel are called on as peculiarly indebted to Jehovah, yet all saints are joined with them in the triumphant song.

> " *Sing to Jehovah a new song ;*
> *Let his praise be in the congregation of saints.*" (Psa. cxlviii. 14.)

The theme. Are we not carried away to the scene in Rev. v. 9, to the " new song" to the Lamb who takes the book and opens its seals, and claims possession of earth ? Let all saints accord in this great hymn of triumph. Yet let Israel not fail to lift up their voice above all others, for they have been peculiarly honoured, and are above all others exalted. " *Let Israel rejoice in him that* MADE HIM," *i. e.*, made him what he is, as Deut. xxxii. 6 ; Isa. lvi 5. ; Job xxxv. 10. " *Let Zion's children rejoice in their King,*" who takes them under his special protection, and deigns to be specially called " *King of the Jews.*"

> " *Praise His name in the dance,*
> *Play to Him with timbrel and harp ;*"

as David before the ark (2 Sam. vi. 5, 14, 15), and as Jephthah's daughter welcoming her sire, (Judges xi. 34). For the Lord "gloriously helps the wretched" (say some), or better far, "*Beautifies the meek with salvation,*" *i. e.*, with all the spoils of that victory which he has achieved.

> " *Let his saints exult in joy !*"

No longer obscure, despised, the offscouring of all things, but glorious in the glory of their King, let them joyfully exult. And " *on their couches,*" when resting from active work and meditating on the Lord's ways (not as Psa. xxxvi. 14, nor Psa. iv. 4 even ; but in loftier and happier themes) "*let them sing.*"

> " *High praises loudly sung,*
> *The two-edged sword waved aloft !*"

The " exaltings" or " *extollings*" seem to refer us to all pre- vious psalms wherein worshippers have said—" I will *extol* thee, O God," for the root is the same ; and here, " *in their throat,*" as it is in the Hebrew, is equivalent to *speaking aloud,* like Isa. lviii. 1 ; the very opposite of the heathen's dumb idols, Psa. cxv. 7. And what is the " Two-EDGED SWORD ?" Is it not the peculiar symbol of *Messiah ?* As Bunyan represents his captains with their escutcheons—Captain Boanerges, with three burning thunderbolts ; Captain Execution, with the axe lying at the foot of the tree—so we may say that the escutcheon of the King that cometh to avenge his Father's honour, is *the two-edged sword :* for thus we find it in Rev. i. 16, ii. 12, as well as Heb. iv. 12 ; and we may add Rev. xix. 15. It is the Ehud-dagger (Judg. iii. 16) that slays the oppressor. The time is come for this now. " The *meek*" (ver. 4) put on salva- tion-strength ; and their King associates them with himself in the battle. It is like Rev. ii. 26–27, and iii. 21, even as " *beau- tifying with salvation*" is like Rev. ii. 28. Some, indeed, con- fine this to Israel, and compare Jer. li. 20, 21. But as we find " *all the saints*" associated in the work, we prefer the view that makes verses 6–9 to refer to "*the saints judging the world.*" They are figuratively said to lift up the " *two-edged sword,*" be- cause they join with Messiah in inflicting the fourfold vengeance, (Deut. xxxii. 41). At the same time, Israel in the flesh shall

be acting a part analogous to that of their King and his
heavenly hosts, (Ezek. xxxviii., Zech. xiv.).

Prophetic
reference.

What an echoing back of this song is Rev. xix. 1–6, with all
its " *Hallelujahs* !" Israel is the chief musician, or rather,
their King. Messiah himself leads the praise ; but it is for the
lips of the whole congregation of his redeemed—" *This honour
is to all his saints.*" Still, sovereign grace puts Israel prominently forward ; so that we cannot fail to see in this Psalm,

*Triumphant praise from Israel, because of their King and
all his saints subduing the nations.*

Psalm 150

1 PRAISE ye the Lord!
Praise God in his sanctuary:
Praise him in the firmament of his power.
2 Praise him for his mighty acts:
Praise him according to his excellent greatness.
3 Praise him with the sound of the trumpet:
Praise him with the psaltery and harp.
4 Praise him with the timbrel and dance:
Praise him with stringed instruments and organs.
5 Praise him upon the loud cymbals:
Praise him upon the high sounding cymbals.
6 Let everything that hath breath praise the Lord.
Praise ye the Lord.

This the closing
Psalm.

WHEN men presume to dictate to the Spirit of God, how deep
their fall ; as we see in the apocryphal attempts at writing
books of scripture to be added to the genuine word of God.
So it happens here, also ; for the Septuagint have not been
content to close the Book of Psalms with this most lofty and
sublime doxology, but have added a psalm about David's history—a tame piece of prose* that surprises every one by its in-
appropriateness in such a position. But the true close is the
150th Psalm, of which it may be said, that as the preceding

* It begins thus
"I was little among my brethren, and the youngest in my father's house.
I fed the sheep of my father. My hands made the organ."
and ends with
"I went forth to meet the uncircumcised, and he cursed me by his idols.
But I, drawing his own sword from him, cut off his head, and took away reproach
from the children of Israel."

one ushered us into the presence of the King, and placed us
with him in his kingdom, this leaves us in it, singing endless
" *Hallelujahs.*"

Augustine ingeniously notices, that "Psalm 50th was one
of *repentance;* Psalm 100th" (*i. e.*, in the Septuagint-reckoning
our 101st) "is about *mercy and judgment;* but the 150th is
the *praise of our God* in his sanctuary ; for there we arrive at
life eternal and blessed." Hengstenberg remarks—"As the
life of the faithful, and the history of the Christ, so also the
Psalter, with all its cries from the depths, runs out in a *Hallelujah !*" Dr Allix says of it—"It relateth to Messiah's
reign, when every thing that has breath, or was made by him,
shall be subjected to him." Horsley says of it—"A grand
chorus of all voices, and all instruments ! "

Patrick has a not uninteresting note on the many instruments of music in Psalm cxlix., which we quote here. "The
ancient inhabitants of Etruria used the trumpet ; the Arca-
dians, the whistle ; the Sicilians, the pectid ; the Cretians, the
harp ; the Thracians, the cornet ; the Lacedemonians, the
pipe ; the Egyptians, the drum ; the Arabians, the cymbal."
(Clem. Pædag. ii. 4.) May we not say that in this Psalm's
enumeration of musical instruments, there is a reference to the
variety which exists among men in the mode of expressing joy,
and exciting to feeling ? All nations, come and praise ! Use
every energy, for praise ! Men in every variety of circumstances, men of every various mood, men of all capacities, come
and praise ! Each in his own way, sing "*Hallelujah !*" And
in the words of another—"The Church composed of many
different members, all actuated, like the pipes of a well-tuned
instrument, by the same spirit, will become one great instru-
ment, sending forth the praises of God Most High." The instruments of music here.

"*Praise ye* יָהּ "—the peculiar name of God in covenant with Israel. The theme.

"*Praise ye* אֵל "—the name that implies dominion over all the earth.

I. Where shall His praise be uttered ? In his *sanctuary*,
where every thing speaks of *redemption;* and in the *firmament,* which his might has spread forth between earth and
heaven, on the platform of creation. The plan.

II. Why? Because of his deeds as the *Mighty* One*—those beams of glory inexpressible ; and because of the " *multitude of His greatness*"—that Source of all these beams, his own nature in itself.

III. Wherewith? With every instrument—with trumpet, psaltery, harp, soft timbrel, pipe, stringed instruments, and wind-instruments ; with cymbals, softly played (שָׁמַע that do not overpower the voice of the singer) ; and with cymbals of jubilee, (2 Sam. vi. 5). Not merely an instrument of ten strings, as at other times, but ten distinct instruments are called for ; and twelve times is the call uttered, " Praise ye !" הַלְלוּ. Twelve times ; so that each tribe is summoned, and then all the universe besides, to use their voice.

" Let every thing that hath breath, praise Jehovah ! "

All creation is summoned to take part, and angels too ; for they have interest in our redemption scenes—since He is to " reconcile all things to himself, whether they be things on earth, or things in heaven," (Col. i. 20).

What magnificence and majesty in this close! Praise gathered in from every creature ; every instrument of joy, and gladness, and triumph, and jubilee, summoned to sound loud praise ; and every heart and voice engaged to help the choir. " Every voice teems with praise ; every thought is about praise ; every object awakens it ; every power uses itself for His service " (Meditat. on Psalms). And no wonder, when we remember that we are ushered into the kingdom. " The Levites have changed their service now ; no longer have they burdens to bear through the wilderness ; but they lift up new songs in the house of the Lord. The heavens have changed their glory too ; they have ended their laughter at the proud confederates (Psalm ii. 3) ; and are now filled with joy and singing, and with that glory which is to break forth from them, and be a covering

---

* The note, in the Version of Junius and Tremellius, on the 13th verse of Psalm cxlviii., applies here also, a note wherein they say, " that the cause of praise is both God's own great name, and also his doings to his Church :" *Cujus restitutionem res omnes creatæ expectant exerto capite, et angeli ipsi cupiunt introspicere.* Rom. viii. 19 ; 1 Peter i. 12.

over all the dwellings of Zion, (Isa. iv). These are days of heaven upon the earth! The kingdom has come; and the will of the Blessed is done here as there. The mystic ladder connects the upper and the lower Sanctuaries. Praise crowns the scene. The vision passes from before us with the chanting of all kinds of music. *Man has taken the instrument of joy into his hand;* but it is only to God's glory he strikes it. The creature is happy; God is glorified; yes, praise, all praise! untiring, satisfying fruit of lips uttering the joy of creation, and owning the glory of the Blessed One," (Medit. on the Psalms, p. 195).

We close the Book with something of the feeling with which we suppose John came away from hearing "the voice of much people in heaven, saying, Hallelujah!" We seem to have been brought within hearing of heavenly melody, from heavenly harps and voices. Is not the closing verse taken up in Rev. v. 13— " And every creature which is in heaven, and on earth, and under the earth, and such as are in the sea, and all that are in them, heard I saying, Blessing, and honour, and glory, and power, be unto Him that sitteth upon the throne, and unto the Lamb for ever and ever!" And again, in Rev. xix. 6, 7, when the great multitude, with voice " as the voice of many waters, and as the voice of mighty thunderings," cry, " Hallelujah : for the Lord God omnipotent reigneth. Let us be glad, and rejoice, and give honour to him ; for the marriage of the Lamb is come !"

The end.

May my voice be raised in that mighty thunder of praise, in the great congregation! rapturously uniting with Israel, and all the saints, in this grand chorus of the universe, this full-toned

Call upon the universe at large to praise Jehovah with heart, and soul, and mind, and might!